Battling Bella

Battling Bella

THE PROTEST POLITICS OF BELLA ABZUG

Leandra Ruth Zarnow

Harvard University Press

CAMBRIDGE, MASSACHUSETTS
LONDON, ENGLAND
2019

First printing

Publication of this book has been supported through the generous
provisions of the Maurice and Lula Bradley Smith Memorial Fund.

Library of Congress Cataloging-in-Publication Data

Names: Zarnow, Leandra Ruth, 1979– author.

Title: Battling Bella : the protest politics of Bella Abzug /
Leandra Ruth Zarnow.

Description: Cambridge, Massachusetts : Harvard University Press, [2019] |
Includes bibliographical references and index.

Identifiers: LCCN 2019014313 | ISBN 9780674737488 (alk. paper)

Subjects: LCSH: Abzug, Bella S., 1920–1998. | Women—Political
activity—United States—History—20th century. | Civil rights
movements—United States—History—20th century. | Democratic
Party (U.S.) | United States—Politics and government—20th century.

Classification: LCC E840.8.A2 Z37 2019 | DDC 320.082/0973—dc23

LC record available at https://lccn.loc.gov/2019014313

For my parents, boundless believers.
And Juan Cisneros, for whom New York's
city lights dimmed too soon.

CONTENTS

PREFACE

This book began with two moments in the past. As a student at Smith College in the late 1990s, I worked at the Sophia Smith Collection, a women's history archive. There, I came across a swirly signature, "Bella," when I was cataloging correspondence in a collection Gloria Steinem had recently donated. Curious, I learned Bella Abzug was the mystery scribe, and that First Lady Hillary Clinton was not the only woman in politics to be at once revered and reviled. This discovery brought me back to an earlier memory of a story my father had told. It was August 1970. He was twenty-four years old, an organizer for Students for a Democratic Society and the Vietnam Vets Against the War, and was visiting relatives in New York City. Proud members of the National Organization for Women, they led him into a stream of women marching in the Women's Strike for Equality, a historic mobilization held on the fiftieth anniversary of women's suffrage. The day was unforgettable. Most vivid in his memory was the impassioned oratory of a lady with a hat. This was Abzug, and this book is as much for the young people she inspired then as it is for a new generation untouched by her vibrancy.

My narrative came to form in the wax and wane of the George W. Bush and Barack Obama presidencies as they grappled from different angles with an elusive terrorist target, global economic strains, and the complexities of a more diverse nation. It reaches readers at a historic political impasse amid Donald Trump's presidency. Some Americans have gained comfort in the hope of recovering an imagined great America, while others have protested and resisted this new nationalist idiom.

Bringing protest to politics, Congresswoman Abzug may be a visionary for our times as much as hers. The will to resist became a central posture in 2017, a year of protest unlike any in the early twenty-first century. Fifty years prior, Abzug blazed onto the national scene as a potent force of protest and resistance. Working on the edges of the political mainstream, she stretched its epicenter closer to her. Her thinking was radical, though some of her most outrageous ideas and goals have since become the norm.

I place Abzug as a participant in the American Left, a broad political community to which she proudly belonged. As I completed interviews for this book, some individuals close to Abzug expressed discomfort with my choice to focus on her leftist past and to use the term Left alongside the more ambiguous radical. They are understandably fearful that being truthful about Abzug's history will provide fuel for the partisan fire that continues to swirl. Yet, to deny her self-labeling would be ahistorical. It would also limit understanding of the interactive relationship between leftists and liberals, and particularly how Abzug helped extend progressive pressure within the Democratic Party and Congress in the early 1970s.

Abzug was not one to save much before she held political office. I am beholden to others for valuing what she did not preserve on her own. One close friend, Amy Swerdlow, can be credited for keeping legal pads from the 1960s filled with ideas Abzug tried out in Women Strike for Peace and formalized in Congress. Sitting down with those who knew her, hearing moving and wild stories about this vivacious woman, has been a joy of this project. Oral interviews colored the inert remnants of life stored in archives and allowed me to imagine Abzug in action. I have also taken care to dwell on the occasions when she paused to jot down her reflections.

I am quite deliberate in my attempt to write women into the more conventional annals of political history, a genre that remains partial to "great men." Early women's historians brought attention to the domestic and intimate aspects of life when all of history seemed to be about business and politics. I work in this tradition, while also exploring Abzug's high-velocity political life. What fueled her passion, how she crafted her politics, and why she saw such promise in the democracy she critiqued so deeply is what I have sought to capture here.

Battling Bella

INTRODUCTION

OUT FRONT

I come out of the peace movement and women's rights.
They thought I was a lunatic. Now these causes are being
supported by a majority of the people. I've been out front.
Everybody's caught up.

—BELLA ABZUG

ANDY WARHOL HAILED A CAB down to his studio overlooking Union
Square, where Bella Abzug waited for a portrait sitting commissioned
by *Rolling Stone* magazine. Warhol took special delight in this assignment.
He thought Abzug had panache. He appreciated her steadfast advocacy of
gay rights at a time when few politicians would touch the issue, and he
enjoyed running into her at parties. Warhol chronicled these exchanges
in his diary along with Abzug's media appearances and her electoral losses
and wins. "What do you think New York needs most?" a journalist asked
Warhol in September 1977. "A woman mayor. Bella Abzug. She'd be great,"
he replied.[1] Abzug kicked off her candidacy earlier that June by cruising the
streets of Manhattan in a gold convertible with the swagger of a victor on
the make. A week after her announcement, Warhol was tasked with creating presumably the earliest portrait of New York's would-be woman
mayor.

Warhol loved "a certain kind of outrageous nerve," a quality Abzug did
not lack.[2] When crafting her portrait, he rendered "battling Bella" as a blithe

spirit, forward-looking and radiant. Snapping dozens of Polaroid photos, he caught her mid-grin, delighting in the scent of a rose the same shade as her lipstick, tipping her brown hat just so.[3] In the final silk screen, the rose did not appear. Instead, Warhol opted to focus on his subject's hat, depicted in jet black and accented by a backdrop of blue, purple, turquoise, and coral pastels. The resulting halo effect invoked religious iconography, a nod to Abzug's self-confidence and fame.

Actress Shirley MacLaine loved Warhol's screen print of her friend so much that she displayed it on her bureau. Warhol's portrait elevated Abzug, the most influential woman in US politics at the time, to the realm of an American cultural icon. It also served as a counterpoint to the usual portrayals of Abzug as an uncouth, bossy loudmouth. But the image did nothing for her election prospects. In a twist of fate, Abzug's *Rolling Stone* cover shot did not run in September as scheduled, pulled for a memorial to Elvis Presley, who had died in August. Instead, Warhol's portrait appeared in October as a coda underscoring Abzug's defeat in the mayoral primary the previous month, in which she finished fourth behind Ed Koch, Mario Cuomo, and the incumbent, Mayor Abraham Beame. It would be the latest setback Abzug faced after giving up her seat in the House of Representatives to try for the Senate in 1976.

"More than a congresswoman. She's a *Symbol*," a 1972 profile of Bella Abzug in *Life* magazine pronounced.[4] In the refraction of cultural memory, it is not her words or actions but the image she projected—the symbol she became—that endures. She reappears in the twenty-first century in sporadic cultural portraits: a tattoo on the arm of Lily Tomlin's character in the comedy *Admission* (2013) and among municipal bureaucrat Leslie Knope's photo gallery of heroines in the sitcom *Parks and Recreation* (2009–2015). Humorist Paul Rudnick tweeted followers during the 2016 general election, "I may have converted a cranky Upper West Side cab driver, who wasn't voting, into a Clinton supporter, by invoking Bella Abzug."[5] She remains a luminous spirit in the city she loved, watching over a small stretch of Hell's Kitchen greenspace, renamed the Bella Abzug Park in 2019.[6] There New Yorkers pause to enjoy its cascading fountains and rush off to enter the Hudson Yards subway station. Abzug would have delighted in this feature for she was most at home chatting up constituents at subway entrances. For those who are old enough to recall Congresswoman Abzug in action, she still conjures passionate reactions. Some remember her as a fear-

Figure I.1 Andy Warhol's affectionate portrait of Bella Abzug on the cover of *Rolling Stone* in October 1977 denoted her status as a cultural icon as much as a political force. (Credit: Copyright © Rolling Stone LLC 1977. All Rights Reserved. Used by Permission)

less trailblazer, and others as a meddling menace. Most agree that she pushed the limits because she wanted to achieve meaningful change.

References to Abzug have most often been employed to measure where we stand as a nation in cracking the durable political glass ceiling. "Behind Clinton—and, really, every woman who has run for U.S. political office in the last four decades—is Bella Abzug," Eliza Berman of *Time* magazine reminded us just days before former secretary of state Hillary Clinton announced her presidential candidacy in April 2015.[7] If power is measured by the march to the presidency, Abzug did not get very far. When she entered Congress in 1971, she was one of fifteen congresswomen, a four-seat jump big enough that journalists noted women's increased clout. Each election cycle in the 1970s was billed as a potential "year of the woman," and each one fell short of expectations. In 1972, Abzug appeared on the cover of *Life* magazine as the embodiment of women in politics just days before she lost a primary that nearly ended her political career. Though the death of her opponent, Representative William Fitts Ryan, gave Abzug a second chance, women picked up only three seats in the House and lost two seats in the Senate during this midterm, increasing their overall number in Congress by one. At the nation's bicentennial in 1976, Abzug tried her hand at becoming "*more* than one in a hundred" in the Senate.[8] Entirely male then, it remained so for that election cycle.

Political change has moved considerably slower than expected. The 1970s—a time notable for its groundswell of feminist mobilizing—closed with fewer women in Congress than at the beginning of the prior decade. Projecting far ahead in 1971, the National Women's Political Caucus believed it would not be a stretch to predict that half of the members of Congress would be women by 2020.[9] Bella Abzug's story brings into fuller view this persistent and arduous campaign to make women more visible in American politics.[10]

Abzug attained the limited vestiges of power she could. House majority leader Tip O'Neill designated Abzug as a Democratic at-large whip, making her the first woman in the history of the House of Representatives to hold a whip position.[11] Simultaneously, she chaired the Government Information and Individual Rights Subcommittee, a critical oversight body of the House Government Operations Committee. These accolades led *U.S. News & World Report* to rate Abzug the third most influential member of Congress in 1976.[12] Within the Democratic Party, she helped solidify a feminist bloc that held such sway that one aide to President Jimmy Carter characterized Abzug as "the political Rabbi and Godmother of the Women's Movement."[13] Recognition was reluctantly bestowed. As journalist Mary McGrory observed, "She is called 'madame chairwoman' with pained correctness by government officials who, like her colleagues, once hoped to ignore her out of existence."[14]

Blurring the line between politics and entertainment, Abzug made sure she could not be ignored. She hobnobbed with celebrities and became one. She came to be known simply as Bella, a term of endearment reserved for someone familiar, approachable, and compassionate.[15] She appeared in a portrait by the painter Alice Neel and as the sole cameo in Woody Allen's 1979 film *Manhattan*. Newspapers ran photographs of Abzug without captions, her hat alone giving away the woman it crowned. Her name became a way to describe doing something with gusto: "One could not say a lady bakes a pie with abzuggery but one could say a PTA vice president argued her point before the Board of Education with abzuggery."[16] Avid fans traded Bella keepsakes and asked for her autograph. Abzug loved the public attention and reporters-in-waiting, but being a media magnet exposed her to a high level of scrutiny. She was often cast as an archetype of a pushy, shrill woman politician.

Abzug was not allowed the space in politics to be herself. "Sure. I say things straight out, but so do a lot of men. When a man is that way, they say he is a strong, forthright individual and leader. When a woman is that way, she is 'abrasive' and 'belligerent,'" she explained of the double standard.[17] Abzug was a full-throttle, high-volume, commanding presence. She could be impatient and unyielding. She demanded too much of herself and her collaborators. She dished out fire and fury. But she spoke forcefully so that more women could be heard. And she pushed forward relentlessly so that it would be easier for more women to follow.

CONGRESSWOMAN ABZUG RALLIED OUT front on issues that have since achieved heightened importance: she introduced the first federal gay civil rights bill; sponsored legislation for clean energy and water as an early environmentalist; advocated for urban revitalization and mass public transportation; called for universal child care, universal health care, equal pay for equal work, and a living wage; and raised privacy concerns in the face of technological advances and increased state secrecy. Always on the cusp of change, she spent years before her time in Congress marching in student protests, advocating in courtrooms, and lobbying congressmen. She joined movements before they reached a critical mass—racial civil rights before Montgomery and Selma, peace activism prior to the Vietnam War, feminism in anticipation of the later United Nations Decade for Women, and LGBT rights in an era when homophobia prevailed.

By the mid-1960s, Abzug had decided it was time to transition from being an outside agitator to an outsider agitating on the inside. An "instinctive radical," she detected an opening for leftists to enter electoral politics that had not been present since the 1930s.[18] Advocating "pragmatic radicalism," she modeled a practical, reasonable resistance.[19] She sought to reconstruct US society and politics using the instruments of democracy instead of starting from scratch, promoting rebellious reform over revolution. As one former aide observed, Abzug "always wanted to take the far forward position, and would do that time and time again to give other people the room to move."[20] She pushed from the left to shift the center. This story of how she and others brought protest to politics as the sixties moved into the seventies has been the most underplayed chapter of those nostalgically memorialized "days of rage."[21]

Abzug was among the boldest of visionaries during a period of unsettling uncertainty brought on by great structural and societal change. When she served in Congress between 1971 and 1976, the nation teetered on the brink of either destruction or rebirth. Americans faced tightening pocketbooks, globalizing industries, stalling wages, closing factories, shifting family structures, deep-seated inequities, tense urban unrest, an unending war, and political corruption. At the same time, since 1960, Americans had witnessed the end of public segregation, the introduction of the pill, an expanded workforce, and diverse Americans advocating for a more inclusive democracy. These changes caused great concern but also the continued will for reform. Yet Americans across the political spectrum—left, right, and center—vacillated on how to respond to societal problems and could not come to agreement. Cleareyed, Abzug soberly assessed in 1971, "Americans, men and women, young and old, recognize that our nation is caught up in a crisis of soul and purpose." Idealistically, she predicted, "Americans want change, and I believe they are far ahead of the leadership of both the Republican and Democratic parties in their willingness to accept the necessary solutions, to restore America to health and sanity."[22] She could imagine a different future because of her past.

Abzug believed that the problems facing the nation during the Vietnam War had been unmatched since the Great Depression. She came to her politics during this earlier period when Americans responded to devastation with openness to greater political experimentation. For Abzug, this meant finding solace in Conservative Judaism, answers in Socialist Zionist utopianism, and belonging in the wider US Popular Front.[23] In this milieu of 1930s left-liberal progressivism, she could be a Zionist and still find common cause with civil libertarians, New Deal liberals, unionists, anti-racists, pacifists, and Communists, working toward a collectivist future. Abzug continued to be motivated by the politics of her youth well after the idealism of this moment faded, the political ties became suspect, and the electoral field and cultural mood narrowed to a "vital center."[24] She would always be a Socialist Zionist first, carving out a singular identity as a deeply devout Jewish politician who sided with most leftists on every count except Israel.

Political change in the 1970s has been considered mainly as a precursor of our times, but Abzug looked backward as much as forward.[25] Living in the shadow of the McCarthy period, she refused to let bygones be bygones. She saw President Richard Nixon foremost as "tricky Dick," who had once been a member of the House Un-American Activities Committee. Abzug was unable to shake memories of navigating unfriendly territory as a young lawyer representing workers, racial minorities, immigrants, women, and political dissenters deemed "un-American." Once she became a congresswoman, she forged a redemptive campaign to scale back the midcentury expansion of the national security state. In doing so, she highlighted how the US government vacillated between its role as a noble protector of cherished democratic values and a coercive agent encroaching on Americans' civil liberties.[26] Her example underscores the need to assess how earlier debates about the US government's jurisdiction and responsibility to its people reached fever pitch during the 1970s. The Equal Rights Amendment and family values, oil crisis and stagflation, busing and affirmative action, Watergate and the end of the Vietnam War all take on a different light when viewed not merely as harbingers of a more conservative, if diverse, future America. These concerns were mired in earlier tensions and reflective of long-standing allegiances and impulses foundational to this contested nation. Cold War battle lines continued to be drawn, as did reactions to the end of Jim Crow and the forced retreat of Rosie the Riveter.

When progressive protest politics achieved momentum in the early 1960s, Abzug fed off this energy while sustaining earlier allegiances and concerns. She became a generational bridge, encouraging radicals old and young to learn from and welcome each other. In the Vietnam War era, she urged left-ists to gain persuasive power in the policy arena as they had during the New Deal–Popular Front era she idealized. Hers was a revival project as much as an aspirational endeavor. She uniquely fused the multi-issue collectivist concerns of the 1930s with the identity-focused and antiauthoritarian im-pulses of the 1960s and 1970s. She drew young idealists in without displacing those whose political awakening closer matched her own. But this union was always fragile, with skepticism and righteousness exhibited by both sides. Age complicated differences in strategy, emphasis, and style. Younger activists believed their elders were too apolitical, sectarian, puritanical, and moderate, while older activists judged youthful organizers as naive, impre-cise, outlandish, and impractical.

Transcending these divisions better than most, Abzug listened to fresh voices on the scene and was able to articulate their concerns to a wider au-dience. She was among those who led the siren call for new politics, a term that was introduced to the political lexicon in 1966 and served as short-hand for the rebellious, imaginative mood of Americans as they dreamed up what US democracy might look like in the final quarter of the twentieth century.[27] Abzug captured this restive spirit boiling over from antiwar, civil rights, gay liberation, antipoverty, environmental, and feminist organizing. She saw great potential in the loose coalition that formed to challenge the Vietnam War and translated the myriad demands of a "movement of move-ments" into clear policy goals.[28] She railed against "the system," as she urged young people to put Yippie silliness and Weather Underground criminality aside for activism through the ballot box. She reminded self-regarding proponents of the New Left that they were not so original but instead were building on the ideas and efforts of many who came before them.[29] Though some activists did not take kindly to this reprimand, others shared her vision for augmenting radical change through a progressive insurgency in electoral politics. Capitalizing on this momentum, Abzug helped the pro-test energy of the 1960s mature into a demand for power through public office, legal action, and institutional control.

On Capitol Hill, Abzug treated her office as an extension of community-level, frontline activism for a wide range of causes. Bringing the state closer to the street, she opened her doors to advocates, creating a direct channel to federal policymaking. An urban populist, she drew attention to city dwellers as resources shifted to the suburbs. An ambassador of underdogs, she highlighted the myriad ways the US government failed underprivileged populations. An antiwar internationalist, she helped reset foreign policy focus on human rights at the end of the Vietnam War. A civil libertarian, she expanded the idea of privacy rights to include protections from government surveillance alongside reproductive and sexual freedom. A feminist power broker, she used her position among a male-dominated political elite to question the patriarchal underpinnings of democracy.

Abzug was not of "the people" she aspired to represent. Her understanding of want was politically inspired more than personally experienced. Once a labor lawyer, she represented blue-collar workers without being one. Although not rich, she was well-off, with a stockbroker husband and a brownstone they called home in Greenwich Village. Engaged in a kaleidoscope of causes, Abzug thought deeply about the interplay between race, class, sexuality, and gender well before intersectionality became a vogue political term. But at times her position as an affluent, white, heterosexual woman caused her to misread or minimize the needs of others. Likewise, her personal ambition did not always square with her commitment to collectivism, for it was easier to organize around democratizing politics than to share the stage.

AMONG THE GREATEST political bellwethers of her time, Abzug elicited visceral reactions from observers near and far. She reflected the conflicting moods of the nation: impatient and enraged, but also teeming with expectation. And she pushed her leftist agenda as if it were middle-of-the-road. Looking at how Americans responded to her actions is important for understanding her story. As one of the most reviled and beloved political figures of her day, she was "the conservative's devil" for some and "sister Bella" for others.[30] Much of this response was tied to being a woman trailblazer pushing into male domains, compounded by being among the few overt radicals in federal office. Abzug was a polarizing figure during polarized times, and these feelings continue to fester. Many of those she alienated were members of her own party.

More than a story of the Left versus the Right or Democrat versus Republican, an account of Abzug's political years reveals an ongoing internal conflict within the Democratic Party.[31] Not unlike the more recent Tea Party insurgency within the Republican Party, this was a battle fought for the soul of the Democratic Party. The contest pitted New Politics Democratic reformers against entrenched powers that included southern Democrats and Cold War liberals. With the force of movements behind them, New Politics Democrats gained ground within the Democratic Party and Congress between 1968 and 1976. Abzug's campaign pledge revealed which side she was on—she would "give the power back to the people."[32]

Abzug was a relative newcomer to the Democratic Party in the 1960s, having been a member of the American Labor Party previously. Once a Democrat, she directed a fierce campaign to steer the party past its exclusive New Deal base and its Cold War labor-liberal accord. She challenged it, ensnared by an anticommunist us-versus-them mentality, to reconstitute itself as the party of human rights and diplomacy first. She urged Democrats to enlarge their conception of economic security to address the needs of a more inclusive workforce and the inequities brought on by a globalizing capitalist economy.[33] The way of the future, in her view, was to build a green, technology-driven economy that penalized the offshore flight of US corporations, took better care of families, and responded to the needs of all workers. Democrats, she argued, should be ahead of this change, thinking about ways to appeal to the working class broadly defined.

Real change, as Abzug saw it, would require bringing more women into the Democratic Party. With so few women in office, she could argue the untested point that they were most capable of cleaning up the mess in Washington. In making this case, she drew upon early twentieth-century suffragists' claims that women would be the most pious housekeepers of politics. Abzug, however, did not want women to edge into politics in the name of women and children. Rather, she assumed mistakenly that most American women leaned progressive and would be predisposed to help realize a multifarious new Democratic order. More achievable, Abzug helped ensure women's rights would be a central tenet of Democratic New Politics, and since the early 1970s, the Democratic Party has maintained this feminist edge.

New Politics Democrats were a loosely aligned faction that never achieved majority control of the party's agenda, ranks, or leadership. Nonetheless, Abzug and her peers gained outsize influence on the shape of the Democratic Party and the policy agenda of the Democratic-controlled Congress in the early 1970s. These progressives pressed for reforms in areas including foreign affairs, executive power, human rights, civil liberties, consumer protection, women's rights, and environmentalism.[34] New Politics Democrats demanded greater party democratization and congressional representativeness, changing the rules of belonging. The party of Andrew Jackson became the nation's most inclusive and most concerned with rights. These noticeable shifts were not totalizing, but they were consequential. Leftists' resounding critique of liberalism exposed its deficiencies, deepening Americans' heightened distrust in government. Opening the ranks of the Democratic Party decentered its traditional white, male base. Prioritizing civil rights, reproductive justice, and détente troubled white supremacists, social conservatives, and defense hawks who once felt at home as Democrats. Abzug did not worry about backlash when running as a New Politics Democrat in 1970 or promoting bold progressive reforms during her three terms in the House of Representatives. She recognized that the political terrain was shifting, but along with many contemporary political pundits, she could not foresee which "real majority" would triumph.[35] With the jury still out, she made the case vigorously for a social democratic turn in US politics.

BELLA ABZUG STROVE TO ENSURE that this fateful political moment was remembered. In Congress, she took on the role of documentarian, hyperfocused on establishing new procedures to expand preservation of and access to records. She treated the activity of her congressional office as a form of witnessing, and for this reason instructed congressional staff to keep every office memo, speech draft, unsolicited pamphlet, and constituent letter. Yet, before she had congressional staff, she could not be bothered with the act of archiving. Nor did she often take time to record her thoughts, send copious letters, or dependably keep an appointment book. Her secretary was her scribe, while activist collaborators and her husband, Martin, doubled as typists. Late in life, she did not get around to finishing the memoir friends Shirley MacLaine, Gloria Steinem, and Robin Morgan had prodded her to write.[36] "I'm an activist. I want action—not talk," Abzug said of her constant motion.[37] Her story is one of the confluence of movements and the impact of bringing truth to power as much as her own inability to stop.

1

POLITICAL TIES THAT BIND

ZIPPY **AND UPLIFTING**, the theme song of Bella Abzug's 1976 Senate campaign had the crowd-pleasing dynamism of a Broadway musical. Written by theater veteran Jay Gorney, the tune transported audiences gathered in community centers, union halls, and school auditoriums across New York's hinterland to Forty-Second Street. One could almost imagine the house lights dimming as the first note sounded on the piano and a male singer began:

> With a senator from New York state, whose ideas belong to 1908.
> Let's switch to one who answers to the people and not the privileged few.
> We know what Buckley is and we don't need him.
> We also know the best to succeed him.
> Let's all unite around Bella. She's the popular choice.
> Give your ballot to Bella, and give the people a voice.[1]

This populist jingle carried forward the economic parity and rights-focused platform Abzug first campaigned on six years prior. It signaled to voters that Abzug, although now prominent, had not reneged on her commitment to serve everyday people. But there is more to the meaning of this song.

Not only a talented composer, Gorney was also Abzug's former legal client. He never forgot her willingness to appear by his side when he testified before the House Un-American Activities Committee (HUAC) in 1953. He remained appreciative of her futile effort to find him work, unemployable after he was an unfriendly witness who told committee members the Bill of Rights "is not musical comedy" and he would not be their "trained stool pigeon."[2]

Jay and his wife, Sondra, had been active in the Hollywood Left for years. He wrote the hit Depression era tune "Brother, Can You Spare a Dime?" before helping make Shirley Temple a star. Sondra acted in the Federal Theatre Project before balancing work at *Pic* magazine and fund-raising for progressive causes. In 1947, they moved to New York City, tuning in during their cross-country drive to hear the Hollywood Ten, "dear friends with whom we had spent many hours," testify before HUAC.[3] By 1950, the blacklist had caught up with the Gorneys. CBS fired Jay shortly after *Counterattack* published their names and affiliations on a list of alleged Communists. When subpoenaed to appear before HUAC, they called Abzug because "she was a well known progressive lawyer" recommended by show business friends.[4]

Thirty-three at the time, Abzug had secured a reputation as a shrewd, fearless advocate in and out of the courtroom. In a period in which loyalty oaths were government sanctioned, she refused to ask potential clients the dreaded question, "Are you, indeed, a Communist?" She established a career representing unionists, underprivileged people, and political dissenters at the cost of losing business, facing personal threats, risking her health, and living under government surveillance. She was driven by the belief that civil rights, civil liberties, and one's economic well-being should not be constricted in the name of national security. While she never joined the Communist Party, to critics, she may as well have. Her willingness to associate with known and suspected Communists made her guilty by association. As her opponent Republican Barry Farber reminded people when running against Abzug in 1970 for Manhattan's Nineteenth District seat, "Mrs. Abzug does have a political past . . . and if more people knew it, she would have no political future!"[5]

This layered past reveals how early Abzug became an oppositional reformer determined to expose and reshape what she saw as the structural and cultural "clutches in which democracy is suffering."[6] It reveals how much the social and professional relationships she first cultivated as a student activist and political lawyer continued to be an influence. These were

Figure 1.1 Republican Barry Farber distributed this flyer highlighting Bella Abzug's long-standing leftist ties during their contest for New York City's Nineteenth District seat in 1970. What Abzug staff saw as a dirty smear campaign, Farber aides believed to be vital voter education. (Bella Abzug Papers, Box 1032, Rare Book and Manuscript Library, Columbia University)

the political ties that bind, endearing her to her past, shaping her present, framing her vision of the future.

In a sense, Abzug's appropriation of "new politics" as an antiwar activist-turned-politician in the 1960s was a matter of convenience. Claiming novelty, she repurposed older ideas, postures, and goals promoted by the US Popular Front that continued to motivate her actions. Once a politician, she did not closet her leftist past as did her contemporaries, writer Betty

Friedan and former US Women's Bureau head Mary Dublin Keyserling.[7] Even so, Abzug selectively portrayed her radical history, rendering it more palatable to voters.

"In the early fifties," Abzug wrote, "I concentrated on labor law and spent a lot of time fighting McCarthyism. By 1960 (strange how my life has been divided into decades) I became a peacenik."[8] This imprecise description obscured the layers of connections and commitments that continued to be meaningful. What is so striking about Abzug's political journey is how consistent she was, stubbornly so, in working to realize a socialist vision of democratic rule. She drew energy from being part of causes and movements bigger than herself, but was always driven to challenge injustices as she saw them.

A Socialist Zionist Is Not a Communist

Abzug did not join the Young Communist League, as would her husband, Martin, and her childhood friend and speechwriter Mim Kelber. As a student activist and lawyer, Abzug formed alliances with Communists, becoming what Kelber affectionately called "our broad element."[9] But she refused to join the party, which she saw as rigidly dogmatic, xenophobic, and secular. To do so would have denied her practice of Judaism, her identity as a Diaspora Jew, and her political orientation as a Socialist Zionist.

Abzug's political passions were fired by a deep sense of faith. She liked to say she was "born yelling" in 1920, perfectly timed to come into the world the year women got the vote.[10] The Savitzky family home was typically filled with the sounds of music and prayer. While Sabbath night each Friday was a sacred tradition, it was also festive. Mother Esther blessed the bread and wine, lit candles, and laid out a Kosher spread. After dinner, grandfather Wolf Tanklefsky, an Orthodox Jew, provided a Torah reading. This religious meditation would often be followed by father Emanuel singing Yiddish melodies, with Bella accompanying on the violin and sister, Helene, on the piano. Sometimes Wolf told bedtime stories from the book of Isaiah. Teachings such as "Cease to do evil; learn to do good. Devote yourself to justice" resonated with Bella most.

Through Judaism, Abzug gained a moral compass. Her parents were the first to model this connection. Emanuel and Esther emigrated from Russia to the United States in 1902 and 1907, respectively, searching as most immigrants did for better economic circumstances and greater religious freedom. While Abzug remembered them as simple, hardworking people of humble means, they were well-off enough to leave the tenements of Manhattan's Lower East Side behind for the "blocks and blocks of handsome flats and residences" in the Southeast Bronx.[11] As an adult, Abzug underplayed this social advancement, describing their first railroad flat at 1038 Hoe Avenue as overcrowded by extended family.[12] This would only be for as long as it took for Emanuel to transition from a bookkeeper in the meatpacking industry to owning his own butcher shop. The year after the stock market crashed, the Savitzkys kept on an African American maid, Myrtle Thompson, to tidy their multiroom apartment at 3065 Roberts Avenue.[13]

Living comfortably, Emanuel and Esther instilled in Bella the understanding that it "was not enough to seek a way out of poverty or a way out of discrimination for ourselves, but for others." When Bella visited her grandparents in an adjacent apartment, she gained further instruction on going past *tzedakah,* or charity, to pursue a "very simple sense of justice" in one's life's work, and commitment to *tikkun olam,* the Jewish ethical challenge to better one's world.[14]

Judaism introduced Bella to injustice. She soaked up her first Hebrew lessons from Wolf, who glowed when his granddaughter recited Hebrew prayers in perfect tone before his friends.[15] He encouraged her education, perhaps making amends for having pulled her mother, Esther, a promising student, out of school to keep the books at his butcher shop. Picking Bella up after school, he brought her with him to the synagogue. Once there, she left her grandfather to pray behind the *mechitzah,* the curtain separating women from men. In these sectioned-off quarters, Bella learned that women were treated "as another constellation" in Orthodox Judaism.[16] This spatial segregation carried over to religious study. Women could learn Hebrew, but they could not read from, touch, or dance with the sacred Torah scrolls.

In synagogue, Bella gained her first exposure to institutional sexism upheld in cultural practice and reinforced through architectural design. She also learned that she could cross the gender divide in Judaism and get away with it. When her father died from a heart attack in 1934, Bella, full of remorse, made a gut choice to say Kaddish, a ritual reserved for sons. She tried to be discreet, selecting an inconspicuous corner in the Orthodox synagogue, but it was hard to miss this young girl praying among men.

"I will never forget your sister, eleven or twelve years, how she came to the synagogue every morning," one astonished observer told her sister Helene.[17] Abzug later described this instinctive challenge as "one of the early blows for the liberation of Jewish women."[18] More so, it reflected the influence of her training in the Socialist Zionist youth organization Hashomer Hatzair, which emphasized gender egalitarianism alongside labor collectivism.

Bella's zealous enthusiasm for Hebrew led her to become "a hot Zionist" dedicated to the cause at twelve years old.[19] When her grandfather had taught her all he could, she enrolled in Talmud Torah instruction at the Kingsbridge Heights Jewish Center. Founded in 1924, the religious center was part of a synagogue boom the decade before the Great Depression.[20] An outpost of Conservative Judaism, the denomination's slightly relaxed gender code allowed Bella to learn Hebrew alongside her male peers. Bella's Hebrew teacher, Levi Soshuk, enlivened lessons with Jewish history, folklore, literature, and discussions of Zionism. A "handsome young man," Soshuk encouraged Bella to see Hebrew as "the linguistic coefficient of territory," and her language training as the first step in preparing for immigration to Palestine.[21] Bella got an initial taste of Zionist kibbutz living at Camp Achvah, a summer camp Soshuk once attended run by the Bureau of Jewish Education in Godeffroy, New York. Fully immersed, Bella spoke only Hebrew as she hiked, paddled, danced the hora, and studied the geography of Palestine.[22] Hashomer Hatzair scout troops complemented this experience after campers returned home. Soshuk encouraged Bella to join her local Hashomer Hatzair club, Ken Bronx. Eager to please, she would dutifully "get dressed in this gold outfit with an orange tie and go to meetings and come back late."[23]

When Bella joined the youth group in 1932, Hashomer Hatzair had entered a golden period, with 1,500 members in North America and 42,420 members internationally.[24] Founded in Vienna in 1913, the movement gained a boost after Britain issued the Balfour Declaration in 1917, which "viewed with favor the establishment in Palestine of a national home for the Jewish people."[25] In a time when labor Zionism "became *the* Zionism of mainstream American Jewry," Hashomer Hatzair remained its most radical wing, espousing "utopian-Marxist socialism."[26] The rebel youth of Israel's future, Hashomer Hatzair members were Zionist renegades who wore their "independent political trend" as a badge of pride.[27] The group participated in the International Working Union of Socialist Parties, while critiquing European worker parties for their reformist concessions and appeasement of fascism. Flirting with Trotskyism, Hashomer Hatzair leaders vowed they would not "wait for the Comintern to 'permit'" immigration of Jewish radicals "to the land of its past."[28] Hashomer Hatzair advocated the establishment of a binational Jewish-Arab workers state "based on the principles of non-domination and political parity."[29] Yet despite this expression of solidarity, the group's "pioneer dreams" of establishing cooperative agrarian compounds on uncultivated "new wilderness" overlooked the presence of Arabs on this land.[30]

Bella was too young to fully comprehend the intricacies of Hashomer Hatzair's political positioning, but she nonetheless developed a lasting class consciousness and ethnic nationalist identity. Bella's reading of philosophers Martin Buber, Aaron David Gordon, and Ber Borochov nurtured her awareness of organic agrarianism, proletarian binationalism, and Jewish self-determination.[31] But it was the fun she had socializing with other scouts, attending free cultural events, learning farming techniques, and discussing "collective living, collective production and collective distribution" that held her interest.[32] These teachings often came in the form of a song. "Good-bye America / Good-bye Yankee fashion / We are going to Palestine / To hell with the depression." As an adult, Abzug could still belt out this tune "with a dramatic voice, and close to perfect pitch."[33]

Hashomer Hatzair gave Bella a framework for understanding the economic devastation of the Great Depression, which did not leave her family untouched. By 1933, one-third of all New Yorkers were out of work.[34] Her father's business, the Live and Let Live Meat Market on Ninth Avenue, failed, unable to compete with the rise of chain grocery stores and tightening of family budgets. Still, the Savitzkys' worst economic setback did not lead them to join the breadlines at Jewish aid societies. Participation in Hashomer Hatzair helped Bella understand this difference. Having "never missed a meal or worked really hard," she could see that "going to kibbutz would be roughing it." She came to this realization by comparing herself to her scouting friends, who "were really poor" and dreamed of cooperative farming in Israel, "where they would be better off economically."[35] Moving past empathy to action, she delivered her first offering as an ally in the class struggle. Unbeknownst to her father, she carted his prized record player to her scout meeting and gave it to her troop.

Bella often clashed with her father, Emanuel, whom she remembered as a strict disciplinarian. He found it troubling that his daughter rode subway cars while fund-raising for the Jewish National Fund, believing that Hashomer Hatzair encouraged her wild streak. The Zionist group, quite deliberately, gave "girls who felt frustrated in the atmosphere of their families, or of general society," an "immediate freedom to express themselves."[36] Her mother, Esther, reinforced this message at home, granting Bella permission to roam when Emanuel was at work. Bella found that her preferred attire of shorts and sneakers provided greater ease to play sports, shoot marbles, and ride "every boy's bike in the neighborhood."[37] On her rounds, she studied the oratory of ardent street lecturers promoting a range of causes. They "could keep on for three-quarters of an hour, gathering a crowd of 150 people and bringing it all to a climax with a good sale of literature and an exciting question period."[38]

Bella imitated soapbox speakers as she perfected her thirty-second pitch to donate funds for Israel. But the father she was rebelling against influenced her even more. Emanuel shied away from socialist and anarchist ideas and allegiances and avoided the paternalist patronage of Tammany Hall machine politics. Yet, World War I had left him deeply troubled. He made his pacifist critique of militarization clear by naming his business the Live and Let Live Meat Market. His social entrepreneurship modeled for Bella the possibility of principled consumerism and the power of issue-driven, everyday organizing. Her father's example spurred her to keep at Zionist fund-raising, staying out "until her blue jar was completely full."[39]

Becoming a Socialist Zionist nurtured Bella's ties to people beyond her family. Cultivating diasporic belonging, Zionism was a form of pan-nationalism for a people without a nation. As a Zionist, Bella developed a sense of her difference and worth through the process of self-realization, in which she studied Jewish culture and history but also the sources of anti-Semitism. Hashomer Hatzair members were taught that their position as a "perpetual minority" made them susceptible to displacement, encouraging vigilance and group insularity.[40] Bella's ethnic particularism made her hesitant to take up coalitional politics. Her older sister, Helene, led the way, joining Hunter College friends who took the Oxford Oath for peace and marched in the National Student Strike Against the War in 1935.[41] Bella followed suit once the Spanish Civil War erupted in 1936, for she believed fascism's rise in Spain was "the beginning of the end" for democracy.[42] Once in high school, she joined Avukah, a Zionist club with fifty-nine chapters by 1939 that encouraged its members to prioritize Jewish interests while working toward the greater goal of establishing a "progressive social order."[43]

Abzug's involvement in Hashomer Hatzair and Avukah primed her to be sympathetic to the ethnic particularism that complicated coalitional social movement politics in the 1960s and 1970s. When she later encouraged women to work toward a common cause, she understood more than many white feminists why differences among women must be considered. She cultivated connections with ethnic nationalists, seeing their ethnic pride and prioritization of self-determination as like that of early Zionists. At the same time, her religious identity and idealization of the pre-Israel articulation of Socialist Zionism espoused in Hashomer Hatzair later strained her leftist and feminist alliances.

Once arriving at Hunter College, Bella shed any lingering reluctance to become a student activist committed to wide-ranging labor, anti-imperialist, antiracist, pacifist, and civil liberties causes. In 1938, she joined the American Student Union (ASU), which served as the student arm of the US Popular Front.[44] Hunter had one of the organization's biggest chapters, reflective of the largely Jewish, Italian, and African American working-class student body at this all-women, tuition-free public university. Part of branching out meant forming friendships she would not have otherwise. Young Communist League (YCL) devotee Helen Bierman (later Shonick) expanded Bella's thinking as they canvassed while "talking about everything."[45] Toussaint L'Ouverture club officer Patricia Williams (later Garland Morisey) "really move[d] the issues" for Bella, encouraging her to consider Black-Jewish connections.[46] Bella stood out as different to secular friends, seemingly going "to temple all the time."[47] These political friendships lasted. Hunter friends later joined her in the peace movement, worked on her campaigns, and served on her congressional staff.

Known at Hunter College as "Bella Savitzky, All Around Girl," she cut a distinct figure as a "dynamic type" who "makes full use of 5'6" with an "athletic body, nice hands, and hypnotic eyes."[48] In college, she shed her short bob and her favorite men's shoes for a new look of tailored suits, a change encouraged by her mother, who impressed upon her that leaders should look distinguished. While at Hunter, Bella moonlighted at the Jewish Theological Seminary, Conservative Judaism's flagship institution, pursuing an Israel Friedlaender Jewish education certification at its Teachers Institute. She desired to move on from teaching Hebrew to become a rabbi, a profession closed to women.[49] Recognizing this pursuit was futile, she left the program short of a degree once her secular path as a political science major was secure and her work as a student leader at Hunter took priority. There, professors such as Margaret Spahr, the first woman to graduate from Columbia Law School, groomed Bella to carry the suffrage torch forward in a career in law and government.[50]

At Hunter College, women were leading decision makers in every capacity. In these years, Bella made her first lobbying trips to Washington, engaged in an all-women model Congress, and learned how to translate social movement concerns into campus policy. Bella emerged as a leader because she had a well of enthusiasm and a committed network behind her, and she made time for extracurricular activities on a campus where most students had to work full time to get by. Elected as freshman class president, she rose through the ranks of student government to become student body president in 1940–1941. In this highest office, she promoted democratization in student government by introducing mandatory class meetings. She also encouraged interracial alliances by championing campaigns to introduce black studies and Jewish studies.[51] Some judged her leadership "fair and square," noting that "everyone with an axe to grind or a chip on her shoulder gets a chance to be heard."[52] But an anticommunist faction on campus believed she was heavy-handed, and prioritized the interests of a progressive bloc dominated by ASU members. This opposition did not stop Bella from winning the presidency by 400 votes, but it made her tenure difficult.[53]

Bella led Hunter College during a politically fraught moment as the United States prepared for war and New York became embroiled in a red scare. Taking sides as president, she amplified the messages "Keep America Out of War" and "Save Our Schools." This posture made her doubly suspect once the New York legislature's Rapp-Coudert Committee, which began as a budget inquiry, shifted its attention to Communist indoctrination in city schools. Students like Bella saw Rapp-Coudert as "an effort on the part of very significant, powerful and rich economic forces in this city to do away with the city college system."[54] Supporters of Rapp-Coudert, in contrast, deemed students like Bella either dupes or devious collaborators. In March 1941, the New York Post characterized her as a "campus pink" in a front-page profile. In it, Dorothy Schwartz, who led Hunter's anticommunist Thomas Mann Club, noted of Bella's campus leadership, "The girls got too much, from a minority group, of what represented the Communist Party line."[55]

Schwartz was not incorrect, but she missed how the Communist line could also be the Zionist line, a point Bella raised in her defense. Paying greater attention to the nuanced complexity of positions within the US Popular Front milieu reveals participants' independence and diversity. In August 1939, Joseph Stalin and Adolf Hitler entered a nonaggression pact that required Communists to shift their stance from one of collective security to anti-intervention. Communist-dominated organizations changed course so quickly it shocked many non-Communist progressives, causing left-liberal partnerships to fracture.[56] Bella later suggested she had been stunned and confused in this moment, but "there was no transition" for her after the Nazi-Soviet Pact as she had been more focused on Zionists' anti-imperialist critique of Britain.[57] Her anti-interventionist position was indeed a response to the British government's 1937 retreat from the Balfour Declaration after the Peel Commission recommended that Palestine be partitioned into separate Jewish and Arab states. Avukah leaders stressed the need to "fight British Imperialism," yet after 1939, they also critiqued the Soviet Union and distanced their club from the ASU.[58] Not following suit, Bella elected to keep one foot in each door. In antiwar debates on campus, she spoke as an anti-British Zionist, asking, "Does suppression of all democratic processes at home, and consistent exploitive policies in Palestine and India paint England unblushingly as their 'saviour of democracy'?"[59] But she did so also as a representative of the ASU, sticking with the group to which most of her friends still belonged, despite the club's membership dipping by two-thirds.[60]

Bella would repeat this pattern as the Cold War set in, affirming her loyalty to an organization marked as subversive just as they reached their most beleaguered state. An instinctive contrarian, she was attracted to arguing unpopular positions. Her entanglement in the New York Red Scare of 1940–1941 turned this sporting disposition into a reflexive political posture and made a staunch civil libertarian out of her. After this point, she railed against political and economic elites who used anticommunist censure to maintain "the status quo." She was not incorrect, but she failed to acknowledge how Communists too were motivated by self-interest. Under the leadership of William Z. Foster, the US Communist Party abandoned its "Communism is twentieth-century Americanism" appeal in favor of a more rigid reflection of Soviet policy.[61] As a student activist and lawyer, Bella had more to say about US leaders' abuse of power than the domestic totalitarian practices and geopolitical subterfuge of the Soviet Union. This is the reason the New York Post directed a negative spotlight on her, and why anticommunist researchers, government agents, and political adversaries later kept this clipping in their files.[62]

Frustrated by the effect, Abzug protested, "What difference does it make what I thought when I was eighteen years old?"[63] She made this statement in the final years of her life, still seething over how often the New York Post article had been replayed during her political career. Her early student activism cast a long shadow because she never abandoned the social democratic vision for change she exhibited at Hunter College. As a politician, she maintained a deep attachment to the ideal of Popular Front collectivism despite the Communist Party's authoritarianism. She believed US Communists' vigorous attention to racial, economic, and gender disparities outweighed their allegiance to a foreign entity and the Soviet Union's deleterious motives. Her willingness after 1939 to still work with Communists placed her among a dwindling minority of American progressives.

After World War II, the challenges of rebuilding Europe and the decolonization of its former empires were compounded by heightened tensions between the United States and the Soviet Union. At home, fear of Communist infiltration in US organizations and institutions mirrored foreign policy concerns over unstable nations falling, like dominoes, into the Soviet orbit. Following the introduction of President Harry Truman's Federal Employee Loyalty Program in 1947, government-led and independent anticommunist inquiries had the lasting effect of flattening out both the perception of the American Left and its real definition.[64] To outsiders, all radicalism looked and was judged the same. For reformers falling under scrutiny, it became riskier to promote wide-ranging social change. As a result, the US political landscape at midcentury leaned centrist, but politics, in these years, were not tame or free of dissent.

During the early Cold War, the American Left became more insular, anxious, and embattled, but it still maintained greater variety and wider concerns than its Communist wing. Bella sustained her independent radicalism, though her Socialist Zionist identity became less pronounced as she aged.

This fading of emphasis occurred, in part, because of the realized goal of Israel's founding in 1948. After her involvement in the US Popular Front, she continued to prioritize coalitional politics as a way to maximize her impact. For this reason, she quickly advanced from a singular focus on labor law to become a legal advocate willing to take cases on all fronts—civil rights, civil liberties, immigration, criminal justice, business, and family law. Defending the downtrodden, deviant, and defiant, she countered a "creeping paralysis" taking over the legal profession preoccupied with respectability and status.[65] In the process, she became both a believer in the law's potential as a tool of dissent, and a critic of its coercive and procedural trappings.

Defending "Un-Americans"

Bella never fit in at Columbia Law School, where she was one of nine female students admitted to the class of 1942. It had not been her first choice. Harvard Law School, predictably, rejected her because it did not admit women. Columbia Law was her mother's preference, for Bella received a scholarship, the Ivy League school was a short subway ride away, and she could still live at home. After four years at Hunter College, Bella had trouble adapting to Columbia Law's subdued, erudite, and male-centric atmosphere. She excelled scholastically, receiving a coveted spot as an editor of the *Columbia Law Review,* but working toward deadlines became a "form of torture."[66] Her deportment as a former campus organizer made her stand out, as did being Jewish, an ethnic group Dean Young B. Smith actively limited to one-third of the student body.[67] Bella and female classmates also faced daily reminders that they were barely tolerated on campus "for the duration" of the war.[68] The door of the bathroom Bella used had "wo" haphazardly penciled in before "men."[69] Esteemed professor Julius Goebel Jr. only called on women on "ladies day," when he forced them "into describing cases in which women were treated as chattels, treated as property, and denigrat[ed]."[70]

Bella refused to adapt. Instead, she urged her female classmates to go beyond their hushed conversations about unfair treatment to lodge formal grievances, an encouragement that did not gain traction.[71] Bella and her peers' growing awareness of the institutional sexism that encumbered their legal education reflected women's heightened expectation that wartime work would lead to social advancement. After World War II, the US government, in partnership with business interests, prioritized returning veterans' reconversion and valorized domesticity, thereby stifling women's wartime gains.[72] Yet, this narrowing of opportunity did not diminish the ambition of women such as Bella who refused to relinquish wartime access to jobs and education. She increasingly saw her individual push for professional recognition as part of a greater, unannounced collective struggle. Frequent check-ins with law school friends—National Association for the Advancement of Colored People (NAACP) staff attorney Constance Baker (later Motley), National Lawyers Guild colleague Gloria Agrin, and Washington, DC, lawyer Francine Salzman (later Temko)—made this lonely challenge as a minority in the profession more bearable. So, too, did her marriage to Martin Abzug in 1944.

Bella's nights with Martin softened her days, helping her brace routine discrimination such as being called a "menstruating lawyer."[73] Martin met Bella by chance when both vacationed with relatives in Florida. A Jewish student radical active at City College of New York, he had admired her from afar, hanging on to a clipping of her profile in the *New York Post*. While in the service, Martin courted with Bella by mail, each of them writing with unusual frankness about their expectations for a life partner. Bella made clear she wanted children but not at the cost of her legal career. Martin joined the family business, the Albetta Blouse Company, but set his heart on becoming the next great American novelist. He romanced Bella by typing up her legal notes late into the night, a skill she elected not to acquire.[74] Martin's intellectual encouragement, caregiving, and deep loyalty, already apparent during their courtship, would be the bedrock of their partnership rooted in a mutual commitment to radical politics. Uninterested in being on the front lines, Martin created the space and security that allowed Bella to take on taxing, underpaid, politically charged cases.

Although law school was "to the grindstone" and largely apolitical, Bella Abzug's exposure to legal realism deeply shaped her approach to legal practice.[75] Studying with legal realists including luminary Karl Llewellyn, Abzug learned that law, not sacrosanct, could be used for coercive and generative purposes.[76] This idea powerfully challenged legal formalism while still working within the parameters of procedure and precedent. To critics of this renegade school of thought, legal realists "sounded like the bar's

Bolsheviks."[77] For Abzug, legal realism provided greater direction, convincing her of the importance of studying case law to learn how it could be manipulated. Proponents of legal realism encouraged lawyers to work in the service of others in government, legal aid, and the burgeoning field of labor law, reinforcing her decision to pursue the latter. "I always felt that law was a social instrument for change," she often noted, reciting a central legal realist tenet as her own.[78]

Abzug had an opportunity to put her legal education to immediate use when she landed a coveted staff attorney position at the leftist labor law firm Witt & Cammer. She later suggested she took the job simply because they did not ask if she could type, but there was more to it than that. Partners Nathan Witt and Harold Cammer had impressed Abzug while she was at Hunter College when they represented professors she adored before the Rapp-Coudert Committee. Former students of Felix Frankfurter at Harvard Law School, Cammer and Witt developed reputations as prominent New Deal lawyers (Witt was especially notable for his role in drafting the Wagner Act). In 1936, they also helped found the National Lawyers Guild, a bar association in which Abzug became heavily involved that offered an inclusive, left-liberal alternative to the American Bar Association.[79]

Working at Witt & Cammer from 1945 to 1948 taught Abzug that even the most enlightened unionists and their lawyers could harbor deepseated prejudices in spite of being good on class. Although Cammer and Witt gave Abzug encouraging guidance, she had few fond memories of her time at the firm. "I was breaking my neck, working for them day and night," and striking unionists "were getting arrested all the time." One partner in the firm, former Congress of Industrial Organizations general counsel Lee Pressman, "would have me go to court with him and carry his briefcase." When a collective bargaining session "didn't go right," they would say, "it's because of the *maidel*," meaning woman in Yiddish.[80] Abzug's accounts of these unwarranted episodes of workplace discrimination were not imagined. She stood out as one of a handful of women staff attorneys working at labor law firms in New York City. Within the entire profession, the number of women in law schools increased from 3 to 12 percent during World War II but dropped back down to its prewar presence after.[81] Her firm's clients were tough guys—mine workers, autoworkers, steelworkers, longshoremen, furriers, bartenders—in the most radical locals in New York, unaccustomed to dealing with women lawyers. Pressman, a silent partner who returned to the firm full-time in fall 1947, did not distinguish Abzug from a secretary and treated all staff as "just part of the help."[82]

In her first days of lawyering, Abzug developed strategies that carried her forward professionally when navigating this difficult work environment. She began to wear hats to court so that, as she explained, "They knew I was there for business."[83] She ate candy and comfort food to get through long waits for client hearings at night court. She schooled clerical staff to treat her as an equal to male lawyers, directing, "If you call Harold Mr. Cammer, you will not call me Bella, you will call me Mrs. Abzug." And, according to lawyer Ralph Shapiro, who shared an office at Witt & Cammer with Abzug, she talked on the phone a lot, loudly, and "had a low trigger for getting upset and excited."[84]

Abzug angered easily, but she had reasons to be angry. Pressman, whom she felt "treated me like I was a non-entity," thwarted her opportunity to become a partner in the firm, and she left in 1948.[85] Abzug also read the writing on the wall, watching a conservative turn in the labor movement take hold. She entered the field of labor law during an exciting and busy postwar upswing of union activity. She left as her bosses braced from the aftershocks of the 1947 Taft-Hartley Act, which constrained collective bargaining and required union leadership to sign political loyalty oaths.[86] Abzug expanded her specialties beyond labor law, taking on estate, contract, and divorce cases to offset pro bono and low-paying political cases. She favored solo practice thereafter, making only one exception in 1953–1956, when she entered a partnership with fellow Guild member Howard N. Meyer. The firm became Abzug & Meyer because she had convinced him that naming her first would achieve a small measure of equity for the injuries she and other women lawyers suffered as minorities in the legal field. She further argued, in case Meyer needed more convincing, that *A* appeared before *M* in the alphabet.[87]

Abzug personalized a broader political fight for women's recognition she helped advance within the National Lawyers Guild. As a member of the New York chapter's Constitutional Rights Committee, in 1948 she helped draft an incisive report on women's experience in the legal profession. Noting how women worked "in the offices of progressives but are lost in the background," its authors emphasized that the "struggle for equality for women . . . is still going on." They urged women to "take their places as leaders" but also faulted men in progressive circles for their bias and inaction, arguing, "This fight can only be won if in the course of the struggle all traces of male chauvinism are removed."[88] This report, drawing on Abzug's experience, reflected leftist lawyers' feminist orientation. Although, they did not self-identify as feminist, a classification they associated with elite women in the National Woman's Party, they contributed to a legal vanguard that laid the foundation for the specialization of women and law that developed in the early 1970s. Unfortunately, while women lawyers had a visible presence in the Guild, little came of their agitation after 1948, when the group prioritized defense of civil liberties and its own organizational survival.

Abzug became a Guild lawyer because the bar association's principles reflected her worldview and she was comfortable in the company of its largely Jewish members. She joined during a postwar membership drive that increased the number of affiliates from 803 in 1946 to 3,188 in 1948 and stuck with the National Lawyers Guild during its subsequent deep dive, with membership hovering near 500 for the next decade.[89] Before the Nazi-Soviet Pact, New Deal Democrats and Popular Front leftists coexisted in the bar association. After 1939, frequent attempts to introduce loyalty oaths failed, and those uncomfortable with open membership exited. This pariah status grew as Guild lawyers were increasingly targeted in public and clandestine domestic Communism containment efforts. In 1947, FBI director J. Edgar Hoover ordered wiretaps to be installed at National Lawyers Guild headquarters, taking a special interest in monitoring the lawyers who represented the bulk of "un-Americans." In 1950, HUAC characterized the group as the "legal bulwark of the Communist Party."[90] And in 1953, Attorney General Herbert Brownell announced he might add the Guild to his "quasi-official blacklist," the List of Subversive Organizations, an action the bar association stalled by suing Brownell.[91] Abzug could have left at any of these moments. Instead, she doubled down, identifying as a Guild lawyer financially and professionally committed to its counter-challenge of state secrecy and political repression.[92]

Abzug did not think twice about forging a career in these quarters, despite the repercussions, because she felt most at home among these imperiled, defiant attorneys. As one colleague noted, it was the "only bar association in which a political left winger who was a lawyer could live."[93] Guild lawyers formed an intimacy heightened by the shared struggle they faced as anticommunist attacks threatened their organization's future. During the McCarthy period, defense of oneself accompanied the professional obligations of defending others. Most Guild lawyers were under surveillance; had difficulty staying financially solvent; worried about potential contempt citations, disbarment, and jail time; and experienced family and friends who pulled away, fearing guilt by association. In this isolated state, Guild lawyers depended on each other for case referrals, social connection, career mentorship, and legal representation.

Abzug's early legal career mirrored this pattern of professional rebellion and dealing with the residual damage. High-profile cases she took on in the late 1940s and early 1950s secured her reputation as a tenacious lawyer admired within leftist circles, but at the cost of new clients and ostracizing family. Martin's brother Malcolm would not associate with Bella and Martin after government agents questioned him about their politics. Bella was convinced that "people were scared to come to the office."[94] It is difficult to measure the extent to which Abzug's political cases limited the growth of her practice, since her office records and case files have not been preserved. Unsatisfying as it is, her appearance in Guild organizational records and the paper trail of her most prominent cases provide a window into how she approached the law during these years. What is clear is she became a maverick among renegades.

In the 1950s, Abzug waved the banner of First Amendment rights when it was extremely risky to do so. When called before committees, a witness could admit or deny Party membership, testify about political affiliations, object on procedural grounds, or refuse to name names (referred to as "the diminished fifth"). Civil liberties lawyers hotly debated which strategy to recommend. Within the National Lawyers Guild, the presence of lawyers openly defending US Communist Party leaders and affiliates facing Smith Act violations added a further layer of tension. Abzug worked with these Communist lawyers, but she was not part of their inner circle and was not invited to their strategy sessions that often occurred before Guild conventions.[95] Nevertheless, she was highly influenced by one such lawyer, Abraham Unger, who argued in testimony before Senator Joe McCarthy, "As a legal question you have no right to inquire into the political beliefs and opinions of people."[96] Abzug acknowledged lawyers who promoted Fifth Amendment defenses "pilloried Unger" for his stance, which, on this occasion, led the McCarthy Committee to hold him in contempt of

Congress.[97] Abzug sided with Unger and likely received the same criticism. Civil liberties attorney and Guild heavyweight Leonard Boudin believed a Fifth Amendment defense was "the safest course to follow, if a person did not want to have to either go to jail or name other people eventually."[98] This line of defense protected testifiers against self-incrimination, but it also became an implicit admission of guilt. To encourage the opposite, as Abzug did, demonstrates how she favored principle over pragmatism as a civil libertarian. It also suggests her civil liberties practice was small, attracting only clients willing to consider the precarious path of being an unfriendly witness.

Abzug recommended that clients take risks she personally faced. She was questioned as a witness before grand juries in both 1949 and 1951.[99] Because these records are sealed, it is not possible to know if she argued definitively then, as she would later, that "the Constitution permits any kind of ideas and thinking you please to have, and that no government has a right to interfere, ask questions, or challenge that thinking."[100] She eluded contempt citations when testifying on these occasions. Still, the experience unsettled her to the point she never talked about it.

Challenging the Sexual Color Line

Abzug recalled more readily how she had played a small part in building momentum toward dismantling de jure segregation. Her defense of African American Mississippian Willie McGee during 1948–1951 secured her reputation as a rights advocate, but also as a suspect lawyer. The black-on-white rape case began when McGee was convicted in 1945 by an all-white, male jury in less than two and a half minutes, and ended with McGee's state-administered execution on May 8, 1951, a lethal punishment reserved overwhelmingly for black men. Abzug highlighted this race-based discrimination when she helped lead McGee's defense during his appeal.[101] More unusual for the time, she and cocounsel openly discussed the sexual politics at play late in McGee's appeal. In 1950, when all other arguments had been exhausted, Abzug advocated that McGee's contention that he had a consensual extramarital affair with his accuser, Wiletta Hawkins, be introduced. The veracity of McGee's and Hawkins's claims remains unverifiable, leading investigators then and since to uncover a web of inaccuracies in the public record that cast a shadow over the case.[102] Abzug believed her client to be innocent, and she saw Hawkins and McGee as equally victimized by a southern criminal justice system that did not afford them sexual agency.

Abzug recognized, quite simply, that rape law had moved far from its original intent to protect women to become the leading mechanism to police the sexual color line. Forming this understanding, she drew on the arguments presented by antilynching activists Ida B. Wells and Jessie Daniel Ames, as well as those of contemporary leftist and black women who theorized about the interlinkages of race, class, and gender oppression.[103] It is clear Abzug hoped the legal challenge of the sexual color line delivered during McGee's appeal would extend further than male cocounsel were prepared to go. In one draft, she wrote that the case was tainted "by the distorted mores of the State of Mississippi which makes sex relations voluntarily entered into between a Negro man and a white woman a greater offense than the crime of rape itself."[104] Final briefs delivered a more palatable, less feminist critique, generally highlighting the existence of an interracial, extramarital affair, but shying away from deconstructing the full implications of McGee's criminalization. Even so, Abzug's attention to sexual freedom alongside racial justice reveals how deeply she understood "the personal is political" before this concept came into wide use. Her McGee defense nurtured her belief that people should have a right to love whomever they please, a view she extended to gay and lesbian rights during her time in Congress.

Unfortunately for McGee, Abzug's role in his case did not aid his chances of survival. She and cocounsel John Coe attempted to frame McGee's defense within the parameters of Cold War foreign policy interests, writing to President Truman, "We cannot deny the significance of our civil rights record as an issue in world affairs. . . . We dare not preach freedom abroad and tolerate its absence at home."[105] In the early 1950s, the US government increasingly, if reluctantly, intervened in civil rights matters as a strategy to offset the negative impact of Soviet Union propaganda highlighting public segregation and racial violence. Yet, the Truman administration and the US Supreme Court drew a line between acceptable and unacceptable civil rights advocates and civil rights claims. The McGee case, dealing with the most intimate, taboo concern of racial intermixing became a global cause célèbre of the American Left. The Civil Rights Congress (CRC), which HUAC

Figure 1.2 Life magazine published this image of Bella Abzug and Florida lawyer John Coe after their client African American Willie McGee was executed in Mississippi in 1951. The accompanying article blamed McGee's "imported" lawyers for his death rather than racist prosecution and sentencing practices. (Robert W. Kelly / The LIFE Picture Collection / Getty Images)

characterized as a Communist front in 1947, led McGee's defense during a time when the NAACP was seen as suspect, yet more tolerable.[106] These characteristics made the McGee case untouchable.

Recruited through Guild channels, Abzug did not fully comprehend how much Cold War politics constricting civil liberties had also narrowed the spectrum for civil rights. Only a few years into her legal career, her inexperience mattered less than her legal ties. This career-making case was her big break and, she hoped, her first chance to argue before the Supreme Court, a dream unrealized. Only Justice Hugo Black voted to hear the case, and he intervened once, providing McGee a stay of execution after Abzug and others met with him in chambers.[107] During the course of McGee's appeal, Abzug often reached out to her law school friend Constance Baker Motley, hoping she might compel the NAACP to be more involved. Thurgood Marshall, however, had little interest in being tarred by the CRC's leftist reputation. The "Save Willie McGee" campaign grabbed headlines with demonstrations such as one in which protesters chained themselves to the Lincoln Memorial. Although Abzug appeared at CRC events, she criticized its leaders William Patterson and Aubrey Grossman for prioritizing direct action at the cost of legal action. While she challenged this strategy internally, she reserved public animus for Mississippi journalists and state officials, whom she faulted for creating a culture of fear and violence.[108]

Representing McGee required considerable nerve. Several of his local trial attorneys abandoned the case when they faced the risk of disbarment and threats to their lives. Governor Fielding Wright made clear, "We will not tolerate a wild-eyed, howling mob of Communists and sympathizers, gathered by the CRC to stage a demonstration in Mississippi."[109] He refused to provide Abzug and cocounsel with police protection, leading Abzug to publicly warn, if "harm comes to anyone, we will hold you personally responsible."[110] Abzug also sought federal intervention, writing the State Department on one occasion to ask for assistance, a request denied. The US government monitored development in the McGee case on the ground, but not for the reasons Abzug had hoped. The FBI cited her defense of McGee and membership in the National Lawyers Guild as reasons to open an internal security file on her in January 1951, a few months before her client's death.[111]

Government agents were in Jackson when Abzug experienced her most traumatic run-in with local vigilantes in March 1951. She arrived in town a day before a hearing on new evidence before Judge Sidney Mize of the Southern Mississippi District Court. The hotel where she had a reservation refused to house her, concerned that its business would be harmed. Exhausted and very pregnant, Abzug opted to wait out the night awake in a bathroom stall at the bus station. Hearing her name called out on the intercom in the middle of the night sent a shiver down her spine. The next day, she delivered a rousing argument on behalf of McGee, her defense of his bodily rights amplified by the threat to her own body.[112] Once home, Abzug learned that *Jackson Daily News* editor Frederick Sullens had warned in print, "If Mrs. Abzug ever again appears in Mississippi, either as a lawyer or as an individual, it will be one time too often. . . . Too bad the courts don't have authority to send some lawyers to the electric chair along with their clients."[113] Distressed, she passed the clipping along to Abraham Unger, writing him, "Abe, see what I mean."[114]

Abzug's inability to move the higher courts to intervene on behalf of Willie McGee dampened her faith in court-centered legal activism. She believed Judge Mize to be "the most enlightened but not very" of Mississippi judges, but it did not surprise her when he elected not to give McGee's case new life, instead determining, "There must be an end to litigation."[115] Working one last legal angle elsewhere, Abzug was not on-site when McGee was executed in a traveling electric chair set up in the very courtroom of his first trial in Laurel, Mississippi, an episode covered by local news stations as if it were a sporting event. Listening by phone, Abzug felt forever unsettled by the approving "bloodcurdling screams" that lit through the large crowd.

This civil rights loss, coinciding with fruitless civil liberties defenses, reinforced Abzug's feeling "that there was something so terribly, terribly wrong with our democracy."[116] She connected McGee's death to a personal tragedy, having suffered a late-term miscarriage shortly after her sleepless night in the Jackson bus station.[117] She often recounted this string of losses sorrowfully to friends, congressional staff, and her two daughters, the imprint of McGee's life clear from the portrait of her client that hung in her home.[118] In the immediate aftermath of his execution, *Life* magazine profiled Willie McGee's case and placed the greatest blame for his death on his "imported" lawyers.[119] Furious, Abzug fired back, "You attempt to convey the impression that there was no question of McGee's guilt. The very opposite is true, and that is why so many people (not solely the Communists) believed in his innocence and will always believe McGee was framed by the State of Mississippi because he was a Negro."[120]

Denying the force of anticommunism, Abzug idealistically and incorrectly believed that a shared commitment to civil rights would compel lawyers of different political persuasions to build this legal specialization together. She hung on to the wishful belief that "Thurgood [Marshall] actually intended to play a role" in McGee's defense.[121] Yet, her friendship with Constance Baker Motley was not enough to bridge an organizational left-liberal divide, and overtures the Guild made to the NAACP, particularly after its success with *Brown v. Board of Education* (1954), were not reciprocated. Abzug was a "prime mover" in the Guild, pushing for the establishment of a national interracial network of civil rights lawyers that, quixotically, would work without "conflict with the actions of any existing organization."[122] In October 1952, 277 lawyers from twenty-seven states attended a Guild-sponsored civil rights conference in New York City. Although a historic gathering, this one-off event did not amount to a sustained civil rights legal network. The venture fizzled in 1953, when the filing of *NLG v. Brownell* captured Guild leaders' attention and the bar association subsequently prioritized civil liberties over civil rights. Likewise, Abzug's challenge of state regulation of sexual intimacy during McGee's appeal was not a sustained feature of her civil rights practice.

After McGee's death, Abzug made a conscious decision not to return to the South, promising her husband, Martin, she would engage in local civil rights activism while their family was young. In 1952, Bella and Martin purchased his parents' home in Mount Vernon, New York, where they raised their two daughters—Eve (Egee), born in 1949, and Isobel Jo (Liz), born in 1952—away from the city bustle. Reluctant to contribute to "white flight," Bella and Martin were attracted to this bedroom community just beyond the Bronx because it was relatively diverse, with Jewish, Italian, and African American residents. In many ways, this suburban existence was idyllic. Their brick colonial home, a duplex that brought in extra income, sat on a corner lot overlooking a quiet, tree-lined street. Bella never found comfort in these quarters, however, wary of the cult of domesticity many neighbors embraced. The Abzug home remained a politicized space, where she and Martin hosted political friends and taught their daughters not to believe everything they learned in school. Bella was noticeably absent for long stretches, leaving Eve and Liz in the care of African American housekeeper Alice Williams, who had moved with the Abzugs from Manhattan. Williams's presence in their lives for more than twenty-five years reflected the family's affluence, as well as their dependence on her home management skills down to mastery of beloved Jewish recipes.[123] Williams's domestic labor enabled Bella and Martin to become heavily involved in the Graham Neighborhood Association, through which they supported residential and school integration campaigns.

Deeply engaged in the integration struggle in the 1950s, Bella Abzug believed *Brown v. Board of Education* to be a tepid, inadequate decision that left much of the Jim Crow system intact. In a 1955 law review article, she argued that justices' imprecise directive that school integration occur "with all deliberate speed" opened the process to southern legislatures' "legal bottlenecks to forestall the inevitable."[124] She estimated only localized mass mobilization coupled with robust federal enforcement of *Brown* would thwart antisegregationists' crafty maneuvering. Essentially, by this point, Abzug's view that court action was the surest and quickest route to radical change had soured.

BELLA ABZUG'S FIRST DECADE of legal practice had been riddled with losses, deepening her feeling that litigation could be tedious, sluggish, and futile. Disappointment and pragmatism compelled her to look past the courts to other theaters of engagement. The US Congress was one such arena. In the early 1950s, Abzug joined a team of Guild lawyers who drafted a comprehensive civil rights bill, a process she found stimulating.[125] Thereafter, she argued in these quarters that lawyers should be involved in statutory development alongside litigation. Additionally, Abzug softened her critique of direct action, deeply moved by what unfolded in Montgomery and Little Rock. Court-based activism, she determined, would gain little momentum if lawyers did not partner with grassroots organizers and sympathetic politicians who could apply social pressure on judges. While she continued her legal practice, she increasingly used her off-hours to support issue-focused campaigns. Abzug had little patience for incrementalism, the case-by-case strategy civil rights lawyers favored by the mid-1950s to dismantle racist and sexist laws using the standard set by *Brown*. Approaching law as a leftist, she remained skeptical that ameliorative fixes to achieve "equality before law" would greatly change the underlying structures of power that drive inequality.[126]

Later, in Congress, Abzug delivered a biting critique of US postwar affluence and militarization rooted in her experience as a cause lawyer during the early Cold War. In the thick of the Red Scare, she had professionally defied anticommunist fearmongering and personally resisted the trappings of domesticity. Seeing McCarthyism as a bigger threat than Communism, Abzug underplayed the national security concerns brought on by US-Soviet tensions and the damaging presence of domestic spies. Nonetheless, she correctly recognized that economic and political elites had brandished anticommunism too widely as an operative tool used to control marginalized people, maintain social norms, and limit dissent.[127]

Few lawyers overtly countered Cold War policy in the courts, and doing so made Abzug susceptible to violence, censure, and surveillance. While she exhibited an outward fearlessness, living in a constant state of vigilance and noncompliance left her with battle fatigue and a lasting paranoia about being watched. Abzug did not know the extent to which FBI and CIA agents kept tabs on her, including interviewing her neighbors, frequently calling her home, securing her educational records, tracking her movements when traveling, following her employees, interviewing informants, and opening her international mail. J. Edgar Hoover overrode the FBI New York field office's recommendation to remove Abzug from the bureau's Security Index in 1955 on account of there being "no evidence of CP membership," for the director reserved special animus for Guild lawyers.[128] Likewise, Abzug's preoccupation with "spooks" continued, perplexing acquaintances who met her after the 1950s. Political adviser Ronnie Eldridge would never forget how Abzug stopped by her apartment for a debriefing session during the 1970 campaign, and insisted that the conversation take place in the bathroom with water running just in case someone was listening.[129]

Pressure on radicals eased after June 17, 1957, when the US Supreme Court issued its "Red Monday" decisions indicating it would no longer uphold Smith Act convictions.[130] Guild lawyers Abzug knew had fielded most of these cases. The National Lawyers Guild took the Supreme Court's action as a personal win further sweetened by newly appointed Attorney General William P. Rogers's announcement he would not designate the group as a subversive organization.[131] Despite this reversal of fortune, Abzug never shook the feeling that the prejudices and anxieties that stirred the Red Scare remained an indelible feature of US culture. Likewise, she reminded those who battled an encroaching Red Menace of the rabble-rousers they had once faced. Both sides described these years as a fight for survival, one that uprooted relationships, tested beliefs, and left the future uncertain. The experience would not be easily forgotten, reverberating in American politics going forward.

While Abzug remembered the difficult times that leftists faced during the Red Scare, she preferred to dwell on the principles and passions that first animated her politics. Her thoughts returned to the excitement she experienced as a student organizer at Hunter College, where she found common cause with other progressives working toward a social democratic future. Recalling this example of women-centered collectivism, Abzug realized she was ready for a change. As the National Lawyers Guild focused on rebuilding in the late 1950s, she questioned if this group to which she had devoted great energy fully appreciated her talents and commitment.

This radical bar association, she found, had a glass ceiling. She had gained influence in the New York chapter, elected to its executive board in 1952, but had difficulty advancing further.[132] It took until 1970 for San Francisco lawyer Doris Brin Walker to be elected as the Guild's first woman president. Restless, Abzug decided not to wait for this change. Instead, she became a "key woman" in Women Strike for Peace, a nuclear disarmament group formed in 1961. This volunteer work primed Abzug for her political career.

2

A NEW POLITICS

BELLA ABZUG WAS NOT A FOUNDER of Women Strike for Peace (WSP), though she rarely corrected those who assumed she had been there from the start. Instead, she arrived a week late, spurred on by stories of the group's inaugural strike on November 1, 1961. After the fact, she learned how exciting and meaningful it had been to march with other women in protest of US-Soviet nuclear brinkmanship.[1] On November 9, Abzug participated in WSP's second action in New York, a picket outside the United Nations complex. She fell in line, marching while holding a yellow balloon inscribed with the message "Women Want Peace," but she grumbled as she traipsed along. One demonstrator, Claire Reed, asked Abzug what was wrong. "This is all very good, but this is not the end of everything," she responded, "there's much more to be done."[2] Reed concurred, highlighting how much they could do in neighborhoods, in political clubs, and in legislatures. Pleased, Abzug brought Reed back to her law office near Bryant Park. There, she worked through her Rolodex, spouting off names that Reed hurriedly jotted down. And so commenced Abzug's efforts to turn WSP, an impromptu women's disarmament mobilization, into a decisive lobbying powerhouse.

During the 1960s, Abzug emerged as the principal political director of Women Strike for Peace and an influential grassroots coordinator who Democratic candidates from local offices to presidential hopefuls called on to get out the vote. At decade's end, Abzug squarely identified as a progressive Democrat committed to promoting radical change through electoral politics. She became a leading New Politics Democrat, voicing the concerns of this loosely aligned reformist faction that pushed from the left within the Democratic Party and gained influence by 1968. At the opening of the 1960s, however, she did not identify as a Democrat, had devoted limited attention to electoral politics, and had not yet cultivated a political base.

Abzug's gradual, deliberative move toward a "new politics" is emblematic of American leftists' reevaluation of priorities, reworking of strategies, and reassertion of presence during the early 1960s. The decline of anticommunist fervor provided an opening for more robust political expression of radicalism. Sit-ins at drugstore lunch counters in the South reminded the nation that the desegregation struggle was far from complete. Peace activists too felt a heightened sense of urgency as Cold War tensions resumed, brought on in 1961 by the construction of the Berlin Wall and the Soviet launch of "Tsar Bomba," the most powerful nuclear weapon ever tested. Facing longstanding crises once more, progressive activists determined that the nation's social, political, and economic problems would not be solved without new organizations, new concepts, and new blood. Yet, the idea that the "Old Left" died and a distinct "New Left" appeared at this juncture discounts how prior political objectives and organizing styles were carried forward.[3] Trying to delineate a clear break downplays the exchange among activists across and within age-groups over which issues and tactics to abandon or newly pursue.

Contrary to popular memory, sixties radicals were more than rebel youth. Abzug, a rebel still, saw the passing of McCarthyism as an opportunity for leftists to reassert a social democratic vision for change through political engagement at the community level and in Washington. Some leftists in her age set, fearing a "generational gap" in leadership, judged new groups like Students for a Democratic Society (SDS) and the Student Nonviolent Coordinating Committee (SNCC) to be amorphous, antagonistic, and underdeveloped.[4] Abzug's involvement in Women Strike for Peace made her more receptive to new emphases in political organizing and made it clear this repositioning did not occur solely along generational lines. WSP affiliates, young and old, rejected what they saw as a masculinist model of centralized leadership, instead developing a fluid, nonhierarchical decision-making style that came to be known as "participatory democracy."

Abzug's work in WSP alongside dear Hunter College friends opened her to greater influence. In the company of familiar collaborators, she tried out new organizing approaches, while also critiquing them. She embraced the demand for greater democratization without abandoning the view that movements needed leaders and she was equipped to be one. She participated in street protests, while arguing that mass mobilization would be ineffective if demonstrators did not link direct action to political action. Radicals, she believed, must bring "protest to power."[5]

Idealistically, Abzug envisioned that leftists could build a powerful alliance that matched the creativity and potency of the Goldwater coalition, the hard-right grassroots insurgency that secured Senator Barry Goldwater's nomination as the Republican presidential candidate in 1964. She believed that if workers left out of the New Deal coalition (women and racial minorities) joined with issue-focused progressives (those against poverty and for peace) they could create an expansive Democratic coalition that checked the influence of liberal Cold Warriors and southern Democrats. In 1970, Abzug ran as a progressive urban populist who sought to realize this "new politics" drawing on the power of "the people." In the early 1960s, although hugely ambitious, she hardly had the clout to spur a progressive Democratic insurgency, but it did not stop her from thinking imaginatively about how to achieve this goal.

Participatory Democracy

In Women Strike for Peace, decisions were made by phone tree, with one woman calling the next to spread the word that an action had been planned. Abzug excelled in this format as an avid debater who loved to talk on the phone and carried on until those on the receiving end were persuaded. Often these calls, placed to forgiving friends, occurred after bedtime. Aroused from slumber, they would whisper to their husbands, "She does her best work at night. Go back to sleep. I'll talk soft. Bella, don't yell."[6] Effective as she was in moving her agenda forward, Abzug had trouble adapting to this undefined style of decision making, preferring the bureaucratic pyramid of local and national boards delineated in the National Lawyers Guild. Abzug appreciated how WSP's dispersed model of "un-organization" sped up the time from idea to execution and allowed for greater innovation, but she also saw WSP's purposeful "unparliamentary way of proceeding" as a leadership gap.[7] Abzug took advantage of this opening, immediately asserting that WSP should engage in lobbying in addition to rallies. She first presented this position in New York, where she had an established web of influence.

Abzug's participation in WSP marked her return to the women-centered organizing that had animated her college years. Living separate, parallel lives, many women veterans of the 1930s student movement revisited their earlier concerns of antifascism and peace when working toward nuclear disarmament. Abzug's Hunter circle in WSP included Judy Lerner, who often carpooled with her to the city, where they met up with Amy Swerdlow and Mim Kelber at meetings. Her social network soon expanded, including Barbara Bick and Eleanor Garst in Washington, DC, Mary Clarke in Los Angeles, and Claire Reed, Shirley Margolin, and Lorraine Gordon in New York. These activist friends stimulated Abzug. "How many times did we sit talking 'till 2–3 in the morning after a meeting?" recalled WSP collaborator Elaine Kuntz. "You did a lot of talking, you also listened—and what's more, paid attention."[8]

Abzug's volunteerism diverted attention from her legal practice, making it easier over time to imagine taking the professional leap from lawyering to public office. Daytime meetings were not an inconvenience for many participants who did not work, but for Abzug, attendance diverted her attention from paying legal clients. She made this sacrifice because she saw her disarmament work as an expression of her motherly love and an extension of her parenting. WSP consumer boycotts altered how her family ate, with powdered milk introduced as a replacement for potentially radioactive milk. Daughters Liz and Eve knew they were not allowed to participate in duck-and-cover drills at school, a reflection of WSP's rejection of civil defense preparation. These choices ran counter to normative cultural practice. Defying convention took strength, which they drew from each other. As Eve observed, "They really did enjoy themselves. I think that's a huge thing that may be overlooked."[9]

The New York wing of WSP was its most left-leaning and most immediately on board with the political program Abzug envisioned. She attended her first planning meeting in early December 1961. There, she emphasized that "in addition to showing outrage, despair and other important emotions," women peace activists should "influence change through existing procedures" and change policy as they could.[10] Abzug's critique sounded familiar to this audience, gathered at the Upper West Side apartment of

Roberta Cohn, a longtime radical married to labor lawyer Sidney Cohn and formerly blacklisted actor John Garfield. New York WSP formed a Central Coordinating Committee to bring more structure to their organizing than WSP had imposed nationally. Abzug convinced this receptive body to create a legislative committee with her at its head.[11] From this new post, she expeditiously set in motion WSP's first full-scale lobbying campaign.

Abzug believed this effort must emanate from New York, unfairly judging WSP founders based in Washington, DC, to be political amateurs. Yet, it was their overt stance against anticommunism that had encouraged her to join. WSP cofounder Dagmar Wilson had been active in the National Committee for a Sane Nuclear Policy (SANE) and left that group after formally critiquing its decision in 1960 to revive its loyalty oath policy and purge suspected Communists. On September 21, 1961, she convened a meeting with Eleanor Garst, Margaret Russell, Folly Fodor, Jeanne Bagby, and others to form a different kind of organization. WSP was the antithesis of SANE—women-centered, nonhierarchical, and politically inclusive. In this spirit, WSP cofounders wrote an open letter to Jacqueline Kennedy, in which they proclaimed, "It is not better to be dead than Red."[12] They also decided not to have formal membership or create members lists, out of fear they could be used by government or private entities to harass and prosecute their affiliates. This openness attracted Abzug, who had been active with Martin in SANE up to the organization's anticommunist turn.[13] Recognizing that Wilson did not share her leftist ties, Abzug saw WSP as a politically diverse group that could help foster a return to left-liberal partnership thwarted during the Red Scare.

Abzug noted how disarming WSP's moralistic performance of respectable motherhood could be, but she rightly anticipated that this image would make it harder for peace women to cultivate a reputation as adept political operators. She begrudgingly showed up at protests in the designated uniform of tailored suits and white gloves. She had little patience, however, for Folly Fodor's story line related in the *Saturday Review* after WSP's initial strike: "We were overwhelmed . . . we were not organizers . . . we've got brains and no experience."[14] Formerly active in the Young People's Socialist League, the Democratic Party, and SANE, Fodor had plenty of political experience. Abzug believed it was a mistake to underplay the longstanding activity and cultivated expertise of strikers who spent much of the 1950s active in PTAs, neighborhood associations, party clubs, unions, religious groups, and professional associations. Rather, she sought to augment the political edge present in WSP's first call to action, which urged women to "tell our elected representatives that they are not properly representing US by continuing the arms race and increasing the threat of total destruction."[15]

The success of the organized lobby orchestrated by Abzug on January 15, 1962, convinced WSP participants to follow a "demonstration/lobbying format" in all subsequent major actions.[16] Media sources—and President John F. Kennedy—paid the most attention to 2,000 soggy demonstrators standing in the rain with homemade signs with messages such as, "When it rains, it pours—strontium 90." Noting the protesters outside, Kennedy publicly commented, "I think these women are extremely earnest, and that they are concerned as we all are at the possibility of a nuclear war."[17] Representatives on Capitol Hill personally learned how earnest WSP lobbyists were when they came calling unexpectedly. Abzug's team, equipped with incisive, well-researched talking points, met with more than thirty congressmen and high-ranking officials, including Adrian Fisher, deputy director of the Arms Control and Disarmament Agency. Delivering four clear positions, they argued, "The differences are not insurmountable between the U.S. and Soviet Union to bring both sides to a disarmament agreement; the appropriations and powers of the Arms Control and Disarmament Agency should be extended; U.S. support of the United Nations should be improved; and nuclear tests should cease."[18] Unsurprisingly, not all members of Congress were receptive to their visits. Even so, Abzug was heartened by the "determination on the part of the women not only to continue their work but to improve and intensify it."[19]

Abzug's next venture, a campaign to collect "a million votes pledged to peace" during the 1962 midterm election, reflected her attention to developments in the black freedom movement and her analysis of past women's rights organizing.[20] Transitioning from sit-ins to voting drives, the NAACP, SNCC, Southern Christian Leadership Conference, and Congress of Racial Equality collaborated to form the Voter Education Project. Abzug kept abreast of this effort through the National Lawyers Guild, which increasingly fielded lawyers to defend these civil rights protesters. This activity heightened her focus on political citizenship and made her think more deeply about the power of the vote. Even so, she elected not to join the frontline challenge of racial disenfranchisement, instead focusing on activating largely white women with access to voting. Her legislative committee studied polling data from the 1960 presidential election, and found that women were a swing vote of "as little as 2%" in some districts. "Should the time come when we controlled that 2% our power would be enormous and we could use it without taking sides politically or endorsing candidates in the ordinary sense of the word," Abzug reported at WSP's 1962 convention.[21] She came to this conclusion after reading Eleanor Flexner's *Century of Struggle,* a moving account of the long campaign for women's suffrage published in 1959.[22] A political field guide for Abzug, this book offered her an outline of how to build a multilevel lobbying campaign and solidified her commitment to a long game working toward gender parity in politics. Thinking of WSP differently thereafter, she urged her colleagues to see their disarmament work as part of a continuous and interrelated struggle for women's civil rights, economic independence, and world peace.

Recommending that others read Flexner, Abzug found it easier to convince WSP participants to contribute time to electoral politics than to stimulate their political awakening. At the first "Wispuree" in Ann Arbor, Michigan, in June 1962, WSP affiliates voted to move forward with a national peace pledge campaign. "Willy nilly we are a political factor and . . . no amount of study or demonstrating will achieve our ends unless we can force the issues on to the floor of the House and Senate," wrote Elsa Knight Thompson, thoroughly persuaded by Abzug's swing vote pitch.[23] The group's "Guide to Legislative and Political Action" outlined characteristic features of issue-focused grassroots campaigns: canvass shopping centers, penetrate party clubs, create separate peace action committees, draft voter guidelines, and interview and endorse peace candidates. What set WSP apart was the women's rights framework that Abzug helped introduce immediately and overtly. One early press release she wrote noted, "It took the suffragettes fifty years to get the vote. With the threat of nuclear disaster hanging over our heads, we have to use our votes to get peace within the next few years."[24] In doing so, she cast WSP's activism as part of women's unfinished struggle to attain full political citizenship.

During this first peace pledge campaign, WSP did not advocate increasing the number of women running for office. Abzug's pragmatic assessment of women's viability as candidates narrowed her focus horizontally to maximizing women's use of "the political power of the vote."[25] Yet, even with greater political clout, WSP—and women—had no guarantee

Figure 2.1 In Women Strike for Peace, Bella Abzug encouraged participants to promote the goal of gender parity in electoral politics alongside disarmament, beginning with the first peace pledge campaign she oversaw in 1962. As seen here, WSP sustained this dual emphasis throughout the 1960s. (Syeus Kottel, Martha Baker Papers, Box 13, Rare Book and Manuscript Library, Columbia University)

that their pressure tactics would persuade men in power to be responsive to their demands. WSP's first peace pledge fell 900,000 signatures short of its "million votes" goal, but it was heartened that 100,000 was not much less than President Kennedy's marginal win in 1960 by 112,881 votes.[26] Abzug hoped these results would put WSP "in a position to evaluate and encourage potential peace candidates for 1964" and to exact influence on President Kennedy.[27] Instead, as Abzug feared, WSP's maternalist rhetoric and image gave the Kennedy administration and male-led peace groups the excuse to dismiss them "as politically unsophisticated wives and mothers."[28]

The Cuban Missile Crisis during thirteen tense days in October 1962 delivered an unexpected jolt that heightened public pressure for a nuclear disarmament agreement between the United States and Soviet Union. On May 7, 1963, a few hundred WSP lobbyists led by Abzug visited seventy-eight senators and more than half of the representatives on Capitol Hill, "hour after hour, footsore but determined," during their "Mother's Lobby for a Test Ban."[29] The Kennedy administration found it useful to highlight this grassroots arms control pressure to counter military and congressional pro-arms pushback during treaty negotiations, but WSP was nonetheless left in the dark during high-level talks. The closest it came to this theater of influence was a briefing in January with Robert Matteson of the Arms Control and Disarmament Agency, who adhered to the administration's strategy of making WSP feel integral to the process, while keeping the specifics of test ban negotiations vague. Sequestered to the halls, peace women cheered British, Soviet, and American diplomats on as they exited talks at the State Department, showering them with bouquets.[30] In contrast, President Kennedy approached SANE leader Norman Cousins to facilitate unofficial talks between Soviet and US emissaries in December 1962 in New York, which led to formal diplomatic negotiations in January. In March 1963, Cousins met again with Kennedy. In April, Cousins drafted a strategy memo the president consulted. And in June, Cousins helped write, "A Strategy of Peace," a speech Kennedy delivered at American University that helped persuade Soviet Premier Nikita Khrushchev to endorse an atmospheric test ban on July 2. This level of access and influence was what Abzug desired and never achieved. The resulting "half-treaty" ratified by Congress on September 24 fell short of WSP's desired comprehensive ban, a goal SANE initially supported, but one that was tempered once Cousins was invited to the table.[31]

Abzug's effective supervision of WSP's test ban treaty campaign elevated her stature as a "key woman," but she remained one among a circle of leaders. She learned her persuasive power was not absolute during a debate over the group's future direction at WSP's second convention in Urbana-Champaign, Illinois, in June 1963. "The weather and discussion were hot—and 3 weeks later we were demonstrating against the war in

Vietnam," recalled Mary Clarke.[32] At the conference, WSP screened a film they had procured depicting US military advisers engaged in combat in Vietnam, which convinced them that this hot spot should be their next focus. On board with this decision, Abzug helped draft a statement that noted "the possibility that this undeclared war may escalate into nuclear conflict, and to the specific ways in which basic human morality is being violated by attacks on civilian populations—women and children."[33] It would be among the first delivered by a peace group.

Where Abzug, surprisingly, broke with her WSP colleagues was in arguing against expressing formal solidarity with the black freedom movement, which she believed would muddy their focus on peace. Her position surprised those that knew of her work as a civil rights lawyer. This debate had been brewing since WSP's first convention in Ann Arbor in 1962, held days before SDS drafted, "The Port Huron Statement" nearby. There, young activists involved in SNCC—and soon SDS—made the case for WSP to broaden its interests to include civil rights.[34] In Urbana-Champaign, Casey Hayden reiterated this point, relaying how the Ann Arbor group participated in local sit-ins and fair housing campaigns. Abzug spoke next, challenging Hayden vigorously. Recognizing that "all struggles for freedom and equality create a better atmosphere in which to struggle for the freedom to live in . . . a world free of war," Abzug nonetheless encouraged WSP to "zealously guard and carefully avoid" draining its resources and becoming "a resolution policy position paper organization which resolves on all issues." Speaking to this predominantly white audience, she encouraged the group to reach out to African American women to discuss their parallel causes, "each from our own vantage point." But she nonetheless urged WSP to limit civil rights engagement to individual action "in our personal lives." Not stopping there, she gave these activists permission to direct their time solely to peace, assuring them they could "feel secure that many others, growing in numbers each day," had joined the racial civil rights cause.[35] As Abzug wrapped up her remarks, Ann Arbor affiliate Mickey Flacks whispered to Amy Swerdlow she did not agree. Swerdlow "told the whole room," and "Bella hit the roof." "I'll put my civil rights credentials against anyone," Abzug shouted before storming out, directing her husband, "Martin, we're leaving." She had a will to lead so expansive she had trouble recognizing moments when it would be prudent to follow. "Don't worry, it will pass," Martin assured Mickey's partner, Richard Flacks, upon exiting.[36] So did the resolution, affirming, "As a movement working for an atmosphere of peaceful cooperation among nations, we support the movement for integration in our own nation. Our goals are inseparable."[37]

Ironically, Abzug made the opposite argument in the National Lawyers Guild—still involved in this bar association in the early 1960s—at the very same moment. The Guild flirted with the idea of taking up disarmament, hosting a "world peace through law" conference in New York City a few days before Abzug joined her first WSP picket. Initially, she committed time to both causes, attending WSP organizing meetings in the morning and Guild integration committee meetings at night. It was not unusual for her civil rights and peace networks to cross, such as when she called on SNCC executive secretary James Forman to help secure WSP friend Claire Reed work at a poverty center in Harlem.[38] However, Abzug increasingly believed peace, not civil rights, had the greatest potential of tying all currents of the Left together. Operating from this point of view, she pushed peace in the Guild alongside WSP.

Abzug made this point as the Guild entered a rebuilding period in which the bar association became an auxiliary of social liberation and ethnic nationalist movements. Guild members' legal aid during SNCC's Freedom Summer in 1964 solidified this reorientation. Resisting this change, Abzug contributed to the Guild's disarmament committee and joined those who worried "the guild would turn into a one-issue organization" and become solely "the legal arm of the civil rights movement."[39] Recognizing the stakes, she made sure to be at "one of the stormiest meetings" in the Guild's history in November 1963.[40] There, she argued vehemently that "peace . . . will make possible the successful objectives that the integration movement requires." Deconstructing what she saw as the far reaches of the Cold War military-industrial complex, she urged Guild members to return to their economic roots. Highlighting the inadequacies of American capitalism, she articulated how part of the call for peace must be a reconversion of the economy to facilitate reforms "providing jobs, schools, and other basic needs." While she recognized the Guild should "influence the bar towards integration," she believed it should diversify its interests. In her view, its decision to focus almost singularly on civil liberties over the last decade at the cost of developing a civil rights program had been a misstep, and "it would be a mistake" again to "leave out other people who are interested in other fields."[41] Considering the Guild's origin as a multi-issue legal advocacy group, she did not see her push for the bar association to stretch its interests as incompatible with her call for WSP to sustain its narrow programmatic focus.

On the losing side of the Guild's fight, Abzug pulled away from the bar association while never abandoning close social ties with many of its members. She pivoted toward the place where she believed she was most heard. In WSP, when she learned that some thought her approach overbearing, she overcame this obstacle by sending emissaries to meetings to present her ideas "in a softer way."[42] She found it more difficult to tolerate being passed over in the Guild than having her leadership tested as she built a network of backers in WSP. While she volunteered her services as part of the Committee to Aid Southern Lawyers, formed in 1962, she never got over the instant praise bestowed on its initiators, Detroit attorneys Ernest Goodman and George Crockett. That their concept essentially replicated the network Abzug had tried to launch unsuccessfully in the early 1950s deepened the animus she felt for Goodman, who overstated his contribution to Willie McGee's defense as the case concluded. "I would push Bella in front of me every time" we exited the Mississippi state capitol, Goodman kidded, an act she did not find funny.[43]

Abzug's decision to devote her greatest energy to building a peace movement was a strategic choice, but one that reflected her orientation as a white woman who did not live under the shackles of Jim Crow. US Popular Front activists including Abzug had once framed the fight against fascism as an antiracist, democratic cause. Likewise, she believed that challenging nuclear warfare and US involvement in Vietnam was a pressing antiimperialist, social justice concern. Civil rights organizing, she estimated, had reached a critical mass expansive enough to move the US government toward substantial policy change, and thus some radicals could afford to direct their energies elsewhere. This is not to say that she did not take her work as an ally seriously. She deeply regretted her absence at the March on Washington for Jobs and Freedom on August 28, 1963, staying home at the last minute after her husband urged her to prioritize the health of a sick daughter as her temperature spiked.[44] Yet, Abzug's prioritization of peace over racial civil rights encouraged parallel organizing on different paths.[45] This separation of social movement interests complicated her quest for a loosely unified new Democratic order and reduced the cross-pollination of progressive campaigns going forward.

Becoming a Democrat

Abzug's reluctant gravitation to the Democratic Party soon followed her pivot toward peace organizing. This was the greatest leap to make, for she had spent more time over the last two decades criticizing Democrats than thinking about joining them. She had also wholeheartedly signed on to WSP's strategy of nonpartisanship. "We are not a political party. We are a movement . . . a pressure group appealing to *all* voters, *all* candidates, *all* political leaders, and *all* political parties," the 1962 political field guide she helped write directed.[46] Yet, in 1964, she strongly urged WSP to support Lyndon B. Johnson, whom she believed to be the surest bet for peace. Goldwater, who advocated a "win-policy" in Vietnam and renewed nuclear stockpiling, was too scary an alternative.

Deciding to go "part of the way with LBJ" required Abzug to shift her leanings away from third-party politics.[47] Abzug was in high school when the National Labor Relations Act (Wagner Act) and the Social Security Act passed in 1935, President Franklin D. Roosevelt achieved a resounding re-election victory in 1936, and the "Roosevelt Recession" took hold in 1937. During this period, leftists and liberals aligned to support Roosevelt's New Deal agenda, spurred on by the president's commitment to establish a safety net for "the forgotten man." Yet, the Popular Front–New Deal alliance had always been a matter of convenience, and by the time Abzug entered college, the honeymoon had ended. The year 1938 was a bad one for Democrats, with Republicans gaining seventy-five seats in the House of Representatives, leaving its liberal bloc much diminished.[48] As the Depression persisted and global fascism expanded, US leftists moved from Democratic allies to adversaries, critiquing Roosevelt's acquiescence to southern Democrats in Congress and allies in Europe.

Too young to vote, Abzug nonetheless decided this was not the party she planned to join. In 1938, she canvassed for Hunter College alum Bella Dodd, who ran unsuccessfully for New York State Assembly on the American Labor Party ticket. In Abzug's view, Dodd was "full of personality, full of ideas, full of guts," whereas Eleanor Roosevelt was "pretty outrageous."[49] Abzug exhibited little love for the First Lady because she had taken sides when the student movement divided after the American Student Union's anti-interventionist turn. Thus, Abzug spent more time as a student activist thinking about what the New Deal did not do rather than what it accomplished. In February 1940, she joined a brigade of 200 Hunter College women at the American Youth Congress Citizenship Institute. President Roosevelt met with the group, engaging in a tense back-and-forth about his policies when pressed, especially on why the United States offered military aid to Finland after a Soviet invasion in November 1939. In the crowd that day, Abzug later reported back on campus, "We demanded that all loans to Finland and money for rearmament be used to alleviate the misery of the unemployed in America, and to extend NYA, WPA, housing and Social Security programs."[50] In the balance between guns and butter, Abzug always prioritized the latter, seeing the reconversion of military aid into domestic social spending as preferable.

After World War II, Abzug wanted no part of the Democratic Party's turn toward anticommunist and centrist politics or its continued appeasement of a racist faction. Instead, she became a rank-and-file member of the American Labor Party (ALP). Fleeting and limited in its impact, this New York party, founded in 1936 by former Socialist Party of America members, attracted pro-Roosevelt social democrats in the 1930s and those hanging on to the coattails of the Popular Front in the 1940s. Locally, Abzug volunteered as a poll watcher for Representative Vito Marcontonio, the ALP's greatest success story. Nationally, she supported the Progressive Party, established in 1946 to deliver a resolute, if fleeting, challenge to Cold War liberalism. A "Woman for Wallace," Abzug cast her confidence in Progressive Party presidential candidate Henry Wallace.[51] Vice president under Roosevelt, Wallace emerged as a counterpoint to President Truman, who fired him as the secretary of commerce when he publicly critiqued US containment policy. To leftists, Wallace was a light in the darkness, and his pummeling deepened their impression that the United States had taken a destructive conservative turn, with Democrats not much different than Republicans. The ALP folded in 1956, leaving Abzug without a party. That year, she did not support Democratic presidential nominee Adlai Stevenson, whom she characterized as half-baked. And in 1960, she thought John F. Kennedy to be a more rampant Cold Warrior than Richard Nixon.[52]

Abzug's view of President Kennedy had softened by the time of his tragic death on November 22, 1963. Like most Americans, she remembered exactly where she was when she learned of his assassination. She was at her law office, listening to the radio as she worked on a brief highlighting the importance of free speech.[53] Abzug had been moved by Kennedy's evolution during test ban treaty negotiations, and she worried his successor, Lyndon B. Johnson, would slow momentum. "If our small voice was heard before," she told WSP activists, "it must be heard again more widely, more effectively, and more decisively."[54] WSP's first test came when Johnson revived Kennedy's effort to help the North Atlantic Treaty Organization build a nuclear fleet armed with Polaris missiles. In December 1963, Johnson signaled his support for congressional hearings on a multilateral force, which he described as a controlled shield of deterrence "as Europe marches toward unity."[55] For Jewish participants in WSP, the prospect "that German fingers might come near the nuclear button" was too much to bear after the Holocaust.[56] Abzug shared this worry, which WSP activists presented forcefully during an international action at The Hague in May that drew women from across the Iron Curtain. Still, she did not attend this international lobby, or any other, seeing WSP's domestic program as the greatest priority.

Abzug believed Johnson's move to establish a multinational force called into question the balance of democratic powers. She made this case in an intricate analysis of the Atomic Energy Act of 1946, or McMahon Act, which prohibited the exchange of atomic technology, material, and components between states and established nonmilitary oversight through the Atomic Energy Commission. Writing draft after draft, she worked out her first extended comment on the importance of active congressional oversight of executive power. She would echo this earlier argument when forcefully contributing to the War Powers Act debate in 1973. One decade prior, Abzug faulted Johnson for promoting the multinational fleet without prior approval by the Joint Committee on Atomic Energy, which she saw as disregarding "appropriate congressional procedure."[57] Under Abzug's direction, a "smallish lobby" made this case in March 1964 during visits to eighty congressional offices, fourteen embassies, and multiple agencies.[58] The effort did little to persuade the Johnson administration to shift course, however, with officials pushing aggressively that spring through diplomatic channels and in closed congressional sessions for the multilateral fleet's creation.

Abzug's early critique of President Johnson's liberal interpretation of presidential power did not stop her from urging WSP to suspend its nonpartisanship in support of his election. She took this unexpected and controversial action because she determined a Goldwater presidency would be appreciably worse. Abzug watched in wonder as the hard-line senator se-cured the nomination at the mid-July "GOParty 1964" in San Francisco.[59] Since January, his promise to "offer a choice, not an echo," steadily stirred conservatives across the Sunbelt and Rocky Mountains.[60] The slow-burning match kindled such a fire Goldwater squeezed out a wide pool of moderate contenders ensconced in the party's Northeast establishment. Dedicated Goldwaterites indicated they would "rather lose fighting for conservative principles than win with another 'me-tooer.'"[61] At the Republican National Convention, Goldwater affirmed his commitment to renewed nuclear brink-manship, rolling back the 1964 Civil Rights Act, and nationalizing "right to work" policies.[62] It was enough to encourage Abzug to shed her past hesitation about Democrats. "Anything less than an enormous defeat for Goldwater," she predicted, "will mean a setback for whatever progress has been made toward unfreezing the cold war."[63]

Other elements encouraged Abzug to steer WSP toward the Democratic Party in 1964. She observed that the force behind Goldwater was more powerful than the candidate himself. She recognized that women helped secure his rise, noting the presence, as one *New York Times* reporter ob-served, of "smiling women who wear Goldwater corsages, Goldwater hats, and dress their children in Goldwater banners."[64] The group Abzug called the "radical right" were a familiar cast of characters to WSP activ-ists; members of the John Birch Society and Young Americans for Freedom ran antagonistic counteractions at WSP demonstrations. They were also "active letter writers" and tireless campaigners. "The mail must be swung in favor of peace interests," Abzug challenged, urging WSP to help mobilize a progressive counterweight to this organizing.[65] Conservative women made inroads with Goldwater, but she believed they had not necessarily done the same with all women voters. The "51 percent factor" could still be a Democratic majority.[66] In a sense, Abzug both admired the organizing efforts of conservative women and maintained the view that women natu-rally leaned progressive and "Goldwater girls" were misled. For this reason, she quickly focused on peace women's organizing to make inroads in the Democratic Party.

Already thinking beyond WSP in 1964, Abzug estimated that left-liberal alliances in electoral politics could be rekindled because the domestic Red Scare had finally passed. WSP's effective shaming of the House Un-American Activities Committee on December 11, 1962—what one reporter called "ladies' day at the ball park"—cemented her feeling.[67] Abzug had been the first name on the list HUAC prepared of twenty New York WSP affiliates to subpoena, and her first lobbying action was highlighted as a sign of suspected Communist influence.[68] Why she was spared when fourteen subpoenas were issued in November is unclear. Sitting among 500 others in the gallery that day, Abzug watched as fellow activists testified, showered with flowers and cheers as they took the stand, "befuddling grim-faced committee members."[69] "The women won—hats down," SANE leader Homer Jack judged.[70] Abzug agreed, yet it had been hard for her to sit silent. As Amy Swerdlow recalled, "It was not her day."[71] Despite Abzug's offer to represent the subpoenaed women, the group decided to go with big-name civil liberties lawyers Thurman Arnold, Telford Taylor, Leonard Boudin, and Victor Rabinowitz. As WSP's default resident lawyer, Abzug offered advice behind the scenes and delivered an affirming postscript. HUAC failed its goal of "'public exposure' of individuals" and "disapproval of the peace movement," she wrote, presenting "no proof of any kind of Communist influence in the WSP in New York or elsewhere."[72] McCarthy antics, she happily noted, had finally been put to rest.

Anticommunist probes had indeed fallen out of favor, but the US government reoriented, rather than rescinded, its surveillance of dissenters. Under COINTELPRO, the FBI's directive to "expose, disrupt, misdirect, discredit, or otherwise neutralize" radical organizing, the bureau amassed forty-nine volumes on WSP, and Abzug's file shifted in 1961 from concern over her Guild ties to her involvement in WSP.[73] HUAC had also capitalized on an ongoing internal fight in WSP. Although Dagmar Wilson did not name Abzug in her testimony, she openly criticized Abzug's organizing style, WSP's shift toward lobbying, and the New York branch's preference of greater structure. Exasperated at one point during the HUAC hearing, Wilson remarked to her questioner that New York had created a Central Coordinating Committee "over my dead body."[74]

After this HUAC appearance, jockeying over which half of the "demonstration/lobbying format" to prioritize continued within the group. Abzug's angling toward Democratic Party politics exacerbated this tension. She held enough sway to steer WSP toward support of Johnson, but not without some affiliates rightly noting the alliance was an irreparable programmatic reorientation.[75] In her push toward the Democratic Party, Abzug did not heed the warning signs that Johnson would be a wartime president. On

August 2, three North Vietnamese patrol boats opened fire on the USS *Maddox* after the destroyer edged into their territorial waters. With election results in play, Johnson calculated Congress would not stall a resolution allowing the president to "take all necessary measures to repel any armed attack" that the United States held "vital to its national interest."[76] He was correct. The Gulf of Tonkin Resolution passed quickly, despite strong objections from Senators Wayne Morse and Ernest Gruening.

In late August, Abzug made her first appearance at the Democratic National Convention (DNC) in Atlantic City, joining 300 WSP demonstrators there to protest the Gulf of Tonkin incident and collect 15,000 "Stop Goldwaterism" signatures within an hour.[77] Delegate Paul O'Dwyer, a lawyer she knew from the Guild, was surprised to see her marching on the boardwalk. "What are you doing here Bella?" he asked. "We're lobbying on peace," she replied, handing him a fortune cookie with the prophecy, "Negotiation, no annihilation." "Peace! Civil rights is the issue at this convention," he countered.[78] O'Dwyer was right. The 1964 DNC is most remembered for the Mississippi Freedom Democratic Party's delegate challenge and sharecropper Fannie Lou Hamer's moving voting rights appeal. The presence of peace activists is less remembered, and Abzug's debut before the Platform Committee did not make the splash she had hoped. "In the name of women everywhere we urge that this election not be turned into a competition in brinkmanship, but rather a competition of sound foreign policy that will build a world free from war and poverty," she and Audrey Fain noted, representing WSP.[79] Using Lyndon B. Johnson's Great Society rhetoric, they openly pandered to the president.

The move did not capture the attention of Johnson, who was preoccupied with subduing the Mississippi delegate challenge. Being overlooked frustrated Abzug, who had taken a substantial personal leap and significant strategic risk steering WSP toward the Democrats. She came home feeling like "our Atlantic City action was good but could have been better."[80] Women peace activists were noticed by the Johnson campaign enough to take advantage of an image they helped create. On September 7, Americans tuning into NBC's *Monday Night at the Movies* viewed a startling ad that had only one airing. The camera zoomed in on a young girl sitting in a placid field innocently plucking petals from a daisy. All the while, an ominous male voice counted down to zero until, unexpectedly, the screen went blank, then returned to a mushrooming atomic cloud. "These are the stakes," the president warned viewers, "to make a world in which all God's children can live, or go into darkness."[81] That month, Goldwater insiders polled national support for Johnson at a hefty 61 percent to Goldwater's 27 percent, foretelling Johnson's imminent landslide.[82]

By October, most within WSP shared affiliate Alice Hamburg's view that they should "expose LBJ's blatant hypocrisy."[83] Waiting until Abzug was not present, the group debated whether it wanted "to be a lobby group" or "bring in total concern of women all over."[84] Abzug agreed that the Vietnam War made it difficult to support Johnson, but once committed, she urged others not to resign from the Democratic Party in protest. Stubborn and running a long game, she dug in further, arguing, "You cannot withdraw from work which you have not already done."[85] Abzug viewed Johnson "as an *instrument* rather than the *steward* of the public welfare," a rationale that allowed her to align with the president on some issues while remaining critical of him on others.[86] She had hoped that an anti-Goldwater vote would improve domestic conditions and stall war, not hasten its course.

In November, WSP declared a state of emergency when it learned of US air attacks on North Vietnam, unaware that Johnson also planned "larger and stronger use of Rangers and Special Forces and Marines."[87] On February 7, 1965, National Liberation Front forces of North Vietnam attacked a US army site in Pleiku, and the Americans swiftly responded by bombing the North Vietnamese army at Dong Hoi. Two days after Operation Rolling Thunder commenced, 300 WSP lobbyists fanned throughout Capitol Hill to distribute thousands of shopping bags filled with peace pledges.[88] The effort was WSP's first undertaking in the most extensive hearts and minds campaign directed at Congress during the Vietnam War. Unfortunately, it had little immediate impact. On March 16, as Johnson rallied Congress to get behind the Voting Rights Act, reciting Selma marchers' anthem, "We Shall Overcome," the first US Marines moved in at Da Nang. That same day, WSP experienced its earliest wartime casualty. Eighty-eight-year-old Alice Herz of Detroit set herself on fire at a shopping center, mimicking the self-immolation of Buddhist monks in Saigon protesting US bombing. Seeing this form of civil disobedience as futile, Abzug focused on pressuring the White House to grant WSP an audience. In April, 40,000 more Americans troops were deployed to Vietnam. In May, WSP lobbyists made it past the White House gates to meet with National Security Council member Chester L. Cooper for three hours. It would be the closest WSP ever came to President Johnson, whose team decided thereafter, "If anyone sees this group they should be well down the totem pole."[89]

Initially, Abzug believed Johnson to be a reluctant warmonger. She took this position in a report on Vietnam she wrote after the election. She acknowledged that the "US gets on the escalator" in Vietnam in 1964, but she let Johnson off the hook, suggesting "election promises forgotten" were the casualty of a war he never wanted.[90] Although, it became increasingly difficult for her to square Johnson's campaign pledges or his favorable domestic program with the actions being taken in Vietnam. In July, Medicare and Medicaid passed while 50,000 troops left stateside for combat. By August, Abzug was done with the president, but not with Democrats. The Great Society could "have turned their back on man's ability to use nuclear power to clothe the poor, feed the hungry, and cure the diseased," she observed. "Instead, its power has been used to clothe the failure of diplomacy with military security, to feed stockpiles . . . in an escalating undeclared war of a particularly ugly kind."[91]

Coming to this viewpoint by the summer of 1965, Abzug fell in step with most activists in WSP. Yet, she remained singular among WSP's "key women" in her determination to position their affiliates as an influential bloc within the Democratic Party. In becoming a Democrat, she did not temper her radicalism. Rather, she calculated that leftists could draw the energy from street-level protest into the party structure to become inside agitators. Progressive social movements during the 1960s did not simply spin out from respectable, integrationist politics to a maelstrom of civil disobedience, separatism, violence, and destruction. Activists also swung into the Democratic Party and toward political power centers, seeing an opening for radical resistance of "the system" within the system. These two strands of engagement, while often in tension, developed in conversation.

Bringing Protest to Power

Abzug never apologized for being wrong on Johnson, though it set her back a bit. She found 1965 to be a year of searching and a year of change. The steady commute to the city for work and organizing meetings had begun to wear. She wanted to be closer to the heart of antiwar activism and hoped to augment her influence. After thirteen years in Mount Vernon, she longed to get back to the city. She had never adjusted to suburban life, which she described as a "1950s cocoon approach to living . . . of prosperity, of having children, of having a happy life."[92] When it was clear that her daughters, Eve and Liz, budding sculptor and singer, would happily attend the High School of Music and Art in Manhattan, Martin consented to the long-awaited homecoming.

The Abzugs found a 1920s brick walk-up at 20 West Sixteenth Street, near bustling Union Square. Making this move to Greenwich Village reflected their interest in being at the cultural and political epicenter of New York progressives, but also their hope as city people to reverse a troubling trend. The systemic ramifications of white flight, a migration pattern to which they had contributed, were on display during the riots that erupted in Harlem in July 1964 over an incident of police brutality. Empathetic, Bella and Martin reembraced urbanism as residents, developers, corporations, and politicians increasingly focused elsewhere, seeing cities as "more and more unsettled, uncomfortable and downright dangerous, less and less pleasant."[93]

Before leaving Mount Vernon, Martin and Bella made a final parting contribution to local integration efforts, selling their house to Malcolm X's widow, Betty Shabazz. Their friends, actors Ruby Dee and Ossie Davis, had approached them with this prospect, and they did not think twice about the sale despite the objection of some neighbors. Bella had admired Malcolm X, when he severed ties with the Nation of Islam. She shared his perspective presented in "The Ballot or the Bullet," calling on African Americans to "become more politically conscious, more politically mature," and engage in electoral politics.[94] At first, Shabazz hesitated on the sale, unsure she wanted to take on the headache of renting out a basement apartment. Once she was persuaded, the Committee of Concerned Mothers commenced fund-raising, including a concert at Sidney Poitier's estate, which helped offset the $40,000 purchase. Thereafter, the Abzugs took pride in providing Shabazz, mother of five and pregnant, with a place to begin anew.[95]

Although thrilled to be back in Manhattan, Bella entered a period of adjustment. Moving her legal office home, she eliminated her hour commute and blurred the delineation of her personal, political, and professional lives. Increasingly, she took to parlor politicking. "She would do a lot of her talking in the kitchen, on the phone—on a director's chair—and she would hit the countertops" hard with her fist, recalled her daughter Liz.[96] Bella often worked late into the night, her mind whirring as the city's rumble quieted. It was liberating to organize at all hours without limits, but when her home became mission control it was difficult for family members to get enough sleep.

Thankfully, for all involved, Bella Abzug paused more often than usual in this moment. Typically a thinker on the move, she became a doer who took time to reflect. She jotted down her ideas on yellow legal pads, and these notes written as quick scribbles and long-winded soliloquies, served as first drafts of circulated position papers, slogans, and speeches.[97] They capture Abzug's thoughts at a defining transition in which she expanded focus beyond Women Strike for Peace to position herself as a national antiwar movement leader and influencer in Democratic politics. She contemplated a great deal about where to next direct her energies, how leftists should influence the political process, and what the political direction of the nation should be.

Frequently, Abzug dwelled on how to close the seeming gulf between direct action—immediate, palpable, insubordinate—and political action, which tended to be plodding, elusive, and legalistic. She believed political engagement was not merely an extension of protest but a necessary corollary. Mobilization pressure drew attention to a cause, but access to power was more precious. Radicals, closed out of power centers, needed to think and act strategically about how to break in. Critiquing civil disobedience and separatism, Abzug believed it more effective to "use conventional political techniques for radical goals." Essentially, she articulated a reasonable radicalism, one that posited that "radical goals do not require radical techniques."[98] In making this case, it is clear how much faith Abzug had in the US democratic system. We do not need a revolutionary "next America," she assessed, but rather a transformative reimagining of the democratic system that exists.[99] She did not trust liberals in power to correct its current path. She believed, quite grandiloquently, that leftists had the greatest moral compass in US society. They were best suited to direct critical focus on the expansion of US imperialism and global capitalism, and the persistence of domestic racism, sexism, and class inequity. Naming social problems did not solve them, however, and progressives could not greatly effect change from the political fringes.

Abzug believed leftists should prioritize building collective "pressure upon political parties to channelize these protests into political action."[100]

Considering the 1964 election, she determined that Democrats were "led and pressured into serious rightest directions, in foreign policy particularly," because the party had "been abandoned by those left of center." In her estimation, the nation would have been a lot better off if the Left had grabbed hold of the party akin to the Republican Party's "seizure by the Right."[101] She faulted leftists, including herself, for being disinterested for too long in two-party politics and ceding too much territory to others. "Overnight, while we all slept, for several years, very quietly they steadily, carefully, very correctly, the people who cared to exercise their rights to participate in the electoral process" came out for Goldwater, she noted with a mix of admiration and concern.[102] Leftists, she envisioned, could activate the same fervent organizing energy and deliver the same obstructive reorienting jolt to the Democrats.

Abzug did not form these ideas in a vacuum. At middecade, a group of political activists on the Left theorized how to move "from protest to politics," a shift articulated by civil rights leader Bayard Rustin in his so-titled 1965 article. Once a Communist, Rustin renounced this party, joining the Socialist Party of America (which reorganized in 1972 as Social Democrats, USA). As a key coordinator of the March on Washington, Rustin had little patience for black nationalism and its militant "moralists." True revolution, he argued, came about with "the qualitative transformation of fundamental institutions . . . where the social and economic structure they compromised can no longer be said to be the same." He believed a New Deal–esque "coalition of progressive forces which becomes the *effective* political majority of the United States" could accomplish this goal.[103]

Abzug agreed with Rustin in many areas. She too waxed nostalgic about the "tremendous protest" and sweeping reforms of the 1930s. She believed the Vietnam War could have the same activating effect as the Great Depression, and imagined the United States to be on the verge of another era of reinvention. It was time, she calculated, "to move a particular party if it will be influenced."[104] But she parted ways with Rustin, and his Socialist Party counterparts, on a fundamental point.[105] Abzug saw the New Deal coalition as a failed enterprise once it morphed into a Cold War alliance between anticommunist liberals and organized labor. She had little love for the hawkish and protectionist wing of the labor movement steered by leaders such as AFL-CIO president George Meany. It was this faction Abzug faulted for the late 1940s purge of left-led unions, the development of a military-industrial complex, and the cold shoulder that women workers received once the troops came home after World War II.

Abzug envisioned a newly constituted Democratic coalition more egalitarian and libertarian in form and more driven by a quest for peace. She also believed it essential to tap into the new currents of social movement organizing that Rustin and others were quicker to dismiss. While she critiqued civil disobedience as a tactic, she was less concerned about the shift toward social liberation and ethnic nationalism. Coming to her politics through her Jewishness, she understood the attraction of self-realization and self-determination. She believed that identity-based activists could be encouraged toward a broad "people's coalition" as she had once extended her Zionist allegiance to participate in a wider US Popular Front.

BELLA ABZUG EXPRESSED THIS VISION in the early 1960s, when her audience was limited primarily to the few thousand women in Women Strike for Peace. Nevertheless, it is important to return to her ideas in this moment to understand the genesis of the political agenda she forwarded in Congress. Her conceptualization of a new Democratic order was expansive and ambitious. She wanted to stimulate what political theorist Arnold S. Kaufman called a "new politics of radical pressure that synthesizes in mutually reinforcing ways welfare politics, coalitional politics, and participatory democracy."[106] Kaufman's antiwar and civil rights organizing on college campuses led him to believe the time was right for a new "radical liberalism" that drew movement politics into the Democratic Party. Abzug could not agree more.

This call for a "new politics," first sounded during the 1966 midterms, became the drumbeat of a breed of dissident partisans in the Democratic Party that never gained control of the party, but exacted enough influence to change its appearance, organization, and agenda. New Politics Democrats had a clear reform mission that they executed most strikingly between 1968 and 1976.[107] But the mood of new politics went beyond these renegade Democrats, taking on a cultural meaning and style. For political scientists, new politics connoted an age in campaigning characterized by direct mailing, computerized polling, multimedia marketing, and celebrity politicians.[108] The term new politics became a populist shorthand for change connoting the will of "the people." For those resisting change, it became a term of disparagement, a way to conflate the mass of demonstrators in the street and reformers working through political clubs. And for the radical purists, new politics was a sign of selling out on the way to coalition and consensus.

Abzug worked in the vanguard of Democratic New Politics. She anticipated this insurgent development, helped define its goals, capitalized on its momentum, and broadened its reach. She began this effort as most organizers do, working locally. In 1966, her apartment at 20 West Sixteenth Street buzzed with activity, political collaborators steadily streaming in and out of Abzug's home office alongside her clients.[109] From this outpost, she worked two angles at once. She sought to draw more progressive women into Democratic politics, while expanding antiwar influence in local reform Democratic clubs and the national Democratic Party structure. Urging the former group to take electoral politics seriously, she asked the latter, "Where are the women?"[110]

3

OFFICE BOUND

B **ELLA ABZUG SPENT** much of the late 1960s preparing for office, though she did not announce or perhaps even recognize that this was her intention. Her plodding transition from a political strategist to a political candidate reveals how unimaginable it was for most women to see themselves in elected office. She could dream big about actualizing a Left-led New Politics Democratic resistance. Although, even as she expanded her base, moved into party politics, and tried out campaign strategies, she did not immediately cast herself in the role of a Washington change maker. It took mounting frustration to propel her forward. Between 1966 and 1969, she watched as women-led antiwar efforts were credited to men and campaigns inadequately reached out to women. She boiled with anger each time she thought her ideas were unfairly dismissed and her contribution was undervalued. She found it deeply unsatisfying to be working in the hidden backrooms of campaigns as antiwar male candidates she supported in local and national races promoted their vision for change out front in full view.[1]

When running for Congress in 1970, Abzug urged other women to make the journey she had just completed, going from being office bound to being bound for office. It took four years of intentional grassroots organizing, network expansion, and platform development to ready herself for a political run. Likewise, forces beyond Abzug in the antiwar, antipoverty, and feminist movements expanded, augmenting her chances as an activist candidate who might win in New York City. By 1970, with New Politics a defined progressive posture within the Democratic Party, public support for the Vietnam War continuing to erode, and women's liberation gaining national media attention, the possibilities for Abzug as a candidate heightened.

Women's antiwar activism, observes historian Rhodri Jeffries-Jones, "went hand in hand with legitimization of women in politics."[2] Abzug certainly sought to draw this connection, as she pressed simultaneously for an end to the war and for women's inclusion in politics. She parlayed her leadership role in Women Strike for Peace into becoming an asset to candidates—from local reform Democrat Jerome Wilson and Mayor John V. Lindsay to presidential hopefuls Senators Eugene McCarthy and Robert F. Kennedy—seeking the support of antiwar interests and women voters. In between advice on the issues, Abzug offered counsel of a different kind. As McCarthy aide Curtis Gans remembers, Abzug was persistent in prodding, "Where Are the Women"?[3] When supplying Democratic campaigns with dependable teams of grassroots organizers, she made clear that antiwar women expected something in return for their womanpower. She pushed for the advancement of women on campaign staffs, in party leadership, and among convention delegates, and in turn, she augmented her own visibility and influence.

In the late 1960s, Abzug continued an uncomfortable dance with leftist activists who veered toward confrontational politics and separatism. In her view, the Democratic Party was primed for change, and progressives had a real shot at a party takeover. For this reason, Abzug devoted considerable energy to building antiwar political action committees and creating a political bloc of progressive women beyond the ranks of WSP. Expanding her web of influence in the antiwar movement proved more immediately successful than her effort to steer the direction of "new feminism."

Abzug's call for recognition of campaign's dependency on "womanpower" did not signal her embrace of "women power" as defined by proponents of women's liberation. She delivered a critique of women's subordination in electoral politics quite similar to the grievances addressed by Casey Hayden and Mary King in a 1965 memo they circulated within the Student Non-Violent Coordinating Committee. In it, they took men in the civil rights and student movements to task for casting women as domestic, clerical, and sexual helpmates in the struggle.[4] And yet her challenge came from a different place rooted in her longtime frustration with institutionalized sexism.

As the rumblings for women's liberation Hayden and King expressed grew, Abzug responded favorably, incorporating feminist rhetoric into her antiwar messaging, but she wanted to define women power on her own terms. She urged women's liberationists to see ending the Vietnam War as the most pressing women's rights concern. And while she understood the importance of self-realization as a first stage of politicization, she believed women should move quickly from naming "the problem" to pressuring for change in politics. Patriarchy, she emphasized, would not be dismantled so long as it remained alive and well in the halls of government. While she was not fully successful in making this case, the process of trying helped convince Abzug she should lead by example.

Women Power for Peace

The 1966 midterms provided Abzug with an opportunity to expand her reach beyond WSP and further into the realm of New York reform Democratic politics. During this election season, she drew on her notoriety as an antiwar field organizer to become a leader in issue-oriented political action coalitions. Through this work, in turn, she gained an inside track as an adviser to political candidates seeking endorsements, field support, and advice. While this attention was gratifying, she soon realized that there was no guarantee that the counsel she gave would be taken or the work that she did would be credited.

In February 1966, Abzug co-organized the Seventeenth Congressional District Peace Action Committee (17th CD PAC), an alliance of district residents active in groups such as SDS, WSP, SNCC, and SANE who sought to bring local politicians around to the antiwar cause. While claiming the mantle of nonpartisanship, the 17th CD PAC was singular in its intent of "stacking the meetings" of reform Democratic clubs.[5] New York's reform Democrats were already rebels in party politics, characterized as "emotional, idealistic, impractical and usually successful."[6] These clubs, first established by supporters of 1952 and 1956 Democratic presidential nominee Adlai Stevenson, had delivered a challenge to Tammany Hall incumbents. Their early victories—William Fitts Ryan's congressional win opposing Herbert Zelenko in 1961, and Ed Koch's unseating of Carmine DeSapio in 1963—secured the staying power of this liberal reformist wing.

The 17th CD PAC saw reform Democrats as potential allies, but nonetheless vowed to work "within and without the party structure" by putting antiwar interests before partisan ties.[7] The PAC's endorsement soon mattered to candidates who wanted peace on their side.

Through the 17th CD PAC, Abzug expanded her web of influence, forming a network of politicos she would draw on in future campaigns. One such participant, Doug Ireland, became her campaign manager in 1970. A budding journalist and assistant national secretary in SDS, Ireland decided "attaching myself" to Abzug would be an invaluable political education. "Right away I was quite impressed" with her "political strategy and with her pragmatic radicalism," he recalled. He shared her view that it was time to "get the arteriosclerotic Dixiecrats evicted from positions of power and renew the Democratic Party with an infusion of activism from the various social movements that were burgeoning at the time."[8]

Abzug became the gatekeeper of the 17th CD PAC. "Call Bella Abzug. . . . They're interviewing candidates. I want to meet her," electoral hopeful Allard Lowenstein told aide Ronnie Eldridge. She met Abzug at Granson's Restaurant, owned by Lowenstein's family, and Eldridge and Abzug "hit it off right away."[9] Even so, Abzug would not support Lowenstein, whom she later described as "brilliant," but "a believer, largely in himself."[10] While she later supported Lowenstein's "Dump Johnson" effort, his long-standing anticommunist views strained their relationship from the start. "You cannot expect liberals in this country to support the civil rights movements when you are using people who don't really believe in freedom," Lowenstein had told organizer Ed King after lawyers from the National Lawyers Guild were recruited to defend arrested protesters during the 1964 Freedom Summer voting drive.[11] Abzug did not take kindly to Lowenstein's opinion. Likewise, he was "uncomfortable with ideologues" and thought her to be one.[12]

The candidates Abzug got behind tended to be younger, more malleable, and more sympathetic to her politics. One such candidate was thirty-four-year-old Democratic state senator Jerome Wilson, a three-term legislator who ran for the Seventeenth District congressional seat in 1966 after being redistricted. "This district needs a bellringer, a whistle-blower and a champion, if necessary, of the unpopular," Wilson declared.[13] His zealous reformist posture appealed to Abzug, as did his role in reforming New York divorce law to expand rightful cause beyond adultery, which benefited her family law clients.[14] She recognized he "had to be convinced that a dissent from the Administration position would mean campaign workers and votes," but there was more to it than that.[15] Her leftist ties made some Wilson aides nervous, and they worried her support would hurt his chances in the primary. He decided it was worth the risk.

Abzug delivered 17th CD PAC support and abundant counsel. Yet it was her deep well of women volunteers drawing from the antiwar movement that made the greatest impact for Wilson and like campaigns. Abzug stacked the ranks of East Side Women for Wilson and ran a tight operation out of an area reform Democratic club. Women were "80% of his telephone canvassers, 98% of his clerical workers and 75% of distributors of leaflets on street-corners, at subway stops and supermarkets."[16] Also valuable, Abzug helped shape Wilson's foreign policy program, providing advice at length. "She would talk and talk and talk. If one needed to go the bathroom, you could do that, come back, and she'd still be talking," recalled Wilson.[17] Abzug's strategy was to push until she persuaded. "Gradually," she noted, Wilson moved to "a strong position, endorsing a cessation of the bombing of North Vietnam without pre-conditions, as U Thant had proposed, ending the buildup of U.S. troops in Vietnam, and a declaration of our readiness to participate in a cease-fire supervised by an appropriate international body."[18] As Wilson affectionately remembered, "She used me as the spokesperson for her beliefs. She was the tutor and she was the inspiration for my positions against the war."[19]

The combined force of antiwar and reform Democratic support, along with an endorsement from New York's Liberal Party, helped secure Wilson's substantial primary upset beating "regular" Democrat Peter Berle.[20] Taking on incumbent Republican Theodore Kupferman proved more difficult. One Wilson canvasser confronted Kupferman on Vietnam, leading him to coyly respond within earshot of a reporter, "I'm not a hawk . . . I'm not a dove. I'm a wise old owl."[21] Wilson believed an unexpected Internal Revenue Service (IRS) audit initiated in the final days of his campaign made the difference in the "closest and most sharply contested" general election in Manhattan during the 1966 midterms.[22] Kuperfman's slim 1,400-vote victory over Wilson heartened progressives, who saw his near upset as something they could build on before the 1968 campaign season. In Abzug's view, it was "only a beginning."[23]

Alongside Wilson's race, Abzug helped thirty-four-year-old councilman Theodore Weiss take on her future opponent Representative Leonard

Farbstein in the Nineteenth District. Fifty-three percent of district voters polled favored Farbstein, the five-term incumbent who became reformers' "one sore thumb."[24] He lost the first vote, contested the victory, and was declared the winner after the recount. Weiss sued, claiming "wholesale fraud perpetuated by Tammany."[25] The court agreed. Weiss's staff reached out to Abzug again, believing that "the cutting edge organization, and the agent of change was Women Strike for Peace."[26] As Weiss's campaign manager Bill Chafe recalled, this choice was strategic but challenging because Abzug and WSP were a package deal, and "you needed her support, but you did not necessarily welcome her style."[27] In the end, Abzug's team of canvassers could not secure a win for Weiss, who lost by 1,092 votes. Some WSP volunteers felt remorse, believing, "If we had worked just a little bit harder, he could have won."[28] Farbstein had argued that being antiwar was anti-Zionist, undercutting Weiss's lead in this heavily Jewish district. Having analyzed this race, Abzug would be better able to anticipate Farbstein's appeal to Jewish voters when running against him in 1970.[29]

WSP's volunteer brigade stretched beyond New York and was, as Abzug called it, "one of the best peace-force efforts mounted anywhere in the country."[30] Creating this unit required the labor of many organizers, phone tree blasts, and action plans. However, Abzug set the tone. "The protest against the war will remain a poll, a statistic, a fly in the ointment to 'consensus,' but nothing more until there is recognition by peace pressure groups that the public support they build for change must be channelized directly into the American political party structures," she urged.[31] Thousands of peace women responded to this dispatch, helping roll out campaigns in a breakout year for antiwar candidates. More than a hundred "dove" candidates ran obstructionist campaigns in twenty states, splintering the Democratic Party enough to help Republicans gain forty-seven seats in the House and three in the Senate.[32] Political analysts at the time credited the 1966 election results to "a combination of regular Democratic atrophy and a pervasive dissatisfaction with the Johnson Administration centered on Vietnam."[33] What they could not yet see was how this election previewed a party rebellion coming to form and one in which women played a decisive role.

Peace women's self-awareness that they had put in considerable hours for antiwar candidates during the 1966 midterms made their erasure more difficult. Abzug was particularly incensed that reporters overlooked WSP's role in crafting and executing that year's peace pledge. Journalist Jack Smith of the *National Guardian* incorrectly credited SANE with initiating the campaign, when many in the antiwar movement knew that the pledge "started as a New York activity, became a national WSP activity and finally, a national peace activity."[34] In Abzug's district, canvassers had collected sixty signatures an hour in April. Nationally, 3 million pledges had been distributed by May, at least half by WSP affiliates. Beyond Smith's oversight of this activity, he suggested the peace pledge tactic muddled antiwar focus on direct action. In doing so, he picked at an open sore as antiwar activists continued to debate whether electoral engagement would increase their influence or drain their resources. Defensive on both fronts, Abzug could not help but fire back. "Gentlemen, I wish to differ with the facts and conclusions of Jack Smith's article," she wrote, asserting that the peace pledge was led by WSP, was far from moderate, and injected a full-throttle antiwar edge in politics with the goal of "a change of policy."[35]

This letter to the editor, which was not published and may not have been sent, reveals how angry Abzug felt when her leadership was called into question at the same time it went unrecognized. Increasingly, she voiced the opinion that women were not merely an untapped resource in politics; they were a vital asset already employed and unfairly taken for granted. Men who worked with Abzug sensed her personal dissatisfaction with a support role. As Jerome Wilson observed, "Bella was counseling people like me to carry her anti-war message rather than doing it herself."[36] For those politicians who listened, she worked tirelessly to help them achieve greater inroads with the interest groups she bridged: antiwar and women. Abzug committed to this indirect role of counselor, but channeling her ideas through others was not her natural posture. Still, she was not yet prepared to break through as a political candidate.

During the next election season, Abzug focused threefold on drawing antiwar interests further into Democratic politics, building a progressive women's voting bloc, and supporting democratization efforts in the party. She worked toward long-term aims as well: reorienting congressional power and priorities, remaking the structure and program of the Democratic Party, and stimulating a leftward turn in the United States. Having devoted a great deal of time to thinking through these goals, she found it frustrating that many activists she worked with were not immediately on board. Still, Abzug emerged as an influencer among the wing of movement actors who believed, as she did, that protest must be brought into the halls of power.

Abzug understood why some peace activists felt that civil disobedience was warranted. News of more body bags coming home from Vietnam continued, with 72 Americans dead and 337 wounded in January 1967, and 282 more dead and 1,576 wounded in February.[37] In response, she joined 1,500 protesters camped outside the Pentagon on February 15, some women using their heels as door knockers to press for admission to this inner sanctum of military operations. Defense secretary Robert McNamara, who watched the scene unfold as his helicopter landed on the building's rooftop tarmac, was so moved that he granted WSP affiliates a hearing in which they recited a "Declaration of Conscience."[38] Alongside this promising response from McNamara, Abzug believed recent antiwar statements by Reverend Martin Luther King Jr. and Senator Robert F. Kennedy signaled that peace activists could "convert what well may be a majority sentiment . . . into a majority *movement* against the war."[39] She found it disconcerting that many within WSP discussed "where and how" civil disobedience "would . . . be most effective," instead of thinking about how to build this antiwar majority.[40] She believed correctly that ratcheting up confrontational and violent forms of protest would stall public support to end the war.

Abzug's ambition to build a progressive women's voting bloc in 1968 was compromised by the turn toward civil disobedience and the rejection of her leadership within WSP. She introduced her plans for a "'campaign of women' to end the war in '68" at the group's annual convention in Washington, DC, in September 1967, hoping to rally her colleagues to take up the unfinished suffragist project of forming a women's voting bloc. She called on peace women to assemble "a Convention of Women" that bridged all "areas where women function—education, arts, professions, housewives, working women, black women, women of deprived areas." "The struggle to unite the women of this country to end the Vietnam War is the most significant single thing we can pursue," she asserted. "We have never pushed it to its logical lengths."[41] This intersectional goal was a strategic shift for Abzug, who in WSP's infancy had argued for singular focus when others wanted to bridge peace and racial civil rights activism.

Abzug expected that her idea would be a tough sell because the mood of the moment was to fight, not peacefully mobilize. She believed that more would be gained through measured resistance. In the days leading up to the WSP convention, she spent considerable time pleading with her peers to keep their cool at a planned antidraft demonstration, but she understood why they were upset. The Department of Interior had issued an ordinance limiting the number of protesters to 100. In challenge, Abzug argued that WSP's "right to dissent" would be "another casualty of the war in Vietnam."[42] At the same time, she brokered a deal with the White House police she thought pretty reasonable—a revolving picket of 100. Even so, shortly after the demonstration got underway, "the crush started." Police reacted, "hitting women, punching grandmas, shoving children," and handcuffing demonstrators.[43] Abzug rushed forward, beseeching the police to stop the assault, and the protesters to abide by the revolving picket. But with arrests already made, the damage had been done.

And so it was that consideration of Abzug's proposed women's bloc was subsumed by a wider debate over civil disobedience. On one side, Abzug questioned, "Is jail necessary?"[44] On the other, Dagmar Wilson countered, "Although we don't plan to get ourselves arrested, sometimes things happen."[45] Abzug saw the confrontational tactics of white draft resisters as not only a foolhardy, "narrow" approach that did "not spur the masses of people to action," but also an expression of privilege.[46] African Americans used civil disobedience to combat a "feeling of powerlessness, frustration and isolation," while "brave young draft resisters" felt "neither powerless nor isolated from the American people."[47] Abzug's biting critique was one that few in her antiwar circle were willing to make, but it did not endear her to fellow activists. She increasingly felt like a leader who had lost control of the movement she led. As WSP collaborator Martha Baker recalled, "The idea that any of us would voluntarily go to jail drove her crazy."[48]

Nothing demonstrated Abzug losing ground more than the formation of the Jeanette Rankin Brigade (JRB), which mirrored her proposed "Convention of Women." The JRB mobilization was a masterful feat, drawing together civil rights, antipoverty, antiwar, and feminist concerns. On January 15, 1968, some 5,000 women dressed in black, the color of mourning, arrived on Capitol Hill to protest the war and deliver the brigade's petition to House and Senate leaders. It was here that the women's liberation anthem "Sisterhood Is Powerful" debuted.[49] And it was here that Jeanette Rankin, the nation's first congresswoman, urged forward three generations of women across race and class lines. A coalitional endeavor, the JRB steering committee joined civil rights activists including Rosa Parks, Coretta Scott King, Fannie Lou Hamer, and Ella Baker with peace leaders including WSP's Dagmar Wilson, Cora Weiss, Amy Swerdlow, and Mary Clarke.[50]

Abzug was markedly absent, staying away in part because JRB would not prohibit civil disobedience, but even more so because she felt rejected. The group had appropriated and augmented WSP's 1968 political campaign strategy. The JRB used the same slogan, "Make Women Power Political Power," called for a new women's political bloc, and billed their demonstration as "A Congress of American Women." What her friends on the steering committee saw as an elaboration of her good ideas, Abzug believed to be a usurpation of her concept in a diluted form. The JRB presented her with the best opportunity she encountered to help build a diverse progressive women's political coalition, and stubbornly, she passed on its potential.

The JRB's greatest failure, in Abzug's estimation, was that its organizers expectantly urged women to "make women power political power" without providing them the skills or infrastructure to realize this goal. She criticized JRB leaders for sending participants home with the "highly cavalier and questionable advice for women to run as candidates in every congressional district."[51] This may come as a surprise that one of the leading co-founders of the National Women's Political Caucus (NWPC) in 1971, the first women's political patronage organization of its kind, would not support a full-scale attempt to draw women into office in 1968. Abzug's reluctance expressed just a few years prior to her own campaign shows how gradually she shifted her own thinking in this area and how futile she still believed women's election prospects to be. Instead, she pressed her counterparts to organize a voting coalition as the surest way to get "real mileage" and help "create the beginnings of a change."[52]

Additionally, Abzug did not fully appreciate the political approach of women's liberationists who participated in the Jeanette Rankin Brigade demonstration. The newly formed New York Radical Women staged a "burial of the weeping womanhood" at the Arlington National Cemetery, in which they cast off accoutrements of beauty culture to criticize femininity alongside war.[53] Abzug believed this style of protest was ridiculous and ineffective, and that it diminished the severity of the Vietnam War. After the JRB, New York WSP participants returned home buzzing about the "heated debates about traditional sex roles" that had unfolded, "the meaning of woman power and women's liberation, and whether or not affluent young radical women had the right to push their demands forward when our sisters were dying in Vietnam."[54] Abzug could not ignore this major shift.

Women were increasingly coming together to talk about their lives on college campuses, in community centers, in breakrooms, and in living rooms. The National Organization for Women, formed in 1966, pressed for a full-scale reevaluation of American institutions, laws, and cultural behavior.[55] Abzug could get on board with this organizing spearheaded by professional women more readily than she could the consciousness-raising exercise practiced in women's liberation groups. Although sharing personal experiences dealing with taboo issues like abortion, rape, and domestic violence evolved into political campaigns she later supported, she did not think much of this style of organizing as it first took hold.

Deconstructing femininity, in Abzug's view, was a low priority next to ending the Vietnam War. She saw younger feminists' conceptions of patriarchy as rooted in earlier leftist analysis of male chauvinism, an inheritance that was unacknowledged. She also judged their "mystical or archaic interpretation as to what is the role of women in our society" to be unsophisticated. At the same time, she was aware that these activists saw her approach as "too tame because it relates to the electoral process."[56] These different emphases and shared skepticism created distance between Abzug and proponents of women's liberation. Even so, she recognized the common cause she had with these budding activists and would adopt their rhetoric and demands with relative ease when becoming a New Politics Democratic candidate.

The National Conference for New Politics (NCNP) held in Chicago over Labor Day in 1967 was a galvanizing moment for women's liberationists in attendance. The NCNP, which formed in 1966 to bring New Left energy into Democratic politics, backed candidates like Jerome Wilson during the midterms.[57] The group's founding conference in 1967 sought to draw together progressives across the left-liberal spectrum, a joining represented by Dr. Martin Luther King Jr. and Stokely Carmichael's shared time onstage. Regrettably, the "fruitful dialogue" between movement activists engaging new constituencies and "searching" liberals did not come about.[58] Instead, the conference devolved into a series of demands for recognition, with ethnic nationalists gaining more ground than feminists. Although accounting for only 20 percent of attendees, the Black Caucus persuaded the full delegation to grant its affiliates 50 percent voting representation. Responding to the six-day Arab-Israeli War that June, attendees indicated their shift toward an anticolonial and pro-Palestinian position by passing an anti-

Zionist plank.[59] These issues moved NCNP's full body to act, while women's rights did not. Women's NCNP presence was broad enough to convene three breakout groups—the WSP Caucus, Women's Caucus, and Women's Liberation Caucus. Florynce Kennedy and Ti-Grace Atkinson led an effort to call for "adequate emphasis" of "issues as affect women in the home and outside the home" and the "right to self-determination" in NCNP's platform.[60] Shulamith Firestone and others rushed the stage to demand a hearing. NCNP chair William F. Pepper refused to hand over the microphone, telling her, "Cool down, little girl. We have more important things to talk about than women's problems."[61]

For feminists on the receiving end of this condescending rebuke, this moment served as the "final precipitant to an independent women's movement."[62] Abzug believed the silencing of Firestone to be shameful, and she left the conference early out of disgust.[63] But she failed to approach these feminists in solidarity and remained perturbed by the splintering of groups "set in their own views" at NCNP. She worried identity politics could create a silo effect, skewing focus away from the collective goal of defining a comprehensive progressive agenda. Focusing on this disruptive current, she underplayed the successful passage of antidraft and immediate-withdrawal resolutions, suggesting there was not "much for WSP to go along with."[64] Abzug found it disappointing that the convention did not amount to a defined New Politics movement, but still thought that the call for "new politics" could be sustained beyond this single event. Peace more than feminism, she believed, would be the connective glue that brought Democratic New Politics together. She expected the presidential race of 1968 would be a prime mobilizing moment.

Rebel Partisans

New Politics resisters were a visible presence, but not a dominating power, at the 1968 Democratic National Convention. The demand for an open Democratic convention and debate over "new priorities" reflected the purposeful, plotted infusion of social movement organizers and affiliates into the Democratic Party.[65] The combined force of outside agitators and disillusioned party reformers spurred the greatest reevaluation of party structure and purpose since the Roosevelt years. The upset complicated the selection of delegates and disrupted Vice President Hubert Humphrey's easy path to the presidential nomination. Rebel partisans like Abzug were disappointed that their immediate impact was not more totalizing, but they had a noticeable effect that continued to build thereafter.

Abzug had temporarily abandoned her focus on influencing the Democratic Party when she backed a short-lived Dr. King–Dr. Spock presidential campaign promoted by the National Conference for New Politics. The 17th CD PAC divided over support of this ticket, as did the wider Metropolitan Council for Peace Politics, a citywide alliance of around 500 that Abzug helped found in 1967 with the aim of creating "a caucus in every Democratic club."[66] Doug Ireland, arguing one side, contended that "the defeat of Lyndon Johnson and the possible ending of the Vietnam War was so crucial that the moment was not ripe for a third party."[67] Abzug countered that "between two equals the choice should go not to the Democrat ipso facto, but to the candidate who will go down the line anti-war."[68] As her critique of President Johnson mounted, she reverted to her third-party leanings. Her personal ties to Benjamin Spock motivated her position. Dr. Spock and his wife had moved to Manhattan from Cleveland shortly after Bella and Martin returned to the city. Common antiwar interests kindled the couples' friendship, but they also enjoyed dancing and traveling together. A "prototypical New England WASP," Spock may not have been an obvious match for the very Jewish Bella Abzug, but their connection embodied the confluence of liberals turning toward radicalism and leftists moving toward respectable politics in 1967–1968.[69]

Unsurprisingly, the King-Spock ticket fizzled, as did the organization that backed it. The NCNP folded in April 1968, unable to overcome financial woes, leadership jockeying, programmatic incoherence, and an investigation by the Senate Internal Security Subcommittee.[70] However, the end of NCNP did not halt the push toward a Democratic New Politics. Abzug devoted considerable attention to a grassroots campaign to pressure Johnson not to seek reelection. The Dump Johnson campaign was initiated by reformers connected to the liberal engine, Americans for Democratic Action. Al Lowenstein, a board member, and Curtis Gans, on staff, convened informal discussions on how to deal with Democrats' "Achilles heel . . . the unpopularity of Lyndon Johnson." Their conclusion was to recruit an alternative candidate and to mobilize grassroots support. Abzug joined the campaign to help drum up peace movement involvement. Gans characterized her behind-the-scenes work as vital, if "not generally recognized by history."[71]

The Dump Johnson movement provided Abzug with an opportunity to expand her acquaintance with antiwar Democrats outside of New York and beyond those she lobbied in Washington. Abzug helped map out the campaign's primary strategy. Studying election procedure state by state, she determined that Wisconsin was the only state where "the electorate will have an opportunity at a primary election to vote 'yes' or 'no' for Johnson."[72] To coordinate a challenge, she reached out to Donald Peterson of the Concerned Wisconsin Democrats and enlisted local women's peace activists to collaborate with his outfit. In New York, she rallied her network to register voters before the October deadline for eligibility to vote in the primary. This effort built on the Vietnam Summer voting drive of the previous year, which sent "hundreds of new people out ringing doorbells."[73] This nationwide pressure helped push Johnson toward a decision that Dump Johnson campaigners had not anticipated. On March 31, during a live television broadcast, he stunned Americans when he announced he would not seek reelection.

Before this point, two worthy opponents had already jumped into the race, encouraged informally by leaders in the Dump Johnson movement. Abzug was not particularly enthusiastic about the first, the professorial Senator Eugene McCarthy, who announced his candidacy as "a vehicle for protesting against the war" in November 1967.[74] Still, she delivered WSP support, while alerting McCarthy to the considerable hurdle he would face attracting antiwar interests, since "many people working for peace in Vietnam are skeptical and pessimistic about the electoral process."[75] Abzug helped recruit canvassers to make the trip from New York to New Hampshire, where Curtis Gans ran McCarthy's field office. Gans's grassroots operation helped McCarthy come close to beating Johnson, 42.4 percent to 49.5 percent in the New Hampshire primary on March 12, a surprise finish Senate majority leader Mike Mansfield called a "warning signal."[76] Four days later, Senator Robert F. Kennedy jumped into the race, a decision McCarthy did not appreciate.

Kennedy's announcement required progressive Democrats to pick sides. Abzug feigned neutrality, calling Kennedy's campaign another "crack in the door."[77] But she chose like everyone else. In March, Kennedy's campaign manager, Stephan Smith, called Abzug and asked her to support the

Figure 3.1 Senator Eugene McCarthy is pictured wearing a "Bella Abzug for Congress" button in support of her bid for office in 1970. McCarthy was among the male "doves" Abzug backed in the 1960s, drawing womanpower and women power into their campaigns. (Uncredited, Bella Abzug Papers, Box 1088, Rare Book and Manuscript Library, Columbia University)

campaign. Summoned to Kennedy's midtown suite on Saint Patrick's Day, she brought with her a cadre of women organizers who briefed the new candidate on antiwar activities under way. This was not the first time that Kennedy had met Abzug. Kennedy adviser Ronnie Eldridge, still friendly with Abzug, had secured a meeting for WSP lobbyists with the senator one year prior. On that occasion, Kennedy had jested before the entourage arrived, "Did he need a helmet? Were they coming on their motorcycles, and did he need protection?" Their demure demeanor disarmed Kennedy. As Eldridge recalled, "Everybody stood around waiting for this tirade, and there were all these nice ladies."[78] Abzug had exhibited reservations about Kennedy's views earlier, writing in 1966, "Too soon to tell but doubtless liberal a la his brother. Nothing yet re Vietnam."[79] Yet, Kennedy's reaction to the Tet Offensive on January 30, 1968, demonstrated his level of conviction. That day, the National Liberation Front (NLF) and the North Vietnamese Army targeted "thirty-six of forty-four provincial capitals, five of the six largest cities, fifty hamlets, and, most notably, the U.S. embassy, presidential palace, and South Vietnamese Army headquarters."[80] While the attack failed to incite an uprising against US-backed President Nguyen Van Theiu, and the NLF suffered the brunt of casualties nearing 40,000, the unexpected action brought into question the prospect of winning this war. "We are mired in a stalemate," Walter Cronkite told television viewers after returning from Vietnam.[81] Senator Kennedy went one step further, asking, "What has happened to America?"[82] This was the question Abzug believed needed to be asked.

As Abzug became "very important" to the Kennedy campaign, she feared that the McCarthy-versus-Kennedy fissure would divide progressives irreparably.[83] She contributed to a minor "Stop Humphrey" effort after Vice President Hubert Humphrey, an establishment Democrat, announced his candidacy on April 27. Unrealistically, Abzug hoped McCarthy and Kennedy supporters would engage in "creative competition for specific programs to reconstruct American foreign policy and reconstruct our cities," and become a united front in the effort to stave off Humphrey.[84] Projection of the New York Democratic primary had McCarthy and Kennedy dividing the vote in all but two districts, awarding Humphrey a win.[85] Abzug was deeply worried about this potential. She pressured Gans to build bridges, and she worked with Eldridge, Sarah Kovner, and others through the Coalition for a Democratic Alternative to develop an issue-focused agenda outside the campaigns.[86] Tensions got worse instead of better. Gans suspected Abzug was for Kennedy, while those in Kennedy's campaign were convinced Abzug was with McCarthy. She called Eldridge under an assumed name to get through on the line. It was enough to stir Abzug's doubts. Scribbled amid phone numbers, polling statistics, and lighthearted doodles, she recorded her uncertainty, writing, "Can't imagine it—impossible—we'll take a strong stand v. the power—can't tell what can happen between now and June. I can't tell."[87]

No one could foresee the tragedy that befell on June 5. Kennedy, on tour in California, where he met with African American residents in Watts, Mexican American farmworkers in Delano, and draft-weary students at Cal State universities, was assassinated at a Los Angeles hotel. His funeral at

Saint Patrick's Cathedral replaced homecoming rallies planned in New York to proceed the June 18 primary. Like many Kennedy followers, Abzug sorrowfully reflected, "I had just gotten to influence him about the war in Vietnam," and wondered what could have been.[88] It was a difficult blow after Martin Luther King Jr.'s assassination in April, which Abzug described as "a tragic reminder of his warning that the fate of our people at home is bound inevitably with American withdrawal from Vietnam."[89] She hoped that people would come together after the loss of King and Kennedy. Instead, McCarthy and Kennedy supporters worked for parallel concerns in separate quarters. In New York, all progressives came over to the stop Humphrey camp, with Humphrey gaining only 11 of the 123 delegate slates.[90] Nonetheless, lawyer Paul O'Dwyer, running for the New York state senate, had a staff so divided between McCarthy and Kennedy factions, they set up separate offices.

For Abzug, everything after Kennedy's assassination proved to be a disappointment. She did not believe that McCarthy, who lacked charisma, could carry a progressive insurgency forward and expected his stature would fade after the election. "The best we could have done had we gotten Kennedy into the presidency would have been to establish a people's victory that might have enabled us to build a broader, deeper political movement. But we were routed, as usual, and we fell apart," she lamented.[91] In making this judgment, she dwelled on the fragility of progressives' alliance and the loss of the presidency. What she undervalued was how the New Politics force, while fragmented and imperfect, had gained traction.

Part of the reason Abzug missed the inroads a growing New Politics faction made in 1968 was because she was not a major player at the Democratic National Convention. She largely advocated from the wings, cornering delegates in the hall before a vote, urging them to do the right thing. In the lead-up to the DNC, she again addressed the Platform Committee. Speaking after Al Lowenstein, she read off a litany of offenses that occurred on Johnson's watch: the "horror of Vietnam . . . a monstrous military behemoth . . . futile peace talks . . . a punitive draft system . . . the weakening of the United Nations . . . and, a national atmosphere of despair and violence." It was not good enough, she told this committee, to recognize these failures. "The Democratic Party must restructure itself to restore political power to the people," she urged, "by the guarantee of full franchise and representation for those who thus far have been barred from decision making by reason of race, poverty, class or sex."[92] While

Abzug's remarks uniquely highlighted the perspective of women activists, her testimony is most compelling because of its similarity to that of others. She worked in step with a growing progressive faction focused on democratizing the Democratic Party alongside setting a new agenda.

The 1968 DNC stands out for the visible "open convention" challenge launched by racial minorities, women, antiwar advocates, and others to contest the white, male liberal establishment that propped up the party's exclusionary practices alongside its Cold War imperative. This challenge was preceded by the Mississippi Freedom Democratic Party's delegate seating campaign in 1964 and would be succeeded by the National Women's Political Caucus's effort to expand women's delegate strength in 1972. The 1968 DNC served as a pivotal midpoint, the moment of realization by party leadership that they must respond to grassroots pressure for democratization or face a greater moment of reckoning. Coming around to this position did not occur without tense internal resistance to change.

The organizing Abzug did in New York to mobilize a "people's" challenge at the DNC reflected a pattern that played out nationally. New York State Democratic chairman John J. Burns dodged McCarthy operatives' demand for delegate control, opting instead to award only fifteen and a half delegates, or less than one-fourth, to McCarthy backers. "If I ignored the people who have helped me with the organization's work and appointed strangers just because they were for McCarthy, I'd have a revolution on my hands," Burns insisted.[93] That attitude was enough to encourage a walkout and spur grassroots mobilization to democratize state party procedure. The Coalition for Politics of the People, which Abzug helped found, demanded "an open convention." Most immediately, they aimed to deliver "meaningful pressure" on the Democratic Party, but they also sought to become "a permanent coalition" within the party advocating "peace abroad and . . . new priorities of the black, the poor, the minorities, and our cities."[94] Attracting only a few hundred members, this New York–centered alliance gained little traction on its own, but augmented its force by joining up with the wider National Coalition for an Open Convention, which had thousands of participants. This outside pressure boosted the McCarthy campaign's effort to push for structural reform. Most consequentially, they leaned on Iowa governor Harold Hughes to chair an informal commission to evaluate delegate selection rules. The commission report affirmed what grassroots forces had already declared: "This Convention is on trial."[95]

The Democratic Party's Rules Committee determined this charge would be fatal to ignore. Accordingly, it established a formal commission chaired by Senator George McGovern and Representative Donald M. Fraser, tasked with evaluating and reforming party procedure by the next convention. The reforms the McGovern-Fraser Commission oversaw, in place by 1972, would enact "the greatest systematically planned and centrally imposed shift in the institutions of delegate selection in all of American history."[96] New rules would make the Democratic Party more inclusive, transparent, and responsive to its members, and in turn, would open party leadership to new influences as women and racial minorities gained a greater presence. This procedural reform was a direct response to the mounting pressure directed at the Democratic Party from progressive social movement activists working in common cause with partisan reformers. In the swirl of unrest that consumed the 1968 DNC, it was easy to miss this undramatic yet transformative action.

Television cameras zeroed in on the tense face-off between protesters and police in Chicago's Grant Park. Inside the convention hall, the ruckus on the floor was not violent, but neither was it tame. The New York delegation was among the party's most rebellious. Unsatisfied with Humphrey, still divided into McCarthy and Kennedy camps, New York delegates attempted to nominate Senator Edward Kennedy for president in honor of his deceased brother. Once this defiant move was quashed, focus turned to the issue that Abzug watched most closely. After 1:00 a.m. on August 28, Platform Committee chair Hale Boggs opened the Vietnam debate as oppositional delegates chanted angrily, "Let's Go Home, Let's Go Home." Party leader Carl Albert made a rare concession, calling it a night. When debate returned to Vietnam the next day, a minority faction called for the adoption of a plank demanding an unconditional halt of bombing in North Vietnam and a phased mutual withdrawal. Instead, a majority plank sustaining Johnson-Humphrey wartime policy passed 1,567 to 1,041. Unwilling to accept defeat, New York delegates immediately jumped to their feet, donned black armbands, and sang "We Shall Overcome." That night, Humphrey secured the nomination as mayhem erupted outside. The tear gas was so thick it came in through the vents at the Hilton hotel, where police officers indiscriminately evicted campaign workers from McCarthy headquarters.[97]

This confrontation led many Americans, including Abzug, to feel like the nation had reached a tipping point and everything was unraveling. This view of "1968-as-peak" has captured popular imagination for too long, skewing focus away from what came next.[98] For New Politics Democrats, 1968 marked an opening salvo of a progressive political resistance that impacted the tenor of electoral politics, the shape of the Democratic Party, and the direction of congressional action through the mid-1970s. In November 1968, with President Richard Nixon elected, Robert F. Kennedy slain, and Eugene McCarthy sidelined, it did not feel like new politics would take flight. And yet, what began in 1966 had established surer footing in 1968 and would continue thereafter. In the moment, New Politics Democrats could not foresee how their organizing at the grassroots and within the party would enable a small cadre of reform candidates like Bella Abzug to gain office in 1970. They did not anticipate antiwar reformer Senator George McGovern would secure the Democratic presidential nomination in 1972. And they could not predict how the Watergate scandal would rock the nation, triggering a wave of post-Watergate reformers to sweep the 1974 midterm elections and carry the New Politics mantle forward. They also could not foresee how their critique of Cold War liberalism and their increased visibility as a progressive Democratic faction with clout would invariably foment resistance by conservatives within their party and by Republicans.

Women, too, did not anticipate how they would emerge by 1972 as a noticeable "breakthrough" force in electoral politics. The 1968 election was a turning point for left-liberal women in politics. Their involvement in insurgent presidential campaigns and open convention challenges stirred their political will and personal ambition.[99] Inside the Democratic Party structure and through issue-centered organizations, women offered a groundswell of support for political campaigns as they had historically. What shifted at this point was how vocally women such as Abzug demanded recognition and encouraged others to do the same. These solo quests for respect grew into collective pressure for a systemic reevaluation of women's opportunity and advancement in electoral politics.

The Taxpayers Campaign

After the 1968 DNC, Abzug was still not prepared to run for office. If anything, she thought she needed a break from politics, disillusioned with how the McCarthy and Kennedy campaigns turned out. Abzug decided to refocus her energies on Women Strike for Peace and return her organizing attention to New York City. She gained most inspiration from the growing welfare rights movement, heartened by this women-led poor people's campaign to stave off cuts in benefits and challenge paternalistic surveillance of recipients. She was convinced, as welfare rights activists argued, that public aid should be a guaranteed right and that women's reproductive labors should be valued. Under the direction of Beulah Sanders, the City-Wide Coordinating Committee of Welfare Groups framed urban poverty as an antiwar issue.[100] Abzug had worked with Sanders, considered her an incredible speaker and gifted organizer, and sought to coordinate efforts across class-race lines around economic justice and peace.

WSP's National Taxpayers' Revolt against Military Spending, launched on April 15, 1969, reflects this connection. Abzug spearheaded this venture with antidraft organizer Irma Zigas. Evoking the Boston Tea Party, women hosted antiwar, antitax "tea parties" in their homes and delivered tea bags to Congress members. They urged those who opposed the war to see the federal budget skewed toward military spending as "a situation of taxation without representation."[101] Abzug set the tone for this "tax revolt" at WSP's Tax Day picket outside the IRS building in Manhattan. "Americans on every level of society—blue collar, white collar, Black, poor, and middle class—conduct a bitter struggle, daily, to secure their unfulfilled right to adequate income, good schools, decent homes, and medical care," she remarked.[102] She had watched President Nixon's first moves to continue the devaluation of gold, escalate military action, and consolidate and privatize government services.[103] And she believed that his wartime spending further redirected federal funding away from the nation's cities. The antitax campaign sought to encourage women to use their purchasing power as a protest tool, while raising awareness of this diversion of funding. Ambitiously, Abzug envisioned an antitax march on Washington akin to the March on Washington for Jobs and Freedom, but it never materialized. Before moving forward with this concept, or allowing the WSP antitax venture to fully flourish, Abzug redirected her focus toward the reelection campaign for Mayor John V. Lindsay.

The year Abzug returned to Manhattan, Lindsay achieved an upset win over New Dealer Robert F. Wagner, whom he criticized for his "tired management."[104] Casting himself "as a progressive more than a Republican," Lindsay ran a fusion campaign boosted by a well-oiled field operation that included 122 storefronts and 24,000 energetic volunteers.[105] Once in City

Hall, he sought to stymie the effects of deindustrialization and suburban-ization that were manifest in growing crime, drug use, unemployment, and poverty. By the time he was up for reelection in 1969, enthusiasm for Lindsay had worn thin. The city remained divided after the contentious Ocean Hill–Brownsville teacher's strike and budgetary problems at the City University of New York had marred Lindsay's reputation. Embroiled in both of these issues, Abzug had taken unpopular positions that would con-tinue to haunt her once in elected office. During the 1968 teacher's strike, she sided with the African American–led school board seeking control over curriculum and staff hires rather than with the teacher's union. And in 1969, she represented black and Puerto Rican City College students during their campaign for ethnic studies and open admission.[106] Lindsay's struggle during the election because of both issues drew Abzug's sympathy. The mayor also gained criticism because of escalating welfare and pension costs, strained negotiations with municipal unions, and a police force on edge after he established the Civilian Complaint Review Board to rein in police brutality.

This period, Lindsay later reflected, "had been the worst of my public life."[107] While he recognized his reelection chances were uncertain, he was still caught off guard by his "squeaker of a loss" in the Republican pri-mary.[108] State senator John J. Marchi supplanted Lindsay, and quelled a return attempt by Wagner, by drawing on Italian patronage and engaging in "law-and-order" fearmongering. A parallel upset occurred on the Demo-cratic side, where anticrime candidate Mario Procaccino beat out Bronx borough president Herman Badillo and writer Norman Mailer, whose spoiler campaign promoted the idea of New York City becoming the fifty-first state. But Lindsay received a way forward after the primary, gaining support from the Liberal Party, a New York–based third party, to run as its candidate.

Lindsay's aides presumed they could develop another fusion campaign attracting progressive Republicans and Democrats, but they needed the help of Democratic organizers to achieve this feat. Their outreach effort was fast and furious. "We went on a rampage. We saw an opportunity to orchestrate a scenario that exploited the divisions in the Democratic Party before they had an opportunity to unify," recalled Lindsay's campaign manager Richard "Dick" Aurelio.[109] In search of a "Democratic guide," Lindsay aide Barry Gotteherer recruited his friend Ronnie Eldridge, who in turn reached out to Abzug.[110] Eldridge had worked for Mailer and did not know Lindsay, but she thought the prospect of Procaccino as mayor "so ludicrous" she agreed to lead Democrats for Lindsay.[111] While Eldridge could pull in endorsements, she believed she needed help harnessing social movement energy and drumming up block-by-block support. For this reason, she thought to bring Abzug in as she had for Kennedy's campaign.

It took some time convincing Lindsay and Aurelio. Both had been on the receiving end of Abzug's lobbying visits when Lindsay served in the House of Representatives and Aurelio worked as chief of staff to Senator Jacob Javits. They knew she could be relentless and disagreeable, and worried if they could keep her in line. Additionally, they did not want to alienate Lindsay's Wall Street backers or further ostracize New York's business elite, already on edge because they believed the mayor's social spending and tax policies made the city less hospitable to corporations. All this was weighed against Abzug's mobilizing skills and ability to deliver an endorsement from the New Democratic Coalition, a group she helped form in 1968 to carry New Politics forward. The trick, Lindsay aides decided, would be to keep Abzug "in the tent, but . . . figure out a way that [she] does not become the front page picture"—in other words, to send her out as a surrogate, but "at a time when the news was already put to bed."[112] And so, when Eldridge called, Abzug appeared at Lindsay headquarters the Sunday night after the primary. Her physical presence floored aide Sid Davidoff, who would never forget "Bella . . . on top of the desk with her legs hanging over . . . a big woman in stature, wearing her hat, and shouting her demands." As Davidoff recalled, "She was so firm in who she was and what she was and clearly was a person who was committed to the issues."[113]

Abzug was recruited to pacify social justice organizers and nurture their support, not to give them the reins to the campaign. Movement activists overestimated their impact on the election outcome and underestimated how difficult it would be to move Lindsay in their direction. Abzug proposed reconstituting WSP's antitax campaign as the Taxpayers Campaign for Urban Priorities, an issue campaign that would be overtly for Lindsay but would have an air of independence. New York WSP activists believed they "thrust Lindsay into this [antitax] campaign," but his team had already been exploring angles to critique the "guns and butter" economic approach.[114] The diverse neighborhood clubs and advocacy groups that allied under this loosely defined populist antiwar taxpayers coalition helped Lindsay expand his reach and affirm his progressive credentials. But this initiative also provided Lindsay with a buffer between his campaign and this auxiliary grassroots unit.

Abzug and her allies attempted to exert more control. On Abzug's behest, Lindsay met with thirty WSP activists, who urged him to "actually become an organizer, leader and activist."[115] In turn, they worked as canvassers and researchers. They crunched numbers, quantifying how many more schools, child care centers, and public housing units could be funded if tax dollars stayed in New York. Urging Mayor Lindsay to make this case to President Nixon, Abzug drafted an ad that ran in the New York Times delivering her desired dispatch. "New York spends more on war than on New York. The $9 billion of our tax money that Washington spends on the military each year is more than our entire city budget. It could get us more housing, more jobs, more schools, more hospitals and health care, better public transportation, and cleaner and safer streets," it read.[116]

Lindsay's campaign supported this message even though it complicated his position on tax policy and indirectly highlighted how he had exacerbated New York City's financial woes. During his first term, Lindsay supported tax hikes passed by the New York state legislature on stock transfers, personal income, and business revenues. But increased taxes assuaged the city's budget problems only temporarily. In 1968 and 1969, Lindsay returned to Albany to press the legislature to redirect state income tax funds to the city and give the city more license to determine its own tax figures. Unsuccessful in these efforts, he shifted to borrowing funds, moving revenue between programs, and offering municipal bonds. This cycle delayed the full brunt of New York City's fiscal crisis, while digging the city deeper into its hole. It is not clear if Abzug had analyzed Lindsay's past fiscal program or discussed the extent of his lobbying in Albany or Washington with his aides. The Taxpayers Campaign for Urban Priorities promoted a simple message that explained away New York's economic windfall as federally induced. Pointing the finger at Nixon was an effective maneuver to direct focus away from Lindsay, underplaying the fact that the deep-seated problems facing the city began before the Vietnam War. Accordingly, the Taxpayers Campaign was not designed to offer solutions beyond the general suggestion of rerouting federal dollars from the military to jobs, infrastructure, and social programs.

New York City stuck with Lindsay, but just barely. His coalition "does not even run beyond the East River ot [sic] the Manhattan suburbs," noted one analyst, highlighting that six out of ten New Yorkers did not vote his way.[117] Lindsay's aides thought Abzug's contribution "had to be something that was helpful," but not at the level she did.[118] Expecting an appointment, she floated the idea of leading a new Urban Priorities Division, "planning for human needs and a livable environment . . . and a basic educational and organizational effort in the neighborhoods."[119] Abzug pressed this idea persistently. When she showed up at City Hall on one occasion, ready to discuss her proposal, Lindsay opted to leave rather than hear her out. He told aide Sid Davidoff, "You take her," as he ducked out through a back door.[120] Lindsay did not strongly consider establishing an Urban Priorities Division or giving Abzug a municipal post. He did see the benefit of having a liaison to social movement organizers on staff, and for this role, he hired Ronnie Eldridge as a special assistant. Lindsay wanted to keep progressive Democrats in his corner, and he aspired to meet New Yorkers' needs down to the neighborhood level. What Abzug had proposed would have reversed this directional relationship. She envisioned bottom-up, community-powered policymaking in which constituents had great license to personalize city services. Essentially, she advocated extending the social pact between the city's government and its people just as this relationship began to crumble. In contrast, Lindsay's brand of "urban liberalism" delicately balanced past commitment to providing all city dwellers with a social net alongside greater openness to private sector engagement in government. "He was poised," as historian Kim Phillips-Fein notes, "between an older industrial New York, with its longstanding social welfare traditions, and a new white-collar city that had no such allegiances."[121] Abzug did not recognize Lindsay's predicament or his level of sympathy. He could see her frustration more than she could, and encouraged her to run for office.[122]

IN BELLA ABZUG'S TELLING, her decision to run for Congress came to her as a vision. She went diving while on winter holiday at Club Med in Martinique. Way down in the deep blue sea, thinking without "interference," she decided, "Well, God damn it, I think it's overdue. I will run."[123] This dramatic explanation underplays how Abzug had been moving toward this end for quite some time. Since 1966, she had been gradually forming a brain trust, perfecting campaigning techniques, establishing a platform, and building a base. In 1967, she first encouraged WSP to "promote and elect more women candidates," though she did not believe that this focus should be a main priority and she did not suggest herself.[124] In 1968, her family moved to 37 Bank Street in the Nineteenth District, where Ted Weiss lost to Leonard Farbstein, and she believed she could win his seat.[125] And in 1969, she finally decided to give it a go. Abzug faced what she later described as a "catch-22": "Women lose because they don't have enough support . . . they don't have enough money to conduct effective campaigns," and "they have trouble raising money because people think they're losers."[126] Demanding greatness of herself, she found it difficult to take the political plunge knowing defeat was more likely than winning. Lindsay's campaign gave her the final push she needed, stirred by her frustration that she could not influence him more, and by his encouragement that she could act directly if elected.

Abzug's involvement in Lindsay's campaign was valuable, for it confirmed that bread-and-butter issues matter to voters. While she focused increasingly on antiwar and feminist concerns, she never lost sight of class. Once the Johnson administration was embroiled in the Vietnam War, the experimental energy and resources drained out of War on Poverty programs. Abzug joined a chorus on the Left critiquing this reordering of priorities and participated in local efforts to assuage and expose the federal government's abandonment. Her antitax campaign, in its call for economic reorganization, sought to provide antipoverty, labor, and civil rights activists with an overarching systemic response to growing class inequity. Running John Lindsay's Taxpayers Campaign for Urban Priorities enabled Abzug to test out a leftist brand of economic populism tied to an antimilitarization critique. The campaign made overtures to all New Yorkers, encouraging, "The time has come for everyone to say *stop*—whether he's a Democrat, a Republican, a Liberal, an Independent, a rich man, a poor man, a white man, a black man or Puerto Rican, a Catholic, Protestant or Jew."[127] As one "Manhattan liberal" kindly brought to Abzug's attention, however, "You omitted Conservatives."[128] This letter made Abzug pause, but she never seriously considered this group as part of "the people." Thus, the antitax campaign both encouraged her to think more broadly than her women and antiwar base and solidified her progressive articulation of working-class interests.

By the end of the 1960s, Abzug had fully committed to being a New Politics Democrat. On task, she stayed firm in her position that the Left should not write off the Democratic Party as the party that fortified the national security state, stilted further growth of the welfare state, and propped up a legally enshrined racist, sexist, heteronormative state. After 1965, she shifted from talking about radicalizing the Democratic Party to working within it toward this end. She employed a local-national strategy, helping build a coalitional grassroots network in New York that could feed quickly and effectively into national issue campaigns and support of political candidates.

This kind of reasonable resistance, replicated in pockets throughout the United States, helped shift the conversation at the 1968 Democratic National Convention toward New Politics concerns. Outsider partisans' efforts to take control of the party platform were quashed, but their call for greater democratization influenced the internal reform that followed. More so, this mobilized insurgency inspired individuals such as Abzug to move from the wings into the chambers of federal policymaking. As an activist candidate, she made clear that she planned to bring the fierce impatience of progressive social movements to the staid halls of government.

4

CAMPAIGN FOR THE PEOPLE

I S WASHINGTON READY for Bella Abzug? Is Anybody?" was the title of an article by journalist Jimmy Breslin in *New York* magazine in October 1970. "She is loud. She can also be good and rude." She indiscriminately "fussed and fumed." She had a "wide, clomping stride." "She looked like a fighter in training," Breslin characterized. Bella Abzug's jibes were not only rhetorical. As Breslin told it, her aide Michael Macdonald had stumbled into the Lion's Head bar in Greenwich Village one night, where Breslin was enjoying a pint. Doubling over in discomfort, Macdonald told how Abzug had given him "a whack in the side" when they disagreed about scheduling. Feeling remorse, she phoned the next day, saying, "Michael, I called to apologize. How's your kidney?"[1]

For tough New Yorkers, this image of Abzug "pushing, brawling, poking, striding her way toward the Congress" worked.[2] In the 1970s, New York City was a gritty and ailing metropolis in need of someone who could embody its residents' fury and elevate their hope. "There is nothing beautiful left in the streets of this city. I have come to believe in death and renewal by fire," wrote poet Audre Lorde in her elegy "New York City 1970."[3] The Nineteenth District—where Abzug ran for a seat in the House of Representatives—ran along the West Side of Manhattan up to Eighty-Third Street. Its neighborhoods were as economically varied as they were diverse, with glimmering markers of affluence and woeful corners of neglect. The district was riddled with dilapidated housing, its unemployment rate at 8.7 percent had surpassed that of Harlem, and 200 percent more men from the district were drafted or enlisted in the military than any other in the city.[4] Responding to this grim situation, Abzug promised to be "no humble member of Congress who plays follow the leader and keeps quiet."[5]

Tenacious and tough as nails, Abzug "came into a room like a lumberjack."[6] She stood on street corners, stopped people in their tracks, and vehemently debated them on the issues as she asked for their vote. Her hat and girth drew attention, her voice bellowed and boomed, her finger punctured the air, and her delightful cackle lightened the mood. Abzug encouraged the moniker "Battling Bella," which stuck. Her campaign literature used the word "fight" more than any other. She made it clear women could be "tough Jews" too, joining a long tradition of New York male "prizefighters, gangsters, left-wing heavies, and trade unionists."[7]

Abzug ran for Congress as a leftist urban populist who zeroed in on how the nation's expanded war purse, coupled with the forces of deindustrialization and suburbanization, hurt city people.[8] Her populist message reflected her long-standing commitment to being an ally in the class struggle. Most recently during the Lindsay campaign, Abzug had considered the US economy's waning productivity and innovation alongside the bleeding of capital away from northeastern cities and beyond US borders. Workers were increasingly isolated and vulnerable, facing deskilling, stagnant wages, declining benefits, and "right to work" laws. Many of these problems hit New Yorkers hard, as manufacturing businesses joined residents fleeing northern urban centers. Abzug focused on these structuralist concerns during her 1970 campaign and thereafter, breaking down macroeconomic trends to the level of dollars and cents.

It was not enough, Abzug argued, to think creatively about how to bring average New Yorkers relief during hard economic times. The changing economy, she believed, warranted a fundamental reconsideration of the exclusionary citizen-worker ideal. She sought to recenter focus in Democratic politics on an emerging workforce that included women, homosexuals, new immigrants, racial minorities, and the poor. She made clear Franklin D. Roosevelt's image of the "forgotten man" was an archetype that left out most Americans. Rejecting the valorization of white, male, heterosexual laborers, she argued that women were "the real silent majority."[9]

In doing so, Abzug attempted to connect emerging identity politics with the bread-and-butter issues that mattered most to the Democratic Party's traditional blue-collar base. Running on the slogan "This Woman's Place

Is in the House—the House of Representatives," Abzug put forth a break-through message that signaled her feminist purpose.[10] With her headquarters placed a few doors down from the Stonewall Inn, where gay bar goers resisted a police raid in 1969, her campaign was among the first nationally to embrace gay liberation as well. Hastily scribbled campaign handbills, noting "Give the Power Back to the People!," looked as if they came hot off a mimeograph machine set up at the frontline.[11] The Abzug operation reflected the pace, informality, and zeal of 1960s progressive social movements. And yet, as Abzug appropriated the rhetoric and harnessed the dynamism of antiwar ethnic nationalist, and social liberationist organizing, she remained committed to the ideas and tactics that formed her politics during the Popular Front–New Deal era. Bridging these leftist currents, she aspired to reconcile the "politics of recognition" with the "politics of redistribution."[12] That is, she sought to connect the demand for greater rights and representation with an appeal for wider economic parity.

Abzug's "new politics" articulated a rights-centered, economic justice–focused, and global peace–oriented agenda. She ran to demonstrate how an "activist Congresswoman" could clean up the "high places in Government where cynical men now abuse power."[13] She tried to reform how campaigns were done, working outside patronage channels, challenging incumbency, circumventing party procedure, securing activist endorsements, and employing small-donor fund-raising. She became a candidate because she feared leftists were losing perspective and needed greater direction.

An Activist Campaign

On March 6, a week before Abzug formally announced her candidacy, Leonard Boudin's brownstone blew up in broad daylight a few blocks away from her home. Abzug had known Boudin for years. They had worked together as National Lawyers Guild lawyers, had attended the same dinner parties, and had twirled around the dance floor on occasion. Boudin's daughter Kathy—similar in age to Abzug's daughters, Eve and Liz—got involved with the Weather Underground and had turned her family's home into a bomb factory. Now Kathy was on the run.[14] This was the district Abzug hoped to represent, and the fatalistic, disillusioned young people among those she aimed to reach.

Abzug's political campaign served as a vehicle to reassert her view within the Left that "radical change is a painful struggle requiring education, new and old forms of agitation and organization directed to short and long term goals."[15] The terrorism of the Weather Underground reflected the most extreme current of radicalism, but Abzug observed other troubling developments—Yippies, hippies, communes, and paramilitary groups. Revolutionaries known as the Crazies had recently interrupted her remarks at a peace forum at Saint Marks Church, barging in shooting squirt guns, yelling, and banging on a piano as she spoke. "Their aim is to purge the old guard who are still sick enough to believe in electoral politics, pacifism, and peaceful demonstrations," wrote Joe Flaherty in the *Village Voice*.[16] Abzug thought this was absurd. She worried that the Left had become so intolerant, "hurling words like 'pigs,'" that "we turn against ourselves" and turn off everyone else.[17] She believed the passion of youth stirred this fanaticism, but she did not deliver her critique of this turn toward violence and separatism as a generational slight. Instead, she urged activists to exhibit greater perseverance and to refocus their collectivist purpose.

Those from Abzug's district who were attracted to the Weather Underground, the Young Lords Party, or the Women's International Terrorist Conspiracy from Hell did not become immediate converts to her brand of radicalism, though some participants would join her later campaigns. Nonetheless, she attracted a deep well of high school and twenty-something backers who were inspired by her leadership and whom she affectionately called "the kids."[18] Some youthful volunteers—Jerrold Nadler, Barbara Ehrenreich, Richard Morris, and Scott Stringer among them—went on to do bigger things. Many were veterans traveling a political circuit that led from McCarthy and Kennedy, next to Mailer, Badillo, and Lindsay, and then Abzug. Recruits were sent by Abzug's lawyer friends, movement contacts, family members, and organized groups like the Movement for a New Congress. Others she urged to come along as she made the rounds to community groups, union gatherings, speak-outs, and consciousness-raising sessions, inviting, "Come and join in my campaign. It is new, exciting and daring and meaningful."[19]

New York Women Strike for Peace treated her potential placement in office as a seat of their own. While she ran to get women, "America's oppressed majority" who did the "drudge work of politics . . . out front," they did the bulk of her clerical work and canvassing.[20] Abzug valued the leadership of her activist inner circle, who made decisions when she was not around. Likewise, Guild lawyers were invested in her campaign, serving as poll watchers and political advisers. Sometimes encouragement came unsolicited, such as attorney Abraham Unger's note to his former disciple, in which he counseled, "What distinguishes you from your rivals is that you believe in all the ideas you advocate and are not a demagogue or opportunist. And if you set out determined not to deviate or pussyfoot, not to say all things to all men, and women, you ought to win out, stage by stage."[21] Abzug drew former American Labor Party members into Democratic politics as she called on reform Democratic allies to help her maneuver party channels. She harnessed the support of progressive Jewish organizations as she depended on antipoverty, civil rights, and labor organizers to help her address race and class concerns. Her campaign became a family affair. Martin had urged her not to run, worrying it would be ugly business and a "wasted effort," but he eagerly knocked on doors, delivering his "Bella for Congress" pitch without revealing his personal stake.[22]

Abzug thoughtfully fused the old and the new in her campaign. She harnessed the energy of social liberation but also responded by incorporating an antiestablishment posture and new issues such as the call for abortion on demand. Yet, she continued to exhibit a structural outlook, highlighting the systemic underpinning of social problems, while defining radical ideas and interests in tangible, accessible terms. Navigating activist and traditional party spaces, she drew on the expertise of party players while engaging in a campaign style that mirrored the flexibility, creativity, and immediacy of grassroots organizing. Making things up as they went along, Abzug's staff constantly evolved. Her headquarters was a place where "if you showed up three times, you were a regular," and your contacts were added to the hundreds of three-by-five index cards detailing volunteer information.[23] If that failed, Abzug's campaign manager, Doug Ireland, had a "card file mind for all political events, candidates, and non-entities." Once active in the 17th CD PAC with Abzug, Ireland ran Al Lowenstein's successful 1968 congressional bid in Nassau County. As "the youngest Old Leftist in America," Ireland shared Abzug's vision for drawing radicals into politics and facilitating exchange across generational lines.[24] He handled Abzug's "desk operation," while Steve Max, who had directed SDS's Political Education Project, ran her "groundwork."[25]

The placement of Abzug's headquarters, at 61 Christopher Street off Sheridan Square, reflected her staff's desire to be at the center of progressive action and their self-assured sense that the campaign could be historic.

Taking over the old *Village Voice* office, the Abzug campaign was housed in a weathered outpost of Greenwich Village on a street "like an old parchment that has been written on over and over again."[26] This neighborhood had been the stomping grounds for bohemians and social reformers of all kinds for nearly a hundred years. In 1970, it was a meeting point of politics and the press. Journalists could stop by the Village Independent Democrats office, also housed nearby, for a scoop and continue on to the Lion's Head, city reporters' favorite watering hole. Close by stood the Stonewall Inn, where a police raid on June 27, 1969, set off a three-day confrontation between cops and more than 200 club goers. "They Invaded Our Rights" and "Support Gay Power" were among the messages scrawled on the boarded-up bar, reclaiming the space as a site of gay liberation.[27] The Abzug Campaign added its own color to the vibrancy of Sheridan Square, with canvassers roaming the streets soliciting petition signatures, volunteers inside working the phones, and Abzug shouting over everyone. "Bella Is Beautiful" posters hung on the walls next to those touting McCarthy for president. All this reflected the usual sights and sounds of a campaign. What made Abzug Campaign headquarters atypical was the volunteer-run drop-in child care center on the second floor, free to staff and neighborhood residents and open from 10:00 a.m. to 10:00 p.m.

In creating a different kind of workplace, Abzug modeled what she described as an "acting, not talking," campaign.[28] Universal child care was a central tenet of her platform. She went beyond projecting what it could look like if all parents had access to free, safe day care to experimenting with how neighborhood-centered services could function. Socialistic in its design, the center offered an alternative to the inadequate privatized system in place in the United States, and highlighted the drain of public social services she blamed on the Vietnam War. Not subtle in her delivery, she played up the novelty of this feature of her campaign when reporters came calling. A picture of Abzug, smiling with a baby in her arms, ran in the *Manhattan Tribune* with the accompanying jingle: "Because, while spending sixty skillion smackers on/the war, he [Nixon] tells us he's against starvation./ Bella having heard the song before, is pointing/out another kind of deprivation."[29]

This "acting, not talking" framing was a deliberate strategy to set herself apart from incumbent Leonard Farbstein. A lawyer who had served during World War I, Farbstein served in the New York State Assembly before he was elected to the House of Representatives in 1956. Abzug tried to deflate his argument that he was a tested "progressive Democrat" by demonstrating that he was detached, presumed his seat was his for the taking, and had lost sight of New Yorkers' needs.[30] She took advantage of his weeklong absences while completing his responsibilities in Washington by running a seven-day-a-week, block-by-block campaign.[31] "Once a year he sends out a pamphlet from the Department of Agriculture about how to make potatoes," a reporter overheard her telling mothers in Abingdon Square.[32] Setting up a visible contrast, she brought her constituent services to street corners. On the Lower East Side, observant Jews could report on employers requiring them to work on the Sabbath at tables set up along their walking route, information Abzug's staff passed on to the municipal Human Rights Commission.[33]

As a change candidate, Abzug had little patience for the argument that safe incumbents should not be unseated. She believed incumbency favored men, and it had indeed, the "safe seat" position used historically as a justification to dissuade women from running. Promotion of incumbency prioritized an individual's climb to power over the cultivation of new leadership within the rigid seniority structure that governed the major parties and legislatures. She ran to upset this equilibrium, challenging recruitment and advancement practices that governed all political spaces down to the Democratic Party's most liberal local clubs.

In Abzug's view, reform Democrats adhered to "a closed near secret procedure cooked up by club presidents and district leaders." She believed that reform Democrats were an "elite group of club members" who had liberal leanings but not fair practices, and that "those who participated in the McCarthy, Kennedy, McGovern & King movements" should "coalesce to say 'no deal.'"[34] Abzug lodged this critique in 1969 during the municipal elections as a justification for choosing not to back Carol Greitzer for City Council. Backing Greitzer—a Hunter College graduate, working mother, and advocate of women's rights—seemed like a natural choice. But Greitzer was the heir apparent to Ed Koch's old seat after he moved on to Congress. Abzug did not like the "almost inevitable" closed process in which reform Democrats selected Greitzer as their pick.[35] Abzug advocated gender parity, but not unconditionally, withholding support if a candidate did not match her ideology, could be a potential rival, was not the pragmatic choice, or complicated an argument she was trying to make. In

1969, Abzug elected to forge a principled protest of "the procedure" over endorsing Greitzer, and directed antiwar activist volunteers toward Lindsay instead. This slight would be remembered by Greitzer. Likewise, Abzug's prior critique of "the procedure" primed her for an antiprocedure, "free and open choice" fight during her 1970 campaign.[36]

Abzug overcame reform Democratic gatekeeping by outorganizing her opponents and outwitting club leaders who controlled this process. In January, she began wearing a button that read, "Abzuglutely," her pithy response to the question, "Will she run?"[37] In February, she made her soft debut as a candidate at the New York New Democratic Coalition meet and greet for midterm hopefuls. And at her formal announcement on March 13, she visually demonstrated she would have the force of antiwar, antipoverty, civil rights, and feminist organizers behind her.

Kicking off her candidacy at the Overseas Press Club, Abzug's announcement was a highly choreographed event. Prominent women joined her at the podium, including welfare activist Beulah Sanders; feminist writers Gloria Steinem, Betty Friedan, and Lucy Komisar; Representative Shirley Chisholm; and former city commissioner Elinor Guggenheimer. Abzug put on a show. She threw her wide-brimmed hat into the ring, a stunt her WSP friend Lyla Hoffman put her up to. This performance attracted media attention, "charming the gentlemen of the press," but not in the way Abzug had hoped. One profile described the scene as just "like ladies' day at Yankee Stadium" and devoted inordinate space to describing her "French haircut" and "Bermuda tan" and how "she violently poked the air with her finger, like a cowhand on a toot shooting the shit out of the atmosphere."[38]

These accounts downplayed Abzug's razor-sharp message. "Our Great Society is sick, and the major reason is that our priorities are insane," she charged, running through a litany of concerns: "the heroin epidemic that is slaughtering our children, . . . the garbage-littered streets, broken-down subways, filthy air and rising pollution of noise." She explained how these mounting problems stemmed from national neglect and could be fixed "with a reordering of national priorities." Owning her reputation as "tough, persistent and aggressive," she highlighted these qualities as the mark of New Politics Democrats as opposed to do-nothing politicians in Washington. She and her counterparts were different, closer to the people, and the most "involved with the great issues of our time—ending war, poverty and racial injustice—rather than just those who have come up from the clubs."[39]

Abzug made clear she would run an obstructionist campaign. By March, the contender list had grown to include lawyers Ted Weiss, Ira Glasser, Howard Squadron, Justin Feldman, and Lindsay aide Barry Gottehrer, and all vied for reform Democratic backing with the vote scheduled for the end of the month. Club leaders' unusual step of inviting New Democratic Coalition members to participate in the procedure provided Abzug an opening to challenge the typical process. She sent Miriam Friedlander and Rochelle Slovin, active in reform Democratic politics alongside WSP, to make the case: If the New Democratic Coalition had been invited to participate in the vote, why not "her groups"?[40] As Abzug saw it, "Once my people were in there too, issue people, I had a shot."[41] Abzug signaled she would opt out of the reform Democratic procedure unless club leaders relented, which was an empty threat considering her campaign would be a nonstarter without their blessing. Abzug won this battle with conditions. Groups had to be approved, include registered Democrats, and must make their membership lists available to all candidates.

This wider reform Democratic vote made the process more transparent but also more contested, prompting the "bitterest infighting in the history of the Reform movement."[42] At Abzug's behest, more than twenty groups were added, including tenants' rights, block associations, peace action committees, parent clubs, and feminist organizations. These groups did not raise red flags with the exception of the National Organization for Women (NOW), which Abzug's male opponents assumed to be predisposed toward women candidates. Barry Gottehrer called the whole operation "a ploy destructive to the procedure." Ira Glasser suggested he "was all for mass movements, but now that we have them, we are in a complex situation."[43] Responding, lawyer Saul Rudes, a close friend and adviser to Abzug, promised, "Bella would support the candidate who survives the procedure."[44] A mobilization of support both within and outside the district boosted Abzug's campaign. Brooklyn representative Shirley Chisholm encouraged, "How often I have wished as Congresswoman to have other women help me to speak out for the conservation and preservation of our human resources. We desperately need people with commitment. Bella, Godspeed to you."[45] This organized pressure had the effect of winnowing Abzug's competition. The final holdout, Howard Squadron, dropped out the weekend before the vote. Aware that outsiders were most responsible for her victory, she hoped to mollify any hard feelings club members had by addressing

Figure 4.1 A natural street campaigner, Bella Abzug personally connected with voters in her economically and racially diverse district. Here, she and volunteers passed out "Carry Bella Abzug to Congress" shopping bags in Chinatown. (Uncredited, Bella Abzug Papers, Box 1089, Rare Book and Manuscript Library, Columbia University)

them in an open letter. "We *can* win this year: together with the young, the poor and blue collar workers, the peace movement, the disenfranchised minorities, and concerned women," she wrote.[46]

After the reform Democratic procedure, Abzug took her "campaign into the streets," the politicking space where she felt most comfortable.[47] She was her campaign's biggest asset, a master retail campaigner who had incredible stamina and enjoyed shaking hands. She had been perfecting the art of persuasion since soliciting for the Jewish National Fund as a teenager. Starting at 7:00 a.m., she moved at fifteen-minute intervals from one street corner to another, from a grocery store to the next subway stop. She circumnavigated the district, which originated at the East River, then dipped to the waterfront and Wall Street. It continued through Chinatown and Little Italy and extended past Chelsea and Lincoln Center. Greenwich Villagers saw themselves as the district's new heart after being added during the last round of redistricting, but the Lower East Side, where Representative

Leonard Farbstein lived, remained its historic center. Martin called the district a "gefilte fishhook" after the Passover delicacy, highlighting its sizable Jewish population, but Bella also prioritized outreach to Asian, black, and Puerto Rican voters.[48] Doug Ireland characterized the district as "the most progressive piece of land anywhere in the country," but Bella Abzug had to contend with a noticeable faction of conservatives, including emerging neoconservative intellectuals.[49] Still focused on building a new Democratic coalition, she aspired to bring together her district's disparate groups to model locally what this voting bloc could look like nationally. She envisioned women voters would be the connective glue in this coalition and expected them to be her secret weapon during the 1970 campaign as 60 percent of district women were registered Democrats.[50]

New Yorkers of a certain age may remember Abzug stopping their parents in conversation on their way to school. In this time, when there were only eleven women in Congress, it was a novelty to see a woman out campaigning. Abzug reflexively understood her street campaign was not only a necessity to win but also an opportunity to challenge people's impression that only men looked like leaders. Her strategy was not to play up femininity but to deconstruct it by presenting herself as sincere, confident, and forward. Her magnetic charisma won over many, who often called out, "Hey, Bella," as she made her rounds. She drew passersby into her orbit, sometimes for longer than they expected. "Somebody would challenge her in terms of her ideas and a full-fledged debate would go on right at the subway stop," observed actor Peter Riegert, who described working as Abzug's "body man" as "an up-close master class in politics from one of the best."[51] As much as she loved this back-and-forth with constituents, it also tired her and at times made her short with staff, who counseled her to approach campaigning with levity. As one schedule note advised on how to get through a full day of campaign stops, "Relax, tell a few stories, and enjoy their food."[52]

Abzug had the most difficulty with fund-raising, an aspect of campaigning that has historically been a stopgap for women candidates who faced a "viable candidate" bias and had trouble cultivating party patronage. In 1970, campaign financing by organized political action committees was not as rampant as it is now, and media sources were more centralized, making it possible for change candidates like Abzug to match their competition. Nonetheless, working outside the party structure, she had to use innovative strategies to attract donors. She cultivated small donations, sending canvassers out to collect "dollars for Bella" on the street. Her "Friends of Bella Abzug" operation highlighted the national dimensions of her campaign.[53] And she gained endorsements from figures outside of party channels, including social movement leaders and celebrities.

Abzug's campaign had the razzle-dazzle of showbiz. She made the unusual choice for the time to fund-raise in Hollywood, drawing on her former clients and friends in the entertainment industry to augment her star power. Her list of famous "Bella Boosters" hit just about every letter of the alphabet: David Amram, Warren Beatty, Harry Belafonte, Martin Balsam, Vinie Burrows, Mart Crowley, Ruby Dee, Jane Fonda, Jack Gilford, Yip Harburg, Kim Hunter, Anne Jackson, Ring Lardner Jr., Zero Mostel, George Segal, Dick Shawn, Barbra Streisand, Rip Torn, Eli Wallach, and Shelley Winters.[54] Star-studded fund-raisers like the evening review "Bella on Broadway" made Abzug's campaign the talk of social columns as much as political editorials. During the primary, Streisand promised "stars of stage, screen, and radio" at an Abzug fund-raiser she held at her new Upper East Side townhouse, where she and Belafonte handed out signatures for a twenty-five-dollar donation.[55] This combination of directly solicited small donations and glitzy donor fund-raisers helped Abzug's campaign stay solvent.

The grassroots campaigning strategies Abzug employed were not unique to progressive women. In 1970, conservative Republican Phyllis Schlafly also ran on the slogan "This Woman's Place Is in the House—the House of Representatives" and vowed to end the days in which women were "merely doorbell pushers."[56] She stumped at Illinois county fairs, handing out aprons adorned with elephants and eagles, just as Abzug blanketed Manhattan blocks with "Carry Bella Abzug to Congress" shopping bags. And both Schlafly and Abzug played to their strengths by drawing on the women's associational networks that powered their politics. Schlafly's campaign in America's heartland is largely forgotten, since it did not end with a victory, but journalists at the time picked up on the similarities of their campaigns at "the opposite extreme of the political spectrum." Essentially, women of both parties ran retail campaigns out of necessity. Republican and Democratic women candidates had to think creatively about how to both use and disarm voters' gendered assumptions that precast women politicians as emotional busybodies, but as collaborative innovators as well.

Drawing focus to the challenge both Abzug and Schlafly embodied, reporters predicted 1970 could be a year in which the gender "gap is almost certain to be narrowed."[57]

Running for Liberation and Hard Hats Too

The slogan "This Woman's Place Is in the House—the House of Representatives" was an expression of Abzug's long-standing work to achieve gender parity in politics, an interest of hers predating new calls for women's liberation. She saw the disruption of male elites in power as a necessary measure to upend the grip of patriarchy, a system embedded in US law and government. Looking at how power functioned along connected planes, she focused on the interrelated forces of misogyny, white supremacy, economic control, and national hegemony. This approach—today described as intersectionality—reflected Abzug's Left feminist orientation and former engagement in the US Popular Front.

Abzug's most ambitious goal during her campaign was to establish the foundation for a new Democratic coalition that expanded past its white working-class base to focus more intentionally on the needs of women, racial minorities, gay people, and the poor. She attempted to bridge what was not yet a secure divide between class and identity politics, or white male workers and everyone else. Her antiwar brand of urban populism appealed strongly enough in 1970 to secure her win, attracting some blue-collar voters to her base. But her style registered more readily than her scolding message, urging male blue-collar workers to face the realities of the changing workforce and economy, make room for others, and press collectively for reforms. Abzug cultivated support across a spectrum of progressive issue- and identity-based social movements, but the coalition these groups formed was one of convenience and did not lead to a sustained cross-pollination of engagement.

Garnering the support of women's liberation groups required the most work for Abzug, who needed to prove that her embrace of feminism was not simply opportunistic. In 1970, media outlets discovered feminism, deciding it was "hot stuff this season."[58] Male editors sent out women researchers in search of their first solo bylines as reporters to record what really happened at a consciousness-raising session. The week Abzug announced her

Figure 4.2 Bella Abzug zeroed in on what she called the "un-representativeness" of Congress in her catchy campaign slogan featured on this pamphlet. (Bella Abzug Papers, Box 64, Rare Book and Manuscript Library, Columbia University)

candidacy, women staged a sit-in at the offices of the *Ladies' Home Journal*, hanging a banner outside the window declaring, "Women's Liberation Journal." Abzug, who admired women's quest to equalize the fourth estate, actively drew feminist journalists into her campaign to serve as her emissaries. Gloria Steinem was key among these feminist boosters. Steinem had protectively urged Abzug not to run, worried that she would take a lot of abuse in the ugly game of politics.[59] Once Abzug committed to the race, however, Steinem championed her campaign within feminist circles, their bond familial and Steinem's loyalty deep. Yet, Abzug's connection to Steinem, who media outlets quickly latched onto as the star of the feminist movement, stirred the suspicion of some activists frustrated by this flattening of leadership.[60]

There were reasons why it took time to draw feminists into Abzug's base. The misleading description of her in early campaign literature as a "housewife" and "mother who's raised two kids" and "knows what these burdens mean" could account for some hesitation.[61] In an attempt to portray her as a maternal "everywoman," her campaign staff initially tried to decenter her identity as a working professional. Additionally, Abzug did not find some cultural feminist campaigns to be political, seeing the challenge of American beauty culture as secondary. Her response to the critique that Madison Avenue enslaved women was, "I'm so well liberated for so many years that I can afford to wear make-up. No one can enslave me."[62] This comment fell flat to some feminists, who were appalled that she still wore a girdle.

Abzug likewise felt some feminists took their critique of patriarchy to an extreme, dismissing all men instead of distinguishing individuals from an overarching oppressive system. In *The Dialectic of Sex*, Shulamith Firestone called child rearing the "tyranny of their [women's] biology" and imagined a world of "cybernetic socialism" in which test-tube babies were raised communally.[63] In "Goodbye to All That," Robin Morgan declared, "Any man who claims he is serious about wanting to divest himself of cock privilege should trip on this: all male leadership out of the Left is the only way."[64] Responding, Abzug countered, "I don't believe women are going to get liberated by attacking the male. Women must fight for and win a political structure that mirrors reality, not defies it."[65] This position did not deviate from her wider critique of the confrontational and separatist turn in leftist organizing. But to younger feminists receiving this criticism from a fifty-year-old woman, the dismissal felt parental.[66]

"They will not support you," Abzug recalled writer Susan Brownmiller telling her.[67] Unsatisfied with this response, Abzug tasked her staff with compiling a long list of feminist groups to reach out to, from the High School Women's Liberation Group to Redstockings, and Women in City Government United to the Lower East Side Day Care Co-op.[68] Aligning with groups that prioritized institutional reform, such as NOW and the Women's Equity Action League, came more naturally to Abzug than radical and socialist feminist consciousness-raising groups. Even so, she learned to speak the language of women's liberation, adopting the idea that "the personal is political" in her speeches by highlighting aspects of her biography that resonated. "She got it. She continued to get it, and so many women from the movement worked on that first campaign," recalled Brownmiller, ultimately convinced.[69]

Gay liberation activists signed on to Abzug's campaign more readily, encouraged by her campaign manager Doug Ireland, who although not publicly out, was gay. Abzug initially harbored discomfort about gay, lesbian, and transsexual (now termed transgender) lifestyles, but she intuitively and unreservedly welcomed this alliance.[70] Her cultivation of a "gay vote" was historic, placing her among a handful of major-party candidates nationally reaching out to this constituency. Abzug saw gay rights as an extension of her earlier advocacy, as a lawyer of African American civil rights. Ireland sensed his boss would have this "instinctive response to the need for gay rights" as an aspect of human rights.[71] He facilitated her connection to key gay activists, recognizing the potential electoral dividends of this support, and in turn, how her discussion of gay rights would increase visibility of this cause. Her antiwar commitment endeared her to Gay Liberation Front followers who saw gay liberation as part of an interrelated "paradigm of resistance."[72] However, she formed a closer partnership with the Gay Activists Alliance (GAA), a "more academic, more intellectual, less street oriented, and more white" group formed in December 1969.[73] This organization helped steer Abzug's gay rights platform that encompassed eliminating discriminatory federal hiring practices and security clearances, destroying data on federal employees' sexual activity, removing barriers to citizenship and visas, reforming tax codes, and achieving equal treatment under the law. In turn, GAA president Jim Owles could advertise that the group "played a meaningful role" in Abzug's campaign, demonstrating the difference they could make for others.[74]

Despite Abzug's being out front on the gay rights issue, the limit of her reach was on display during her first campaign. She was fine speaking to gay men in bars, but not in bathhouses. Ireland put the popular cabaret Continental Baths on the schedule without much thought, and the manager agreed to squeeze Abzug in between acts. Afterward, she scolded Ireland, "You cretin. What have you done to me? I'm up here in these fucking baths—filled with guys in towels held up by Bella buttons and some are only wearing the buttons and not the towels!"[75] She also hedged on issues, eluding a clear stance on gays in the military and gay sex education, saying, "I will have to give it more thought."[76] And she was gently reminded by gay observers to stop leaving "gay people—and their votes—in the closet" when talking about her imagined coalition.[77] Yet, despite her oversights and misgivings, she became "a minor folk heroine" to this constituency nationally.[78]

Abzug worked hardest to cultivate an image as a hero of the working class, a group she defined broadly along race, sexuality, and gender lines as "the people." Although she became relatable as "Bella," Abzug was accustomed to the comforts of upper-middle-class living. Her ties in the antipoverty and civil rights movements were strong, but she approached this work as a member of the professional class. In private, she referred to her grassroots activism as working among "the weeds."[79] This distance limited her experiential conception of working-class needs and everyday struggles. But ever since the Great Depression, she remained committed to realizing greater labor rights and economic justice, and continued to theorize how to make US capitalism and democracy fairer. Even as she prioritized other concerns, her class consciousness remained an anchor.

In her campaign, Abzug revised the economic critique of the Vietnam War she had crafted for Lindsay's Taxpayers Campaign for Urban Priorities. Abzug's campaign for Lindsay had been instinctive. During her own campaign, the experts Abzug solicited to assess New York City's financial windfall only reaffirmed her view that, as one advisor suggested, "poverty and discrimination and unemployment are national dilemmas, and the national government should pay the consequences."[80] The trick would be how to convince patriotic blue-collar workers that the war led to inflation and hurt their pocketbooks. Abzug's "hard hat piece" delivered this message simply, asking, "Hey, Buddy. How's about five bucks for a cup of coffee?"[81] Male laborers responded to her "I tell it hard and straight" style.[82] As one cab driver explained, "I just like Abzug's guts: there she was, in the middle of the campaign, shouting in Yiddish practically on Farbstein's doorstep."[83] It was an unlikely affinity, but "she connected on a very visceral sense with a constituency that no one alludes to in the liberal Democratic Party—tough guys who work tough jobs and have tough lives."[84] Despite this rapport, Abzug had difficulty countering the patriotic discourse attached to military service and organized labor's ties to defense industries. As a former labor lawyer, Abzug had deep union connections, but she sided with the antiwar, inclusive wing of the labor movement as it battled its hawkish, protectionist, exclusionary other half. This historic divide, dating before the early Cold War, had been widened by the 1947 Taft-Hartley Act. The Vietnam War rekindled tensions and reaffirmed a left-right ideological split.[85] Government support of affirmative action, ethnic communities' greater demands for control of social services, the growing clout of women- and minority-dominated public and service sector unionism, and the strain of globalization and deindustrialization exacerbated these tensions.

It was this minefield that Abzug entered when her campaign issued a call for an antiwar work stoppage and demonstration on Wall Street on May 6. Abzug had been motivated to act after a spiral of events that began with President Nixon's April 30 address, in which he reneged on the promise to pull 150,000 troops out of Vietnam. Instead, ground forces were sent to Cambodia to wipe out Vietnamese Communist safe havens exposed in the wake of a coup defeating neutral Prince Norodom Sihanouk. Then, on May 4, news broke that four students had been shot to death and more injured by National Guardsmen during a protest at Kent State University in Ohio. The indelible image capturing that tragedy—a wailing college girl crouched over a fallen boy, her hands uplifted—immediately joined the collage of photographs Abzug's staff hung on the walls at her campaign headquarters.[86] Instinctively, she halted her nonstop campaigning, and her staff put together a flyer advertising a noontime rally outside Federal Hall, where Wall Street met Broad Street. "There can be no regular campaigning, no regular business in Congress, no regular business on Wall Street until the United States terminates its actions in Cambodia," the campaign flyer read.[87] In connecting the war with finance, Bella implicated the industry in which her stockbroker husband, Martin, worked and prepared to protest on his doorstep. She told the midday crowd, "It is most important that this activity be held on Wall Street because Nixon is convinced that big business and big money are supporting his policies."[88]

Abzug's Wall Street rally inadvertently helped kick off the cycle of events that escalated to a "hard hat riot." Some participants in the protest called by her campaign continued to march up Broadway, and construction workers frustrated by their presence pelted them with glass. The next day, demonstrators returned to Wall Street, and this time hard-hatted laborers stormed the crowd to rip American flags out of demonstrators' hands. Meanwhile, Mayor Lindsay met with two Kent State students and visited New York University students protesting the war in Washington Square. Calling for a "new majority" in Washington, he urged the public to "elect antiwar Congressmen and Senators"—Abzug was one of two candidates he endorsed in local races.[89] By Friday, the protest on Wall Street had escalated to hundreds of antiwar demonstrators chanting "Peace Now," matched by construction workers countering, "Love It or Leave It" and singing "God Bless America." Stock trading dipped to its lowest point in 1970 that day.[90] In the aftermath, Lindsay condemned the "breakdown of the police," who "had no excuse" to let "marauding" construction workers "take the law into [their] own hands."[91]

Abzug agreed with Lindsay, who received the brunt of conservative backlash after this skirmish. Abzug did not, however, join the chorus of liberals who called the construction workers cowards, bullies, right-wing vigilantes, and fascists. Instead, she answered the call Pete Hamill delivered in his article "The Revolt of the White Lower Middle Class," in which he urged "New York politicians to begin to deal with the alienation and paranoia of the working-class white man."[92] Talking it over with Gloria Steinem, Abzug decided to reach out to construction workers by visiting them in their territory on their terms.[93] Her advance team circulated an invitation, noting, "Construction Workers. The peace movement is not your enemy. The war is your enemy. Let's talk about it." Next, she dropped in at construction sites during the lunch hour, holding impromptu military budget teach-ins. "Our tax dollars go for missiles and bombs," she explained as a laborer chomping on a sandwich replied in between bites, "and to the moon." One worker argued peace activists' defacement of American flags was an affront to veterans. Another countered, "This war is taking from the middle-class. . . . The $40,000-a-year guys can deduct their subway fare." Pleased, Abzug encouraged, "You should join together to tell Washington to stop this nonsense and bring that money back home. You should invite me down to your next meeting. I'd love to come." She thought she was making progress. Reporter Nick Browne believed otherwise, judging, "The persuasive clout of the Jewish mother must be measured in the low megaton range."[94]

Understanding to a point, Abzug would not forgive the prejudices some blue-collar workers displayed. On May 15, two black students were shot to death and more injured outside a women's dormitory at historically black Jackson State College in Mississippi. Three days later, construction workers heckled students protesting the flagrant overuse of police force at Jackson State outside the New York Board of Education, throwing eggs at them. Two days after that, the Building and Construction Trades Council of Greater New York sponsored a pro-war march of 150,000 in lower Manhattan. Abzug believed that racism lurked under the cover of flag-waving nationalism and that some unions condoned both. Concerned by unionists' display after Jackson State, she publicly rebuked, "We have reached the point where we tolerate loss of life; where we accept barbarism in place of civilization; where savagery holds sway over reason and codes of conduct." Recalling Martin Luther King Jr.'s appraisal that "the United States is the greatest purveyor of violence in the world today," Abzug chillingly cautioned, "The consequences of not ending the war may well be the end of our society."[95]

Abzug hoped to stir the better moral senses of the white working class, but her reprimand felt like the ruler delivered by a stern schoolteacher. Liberals loved her overture to the hard hats. "If Richard Nixon is serious about bringing people together, he might well take a leaf from Bella's book—if she'd let him have it," one *Newsday* columnist effused.[96] Yet, it was her personality more than her message that registered. She delivered daily reminders to white male workers of their competition. As the hard hat conflict unfolded, she promoted the grape and lettuce boycotts led by the United Farm Workers, marched with Lower East Side tenants protesting evictions, advocated the demands of the National Welfare Rights Organization, and cashed government bonds to remove money from federal war coffers.[97] Her "labor donated" flyers highlighted that her labor support—unions such as the Health and Hospital Workers Local 1199 and the Hotel and Restaurant Workers Local 89—represented the public and service sector unionism of the future more than its industrial past.[98]

Abzug's dialogue with construction workers may have won her some votes, but her outreach was locally isolated and short-lived, and it achieved limited impact. Her awareness-raising campaign meant to cut through Nixon's misinformation paled in comparison to the president's White House ceremony in which he presented New York trade union president Peter Brennan with a hard hat. Still, Abzug went to greater lengths than many progressives to speak with blue-collar workers, trying to understand their problems, assuage their concerns, and propose reforms that would better their lives. It is assumed that New Politics Democrats placed class last, but for Abzug, class was near first. Although she would not let workers off the hook, and she called out xenophobic, hawkish, and exclusionary strains within the labor movement. Highlighting these blind spots and shortcomings is not the same as leaving class out. Abzug understood this distinction, but perhaps she gave white male workers too much credit, thinking most could set aside intolerance and personal gain to adjust to the demands of an increasingly diverse workforce and multiracial democracy.

Overcoming a Political Past

Abzug's long-standing radical politics served as her biggest hurdle during the 1970 campaign. Her challengers highlighted positions she had taken that specific constituencies from Jewish voters to unionists, and partisans from moderate Democrats to conservative Republicans deemed questionable. Opponents featured damning aspects of her biography incompletely, going back to her student activism and work as a lawyer and drawing on anticommunist research. This obstacle was the most difficult to overcome during the general election, which was not as easy to win as one would assume in her consistently Democratic district.

The inquiry into Abzug's recent past began during her primary fight against Representative Leonard Farbstein and centered on her Jewish credentials. Although Farbstein immediately condemned Nixon's action in Cambodia, Abzug emphasized Farbstein's early support of the Vietnam War and his opposition to unilateral withdrawal.[99] Refuting his claim that being antiwar was anti-Zionist, she identified as a Jewish candidate and she engaged in robust street politicking in largely Jewish neighborhoods. On June 15, a sound truck cruised along Grand Street on the Lower East Side, where Farbstein lived, with Abzug shouting through a bullhorn in Yiddish and Barbra Streisand waving to her fans.[100] Days earlier, Pete Hamill had incorrectly reported that Farbstein voted against the 1966 Civil Rights Act (which did not pass), an error his team suspected arose from bad information passed along by Abzug's campaign. An insider report circulating among Abzug's staff did in fact inaccurately highlight this negative vote.[101] Farbstein's aides did their own digging, unearthing a speech Abzug made in 1967 responding to the Arab-Israeli War where she hedged on unconditional military aid to Israel.

The Arab-Israeli War deeply troubled Abzug. She faulted "both sides" for participating in "an arms race."[102] She defended Israel's right to self-determination but favored diplomacy over military action and still believed

111

in the dimming possibility of a binational workers' state. Abzug's position, in line with that of early Socialist Zionists, became a liability once the spectrum of acceptable Zionist ideology had narrowed. This constriction began in the wake of the Arab-Israeli War of 1967 but intensified after Israeli phantom jets attacked a military base close to Cairo on January 18, 1970. As Egyptian president Gamal Abdel Nasser vied for Soviet support, Israeli prime minister Golda Meir urged Nixon to send more military planes. Knowing Abzug's history, Farbstein centered on the jets for Israel issue, guiding reporters to trace how she "initially shied away from a commitment."[103] Support for jets became an indicator of Zionist allegiance for American Jews in this moment, as well as a sign to Arabs of US support for Israel.[104] Livid, Abzug confronted Farbstein publicly, avowing, "Lennie, this is one Jew you're not going to out-Jew."[105]

Abzug thought it unfair that she and other Jewish politicians increasingly had to pass hard-line Zionists' litmus test on Israel. Nonetheless, she adjusted her Zionist position in 1970 in response to this renewed conflict, embracing unequivocal support of military aid to Israel. In making this choice, she moved against the growing current within the American Left in which Arab American nationalists and non-Arab radical allies referred to Palestine as a colonized place and Palestinians as oppressed people.[106] Seeing Zionism as an anti-imperialist project, Abzug found this anticolonial critique to be troubling. Accordingly, she aligned with the majority of American Jews who shifted with the 1967 war from "Israel was they" to "Israel is we."[107] Her strong Zionist identity disappointed pro-Palestinian sympathizers and pacifist purists backing her campaign.

On primary day, reporters at Abzug campaign headquarters began calling the race after she won the Sixty-First Assembly District on the Lower East Side, but "she kept asking are you sure I've won."[108] "Lemme see the figures—it's an amateur campaign to the end—I still don't know if I've won," she told staff. Then, Al Lowenstein appeared and gave Abzug a big bear hug as he told her, "You're going to be the first on the House roll call." Crying tears of joy, she took in the news and then joined the crowd of supporters gathered in Sheridan Square. Lifted onto a chair, as if a bride at a Jewish wedding, she boomed through a megaphone, "The people have won!" Highlighting the impact of her team of canvassers, she noted, "It's only fitting that this campaign should end in the streets where it began. But this is only the beginning."[109]

Abzug beat Farbstein 17,341 to 14,642; the Jewish vote helped put her over the top, but so did backing from Herman Badillo.[110] Outside of the Bronx, her district had the most Puerto Rican residents, and this group was an emerging Democratic bloc in the city. When Badillo too won his primary, he proclaimed, "Mine is a victory for the new politics. With Bella Abzug, we have proven that the new coalitions can win against the old machines."[111] The *New York Times* called the race a victory for "candidates who held forth a hope for reform leadership, for liberal approaches in impacted areas where racial difficulties are omnipresent, for new efforts to end the war and reorder priorities."[112]

The *Philadelphia Inquirer* likewise predicted, "For the first time in two decades, genuine radicals of the left are coming to the House."[113] Conservatives worried that this might be the case. The day after the primary, members of the Young Americans for Freedom barged into Women Strike for Peace headquarters and "proceeded to deface posters, throw important papers all over the place, dump peace jewelry on the floor, and steal names from our files." Called in, Abzug gave the young men a "thorough tongue lashing," told them they would not be charged, and posed with the group for a photo that appeared in the *New York Post*.[114] She did not think much of the incident, but it was a preview of how she became a galvanizing force for conservatives to rally against. Indeed, the Abzug-Farber race served as a solidifying moment for disconnected factions of New York City conservatism. In this seeming bastion of liberalism, conservative intellectuals sharpened their pencils and grassroots organizers mobilized their followers in challenge of her candidacy. Barry Farber, a nationally syndicated talk show host, encouraged this coalescence by using his radio program as a bully pulpit for a range of conservative causes during the general election. Abzug filed a complaint for equal air time, and WOR-AM acquiesced, giving her a fifteen-minute late night broadcast she never used and advertising spots she did.[115] But she misjudged Farber to be a man of little consequence who hid behind a microphone.

Farber first attacked Abzug's support of feminism. He poked fun at Abzug's Lower East Side tour with Streisand by staging his own atop a garbage truck, addressing the crowd in Yiddish, Chinese, and Spanish (a linguist, he spoke fourteen languages). He ended his playful jaunt outside Abzug's headquarters at Sheridan Square, where he delivered her flowers with the message "May there be no 'rain on your parade.'"[116] Farber referred to plans under way for a Women's Strike for Equality parade planned for August 26 to commemorate the fiftieth anniversary of the ratification of the Nineteenth Amendment securing women's suffrage. An estimated 50,000 marched in New York that day, convening around three demands: free twenty-four-hour child care, abortion on demand, and women's equal opportunity in employment and education.[117] Abzug took time from campaigning to plan this march initiated by writer and NOW leader Betty Friedan, and she did not appreciate Farber's slight. For Farber, Abzug personified the very civil disobedience strain of leftist politics she had long critiqued. Jibing at her, he invited feminists on his radio program and afterward pronounced, "Feminists are the hardest group of people I've ever had to deal with. It's like trying to contain a tornado in a paper bag."[118]

In turn, Abzug tried to contain Farber by exposing aspects of his résumé she thought to be suspect, but the strategy backfired. The profile her researchers put together noted that he received a degree from the University of North Carolina, participated in the National Student Association, reported in Hungary and in Cuba during the revolution, moved to New York City in 1957, registered as a Republican in 1968, and was backed by Roy Cohn, former counselor to Senator Joe McCarthy.[119] Abzug accused Farber of being a "junior Agnew" and a shadowy figure with no past.[120] Taking this bait, he responded by exposing her as an "old-left stalwart."[121] Farber's team proved to be adept researchers. Lawyer Alexander Sacks wrote the US attorney general on Farber's behalf to solicit confirmation of Abzug's suspected Communist ties.[122] Additionally, Farber had the conservative intelligentsia on his side. Penn Kemble wrote in an article in *Commentary,* "While at times she may appear to be the New Politics answer to Abbie Hoffman, Mrs. Abzug deserves to be taken far more seriously. Her roots lie in the Old Left, rather than the new liberalism."[123] A growing anti–New Politics countercoalition solidified that included neoconservatives, anticommunist Socialist Party and Liberal Party members, right-leaning unionists, hard-line Zionists, and Republican partisans. The Liberal Party's endorsement of Farber was an especially difficult blow for Abzug, as the third party backed most reform Democrats but continued to "harbor certain differences" with her.[124] It was neoconservatives' alliance with anti-Abzug unionists, however, that proved most cumbersome in 1970, previewing the trouble ahead during her future Senate bid.

The troika of Israel, affirmative action, and perceived liberal elitism caused neoconservatives to drift from the Democratic Party, a movement Abzug helped along. Her role in the 1968 Ocean Hill–Brownsville teachers strike, a sign according to critics of "all that was wrong with the Great Society but more broadly with twentieth century urban liberalism," encouraged this animosity.[125] It also made United Federation of Teachers (UFT) president Al Shanker a dedicated enemy. After this tense strike, New York City politicians were asked: Which side were you on? Abzug could not deny where she had stood because a photograph circulated of her unlinking the chains prohibiting entrance to her daughter's school, the High School of Music and Art, closed during the strike.[126] The conflict began on May 9 when a black-led school board, focused on community control of curriculum and hiring, reassigned a white teacher in the district on precarious grounds. This act set off a heated, extended face-off pitting the local school board, the supportive citywide Board of Education, African Americans, and leftist sympathizers against largely Jewish teachers, the UFT, and those frustrated with racial politics. By October, Abzug, who deeply sympathized with the school board, decided to help convene an "emergency school" with a few dozen parents.[127]

During her 1970 campaign, Shanker told UFT members, "Bella Abzug is in favor of total community control of the schools (and of police and hospitals as well)."[128] She tried to reason with teachers, explaining her view that underprivileged parents should have the right to be a "consultative voice" in public school decisions, including the transfer of teachers "not sympathetic to experimental programs."[129] Uncomfortable being cast as a strikebreaker, though she was one in this instance, she wavered on which version of the truth she wanted to tell. At her most genuine, she admitted, "I went into the school briefly only to determine whether physical conditions were safe for the students."[130] For Shanker, this was too much. His opposition to Abzug, however, went beyond this strike. He reflected the hawkish, anti-integrationist wing of the labor movement that viewed the New Politics Democratic agenda, as he characterized it, as a "dilettantish approach to economic problems, reverse racism, and anti-American foreign policy."[131]

Being characterized as antilabor hurt Abzug immensely, for she began her career as a labor lawyer. Although, Farber's replay of the jets for Israel issue devastated Abzug most. He portrayed her as the enemy of an "encircled, dauntless nation" America must defend to win the Cold War.[132] There was a gendered aspect to this argument as well, for the soft diplomacy versus tough national security debate spoke to the nagging concern that having more women in Congress would lead to the nation's demasculinization. Victor Lasky drew this line in the *Jewish Press,* asserting that Farber had a "chance of defeating a noisy woman candidate with impeccable leftwing credentials" because he was "not ambivalent about Israel."[133] Farber used his radio show as a platform to question Abzug's Jewishness. On October 21, he urged on the air, "If anybody is listening, beginning with Bella Abzug, has any evidence that Mrs. Abzug has ever protest Soviet mistreatment of Jews, please get that documentation to me, I'll pay for the messenger, I'll pay for the train-ride from Syocett, I'll pay for the taxi, I'll pay for everything."[134] Farber followed Abzug around with a tape recorder after this broadcast, urging her to go on the record. His prodding captured the interest of Meir Kahane, leader of the militant Jewish Defense League (JDL), who called Abzug a "disaster . . . for the Jewish people and for the State of Israel."[135] On Kahane's order, JDL demonstrators set up a perpetual picket, camping outside her events, headquarters, and home waving signs that read, "A Vote for Bella Is a Vote for Communism" and "Israel Yes, Bella No." Abzug confronted Farber during debates, had Rabbi Israel Miller of the Kingsbridge Heights Jewish Center verify she had taught Hebrew there, and enlisted Esther Smith of the American Jewish Congress Women's Division to renounce Farber's "'big lie' campaign."[136] This conflict got ugly. Outside the "Broadway for Bella" fund-raiser, Abzug supporters and JDL protesters came to blows.[137]

The general election introduced Abzug to political mudslinging, a strategy she found personally devastating but was not above dishing back. Her purpose was to gain power for progressives, and she needled her way forward as a street fighter for this cause. On Election Day, she called "from every phone booth to yell that Barry Farber was stealing the election."[138] While Abzug despised machine politics, she gave the go-ahead to lean on Lower East Side district leaders Prospero Viggiano, Louis DiSalvio, and Michael Bloom. One critic characterized the maneuver as having the "residue of the worst of the old Tammany in Manhattan."[139] Abzug's willingness to move into this ethical gray area disappointed volunteers such as Rochelle Slovin, who noted, "There were people involved in the campaign that were not ethically pure for a woman who staked her claim as a principled candidate."[140]

Michael Bloom walked his neighborhood with Abzug on Election Day, but he handed out palm cards for Farber right next to her. Frustrated, she muttered, "The whole thing is a charade."[141] Touch and go to the end, Abzug beat Farber by 8,690 votes, a win to celebrate, but a margin much narrower than expected.[142]

VICTORIOUS, BELLA ABZUG LEANED OVER to her friend Amy Swerdlow to say, "'*Du zest,*' you see."[143] She had reason to be delighted. She had captured a seat as a New Politics Democrat, and she had survived a smear campaign that rivaled Nixon's attack on Helen Gahagan Douglas during the 1950 California Senate race. While civil liberties did not factor heavily in Abzug's campaign, the general election refocused her attention on this issue. She described the onslaught she faced as "like the darkest days of McCarthyism," joining leftists who had begun to speak out about their experience with surveillance and censor during that period.[144] For those on the right, the very potential of Abzug in Congress posed a threat. Just as she bridged old and new currents of American radicalism, her candidacy connected anticommunists who once had a stake in the Red Scare with those who newly believed 1960s progressive social movements had gone too far and the government had given in enough.

Abzug was bound for Congress as part of a visible faction of New Politics Democrats, serving alongside freshmen Ronald V. Dellums of California and Father Robert F. Drinan of Massachusetts. The Ninety-Second Congress had greater diversity, which she sized up as "12 Blacks and 12 women and a couple of Mexican-Americans and a Puerto Rican." But, as she admitted, New Politics Democrats in Congress would not be many, and they needed a wider "political movement behind them."[145] The local base Abzug had established did not equate to a widespread or proven new Democratic coalition. Her campaign manager dwelled on this reality in his postelection assessment. Seeing Abzug as a "notable exception," Ireland judged the midterm results as a "disaster for liberalism." For, just as Manhattan sent Abzug to Washington, Conservative Party candidate James L. Buckley would represent New York in the Senate. This contrast, he believed, was a sign of "the defection of the working class vote from the Democratic Party."[146] Prescient in his estimation, Ireland recognized that Abzug's outreach to blue-collar workers had been largely in vain, but he encouraged progressives to continue this work. Likewise, economist John Kenneth Galbraith, who backed Abzug during her campaign, predicted that if the Democratic Party did not reform "the system" and serve "the people," then "it has no purpose at all."[147]

Despite this sober reality, Abzug had achieved a Democratic upset that signaled the strides made by New Politics Democrats. This growing oppositional faction had galvanized voters in pockets throughout the United States in 1970, building on the ground they had laid since 1966. Abzug figured out how to maneuver within and around the local Democratic Party apparatus, bringing voters a message that fused economic and social concerns. She ran as an overt leftist and still managed to win. She challenged the usual rules of campaigning, while working within the parameters of electoral politics. To some leftists, her willingness to bring protest into the Democratic Party—the party of southern Democrats, the party that launched the Vietnam War—felt like a grave accommodation, even borderline traitorous. As a believer in the virtue of democracy, Abzug saw this attitude as defeatist. "At my age," she promised, "I'm hardly likely to turn and change from tiger to pussy cat."[148] She would find, however, that adapting to Congress, a slow-moving behemoth, would be harder than expected. As Ronnie Eldridge predicted, "She's always been on the outside and now she'll be on the inside . . . and I don't think she's figured that out yet."[149]

5

NOT ONE OF THE BOYS

THE OPENING OF THE NINETY-SECOND CONGRESS was an "unusual day," instead of the typically "staid affair," thanks to Bella Abzug.[1] A flyer promoting her inauguration promised, "Bella Won't Be One of the Boys."[2] She did not disappoint. She sat in the front row of the House chambers to ensure a captive audience. She forcefully read a resolution to "set the date for completing the safe and systematic withdrawal of all American armed forces from Vietnam, Cambodia and Laos . . . no later than July 4, 1971."[3] She later joined an expectant crowd of 500 gathered on the Capitol steps, huddling in the frigid air and chanting, "2, 4, 6, 8—Bella, Set the Date!" All quieted when Representative Shirley Chisholm stepped forward to administer Abzug's oath, accompanied by nine others, including Representatives Robert Drinan, Ronald Dellums, Ed Koch, and William F. Ryan. Earnest and exalted, Abzug recited, "I pledge to devote my time, my energy and my abilities—in and out of Congress—to help end the war in Indochina, to work for new priorities to heal the domestic wounds of war and to use our country's wealth for life, not death."[4] As she spoke, homemade signs swayed in the background, one reading, "Give 'Em Hell Bella!"[5]

Abzug blazed into Congress ready to "push and push and push," but what she found was that "the system" she challenged pushed back.[6] She came to Washington to achieve results, not merely to be a voice for a cause. During her first months in Congress, she faced the sobering reality that "the House of Representatives is a very awesome thing." She idealistically had thought that legislative action might bring about progressive reforms more quickly and more completely than the courts. Once ensconced in the process of lawmaking, however, she faced "layer after layer of complications and procedure which make it a long time to get a bill through or to be heard."[7]

Abzug adapted to this work more readily than to the workplace. An institutional reformer, she invested in the lawmaking process, staying late, reading bills meticulously, showing up for committee meetings and votes, and scheming with allies. Although she complained about the many rules governing federal lawmaking, as a lawyer she delighted in procedural intricacies and enlisted attorneys she knew to aid her hunt for maneuvers. Mining arcane, forgotten rules, she recovered a few that helped her circumvent seniority and thus southern Democrats and Cold War liberals in power. As a result, she was able to get the two issues she worked on most—ending the Vietnam War and sex discrimination—up for debate and into bills. What she refused to abide by was the tradition set by former House Speaker Sam Rayburn, who said, "If you want to get along, go along." She determined not to be "cowed by the atmosphere," seeking to resist the temptation of complacent incumbency and unprincipled compromise.[8] Most centrally, she sought to expose how Congress operated as a patriarchal institution designed to preserve what she called male "power and potency."[9]

Abzug could push more than she would have been able to otherwise because she arrived in Congress amid "a new procedural era" with structural reforms under way since the mid-1960s.[10] Most contested was what Representative Michael Harrington (D-MA) called the "pernicious seniority system."[11] The Democratic Study Group (DSG), a liberal congressional network created in 1959, had long criticized House committee chairs' concentrated power and "virtual monopoly of the most visible communication channels."[12] The 1970 Legislative Reorganization Act established recorded roll call votes, made committee activities public, and gave committee members more influence in setting the policy agenda. That year, Representative Julia Butler Hansen (D-WA) was also tasked with overseeing a committee to review the chair appointment process and committee organization. At the opening of the Ninety-Second Session, the House Democratic Caucus reviewed the Hansen Report findings and, with Democratic leaders' support, determined how to "loosen the seniority knot."[13] House Democrats sanctioned a sweeping expansion of subcommittee power—a reform from which Abzug would soon benefit. Reforms additionally included limiting chair leadership to one subcommittee, increasing subcommittee staff and autonomy to develop legislation, and allowing ten members to contest a chair appointment recommended by the Committee on Committees and demand a vote. Thus, Abzug's agitating for structural reform was not singular but rather part of a collective internal campaign for greater democratization that led to concrete congressional reorganization. But she also broke from the pack, highlighting how even male reformers had blind spots when it came to gender equity among members of Congress. In this area, she adamantly refused to be "one of the boys."

Adjusting to Capitol Hill

As a new legislator, Abzug set out "to be a maverick without becoming a pariah."[14] This balance was tricky to strike. She wanted to be a bridge builder, but many of her peers saw her as an insolent and antagonistic obstructionist. It was her purpose, not simply her personality, that fostered this impression. In time, Abzug figured out how to tone down her delivery and moderate her expectations without losing sight of her radical goals.

Uninterested in superficial niceties, Abzug had trouble adapting to the respectability politics required of legislative work. Openly critical of the "old boys" culture that governed Capitol Hill, she did not participate in the DC social circuit and did not exhibit the deferential reserve expected of junior Congress members. At the same time, she immediately signaled her interest in belonging. She reached out to congresswomen, hoping to build a formal Women's Caucus, but did not anticipate the extent to which ideological differences divided women lawmakers. She pressed to be invited into an informal antiwar caucus known as "the Group," but this male body that doubled as a social mixer was reluctant to let her in. She hired a youthful staff deeply committed to shared progressive interests, but it was not the same as collaborating among longstanding activist friends. As a result, Abzug worked largely in isolation during her first months in Washington, and she felt incredibly lonely, missing her husband, her daughters, and the social network she had left behind.

Abzug found it difficult to adapt to a workplace not made for women. She was accustomed to being a minority in the legal profession, which was

Figure 5.1 Bella Abzug worked late at her office in the Longworth Building. Catching a glimpse of the congresswoman in action became a Capitol Hill attraction, but this women-led workplace was more than a novelty. It visually challenged the patriarchal structure of Congress. (Uncredited, Bella Abzug Papers, Box 1089, Rare Book and Manuscript Library, Columbia University)

just opening up to women after years of discriminatory practices in law school admissions and hiring. Her position as a minority in Congress felt more pronounced because there were only fifteen women among the 535 legislators, and there were no established organizational support networks for women in an institution patriarchal in design. The Capitol building lacked "physical facilities for women . . . an index of their alienation."[15] The gym was segregated by sex, as were the House barbershop and beauty parlor. Most frustrating to Abzug, "There's only one women's room, a very fancy place . . . that we never go to because it's very far away and by the time you go there it takes forever."[16] Offices functioned in a way that reinforced this culture of exclusion. Female staff members often were eye candy, placed at reception, and expected to work as volunteers. They were tasked with "office housekeeping," rarely asked to complete duties like "working out legislation, developing strategy on procedures, and lining up speeches." They were peripheral players in "a large old-fashioned men's club with stultifying rules of behavior" reflecting "deeply imbedded discriminatory practices against women."[17]

Abzug called out this misogynistic culture and modeled a different kind of workplace. Visitors at her congressional office at 1507 Longworth noticed the contrast immediately, interacting with women who filled out every rank on staff. The space was cramped, jamming a lot of activity into three rooms. The walls were peppered "with an assortment of maps, calendars, pictures, caricatures of Abzug, art posters, movement posters and anything else that'll hang on the end of a nail."[18] The work was serious, but the mood remained casual. Staff showed up in hot pants, which "drove Bella insane," but not enough for her to enforce a dress code.[19] She encouraged the topsy-turvy interchange of staff, activists, and everyday people, positioning her office as a renegade conduit for social movements on Capitol Hill. This unusual mélange of engagements combined with Abzug's magnetic personality made her office an instant marvel.

Abzug followed the lead of Shirley Chisholm by hiring a majority of women for her staff. Like Chisholm, she sought to replicate the atmosphere of grassroots organizing by being "deliberate" about hiring "people that had a spirit and an approach to life that I did."[20] For the job of administrative assistant, Ronnie Eldridge suggested Esther Newberg, a Connecticut native in her late twenties who had worked for Arthur Goldberg's campaign for governor and for Senators Robert F. Kennedy and Abraham Ribicoff before then. The interview took place at Abzug's apartment, in her bedroom, the congresswoman-elect grilling Newberg as she put on a girdle. She "said something really interesting that I never forgot," recalled Newberg. "She wanted a congressional staff that would know how to attach to bills irrelevant things," pet amendments, "the way southern Senators did." The exchange indicated Abzug "was out there" but also "ahead of her time."[21] Signing on, Newberg told reporters, "I believe in all the things she believes in."[22] To run her day-to-day operation, Abzug hired seasoned clerical staff such as Howard University graduate Tracy Simmons, who had worked for one-term Representative Al Lowenstein. Abzug went outside congressional channels to recruit young lawyers without Hill experience who brought the fresh currents of public interest law to her office. Interviewing for the job of legislative assistant, friends Nancy Stanley and Judy Lyons Wolf convinced Abzug to let them share the position. Wolf had toddlers at home, and Abzug had campaigned on promoting child care. Accordingly, it made sense to create a flexible workplace. Involved in women's liberation, Stanley compelled Abzug to hire her to focus entirely on women's rights, impressing Abzug during the interview by goading, "'I'm a radical and I don't think you can make it, but I want to watch you while you try.'"[23] The only man initially on staff was not on the payroll. Antiwar philanthropists Martin and Anne Peretz, friends of Abzug's, hired Vietnam veteran and GI Rights activist Jim Crawford to work full-time on veteran's issues.[24] Later, Abzug would relax her hiring preference of women and moderate the youthful energy by bringing on law school friend Fran Temko and WSP friend Eleanor Garst. In contrast to her DC operation, Abzug's New York office immediately drew on her established network, with close WSP collaborators, New Democratic Coalition affiliates, and former campaign aides on staff.[25]

Abzug initiated her first campaign as a legislator to gain a spot as the only woman on the Armed Services Committee. Only three women had served in the past on this committee considered the domain of men—Representatives Margaret Chase Smith (R-ME), Katharine St. George (R-NY), and Mary Farrington (R-HI).[26] Abzug made the unusual choice of going public with her appointment campaign, but not that surprising for this outsider used to lobbying her case from every angle. "I want to get on that committee so I can challenge the Pentagon where it will hurt the most—where its money comes from," she told the Washington Heights Child Care Coalition, just as she enlisted colleagues to press House leaders and personally petitioned members of the Ways and Means Committee.[27] She was not selected because of her oppositional posture. Chair L. Mendel Rivers of South Carolina—whom Abzug described as "the Pentagon's obedient servant"—had promised the seat to Louise Day Hicks (D-MA).[28] When Rivers died during the appointment process, his successor, Representative F. Edward Hebert (D-LA), proved no less receptive. Instead, Michael Harrington (instead of Hicks) and Representative Lee Aspin (D-WI) were appointed. Unsatisfied, Abzug raised the issue before the full House Democratic Caucus on February 3. Announcing "we are here," she argued for greater recognition of women while highlighting her expertise as a former lobbyist "involved in a deep study of military appropriations."[29] The performance closely resembled Chisholm's challenge of her "ridiculous assignment" to the Agriculture Committee in 1969 and Herman Badillo's parallel fight to be added to the Armed Services Committee in 1971.[30]

These appeals were ineffective, but they embodied the spirit of New Politics Democrats no longer willing to quietly concede to seniority practices they deemed unfair. Individual challenges of seniority added greater weight to an effort led by the DSG to destabilize the "exclusive, semi-exclusive, and non-exclusive" organization of committees and to slate more liberals for powerful congressional positions.[31] Seeing their efforts as largely unsuccessful, Abzug complained, "We got routed." While aligned with the DSG faction, Abzug found their failure to completely unseat aging southern Democrats frustrating.[32] Yet, their growing clout was evident in the closeness of the votes.

Abzug's assignment to the Government Operations Committee, which she called "an outrage," nonetheless well placed her to be an influential participant in the post-Watergate congressional push to expand oversight of executive power. This committee work, more so than that of Armed Services, was in line with her expertise as a civil liberties lawyer. Abzug recognized as much and privately acknowledged when assigned to "this vital committee" that she was pleased.[33] She vied for placement on the Foreign Operations and Government Information Subcommittee, which she would later chair, scribbling two stars next to this choice and only one next to the Military Operations Subcommittee.[34] Instead, chair Chet Holifield initially assigned her to the Conservation and Natural Resources Subcommittee. Although an environmentalist, she thought the placement redundant, since this concern fell under the domain of her second committee assignment, the Public Works Committee. Abzug credited Representative Martha Griffiths (D-MI) for her appointment to this prestigious committee, which provided her with a way to channel money for infrastructure projects in her district, a "key distressed area."[35]

Committee appointments positioned Abzug to make a dent in specific policy areas, but she was after more wide-scale impact. She brought the urgency of the antiwar movement to Congress, determined with other "doves," from Representative Robert Drinan to Pete McCloskey, to bring about a speedy withdrawal from Vietnam. She felt increasingly dedicated to the feminist movement, which had reached a critical mass when she entered office. And she advocated a full New Politics Democratic reform agenda that included environmentalism, urban revitalization, public welfare, civil rights, consumer protection, civil liberties, disability rights, education and workplace protections, and diplomacy-first foreign affairs. Still, to establish a policy program and effectively execute it were two different things. Deeply aware of this reality, Abzug directed most attention during her transition to office to learning the rules that governed the House of Representatives.

As a political lawyer, Abzug understood how to use legal procedure as a tool of reform—a means to disarm her opponents and thwart their moves on behalf of her client. She believed she could do the same in Congress. She tasked Miriam "Mim" Kelber, her closest adviser and speechwriter, to recruit help from her contacts in the National Lawyers Guild. "She wants to find a way to raise the Vietnam issue on the floor every day; she wants to find ways to guarantee extended debate of military appropriations bills which now whiz through the House," Kelber wrote. "She wants to know how to attach legislation that she's interested in to pending bills . . . how to obtain special orders; how to block or speed up legislation; and probably the most elementary point of all, how to be recognized to speak."[36] Lawyers Abzug consulted with, as well as those on staff, helped her build a procedural tool kit she could turn to on a moment's notice. Majority whip Tip O'Neill handed out quick voting guides in 1971 designed to perfectly fit a man's wallet. Abzug improvised, tasking her staff with creating a longer list of procedural tactics sized for a woman's purse. Whenever she needed a new angle to swing debate, she brandished this quick guide from her handbag.[37] By working within the parameters of House procedure, Abzug made clear that she respected the tradition of federal lawmaking even though she critiqued congressional culture and law as a mechanism of elite power. Instead, the maneuvers she tried frustrated those colleagues who believed she did not respect convention and spoke out of turn.

House Speaker Carl Albert remembered Abzug as a vexing force, suggesting, "New York's Bella Abzug, for one, took the floor at every early meeting to urge this or that motion against the war."[38] However, Abzug addressed the Democratic Caucus infrequently and for the first time in late April only after it was clear the body had been shifting toward an antiwar position. Before then, she reserved her insider antiwar activism to needling members informally and making bold, quotable statements to reporters. She advocated the most extreme antiwar goal of immediate, unconditional withdrawal to give movement demands a wider audience. More so, she wanted to create a stark contrast with moderate Democrats and Republicans who supported de-escalation.

Abzug's sense of urgency increased on February 8, when the US military aided South Vietnamese troops' invasion of Laos to disrupt the supply chain along the Ho Chi Minh Trail. Among those who saw Laos as a "third Vietnam," Abzug called for "on-the spot" investigations of US involvement and was the only Congress member to join immediate protests.[39] The Senate responded to the Laos incursion first, passing a resolution on February 25 to withdraw all troops from Vietnam by January 1973. Abzug found it frustrating that House members were more reticent to act, but she lacked clout to trigger a response. Momentum came after five moderate Democrats, with Hawaii representative Spark M. Matsunaga taking the lead, brought a withdrawal resolution to the Democratic Caucus meeting on March 31. The debate was tense. The room divided between those who saw the December 31, 1971, exit resolution as "destroying the country, to the other extreme" of not having a set-the-date deadline as "betraying the country."[40] Despite Tip O'Neill's support of this end-of-the-year pullout, the resolution was defeated by one vote in favor of a compromise vaguely calling for withdrawal. Father Drinan called the result "another Gulf of Tonkin Resolution." Ron Dellums characterized it as "weak-kneed." Abzug deemed it "a disaster."[41] The fact that a resolution was debated at all reflected the turning tide.

At the Democratic Caucus meeting on April 21, Abzug took fellow Democrats to task, condemning "our own inaction out around the Capitol" and complaining that "you people are helping to insure" Nixon's reelection.[42] Although Speaker Albert had recognized Abzug to address the body, he immediately quashed her attempt to lodge a December 31 exit resolution and reopen debate. This would be the only time she brought forward a resolution on her own. Becoming wise to the tactics employed by this cadre of antiwar Democrats, House leaders changed the rules so that they could redirect debate in the Democratic Caucus at any time and request quorums be confirmed to thwart discussion on a matter. This left Abzug and her counterparts resolved to take their antiwar cause directly to the House floor. There, other "skullduggery" occurred, such as calling up Abzug's antiwar resolution and tabling it before she arrived and, on one occasion, physically holding her down so that she could not rise to force a vote.[43] Still, after the set-the-date effort in March, antiwar Democrats and Republicans did not move the de-escalation target significantly forward. It would take Nixon's acceleration of bombing in April 1972 to compel the Democratic Caucus to request that the House Foreign Affairs Committee propose a reasonable exit date, which it set at October 1. This resolution did not pass when it came up for a vote on the House floor in August.[44]

By Abzug's second term, she began to shed the reputation of being a sideline troublemaker, emerging as a figure who could rally progressive Democrats during key votes. But shifting from pariah status to that of a maverick took time. During her first months in office she had difficulty gaining acceptance even among antiwar Democrats who convened as the Group. Abzug indicated her interest in joining by offering to make a congressional antiwar barnstorming tour she was planning with Common Cause a "Group" activity.[45] But this cohort opted to keep its membership tight and passed on sponsorship of the "peace and priorities" tour launched by a few dozen Congress members that spring.[46] The men involved in the Group—Abner Mikva, Donald Edwards, Robert Kastenmeier, Phillip Burton, Donald Fraser, Benjamin Rosenthal, William F. Ryan, Robert Eckhardt, John Conyers Jr., Edward Koch, Michael Harrington, John Dow, and Henry Helstoski—often met for drinks or dinner. Their social bond went beyond a common interest in pressuring the DSG to do more to end the Vietnam War. In June 1971, when the Group decided to increase its membership by five, it passed on Abzug. Disappointed, she nudged Ben Rosenthal to advocate for her entrance further, and by October, she was invited to her first meeting as the Group's sixth new pick.[47] Phil Burton had resisted her admittance, arguing, "Even our institution will be too straight for her."[48] Gender had something to do with this delayed welcome. One member, Abner Mikva, did not think women in Congress "were leaders on the kinds of issues that came about."[49] In his view, Abzug forced her way in, criticized the Group's actions once there, and helped hasten its quick demise at the end of 1971.

Abzug had difficulty gaining an invitation to the Group in part because male colleagues resented her indictment of male leadership. While she directed most vitriol toward Cold War liberals and Republicans, her critique of male governance sliced more widely. She instructed her staff to focus on the Vietnam War above all else because it was the linchpin to dismantling what she called the "male military megalomania."[50] She made it clear to her male colleagues that she did not believe the Vietnam War would have happened on women's watch. In testimony before the House Foreign Affairs Committee, she charged, "A few men in high places played war games, manipulated governments and leaders, contemplated employing nuclear weapons, ordered the use of flesh-searing napalm and the destruction of the Indochinese countryside with poisonous chemicals, expanded the war in Laos, turned the skies over Southeast Asia into arsenals of terror against entire populations—and never paused to ask themselves who gave them the right to kill and mangle and displace a million people."[51]

This pointed critique of men in power did not win her many friends among men. Nor did it make women members more likely to sign on to Abzug's idea of a formal Women's Caucus akin to the Black Caucus established by African American members. Abzug incorrectly assumed that congresswomen as ideologically different from her as busing advocate Louise Day Hicks would be willing to set their issues aside to prioritize a shared identity. While Representatives Chisholm, Patsy Matsu Takemoto Mink (D-HI), and Ella Grasso (D-CT) often joined Abzug, other women members more supportive of the Vietnam War were reluctant to collaborate. Representatives Julia Butler Hansen (D-OR), Edith Green (D-OR), and Leonor Sullivan (D-MO) waited until Abzug left Congress to formally convene a caucus in 1977. The war issue, but also Abzug's forward personality, made it difficult for her to achieve her desired end.[52] "I know we're all very different," Abzug acknowledged, after failing to rally all congresswomen to issue a joint Mother's Day statement against the war, but she never came to terms with this reality.[53]

Abzug quickly became isolated upon joining Congress because she blazed in as a change candidate announcing her displeasure and gaming for a fight. She walked a tricky path of seeking inclusion and political capital in the very institution she brazenly deconstructed. Her dual challenge to the structure of Congress and thrust of policy felt like a personal affront to many of her new colleagues. Received coldly, Abzug believed she was unduly dismissed. Two months into office, she lamented, "I haven't felt any power at all."[54] Learning one's limits was a sobering process quite typical for congressional newcomers. Abzug's troubles were compounded by her minority status as a woman and a leftist. Still, she influenced debate more than her rank should have allowed because of her savvy use of congressional procedure. She had two tricks up her sleeve. Her rediscovery of the resolution of inquiry helped her draw attention to state secrecy during the Vietnam War, and her discreet employment of bill riders focused on sex discrimination helped her address gender inequity in US law.

Procedural Moves

In early February 1971, New Jersey lawyer Daniel Crystal answered the call for help Abzug issued through National Lawyers Guild channels. Combing through *Hind's Precedents* and *Canon's Precedents*, Crystal discovered a forgotten technique last used during the Korean War. The resolution of inquiry, he explained, "is a legislative device resembling in some respects the interrogation of the Prime Minister and Cabinet in Britain by Parliament." Crystal traced out how the resolution of inquiry had been used since the Civil War, noting, "It does not appear to have been used often, but it is there as a precedent." Essentially, the resolution of inquiry provided Congress with a tool for discovery that required the executive branch of government to answer questions and produce documents. A congressional committee could use this mechanism to gain internal and often confidential information relating to a wartime measure or any questionable executive action. Any House member could initiate this appeal, calling upon the appropriate committee to vote through a resolution of inquiry he or she drafted. The difficulty, however, would be convincing a committee to take this form of aggressive action. "There may be a sleeper here," Crystal encouraged, recognizing that the infrequently used device could catch the Nixon administration off guard.[55]

When the *New York Times* and the *Washington Post* published parts of Robert McNamara's report *United States–Vietnam Relations, 1945–1967: A Study Prepared by the Department of Defense,* leaked by former RAND Corporation analyst Daniel Ellsberg, Abzug decided it was time to strike. On June 21, she issued her first resolution of inquiry, cosponsored by seventeen colleagues, requesting that the Nixon administration produce McNamara's entire classified report to Congress within fifteen days.[56] Abzug kept abreast of Ellsberg's moves before the Pentagon Papers' first pages were set to print. On February 17, she cohosted a Rayburn mixer for Ellsberg with Henry E. Niles of Business Executives Move for Vietnam Peace, giving the disillusioned analyst an occasion to mingle with House members.[57] This event occurred as Ellsberg was discretely testing if he would hand over the classified report to Congress instead of the press, which his lawyers advised would more likely lead to jail time. Senators William Fulbright and George McGovern passed on introducing the Pentagon Papers using the filibuster technique. Employing a representative was a less compelling option, since House rules allowed only portions to be inserted into the *Congressional Record*.[58] After the Pentagon Papers were made public, Abzug believed the resolution of inquiry would remedy this limitation.

Abzug sought to shift public debate and jolt her peers into seeing Congress's potential as a dominant counterforce that could check executive power. "We have a right to know," she told members of the House Foreign Affairs Committee, trying to persuade them to act. The public, she suggested, has been more proactive in the "long journey of discovery from initial detachment to skepticism, questioning, disillusionment, moral outrage, and at last, repudiation of the longest war in our history."[59] On this occasion, committee members were not so moved. Inside the White House, Nixon aides deliberated over how to "cut off" Abzug's request, worried about the effect of getting "these things in the congressional record and all that stuff."[60] Pressed by the administration, the House Foreign Affairs Committee decided not to act on the resolution of inquiry within the required fourteen days. While Abzug did not achieve her desired result, her reintroduction of the resolution of inquiry was a provocative move that did garner the attention she had hoped. She reminded the public of Congress's responsibility, as their representatives, to flex their "right to know" about the executive's dealings. And she encouraged fellow federal legislators to be demonstrative in fulfilling this role.

The Pentagon Papers leak, and Abzug's resolution of inquiry attempt, conjured up a longer past than the Vietnam War. Nixon conflated Ellsberg with Alger Hiss, a State Department official accused of being a Soviet spy in 1948 and convicted of perjury in 1950. Likewise, Nixon knew Abzug as a former lawyer of rogue dissidents during the McCarthy period who had remarkably advanced to Congress. "They're Communists. You know that. Shit that's what they are. No question what Abzug is," Nixon characterized Abzug and New Politics Democrats during one conversation in the Oval Office in May 1971.[61] Similarly, Abzug believed Nixon had not shed his orientation as a former member of HUAC, bringing the repressive practices and subterfuge associated with the postwar Red Scare into the White House. The FBI, she learned from her old law partner Howard N. Meyer, had aided the prosecution in the case against antiwar activist Father Daniel Berrigan, arrested for defacing draft records.[62] Representative Hale Bogg's disclosure that the FBI had active wiretaps on Congress members further worried Abzug.[63] In April, she called for a full investigation of the FBI's surveillance techniques.[64] In May, she charged that mass arrests of antiwar protesters, condoned by the president, "reinstat[ed] the era of the witchhunt."[65] And in June, she urged her House colleagues to "demand that decision-making be done openly."[66] As a "new internationalist," she sought to uproot "old concepts and outmoded policies" endemic to Cold War doctrine and its coinciding intelligence and military apparatus.[67] Her restoration of the resolution of inquiry reflected her interest in "end[ing] government by stealth and secrecy."[68]

Abzug used the resolution of inquiry more successfully after her first try, most notably to compel President Gerald Ford to explain before Congress in 1974 why he pardoned Nixon.[69] This procedural tactic became Abzug's most used oppositional tool, and an immediate favorite of others as well. House members lodged a resolution of inquiry eighty-seven times between 1971 and 1976, a historic high point for its use.[70] During this period when Congress reasserted its might and tested the boundaries of presidential power significantly, the resolution of inquiry became one effective technique to do so. It was a particularly potent way to draw attention the overreach of executive privilege in the area of national security.

The resolution of inquiry delivered a noticeable challenge of executive power. The second procedural tactic Abzug frequently employed during her first days in Congress was subtler. Daniel Crystal had advised her that attaching antiwar riders to every bill would not pass the germane test.[71] While taking his point to heart, Abzug still thought she could effectively use this strategy for feminist purposes since sex discrimination was pervasive. She expected she could convincingly argue that every government service and regulatory law should include a mechanism to address sex discrimination. Additionally, she could employ this amendment-attaching strategy broadly and largely under the radar because riders would be added to disconnected bills being developed by different congressional sponsors and committees. Although critical of rights lawyers' incrementalist approach to changing civil rights doctrine, she employed a parallel tactic when adding sex discrimination clauses to bills, using her position on the Public Works Committee to test out this strategy. She persuaded fellow committee members to support her effort to add a sex discrimination clause to the Accelerated Public Works bill. During negotiations of this bill, this addition did not raise any red flags. Even so, this first try failed along with the bill, which President Nixon vetoed on June 29. Abzug's second attempt worked. On July 12, Nixon signed into law the Emergency Employment Act with Abzug's sex discrimination clause still intact. "We put sex discrimination provisions into everything. There was no opposition," Abzug later proclaimed.[72] While this development was not as totalizing as she suggested, her office was "directly and solely responsible for the first sex discrimination prohibition in a federally-assisted program."[73]

Abzug's mastery of congressional procedure led unlikely congressional allies to recognize her aptitude and savviness as a legislator. Her willingness to use the rules of Congress to disrupt its business and culture led some activists to incorrectly characterize her as a liberal focused on integration. More on point, Abzug was a pragmatist whose radicalism was measured by the desire to realize tangible results. She remained committed to progressive policy goals beyond the pale for most members of Congress. However, once an outsider working within this powerful institution, she had to convince those still toiling at the frontlines that she remained one of them and her office was theirs. This task was tricky because she also sought to distinguish herself as an elected woman of stature.

Representing Social Movements

Abzug came to Washington to give progressive organizers a direct channel to the federal policy arena, but her move into Congress separated her from the activists she aimed to represent. As a leftist focused on institutional influence, she remained committed to the idea of bringing protest to power. Though she was unsure about the extent to which she should protest as a member of Congress, for she believed elected officials should exhibit decorum and civility out of respect for the office. While she continued to show up at Women Strike for Peace actions, she declined to join demonstrators outside Senator James Buckley's office, explaining it was "beneath my dignity."[74] Abzug increasingly elected to address protestors, but not participate as one. She refined her relationship to progressive organizers with whom she had long collaborated. WSP affiliates believed Abzug should feel indebted to them for their role in her victory, and she resented this sense of ownership.[75] While she placed WSP friends on her staff, she saw her work on Capitol Hill as more consequential than the organization that helped launch her career as a politician. Her office became an auxiliary unit for an array of social movements, offering technical assistance, access, and collaborative engagement in developing policy, but it did not drive grassroots activism.

Abzug brought an activist edge to Vietnam debate on Capitol Hill, framing the "illegal and immoral war" as antidraft and civil rights activists did.[76] She railed against the interests of big business in the war industry, highlighting the oil industry's offshore drilling near Vietnam. She challenged Nixon's request for a two-year draft extension, passed by Congress in April, calling conscription "involuntary servitude" unduly impacting men of color.[77] Yet, she was late to answer the Vietnam Veterans Against the War (VVAW) request that she hold ad hoc war crime hearings in Congress, despite lobbying by VVAW cofounder Jan Barry Crumb and her aide Jim Crawford. In late January, Abzug passed on attending the Winter Soldier Investigation hearings in Detroit, funded in part by actress Jane Fonda, with whom she had frequent conversations. Instead, Abzug prioritized her campaign to be appointed to the Armed Services Committee. After this galvanizing moment for GI Rights activists, Representatives Ron Dellums and John Conyers Jr. took the lead in organizing a forum on Capitol Hill for antiwar veterans to deliver their testimonials. Abzug joined this effort, but she had missed the opportunity to be with VVAW from the start.[78] She admired Dellums, a "marvelous speaker" who shared her interest in promoting "our goals from the left wing of the Democratic Party, rather than from outside the party altogether."[79] Over meals they debated jovially about who was more radical. Although frustrated with her support role, she judged Dellums's outreach to veterans unfairly, suggesting his visits to military bases "without consulting anyone" reflected his "personal use" of the issue.[80]

During the VVAW's five-day action in April, Operation Dewey Canyon III, Abzug made sure to have a stronger presence, seeking to make amends. On April 19, she did not join Representative Paul McCloskey when he marched with more than 1,000 veterans and Gold Star mothers to Arlington National Cemetery. Instead, she waited to address the crowd once it had gathered on the Capitol steps. National newspapers that day printed a photograph of her surrounded by soldiers, her hat hovering above the men suited in combat fatigues.[81] It was an emotionally fraught week for VVAW members. This was the moment that decorated soldiers cast away their medals, and Lieutenant John Kerry pointedly queried before the Senate Foreign Relations Committee, "How do you ask a man to be the last man to die for a mistake?"[82] Senator Edward "Ted" Kennedy and Representatives Chisholm, Dellums, and Abzug visited the veterans' encampment on the National Mall. Abzug offered her congressional office as a backup barracks if police initiated protesters' removal. In return, veterans expressed their appreciation. Vinny Giardina of Astoria, New York, stopped with a gift and a note, reading, "Dear Bella, I would like to thank you with these ripped off flowers, from the Capitol lawn, for coming out to the lawn when they try and move us. You are really dynamite!"[83] A VVAW insider, Jim Crawford openly "used Bella's office to help" the group, fielded more than a hundred

Figure 5.2 Bella Abzug blurred the line between protest and politics, speaking here to demonstrators gathered at the US Capitol during the May Day action against the Vietnam War in 1971. (John Bowden, reprinted with permission of the DC Public Library, Star Collection © Washington Post)

veterans' cases during her first term, and instructed others on the Hill how to do this work.[84] Crawford tried to get a new veterans legislative task force going, to mixed reception. Backing this idea, VVAW's Arthur Egendorf emphasized that this was "not going to be a group to back Bella, but her lawyers, her connections in the community, her voice in Congress, and her concern for us, which she made evident long before it became fashionable to jump on the Veterans' bandwagon, will be invaluable aids."[85] Even so, most VVAW activists were skeptical of authority and critical of the government, and they did not want to be beholden to Abzug.

The congresswoman further distinguished herself as close to but not one of the protesters during the Spring Offensive demonstration on April 24 and the May Day Collective mobilization that followed. Abzug was among the eleven senators and forty representatives who made an appearance before 200,000 gathered on Capitol grounds. "Well it looks like everybody is here today. Except Richard Nixon. He is at Camp David," Abzug told the crowd, criticizing the president for retreating after VVAW "brought the war to Washington." She supported this demonstration planned by the National Peace Action Coalition, but worried the subsequent protest would be more problematic. Her own antiwar actions were hardly tame, but she did not want to give members who called these protests a "Communist propaganda project" any ammunition.[86] May Day Collective organizers promised to bottleneck major thruways if Congress did not adopt the People's Peace Treaty signed by US and Vietnamese students by May 1. Although Abzug introduced a resolution in support of this treaty, she did not condone civil disobedience. When she came out to speak to protesters on the Capitol steps, she told one of her former campaign aides, "You're going to get arrested."[87] While the arrests were expected, she was shocked that they began as she addressed the demonstrators. She stopped midsentence to scold the officers, "Don't you guys believe in the Constitution?"[88]

Abzug had not significantly shifted her position on what kind of protest she favored, or who she would defend if pressed to side with protesters or police. For this reason, she easily made the choice to inspect makeshift lockups at the Washington Coliseum and RFK Stadium. Representatives James Corman, Ben Rosenthal, and Don Edwards also inspected holding areas, but Abzug's entrance was the most dramatic, with her arriving via local news helicopter. Nervous to fly in this transport, she willed herself aboard, deciding it would be marvelous to "arrive that way por la cause."[89]

Once inside the stadium, "everyone crouched down around Bella so she could see and be seen and could hear the stories being shouted at her from all directions."[90] The scene, which she later described as "like a concentration camp," was the worst roundup of protesters Abzug had witnessed since the beginning of the war. She used her office and legal contacts to draw attention to the "breakdown of due process," supporting suits initiated by the American Civil Liberties Union (ACLU) and the Center for Constitutional Rights.[91]

Congresswoman Abzug's office linked the antiwar and feminist issues in its policy agenda and constituent services. Women in the military—nearly 10,000 during the Vietnam War—prompted her to follow through on her prior efforts to bridge feminist and antiwar concerns. She received poignant letters from women on active duty and veterans alerting her to how they were expected to "'service' the fighting men of the U.S.," how difficult it was to gain abortions while deployed and on base, and how sexist the military was as an institution.[92] Responding to these direct appeals as well as pressure from Planned Parenthood, Abzug publicly criticized President Nixon's action in April 1971 to tighten regulation of therapeutic abortions performed at military hospitals.[93] She echoed the argument increasingly made by activists pushing for decriminalization of abortion that the thousands of women and children killed in Vietnam far overshadowed any loss of life through abortion.

Abzug strongly supported the decriminalization of abortion, instructing her aides to collaborate with groups like the Women's National Abortion Action Coalition to draw attention to egregious cases and draft legislation.[94] Yet her framing of this issue, reflecting her own reproductive experience, was not as expansive as that of some proabortion activists. In the late 1940s and early 1950s, she had complicated cesarean births and multiple late-term miscarriages. She sought guidance from doctors, including Dr. Fernand Lamaze, the French obstetrician famous for his prepared childbirth technique. Abzug's abortion bills reflected her deference to medical professionals, qualifying that medical abortion, sterilization, and family planning services should be rendered only after "written request of the patient and the decision of the operating surgeon."[95] This language in her military abortion bill and subsequent Abortion Rights Act of 1972 helped set the tone for the medicalized path ultimately consecrated in *Roe v. Wade* (1973).

Feminist and gay rights supporters monitored Abzug's first moves in Congress and held her accountable. They wrote her when they thought an action she took was too timid or contradictory to her principles. She received letters like one from Mary Vasiliodes, a lesbian who expressed her frustration to Abzug that she had attended a NOW cocktail party, knowing full well that Betty Friedan sought to purge the group of its "lavender menace."[96] These letters, read by Abzug, caused her to pause, kept her anchored to movement interests, and fueled her determination to act. She quoted one anonymous letter at length when appearing before the New York City Council to advocate for Intro 475, a municipal antidiscrimination ordinance addressing sexual orientation. It read, "Maybe one day I will be able to sit in a bar in the Village and order a drink, without paying twice as much for it, and without the paranoia that comes over one when a police officer walks in . . . without the fear of being taken to the Women's House of Detention for congregating with people who understand me."[97] Calling police enforcement of sodomy laws a "practice of entrapment," Abzug continued to work ahead of most politicians in her support of gay and lesbian rights.[98] She was uninhibited in her advocacy, taking Mayor Lindsay to task for his "tacit support" of "very real discrimination" during the Intro 475 campaign, an effort that was unsuccessful until 1986.[99]

Abzug believed it was her role to step in when she felt New Yorkers needed more support than the municipal government provided. Her office worked in liaison with officials in City Hall, but it often worked around them as well. Establishing "mobile units" that popped up throughout her district, she sought to sustain the "acting, not talking," posture of her campaign by offering wide-reaching, experimental constituent services. During her first term, she was recognized for offering "the broadest package of community services ever . . . by a member of Congress," setting up the Legal Guidance Center, Consumer Information Service, Social Security Guidance, and Military Reference Library.[100] She actively encouraged anyone with a problem to seek out her staff, but her aides were still amazed and overwhelmed by the sheer volume of cases they handled—1,000 in the first six months and more than 2,500 at nine months—as well as their range: "Draft, immigration, passport, welfare, social security, missing persons, Medicaid, travel refund, transportation, Internal Revenue, employment inquiries, police matters, discrimination, Workmen's Comp., special education, health & hosp., problem, prison, Con Edison, telephone, dept. of Parks, legal referrals, housing, housing maintenance problems, Veterans Administration, drug referrals, abortion, emergency loans, welfare, unemployment insurance, environmental controls, union problems, senior citizen problems, mental illness, personal problems, Medicare, civil liberties, household help and nursing."[101]

Abzug deemed it her responsibility as an urban representative to "funnel federal legislation and federal funds into the city," and she immediately tasked her staff to focus on this goal.[102] But even more, she sought to narrow the distance between federal policymaking and the people she served. The community conferences on child care, crime, and economics she hosted were vibrant brainstorming sessions that brought district residents into the policy conversation and carried their ideas forward. As Joan Gregg, a resident of Chinatown, wrote Abzug, "I have heard you speak and you always made a lot of sense to me in your statements about the effectiveness of local groups and your interest in supporting them in their various struggles."[103]

Promoting an expansive policy program, Abzug attempted to be an advocate for all strands of progressive activism. She drew attention to the municipal and national governments' retreat from providing citizens with a basic social safety net, while supporting local efforts to fill the service gap and demand accountability. Her staff devoted considerable attention to tenants' rights, creating building-by-building complaint files and facilitating cross-district dialogue on fair housing. Similarly, her staff collaborated with local welfare rights activists, and Abzug addressed the National Welfare Rights Organization at its national conference in July 1971. An environmentalist, she contributed to the call for clean water and air, making the case that urban spaces would be more livable if they were healthier and greener. Reinforcing her "new labor" alliances, she met with women unionists making inroads in the hospitality, health, caregiving, education, and retail industries that she recognized to be growing sectors of unionism.[104] Abzug was committed to these concerns, but women's rights gained her greatest attention after the Vietnam War, a reflection of her staffing choices and her feminist identity.

Abzug's office became an engine driving legal feminism forward on Capitol Hill, but she did not endeavor to advance women's rights legislation alone. She worked most collaboratively and effectively with Representative Patsy Mink, who although coming from a different background as a

Hawaiian of Japanese descent shared her sensibility as a lawyer. Similar to Abzug's experience at Columbia Law School, Mink attended the University of Chicago Law School among a handful of women, graduating in 1951. Her path to politics was more traditional; she founded the Oahu Young Democrats in 1954, was elected to the Hawaii state legislature in 1956, and moved on to the House of Representatives in 1965. Mink critiqued the Vietnam War as passionately as Abzug, and likewise believed more women in politics could be a generative "spark plug for an issue."[105] They became frequent lunch companions and close friends, Mink caringly guiding Abzug as she acclimated to Congress. Abzug learned the ropes alongside "freshwoman" Ella Grasso, close to her in age, with a strong sense of family and deep ethnic ties as the daughter of Italian Catholic immigrants. Through their conversations, Abzug knew that Grasso had once led the chapter of the American Student Union at Mount Holyoke and wrote her undergraduate thesis on the Knights of Labor. Abzug could trace a continuous line back to her student Popular Front beginnings and thought that she might be able to conjure up Grasso's inner radical, encouraging her toward bolder action on women's rights and the war despite her being "a real party regular." Marking this distance from Abzug, Grasso often jested, "I'm voting with you today, but how long is this going to go on?"[106]

Shirley Chisholm was the most aligned with Abzug politically, but they clashed most as well. Raised in New York City and Barbados, Chisholm drew on this Caribbean heritage as a politician. Her dual attention to race and gender issues was already apparent when attending Brooklyn College in the early 1940s, where she helped form an African American women's club, In Pursuit of the Highest in All. Earning a degree at Columbia University's Teachers College, she left education in 1964 to represent the Seventeenth District in the New York State Assembly. While in the state legislature, Chisholm introduced bills on sex discrimination, maternity leave, domestic workers' benefits, legalizing therapeutic abortions, and subsidizing child care. Chisholm initiated action in many of these areas when joining the House of Representatives in 1969. Competitive with Chisholm, Abzug resented her head start as a feminist trailblazer in Congress, just as Chisholm questioned the authenticity of Abzug's commitment to women of color and poor women. Their distance was hardly veiled. Chisholm publicly jibed, "Next to Bella Abzug, I'm like Shirley Temple," as Abzug privately suggested, "I'm trying to build a women's movement with Shirley Chisholm, and as far as she goes I gotta let her go with me."[107] Despite these misgivings, they recognized the political value of aligning to move their common causes forward.

While child care policy reform preceded Chisholm's and Abzug's involvement, their collaboration on the Comprehensive Child Development bill helped accelerate its passage with bipartisan support in 1971. Child care advocates approaching this issue as an antipoverty, labor, and feminist concern "channeled their ideas through representatives Shirley Chisholm and Bella Abzug's alternative childcare bill."[108] Their "women's amendments" introduced in May added teeth to the original bill introduced by Representative John Brademas (D-ID) in the House and Senator Walter Mondale (D-MN) in the Senate. Abzug came to the child care issue from a place of privilege, having had the financial means to employ a caregiver to watch her children since infancy. But she recognized the widespread economic disadvantage other women faced when weighing employment against parenting responsibilities and the cost of child care. As a socialist, she believed government had a societal responsibility to ensure all Americans' access to this basic service that would enhance familial well-being and benefit market productivity. As a feminist, she saw the emphasis on privatized child care as a product of "male prejudice and the male fear of competition."[109]

Abzug's approach to developing child care policy reflected her commitment to bringing the federal policymaking process down to the neighborhood level. In February 1971, she held an open hearing in her district that reflected her promotion of "maximum participation in planning and policy . . . by parents themselves."[110] Returning to this implementation posture practiced in early Great Society programs, Abzug demonstrated her affinity with antipoverty organizers. Representatives of groups such as Head Start, the Committee of Community Control, Catholic Charities, and NOW testified, but the more poignant speakers were individual workers sharing the circumstances of their lives. Postal workers on the overnight shift discussed being "constantly caught in the squeeze of trying to find adequate" twenty-four-hour drop-in centers, and public housing residents and department-store workers brought up the need for on-site child care facilities.[111] The conversation intensified as audience members highlighted racial and economic disparity in child care services. Abzug mediated with cool resolve, arguing that a universal child care program could transcend barriers by balancing collective access to and individual choice of services.[112]

Chisholm and Abzug each gave a little as they drafted their amendments. They were united in the view that child care services should be locally controlled and child care centers should be equitable workplaces. Where they did not completely agree was on funding. They laid out two graduated scales of spending ($5, $8, and $10 billion over three years) and participant parameters: the "economically disadvantaged" would receive 65 percent of funds in the first year, 60 percent in the second, and 55 percent in the third. This scale reflected concessions Abzug and Chisholm made; Abzug favored an immediate reduction to 50 percent whereas Chisholm, seeing "the bill essentially as a poverty bill," favored a 65 percent scale for all three years.[113] The final bill that passed in Congress mirrored this compromise, slating $2.1 billion for a national program offering free services to impoverished parents and supplemental assistance for those in higher income brackets. Yet, it was Abzug's preferred framing of national child care as universal that set off alarm bells for conservatives who recognized, as historians have since noted, that this legislation "redefined the social contract itself."[114]

Vetoing the act in December 1971, President Nixon pushed back, arguing that the government's role should be "one of assisting parents to purchase needed day care services in the private, open market."[115] Kicked back to Congress, legislators did not muster enough votes to override Nixon's veto and this issue has largely been dead in the water since. How close advocates came to achieving comprehensive child care legislation demonstrates the persuasive edge progressive legislators achieved in Congress in the early 1970s. But just as one faction of American society pushed for the expansion of public benefits, another pulled back, welcoming privatized health, education, and social services. With Nixon in the White House, he tilted the balance toward the latter, helping hasten the federal government's embrace of neoliberalism.

This setback was devastating for Abzug, but it came alongside the passage of Title IX of the 1972 Higher Education Act Amendments—a law Patsy Mink took the lead on and Abzug cosponsored—which opened the world of sports to women. The mixed outcome of the first feminist legislative campaigns led Abzug to believe that feminists in Congress could gain an outsize impact because they had the power of a mass movement behind them. Additionally, the legal momentum to expand civil rights law had dissipated, but not disappeared, after a decade of courtroom and legislative action to dismantle Jim Crow. Abzug and her feminist peers in Congress sought to capitalize on this lingering momentum by making the case to their largely male cohorts that the rights revolution should extend to gender as well.

As a lawyer, Abzug was most interested in creating synergy between court-based legal feminist activism and federal legislative development. Her staff aided lawyers in their suits, wrote amicus curiae briefs, publicized test cases, and collaborated with legal advocates to draft bills. This joint effort ensured a confluence between legislative and courtroom action, and an interconnection between staff in congressional offices, in government agencies, and in newly established women's rights legal defense organizations. Significantly, Abzug's office became a generator of feminist lawmaking as the field of "women and law" formed. She created a space where some of these first legal specialists tested out their ideas, encouraged by Abzug's example and mentorship. Indeed, working in her office became a formative "point on the continuum" for feminist lawyers who then moved on to the Equal Employment Opportunity Commission (EEOC), feminist legal defense groups, and law school professorships.[116] This web of engagement helped lay the foundation for feminist jurisprudence.

Abzug's promotion of the Equal Rights Amendment (ERA) highlighted her collaborative legal activism and her prioritization of statutory development. For much of her adult life, Abzug had not supported the ERA, siding with women labor unionists who viewed the National Woman's Party's campaign for the constitutional amendment as an assault on their hard-won protective legislation that covered women in the workplace uniquely. Once Title VII of the 1964 Civil Rights Act addressed sex-based workplace discrimination, the point became moot. Appearing before the House Judiciary Committee in March 1971, Abzug urged women, "divided too long," to use their "real political muscle" and make the ERA, once "a legislative joke into a political reality."[117] In contact with Ruth Bader Ginsburg, Abzug knew the ACLU Women's Rights Project had been developing test cases to steer the Supreme Court toward applying strict scrutiny when determining whether a law treated men and women fairly and neutrally. These feminist litigators believed a *Brown*-like ruling on sex discrimination could effectively address gender bias in law. Abzug did not have such faith in the Supreme Court. Instead, she sided with legal scholar Thomas Emerson, who argued in an influential *Yale Law Review* article coauthored with his feminist students Barbara Brown, Gail Falk, and Ann Freedman, that the Supreme Court exhibited an "offhandedness and tolerance for inconsistency."[118] Legal personhood, Abzug correctly assessed, would be achieved most definitively through a constitutional amendment.

Abzug was not a driving force in the ERA campaign on Capitol Hill, led largely by Representative Martha Griffiths, a leading Democrat from Michigan first elected in 1954. While offering her support, Abzug highlighted how gender-neutral laws would provide empty equality for many women if material betterment continued to lag. For this reason, she simultaneously promoted the Women's Equality Act, designed to expand the EEOC's enforcement capacities. Diverse women workers wrote to and visited Abzug to seek her guidance and urge her to hold the EEOC accountable, reinforcing her view that the workplace discrimination she had experienced as a lawyer was pervasive in every industry. In March, she noted before the House General Labor Subcommittee, "Women and minorities are still castoffs of the American economy." Her staff collaborated with activists to bolster this point with data: women of color filed more than one-quarter of all sex discrimination grievances with the EEOC during its first four years, but only one case the EEOC acted on involved a Latina. Highlighting this case, Abzug faulted legislators more than the EEOC for creating "a watchdog without teeth."[119] She joined advocates and Democratic legislators who argued that the commission should have the power to issue cease-and-desist orders like the National Labor Relations Board.

As telephone operators picketed with signs stating, "Dial O for Oppression," Abzug lambasted the US government for rewarding the American Telephone and Telegraph Company (AT&T)—the nation's largest employer and its most "blatant, rampant, and pervasive" discriminator—with more than $931 million in defense contracts.[120] As a federal legislator, she saw her role assisting discrimination suits to be threefold: apply pressure on government agencies, augment public attention, and rally support among fellow congress members. AT&T's 1973 settlement of $15 million in back pay and $23 million in raises to 15,000 women and minority workers was a landmark victory that reflected the combined effect of union, public, legal, and federal pressure.[121]

Abzug's reformist purpose stretched beyond legal feminism. She saw law as the primary mechanism to reinforce or remedy the systemic inequities built into American institutions and reinforced through cultural practice. For this reason, she directed focus on Congress, drawing attention to its sex-segregated spaces by forcing her way into them. An avid swimmer, she requested lane times at the congressional pool, dismissing the suggestion that this men-only domain had to remain so because some male legislators liked to swim in the nude. Abzug's integrationist everyday protest triggered like efforts, with women on President Nixon's staff pushing for access to the White House gym.[122] Additionally, Abzug helped introduce gender-neutral language to the federal arena. She insisted that she be designated as Ms. Abzug in the *Congressional Record,* a prefix the "unconvinced proofreader" kept correcting to "Mrs."[123] And she scolded letter writers who mistakenly wrote, "Dear Mr.," setting them right with, "First of all, it is Congresswoman, not Congressman Abzug."[124] Collaborating with the ACLU, Abzug introduced a Ms. bill in July prohibiting the use of prefixes in all government correspondence and publications.[125] Dual courtroom and legislative activism achieved the desired effect as the federal government ultimately responded by adopting this new standard.

BELLA ABZUG CAME TO WASHINGTON to be more than a voice for progressive causes. Speaking in Congress was in itself a defiant act. During the Ninety-First Congress, women members addressed the full body decidedly less than their male counterparts—ten times in the House and once in the Senate by one count.[126] Women in the Ninety-Second Congress totaled only fifteen members, five fewer than ten years earlier.[127] Although dipping in numbers, Abzug and her allies in Congress embodied a demographic shift toward professional women elected to their own seat, not that of a deceased husband; they also focused on women's rights more than the innocuous concerns of women and children. By February 1971, thirty-five bills had already been introduced addressing women's rights issues, a reflection of this change in priorities.[128]

In September 1971, journalist Mary McGrory observed "two Congresses: one docile, the other seething."[129] Abzug encouraged this separation, stirring the pot more easily because the old ways of doing things were already unbalanced. She worked among progressive reformers who seized on an opening for reform in the early 1970s, and she effectively positioned feminist policy to be a key aspect of New Politics Democrats' agenda. Buoyed by the force of a mass feminist movement, she and a small cadre of women's rights–focused legislators aimed to achieve transformative legal remedies for women akin to the race-centered civil rights legislation passed during the previous decade. The male-majority Congress, already primed for internal congressional reform, responded by supporting many of the measures women and male allies brought before them. Yet, feminists' two major legislative goals—universal child care and the ERA—ultimately failed, a testament to the counterorganizing force of those who preferred small government and cultural traditionalism. Assessing the political climate realistically, Abzug understood that New Politics Democrats and bipartisan feminists' window of opportunity might be slim and opposition would be fierce. In 1971, she noted, "The country is in serious crisis, it's bursting at the seams, it has an opportunity for social change like never since the [19]30's. It can go either direction."[130]

Abzug came to Washington with measured optimism about the nation's potential to swing left and Congress's ability to enact progressive reforms. The resistance she faced upon arrival, while expected, was staggering. She predicted hopefully that public opinion had shifted against the Vietnam War to such an extent that "the Cold War is being liquidated."[131] Her new colleagues in the House of Representatives, however, lagged far behind their Senate counterparts in opposition.

Drawing on her "Battling Bella" persona, Abzug entered Congress fired up to challenge the Democratic establishment and Republican minority in the House. Most of her early attempts to get her bills moving and to shift policy debate failed. Her mastery of procedure and her purposeful disregard of House decorum enabled her to achieve a presence unusual for a junior member. Still, her ambition to achieve considerable clout led her ultimately to downscale her defiance and work on building interparty and bipartisan alliances. She learned to cede ground to others who shared her politics, strategically considered how to frame her issues in a manner palatable to moderates, and opened herself to the possibility of trade-offs and concessions. She quieted her leftist critique of incremental fixes, settling for small reformist victories she believed would build momentum toward systemic structural reordering. She did not believe this was selling out, but rather pragmatic radicalism.

Abzug's gendered challenge of structural power elicited the greatest resistance from legislators deeply invested in the patriarchal order that governed Congress. This institution was not simply unrepresentative; it was established with an endemic preference for men in power. Facing systemic reforms, those who benefited most pushed back. As one editorial noted,

"Ms. Abzug Finding Mr.'s Rule House."[132] She felt the enormity of this reality most acutely when first acclimating to Congress. Once inside this power center, she focused on drawing more women in with her, for she recognized that a gendered dispersion of power was required to destabilize the patriarchal bedrock of US government and society.

6

YEAR OF THE WOMAN

BELLA ABZUG BEWARE," warned Robert W. Dietsch in the May 29, 1971 issue of the *New Republic*. The population dip recorded in the 1970 census required one Manhattan district to be eliminated. Abzug, only four months on the job, was the most vulnerable. In accordance with *Baker v. Carr* (1962), districts had to be proportional to the population following a "one man, one vote" rule, but their boundaries did not have to make sense. As Dietsch explained, they could be "drawn between city blocks or even through the middle of an apartment house."[1] Republicans in control of the New York state legislature had every incentive to jettison Abzug's home turf, which they did in February 1972, eliminating the Twentieth District. Her attempt to run in the Twentieth District against longtime ally and ailing Representative William Fitts Ryan felt like a betrayal to his supporters, many of whom had backed Abzug in 1970. This primary race pitted friend against friend. Ryan surrogates accused her of being unfeeling, but Abzug believed her redistricting could be judged the same.

Abzug's personal make-or-break moment in 1972 occurred during a breakthrough year for women in politics. In this early "Year of the Woman," seventy-five women ran for Congress, and three women—Shirley Chisholm, Patsy Mink, and Linda Jenness—ran for president.[2] In the prime-time special "The Hand That Rocks the Ballot Box," ABC News highlighted how congresswomen's greater visibility, increased feminist activism, and frustration over the country's direction led to this surge in interest. Political commentators suggested feminist demonstrations could only go so far, and "it is on the political front that the best hope lies."[3] Abzug agreed. Once in Congress, she felt more acutely how elite power was male power and sought to rectify this gender imbalance.

Universalizing her personal fight to remain in Congress, Abzug forwarded a multipronged campaign to bring women into politics. She argued forcefully that gerrymandering could adversely impact women, critiqued the Nixon administration's lackluster promotion of women, and pressed party leaders to do the same. Most consequentially, she helped cofound the National Women's Political Caucus in spring 1971, a nonpartisan progenitor of groups like Emily's List, the White House Project, and She Should Run that recruited, trained, and backed women candidates.[4] However, Abzug's calculated choice of whom personally to back were highly influenced by her ideological leanings and pragmatic assessment of their viability.

Abzug's purpose was decidedly partisan. She used NWPC as an engine to boost women's collective clout and her individual power in the Democratic Party. As a nod to nonpartisanship, she urged NWPC to focus immediately and extensively on maximizing delegate strength within the Republican and Democratic Parties as "the most fruitful arena for a quick impact."[5] NWPC brokered results: at the Democratic National Convention, the proportion of women delegates increased from 13 percent in 1968 to 39 percent in 1972, and at the Republican National Convention, from 16 to 30 percent.[6] Abzug focused most on the formation of a left-leaning new Democratic coalition with women at its center. Capitalizing on democratization reforms mandated at the 1968 DNC, Abzug helped ensure an organized feminist bloc would emerge in 1972, checking the influence of organized labor. This change—along with a parallel push for racial minority representation led by the Reverend Jesse Jackson—came so swiftly and unexpectedly, AFL-CIO president George Meany lamented, there are "no steelworkers, no pipefitters, and worst of all, no plumbers."[7]

Although Democratic nominee George McGovern lost to Richard Nixon by a landslide, his campaign reflected how much influence New Politics Democrats had gained within the party since 1968. Abzug helped ensure that the "McGovern moment" was a moment for women. But this marriage was one of convenience, for McGovern welcomed the boost of women's electoral support more readily than he did feminist politics. Abzug's pursuit of greater influence came with costs. She did not endorse NWPC cofounder Shirley Chisholm for president, calculating she would gain more for herself and for women if she hedged her bet on a viable male nominee. At the same time, Abzug argued it was unfair that she was expected to step aside for a male congressman when her district was eliminated. Prioritizing building a national women's political base over local campaigning, she could not match William Fitts Ryan's well of support and lost her primary just before the DNC. Fate interceded, however, when Representative Ryan succumbed to cancer in September 1972, Abzug was selected as his replacement on the Democratic ticket, and she went on to win the general election. Her emergence as an influential feminist power broker within the Democratic Party as her own standing in Congress hung in the balance reflects how precarious women's foothold in politics was during this pivotal period.

More Than a Burlesque Show

In May 1971, as news that Abzug faced potential redistricting first broke, she helped launch an organization that immediately enhanced women's visibility and might in electoral politics. The National Women's Political Caucus, she stressed, should be a "practical, realistic political movement." In framing this enterprise as such, she broke with cofounders who favored participatory democracy. Once a federal legislator, Abzug shed any lingering interest in promoting horizontal leadership. While she believed NWPC's national leaders should be diverse, she did not think it wise to have dispersed decision making. She reverted to her preference for centralized bureaucracy, believing women must mirror the structure of political parties to match their patronage system and become party influencers. NWPC would fall apart, she argued, without a Policy Council, national paid staff, and "constructive leadership."[8] Abzug achieved influence in NWPC, but she did not singularly shape its programmatic direction or impede the creation of a dispersed structure of local and state chapters. Though, as in Women Strike for Peace, NWPC's structure exhibited enough flexibility for her to pursue her own agenda and draw on the clout that accompanied the group's speedy growth.

The first official meeting of NWPC occurred in Rayburn 2253 on June 9. There, two efforts to organize a caucus coalesced, one led by Betty Friedan and the other by Abzug. Throughout the spring, Friedan had hosted journalists, activists, academics, and political aides at her New York City apartment to discuss making a leap into politics. To a similar end, Abzug collaborated with Ronnie Eldridge, Sarah Kovner, Gloria Steinem, and Elinor Guggenheimer to draft a Democratic Party Policy Council resolution highlighting women's secondary status within the party structure.[9] The June 6 meeting in Washington brought together a wider swath of players, including Congresswomen Mink and Chisholm, peace activists, civil rights organizers, women's organization lobbyists, "young women with their backpacks, fresh from the marches against the Vietnam War, black women, Hispanic women, and representatives of the new women's groups."[10] Sixty women with different interests brought their particular concerns to the table at this meeting convened to set the agenda for a larger conference the following month. Discussion turned to structure and purpose; "Do we want to organize on the *issues* apart from women's interests?" Did they want to press for quotas? Could they meet a goal of one hundred new women in office in 1972? Should they have a "specific posture on race, poverty, urban decay, welfare, education, housing, employment transportation and of course, The War?"[11] African American and Republican women made respective appeals for greater representation. Gloria Steinem and Letty Cottin Pogrebin introduced a mission statement they had stayed up all night to draft.

Abzug, who had served as moderator, remembered this to be a "hard meeting." Vying for power, she clashed most with Chisholm and Friedan, whom she unfairly dismissed as making "large speeches." Abzug downplayed Chisholm's role in shaping the NWPC as an intersectional political action group. Chisholm was most responsible for ensuring that prominent women of color would be recruited as founding leaders, and with Fannie Lou Hamer on board by July, that NWPC would be a natural link to the Mississippi Freedom Democratic Party. Friedan also sought to broaden NWPC's appeal, arguing that the group from its inception should welcome women across the ideological spectrum. Abzug did not agree, countering that this catchall approach "flattened out differences about important issues."[12] She suggested Friedan was both out of her element and "obsessed with the business of being *the* sole leader."[13] This animosity was personal but also political. Abzug knew that Friedan had once been a cub reporter under Mim Kelber at the *Federated Press*, a leftist labor news service.[14] Both Abzug and Kelber had been critical of *The Feminine Mystique* (1963), seeing the influential book as purposely avoiding a racialized class critique of domesticity in which Friedan was well schooled. By 1971, Friedan believed that if feminism did not "become political it will peter out, turn against itself and become nothing."[15] Abzug and Kelber wondered what took Friedan so long.

The historic founding conference of NWPC in Washington, DC, on July 10, 1971, proved equally vibrant and conflicted. More than 300 women from twenty-seven states came together to flesh out the contours of a women's political caucus. At this gathering, "Bella was far more in control. Betty didn't stand a chance," according to Eleanor Smeal of the National Organization for Women.[16] Friedan ostracized women of color when she claimed, "Women's participation in political power will change the politics of this whole nation far more and more basically than the black movement or any minority movement or ethnic bloc of the past."[17] Chisholm, in response, introduced a "Position on Racism" drafted by movement veterans Myrlie Evers, Hamer, and others. In it, they encouraged NWPC to "commit ourselves to the awesome challenge of closing the widening gap between white, black, brown, and yellow American women."[18] Abzug's remarks echoed this concern, noting that they should not "replace or supplement a white, male, middle class elite with a white, female, middle class elite." At this founding moment, she was clear how she wanted to shape NWPC. It would be a coalitional project that included the "doubly and triply disenfranchised," but it would not include women who "have screamed for war" or who "are prejudiced, narrow-minded, reactionary, even violent."[19]

The NWPC conference gained widespread attention because it was so unusual. Democratic political hopefuls reached out with their congratulations. "Right on!" Senator George McGovern wrote Abzug. "You are making an important contribution both to equal representation and the treatment of women, and towards insuring a more open and Democratic convention in Miami Beach."[20] McGovern's flattering felicitations signaled the McGovern-Fraser Commission would be receptive to NWPC's appeal for proportional delegate representation at the DNC. Seizing on this opening, Abzug pressed Representative Donald M. Fraser the week after NWPC's founding conference to take the group's request to the full commission: "Each state delegation should be comprised of no less than 50% women" as well as racial minorities and youth proportional to state populations, she wrote, for anything less would not meet the new party standard of "reasonable representation."[21] In response, Fraser assured Abzug that the NWPC and the McGovern-Fraser Commission had a "mutual interest" in holding state party officials accountable.[22]

NWPC made immediate inroads with the McGovern-Fraser Commission because this "mutual interest" was reinforced through personal ties. Fraser's wife, Arvonne, was active in NWPC from its inception. The marital link of NWPC aide law student Phyllis Segal and McGovern-Fraser Commission lawyer Eli Segal further solidified this connection. Commission consultant Anne Wexler and NWPC director Doris Meissner were in conversation, sharing electoral data and advice. Finally, "Friends of the Caucus" participant Fred Dutton, a longtime Democratic adviser, counseled Fraser, "A majority cannot be made into a minority."[23] Abzug recognized these interconnections and encouraged Meissner to parlay these personal relationships into a political alliance. Likewise, with the Policy Council, Abzug reiterated her view that the Democratic Party was where NWPC could achieve the most immediate clout. These internal and external conversations developed during the fall. Meanwhile, Abzug directed attention to an NWPC spin-off venture, helping establish a delegate selection taskforce to educate women about this process in October 1971. With fledgling NWPC chapters just taking shape, she wanted to make sure a grassroots effort to recruit delegates was in place.[24]

NWPC parlayed its access to the McGovern-Fraser Commission into greater influence on Democratic Party leadership. On November 18, DNC chair Larry O'Brien brokered a delegate deal with Abzug, Patsy Mink, Ella Grasso, Shirley Chisholm, Mildred "Millie" Jeffrey, Fannie Lou Hamer, Anne Wexler, Phyllis Segal, and Coleen Waller. It had taken some coaxing to bring O'Brien to the table. NWPC used the power of the media to urge him along, releasing its November 9 letter to O'Brien to the press. Abzug signed this firmly worded letter drafted by Meissner and co-signed by Hamer, Jeffrey of the United Auto Workers union, and former President Johnson aide Liz Carpenter.[25] Joining O'Brien were Donald Fraser, DNC vice chair Mary Lou Burg, and temporary Credentials Committee chair Patricia Harris, an African American lawyer who worked in the Kennedy and Johnson administrations. Abzug "did most of the initial talking," but Harris soon chimed in. She made it clear that the new reform guidelines outlined by the McGovern-Fraser Commission would hold in noncompliance any state delegation that did not mirror its population. As the meeting progressed, Harris spoke "in caveats" and O'Brien remained hard to pin down, avoiding an exact numerical definition of "reasonable representation."[26] "You've got a prima facie case," Fraser asserted. "Why don't you put that in writing?" Mink challenged.[27] Unprepared to do so right then, Burg nonetheless offered a specific figure during the press conference she and Abzug held after the meeting. Reporters confirmed, "50 percent representation of women will be considered prima facie evidence that the slate of delegates has been chosen in a non-discriminatory fashion."[28] Meissner could not believe NWPC's luck, noting, "We would have gone for 10 percent, but they gave us 50 and allowed us to make the challenges."[29]

NWPC had emerged as a decisive political force, landing a substantial victory in a matter of months, although not all men welcomed this new, well-organized drive for more women in politics and government. The overt resistance of this new political group inside the White House was telling. In July, President Nixon summoned his close advisers to his vacation home in San Clemente, California, after national security adviser Henry Kissinger's returned from Paris peace negotiations. On this occasion, the president was debriefed about the NWPC founding conference. As Secretary of State William F. Rogers scanned the headlines, the banter derailed into a blatant, public display of misogyny by Nixon's top brass with journalists taking notes on the scene. Rogers began to describe the photo of NWPC founders sitting onstage that ran in national papers. Kissinger chimed in, noting that Gloria Steinem was among the leaders pictured. Next, the president interjected.

> *Nixon:* "Who's that?"
> *Rogers:* "That's Henry's old girlfriend."
> *Nixon:* "What did it look like?"
> *Rogers:* "Like a burlesque."
> *Nixon:* "What's wrong with that?"[30]

Learning of this exchange, NWPC founders were deeply insulted, and Abzug responded publicly on behalf of the caucus: "Obviously, the President and his advisers are accustomed to viewing women only in terms of flesh show. . . . The President has never said or done anything to indicate that he has the slightest understanding of women, their power, diversity, potentiality or needs."[31]

Figure 6.1 Journalist Gloria Steinem, Representative Shirley Chisholm, and writer Betty Friedan appeared with Bella Abzug at the founding conference of the National Women's Political Caucus in Washington, DC, in July 1971. One of President Richard Nixon's aides characterized this picture, printed in national newspapers, as akin to a burlesque show. (AP Photo/Charles Gorry)

In 1972, NWPC leaders called out this bad behavior but used this occasion to draw attention to Nixon's poor appointment record more than the sexual license men exhibited in the political arena. Republican women had already lobbied Nixon to do better on appointments, and he believed he had done enough. In 1969, his Task Force on Women's Rights and Responsibilities had drafted "A Simple Matter of Justice." And, in April 1971, he hired Barbara Hackman Franklin, a thirty-one-year-old Harvard Business School graduate in banking, to help recruit women.[32] Doubting Franklin would make a difference, Abzug continued to press, particularly for a woman to be appointed to the Supreme Court. Nixon was not amused. "Did you see Bella Abzug is still kicking us around on that?" an aide noted on July 20, to which the president replied, "What we need is a Mexican woman Jew. How would that be?"[33]

In the White House, Franklin was tasked to deal with the "Bella Abzug issue." While Nixon's male inner circle saw Abzug as a pest, Franklin was sympathetic. Although partisan, she agreed with Abzug that "discrimination by the Federal Government is hypocritical and heinous" and that "Executive Orders and Presidential Proclamations have had virtually no effect on the practices of the bureaucracy below."[34] Meeting with Abzug, Franklin saw her as "someone who was inclined to be more supportive than some of the other folks who were on the outside of the government establishment."[35] And she thought Abzug was unfairly maligned in the press. She saved Warren King's cartoon picturing Abzug dressed as a witch, holding a sign that read "A Woman for President." Under the caption, "So What's Wrong with Me?," Franklin wrote, "Nothing! Does King think there is?"[36] Franklin did not appreciate being assigned to clean up after the burlesque incident. She found the "'political power for women idea . . . extremely appealing" and believed the "moderate portion of the women's movement" could be an essential part of "RN's 'new majority.'"[37] But she never made headway convincing Nixon's male advisers that women, like working-class men, could be a key part of his realignment strategy. She leaned on NWPC to elect Nixon's former task force head Virginia Allan to cochair its Policy Council with Abzug; in return, she secured First Lady Pat Nixon's signature for an NWPC campaign letter.[38] When Franklin asked to attend NWPC's second conference, however, the request was denied. Special counsel Charles Colson, who "wouldn't be caught dead in the place," jokingly encouraged Henry Kissinger to go instead, telling him, "Don't go halfway. . . . Buy 8 tickets and take 7 girls."[39]

Resistance from the White House did little to quell the growth of the NWPC, which quickly became the leading feminist political organization. Despite being nonpartisan, its more active outreach to the Democratic Party pegged the group as progressive, a linkage Abzug encouraged by pushing hardest for delegate strength at the DNC. This early win on delegate representation would be NWPC's biggest boon in 1972, and one they capitalized on beyond this election season. The commitment the group secured from the Democratic Party, in line with the party's internal reform mandate, enhanced the connection between feminists and Democrats. In turn, Abzug's role as a broker who helped secure this deal with Democratic leadership elevated her national stature. In 1972, she emerged as a feminist political icon, selected to embody the "Year of the Woman" on the cover of *Life* magazine's special issue recording this phenomenon.[40] However, this increased clout did not assure local electoral victory.

One Woman, One Vote

Abzug forged two campaigns before the 1972 general election—one to save her seat, and one to unseat a congressional ally. To Ryan surrogates, her decision to take on the well-liked reform Democrat was coldhearted and did not make sense. Families, political clubs, and unions divided during "the battle of Bella & Bill."[41] Journalist Pete Hamill characterized the race as "a tragedy" and Abzug's decision to challenge Ryan as "a terrible thing."[42] Abzug lost backers, including Ryan's campaign manager, Henry O'Hagan, who had worked on her 1970 race.[43] "I deplore your decision to run against Rep. Ryan—its seems to me the important thing is to keep good people in and get the 'bad guys' out," wrote one former supporter.[44] "Bella Abzug is threatening to split the reform movement wide open by running against its leader when she has her choice of two machine politicians to fight," worried another.[45] Abzug did not welcome this contest. Her choice to run cannot be understood without exploring her prior failed effort to prevent the elimination of the Nineteenth District. Believing gender bias was behind this gerrymandering, she was not persuaded by those who maintained she should defer to a "good" male incumbent in the primary.

Abzug delivered a political challenge of redistricting that paralleled the argument ACLU lawyer Ruth Bader Ginsburg had been testing in sex discrimination cases. Two Supreme Court seats were vacant after Justice John Marshall Harlan retired on September 23 and Justice Hugo Black died on September 25. Nixon toyed with the prospect of nominating California appellate judge Mildred L. Lillie, even though the American Bar Association had deemed her unqualified. In October, a White House spokesperson announced they had moved on, commenting, "Heaven knows we tried. . . . First Mrs. Nixon talked to him about it, then Martha Mitchell and finally Bella Abzug. But it just wasn't in the cards."[46] Abzug believed the exercise to be a ruse and found Nixon's picks, conservative southerner Lewis F. Powell Jr. and Goldwater's former campaign counsel William Rehnquist, to be deeply problematic. Not only was Rehnquist a critic of the ERA, but the brethren would continue to reign. Abzug knew that when cases addressing women's issues had come before the court, the hearings were riddled with "frequent interruptions for laughter." "I doubt that a woman Supreme Court Justice, who has had to fight her way through all the obstacles of a male-dominated profession, would find anything very funny in the efforts of women to get legal redress of their just grievances," she told a group of attorneys in November.[47]

When Abzug spoke on the House floor during the final ERA debate, her remarks reflected how influenced she was by Ginsburg's parallel work in the courts. Ginsburg had been developing a strategy of "reasoning from race."[48] In one case, *Reed v. Reed,* her client Sally Reed challenged an Idaho law that favored her estranged husband as the executor of her deceased son's estate. In a brief for this case, Ginsburg argued that "sex and race were both 'congenital, unalterable trait[s] of birth.'"[49] This line of reasoning led the Supreme Court to its ruling issued in November 1971, in which it acknowledged that sex discrimination fell under the equal protection clause of the Fourteenth Amendment. While the justices stopped short of applying the same level of strict scrutiny as employed in race-based cases, feminist lawyers were pleased with this outcome.[50] Abzug, like Ginsburg, treated race and sex as analogous in order to lead congressmen toward seeing the passage of the ERA as the next natural step in civil rights change. The ERA, Abzug argued, was necessary "to insure the rights of women just as the 14th Amendment provided the basis for civil rights legislation," for "stereotypes which punish women for their chromosomes, much as blacks have been punished for their unalterable trait of color," were entrenched in law.[51] The difficulty with this line of argument was twofold: in suggesting similarities, one could lose track of difference; and in highlighting parallel injustices, one could problematically rank either sex or race discrimination as worse than the other. Abzug found herself stumbling into this very trap.

When developing an argument against redistricting, Abzug and staff looked at the latest legal scholarship considering *Baker v. Carr.* Thinking a great deal about this issue, Abzug wondered if the "one man, one vote" test created to address racial disenfranchisement could be applied to gender as well. She recognized that "minority groups and urban interest have been given the short shrift" in apportionment decisions, which necessitated a new "equality standard" in *Baker* that was "fair, equitable, reasonable, and representative."[52] It was harder to make a case for "gender gerrymandering," for women lived in all neighborhoods and belonged to all political parties.[53] For this reason, political scientists and theorists have only recently begun to explore how gender impacts voter suppression and redistricting politics. Abzug moved toward this conclusion because she had a hunch it mattered to the predominantly male Republican legislators in Albany that she was both a leftist and a woman. Abzug publicly introduced her view that she was a victim of gender gerrymandering in February 1972. With 150 NWPC supporters around her, she charged male legislators with making a "grossly discriminatory . . . move against me." "In New York State, where women also account for more than half the population, we have been almost totally excluded from elective and appointive office," she asserted.[54] Working the media circuit, she pressed that *Baker* should be extended, arguing, "We'd like to make sure that it's also one woman, one vote."[55]

This argument was a tough sell politically and even more so legally. Patrick Watson of Channel 13 took Abzug to task, asking, "Isn't it, in fact, just a coincidence that you're a woman and that this is happening to you and that the real discrimination is based on the fact that you're a pretty damn difficult person to get along with and that you don't have many friends among the regular Democrats and you don't even have many friends among the Reformers?"[56] Abzug was adamant that gender had something to do with it, and she wanted to test this theory in court. Her adviser Mim Kelber counseled otherwise. In her view, court action would take too long. She recognized the only litigable angle at that point was "ordinary gerrymandering with a partisan motive."[57] For this reason, Abzug resolved to try her case in the court of public opinion, and here she failed. In an article dated March 8, reporter Flora Lewis favorably highlighted the congresswoman's call for legal recognition of gender gerrymandering. But the story was still damning because it included a quote from Abzug that rang as tone deaf. In it, she tactlessly argued, "If they were doing this to a black, they would never get away with it."[58]

Abzug's remark, while callous and indefensible, highlighted how she compared racial and gender bias along a parallel axis. She maintained a leftist understanding of how white supremacy and male supremacy were connected, and yet, when pressed, she exhibited frustration that sex discrimination seemed more intractable. She prioritized fighting gender injustice in this moment, believing the Jim Crow system to be largely deflated. Public observers picked up on this privileging. As one constituent wrote, "Of course, the blacks will consider what you said a racist-oriented remark, insensitive to the needs of the 'black revolution,' but I appreciate your anguish and I hope you will be successful in your efforts to retain or regain your seat in Congress. I'm waiting to see how many black organizations rush to your assistance."[59]

Abzug exhibited the limits of her antiracist, feminist solidarity when she chose not to endorse Shirley Chisholm, who first publicly discussed running for president in July 1971. Abzug's decision contradicted her goal of building a diverse, progressive new Democratic coalition, an outcome Chisholm actively advocated for when campaigning nationally. Instead, Abzug focused on the quickest path to influence and did not expect Chisholm to be able to galvanize voters to the level of Eugene McCarthy or Robert F. Kennedy. This choice was not surprising, for Abzug had questioned the usefulness of symbolic women's presidential campaigns since the early 1960s. Noting publicly, "I don't know that she has suggested that she plans to win," Abzug revealed her pragmatic calculation that Chisholm was not electable due to her progressive politics and even more so because of her race and gender.[60] For this reason, Abzug strongly lobbied against endorsing Chisholm within NWPC. Instead, Abzug encouraged the group to maintain "an overall view of the political campaigns," not to back "just any women," and not to "put themselves in the position of running against each other."[61] Persuasive and powerful, Abzug compelled NWPC to offer only enthusiasm to Chisholm, leading individual members—most notably Betty Friedan—and individual chapters to defy this neutrality policy and endorse anyway. Chisholm never forgave Abzug for her lackluster support, frustrated by her "strange statement" at the press conference when Chisholm formally announced her candidacy in January. Abzug called Chisholm "a lightning rod" and a "rallying point on the issues" and offered her "encouragement," but no more.[62]

Additionally, Abzug contradicted the position she presented in NWPC that women should "avoid running against men incumbents who are good on our issues" by running against William Fitts Ryan.[63] Before she made this choice, Abzug received an outpouring of sympathy. "Look What They Did to Bella Abzug!" the *New York Times* announced on March 12, with Francis X. Clines calling the act one of "vengeance of oedipal proportions driving the anonymous male mapmakers who disposed of the 19th like a rag, a bone, and hank of hair."[64] Democratic state legislator Mary Anne Krupsak suffered a similar fate, but the redistricting of Abzug's seat felt more premeditated. "Dear Bella, My heart goes out to you. Whatever you decide we are with you, believe in you and have faith in your magnificent courage and spirit. Dearest Love," wrote friend "Millie" Jeffrey.[65] "We're sorry you got screwed," wrote J. Richard and Michele Forman of Vermont.[66] The terror for some changed when Abzug announced she would challenge Ryan.

Abzug ran against Ryan because she calculated she would have more difficulty winning the general election in other districts. Abzug agonized over where to run. Her staff created hypothetical maps, speculating on how the lines would be drawn. Until late February, they thought the Lower East Side would remain intact.[67] Then, rumors hinted at an incoherent redesigned district that would slice through lower Manhattan and include conservative-leaning Staten Island. Abzug made her rounds to party clubs in every borough. "People on the West Side wanted her to go to the East Side, and those on the East Side wanted her to go to the West Side. . . . People in Manhattan thought she should certainly run in Brooklyn or Staten Island without bothering to find out whether the people there wanted her," Mim Kelber recalled. Liberals in Staten Island urged her to run against Representative John M. Murphy, but she saw this borough as "totally unfamiliar terrain." Abzug unsuccessfully tried to convince Al Lowenstein, also district shopping, to let her take on Representative John J. Rooney in Brooklyn, whom she thought she could beat. It came down to Ed Koch or William Fitts Ryan. Koch "was the one she wanted most to contest because she regards him as a fake liberal," Kelber noted, but "she was getting all kinds of flak from reformers who support Koch."[68] That left Ryan.

On March 21, 1972, Abzug announced that she would challenge Ryan because she lived in the redrawn Twentieth District and it was the "only sensible place" to run.[69] The reservations Abzug had about taking on Ryan had waned in the final days of her redistricting campaign. Women office-holders and presidential hopefuls George McGovern and John V. Lindsay had publicly urged New York state legislators to give "Bella . . . a fair shake."[70] Abzug's male colleagues in the New York congressional delegation, Ryan included, had remained silent. It is "hard to develop a united feeling about it," Abzug wrote privately, relaying her frustration.[71] She leaned on Lindsay and Governor Nelson Rockefeller to tempt Ryan with appointment offers, placing him, as one reporter observed, "under what is probably the hottest gun in New York politics."[72] He was not about to step aside, for aides had polled reform Democratic clubs to see if they swung toward Abzug, and while respondents thought she had been given a "raw deal," they largely favored him.[73] Ryan, who publicly commented that running against him would not be "the right thing" to do, found it "difficult to believe" when she did not abide. He was personally offended, since she had consulted him "on issues and problems," and he saw her move as inconsistent with her prodding on the "need to build a meaningful coalition to defeat reactionaries."[74]

Abzug's decision to take on Ryan reflected her determination in 1972 to shift the gender imbalance in Congress and in the Democratic Party. Days after her announcement, she penned an op-ed that candidly quipped, "If a man from Mars was to visit Capitol Hill and take the term House of *Representatives* literally, he would conclude that the United States is a prosperous land of small towns, farms and suburbs occupied by middle-aged and elderly white men who are lawyers, bankers, businessmen, farmers and occasionally teachers and journalists."[75] She found it frustrating that women, more than men, were expected to defer to incumbents. It would be nice if some "men move up, down, out, or over," she pronounced in one interview.[76] What Abzug's feminist supporters saw as a challenge of the "male power structure," some of Ryan's backers believed to be undeserved entitlement. Male journalists questioned why Abzug had to run. Nat Hentoff called Abzug's challenge of Ryan "plain old predatory" and asked, "Is it worth it, Bella? Is it really worth it?"[77] Phil Tracy assessed, "The only clear-cut distinction between Bill Ryan and Bella Abzug is their sex."[78] For her part, Shana Alexander observed that Abzug had become a target of "a genuine male backlash, the first in American political history," and accused male reporters of "gusts of locker-room sentimentality."[79]

Gender became a central point of tension in the Abzug-Ryan primary because the candidates were so ideologically similar. Ryan's camp, anticipating that he might have a female challenger, encouraged him to get ahead of gender by developing a women's rights platform early, paying female staff equitably, and mentioning women often during the campaign. Ryan supported the ERA, abortion for all, universal child care, a guaranteed annual income, and equal opportunity in work, education, and politics, yet Abzug's backers saw his late embrace of these positions as "something less than total commitment to our unequal status."[80] Abzug argued she was "the greater of two goods," which was a tough sell, since at different points in 1971 she had called Ryan outstanding, intelligent, effective, and one who took the "purist position."[81] Ryan and Abzug were both graduates of Columbia Law School, often voted together, and had 100 percent voting records according to the Americans for Democratic Action.[82] Abzug's image appeared next to McGovern's on a flyer that said, "A new politics: This year we can make it happen!"[83] Yet, Ryan supporters could effectively counter that he had been a leading progressive in Congress "long before the term 'new politics' entered our national vocabulary."[84] Elected in 1960, he went to Albany, Georgia, to visit jailed civil rights protesters in 1962 and led the first House appropriations challenge of the Vietnam War in 1965.[85] Like Abzug, he believed a "progressive coalition" was "necessary to get this Nation back on the right track" and similarly asserted, "We must have a people's Congress."[86]

Ryan and Abzug spent much of the primary vying for the "most progressive" title, but Abzug was willing to go to greater extremes. In 1971, Ryan and other city leaders backed Abzug's effort to launch a Committee to Make New York City a State, an early, unrealistic response to the city's fiscal crisis. By the time of the primary, the idea that the city "in bondage" should secede fell out of favor, and Ryan quieted his support.[87] Similarly, he delivered "serious challenges to the leadership" on the war but limited most of his antiwar activity to Congress.[88] In contrast, Abzug used her office to bring antiwar movement campaigns into the federal arena that few legislators would touch. On March 29, she introduced unconditional amnesty legislation her staff drafted with organizers of the National Committee for Amnesty Now, and that same week, she facilitated soldier John Herndon's return after going AWOL in 1970.[89] On April 20, Abzug and Patsy Mink met with National Liberation Front foreign minister Madame Nguyen Thi Binh for six hours in Paris, adding to the feeling that Abzug was a radical and possibly a Communist. The congresswomen had hoped their public overture outside of diplomatic channels would help reboot peace talks, but little was accomplished since NLF "put Bella and Patsy squarely in the administration camp."[90] Instead, the trip provoked mockery at home. Most strikingly, Francisco "Corky" Trinidad's cartoon portrayed NLF male negotiators discussing Binh's meeting, noting, "I knew letting her talk to Patsy Mink and Bella Abzug was a mistake. She calls me Comrade Chauvinist Pig already."[91]

Ryan and Abzug's campaign shuffle to best each other spilled over to the House of Representatives, where their contest threatened to divide New Politics Democrats. On May 8, the US military escalated its bombing in North Vietnam. A small cadre of antiwar Democrats, Abzug and Ryan included, decided that the magnitude of this action warranted issuing a first call for President Nixon's impeachment. Abzug worked with the Lawyers Committee on American Policy toward Vietnam on a solo resolution. John Conyers Jr. convinced her to hold off from issuing it, arguing that collective action was best. She agreed, but Ryan "broke ranks," introducing an impeachment resolution on May 9.[92] Coming to Abzug's defense, Conyers publicly criticized Ryan's singular action.

Supporters of Abzug and Ryan both used misleading tactics. An anti-Bella group titled Women's Political Caucus, Inc., sounding like the NWPC, confused voters, while Abzug's campaign literature referenced a Nat Hentoff article in the *Village Voice* to make it seem like he endorsed her.[93] The Abzug campaign dug lower than Ryan by making his poor health an issue. Ryan aides stewed over how to address his ailing health, for it was clear to all observers that he had not recovered from throat surgery. Ryan knew his failing health would be a problem. He tasked an aide to compile a report on how elections back to 1944 had handled health concerns. Ryan was advised, "Attack the issue frontally, candidly, casually, and if possible, humorously."[94] Trying out what to say, he jotted down possibilities, one reading, "since operation, usual 14/16 hr day, family, & staff can't restrain me, or voice would have improved faster."[95] His campaign tried to make the most of his condition, poking fun in one flyer, "Our Congressman Ryan. His record speaks louder."[96] Abzug campaigned as she usually did, speaking at full volume in debates and at campaign stops, which Ryan, with his diminished voice, could not match. Abzug believed that treating Ryan as an equal competitor was the right thing to do. But he was not at full capacity, and those sympathetic to him could see the imbalance. While Ryan's campaign was not forthright when it suggested that he had "demonstrated his full recuperation," Abzug campaign workers who intimated that Ryan had a terminal illness crossed the line.[97]

Abzug's treatment of Ryan's health did not play well with voters, but three additional factors narrowed her chances. Foremost, Abzug did not have reform Democrats' essential backing once she took on an early leader in their movement. In 1957, Ryan had helped found the Riverside Democrats and achieved an upset victory as a district leader. Abzug, by contrast, had received the reform Democratic designation in 1970 by powering through their procedure, emerging as a winner by channeling outside support into the party clubs. Additionally, the Liberal Party went for Ryan, as did the faction of New York City unions Abzug had already lost in her 1970 election.[98] Second, Abzug had difficulty overcoming the power of incumbency. Ryan ran on experience, comparing his twelve years in office to Abzug's year and a half.[99] She tried to match this argument by highlighting how she was a national leader in the antiwar and feminist movements, whereas Ryan was a neighborhood deputy. Abzug, however, made the error of not doing enough to highlight the expansive constituent services she had introduced in her district. Accordingly, she was susceptible to the critique, put forth by Judith Michaelson, "What do Wagner, Spock, Myrlie Evers, Marlo Thomas, Shirley MacLaine, Alan King and Councilman Carter Burden have in common besides their approval of Bella? They don't live in the district."[100] Finally, unlike during her 1970 campaign, Abzug prioritized identity politics above all else. Feminists and gay rights activists asked Ryan, as Peter Fisher did, "Where have you been all along?"[101] But for those more reluctant to sign on to social liberation, and for those who believed it had already gone too far, Abzug was the more problematic candidate. Her loss reflected just how much the Twentieth District was with Ryan, who beat her two to one. While his support was strongest on the Upper West Side, he also won in Abzug's neighborhood, Greenwich Village.[102]

By 1972, voters in New York City believed they had a strong sense of what Abzug stood for, the change she was after, and who she represented. Additionally, the gendered campaign she lodged to challenge redistricting hung over her primary race against Ryan. Directing most focus on gender early on, she narrowed voters' perception of her interests to identity politics. In the "Year of the Woman," this posture made it seem like women's central purpose was to demand inclusion more than to reframe national priorities. Abzug encouraged this perception, noting in her concession speech, "Not only will I be around, but I think many other women are going to be visible in politics, too."[103]

Changing the Face of the Democratic Party

During Abzug's primary contest with Ryan, she devoted considerable attention to developing NWPC's Democratic National Convention strategy. The promise NWPC achieved from Democratic Party leaders to work toward proportional delegate representation gave the group a clear presence as watchdogs of the implementation process at the state level and on the DNC convention floor. Abzug's influential role in negotiating NWPC's deal alongside her position in Congress led to her appointment on the Platform Committee. She delved into this work in late June, the week

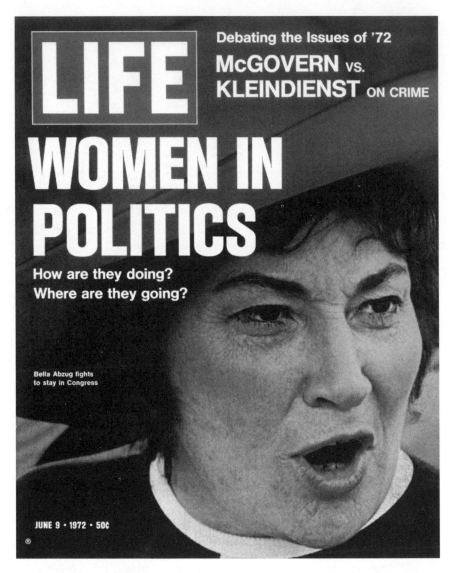

Figure 6.2 Declaring 1972 the "Year of the Woman," *Life* magazine selected Bella Abzug to symbolize this breakout year of women running for office. (Leonard Mc-Combe/The LIFE Picture Collection/Getty Images)

after losing her primary, with her career in public office seemingly over. Ironically, just as her influence in the national Democratic Party widened, her local footing in electoral politics closed. As a result, what Abzug primarily offered the McGovern campaign was the growing clout of women as a voting interest group.

Abzug believed she would have considerable sway during platform negotiations because, in her view, McGovern's nomination made clear that the party establishment was "out of touch this year" and clearly "threatened."[104] She was correct. McGovern gained the Democratic Party nomination because moderate Democrats who had supported the Americanization of the Vietnam War had been effectively countered by antiwar interests. The war issue had become an umbrella that tied together the loose web of progressive causes that fell under the mantle of New Politics. And enough progressive voters had mobilized effectively to steer party clubs, districts, and state delegations toward the New Politics program, transforming this outsider grassroots pressure bloc into a party wing. This was the Democratic upset that Abzug had been working toward since she first urged leftists to bring protest into politics in the mid-1960s. Yet, she came late to the McGovern camp. She became a McGovern surrogate when she realized progressive forces were coalescing around him. Ultimately, she decided that McGovern could achieve for the Left what Barry Goldwater had in 1964 for the Right. Abzug endorsed McGovern because he was the last reform candidate standing, her half-heartedness apparent when she finally encouraged in May, "Maybe the peace movement should join up in the political campaigns of peace candidates like McGovern."[105]

The progressive grassroots mobilization that secured McGovern's nomination reflected the maturity of Democratic New Politics, but this leftward push came alongside a rightward pull on display at the 1972 DNC. On the Platform Committee, Abzug sat next to backers of presidential hopeful Alabama governor George Wallace, demonstrating that the party's segregationist faction still had a presence. After the ERA passed the Senate in March 1972, a ratification challenge ensued that social conservative Democrats and Republicans both forwarded. Meanwhile, labor unionists who saw the expansion of rights and protections for nonwhite, nonmale workers as a threat remained vocal within the party, if out of step with McGovern's wing. For all ideological and identity groups, including the New Politics victors, the 1972 DNC was an uncomfortable place to be as the party divided and different factions vied for control.

Drafting the Democratic Party platform was a particularly tense and consequential exercise. As an antiwar candidate, McGovern condoned an antiwar plank that incorporated the wishes of the party's Left. Abzug would have preferred a thirty-day timeline, but the plank called for immediate, complete withdrawal from Vietnam and amnesty for draft resisters.[106] Identity issues proved trickier to negotiate. Abzug strongly backed a gay rights plank, which called for the "repeal of all laws, federal and state, regarding voluntary sex acts involving consenting persons in private, laws regulating attire, and laws used as a shield for police harassment."[107] She encouraged Democrats to lead on this issue, stressing to her peers that it is "sheer hypocrisy" not to recognize "that there's a total society" and there are "homosexuals who believe that they should get the protection of a party like this."[108] The plank failed 34 to 54, for McGovern aides were not supportive, seeing the issue as one that could be easily distorted. The fifteen-point women's plank—the most comprehensive considered by the Democratic Party—did pass, but not with the abortion plank that feminists wanted to be included. Backed by NWPC leaders, Abzug introduced a plank modeled after the Abortion Rights Act she sponsored in Congress that advocated for women's "freedom to choose."[109] Once it was on the table, it was clear that abortion posed "more of a problem with the mc govern [sic] people than any of them will admit."[110]

NWPC found resistance from party leadership when it moved from negotiating a presence at the DNC to pressing for programmatic changes. McGovern's women's rights coordinator Amanda J. Smith had suggested "it's a whole new ballgame" for women after McGovern secured the nomination.[111] NWPC leaders sought to hold him to task, and abortion was their primary concern after delegate strength. In this moment, when abortion was still illegal in most states, being pro-choice was not yet a litmus test for Democratic candidates. McGovern believed he could gain feminist support while holding out on the abortion issue. In a May press release, he made clear, "I have never advocated federal action to repeal those [state] laws and if I were President, I would take no such action."[112] Even so, he invited NWPC leaders to his home to listen to their position. "We women look at this subject as our Vietnam, since there are more women dying from butchered abortions than servicemen killed over there," Gloria Steinem explained in stark terms. Actress Shirley MacLaine, a McGovern confidante, noticed his discomfort. "Nothing can make a man . . . more nervous than a group of demanding, forsaken, intelligent, unheeded women who are . . . responsible for a bloodless revolution that is already reversing some of the country's priorities," she observed. She counseled him to avoid the subject of abortion, but he encouraged her "to work something out" with Abzug.[113] MacLaine and Abzug met over a round of late night hamburgers at White Castle. MacLaine "was willing to put the question of a woman's right to her own body on the back burner for five more months." Abzug would not, arguing that the "laws needed changing so badly," and "Nixon would make it a campaign issue anyway."[114] At an impasse, they revisited their positions before the full Platform Committee. At 1:47 a.m. on June 27, deliberations over the abortion issue commenced, continuing for two hours. Abzug advocated "abortion on demand," while MacLaine suggested abortion should not be "mixed up in partisan politics."[115] Although sympathetic to feminist interests, MacLaine was pleased that the committee swung her way, announcing, "We're not going to say anything to hurt George's chances."[116]

Platform negotiations between McGovern surrogates and NWPC leaders previewed further conflicts that unfolded at the DNC in Miami in July. There were more than 1,000 women among the delegates, a threefold jump since 1968, and at least 300 were actively engaged in NWPC. The caucus's role in expanding women's delegate strength led the McGovern campaign to see the group as the primary representative of Democratic women. Thus, feminist Democrats' clout surpassed that of traditional women's auxiliary units established in the party. This "really infuriated" Women for McGovern affiliates, who made up at least 200 delegates. As Anne Kunze of this organization scolded, "After all the damage Bella and Shirley had done to your situation, they were able to get your ear on a busy morning the Women who wanted to work for your best interests couldn't even get to you, period."[117] McGovern, however, was not beholden to the NWPC. Top McGovern aides believed they could draw on NWPC—and Democratic women—advantageously without fully committing to feminists' demands.

Delegates at the 1972 DNC reflected the shifting demographics and interests of the Democratic Party. Next to John V. Lindsay, Abzug, as a delegate at large, was the most recognizable member of the New York delegation who went from "'Who's Who' in the state party" to "Who's That."[118] Abzug welcomed this visible change, having been a part of the 1968 open convention movement and having strongly advocated for the democratization of the Democratic Party since. Still, she was not of the rank and file, as was evident from her stay during the DNC at the luxurious Diplomat Beach Resort in Hollywood, Florida, a level above NWPC's headquarters at the Betsy Ross Hotel in Miami. While the DNC program proudly featured "the new delegate" and highlighted the party's "special efforts to reach women, young persons, minorities and others who previously have been shut out of the process," Democratic leaders braced for a floor fight.[119] As floor manager, "Bella was the captain" of NWPC's whole operation. "She would plan how we would get microphone time the next day. She would plan who would speak. And she would plan how and when we would vote on the floor, and whether or not we would disrupt it," recalled party insider and NWPC affiliate Midge Costanza.[120] Running a tight ship, Abzug promised NWPC delegates at an opening rally, "Whatever happens, we are not going to be the sacrificial lamb of this convention."[121]

This is exactly what occurred. Worried about keeping anti-McGovern delegate factions in line, McGovern's top aides reneged on what NWPC leaders had thought was a firm commitment to support their planned challenge of the male-dominated South Carolina delegation. Only 9 of 32 delegates were women in this state delegation, falling short of the new "reasonable representation" standard. NWPC spent the weeks before the DNC delivering credential challenges in thirty states. Betty Friedan had wanted to make Illinois—with only 29 of 160 delegates elected women—"our Mississippi Freedom fight" at the 1972 DNC.[122] McGovern supporters within NWPC steered the group toward South Carolina instead once McGovern made it clear he wished to have the Credentials Committee handle Mayor Richard J. Daley. After making this concession, NWPC leaders expected McGovern to back their South Carolina challenge, especially because on the opening day of the DNC he had reaffirmed his "full and unequivocal support."[123]

McGovern had made a commitment to NWPC his aides did not think wise to entertain. Eli Segal had counseled early on to stay "hopeful that remedies can be worked out" without talking of "mathematical equality."[124]

The evening of July 10, it was clear that they would need to abandon McGovern's deal with the NWPC. An Ohio delegation that supported Hubert Humphrey kept passing during roll call. McGovern campaign staff worried this isolated protest could spread to winner-take-all California, where anti-McGovern delegates threatened to withhold support. Assessing the situation from a nearby trailer, McGovern's floor manager, Richard G. Stearns, began calling floor leaders to tell them to dump yes votes to tank the South Carolina challenge. He calculated, with 1,509 delegates, McGovern could "either win decisively or lose decisively" and needed to show that he could outorganize his opponents.[125] Meanwhile, NWPC leaders suspected Humphrey's faction to be behind the circulation of a forged affidavit signed by director Doris Meissner, inferring NWPC's support for a "Stop McGovern" effort.[126] Distracted, NWPC leaders were caught off guard when delegations began voting against their effort to unseat the South Carolina delegation. Abzug and Steinem ran into McGovern's campaign manager, Gary Hart, shortly after, and he received their wrath. You "sold women down the river," they fumed.[127]

McGovern's male aides depended on women's delegate strength, but they found it frustrating that this developing feminist bloc would not fall in line. They needed NWPC's assistance in mobilizing women delegates as a counterweight to Humphrey's organized labor backers but found it cumbersome that women expected something in return. "They were focused totally on South Carolina as a symbol, and they could have, it seemed to me, cared less about the nomination," Hart later complained.[128] Equally perturbed, Stearns reasoned NWPC could have picked any state after California to test credentials and should have been satisfied by having achieved "the same chance of election [as delegates] that men had."[129] Beyond this suggestion that women's increased presence should be enough, Democratic men observing the failure of NWPC's first South Carolina campaign assumed these women were political novices and unskilled negotiators. Along these lines, South Dakota lieutenant governor Bill Dougherty suggested that NWPC failed because the political process was "so complicated that they haven't figured it out."[130]

The failure of the South Carolina challenge freed NWPC leaders from the grasp of the McGovern campaign, and for the rest of the convention they largely acted in their own interest. On day three of the convention, at 4:00 a.m., a "most severe" debate considering abortion erupted like "vitriolic lava over the convention floor." First to the microphone, St. Louis attorney Eugene Walsh averred, "We want our young to live to be born." Surprised an "anti" had been selected to start the debate, Gloria Steinem reproved Gary Hart, "You bastard, you promised us." Next up, MacLaine encouraged delegates to vote their conscience, saying, "Do what's right for women, do what's right for the candidate and do what's right for the party." Livid, Abzug retorted, "Listen, goddammit, you listen, we want a vote on abortion and we're going to get it."[131] The abortion plank failed, 1,572 to 1,101.[132] Being pragmatic, Abzug commented the next day, "It's not the end of the world that plank didn't get thru. McGovern represents the changes we've needed in the party for a long time."[133]

NWPC made one final gesture at the 1972 DNC that drew attention to feminists' critique of a political glass ceiling and thwarted the smooth nomination of McGovern's initial pick for vice president, Senator Thomas F. Eagleton. Internally, NWPC leaders had decided that they would put forward a vice president nomination of their own, Sissy Farenthold, who had made a strong showing during the Texas governor race that spring. When the time was right, "Congresswoman Bella Abzug activated the NWPC's floor operation," and "dozens of women began to lobby their delegations."[134] "Maybe this is a futile gesture, but anyway, it's the last night of the convention, so let's try," rallied one supporter, waving a "Farenthold for VP" sign.[135] With more than 400 votes cast for Farenthold, the impact of this insurgent nomination surprised Democratic leadership. It also stalled the nomination schedule considerably, with McGovern delivering his "Come Home, America" nomination speech after TV cameras stopped rolling at 3:30 a.m. Even so, the daytime panoramas of the convention hall showcased to home viewers how much the face of the Democratic Party had changed.

Not all involved thought these shifting demographics and the accompanying reorientation of party power were a good thing. As one Boston observer wrote Abzug, "I believe you and your woman cohorts did McGovern a disservice last night by fiddling around with Farenthold symbol vice-pres candidacy and keep McGov off prime time, a bit of evil (revenge for S. Carolina del. Defeat?) or stupidity."[136] Those who benefited most from Democrats' postwar reconversion program, centered on white, heterosexual men's needs and Cold War national security concerns, now found their presence tested. This shift in the Democratic Party especially worried establishment Democrats whose power was displaced by the New Politics turn. A group of "old labor" unionists, political aides, and neoconservative writers banded together to take back the party, forming the Committee for a Democratic Majority (CDM) in the alcoves at the 1972 DNC. This CDM faction contended, as Norman Podhoretz wrote in *Commentary*, that New Politics Democrats were elitists who offered "self-gratulatory speeches about the unprecedented 'representativeness' of the 1972 convention."[137] Yet, it was the visible opening of the Democratic Party to previously disenfranchised and peripheral people of color and women, and the shift toward anti-interventionist human rights interests that concerned CDM most. The committee's founders had an inflated sense of New Politics Democrats' power, for moderate Democrats were still the party's majority. Likewise, Abzug underestimated the development of CDM, suggesting the group's presence at the DNC was nothing more than "a feather."[138]

After the DNC, Abzug instructed her staff to begin packing up her office, but then news broke on September 18 that William Fitts Ryan had died of cancer.[139] With this unforeseen opening, Abzug received a second chance at a congressional seat. She enlisted Ronnie Eldridge to run a rehabilitation campaign to reach out to influential former Ryan supporters. Not taking any chances, NWPC offensively attacked widow Priscilla Ryan's run as "coffin route" entitlement.[140] Similarly, the Abzug campaign suspected Ryan's camp was responsible for a newspaper story published right before Democratic Party county leaders met to vote on their replacement nominee. The article inaccurately alleged that Bella's elderly mother, Esther, whom she supported financially, was on welfare.[141] And still, Abzug won the closed county leadership vote, causing Priscilla Ryan to lament, "This is no way to choose a member of Congress."[142] Determined to stay in the race, she challenged Abzug as the Liberal Party candidate.

The general election face-off between Abzug and Ryan was ugly and served as a first electoral contest between New Politics Democrats and the emerging CDM faction. Al Shanker rallied labor unions who had backed Bill Ryan to support his widow; Podhoretz encouraged CDM followers to do the same. "Mrs. Ryan is being supported by Nixon union money . . . Ray Corbett from the AFL-CIO. Al Shanker gave her $100,000," Abzug charged, casting her opponent as a pawn. Priscilla Ryan refuted this claim, noting, "Sure there were people who supported me who were hawks. But that didn't mean that I was. Which is what she tried—guilt by association."

Abzug ran "like an incumbent Congresswoman" and characterized Ryan as an amateur, while Priscilla Ryan, grieving and never a fan of Abzug, called her an ungrateful mentee who "never did her homework" and could be graded "not just a zero, she's minus."[143] This caustic back-and-forth continued up to the final vote, which Abzug won two to one, the same margin by which McGovern lost nationally.[144]

McGovern had, indeed, become the Democratic Party's Goldwater. Having campaigned for McGovern during the fall, Abzug did not welcome his landslide defeat, but nor did she see it as a complete loss. McGovern's nomination reflected the level of power New Politics Democrats had achieved within the party, which she believed reflected Americans' move toward a more progressive outlook. She did not expect to achieve a national majority immediately and thought that this mobilization was bigger than and irrespective of the candidate who had harnessed its power. McGovern, understandably, tried to cut his losses by distancing himself from the New Politics faction that had secured his rise. He ceded territory to a "recapture coalition" set on restoring the way things were. "We don't want that to happen again," one coalition member explained. "We don't want a party that just consists of Bella Abzug on one hand and Jesse Jackson on the other."[145] Similarly, McGovern retreated from his commitment to "reasonable representation" in delegate selection. Nor did he stand in the way when powerful party members moved to replace his pick for DNC chair, Utah party figure Jean Westwood, with Texan Robert Strauss (Westwood resigned to preserve her dignity). Troubled by these developments, Abzug worried that party leadership could quickly "return us to the days of tokenism."[146]

The McGovern campaign had not in fact moved the bar greatly past tokenism. After the DNC and looking toward the general election, McGovern had appointed Abzug and Shirley MacLaine to lead his National Women's Advisory Council. When she signed on, Abzug expected in return a commitment from McGovern to promote women at every level of his campaign.[147] Gary Hart felt the McGovern campaign should only have to "make up somewhat for past abuses" because 1972 was a "transitional" moment.[148] He selected Ann Martindale as deputy campaign director, Sissy Farenthold as cochair of the National Citizens Committee, and Anne Wexler as executive director of voter registration, but he did not go further. "I think it is a damn waste of effort to have to monitor the formation of each committee within the campaign" for gender equity practices, regional coordinator Judy Brown Sheerer wrote Abzug.[149] She agreed. "Women must be fully integrated" at every level, she told Hart. They must be recruited from "a broad spectrum . . . consumer groups, peace groups, feminists, professional groups, welfare groups, child care, unions, women's clubs, women ethnic groups PLUS regular party types."[150] To reiterate this point, she and Steinem showed up at McGovern headquarters unannounced to check on conditions, with women aides "cheering them on."[151] Bending a little, Hart allowed Abzug and MacLaine to recruit women to team up with men as state coordinators. Additionally, campaign staff were newly encouraged "to utilize women to convert and win votes" that they hoped would make a difference for McGovern.[152]

As Abzug lobbied McGovern to promote women within his operation, she compelled the NWPC to create separate Democratic and Republican task forces, which made it easier for her to siphon energy from the group to fulfill her partisan agenda.[153] Frustrated by this shift away from nonpartisanship, Betty Friedan characterized Abzug and Gloria Steinem as "female chauvinists" in *McCall's* magazine, charging, "Gloria preaches this ideology but Bella practices it."[154] This publicly exposed internal rift revealed the intense debate that ensued within NWPC over the organization's future direction. At NWPC's 1973 conference in Houston, the hall divided into "we-they," or those who favored chapter autonomy versus a "Policy Council dominated by superstars."[155] Abzug, unsurprisingly, advocated centralized leadership, was outvoted, and unsuccessfully demanded a recount. Thereafter, NWPC was less her organization. As delegate Martha McKay reflected, "We're at this point where there has to be a midwife, where the cord must be cut. We don't have the time or money in North Carolina to run to Washington on someone else's ego trip."[156]

AFTER THE 1972 ELECTION, Bella Abzug was the most recognizable woman in US politics. The National Women's Political Caucus brought greater visibility to the individual campaigns of women who ran for office in record numbers during this breakthrough year. Running for president, Shirley Chisholm garnered 152 delegates, and Patsy Mink received 28, but rank-and-file delegate strength extended past the protest candidacies of these NWPC founders. Abzug parlayed NWPC's immediate presence into individual power, emerging as a lead negotiator representing feminist interests within the Democratic Party. This alliance, now very secure, started out shaky, with male Democratic leaders expecting that they could gain maximum feminist support with minimal promises. Abzug also found herself on shaky ground in 1972. She achieved heightened national clout just when it seemed she would be a one-term representative. Her prominence as a national antiwar and feminist leader made it increasingly difficult for her to convince district voters that she cared about their local concerns. Likewise, her desire to be a power broker for progressives led her increasingly to prioritize her individual career over the collective interest of promoting other women in politics.

Political scientist Byron E. Shafer has characterized the NWPC's democratization efforts at the 1972 DNC as "one of the major events . . . in the overall politics of party reform and perhaps, depending on the fate of its products, in American political history."[157] And yet, this feminist triumph has been portrayed as a tragedy in most political histories, which echo the verdict critics of the effort delivered at the time. As Penn Kemble and Josh Muravchik judged, the "counterrevolution in November left one of the major institutions of American democracy in shambles."[158] As this line of reasoning went, women—along with antiwar activists and people of color—were to blame for the mass exodus of white male voters from the Democratic Party and the election of Ronald Reagan in 1980. This framing of 1972 as a tale of loss and abandonment is one that centers on whiteness and maleness. Neoconservative intellectuals coded their gender and racial bias as a lament of an elite takeover of the Democratic Party. Abzug was part of this invasion and became a central target to challenge in a take-back-the-party struggle.

The Democratic Party's increased diversity and leftward shift on display in Miami reflected the inroads party outsiders had made since 1968. These new party players were the drivers of, not the product of, McGovern's nomination. This fervor did not implode after his loss, nor was the old order completely dismantled. After 1972, the Democratic Party remained contested ground, with reformers and restorers vying for power. The election results were mixed, with Democrats picking up two seats in the Senate and Republicans thirteen in the House, including the replacement of eight southern Democrats. Increased retirements and the defeat of incumbents, most of whom faced redistricting like Abzug, led to thirteen new senators and sixty-nine new representatives. As one analyst assessed, "New Politics gained as much as the Republicans did."[159] Accordingly, as the *Congressional Quarterly* predicted, the Ninety-Third Congress would be one in which the Democrats took "another step toward congressional clout."[160] With her star rising, Abzug put her near loss during the 1972 "Year of the Woman" behind her and geared up to be part of this force.

7

PERFORMING POLITICAL CELEBRITY

THE FIRST "BELLA" SIGHTING happened when she was on vacation in Luquillo Beach, Puerto Rico, a few weeks after her 1970 election. Martin insisted she get away to repair. Strolling along a distant sea, Bella welcomed the comfort of anonymity, but it would not be so. As her friend Ronnie Eldridge, along for the trip, recalled, "We were at the beach and she's standing there in this big red caftan and a big hat, and somebody's walking by, and they said, are you her?"[1] This stranger on the beach was among the many admirers and some intruders who approached Bella Abzug as one would a celebrity.

Abzug actively cultivated a cultlike following, relishing her overnight fame. While she did not abandon her leftist politics or former network, her greater notoriety gave her entrée into a social circle where celebrities were friends. She remained conflicted about this move into the spotlight, lamenting the loss of a private self. She presented an approachable, everywoman populist persona, and in return strangers expected interaction and thought they knew her. With idol appreciation came degrees of hate: abusive mail, death threats, lampooning, and weight shaming. Some questioned her authenticity as an activist, feminist, heterosexual woman, devout Jew, and loyal American.

The political overtook the personal, for Abzug had always had difficulty creating boundaries. It was impossible, daughters Eve and Liz complained, to get through a meal at a restaurant without interruption. It was frustrating, Martin reproved, to have their Bank Street home overrun with outsiders. It was unsettling, all agreed, to have garbage stolen to be dissected for skeletons among the sundries.[2] Bella did not practice self-preservation, leading an all-access, event-driven lifestyle. As a result, she could not kick colds, dieted erratically, and collapsed in the car in between appearances. Her speaking schedule was so demanding that she required throat surgery at the end of her first year in office.[3] Outwardly buoyant, she revealed to close family and friends how exhausted and beleaguered she had become. She demanded greatness of herself and expected the same from others. Never one to check her temperament, she delivered her dissatisfaction, frustration, and elation at all registers.

Considering Abzug's full humanity—her strengths and her foibles—offers a broader portrait of this charismatic leader who was and continues to be caricatured. Self-aware that she could be difficult, volatile, and sensitive, she did not attempt to keep her emotive personality under wraps (and may have been unable to do so). She sought to overtly challenge the narrower space of acceptable character that women in politics navigated. When she modeled traits most revered in male politicians—being forceful and fearless—she received negative marks. Unsatisfied, she questioned why men in public were allowed "a wider range of ages, sizes, and styles of behavior."[4] The double standard was not lost on her supporters, who showed up at her campaign headquarters toting signs with wording such as, "Speak softly and keep your cool."[5]

The feminist movement launched an extensive reevaluation of how women were represented in culture alongside the legal feminist reforms pursued in Congress and in the courts. Although Abzug's focus was on transforming law and politics, she contributed to this reappraisal of culture by challenging an entrenched male leadership ideal that made it difficult for voters—and women themselves—to imagine women as elected officials. In the 1970s, congresswomen remained an oddity, never topping twenty until right after Abzug left Congress and only inching past thirty in 1989.[6] Likewise, women had difficulty making inroads in the media business and actively organized to get more bylines and greater workplace protections against harassment and hiring bias.[7] Abzug collaborated with feminist journalists, whom she saw as leading a parallel fight in the fourth estate, but their presence was not enough to shift the kind of coverage women politicians received.

Abzug endured intense media scrutiny because, as she explained, "I believe in the freedom of the press to be wrong."[8] Becoming "exhibit A," she made herself available to the media and received wide coverage in return, but she could not control the message. For every glowing profile, there were others that mocked, "Abzug (pronounced ugh)."[9] Most stories commented on her fashion and figure before the substance of her work. Photographers consistently captured the congresswoman in a smirk, scowl, or shout. In August 1975, *New York* magazine opened Ken Auletta's profile, "'Senator' Bella—Seriously," with a photograph of Abzug's backside.[10] The attention to her body had a purpose. "The Cold War liberal consensus," writes historian Robert Self, "depended on a certain *dis*embodied politics. The 'vital center' consensus depended on denying bodies entry into the political arena . . . and erasing the violence done to bodies in its name from public view." Abzug played a part in bringing "bodies back into politics," making "the violence done to them visible, indeed inescapable."[11] In response, her body (unquiet and uncontained) as much as her actions (multifaceted and imperfect) were dissected.

As a civil libertarian, Abzug staunchly supported the freedom of the press. Although preoccupied with controlling her message and image, she believed strongly that it was a fundamental function of a free, open democracy to have reporters ask hard questions of people in power. For this reason, she actively challenged government secrecy and defended journalists' right to gain access to government records, have their sources protected, and get their unfiltered stories out to Americans. This commitment to a "right to know" helped her endure the constant gaze that accompanied a public life.

The Cult of Celebrity

Abzug's congressional office was a Capitol Hill attraction as much as a workplace. "There were days . . . where we had over a thousand visitors to the office. The line used to form in the Longworth House Office Building for people to just sign her guestbook and hope they'd meet her. I mean the management of the tourism alone was a full-time job, let alone dealing with Bella's personality," recalled former intern Jim Capalino.[12] Abzug actively cultivated this celebrity, signing autographs for adoring fans and shouting back when passersby called out to her. Exhibiting a special affinity for her blue-collar fans, she glowed when she noted, "Cab drivers, truck drivers, they all like me."[13] She entertained the notion that she could reach everyone, suggesting, "When I was in the Bronx, someone yelled from across the street, 'Hello, Bella—from a Conservative!'"[14] As she became "sister Bella" to some, however, to others she became a powerful symbol of a radical woman unleashed. The flipside of being "Battling Bella" was she became a central cultural target to battle against. Likewise, her presentation as a leftist populist who was of "the people" and for "the people" encouraged her followers' sense of intimacy and ownership. The letters her office received reveal how Americans nationally felt a deep connection to Abzug but also were willing to talk back.

The charismatic leadership model attracted Abzug despite her attachment to collectivism. She greatly admired Martin Luther King Jr. for his magnetic, elevating oratory, his ability to inspire, and his effective mobilization of civil rights advocates. Emulating his example, she adhered to a male leadership standard that focused on personality and diverted attention from collaborative organizing. Women in the civil rights movement such as Ella Baker and Septima Clark critiqued King and other male leaders for profiting from and not acknowledging their behind-the-scenes "bridge leadership."[15] Abzug did better, but she benefited from a network of women organizers who helped craft her message, plan actions she led, and filled the crowd.

Speechwriter Mim Kelber, a former labor journalist and medical copy writer, was Abzug's most essential collaborator. High school friends Kelber and Abzug extended their connection at Hunter College, where Kelber served as an editor of the *Hunter Bulletin* while Abzug was student body president. Coming together in Women Strike for Peace once again, Abzug and Kelber rekindled their political partnership. More reserved and contemplative, "Mimi" centered Bella's unleashed spirit and grounded her big ideas. This melding of the minds, a powerful exchange, developed out of a shared worldview, mutual respect, and fierce loyalty formed over years of interaction. At her post in Abzug's New York office, Kelber rounded out the congresswoman's words and often stood in at critical meetings as her representative. Abzug's congressional records reveal their vibrant exchange, firing edits across the telecopy wires. Kelber was more the Marxist, yet she adhered to her friend's pragmatic approach to radicalism, drafting full expositions of Abzug's positions in replies to constituents and speeches. Abzug was not as thankful as she could have been, publicly dismissing the notion that Kelber should be praised for her dynamic prose.[16] Abzug added her own touches, often went off script, and delivered the performance, but it was Kelber, working offstage, who had the greatest influence on the congresswoman's incisive, humorous, and soaring oratory.

Abzug was most in her element when before a crowd. It took her time, though, to adjust to life on the speaking circuit, with events filling up her weekends at home and around the nation. She launched a continuous speaking tour so that she could spread the New Politics Democratic gospel and help build a new Democratic order. Frequently visiting college campuses, she told students, "You've got to go out there and form a coalition, a coalition of young people—on and off campus—women, working people and the minorities who are being sacrificed in this rotten war in Indochina."[17] These tours energized Abzug but also tired her out. She often rose slowly to address whichever club, union, or synagogue she stood before, starting listlessly, her voice often raspy. As she got going, she became increasingly animated. Delivering an opening act, she warmed up her audience with one-liners. Next, she provided a sobering assessment of the nation's problems, who should be held accountable, and how to bring about change. She loved to engage with hecklers in the crowd and soaked in the final applause. "You sense it, something in the waves, the way people look at you and the reaction," she exuded, "converting . . . as I speak."[18]

Abzug recognized that political history did not center on women's voices, highlighting instead the founding fathers to modern presidents. Likewise, male politicians dominated the popular genre of political autobiography. In 1972, Abzug published *Bella! Ms. Abzug Goes to Washington* as a corrective, delivering an "allegory of nation" through a woman's voice.[19] One year prior, Shirley Chisholm had published *Unbought and Unbossed,* which melded autobiography with position pieces.[20] Abzug took a different approach, crafting a diary of her first months in office delivered as if in real time. Like Chisholm, she was aware of how uncommon it still was for a woman to engage in public speech. Abzug's speechwriter Mim Kelber solicitously crafted her most unforgettable lines so that they might be remembered. An audience at the Jewish Center of Kew Garden Hills first heard what became the dynamic opening of *Bella! Ms. Abzug Goes to Washington,* "I've been described as a tough, rather noisy woman, a prizefighter, I've been called Battling Bella, Mother Courage, and a Jewish mother."[21]

This book was not Abzug's idea, and she signed on to the project reluctantly. Literary agent Sterling Lord approached her office, aide Esther Newberg encouraged her to do it, and journalist Mel Ziegler worked with her to get it just right. Interviews between Abzug and Ziegler commenced on January 24, 1971. This project was new territory for both. Ziegler took over the job after leaving the *Miami Herald,* work passed along by his boss, Dick Schapp, who had taught Ziegler at Columbia Journalism School. With little time to write, Abzug agreed to frequent oral interviews. As Ziegler recalled, "I took her spoken language and turned it into written language that sounded like spoken language."[22] Abzug expected Ziegler to keep up with her schedule, study the *Congressional Record,* and follow her on tour. She wanted to be presented as a three-dimensional character in two-dimensional form, requiring careful study of her oratory style because, as she told Ziegler, "nobody talks that way but me."[23]

The remaining transcripts from these book sessions, saved incompletely and in rough drafts, reveal Abzug in unfiltered and tentative form as she first navigated Congress. Additionally, they show how she came to see this book as a distraction and a bother. She felt bound by her contract, and at the same time sought to maintain control of the enterprise by telling Ziegler frequently that she could pull the plug at any moment. Pressed for time, she comes across in these tapes as annoyed by the process and delighted to have the attention. She readily relayed the highlights of her days and had to be coaxed to recount the lows. She would divulge too much and exhibit immediate reservations. "Maybe I shouldn't do this book," she ruminated on tape early on. She had to consider "things that affect my political future," she explained, thinking twice about including her full view of "this thing with me and [Ed] Koch and the race and me and [Betty] Friedan and so on."[24]

Abzug was less concerned about offending congressional peers than she was about how she was perceived. She wanted to come across as mighty, but authentic. "You're inaccurate, actually . . . you kind of miss the sharpness of some of my . . . thrusts on these things," she told Ziegler on one occasion. But he stood his ground, telling her, "All I can say is that you said it although it may not have been an accurate reflection of your feelings." She protested again, "Now, look please, Don't *hakn a tshaynik,*" a phrase that in Yiddish means you are getting on my nerves.[25] Ziegler could not help but chuckle. Still, it was a trying exchange. Abzug's cursing became another point of contention. Ziegler thought it happened habitually enough that he encouraged her to bring this color into print. She believed her slip of the tongue when letting off steam or when delivered as a tool of persuasion did not warrant copy. She did not want to come across as uncouth or give her opponents ammunition. Accordingly, she instructed, "I don't want those four-letter words all over this thing. I have never used those words in the public, and I'm not gonna . . . put them in this book."[26]

Abzug did actively push for her personal life to be part of her political story, reflecting feminists' articulation of "the personal is political." She talked about her daughters and husband as well as how alone she felt during her transition to Congress, and she was frustrated that these sections were edited out of the first versions of her manuscript. She believed it was important for readers to see what it was like for a woman in politics at this granular level. The resulting book offers a mediated glimpse into her interiority, exploring her dieting ups and downs, difficulty keeping staff, isolation in Washington, and the adjustment to having college-age daughters going their own way. Presenting this inside look was in step with the political biography genre that crafted leaders as "at once exceptional and distinctive and intimately and accessibly like them."[27] Yet, Abzug's interest in portraying a fuller image of women in politics guided her framing uniquely.

Abzug's book, published a few weeks before she lost the primary to William Fitts Ryan, was intended to expand her base. Many fans purchased it and stood in line to get their copy signed, "Bella, in sisterhood," but the book was panned in the New York Times.[28] Stephanie Harrington's review delivered an election postmortem that suggested Abzug did not understand "why the progressive wing of her own party will not make itself over in her image."[29] Despite critics' negative response, Abzug's book augmented her name recognition and deepened the fidelity of her devotees.

Congresswoman Abzug's constituent letters reveal the level of personal connection many Americans across the United States felt with her as a leader both relatable and as a luminary they admired. Most correspondence began with salutations such as "My Dear Mrs. Abzug," and "Dear Sister Bella."[30] Many letters crackle with the lingering dynamism of her performances. "Your speech last night at Theta Sigma Chi was truly outstanding. You have the compassion, the intelligence, the fire, and the faith to inspire people to care about our security," wrote one supporter.[31] "I saw and listened to you on the Mike Douglas show. . . . Give 'em hell—you've come a long way baby!" encouraged another.[32] Fans watched the headlines for Abzug, sending her local newspaper clippings to keep her abreast of coverage both flattering and unkind. "I take my hat off to you," praised David Lippman of Los Angeles, who included with his letter a syndicated political cartoon with a caption that read, "To make the tour complete, let's go see the biggest attraction in Washington—Congresswoman Bella Abzug!"[33] Many writers gushed, saying, "You are the beginning of hope," "You're like a voice crying in the wilderness," and "You, Bella Abzug are one of the really beautiful people!!!!"[34]

Thoughtful, emphatic, personal, and endearing, these letters boosted Abzug's determination to deliver results in Washington. They also overwhelmed her and her staff, who initially did not use form responses, had difficulty answering the letters promptly, and attempted to fulfill every request. National followers and district residents were highly invested in tracking her political steps and in helping shape her policy agenda. She encouraged this two-way engagement, campaigning on the idea that government should be powered by its citizens. As organizers like Abzug transitioned into institution building, the standard of engagement and style of communication practiced in grassroots circles carried over. Responsive to the needs and interests of progressive social movements, she contended with highly engaged constituents and activists working with her office accustomed to the immediacy of protest politics.

Talking back was a key feature of participatory democracy and her office was on the receiving end of this dialogue. Abzug welcomed the exchange but felt the weight of expectation. Once in office, she realized her audacity placed her in a bind, for many of the nation's problems were systemic and intractable. "Too many people who are strangers . . . say, 'We're countin' on ya, Bella, You're our hope," she lamented. "I've erected a monster. . . . I've obviously given people the feeling that I can do a great deal, which I can't."[35] As a lawyer who represented blacklisted clients, she knew what it was like to feel as if a person's financial and personal well-being rested on her shoulders. But now, she answered to more people seeking a broader range of solutions and noticeable betterment in their lives.

The vitriolic letters sent to Abzug tell a different story. Tucked away in a few banker boxes, stored separately from notes of "our hope Bella," are "dead letters" Abzug's aides marked as "hate."[36] Her staff shielded her from most of these letters that extended the wrath of angry picketers she occasionally faced. But they are still important, for they were a persistent stream during Abzug's time in office, they highlight what she was up against, and they capture the extent to which she aroused disapproving Americans' intense, visceral reaction. She became a palpable enemy for conservatives, a galvanizing symbol of everything rotten with liberalism. Men and women, named and anonymous, called Abzug a "bi-sexual bitch," a "temporary congress female," a "kike loud-mouthed like you," and a "dirty communist whore."[37] These writers mailed Abzug annotated clippings, often headshots with accompanying commentary such as she "looks like a horse's behind" or "as a pro-wrestler, you could call yourself 'the bedbug.'"[38] They rejected all that Abzug portended, with comments such as "A woman for President? You must be kidding."[39] Anti-Semitic, antiwoman, antigay, and anticommunist or a combination thereof, this body of correspondence exposed how much of a threat Abzug posed to those who benefited from and participated in the politics of exclusion. The congresswoman's calls for peace, equality, and public welfare were seen as disloyal slander by defenders of a patriotic America. For this reason, she received letters such as one from "a military man's mother," who offered Abzug "a definition of you—A-anarchist/B-betrayor/Z-zealot/U-usurper/G-gook."[40] Abzug's politics also inspired longtime Democratic partisans to think differently about their allegiances. As one such Democrat wrote, "You have made a Republican out of me."[41]

This corpus of adoring and abusive mail provides a compelling window into the shifting political terrain. The cult of celebrity Abzug cultivated made her a politician closely watched by fans and foes. As her bulging correspondence attests, numerous observers could not keep their feelings about her to themselves. She elicited gut-level responses that reflected the polarities at play in electoral politics during the 1970s. While polarization did not, in this period, fall along party lines, Abzug's correspondence reveals an ideological schism developing that ultimately became defined as Democrat versus Republican. Fidelity to different belief systems about the family and the nation, religion and the state, and women and their place were increasingly separating Americans. Representative Abzug helped along this separation as Americans divided over the terms of belonging in the United States, the place of government in their lives, and what role the nation should play in the world during the last quarter of the twentieth century.

Being Real

Congresswoman Abzug was known as "Battling Bella" for a reason. She tested people's patience and bent codes of civility. She also came up against the boundaries of respectability considered appropriate for women. While her commanding style turned off some, it was an effective tool of persuasion. Reporters and critics fixated on her lack of propriety, a factor considered when judging the character of leaders. She correctly noted that this was unfair, for emotion is evaluated using gender scripts that culturally distinguish the suitable temperament of men and women. Working within a narrow spectrum of acceptability, Abzug was evaluated as both too womanly, for she was impulsive and impassioned, and not womanly enough, for she was assertive and confrontational. Rage, a quality that could be seen as a show of strength in men, was judged unbecoming in a woman. Abzug instinctively recognized this double standard, complaining, "It's like I'm supposed to be some kinda kooky saint. . . . As if I'm not *real.*"[42]

Representative Abzug became known on Capitol Hill for delivering the "Abzug treatment," a modus operandi of purposeful pestering or "constructive belligerence" that she dispensed when exerting pressure to support a vote or a cause.[43] Sometimes, when she unleashed her "Abzugian temper," staff had to step in to calm people down.[44] Often aides were on the receiving end of this wrath. Working for Abzug was not for the fainthearted. Staffers knew before signing on "that unless you really cared about what she was doing and had an allegiance to her ideas and her politics, you were better off working for someone else."[45] Some lasted longer than others, enduring her reprimands because they recognized her considerable talents and shared a sense of purpose, and because they believed that "between the screaming, she was humorous."[46] For those who knew her well, over many years, this velocity was expected, even endearing. One evening Mim Kelber and her husband, Harry, hosted Bella and Martin at their Brooklyn home. Daughters Karli and Laura wanted to stay up with the grown-ups after dinner but were instead rushed to bed. When they woke up the next morning, they noticed the "long dining room table suddenly was very small." "What happened?" they asked.[47] The leaf had collapsed under the weight of Bella Abzug's firm bang when she made an especially emphatic point. For those without such long-standing ties, her mercurial temperament could be more unexpected and wearing.

Abzug did not greatly mask the pressure she felt. She held herself to the highest standards, and the level of access and responsiveness she encouraged proved unsustainable. She slept four hours a night, chain-smoked, and had a short fuse. "It's very hard to do the job I've cut out for myself," she granted after a few weeks in Congress; the "question is, can I keep up that pace." Some weeks later, she worried, "My schedule is beating me, the constituents beat me—everyone's beating me. I won't last. I have a cycle of ten years. This one I won't make if this goes on." After a few more, she fretted, "I can't take getting up at five in the morning" for the New York–DC shuttle. "I'm so exhausted. I have to start going back Sunday nights. . . . I just can't keep this up."[48] Instead of paring down her schedule, she adjusted and expected staff to do the same. "If the 25-hour day and the eight-day week could be accomplished by legislation Bella would be the floor manager for the bill," Doug Ireland noted of Abzug's workhorse ways.[49]

"It was a trial by fire. I remember looking at the clock constantly because it was ten or eleven at night," recalled aide Elizabeth Langer, who fielded calls from Abzug after leaving the office so often and at such range "we called her 'decibella' at home."[50] Abzug was cast as a nightmare boss in stories detailing her inability to keep staff, and for many who left this was true.[51] But she also faced excessive scrutiny. The office management styles of women in Congress were dissected for indicators of competence and suitability for the job, whereas male Congress members were allowed more room for error. As aide Eric Hirschhorn judged, "Doc Long [Clarence Dickinson Long Jr. (D-MD)] . . . would come in the Rayburn cafeteria and start screaming at his staff in front of everybody. At least Bella would usually shut the door, or if she was in a public place, she would grit her teeth and say, 'You're killing me.'"[52]

As unforgiving as she could be, Abzug had a lot of faith in and respect for her staff and saw her role as that of a captain steering a creative crew. She cut through the formality of Congress, insisting that staff be on a first-name basis. Staff meetings were a space to talk out strategies and tactics, with this dialogue continuing through interoffice memos and telefiles. She spread out substantive work, affording legislative assistants considerable license to create policy in her name. She encouraged, "If you have an idea, there is always a method, procedure—legislative or administrative—to carry it out."[53] But she also expected her staff to have a political sixth sense, often asking aides, "Why didn't you think of that?"[54]

Figure 7.1 Bella Abzug enjoyed lighter moments with her staff, wearing her custom-made "Mad Hatter's Batters" uniform on the field as they competed in the Capitol Hill softball league. An athlete in her youth, she found it difficult to fend off media focus on her fashion and physique. (Uncredited, Bella Abzug Papers, Box 1089, Rare Book and Manuscript Library, Columbia University)

Abzug had a familial touch with staff, her caring evident in concern expressed for an ill loved one. In Washington, she did not have her usual family bearings and had difficulty adjusting. She asked Representative Ella Grasso to be her roommate, but she declined, opting to commute from Connecticut. Keeping her own apartment initially, Abzug could not get used to the "life of great loneliness in personal terms."[55] She opted to live in a hotel, comforted by the constant buzz of travelers coming and going. Most nights, she was one of the last to leave Longworth, working on as the building emptied out. Because she was extremely lonely and hated to be alone, she encroached on her staff's lives more than she should, requesting that they stick around if she did and inviting herself into their homes. Having the congresswoman to dinner left an impression. Once she joined Marilyn Marcosson and husband, Ed, for a late night meal. "What kind of Jewish house is this?" Abzug asked when they did not have sweetener for her iced tea. "What kind of Jewish purse is that without Sweet'N Low in it?" Ed replied as Abzug dug into her purse for that very thing.[56] These light off-hour exchanges made the workday more lively, but they also contributed to a blurring of staff's personal and professional time. As Esther Newberg had to tell Abzug, "I'm your AA, not your super."[57] Abzug overstepped, asking aides to double as a car service, personal assistant, and therapist, but she also sent flowers to aides when sick, gave life advice solicited and unsolicited, and helped staff secure next jobs.[58]

Abzug spent her congressional years off-kilter. She lived two "new lives" in two places "always in the public eye." When she was in town, she did not "feel very related to people . . . outside of my husband and my kids."[59] When she was with family, she raced from dinner to the next event, always on and not fully engaged. Her husband, Martin, continued to be an anchor and a steadfast champion, but Bella was often on her own without his moderating presence and caregiving. In 1972, he talked about moving to Washington, worrying she was "careless about her health, working 18 to 20 hours a day, until 10 or 12 o'clock at night."[60] But he never made the move.

Martin Abzug was a puzzle to reporters. He often sat in the room during Bella's interviews, reading the newspaper, and chiming in from time to time. Photographers captured him standing next to the podium, smiling and holding his wife's purse. This image contributed to new tropes of the "cheerful husband" and the always affable "martyr," but Martin was no pushover.[61] Rather, he openly challenged the view of a mild-mannered

Figure 7.2 Bella Abzug cherished spending Jewish holidays at home, pictured here leading the family Passover Seder, with husband, Martin, and daughters, Liz and Eve. Responding to increased pressure on Jewish politicians to affirm their faith, Abzug invited a photographer to capture this intimate moment. (Leonard McCombe, The LIFE Picture Collection/Getty Images)

man-in-waiting, suggesting, "They say I'm a Milquetoast . . . that's deceptive."[62] "We disagree on almost everything. . . . I'm stubborn," he revealed. When Bella talks too much politics, "I go to bed."[63] Daughter Eve concurred, recalling, "My father could talk about anything even though he was the 'quiet one,' he talked about all kinds of everyday things, about the world, sports, the stock market."[64] Martin wanted to make clear that he had his own talents and his own sense of self. For this reason, unbeknownst to Bella, he invited *Washington Post* reporter Myra MacPherson down to Wall Street to shadow him on the job at C. B. Richard Ellis and Company. As MacPherson observed, Martin told a client, "Listen, either pay up or take the account the hell out of here," exhibiting that Bella was not the only demonstrative family member.[65]

Martin had a tenuous role to play, for he had to assure voters that his wife was happily heterosexual and his masculinity intact. Martin challenged this boxed-in role through humor. "On TV shows . . . he would be ironic . . . when a journalist asked, 'Are you a mutant?' he said, 'No, I'm a Jew.' "[66]

191

Bella's approach was more matter-of-fact. When a constituent wrote her to solicit support for paying political wives a wage, she fired back, "I hope that you would include in your suggestion political husbands as well. After all, as more women are elected to public office we will be creating a new category of political husbands."[67] In kind, Martin was Bella's protector, making sure she was not disregarded. "He would call me up and say to me, 'My Bella,' and then get into what he wanted to say," recalled Mayor John V. Lindsay's aide Sid Davidoff.[68] When Martin thought journalists were being cruel, he would speak out. After reporter Dave Smith described Bella as "that large, loud women," Martin shot back, asking, "Would he use those words in referring to a male politician?" Martin's biting verdict: "In addition to being sexist, it is apparent, he is a jerk."[69]

While treated as a curiosity, Bella and Martin Abzug were also revered as a liberated power couple, reflecting the shifting sense of marriage and family during the 1970s. *New York* magazine featured them in a profile of couples who exemplified egalitarianism in marriage. Confident in their union, both critiqued the "popular fallacy that two strong people can't make it in a marriage." "The key is maturity," Martin reflected, while Bella credited him with making "the major sacrifices in our set up."[70] When Bella and Martin appeared on the *Mike Douglas Show* with John and Phyllis Schlafly, Martin revealed another marriage secret: "great sex!"[71] Although he was jesting, Martin was quite aware of the speculation that Bella must be a closeted lesbian, an assumption made of women who transgressed gender boundaries, including those in politics. The adjective most used to describe Bella was "flamboyant," and her role as an ally of gay people was presumed to be an admission of belonging. At a 1972 fund-raiser, she embraced the drag queen Aurora Borealis in "flamboyant inflowing print, matching turban with shocking pink feather, shoulder bag, beard, mustache, two sets of black eyelashes." When asked by a reporter why she attracted this gender-fluid crowd, the congresswoman remarked, "Everybody is people."[72] In practice, however, Abzug maintained a heterosexual preference. "The way she talked about love, marriage, and family were very traditional, but her political beliefs were obviously more expansive," explained Eve, who would later come out to her parents.[73]

There was, however, a limit to how far Abzug was willing to challenge convention. She spent her early years forging a legal career as a working mother and created a flexible workplace on Capitol Hill that promoted women as professionals. And yet, she had trouble imagining how Colorado representative Patricia Schroeder, who joined Abzug in Congress in 1973, could handle legislating while raising toddlers. "I hear you got young kids. I don't think you can do the job," she told Schroeder.[74] Although Abzug thought the judgment she received to be unfair, she nonetheless delivered some of her own.

Putting on a Whole Regalia

Abzug lived in the public eye more than she had to. She craved media attention and had a great capacity for performance. She believed, as she told one reporter, "TV needs me. The press needs me. Radio needs me. You don't have no story without me."[75] "There isn't anybody that gets what I get," she told another.[76] Seeking a free platform, she devoted considerable time to interviews when acclimating to Congress, averaging three a day during her first two months in office.[77] Appreciative reporters thanked her with imaginative prose. As one journalist attested, "She was very good copy, which meant that she required a lot of adjectives for an adequate description."[78] The adjectives, however, vacillated from praising to damning: aggressive, abrasive, belligerent, bellicose, blunt, blustery, boisterous, bright, bullying, bumptious, captivating, charming, dynamic, flamboyant, loud, overworked, paranoid, peaceful, profane, restless, sensitive, stentorian, tender, tough, and witty.[79]

Part of the reason Abzug granted so many interviews was that she wanted to demonstrate she supported reporters' critical monitoring of government activity. As a legislator in Congress, she believed it was her duty to provide access. She advocated strongly for the power of the press in proposed legislation. In January 1973, as the Watergate story gained traction, she developed a bill echoing action in the Senate that would grant "absolute privilege" to reporters to keep their sources confidential, even "before the Congress, any federal grand jury, or any federal judicial or administrative authority."[80] As the resolution of inquiry enabled representatives to challenge executive privilege, so too did enhancing reporters' right to seek truthtelling about government and business operations from whistle-blowers. At this high point of investigative journalism, Abzug developed ties to reporters such as Daniel Schorr, who thanked her for her "leadership in trying to rally support for me," and for her "general stand in favor of our Constitutional right."[81] Posturing as a civil liberties lawyer, Abzug conveyed a moralistic defense of reporters' First Amendment rights. This purpose outmatched the hesitation she felt to cooperate with journalists.

Abzug attempted to control the spin by granting the most interviews to women journalists, whom she assumed would offer more favorable coverage. Veteran women reporters working the political beat helped Abzug navigate Washington politics when she first arrived on Capitol Hill. Counseling Abzug in private, Mary McGrory wondered in print, "Already it is being asked, 'How long will it take to box Bella in?'"[82] Abzug gained wide, dependable coverage immediately. *Ms.* offered Abzug the most friendly copy with her close collaborator Gloria Steinem at the helm of this popular feminist magazine. Its first stand-alone issue in July 1972, promoting "Wonder Woman for President," reflected the magazine's considerable attention to women in politics. A repeat guest author, Abzug appeared on the December 1975 cover as a female Santa, with the promise, "What Santa Won't Bring You . . . Bella Will!"[83] Journalists who were "private fans" kept her abreast of how her actions were perceived in the newsroom. *New York Times* reporter Grace Lichtenstein relayed her male counterparts' immediate response to the founding of the National Women's Political Caucus, telling Abzug, "When my editors cracked some jokes about it, I warned them that when you're Mayor they'll be laughing out of the other side of their mouths."[84] This kind of insider information heartened the congresswoman, who felt that change was coming to the media alongside politics.

This shifting newsroom culture did not greatly change the tenor of political reporting. Women in Congress were still judged by their looks alongside their message. Some congresswomen attempted to diffuse the media's hyperattention to appearance by toning down their style. Representative Margaret Heckler, for instance, wore a gray flannel suit "to blend into 'the gray Massachusetts sky and the gray male political arena' so the voters would be forced to unconsciously identify her with the issues."[85] Abzug instead tried to use reporters' gendered preoccupation with women politicians' fashion to her advantage. She dressed as if preparing for a stage performance. The day before she met President Nixon for the first time, she bantered with Representative Louise Day Hicks at the House beauty parlor about their respective outfits. "What are you going to wear tomorrow? Long or short?" Hicks asked, referring to the length of her

Figure 7.3 Bella Abzug jetted out to Hollywood during her New York Senate race in 1976 to attend a star-studded fund-raiser hosted by longtime supporter Barbra Streisand at her home. Here, Streisand adjusted Abzug's signature wide-brimmed hat. (Bettman Archive/Getty)

dress. I will "wear a short dress so I could also wear a hat," Abzug decided. "I didn't want to deprive the President of that great event. I figured I'd let him see me in my whole regalia."[86] Her close friend Charita Michaels doubled as her seamstress and stylist. Together, they created Abzug's wardrobe in bold oranges, purples, and golds, patterned with flowers and polka dots, and accompanied by a coordinating hat. The outlandish flashiness of it all was in step with the times but, if too exaggerated, landed her on the "worst-dressed" list.[87]

Abzug used hats as both a symbol and a shield, creating an easy identifier and a natural barrier. She gravitated to this accessory over time, her mother having instructed early on that a lady wears a hat. As a young lawyer at court, she wore hats to distinguish herself as a professional, and returned to this status marker when she entered Congress. Hats also were practical, since there were few women's bathrooms at the Capitol where one could fix one's hair. The range and vibrancy of Abzug's collection reflected her love for milliners' craftsmanship. Shopping for hats became a guilty pleasure, and the absence of a beloved fedora a real loss. One Friday, Ed Koch picked up the phone with Abzug on the receiving end asking, "Can you please fetch my hat in my office and bring it back with you on your flight out of town?" As Koch recalled, "I said, 'Of course, Bella.' And the staff roared. . . . I brought up her hat! Carried it on the goddam plane in a box very careful, brought it to my house and Martin picked it up."[88] Hats distinguished Abzug as an aging woman, among those with "enchanting vintage names like Thelma, Millie, Loretta, Gladys, Nell, Maple, Blanche and Mildred."[89] They became their own story. On election night, she emerged with "the black floppy hat that is her trademark flapping like a victory flag."[90] And they made Abzug a recognizable target. Republican Iso Finzi ran off with her straw panama during a campaign walking tour, and her aide sent to retrieve it discovered a very pleased partisan showing off his catch in a nearby café.[91]

While Abzug's hats helped her gain notice, they immediately offered a way to discount her purpose and resolve. Before Abzug's inauguration, *Washington Post* gossip columnist Maxine Cheshire warned that the congresswoman would cause a "House hat hassle." As the story went, a Democratic colleague asked Abzug what she would do if House doorkeeper William M. "Fishbait" Miller asked her to remove her hat before entering the House floor, a long-standing custom. "Well, I'll tell HIM where to go," she allegedly replied with a few expletives attached.[92] Cheshire's story gained such immediate traction that Abzug felt compelled to respond a few days later, stating, "There've been a lot of stories about my hats—which incidentally I've never worn in courtrooms and don't expect to wear on the floor of Congress."[93] This rejoinder did little to quell the imagination. The *Washington Post* reported on Abzug's hat placement as a feature of the first comings and goings during the Ninety-Second Congress: "The hat went on for her reception where Rep. Abzug seemed annoyed at insinuations she had capitulated to a House rule against the wearing of hats on the floor," and commented, "I'm not here to fight on trivialities. I want to break traditions, but only ones that count."[94] Denying "this crap from the *Associated Press*," she laid on the sugar, saying, "The last guy I'd fight with is Fishbait Miller. He's very friendly."[95] The incident made Abzug immediately notorious and seemingly in need of schooling. As Wyneta Driscoll of Texas wrote her, "A woman can respectfully wear her hat at any time of the day in any room in the house whether it be in a home, church or the White House."[96]

Abzug challenged the self-suffering undertone of feminine respectability, but not the associated physical parameters. In a televised debate with *Cosmopolitan* founder Helen Gurley Brown, Abzug took her to task for promoting "woman as a sex object, as a powder puff, and all of those things that *Cosmopolitan* does so well to market *Cosmopolitan*."[97] Although she delivered this critique, Abzug also succumbed to the leading beauty ideal, and in her fifties yearned to be svelte. She was a stress eater before Congress, and her binge eating escalated. "When I get really agitated on the House floor I go back into the cloak room and I stand at the lunch bar there and I eat things I shouldn't eat," she divulged.[98] She joined Weight Watchers and tried the latest crash diets, her gains and losses reported as news. The physical scrutiny was hard on Abzug, but also on her staff, who had to guess if they should have a diet breakfast or a full breakfast waiting when she arrived.[99]

Because of Abzug's insecurity about her appearance, criticism delivered as a commentary about her body hurt her most. In March 1971, Vice President Spiro Agnew jested at a Republican gathering, "Most importantly, we have to keep Bella Abzug from showing up to Congress in Hot Pants."[100] That same month in *Harper's* magazine, Norman Mailer described Abzug as having "a voice which could have boiled the fat off a taxicab driver's neck . . . full of the vibrations of power as those machines which rout out the grooves in wood."[101] This depiction would become the most quoted characterization of Abzug. Also in March, she was lampooned cruelly at the New York Inner Circle Press Club dinner. Saul Rudes warned her of this possibility and encouraged her to attend as his guest, but she was not prepared for what followed. A male reporter, "shoulders and rear end padded substantially," danced around the stage, trailed by another in a white apron introduced as "Mrs. Martin Abzug." The Bella impersonator broke into song:

> I guess I've never been the high-fashioned kind,
> Mother Nature gave me a big behind.
> Wherever I go, I know I won't fall flat.
> When I just wear my hat . . .
> Oh, I'm filled with jubilation

For women's liberation
We ran our liberty bell
We'll burn a bra and girdle
But dammit there's one hurdle
When we take them off
We all look like hell . . . [102]

All eyes were on Abzug to gauge her reaction. Her presence at the table was a first, as women had previously been excluded from attending, a past discretion that NOW members picketing outside protested. After the skit, strangers came up to Abzug's table to express their disgust. A few friends offered to stage a walkout, but she told them to stay put. She wanted to show she was unfazed by the "rude and crude and vulgar" attack. Afterward, she elected to ignore it, suggesting to interviewer Mel Ziegler, "I don't remember anything about it, it's all in the paper, there isn't anything to discuss."[103] The lampoon at the Inner Circle dinner would be the worst body shaming Abzug experienced while in Congress. And for some women journalists, it was a deplorable reason enough to boycott the event thereafter.[104]

The Inner Circle dinner previewed a pattern of ridicule Abzug would endure over the next five years. Congressional colleagues, it was reported, frequently joked "about the size and shape of her butt—her 'broad base of support.'"[105] Being a persistent target wore on Abzug, but she looked at her situation analytically. She recognized the treatment was a by-product of the change that was under way. As she assessed, the physically focused resistance to her presence reflected "an interesting fight back from males who have fears and insecurity of their own and who have not yet been prepared to accept a real democracy in which both men and women have political power."[106]

A "FIGHT BACK" AGAINST women's advancement in politics did unfold in the media and in popular culture. While a backlash story line that at once declared feminism victorious and dead is most associated with the 1980s and 1990s, these arguments were present in the initial reporting on "new feminism." Early stories differentiated between "good" and "bad" feminists, described internal debates in women's organizations as "catfights," and characterized women's liberation as a passing fad.[107] The political ideas and actions of women legislators were slandered and dismissed using references to their bodies and personalities more frequently than occurred for men. Likewise, the "year of the woman" trope, while a well-intentioned marker of women's upswing in politics, invariably contributed to this backlash. The opening line of *Life* magazine's 1972 article on women in politics declared, "It may not quite be the Year of the Woman, but neither in this election season is the women's movement going to go away."[108] This trendsetting article acknowledged that women's engagement in electoral politics would continue, but it assumed that women's electoral wins would be nominal, exceptional, and provisional.

Bella Abzug was deeply aware of this narrow cultural space allotted for women in politics to succeed. Responding, she noted, "Look. The suggestion that I am . . . that I was . . . some kind of a Happening . . . is outrageous. Like I, Happened once; I don't have to Happen again."[109] She tried to control the story, but her inability to do so was a sign that the fourth estate she sought to protect was doing its job. This positive came with a negative, for coverage of the congresswoman shows how unveiled sexism was in news reporting during the 1970s. Women's greater presence in newsrooms, an outcome of female journalists' organizing, did not greatly shift the tenor of political reporting. Thereafter, political news coverage continued to treat male and female candidates and politicians differently.

In the 1970s, Abzug and her hats were a cultural obsession. Her theatrical style of politicking, coupled with her hobnobbing with celebrities, led her to become a leading figure in popular culture as much as in politics. Yet, her fandom complicated her purpose of building a new Democratic coalition and her interest in being taken seriously as a dedicated, decisive legislator. Her media coverage lent to the argument that, as one surrogate of William Fitts Ryan suggested, she was "the candidate who is there when the cameras are on."[110] Abzug found calls from reporters a distraction and initially voiced this concern, but she continued to answer. She played for an audience, thoroughly enjoying the performance of political celebrity.

8

GOVERNMENT WRONGS AND PRIVACY RIGHTS

ONE OCTOBER DAY IN 1972, Bella Abzug picked up her private line in the Longworth Building and dialed out to New York state assemblyman Albert Blumenthal. They engaged in the usual back-and-forth, followed by a pause. Then the call turned weird. Abzug and Blumenthal unexpectedly overheard a third voice on the line say, "Keep the tape going—I want to get this."[1] One of her constituents, Paul Van Souder, had written Abzug a few days earlier to alert her that her phone might be tapped. "The phone rang perhaps fifteen times with no answer," he relayed, "but 'behind' the rings my friend could hear a dialogue which went something like this: 'How about now? Is it working?' 'No . . .' 'Now?'"[2] Abzug did not want to believe it, but as a McGovern surrogate, she had received an insider report the previous month detailing the break-in of the Democratic National Committee headquarters at the Watergate Hotel in June. She hired the same company, Investigations, Inc., to check her office lines. Its findings were troubling. Her Washington office was bugged, and likely her New York office too.[3]

While no specific evidence linking the Watergate burglary and Abzug's bugging incident has surfaced, newspapers at the time drew this connection. She made the same leap, seeing what happened to her personally as part of a grander, insidious scheme by President Richard Nixon and his cronies. Early to call for Nixon's impeachment, Abzug challenged presidential corruption and expanded executive power in a way that was distinctly informed by her experience as a civil liberties lawyer who was under surveillance during the McCarthy period. The Federal Bureau of Investigation pared back, but did not discontinue, monitoring Abzug after she ran for office in 1970, reasoning that the potential of exposure in this "delicate situation" created a "greater than unusual risk of embarrassment to the Bureau."[4] Having already earned a place on Nixon's "Enemies List," she continued to be meddlesome as the Watergate break-in developed from a sleeper story into a scandal. After Nixon's resignation, Abzug contributed to an extensive, Democratic-led congressional reform drive enhanced by an influx of change candidates—ninety-two newcomers, of whom seventy-five were Democrats and forty identified as progressives—voted in during the 1974 midterms.[5]

In the mid-1970s, Congress reasserted its might. At the beginning of the Ninety-Third Congress, House Speaker Carl Albert accused President Nixon of "wholesale executive invasions of legislative powers and responsibilities" and "creating a crisis that goes to the very heart of our Constitutional system."[6] The Senate and the House of Representatives engaged in a bold challenge of the American presidency carried out over two congressional sessions that reaffirmed the oversight powers of Congress. The War Powers Act of 1973 required the president to notify Congress within forty-eight hours of military intervention and to withdraw troops if not granted approval. The Congressional Budget and Impoundment Control Act of 1974 returned to Congress the final authorization power to cancel or defer federally appropriated funds. The "Year of Intelligence" congressional investigations of 1975 exposed international and domestic covert intelligence operations. The Privacy Act and Freedom of Information Act (FOIA) Amendments of 1974 enhanced individual privacy rights, and sunshine laws passed in 1976 made more of the government's activities public. Together, these reforms highlighted Congress's forceful reconsideration of executive power and delivered the most significant reappraisal of the national security state since its midcentury expansion.

Abzug participated vigorously in this reformist fervor, seizing on the chance to "harass back" in a meaningful way.[7] She sought to bring the "invisibility of the watchers" into view as chair of the House Government Operations' Government Information and Individual Rights Subcommittee (GIIR) during the Ninety-Fourth Congress.[8] In this capacity, she oversaw the implementation of FOIA and the Privacy Act as well as executive agency record-keeping practices. Her attention to government document classification, access, and preservation helped break through the veil of government secrecy. For Abzug, this work was deeply personal, for it came out that her international-bound mail had been intercepted by the Central Intelligence Agency (CIA) since 1953.[9] This revelation deepened her resolve to publicly challenge what she saw as an excessive and damaging intelligence apparatus in which agents skirted the law in the name of national security.

Abzug's committee work during and after Watergate was fired by a desire to gain justice for dissenters long monitored by the government. In the 1970s, leftists opened the wounds of McCarthyism by publicly revisiting their experiences of blacklisting and surveillance through memoirs, lawsuits, and inquiries.[10] Participating in this retrospective appraisal, Abzug used her office to seek retribution for political repression incurred during the early Cold War. Through her example, we can see that Watergate was in part a referendum on the postwar Red Scare. The scandal, as she saw it, became a "shorthand for political espionage, wiretapping, obstruction of justice, conspiracy, lawbreaking, subversion of the democratic process and other criminal actions."[11] And yet, as Abzug characterized the CIA as a "super-snooper," conservative critics reminded that she was "no dewy-eyed innocent."[12] Players on both sides of the Second Red Scare still had a stake in an unsettled debate about whether to prioritize privacy or security.

Congress Should Be a Competing Force

Eighteen members of Congress sat out Nixon's second inauguration, and three members, Abzug, Senator Philip Hart, and Representative Paul "Pete" McCloskey, attended inauguration counterrallies. "We have no intention of uniting around this President," Abzug promised the crowd of around 100,000.[13] She hoped Congress would move from an "impotent" to a "competing force."[14] In making this case during the first months of 1973, Abzug echoed the leading sentiment of congressional Democrats, who shared a "mood of resentment" about Nixon's encroaching powers.[15] On January 2, the House Democratic Caucus resoundingly passed "a pretty resolute resolution" offered by Representative Lucien Nedzi that called for the immediate termination of US engagement in Vietnam and an end to appropriations after prisoners of war returned home.[16] House Democrats wanted to make clear that they would keep the pressure on the president after Paris talks culminated in a formal agreement to end the war signed on January 27. Urged by the Democratic Study Group and Common Cause, they widened internal seniority and procedural reforms. During the Ninety-Third Congress, members established that committee chair appointments be determined by a majority vote and by secret ballot if requested by 20 percent of the caucus; they also mandated open committee hearings unless dealing with issues of national security.[17]

Abzug welcomed these changes, seeing "a basic necessity for establishing the principle of congressional authority."[18] Although she believed that reform efforts meant to counter executive power had moved too slowly during the opening weeks of the new session. According to congressional estimates, President Nixon had impounded $12 billion in funds slated in the last budget, and was making open moves to dismantle the Office of Economic Opportunity.[19] These actions, in Abzug's judgment, reflected an imbalance of power where Congress had allowed economic elites to take unchecked control of a vast administrative state. As she told 20,000 antipoverty protesters gathered in Washington in February, Nixon's "horror budget" was a feature of "dictatorial power" intent to "rob the poor."[20] In step with other reformers, Abzug introduced a bill that gained little traction advocating immediate congressional approval for every presidential move to impound funds. House leadership promoted a less confrontational and more forward-thinking course. The final Budget Impoundment and Control Act reasserted Congress's "power of the purse," while creating new infrastructure—budget standing committees and the Congressional Budget Office.[21]

The War Powers Resolution debate signaled that Congress sought to rein in presidential unilateralism in military decisions. As Representative McCloskey commented, "We better damn well lock the door shut."[22] Abzug joined a small faction of House "doves" who advocated that the resolution go further than it ultimately did. Most legislators agreed that they did not want another Vietnam War, which they blamed President Nixon for prolonging pointlessly. House members divided, however, over the proposed 120-day allowance the president would have for troop deployment and withdrawal while waiting for Congress to issue a formal declaration of war. Republicans felt that the bill encroached on presidential powers, whereas Abzug and other antiwar holdouts delivered "no" votes because of the leeway the resolution granted the president. After the bill passed both houses, Nixon vetoed it in November. Abzug initially stayed firm in her no when the House faced the veto vote, explaining she would "reluctantly" support Nixon's veto "for reasons the opposite." "He feels that this bill would restrain him—I only wish it did."[23] In the end, Abzug demonstrated a greater willingness to go with consensus than in the past. After being lobbied intensely, she switched her vote alongside seven others; this movement put the count four over the required number for overriding a presidential veto. Abzug exhibited flexibility because she believed that a show of congressional strength after Nixon fired special prosecutor Archibald Cox and Attorney General Elliot Richardson was crucial.

Nixon and his team hoped that antiwar fervor on Capitol Hill would distract federal legislators and the public from Watergate, but instead it added to the atmosphere of distrust. "I just wish Bella Abzug or something would get up there. . . . I think they will put a bill up," H. R. Haldeman said during a meeting with the president in February.[24] Abzug did not disappoint, introducing amnesty legislation once again. She used this hot-button legislative issue to directly link the Vietnam War and Watergate. In May 1972, she had advocated for impeachment in response to military action in Cambodia. When she discussed Watergate in early 1973, she situated the break-in within a larger pattern of presidential abuse of power. In her friendlier moments, she suggested conscientious objectors had a stronger ethical core than the president. "It is ironic to hear Henry Kissinger ask 'compassion' for the Watergate burglars, when so little compassion has been shown by the Administration toward men of conscience," she stated at an ad hoc hearing on amnesty in May.[25] At her most extreme, she echoed others on the Left who described Nixon as Hitler, arguing, "We must not be the good Germans who pretended that they did not know the obscene things done to other Germans and other human beings in the concentration camps."[26] Watchful of the rise of European fascism during her youth, she had been among the first tourists to visit Europe after the Holocaust in search of her husband Martin's relatives, who had perished. She believed that the Nixon administration exhibited fascistic qualities and feared what would come next. As she told Jewish antiwar backers at Temple Sinai in Washington, DC, "More and more people are sensing the parallel between this administration and the days before Hitler took over."[27]

During the first months of US disengagement in Vietnam, House Democrats were most focused on stalling additional appropriations. Abzug supported this effort, but she and Senator Ted Kennedy partnered to pressure for further attention to amnesty, veteran reconversion, and human rights violations by Nguyen Van Thieu's regime. Kennedy and Abzug sought to pierce the dominant narrative promoted by the Nixon administration of a seamless withdrawal and patriotic homecoming of POWs.[28] In August 1973, Abzug traveled to Saigon and air bases near Manila, Philippines, and Utamao, Thailand, as part of a congressional delegation. There, she broke away from the pack to visit the prisoners' wing of Cho Quan Hospital in Saigon and met with the family of Madame Ngo Ba Thanh, a scholar who had trained at Columbia Law School and had been arrested for passing out peace leaflets. Back home, Abzug drew public attention to Thanh's case and the broader mistreatment of an estimated 200,000 incarcerated political prisoners.[29] Through this advocacy, she aimed to unsettle Americans' feelings about militarism and presidential authority.

Meanwhile by summer, the Watergate cover-up had become a full-fledged scandal. On August 15, Nixon told audiences during a television address that he had no prior knowledge of the Watergate Hotel burglary. According to one poll, of the 77 percent of the population that tuned in, only one-quarter believed the president.[30] So much had developed since the Watergate bugging trial in January, in which Bernard Barker, Frank Sturgis, Eugenio Martinez, and Virgilio Gonzalez pleaded guilty, and Nixon aides G. Gordon Liddy and James McCord Jr. were convicted. In March, FBI director L. Patrick Gray gave "the little store away" during his interview before the Senate Select Committee on Presidential Campaign Activities, known as the Watergate Committee. As counsel John Dean reported to the president, Gray said "that the FBI records, as far as he was concerned, were available to any Senator in the United States Senate." This worried Nixon. "He's out of his God damned mind," he fumed. "The House will insist on the same rights. . . . You'll have Bella, Bella Abzug asking for FBI stuff. What's he going to say? What in the hell is he going to say?"[31] Nixon could not have predicted that Dean too would turn against him, providing damning testimony before the Senate Watergate Committee in June.

Representative Abzug was not as trigger-happy as Nixon assumed. In March and April, she and her staff deliberated over how best "to nail Nixon" on Watergate and "to move Congress onto the offensive and recoup some of the programs Nixon knocked out."[32] It became hard to keep up with the "seemingly never-ending avalanche of disclosures, charges and countercharges related to the Watergate scandal."[33] On April 30, Nixon fired John Dean and compelled H. R. Haldeman, John Ehrlichman, and Attorney General Kleindienst to resign. On May 18, attorney general–designate Elliot L. Richardson appointed Archibald Cox as special prosecutor. Each day came with a new shock. That month during the Senate Watergate Committee's televised hearings, "witnesses marched across the television landscape, alternately disillusioned, contrite, defiant, obsequious, stonewalling, disenchanted, and steadfastly loyal."[34] Abzug, like many other House members, sent an aide to listen in each day. She spent time deliberating with like-minded colleagues on the DSG Impeachment Task Force and an informal Monday Night Group of progressive Democrats over what to do next.[35]

Abzug wanted to push the impeachment debate in the House faster and farther than most of her peers thought wise. She was frustrated that the House of Representatives remained inactive while the Senate conducted thorough, revealing investigations. In May, she worked closely with Representative John Moss, a senior member of the Government Operations Committee whom she greatly admired, to initiate a call for the House to investigate the president for possible impeachment.[36] In June, House tussles over Watergate became more frequent, prompted by more damaging disclosures, including John Dean's testimony before Senate members that the president knew about the burglary cover-up. Representative McCloskey first attempted to begin a "tempered discussion" of Watergate on the House floor but was thwarted by Republicans using a procedural maneuver.[37] Abzug had better luck one week later, leading off ninety minutes of debate to press for a House inquiry. Her loathing of the president was hardly veiled as she warned of "the Nixon administration's plan to transform our democracy into a police state." Frustrated by House members' reluctance to act, she reprimanded, "One would have to be deaf, dumb, blind or hopelessly intransigent to refuse to acknowledge that the President is under suspicion and thus to condone possible unconstitutional acts, political or other crimes on his part by refusing to carry out our responsibility under the Constitution to investigate his role."[38] Her alarmist tone led colleagues to dismiss her argument. House Speaker Carl Albert called her action "premature."[39]

It seems Abzug took Albert's advice, for she moderated her clamoring. When she issued an impeachment resolution in October, it echoed the points laid out by Representative Robert Drinan, an ally who issued the first formal impeachment resolution in Congress on July 31. In the days before Drinan's resolution, Nixon had refused to turn over White House tapes to the Senate, and Senator Sam J. Ervin Jr. responded by initiating court action to force this outcome. Drinan drew attention to the president's secret tapings and the establishment of a "super-secret security force within the White House," but also his "secret air war in Cambodia" and impoundment actions.[40] Then, President Nixon's audacious firing of special prosecutor Archibald Cox stunned the nation and Congress members. "I felt as if I were living in a banana republic," recalled New York representative Elizabeth Holtzman, who at thirty-one would stand out for her role on the House Judiciary Committee during impeachment hearings.[41] Coming to this conclusion as well, Abzug joined more than fifty colleagues who issued individual impeachment resolutions as a show of force. Simultaneously, Abzug and twenty others active in the reformist DSG, including prominent members such as Morris Udall, Edward Boland, and Robert Eckhardt, urged the House Judiciary Committee adamantly to begin investigation. Minnesota representative John C. Culver led this effort, gaining more than seventy cosponsors for the resolution.[42]

As the impeachment drama unfolded in the House, Abzug delivered her judgment on the president largely as a vocal observer issuing reactive press releases offstage. She was satisfied that the House moved on exploring impeachment but remained impatient as House judiciary chair Peter W. Rodino (D-NJ) moved at a deliberate pace. The Judiciary Committee issued a subpoena for White House tapes in April 1973, following on the heels of new special prosecutor Leon Jaworski's like request. Nixon hedged until the Supreme Court forced his hand on July 24, ruling in *U.S. v. Nixon* (1974) that executive privilege was not absolute and thus the tapes must be produced.[43] That same day, the House Judiciary Committee began televised hearings. On July 27, members charged that President Nixon formed a "course of conduct or plan" to obstruct the investigation of the Watergate burglary, and voted twenty-seven to eleven to send the impeachment article to the House for a vote. "It's only Round One. There'll be a good scramble in the House," assured Representative David W. Dennis (R-IN), but it did little to quell concern.[44] As the Democratic-controlled House prepared for a vote, President Nixon read the tea leaves and resigned at 9:00 p.m. on August 8.

Abzug believed Congress should consider presidential abuse of power beyond Nixon, and her actions after his resignation reflected her view that the office itself had become corrupted. Broadcasting this concern, Abzug helped stir public distrust of Nixon's successor, House minority leader Gerald Ford (R-MI). After Vice President Spiro Agnew's surprise resignation in October 1973 amid a corruption investigation, Ford was next in line. Abzug voiced her opinion that he was an unsatisfactory successor, writing in a *New York Times* op-ed, "Does anyone seriously think that the American people would select Gerald Ford as their President if they had a choice?"[45] Well before Nixon's impeachment was assured, she tried to prime the public and her congressional peers to support holding special presidential elections.[46] This outcome could have been requested by Congress, but the concept was untested and required considerable political capital to achieve. Coming from Abzug, it sounded unreasonable and gained little traction.

When Ford pardoned Nixon on September 8, 1974, Abzug invariably set off the series of events that led to the president's appearance on Capitol Hill to explain his action. Calling the pardon "a total misreading of the American sense of fair play," she rallied thirteen colleagues to join her in issuing a resolution of inquiry posing ten questions to Ford.[47] Lobbied intensely, Representative William L. Hungate (D-MO), chair of the House Judiciary's Criminal Justice Subcommittee, moved forward with the resolution of inquiry requesting information from the executive on the "time, manner and circumstances" of Nixon's pardon.[48] At first, Ford prevaricated, writing Hungate, "We should now all try . . . to heal the wounds that divide Americans."[49] Next, the White House turned over insufficient documentation. Finally, Ford unexpectedly told Hungate he would respond with "direct answers to . . . direct questions" by appearing before the committee on October 18. Against aides' advice, Ford had decided "the best thing for me to do is just go up to Capitol Hill, testify and spell it all out."[50] There would, however, be terms: "no oath, two hours, and no questions from Bella Abzug."[51] This request was easy to oblige, since Abzug was not a committee member, but she still tried to intervene by funneling questions to Hungate. She also delivered her own verdict to the press: Ford's "incomplete and often contradictory" testimony "strains credulity."[52]

One day prior to President Ford's appearance, he vetoed amendments to the 1966 Freedom of Information Act, an action that too would backfire. In 1966, Representative John Moss, a leading member of the Government Operations Committee, had shepherded the landmark bill through the House of Representatives. In 1974, chair William S. Moorhead (D-PA) introduced FOIA amendments that enhanced congressional power to request information, tightened filing response time frames, extended reporting requirements, and increased sanctions for noncompliance. Still, civil libertarians were not thrilled that Moorhead's bill also augmented judges' discretion to review classified documents in camera (or in chambers), keeping security documents out of the public purview. This framing was in line with *US v. Nixon* (1974), which recognized that executive privilege did exist even if not absolute.[53] When the Government Operations Committee debated this feature, Abzug had weighed in vocally, advocating a narrow allowance for executive privilege enumerated in the FOIA Amendments.[54] She worried that if Congress passed the amendments, it would open the door for egregious withholdings of government documents in the future. Despite huge personal misgivings, Abzug followed her aides' advice to sponsor the bill.[55] White House counsel Philip W. Buchen had urged President Ford to do the same, suggesting he sign the law "with certain reservations" because it would be difficult to sustain a veto, since "this is a highly volatile political issue."[56] Buchen's advice would prove prophetic.

In 1974, privacy rights legislation was considered along with the FOIA Amendments, the Watergate scandal heightening concern over government surveillance and record-keeping practices. A relative latecomer to this activity, Abzug emerged as a leading drafter of the Privacy Act on the House side. The American Civil Liberties Union (ACLU), American Bar Association, National Lawyers Guild, and Common Cause had been pressuring for congressional action for some time. Privacy was also a European concern in this decade, with legislation passed in France, Germany, Sweden, Portugal, and Spain better distinguishing the parameters of data collection on its citizens.[57] Seeking to get ahead of the issue, President Nixon had promised Americans during his 1974 State of the Union address that he would create a "personal shield for every American" and tasked Ford to lead a Committee on the Right to Privacy.[58] On the House side, Edward Koch introduced the first privacy bill in 1969, meant as a companion to FOIA to limit how the government obtained and preserved personal data. Abzug signed on to Koch's bill when she first joined Congress. When reviewing his bill as a member of the Foreign Operations and Government Information Subcommittee in February 1974, she no longer believed it to be sufficient. When she introduced a separate bill in April, her House counterparts had already lodged 102 privacy bills with a total of 207 cosponsors, and equivalent activity unfolded in the Senate.[59] Abzug emerged from the pack by highlighting her subcommittee role, the progressive bent of her bill, and her expertise as a civil liberties lawyer.

When marshalling the Privacy Rights Act, Abzug formed an unlikely alliance with Koch, a middle-of-the-road liberal with whom she often sparred, and California representative Barry Goldwater Jr., a libertarian leader of the Republican Task Force on Privacy and son of Senator Goldwater. Abzug's privacy interests were twofold. First, she wanted to protect citizens' "right to the basic protection of privacy which is our birthright."[60] Second, she sought extensive safeguards "for every aspect of an information system" beginning with an "individual's right to know, upon request, whether one is the subject to data in a system." Koch and Goldwater Jr. shared this basic understanding but yielded to business and intelligence interests when defining who should be protected by and exempted from the law. To this point, Koch favored the language "persons" over "individuals," but Abzug's preference won out after she persuasively argued, "The First Amendment was meant to protect individuals, not corporations."[61] Goldwater joined Abzug in the call for an independent review board to ensure multiagency compliance, for both agreed that the reporting process should be streamlined. Abzug proposed a "citizen's privacy index" with contact information and data collection procedures of every agency available at all US post offices. Goldwater did not go this far, but he agreed that Americans should have the right to expunge errors in government records and take legal action against violators.

A successful demonstration of bipartisan collaboration, the resulting bill that made it through committee reflected an amalgamation of features proposed by Koch, Abzug, and Goldwater Jr. Moreover, this bipartisanship showed that Abzug, although reluctant to shed her leftist principles, could make concessions. President Ford made it clear he would not support the establishment of a privacy review board "empowered to define privacy in its own terms and to second guess citizens and agencies," and accordingly, it was excised.[62] More disconcerting for Abzug, the Central Intelligence Agency, Internal Revenue Service, and Secret Service effectively lobbied committee members to allow their agencies to be exempt from the bill because criminal, law enforcement, and intelligence records should remain confidential. Vehemently challenging this position, Abzug argued that rewarding a blanket exemption "almost completely vitiates the safeguard requirements of the bill."[63] She did "not believe it is intelligent to add more yards to the national security blanket so beloved by people in authority."[64] CIA director William E. Colby proved more persuasive, urging Abzug's subcommittee colleagues to exhibit restraint.

In the end, most in Congress preferred to see Nixon's recent oversteps as an unusual case.[65] The Senate bill defined exemptions more narrowly, but the Ford administration weighed in heavily and boosted the prominence of the House version. Abzug joined a final effort to challenge agency exemptions when the bill came to a floor vote in October, but the action proved ineffective. As a *Washington Post* editorial accurately judged, the final law had "no real curbs on intelligence gathering." While a significant milestone, the Privacy Act left "a long agenda of unfinished business in this connection," the editorial board wrote, "and has left us wondering what further offenses must be committed and revealed before enough legislators decide to act."[66] Abzug agreed. She sought to address this "unfinished business" as chair of the Government Information and Individual Rights Subcommittee (which replaced the Foreign Operations and Government Information Subcommittee) during the Ninety-Fourth Congress.

Madame Chairwoman and the "Year of Intelligence"

Abzug played an understated role during the 1975 "Year of Intelligence" by drawing attention to domestic surveillance of American citizens and misuses of government record-keeping practices. As chair of GIIR, she was well placed to contribute in this area because the standing committee had jurisdiction over vast agencies, oversaw the implementation of FOIA and the Privacy Act, and could initiate legislation. She drew most upon her legal background in this area of policy work. Indeed, she saw her subcommittee as a vehicle through which to revisit the legal challenge leftist and civil libertarian lawyers forwarded against government secrecy and anticommunist censure during the 1940s and 1950s. After Watergate, she believed that the tables had turned. Emboldened, she forged an aggressive campaign to expose and destabilize the intelligence apparatus she held partially responsible for this earlier political repression as well as the later monitoring and infiltration of antiwar, civil rights, and social liberation organizations. Abzug's purpose was to trace out this long pattern of abuse, to advocate for reform of the national security state, and to enhance First Amendment protections.

Abzug secured the GIIR chair position because of her due diligence. Over the past term, she had signaled her eagerness and ability to lead by filling in for outgoing subcommittee chair William Moorhead on occasion. Additionally, Abzug's overall clout had grown considerably, as indicated by her selection by House leadership as one of three at-large whips.[67] She gained a residual boost from the progressive sweep during the 1974 midterm elections—"the biggest power shake-up in more than half a century."[68] Many of the new members had entered politics through the Robert Kennedy, McCarthy, and McGovern campaigns, ran in direct response to Ford's pardon of Nixon, and sought to shift the leadership structure and policy priorities in Washington. Journalist Mary McGrory characterized the group as largely "a Bella Abzug Fan Club," and Abzug agreed, proclaiming, "The reinforcements have arrived!"[69]

Although pleased with the progressive infusion of Congress, Abzug had hoped the 1974 midterm elections would be a referendum on male political leadership. In one fantasy, which she jotted down but likely never voiced, she cast first lady Pat Nixon as a secret operative, "converted to women's lib—after having to sit and smile bravely through too many speeches of honor of America," who passed along information to aid impeachment efforts.[70] Abzug acknowledged that women could be corruptible, but she nonetheless believed that women politicians were more risk averse, less prone to secrecy, and less "poker-faced." If she were President Nixon, she suggested at one point, "I'd pick up that phone and raise hell . . . I'd get to the truth if it meant firing everybody."[71] Abzug believed that the women elected to Congress in 1972—Yvonne Burke (D-CA), Barbara Jordan (D-TX), Elizabeth Holtzman (D-NY), Patricia Schroeder (D-CO), and Marjorie Holt (R-MD)—had amply exhibited their decision-making skills. Holtzman and Jordan presented themselves during the House Judiciary Committee impeachment hearings as diligent, hard-nosed questioners.[72] After Watergate, the National Women's Political Caucus sought to capitalize on the mood for change by arguing that having more women in politics would bring decency to the enterprise. While more than 2,000 women sought offices at all levels during the 1974 midterms, their gains were mostly outside of Washington.[73] Only six women joined Congress in 1975, bringing the overall number to nineteen.

Figure 8.1 In 1975, majority leader Tip O'Neill of Massachusetts selected Bella Abzug as one of three at-large whips, a mark of her influence. To her right are deputy whip Jim Wright of Texas, at-large whip John Jenrette Jr. of South Carolina, and majority whip John Joseph McFall of California. (Uncredited, Bella Abzug Papers, Box 1088, Rare Book and Manuscript Library, Columbia University)

The Ninety-Fourth Congress exhibited reformist fervor immediately, extending the prior seniority challenge during raucous House Democratic Caucus meetings as the session commenced. Creating their own New Members' Caucus, first-timers largely brushed off formal ties with veteran House reformers. Still, they were appreciative of prior reform efforts and augmented drives to unseat southern Democrats and Cold War liberals as powerful chairs. As Representative Phil Sharp acknowledged, "We provided the votes in the final step. [Others] plowed the land, and we helped harvest the crop."[74] Abzug was especially pleased freshmen campaigned to dismiss House floor gatekeeper Fishbait Miller, with whom she had tussled over her hat.[75] Newly open committee meetings and increased introduction of floor amendments to edit bills led to a more transparent legislative process, but one that encouraged unguarded haggling and greater political theater.[76] Oversight and hearing activity also increased noticeably, with the number of meetings jumping by two-thirds in the House and close to this amount in the Senate.[77]

As GIIR chair, Abzug capitalized on these trends. She had a singular purpose in mind for her opening act—to take on the CIA. After the election returns were in, Democrats bucked the lame-duck tradition and overrode Ford's FOIA veto. Recognizing he was losing ground, Ford signed the Privacy Act into law on New Year's Eve. Abzug believed that the CIA exemption from this law was deeply problematic, and she made it her mission to reopen the matter. With her jurisdiction highly focused, Abzug got her operation together quickly and scheduled a hearing with CIA director William Colby for March 5. Colby had already made several trips to the Hill, but none had matched his appearance before the Abzug Committee, what one reporter called his "most hostile reception."[78]

Abzug saw her oversight role as a tag-team effort with investigative journalists. In December, Seymour Hersh, with whom Abzug was friendly, broke the story about Operation Chaos, the CIA's "little FBI" program that compiled dossiers on at least 10,000 US antiwar activists using wiretaps, break-ins, and informants. Director Colby suggested of the story, "I think family skeletons are best left where they are—in the closet."[79] Abzug disagreed. Immediately, she publicly urged Colby to notify and provide dossiers to all Americans who were monitored, herself included. As she asserted, "If my right to privacy was violated, I want to know the specifics."[80] The night before his scheduled hearing, Colby unexpectedly obliged. Abzug received an envelope late in the evening marked, "Personal and Confidential." In it, she found a dossier dating back to the 1950s.[81] It was meant to stop her in her tracks, but instead she felt emboldened.

The next day, Abzug engaged in dramatic political theater. She charged into the hearing room, file in hand. Colby tried preemptively to set the tone in his prepared statement, calling for "responsible investigations" of "a few" past indiscretions "exaggerated out of all proportion into a charge that CIA was engaged in a massive domestic intelligence activity."[82] Abzug, however, insisted on a confrontation. She called the CIA an engine of falsehood and exaggeration, as evidenced by "the collection of trivia and inaccurate information" that filled out her own dossier.[83] Highlighting aspects of her file, she resurrected a tactic Guild lawyers used in the 1950s in which they produced portions of FBI dossiers stealthily obtained as legal exhibits to publicly expose the bureau's surveillance methods. These first leaks had in turn prompted director J. Edgar Hoover to double down on surveillance of leftist lawyers, including Abzug. Going through her dossier methodically, she suggested, "I raise this not as a personal matter, but only to reflect a problem we confront." It was clear to observers, however, that this clash with CIA director Colby was undeniably personal, for she aired what it was like to be "victimized by a country in which I was born."[84] In making this show, Abzug turned the political trial perfected by the House Un-American Activities Committee—dissolved during the Ninety-Fourth Congress—on its head. This time, she averred, it would be the spymaster in the hot seat.

While Abzug used this hearing to push back against the idea that surveillance of American citizens was warranted, Colby countered that some of the congresswoman's activities were questionable and fell within the domain of the CIA. Retracing two decades of surveillance, the director confirmed that Abzug's international-bound mail had been opened, the FBI and CIA had passed information about her, Women Strike for Peace meetings were infiltrated, and she continued to be monitored up to 1973. Pressed to justify the inclusion of specific cables, mailing lists, and newspaper clippings, Colby conceded, "A considerable amount of the material in your file should not be in there." At the same time, he asserted that "certain aspects" were "legitimately" there, the agency's domestic and foreign monitoring was "perfectly proper," and it was not Abzug per se but the company she kept and the organizations she belonged to that were suspect.[85] Likewise, Colby argued that it was very reasonable to track Representatives Abzug and Patsy Mink when they met with delegates of the Provisional Revolutionary Government of South Vietnam in Paris in 1972, for this was the enemy.[86] Colby offered a few admissions: four members of Congress had been under surveillance, and the CIA had received one hundred requests for information since the publication of Hersh's article.[87] Overall, Abzug's focus on her personal file, meant to instruct the public about CIA procedure, allowed Colby to stay away from big revelations.

The Abzug Committee engaged in a back-and-forth about privacy rights versus national security interests for four hours with no real winner. In questioning Colby, GIIR divided along party lines, with Sam Steiger (R-AZ) very sympathetic to the CIA and Clarence Brown (R-OH) taking a middle-of-the-road approach. Most Democratic members prodded Colby mildly to draw down the shield of secrecy, while Abzug forced a constitutional debate, delineating "First Amendment rights—to be able to have ideas, to travel, to speak, to write." It was not enough, she argued, to "accumulate all this rotten stuff about people" on the chance that they could be spies or terrorists. Pushing back against Abzug's charge that opening her mail was illegal, Colby delivered the last word, asserting, "We devote our lives to this profession because we believe in freedom, too, and we believe that freedom has to be protected."[88]

Director Colby came away from his "day-long tongue-lashing" before the "redoubtable Abzug" with the dreaded feeling that a more assertive Congress had arrived.[89] "The old tradition was that you don't ask," Colby observed, but Abzug had ignored this standard.[90] The director feared her hearing signaled an unreasonable season of investigation rife with "sensations created by everybody and his brother engaging in cheap TV theatrics at the expense of the CIA's secrets." In this climate, the "CIA was going to have to fend for itself without that long-time special Congressional protection."[91] Still, Colby recognized Abzug had limited jurisdiction, and so far she could only needle him on the CIA's Privacy Act exemption. Abzug was satisfied with her performance. Activist groups singled out in Operation Chaos wrote her in thanks. Satirist Russell Baker sympathetically concocted a scenario of watercooler banter at the CIA:

> "I'm surprised the agency still keeps him [an agent] on.
> What's he do these days?
> They've given him the job of reading Congresswomen's mail.
> And he took it? How low can a man sink?
> He's shot."[92]

Bella and Martin appeared in the image accompanying this piece, locked in a kiss, separated by sterile facemasks suggesting playfully and pointedly how the government sanitized speech. Feeling victorious, Abzug replayed highlights of her exchange with Colby before friendly audiences during the spring.[93]

Abzug did not anticipate how her full-throttle challenge of the CIA would be covered in conservative media. James J. Kilpatrick asserted, "The CIA ought to be commended, not abused."[94] Eugene Pulliam characterized the hearing as a confrontation of good versus evil, not "the big, bold and bad CIA against Snow White."[95] *Human Events* offered its own deconstruction of the congresswoman's dossier, emphasizing her long record of radical activities to show why government surveillance was warranted.[96] Abzug dismissed these stories as "an ultra-rightwing . . . collection of exaggerations and lies of the kind that used to be gathered by HUAC."[97] She was not incorrect, for conservative reporters drew on research that went beyond the tidbits she offered to the public. Nonetheless, the upswing of letters Abzug received after the hearing testified to the growing power of the conservative media to elicit grassroots response. Letters voiced sentiments such as "Leave our CIA alone."[98] The memory of writers ran long, and the vitriol expressed was staggering. Abzug reminded one writer of the "repulsive types in New York during the depression, specifically Union Square."[99] Another wrote, "If I were your milliner, I'd think it appropriate for you to pin a red star to that hat you wear in the wrong place."[100] A third suggested, "We don't like loud mouth women and we don't like communists! We don't like traitors!"[101] Undoubtedly, Abzug's assault on the CIA became a lightning rod for conservatives around which to regroup after the 1974 midterms.

Chairwoman Abzug's challenge of Director Colby captured wide attention in part because the specially created select committees at the center of the "Year of Intelligence" were just getting under way. On March 5, while the Abzug Committee received testimony from Colby, President Ford and his top aides met at the White House with Senator Frank Church and members of the Senate Select Committee to Study Governmental Operations with Respect to Intelligence Activities. A staid World War II veteran and lawyer from Idaho, Church had served in Congress since 1956. He had a nice-guy reputation, but he also had a spine, breaking with former mentor Lyndon B. Johnson when criticizing the Vietnam War on the Senate Foreign Relations Committee. During the White House meeting, Church promised Ford he would "not wreck" intelligence agencies, vowing to "if necessary . . . reform them" and signaling he would focus on past offenses more than present practices.[102] Receptive, Ford pledged he would turn over classified documents on a case-by-case basis and allow CIA employees to be interviewed privately if Church Committee aides signed secrecy agreements. The House Select Committee on Intelligence chaired by New York Representative Otis Pike took longer to get started, holding its first public hearing in July. A World War II veteran, Pike supported the Vietnam War as a member of the House Armed Services Committee, suggesting he might be friendlier than Church. However, "tart-tongued" Pike had a "fearless,

Figure 8.2 News that the CIA had opened Representative Bella Abzug's international mail since the early 1950s attracted attention and sympathy, as this political cartoon attests. As chair of the House Government Information and Individual Rights Subcommittee, she turned her personal experience into an object lesson to highlight the excesses of the national security state. (John Stees, Government Information and Individual Rights Subcommittee Records, 93rd Congress, Record Group 233, Box 18, National Archives and Records Administration)

irreverent personality," making him less willing to consult with Ford and his officials.[103] Unlike Church, Pike had no reservations about highlighting systemic flaws of the intelligence infrastructure or calling out current practices. Both investigative committees, as historian Kathryn Olmsted notes, "were challenging the foreign policy of the Cold War."[104] Essentially, the "Year of Intelligence" broke through the Cold War consensus that had sanctioned covert operations, heightened surveillance, and condoned the expansion of a military-industrial complex.

Abzug welcomed the widespread intelligence investigations that brought critical focus to the national security state, but she did not want to step aside. She developed an internal watchdog approach to keep the heat on these select committees. Her limited clout, narrow domain, and overt leftist, antidefense posture hampered her ability to steer congressional action and debate on intelligence. Nonetheless, she used the mechanisms at her disposal to continue pushing hard. She directed her staff to reach out to the Church Committee often, seeking to mirror Senate investigation of domestic surveillance and government document collection and preservation. Mainly, the Abzug Committee followed. At times, Abzug's staff of just over a handful uncovered leads that the Church Committee, with its staff of more than a hundred and greater authority, could research more deeply and draw attention more widely. In contrast, the Abzug Committee's relationship with the Pike Committee was adversarial. Abzug found it frustrating that GIIR had been reconstituted at the opening of the Ninety-Fourth Congress, losing its domain over foreign affairs. The question came up as to whether there would be anything for her committee to do once the Pike Committee got going.[105] On the defensive, required to cede territory, Abzug competed with Pike for issues to consider and time in the spotlight.

In June, Abzug realized how much Colby had withheld from her committee after reading the report released by the Rockefeller Commission and decided to call him before the committee once more. She had little confidence in this commission established by President Ford to look at CIA activities, seeing Vice President Nelson Rockefeller and his "conservative collection" of corporate elites as having "never shown any concern for civil liberties."[106] Still, they revealed a great deal. Most troubling, it came out that the IRS's Intelligence Division, the Pentagon, CIA, FBI, and the National Security Agency (NSA) shared data stored in a supercomputer network. Abzug called a second hearing to look into this data system on the premise that her committee was still considering a bill to fix the Privacy Act.

Colby had delivered testimony to thirty-seven congressional committees from the first time he appeared before the Abzug Committee in March and his second appearance on June 25. Nonetheless, Abzug still believed there was more to reveal and was the first to question Colby publicly about the Rockefeller Commission report. Both Colby and Republican committee members grew impatient with her needling.[107] Abzug called the CIA's gathering of "millions of pieces" of "scurrilous . . . back fence gossip" an invasion of privacy that violated "every single law in the criminal arena." Sam

Steiger retorted, "The queen has no clothes." He charged her with calling the meeting to "vent your own spleen" and beat down the "most abuse[d] . . . agency in the history of this country." Democrats on the committee steered the focus toward specifics on covert operations. Representative John Conyers Jr. led Colby to confirm that not four, but seventy-five Congress members, "neither a target nor immune," had been under surveillance.[108] Before the hearing wrapped up, Government Operations chair Jack Brooks (D-TX) came in to defend Abzug's right to scrutinize the CIA, reminding Colby that the subcommittee was the longest-standing investigative arm of the House. Her authority reaffirmed, Abzug probed further. She cornered Colby into admitting that Operation Chaos was illegal and some program files had been destroyed.

Abzug was especially focused on getting Colby to outline the Rockefeller Commission's finding most troubling to her as a lawyer. The Department of Justice had entered an agreement in 1954 with the CIA to let the agency handle criminal prosecutions of its employees without DOJ involvement, thereby skirting the law.[109] Abzug and her staff believed this agreement proved that the CIA was not merely a "rogue elephant on a rampage," as Senator Church characterized it, but part of a wider web of collusion between agencies focused on extralegal spying on citizens.[110] As Abzug's investigators assessed, "Watergate cover-up and CIA involvement not much unlike standard CIA cover-up of prosecutions involving its former employees?"[111] The Abzug Committee spent the summer looking into the cases that fell under this CIA-DOJ agreement. Aides flew around the country in search of witnesses and sorted through the DOJ's hefty case index housed at the National Archives in Maryland to find matters referred to the CIA since 1954. Church Committee aide Burt Wides shared information gained from private interviews with CIA counsel Lawrence Houston, author of the 1954 agreement. Additionally, the Abzug Committee directly solicited Director Colby for a full accounting of cases, and the agency turned over a list of thirty cases in response.[112]

The disclosure was a boon, but the last one the Abzug Committee would achieve. Ford administration officials had decided her meddling had gone too far. As CIA counsel George L. Cary alerted White House counsel John "Jack" Marsh, "We have a festering problem with Bella Abzug."[113] Ford aides believed Abzug was acting recklessly and on her own, observing that she "demanded unrestricted access to CIA operational" documents "over the objections of the Republican members of the Subcommittee."[114] They also worried that she might follow Representative Pike's lead, frustrated that he had publicly released NSA documents at the committee's first hearing on September 11. And by this point, the Church Committee had exposed the FBI's harassment of Martin Luther King Jr. as part of COINTELPRO, had probed deeper into the CIA's mail-opening operation, and was beginning to explore the NSA's "questionable propriety and dubious legality."[115] The sum of these investigations had led the Ford administration toward a more combative posture with all intelligence oversight committees. Abzug kept up a letter storm of document requests and reached out to reporters who apprised the public of the situation, but these actions achieved little effect. Stonewalled, she received nothing but "sanitized" versions of documents from this point forward.[116]

Testing Executive Privilege

For the rest of the "Year of Intelligence," Abzug focused on testing the Ford administration to see how far its interpretation of executive privilege would stretch. She directed this challenge through a probe of Operation SHAMROCK, a program in which FBI and NSA agents visited Washington cable offices to read and photocopy private telegrams at night over a period of twenty-eight years.[117] Investigative journalists first uncovered its existence, and Abzug's staff found out about it by chasing the trail left by the press. Church Committee staff had learned of Operation SHAMROCK in May but acted slowly because they were waiting for the NSA to respond to their discovery requests, which it did in September. The Abzug Committee moved on the issue, and its hearing on Operation SHAMROCK in turn compelled Church to pursue the matter further.[118] Abzug's aides learned more than they expected from their interviews with telecommunications company staff and intelligence officers. Operation SHAMROCK began during World War II, extended to New York offices, included the full run of cables to and from the United States, and stopped—at least at Western Union—only, as one interviewee confided, "when your office first contacted the company."[119] Her investigators also identified the FBI's liaison as retired agent Joe R. Craig, who was "in a quandary" when aide Robert Fink arrived to question him and "most reluctant to speak," but confirmed his role.[120]

Although it was just one part of the larger puzzle of intelligence discovery, Operation SHAMROCK became central for Abzug. She devoted considerable resources to investigation of the program because she saw it as another form of collusion, she fiercely defended free speech, and she sought to expose egregious violations of personal privacy. She also personalized the issue. Shortly before her committee's hearing on Operation SHAMROCK on October 23, Bob Woodward wrote an article outlining the NSA's "Gamma" cable interception sweep that included monitoring of antiwar activists.[121] Abzug expected she could be included. For this reason, she was unmovable when "locked in a struggle" with other committee members and Ford administration officials who urged her to back off.[122] President Ford responded to press revelations and building congressional interest by publicly admitting that NSA electronic eavesdropping "though vital, may be of 'questionable legality'" and promising greater oversight.[123] The day before the Abzug Committee's scheduled NSA hearing, White House counsel John Marsh, NSA director general Lew Allen Jr., assistant defense secretary Albert C. Hall, and Deputy Attorney General Harold Tyler all paid Abzug visits. And minutes before the hearing, Attorney General Edward H. Levi stopped by as well. These efforts to reason with Abzug proved futile, as she had made up her mind to hound the NSA publicly. As an oppositional activist congresswoman, this is exactly what she came to Washington to do. Although obstinate, Abzug did not have an offensive advantage, and Ford aides convinced subpoenaed Western Union employees and former FBI agent Joe Craig not to appear. Only the lesser offenders—executives of AT&T, ITT World Communications, and RCA Global Communications— showed up at the hearing. Perturbed by these "sudden, suspicious, last-minute refusals to attend," Abzug handed over her investigators' findings to journalists.[124]

While Abzug was bold and resolute in public, this moment coincided with a period of great personal anguish. Her mother, Esther Savitzky, who had been declining for some time, passed away. Abzug returned home from Washington to attend her funeral at the Riverside Memorial Chapel on October 28.[125] The next day, the Church Committee commenced two days of hearings on Operation SHAMROCK. Most significantly, General Allen revealed during testimony Operation MINARET, where the NSA tracked the cables of 1,680 Americans and distributed information to the CIA, FBI, Secret Service, and army intelligence, among other entities.[126] Abzug still believed the subsequent report on SHAMROCK issued by the Church Committee to be incomplete, for it focused on interception of cables but did not cover telex communications or consider if this style of espionage continued under a new name.[127] As a result, she decided to go forward with preparations for a next round of hearings.

Abzug tried to keep her NSA probe going into 1976, but the "Year of Intelligence" had expired. In January, a Harris poll revealed that 41 percent of respondents did not think "the CIA or FBI have learned their lessons and now will run things properly."[128] At the same time, the public had tired of intelligence investigations, with only 38 percent approving of the Church Committee and 36 percent of the Pike Committee.[129] Many Americans no longer supported the parade of government officials questioned by Congress members or the persistent barrage of newspaper stories that began to sound alarmist. Abzug did not take heed of this shift, in part because she was deeply resolute in her purpose, but also because her supporters continued to cheer her on. Her investigative work buoyed the spirits of progressive Americans for whom she was fighting the most.

In the new year, Abzug tried any remaining patience Ford aides had for tolerating her requests. Abzug took pleasure in being a tempest. She vowed to initiate a FOIA request to make the Pike Report public after the White House used all of its persuasive power to compel House members to vote down its release. Leaked to Daniel Schorr, the report appeared in part in the *New York Times* and in full in the *Village Voice*.[130] In February, the Government Operations Committee signed off on a new round of subpoenas issued by the Abzug Committee in connection with Operation SHAMROCK.[131] Recognizing she would not see classified documents, she moved forward anyway because she remained committed to pressing the Ford administration on executive privilege. The investigation had become an exercise in seeing how far she could take discovery. It was also a means to inflict pain, for her requests required action even if in the form of denials. A forty-four-tab binder titled "Abzug Matter," circulating in the West Wing, tracked the lengthy back-and-forth, demonstrating what a nuisance she had become for the Ford White House.[132] On the advice of counsel Philip Buchen and Assistant Attorney General Antonin Scalia, Ford denied the Abzug Committee's new subpoenas of public employees and private sector witnesses on the grounds of executive privilege.[133] When FBI agents appeared before the congresswoman's committee, they only did so to tell

Abzug that President Ford would not let them talk. She responded, "Executive privilege went out with the American Revolution."[134]

Thwarted, Abzug's staff continued to "keep pecking around the edges" and worked to "prolong this situation." Their line during this final combative phase: "Fight fiercely, burn them whenever and wherever possible, strike a deal only as a last resort."[135] Abzug's legal staff and Ford advisors continued to "haggle over" what material could be seen in public or private committee hearings through June, but the investigation had petered out significantly after April.[136] Attorney General Levi believed Abzug's stubborn insistence on having a public debate about intelligence that involved confidential documents demonstrated her recklessness and naïveté. "I thought what she should do is to have an Executive Session and hear it first. I didn't think she knew what she was getting into," he judged.[137] Far from it, Abzug knew exactly what she was doing during post-Watergate intelligence hearings. She sought to instigate a public confrontation with the executive branch that placed it at odds with public interest in privacy. In a sense, she wanted to make clear how the government's security interests had become so overblown, it had lost sight of its obligations to its citizens.

Abzug joined Congress members equally focused on taking down the curtains screening government. The Abzug Committee shepherded the Government in the Sunshine Act through the House, which required nonclassified agency meetings to be public. Abzug advocated for sunshine legislation because she recognized it would "force the bureaucrats to do the public's business in public."[138] In early 1976, her committee was tasked with consolidating a handful of "sunshine" bills. Negotiations became tense, with committee members dividing over how far the rays of transparency should light up the government's shadows. Republican members seeking to constrict the scope of openness wanted to narrowly define "meeting" and did not support the creation of transcripts for closed meetings. As a compromise, Democrats leading support for the bill allowed that transcripts could be redacted if "the reason and statutory authority for this reason was presented."[139] After these negotiations, the full Government Operations Committee sent the bill onto the Judiciary Committee in February.

The bill that made it out of committee was far-reaching, calling for more than fifty agencies to hold publicized meetings and granting individuals the right to sue if they were unduly excluded. Concerned about this level of exposure, Ford officials leaned on Judiciary Committee members to amend the bill, much to Abzug's consternation. Most significantly, a subtle language change—the addition of "permitted to be withheld"—gave agencies discretion to close any meeting under the guise that sensitive matters would be discussed. Abzug thought this change was "catastrophic," arguing it "would effectively destroy the legislation."[140] While the House bill proved unsatisfying, the Senate bill that more liberally leaned toward transparency became the driver during markup. Accordingly, the final law, which President Ford signed on September 13, 1976, did not have the "permitted to be withheld" clause but did limit closed meetings to only those pertaining to national security, trade secrets, law enforcement, or personal matters. In the end, the Senate version shared the main features of the bill Abzug shepherded through her committee. As a result, the Government in the Sunshine Act served the purpose she had envisioned: creating a mechanism the public could call upon to "sever the seals of secrecy."[141]

Abzug was quite intentional in her work to create watchdog tools for "reporters and citizen groups throughout the country."[142] Her oversight of FOIA and the Privacy Act reflects this deliberate aim. Now Americans lodge FOIA and privacy document requests as a fundamental right. In the 1970s, these "right to know" tools were relatively new and not widely used. Implementation of FOIA's new features and the Privacy Act first occurred during the Ninety-Fourth Congress. Abzug took her role in overseeing this process very seriously. She traveled the talk show circuit to teach Americans how to make FOIA and Privacy Act requests and encouraged viewers at home to solicit her staff's help filing applications. This advocacy campaign conducted via Congress paralleled efforts forwarded by the ACLU, Common Cause, the Center for National Security Studies, and like groups. Americans responded by the hundreds, and her legal staff went to great lengths to follow up on individual cases.[143] Some constituents wrote Abzug to record the progress of their file requests, alerting her about every roadblock experienced or point of subterfuge suspected. Others took a decidedly libertarian tone, asking how they could use these laws to keep the government out of their lives. This is the kind of engagement Abzug had hoped for as she believed that Americans should hold their government accountable.

Agencies facing FOIA and Privacy Act requests were slow to reply and complained about the new workload. These laws had in fact created a mountain of paperwork for agencies. The Department of Justice reported over 30,000 requests for information in its first six months, requiring a whole new department to administer.[144] Abzug dismissed the critique that "federal agencies are being harassed or that a vindictive population . . . engaged in a subtle form of water torture by use of the mail. I view this interest as a logical outgrowth of the last few years."[145] Yet, she knew full well that the FOIA and the Privacy Act provided Americans with a tool of discovery and those who used it most immediately were those who feared that they had been under government surveillance.

Abzug saw the side effect of creating a morass of paperwork for federal agencies as a small price to pay for Americans' ability to gain clarity and peace of mind. She added to the paperwork, taxing agency heads with near-daily letters urging compliance. She wanted to ensure that agencies laid out clear implementation guidelines that set a precedent for the future. As a lawyer, she was also preoccupied with making sure her committee left a thorough paper trail that journalists, attorneys, and historians could follow.[146]

The Abzug Committee's "right to know" efforts reflected her own search for answers. She wanted the government to acknowledge and "remedy the wrongs done to innocent victims by intelligence agencies in the name of national security." The first step, as she saw it, was "to advise" these individuals; the second was to "allow them the option of having every trace of such files destroyed."[147] How much Abzug personalized this process can be seen in how eagerly she aided Women Strike for Peace and the National Lawyers Guild, seeking legal reparations for government surveillance. While Abzug chaired GIIR, the firm Rabinowitz, Boudin & Standard engaged in preliminary discovery for *NLG v. Attorney General,* a suit the Guild filed in 1977 and settled in 1989. Abzug wrote CIA director George H. W. Bush (Colby's replacement) to urge that the agency produce records, and she would be among those featured in the 300,000 pages of government surveillance records ultimately turned over.[148]

Abzug gained the sweetest satisfaction from her posthumous revenge on FBI director J. Edgar Hoover. Unbeknownst to Abzug, Hoover had intervened more than once to keep her FBI file active.[149] Operating from more than suspicion, she was aware that bureau agents had lurked around her law office and had called her home during the 1950s and 1960s. Accordingly, she eagerly joined the line of congressional committees looking at the FBI. In the Senate, the Church Committee reviewed dossier file classifications—from "black bag jobs" to "do not file"—and sought to find out what happened to Hoover's secret files mysteriously removed from his house after his death.[150] Holding hearings in December, the Abzug Committee followed Church's lead. Helen W. Gandy, Hoover's loyal secretary, admitted during testimony before her committee to destroying thirty-five file drawers of documents in 1972 with the approval of Director L. Patrick Gray, which he denied. Responding to this revelation, Abzug suggested, "This matter is reminiscent of the famous 18 1/2 minute gap in the Nixon tapes. Here we have a dozen file cabinets of records maintained by one of the most powerful men in American history, and they are lost—possibly forever."[151] The Nixon tapes were not quite the same as Hoover's filing cabinets. Nevertheless, Abzug highlighted how high officials in US government had prioritized secrecy over the public's "right to know."

BELLA ABZUG'S DEDICATION as a civil libertarian is most evident in her work as chair of the Government Information and Individual Rights subcommittee. Foremost, she sought to enhance First Amendment rights and make it more difficult for the government to encroach on personal privacy. Second, she wanted to augment Americans' oversight capacities by creating new discovery tools and bringing greater transparency to government activities. As Senator Ted Kennedy reflected, "This was a passion that she had. If we got an openness in government, that was truth to power."[152] Abzug sought to diminish elites' control by making it more difficult to govern in secrecy. This call for greater openness in government was part of the progressive push for a more inclusive, responsive democracy that took hold in the early 1970s. But these sunshine reforms had an unintended consequence: more people could watch the government doing its business and did not necessarily like what they saw. The introduction of C-SPAN in 1979 and the growth of cable news further added to this public showcase of policymaking.

Congressional oversight expanded considerably during the mid-1970s, taxing executive officials. They believed that legislators "too often crossed the line that separated constructive oversight from irresponsible intervention in the details of the administration."[153] Among those who crossed the line, Abzug used her committee as a forum to present her views as a self-described "first-amendment addict."[154] She believed her aggressive challenge of the CIA, FBI, and NSA was warranted, for she had been among those targeted in surveillance programs that skirted the law in the name of national security. The post-Watergate climate created greater space for civil libertarians to promote the "right to know" and for dissenters to talk about their experience living under surveillance. Recognizing this opening, Abzug seized on it and used the power of the media and the infrastructure of her standing committee to shed a spotlight on agency practices she believed required reform. Her challenge did little to dismantle the intelligence apparatus or shift Americans' acceptance of the national security state. But she did raise public awareness of the costs incurred with postwar expansion of the US military and intelligence.

By openly using her political past to make her case, Abzug drew greater focus on her radicalism before a national audience. As a result, she reminded conservatives beyond New York why she was a threat to have in Congress. She underestimated how the progressive push after Watergate and at the end of the Vietnam War would jolt those who believed the call for new politics in Washington had gone too far. The crisis mode brought on by political scandal, military defeat, and economic recession led to a reappraisal of executive powers, but also reinforced Americans' tendency to turn away from each other and prioritize security. Abzug challenged this impulse when she ran for Senate in 1976, but she had difficulty convincing Democratic voters to do the same.

9

RUNNING FOR A DEMOCRATIC FUTURE

ON MAY 17, 1976, Bella Abzug summoned her close confidants to 37 Bank Street to engage in a parlor game of "why Bella should not run" for Senate. All agreed that her chances of winning were a "big gamble." One adviser laid out the odds. The political terrain had shifted to "a strong undercurrent of conservatism in [the] electorate, anti-union, anti-welfare, anti–big spending." The "liberal left" increasingly felt "in disarray." Abzug had to prepare for a barrage of "extremely vicious" attacks—"redbaiting, anti-Semitic, anti-big spender, anti-abortion." Her primary hurdle would be differentiating herself from "extremist, anti-male feminists," and her biggest challenge would be attracting the support of "housewives and bluecollar workers." While a victory would give her greater stature and stop the endless campaigning, a loss would create a "big backlash" against Abzug "personally, against the left and against [the] women's movement."[1]

Most of those who were in the room that day look back to this conversation and shake their heads. They contend that Abzug's House seat could have been hers for years to come.[2] This interpretation, however, diverts focus from the political concerns her advisers raised before she entered the race. Those around Abzug cogently and soberly recognized that the political mood in New York and the nation was changing, and her disinterest in compromising her principles to be more electable made her vulnerable.

The 1976 New York State Senate Democratic primary was a nationally consequential, closely watched contest that mattered to more than New Yorkers. This race pitted two sides of the Democratic Party—its New Politics left and its "take back the party" right—against each other at a decisive crossroads in the party's history. These polarities within the party vied for the upper hand in influencing its center. Most treatments of the 1970s political realignment focus on the drift of "Reagan Democrats" to the Republican Party, but the Democratic Party moved rightward too.[3] It is true that Democrats lost their advantage in appealing to the white working class, forfeited their stronghold in the South, and fell out of favor with social conservatives. Focus on a conservative exodus from the Democratic Party, however, draws attention away from how social liberation and family values, diplomacy and defense, and economic parity and personal responsibility split the party first. In the mid-1970s, issues that separate Democrats and Republicans now were already tearing both parties apart.[4]

The 1976 race that played out in New York State to select a Democratic contender for Senate showcased the wider party's ideological and identity-based diversity and its members' deep-seated attachments to divergent interests. By July, the field had narrowed to two major contenders: Bella Abzug and Daniel Patrick Moynihan. Gender became the optic issue in this matchup, a comparison encouraged by both candidates. Abzug's flyers pictured an all-white, male Senate and directed, "Look Closely. There's Something Missing."[5] Moynihan's bumper stickers highlighted his masculinity, noting, "My Man Moynihan."[6] Yet, the race was equally one of "two opposing styles of liberalism: his and hers."[7] Abzug campaigned for expanded equality and Moynihan for a return to liberty. She urged Americans to rethink how the United States structured its democracy, economy, and society in the wake of military defeat, and at a time of increased globalization and pressure from rights movements. He sought to restore strength and order in foreign affairs, factories, and families.

The central preoccupation of voters during the 1976 election was how the United States would dig itself out of a deep recession. Although still a global powerhouse, the nation had experienced its worst slump since the 1930s with more than 8 million out of work, an unrelenting energy crisis, the vexing strain of stagflation, and the lingering costs of war. New York Democrats weighed their electoral options amid a fiscal crisis in which New York City nearly went bankrupt. The *New York Daily News* summed up the federal response with a headline, "Ford to City: Drop Dead."[8] At this tipping point, Abzug placed too much stock in her ability to convince New York Democrats that the answer to the state's and nation's problems was to embrace democratic socialist politics. At this crossroads when Democrats instead veered toward neoliberalism, Abzug directed critical focus on American corporations. Government, she argued, should penalize their self-interested ways, not reward them with contracts and tax breaks. Her proposed program was one of increased taxes on the rich, investment in environmental projects, heavily subsidized higher education, women's equal pay for equal work, and a guaranteed living wage for all Americans. Moynihan, in contrast, praised the multinational corporation, believed Democrats should expand outreach to business, and wanted to responsibly reform the welfare state. Moynihan's program previewed the New Democratic turn in the Democratic Party. Abzug's alternative has become the platform of progressive Democrats in the twenty-first century.

The Moynihan-Abzug contest additionally highlighted Democrats at odds about the role of the United States as a global leader after the Vietnam War. Would the United States expand its military and arms buildup or reduce its operation? Should the United States defend other democracies and lead global human rights efforts? These were the terms of debate that pitted this antiwar leader against the former US ambassador to the United Nations. Their position on Israel was the crucial pivot in this foreign policy discussion, for Jewish New Yorkers were expected to account for 35 to 40 percent of voters in the primary.[9] Abzug and Moynihan were both pro-Zionist but their wider ideological differences on how to manage Cold War foreign policy set them apart.

Abzug remained remarkably consistent during her Senate campaign. She did not greatly change her populist pitch and she continued to call on voters to accept all of "the people" in their communities. She still suggested that the nation's expansive military budget was a root cause of its economic woes. And she still argued the largely untested hypothesis that having more women in government would lead to a more equitable, peaceful society. This tough medicine was too difficult for enough voters to swallow. Her loss—at a close margin of less than 1 percent—left an indelible mark on her career and the future influence of progressives within the Democratic Party.

A Race to Be Watched

Abzug threw her hat into the ring for a shot at challenging the Conservative-Republican senator James L. Buckley shortly after the Ninety-Fourth Congress commenced. On February 5, 1975, she announced she was exploring running for the Senate. "I'm a full-blooded politician," she told the *New York Times*. "I'm in it to stay."[10] By November, she was one of a crowded field of eleven potential candidates.[11] By the time of her formal announcement in May 1976, her competition had narrowed to Ramsey Clark, Andrew J. Stein, Abraham Hirschfeld, and Paul O'Dwyer. One month later, on June 10, Daniel Patrick Moynihan entered the race.

Abzug feared Moynihan's challenge most. She did not expect Hirschfeld, a parking garage developer who urged, "Let a businessman put New York back in business," would be a strong contender.[12] Nor was she particularly worried about New York State assemblyman Stein, who lacked name recognition. Abzug had greater difficulty differentiating her politics from Clark and O'Dwyer. A lawyer from Texas, Clark rose quickly in the Department of Justice under President John F. Kennedy, served as President Lyndon B. Johnson's attorney general, and became a vocal critic of the Vietnam War. While simpatico with Clark, Abzug believed she could outmatch him on the issues, could argue he was untested in elected office, and could point to his recent defeat two years prior when running against Republican senator Jacob Javits. New York City Council president Paul O'Dwyer was an old associate in the National Lawyers Guild virtually in step with Abzug politically, but more willing to cultivate establishment party support. An Irish immigrant, he had worked at the docks and in the garment industry before becoming a lawyer who represented underdogs—striking laborers, civil rights workers, and antiwar activists. Yet, because O'Dwyer had run for the House of Representatives, for mayor, and for the Senate, losing two of these races to Javits, Abzug again thought she had a fighting chance.[13] She was more concerned about Moynihan, since her campaign solicited polling data that suggested he would be a formidable opponent. With Clark and O'Dwyer in the race, her edge narrowed and Moynihan trailed closely behind according to the polling findings. Undecided voters could swing his way, whereas she faced a handicap since a sizable number of respondents had rejected her vehemently.[14] The results presaged difficulties ahead.

For the next two months, Abzug and her aides actively lobbied to keep Moynihan out of the race. Representative Charles Rangel, acting as a proxy for Abzug, characterized Moynihan as a divisive figure in a letter he circulated to legislators in April. Abzug secured endorsements early from Lieutenant Governor Mary Ann Krupsack and from Pamela Harriman, wife of Moynihan's old boss Governor Averell Harriman. Abzug tried to elicit support from Governor Hugh Carey, who steered clear of endorsements even though he was "all for DPM."[15] Abzug's staff worked quickly to reach out to local leaders upstate, hoping to get to them before Erie County Democratic chair Joe Crangle, a central architect of Moynihan's bid. Crangle was not the only prominent Democrat to lobby Moynihan to run. Ed Koch, among those who nudged, thought "it would be a tragedy for the state of New York if she [Abzug] was our Senator, a tragedy for the country and a tragedy for the Democratic party."[16] Moynihan had been quite content teaching at Harvard University since leaving his post as US ambassador to the United Nations, but the encouragement was tempting. Businessman Richard Ravitch, chair of the New York State Urban Development Corporation, proved most persuasive.[17] He convinced Moynihan to seize the opportunity to help shape urban policy within Congress and get New York back on track.

Neither Abzug nor Moynihan were the New York State Democratic Committee's pick when the body voted in mid-June. After six hours of jockeying, the endorsement went to O'Dwyer, who had publicly threatened to drop out of the race if he did not secure this win. Moynihan received "scattered hisses" from the audience when he spoke, but Abzug came in third when the votes were cast. The Abzug campaign responded that it was a good thing not to have the endorsement of the "bosses," seeking to distinguish herself as the New Democratic Coalition pick. Her backers also came armed with flyers they circulated picturing Moynihan next to Nixon with the comment, "What kind of a Democrat do you want for your Senator?"[18]

Meant to be a slight to Moynihan, this question was one Democrats of every persuasion asked about their candidates and their party during the 1976 election season. In the New York Senate Democratic primary, Democratic leaders saw O'Dwyer as the "closest to a centrist right now."[19] Moynihan and Abzug represented the party's right and left poles. Primaries often draw only the most ardent voters, and only one-quarter of registered Democrats in New York would vote in September.[20] The race fueled greater passions and garnered more interest than these numbers imply. By the time the Democratic National Convention was held at Madison Square Garden in July, coverage of the race narrowed to the contest between Abzug and Moynihan. Their starkly contrasting ideology and style, their national prominence, and their enthusiastic fans and vehement foes made this a race to be watched.

Moynihan's path to politics, though marked out in nearby territory, did not resemble that of Abzug. Moving to New York City from Oklahoma at age eight, Moynihan weathered the Depression years raised mainly by his mother in a Roman Catholic enclave of Hell's Kitchen. He attended City College when it was still free. Having served in the navy during World War II, he finished his studies at Tufts University on the GI Bill. He attended the London School of Economics on a Fulbright scholarship, where he acquired a "taste for Saville Row suits, rococo conversational riffs, and Churchillian oratory."[21] Stateside again, Moynihan became acquainted with his wife, Elizabeth, while working for Governor Harriman. The more politically inclined of the pair, Liz "got hooked . . . on the process of government" when first working on Harriman's campaign.[22] While his family was young, Pat Moynihan finished his PhD in international relations at the Fletcher School of Law and Diplomacy of Tufts University. In these years, "in policy terms" he was a liberal, but "he did not share the reformers' visceral suspicion of the bosses."[23]

Liz worked in John F. Kennedy's field office in Syracuse during his 1960 presidential campaign and helped position Pat for the job of assistant secretary of labor when Kennedy won. Staying on as an aide to President Johnson, Moynihan devoted attention to urban poverty and drafted the widely read 1965 report *The Negro Family: The Case for National Action.* Drawing on social science research, this report suggested African Americans faced a "tangle of pathology" due to a pattern of black males' abandonment of their families. This study, which came to be known as the Moynihan Report, received immediate criticism for its "insensitivity, bordering on racism."[24] Leaving the Johnson administration shortly thereafter, Moynihan tried for New York City Council and retired to a professorship at Harvard University. In 1969, wooed by Richard Nixon's invitation to create a Family Assistance Plan, Moynihan put his Democratic allegiance aside to work for the Republican president. Again, in this capacity, he entered controversial territory by suggesting in a 1970 memo leaked to the press that "the issue of race could benefit from a period of 'benign neglect.'"[25]

The battle between Abzug and Moynihan stirred a debate over what kind of liberalism should define Democratic politics going forward. With the Cold War consensus unrepairable after the "Year of Intelligence," the Democratic Party's "vital center" ideology no longer held sway. Pressure from the New Politics Democratic wing loosened the grip of Cold War liberalism on the party and upset southern Democrats' stronghold in Congress. Yet, New Politics Democrats did not emerge as a new establishment, its power contested. The forces that created the Committee for a Democratic Majority (CDM) in 1972 continued to strengthen their organization and got behind anticommunist presidential candidate Henry "Scoop" Jackson in 1976. In New York, Moynihan was their pick. Recruited by CDM founders, he had most recently made a name for himself at the United Nations and, before that, as ambassador to India. He was additionally known for his pointed treatises in the *Public Interest* and *Commentary* theorizing how liberalism should be defined and what role the United States should play globally. His work in these journals, edited by close friends Irving Kristol and Norman Podhoretz, respectively, indicated his alliance with neoconservatives. He did not adopt this identifier introduced by Representative Michael Harrington and meant to be a term of disparagement.[26] Nevertheless, Moynihan spoke neoconservatives' language, believing affirmative action had gone too far and détente had diminished US dominance.

During the 1976 Senate race, Abzug and Moynihan were pilloried by their opposing camps, with past digressions relitigated and current positions dissected. Nationally, they were held up as examples of liberalism at two extremes. This infighting among Democrats proved fruitful for Republicans, who saw Moynihan as an ally and Abzug as a useful adversary to rile up the base. Moynihan had to answer for the Moynihan Report and his explication of "benign neglect," each of which was an "ancient mariner's albatross" around his neck.[27] The Council of Black Elected Democrats voted "without dissent" to oppose Moynihan, and New York state senator Herman Carl McCall warned Moynihan in the *New York Amsterdam News* not to campaign in Harlem, noting, "He may have lived in our community, but he is not one of us."[28] Meanwhile, Abzug had to explain once again why she crossed the picket line during the 1968 Ocean Hill–Brownsville strike, facing picketers in Concord as they sang, "Daniel Patrick Moynihan/ He's No Scab, He's Our Man/Bye, Bye Bella" to the tune of "Bye, Bye Blackbird."[29] Additionally, the Jewish Defense League pickets reappeared to question Abzug's dedication as a supporter of Israel.

In the mid-1970s, Moynihan became the conservative's "warrior intellectual" and Abzug the "conservative's devil."[30] Announcing his candidacy, Moynihan was delighted when Al Shanker and Bayard Rustin unexpectedly stood beside him as he promised "to tell hard truths about national policy in an age of policy ignorance and dishonesty" and "to defend this country and what it stands for in the world."[31] For a number of months, a contrasting image of Abzug had been circulating in the National Conservative Political Action Committee's (NCPAC's) first direct-mail campaign put together by the Right's fund-raising guru Richard Viguerie. Signed by North Carolina senator Jesse Helms, the letter called on conservatives to send in their donations so that they could "out-organize George McGovern and Bella Abzug" and their "sell-America-down-the-drain" forces. "Your tax dollars" are being squandered by "liberals and socialists" to pay for programs that "teach our children that cannabalism [sic], wife swapping, and the murder of infants and the elderly are acceptable behavior," Helms warned.[32] In the *New York Times,* journalist James Roach mocked the letter in "A Nemo to Jese Healms" for its misspelling of cannibalism.[33] Yet, NCPAC had the last laugh, for the letter raised roughly $10,000 per month (a substantial amount for the time).[34]

Alongside McGovern, Abzug proved to be among the strongest galvanizing forces nationally for conservatives during the 1976 campaign season. The Committee for Survival of a Free Congress, backed by Joseph Coors of Coors Brewing Company, sent out a pamphlet that placed Abzug's head at the center of a bull's-eye. In this mailing, thirty-one representatives were pictured on the target around Abzug and measured by how closely each "votes with Bella Abzug."[35] An effective tactic, this litmus test carried over to rhetoric on the campaign trail, where candidates disparaged opponents by calling them "a real Bella Abzug."[36] The extent to which these specific campaigns hurt Abzug in the polls was not quantified, but it is clear that this negative messaging aided her adversaries' critique, rallied conservatives, and encouraged a climate of incivility and unrest. Abzug presented enough of a risk that on June 13, 1975, the FBI informed her that she should not visit Oneonta, New York, for she had received a death threat.[37] Undeterred, she made the trip and delivered her speech anyway.

Abzug and Moynihan added fuel to the fire by zeroing in on each other's associations that their respective backers found disdainful. Liz Moynihan recalled that Pat and Bella agreed to keep things nice, deciding between themselves to focus on the issues. Liz nudged Pat in this direction, for she respected Abzug as a woman who had paved the way for women in politics.[38] Still, both candidates tested this civility. Scoop Jackson aide Elliott

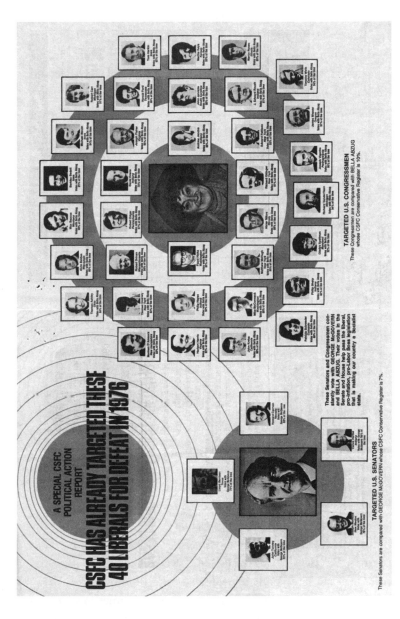

Figure 9.1 This conservative fund-raising brochure distributed nationally during the 1976 campaign singled out Representative Bella Abzug and Senator George McGovern as the leading symbols of liberalism gone awry. House candidates were measured by how close their voting records matched that of Abzug. (Bella Abzug Papers, Box 502, Rare Book and Manuscript Library, Columbia University)

Abrams predicted Abzug would "portray you in two guises: as a Nixon Republican and as an effete intellectual snob from Harvard."[39] Abzug did indeed suggest Moynihan was a turncoat Democrat and "Nixon's man." In contrast, she described herself as a reflection of "the best progressive and humane tradition of the party."[40] Moynihan had no less love for Abzug's brand of liberalism, subscribing to the view that "those who railed against a system that had guaranteed them a comfortable upper-middle class lifestyle" were hypocritical.[41] This antielite critique of New Politics Democrats ran alongside a longer-standing anticommunist view. The whisper campaign promoted by Moynihan confidants was that Abzug had been a member of the Young Communist League at Hunter College and had strong pro-Soviet leanings.[42] Additionally, Moynihan led voters toward the idea that Abzug was the same kind of radical as combative, theatrical countercultural protesters. After Yippie Aron Kay threw a mocha cream pie at Moynihan's face during a walking tour of Lower Manhattan, Abzug called to apologize.[43] Touched by this gesture, Moynihan nonetheless suggested during their last debate that her operatives had paid Kay to pull this stunt.

Abzug tried to disentangle her perceived association with leftist fringe groups by toning down her "battling Bella" persona. She did not want reporters to ask as one did before her formal announcement, "Is Bella as badass as they say?"[44] Her handlers did not think this question set the right tone and encouraged her to soften her image. Doing so was a mistake, however, because it allowed the contest to become a choice between feminine and masculine leadership. "Moynihan is a fighter," his campaign flyers professed.[45] In contrast, her campaign commercials featured a newly refined "Bella Abzug," slimmed down by twenty-five pounds. Showing she could be a good sport, she played the bugle on the *Mike Douglas Show* when asked if she could "toot her own horn."[46] While Abzug played along, she continued to find it frustrating that the measure of women's leadership abilities included attention to their physicality. She was thrilled when Timothy Crouse noted Moynihan's bad body odor in a story in *Rolling Stone*. Abzug wrote Crouse appreciatively, saying, "It's one of the first times anyone has suggested or even hinted" at this unbecoming feature. "You don't think I can use that against him in the campaign?"[47] More than appearance, character was measured in this race and those nationally. Many Americans wanted toughness in their leaders after defeat in Vietnam and amid feminist challenges to traditional masculinity. Leaders seen as either too weak and conciliatory or too bighearted and unrestrained fell out of favor.

At the Abzug campaign headquarters at 130 East Fortieth Street, campaign manager Doug Ireland peppered the office walls with unbecoming shots of Moynihan to remind staff and volunteers who they were up against—the movement organizer versus the policy wonk. Abzug stuck to her usual playbook. "There's no mystery in our plan," revealed Ireland. "All you have to do is get her in front of people."[48] She spent most weekends on the trail after her soft announcement in February 1975. She traveled by a small prop plane to New York's hinterlands, places like Watertown, Poughkeepsie, and Elmira. There, she wooed the crowds "as a celebrity," but "when it got down to specific issues, they did not agree with her on a lot of things."[49] Yet, the face time would pay off as she surprised the Moynihan camp with how well she did upstate. She had more trouble in the bedroom communities surrounding New York City, telling Gloria Steinem knowingly, "I'm everything these people move to the suburbs to escape."[50]

By the summer of 1976, with her operation in full swing, Abzug ran a nonstop retail campaign. Weekdays were reserved for walking tours of New York City, where three-quarters of expected primary voters lived. She could be seen on the boardwalk in Long Island, pitching sun-soaked bathers as Martin stood nearby waving his homemade "Bella for Senate" sign. On Women's Equality Day, the suffrage holiday on August 26 she helped officially designate, she made the case for gender parity locally, urging small donors on the street to "pass a buck to Bella."[51] The stars came out once again for Abzug—Marlo Thomas, Renée Taylor, Walter Matthau, Sidney Poitier, Henry Foner, Joan Rivers, Jack Lemmon, Warren Beatty, Barbra Streisand, Lauren Bacall, Jane Fonda, Candace Bergen, Elizabeth Taylor, Lee Grant, Shirley MacLaine, and Lily Tomlin all offering support.[52] Interest groups were formed to maximize voting blocs Abzug had cultivated since 1970, such as her "Gay Group" chaired by Leonard Bloom and Jean O'Leary and a "Committee of Hispanics for Bella Abzug."[53] Some principles were stretched to prioritize winning. She mandated that field offices be cochaired by a man and a woman, and that these operations be made "as totally representative of your community as you can."[54] At the same time, Abzug was criticized for an action that ran counter to this example; she asked Maggi Peyton, who ran Abzug's exploratory campaign and was a founding member of Manhattan's NWPC chapter, to become deputy director once Doug Ireland signed on to lead as campaign manager.

In contrast, Moynihan's campaign was first run out of former student Richard "Dick" Blumenthal's room at the Biltmore Hotel, and next Liz directed her husband's campaign activities from their New York City apartment. Joe Crangle soon recruited veteran manager Meyer "Sandy" Frucher to take over and build a field operation. An "assembly of Scoop Jackson supporters who suddenly had no work" were recruited as staff.[55] *Commentary*'s Penn Kemble came on board with Norman Podhoretz consulting unofficially, and Irving Kristol's son Bill was among the children of friends who volunteered time. Not one for retail campaigning, Moynihan rolled out his position papers as a hodgepodge of commencement speeches.[56] Most receptions to the candidate were favorable, but student walkouts did occur. Moynihan enjoyed debating, particularly because Abzug was a venerable match. "You cannot beat Senator Buckley by passing yourself off as Senator Buckley, which Pat Moynihan does," Abzug charged at their first televised face-off on August 23, 1976. In the audience, Doug Ireland commented, "This begins the real campaign."[57]

And yet, the campaign had effectively begun before Abzug had announced her candidacy officially or Moynihan had actively contemplated a run. In 1975, Ambassador Moynihan and Representative Abzug became participants in a tense global East-West scuffle to define new standards for human rights. This debate occurred against the backdrop of the end of the Vietnam War and as decolonizing nations asserted their independence. Abzug approached global human rights as an extension of civil rights struggles at home, whereas Moynihan saw the debate as an opportunity to remind the world of US cultural superiority in a continued battle against the Soviet Union. Both challenged the dominant current in the United Nations that declared, "Zionism is a form of racism." But their different postures, platforms, and pasts led hard-line Zionists and promoters of robust defense to see Moynihan as their greater champion.

Human Rights at War's End

A full year before the campaign, the difference between Moynihan and Abzug could not have been starker. One Democrat defended America's global hegemony, and the other called on director William Colby to justify the CIA's continued usefulness. After the 1974 midterms, President Ford's advisers suggested it would be expedient to create alliances with the former kind of Democrat to ostracize the latter. As one aide predicted, the Committee for a Democratic Majority would "play a helpful role in the defense debate we will face this year."[58] Selecting Moynihan as US ambassador to the United Nations was part of Ford's overture to the right wing of the Democratic Party. Moynihan had impressed with an article he wrote in the March 1975 issue of *Commentary* informed by his experience while ambassador to India. There, he had witnessed the nation successfully test a nuclear bomb, and the experience strengthened his "fear that a pinched and resentful British socialist worldview was shaping this Third World rebellion against the West."[59] Upon returning home, he postulated in "The United States in Opposition" that America should strongly defend its traditional role as a global beacon of democratic values. Calling the anti-imperialist bloc of decolonizing nations "the tyranny of the UN's 'new majority'" did not win Moynihan friends on the Left.[60] For others who agreed with Moynihan, including President Ford, he was instantly celebrated. Moynihan was heartened by the hundreds of letters he received, which he believed affirmed that "people are tired of our being ashamed of ourselves."[61]

Equally patriotic, Abzug agreed with Moynihan that American democratic values should be valorized throughout the world, but she faulted the US government for not living up to these ideals. She did not see this critique as a form of self-shame but instead as an important corrective function of democracy. For Moynihan and his followers, the fall of Saigon was a reprehensible humiliation. For Abzug and other antiwar critics, the end of the Vietnam War came one decade too late. In March 1975, she visited Phnom Penh, Cambodia, on a congressional fact-finding tour planned by the Pentagon to win Ford support for a $222 million emergency aid package. She returned "torn up over" the "sight of women and children dying of starvation in the streets," but unconvinced that more military aid would do anything but line "the pockets of generals."[62] Robert K. Wolthuis, a Ford aide on congressional relations, predicted her stance, believing Abzug went into the trip with "a closed mind."[63] In the House, she found herself on the losing side of this contentious appropriations floor debate that stretched to 2:40 a.m. and ended with more support troops sent to South Vietnam.[64] Days later, on April 29, North Vietnamese planes bombed the Tan Son Nhat airport, and President Ford hastily set in motion plans to get the last Americans home. Nightly news broadcasts pictured hundreds of evacuees filing onto the roof of the US embassy in Saigon, clamoring for spots on the final transports out.[65]

In 1975, Abzug committed to such a strong demilitarization and denu-
clearization stance that she reversed her decision not to join demonstrations
while in Congress. In early July, the *Washington Post* published a photograph of the congresswoman holding a sign saying, "Stop the Dooms Day
Clock," as she picketed outside the White House. She offered her staff to
help launch the WSP "Survival Campaign," and joined the protest herself,
because she found President Ford's "maximum flexibility" doctrine on
nuclear arms to be a deeply troubling abandonment of détente.[66] To his
critics on the Left, Ford seemed like he was gaming for another war. On
May 12, Khmer Rouge troops seized the *Mayaguez,* a US merchant ship, off
the coast of Cambodia. Instead of going the diplomatic route, Ford ordered
airstrikes and deployed 1,000 US Marines to the island of Koh Tong "irrespective of the Congress."[67] This blatant disregard of the War Powers
Resolution irked anti-interventionist Congress members such as Abzug,
who insisted, "The last thing we need now is to go back to bombing Cambodia."[68] American soldiers rescued the missing crew, but at the expense of
forty-one soldiers' lives lost and three missing. Peace activists took note that
the same day of the *Mayaguez* rescue, the US military tested a massive
hydrogen bomb underground in Nevada, "jarring the desert over a radius
of 100 miles."[69]

Meanwhile, decolonization efforts embroiled the United States and the
Soviet Union in a geopolitical tango for influence among developing nations. Beyond jockeying in an arms race, these superpowers engaged in a
hearts-and-minds campaign that spilled over to global governance bodies
and shaped their debates. In the 1970s, Americans witnessed a "moral
breakthrough of human rights" across the globe. Local participants strug-
gled for better living standards and drew international attention to their
concerns.[70] The Helsinki Accords, signed by thirty-five nations in 1975,
marked out new terms of engagement between nations in the East and the
West, including in the area of human rights. This issue became a bipartisan
touchstone for US politicians searching for "a way to heal the country by
taming the legacy of Vietnam," but ideological difference shaped their divergent approaches.[71] Abzug saw human rights as an avenue through
which to project US ideals outward while reining in the excesses of super-
power. Moynihan believed US human rights should be the global gold
standard, and when dissenting Americans highlighted their nation's shortcomings, they "hit democracies in the one area where they have the strongest case to make against the dictatorships."[72]

Abzug approached human rights as a Diasporic Jew who exhibited a post-Holocaust sensitivity to acts of discrimination, terrorism, and genocide. Beyond Vietnam, she intervened in foreign affairs most frequently on behalf of world Jewry. Through her subcommittee, she challenged US acquiescence to the Arab boycott and investigated why agencies failed to assign Jewish Americans to Middle East posts. "We cannot begin to say and continue to say we are the greatest democracy in this world, if we continue to allow ourselves to discriminate at home," she asserted, "but we allow other countries to tell us what kind of person that we can bring along, or what kind of policy."[73] Abzug exhibited a special concern for the plight of Soviet Jews. She wholeheartedly supported the 1974 Jackson-Vanik Amendment that enacted sanctions against the Soviet Union for religious persecution of this group, thereby setting a new moral standard in foreign aid decisions. Her alignment with anticommunists on this measure sponsored by Senator Scoop Jackson reflected her willingness to put Jewish interests first.[74]

In the mid-1970s, Israel became the fulcrum of US-Middle East relations in this theater of the ongoing Cold War.[75] Abzug maintained an "Israel exception" to her demilitarization drive in foreign policy. In doing so, she walked a precarious line on the American Left as radicals increasingly echoed the anti-Zionist call in global decolonization movements.[76] Swimming against the stream, she could not stomach the argument that Israel was a neocolonial aggressor in a postcolonial world. Abzug clung to the Socialist Zionist politics of her youth, retaining a utopic vision of what Israel could be even after Hashomer Hatzair shifted its position. In 1970, the group critiqued the rise of a "kind of fanatical and ritualistic Orthodoxy in Israel" that practiced "religious dictatorship" instead of "religious liberty."[77] While out of step with leftists moving toward a pro-Palestinian position, Abzug was in concert with most American Jews who saw Israel's self-determination as an expression of their Jewish particularism and a challenge to global anti-Semitism. After the 1967 Arab-Israeli War, American Jews increasingly believed that the "imperatives of survival superseded all other Jewish ethics," including engagement "in relentless military actions" that brought destruction upon others.[78]

Abzug's adoption of a Diasporic Israeli identity deepened after her August 1971 personal congressional tour of the nation "to see, to listen, and to learn about Israel's hopes, needs and problems."[79] During this trip, she broke bread with prominent women in government, visited an immigrant placement center welcoming 1,000 Soviet Jews per month, and toured institutions including twenty-four-hour child care centers in Jerusalem and Tel Aviv and the Hashomer Hatzair Study Center. The trip affirmed her view that Israel was a successful social democratic experiment and Israeli women were more liberated than American women.[80] Upon her return home, she organized Jewish women's groups to apply pressure on the State Department to resume contract talks with Israel to supply F-3 Phantom jets, thereby echoing the prominent view that the nation's future depended on this military aid.[81]

Abzug saw in Israel the nation she wanted to see. After touring the Golan Heights and West Bank, one of five occupied territories gained in 1967, she reflected, "You begin to realize how serious the problem of . . . the unresolved dispute is."[82] Still, she idealized Israel as a thriving democratic oasis in an otherwise "turbulent Middle East" mired in "implacable hatred for Israel."[83] In contrast, she characterized Arab governments as retrograde, destabilizing forces that "clearly prefer to keep the displaced Palestinians as a source of contention."[84] The Yom Kippur War in October 1973 reaffirmed Abzug's militaristic position that Israel had a "right to exist within secure and defensible borders."[85] She looked at Israel's postwar climate as she had war crime, refugee, and veterans issues at the close of the Vietnam War.[86] Visiting Israel in mid-November, she met with Prime Minister Golda Meir, whom she greatly admired, along with Representatives Ed Koch and Ben Rosenthal. During this session, Meir shared gruesome pictures of tortured Israeli soldiers left for dead by Syrian troops at Wadi Yahudi in the Golan Heights. The disturbing images shocked Abzug, who had advocated for US oversight of Israeli POW exchange before her trip and returned home determined to expose these atrocities to the world.[87] This experience hardened her view that Arab nations surrounding Israel were monstrous warmongers and the Palestine Liberation Organization was a terrorist organization. Accordingly, she framed aid to Israel as a humanitarian response and the targeting of Israeli companies and employees during the Arab boycott as a civil rights concern.[88]

This pro-Israel stance placed Abzug in an uncomfortable position at odds with many leftists and Zionists. She consistently had to defend her views to close friends who saw her Zionist allegiance as incompatible with her radicalism. Mim Kelber, a secular Jew unlike Abzug, accompanied her on her 1971 tour of Israel; having visited the same sites, she returned home convinced that Israelis mistreated Palestinians. While she frequently pressed Abzug on the issue, she nonetheless wrote pro-Zionist letters and speeches in the congresswoman's voice. Strangers and friends alike wrote Abzug to remind her "the Arab people are humans," chastising her for backing what amounted to $9.5 billion in aid by 1976.[89] At the same time, hard-line Zionists saw Abzug's socialist leanings and anti–Vietnam War position as evidence that she was not authentically Jewish. She became suspect by association, such as when the Women's International League of Peace and Freedom sent a letter with her name listed as a sponsor on the letterhead to seventy-six senators condemning Israel's request for $2.5 billion in military aid.[90] Learning about the letter from a constituent, she was livid and promptly resigned. The mishap nonetheless led some Zionists to question her commitment.

Abzug uniquely crafted an identity as a pro-Israel Jewish progressive with a "special responsibility" to promote social justice.[91] For Abzug, this justice work began within Judaism, where sex divisions still governed how and where women could pray and lead in prayer. She actively urged Jewish women to become feminists and Jewish feminists to affirm their Judaism. In one characteristic exchange, she told B'nai B'rith members, "You know what" your name "means in Hebrew? The sons of the covenant . . . you're daughters of the covenant."[92] Speaking before the National Council of Jewish Women, she reflected, "I think it's very constructive that more and more Jewish Women are asking questions about their rights. . . . They are asking how our Jewish tradition . . . can accommodate itself to the changing role of women in our society."[93] Abzug contributed to this change, inviting Rabbi Sally Priesand to deliver the morning invocation on the House floor, the first woman of any religious denomination to do so.[94] To facilitate this first was an honor for Abzug, who had once contemplated going down Priesand's path if only it had been open to her.

While nurturing Jewish feminism within the United States, Abzug engaged in an outward defense of Israel and Jewishness in the global arena. In July 1975, she served as a congressional observer at the World Conference on Women in Mexico City in conjunction with the UN International Women's Year (IWY) initiative. There, Zionism became a hot-button issue as representatives of developing nations expressed solidarity with the Palestinian movement. Abzug had not been greatly involved in the lead-up to IWY, and she swept into Mexico City with great fanfare to attend for three days. While she prepared most beforehand to advocate for a strong disarmament platform and gender parity in global governance, the Zionist debate already under way immediately consumed her. The World Plan of

Action remained neutral on Israel, but the accompanying Declaration of Mexico linked "the struggle of any form of oppression, such as is practiced under colonialism, neo-colonialism, zionism, racial discrimination and apartheid," and called on "women and men together" to eliminate these ills.[95] This equivalency had been increasingly made in the months before IWY, but this UN document would be the first to overtly draw this line. Appalled, Abzug effectively urged the US delegation to not simply abstain but to vote against these "totally irrelevant" resolutions. In doing so, the United States stood alone with Israel.[96]

The Declaration of Mexico served as a rallying cry for marginalized women, but Abzug could not see it as such. She insisted that women's lack of representation on some delegations was the reason this anti-Zionist resolution passed, and romanticized that having more women in the "tower of male supremacy" would produce a different outcome.[97] In making this case, she stretched the gender parity argument she delivered at home to accommodate her pro-Israel aims abroad. While consistent with her critique of hegemonic male leadership in the US government, the argument uncomfortably paralleled US officials' Cold War assumption that women within the Soviet orbit were Communist pawns who did not act for themselves when promoting women's rights.[98] Ironically, constituents accused Abzug of this very thing after she visited China in January 1976 as part of a delegation of US congresswomen, invited for a ten-day tour by the Chinese government. Bella, on a tape recorder, and Martin, on his video camera, captured this significant diplomatic exchange marking the further thawing of US-China tensions. Bella used Martin's film as a fund-raising tool for her campaign, but her presence in China was also an organizing vehicle for anticommunist women in New York who vowed to "defeat you in your coming campaign, for anything."[99]

Despite Abzug's pro-Zionist challenge at the IWY meeting, her anticommunist, pro-Israel critics believed that "she did not get that Russians were behind the 'Zionism is racism' campaign."[100] During the conference, President Ford and Secretary of State Henry Kissinger met with Moynihan to brief the UN ambassador on IWY and about the likelihood that the Israel issue would dominate the General Assembly that fall. He responded, "The only consensus now is screw the United States. The reputation of the US keeps eroding and that reputation is important to us." In the Cold War culture war, "words matter."[101]

In November, it became clear that the United States would not be able to impede the General Assembly's passage of Resolution 3379 declaring, "Zionism is a form of racism." Moynihan charged in a pointed speech before this body that the anti-Zionist resolution was a "terrible lie" that tarnished "the integrity of that whole body of moral and legal precepts which we know as human rights."[102] The performance endeared Moynihan to hard-line Zionists and thoroughly pleased his Jewish neoconservative friends, who defined support of Israel as a central tenet of their pro-defense, Cold War–driven foreign policy agenda. It also impressed Democratic presidential nominee Jimmy Carter, who later consented to Moynihan being "quietly picked" to draft the foreign policy plank as a member of the Platform Committee during June 1976. When Abzug protested Moynihan's appointment, he alleged that she had threatened to withhold support for Carter, which she called a "total lie."[103] The resulting foreign policy plank little resembled the one that she had helped draft when in the same position in 1972. Removed from the process, she could not help but lament that the plank "could have been written in the Pentagon."[104]

While Abzug publicly condemned Resolution 3379 when it passed in late 1975 as "anti-colonialist chic," Moynihan's pro-Zionist challenge at the UN outmatched her own; his pro-defense line gained greater credence in the Democratic Party as it shifted rightward.[105] Sensing Abzug's vulnerability in this area, Norman Podhoretz counseled Moynihan during the Senate race, "I think you have to attack her . . . be more clear and ringing" on defense.[106] Agreeing, the Moynihan campaign circulated flyers that pictured the ambassador in action at the UN and noted, "He Spoke Up for America . . . He'll Speak Up for New York."[107] This powerful imagery enabled Moynihan, a Roman Catholic, to pass the pro-Israel test. In contrast, some New Yorkers called out to Abzug in Yiddish or Hebrew when she was campaigning to see if she could respond and thus was really Jewish.[108] And so, it would be Moynihan's "tough-guy language" and his "politics of patriotic indignation" delivered at the UN during the Zionism debate that set the tone for foreign policy through the Reagan years.[109]

At the IWY meeting in Mexico City, Abzug addressed another concern that would divide Democrats: the rise of global capitalism and neoliberalism. She left the UN conference site to address women advocates at the unofficial Non-Governmental Organization (NGO) Tribune nearby. There, she called for international women's solidarity against the ominous multinational corporation. A "third world of women" exists inside the United States, she reported. "They are economically oppressed . . . and they are losing their jobs to women and young girls in Taiwan, Hong Kong and the Philippines who are employed by our own multinational corporations."[110] This condemnation of US corporate greed and show of sympathy for the working poor played well at the Tribune, but it would be the politics of choice and personal responsibility that became the dominant posture in the United States and the Democratic Party going forward.

Campaigning for More in an Era of Limits

Moynihan and Abzug attempted to outdo each other as populists appealing to working-class voters. She did not believe attracting blue-collar workers or housewives was a lost cause, and directed less attention while campaigning to middle-class interests. She continued to valorize laborers, believing they needed greater champions and that the collective organization of workers would lead to a more social democratic society. As she had in past campaigns, she advocated inclusive unionism that reflected the diversifying workforce and shifting service- and technology-driven economy. Conversely, Moynihan's union backers, recruited by New York AFL-CIO leader Ray Corbett, reflected labor's old guard.[111] Abzug highlighted her time representing dockworkers in night court, walked construction sites in a hard hat, and toured the New York harbor to remind voters that she brought $40 million in harbor cleanup funds to the city.[112] Despite these gestures, Moynihan's working-class origins and short stint as a longshoreman enabled him to better frame his blue-collar overture as stemming from personal experience.[113] For both, economic populism was a performance, for they enjoyed the comforts of upper-middle-class living.

Abzug prioritized attention to class in part because she was aware that New Politics Democrats faced an economic hurdle. The party's efforts to democratize its ranks and leadership along race and gender lines occurred as affirmative action fell out of favor and as second- and third-generation European immigrants, claiming their whiteness, promoted greater ethnic pride.[114] Increasingly, neoconservatives' argument that New Politics Democrats were a bunch of elites crying about identity held sway, and interests like environmentalism and consumer protection became coded as liberal and antilabor. Recognizing these handicaps, New Politics Democrats met in Chicago in March 1975 to assess their agenda going forward. At this gathering, pollsters Louis Harris, Patrick Caddell, and Peter Hart told the group that the public wanted "not simply progressive, but radical, answers to shake the country out of its economic slide." Addressing the crowd, Abzug concurred, calling on her counterparts to "hack out . . . a progressive or radical program for the economy."[115] She used her Senate campaign to model what this progressive economic platform could be.

While Abzug spoke to national economic concerns, the crisis close to home captured her attention. She joined New York Congress members on the Ad Hoc Committee on Aid to New York City that met frequently in 1975 to address how to help City Hall solve its financial shortfall. The situation had worsened, in part, because New York State required New York City to "share substantially in the cost of services" at a level "much greater than any other state placed on its cities."[116] Moreover, New York City paid "a major share—25%—of federal and welfare Medicaid programs" nationally.[117] Facing ballooning pensions and poverty, City Hall scrambled to keep up with this arrangement.

By early 1975, it was clear that something had to give, which first meant cutbacks. Every aspect of city life felt the pinch, with shorter library hours, infrequent trash collection, fewer police on the streets, and hospitals and schools closing doors.[118] Abzug's office scrambled to issue statements of protest, reactive measures that did little to lessen the blow. In May 1975, she amplified her persistent call for federal support, urging President Ford to offer New York City $1.1 billion in aid. In July, Abzug commenced a task force to develop "legislation particularly helpful to the City."[119] However, she did not expect public intervention would be enough. She called for a voluntary bailout, encouraging workers to donate an hour's or a day's wage and city banks to provide more. This solution reflected her interest in neighborhood-driven collective betterment and willingness to turn to private support ultimately if government fell short. Ironically, progressives' instinctive move toward community control invariably created space for private response to this public fiscal crisis, helping pave the way toward a neoliberal future of services delivered in public-private partnership.[120]

On October 17, the crisis was averted when the United Federation of Teachers union agreed to buy municipal bonds to infuse the city coffers with cash. At the time, New York City had only $34 million on hand to pay its debts and $453 million coming due.[121] After this bailout, Ford signaled in December that the federal government would provide $2.3 billion in short-term loans to the city at 8 percent interest.[122]

The national preoccupation with the fate of New York City further stirred an ethical debate about "responsibility" along three axes: personal responsibility to be self-sufficient, government responsibility to its citizens, and US corporate responsibility to workers in a globalizing economy. How Abzug and Moynihan responded in all three areas represented two paths forward in the Democratic Party—the social democratic orientation that was losing its shaky grip and the neoliberal order that took hold.

In the face of economic downturn, Abzug advocated kicking growth liberalism into high gear as most legislators veered away from this big-spending, restorative approach. Abzug and Moynihan both recognized that the promise of more jobs was sweet music to Democratic voters' ears. As an incumbent, Abzug could more easily claim results. Her Public Works Committee appointment had well positioned her to channel millions to New York State—and especially New York City—through infrastructure and environmental cleanup initiatives.[123] She pointed most notably to her support of the Public Works Employment Act, which brought New Yorkers 60,000 new jobs. After House members overrode President Ford's veto, Abzug claimed victory and described the legislative negotiations as a story of David and Goliath.[124] She described her policy accomplishments in terms of dollars and cents. Yet, her inclusive populist message, "Bella Abzug works for *ALL* New Yorkers," had been an easier sell in 1970.[125] By 1976, with the economic slump deeper and longer felt, white male blue-collar workers increasingly trafficked in the politics of resentment, and Abzug's brand of progressive populism appealed mainly to the already converted. She nonetheless attempted to will these laborers out of narrow-mindedness and compel them to see how deindustrialization, deregulation, and globalization hurt all American workers. However, her equally pointed structural critique of suburbanization, urban renewal, and privatization implicated some of the voters she was trying to reach.

Abzug delivered a familiar bread-and-butter pitch to prime her audience for her esoteric deconstruction of the expansion of global capitalism. She tried to make clear how US-based corporations, in their insatiable chase of profit, first left New York for states with right-to-work laws and huge tax breaks, and next moved their production abroad. New York State was becoming the "new Appalachia of America," she warned, an alarmist take that reflected her regional parochialism.[126] Speaking to Americans beyond her state, she urged workers to transcend regional and identity-based differences in a collective challenge of outsourcing and deindustrialization. Conglomerates knew no borders, she argued, and thus American workers' only hope was to challenge the flight of jobs, capital, and resources by overcoming differences and building transregional and transnational labor solidarity. For, as she suggested in one campaign speech, "A displaced garment worker in New York, a shoeworker in New England or an electronics worker in the Midwest does not have the same kind of interest in what happens in the Far East or Latin America as a multinational corporation."[127] In contrast, Moynihan described the multinational corporation as the "most creative institution of the 20th century," emphasizing business innovation as an expression of democratic vigor.[128] In his view, US corporations' global expansion was an important extension of the Cold War foreign policy campaign to stave off Communist rule. Moynihan saw decolonizing nations' move toward state socialism as "a convenient excuse for concentrating power."[129]

Abzug's social democratic leanings were read by some critics as anticapitalist and thus antidemocratic. But it was her determination to realize the best version of the US democratic capitalist system that drove her creative thinking about how to fix America's ailing economy. She believed one necessary path forward was to shift the US economy away from foreign oil dependency and toward greater attention to environmentalism. Abzug became an environmentalist before this movement came into public view with the first Earth Day in 1970. One decade prior, peace women amplified public concern of the health and ecological costs of nuclear testing. Upon arriving in Congress, Abzug authored the 1972 Federal Water Pollution Act Amendments, focused doubly on the social problem of dirty water and unemployment; New York received $1 billion in new construction. She believed environmental jobs bills were not only an ecological necessity but also smart economically.

This viewpoint, popularized in the twenty-first century, was a new way of thinking in the mid-1970s. New York, Abzug argued during her Senate campaign, could be the "lead in becoming the solar energy equipment manufacturing capital of the nation."[130] She recognized that jobs in this new energy sector came at the cost of old jobs in less environmentally

Figure 9.2 Bella Abzug continued to reach out to "hard hats" such as these construction workers during her Senate campaign, proposing an economic program focused on retooling the economy, adjusting to an expanding workforce, and redistributing wealth. (Uncredited, Martha Baker Papers, Box 11, Rare Book and Manuscript Library, Columbia University)

friendly industries, and that new environmental standards impacted production. For this reason, she introduced a bill that sought to protect jobs from elimination in plants shut down due to environmental regulation violations. But she thought this temporary fix must be presented alongside a reeducation effort—convincing laborers that the oil industry was the "real anti-jobs group."[131] These ideas, while forward-thinking, sounded to some like the musings of a candidate who had the luxury not to face immediate economic strains.

A leading advocate of public transportation in Congress, Abzug's support of the construction industry through transportation bills offered the most material example of her booster efforts on behalf of blue-collar workers. She collaborated with Massachusetts Democrat Gerry E. Studds to pass the Interstate Transfer Amendment to the 1973 Highway Act, which allowed cities and states to trade in federal funds slated for highways to build public transit lines instead. In 1976, Abzug also helped quash a repeal effort known as the "Beame Shuffle," which would have cut $100 million in mass transit subsidies. Abzug devoted most attention to repairing New York mass transit, bringing $42 million to the struggling system in 1976. Appreciative, the Metropolitan Transportation Authority gave her a "golden token" for her effort. Her advocacy for the city was so dependable that Deputy Mayor Jim Cavanagh assigned aide Peter J. Kiernan to be her attaché to get legislation moving. He would often accompany her to Washington on the train ride down.[132] Still, more privileged New Yorkers thought Abzug's protection of access to public transportation extreme, and her campaign against increasing New York City subway fares a handout to the poor. She tried to frame mass transit as a "precious natural resource— one of our nation's greatest energy savers, job producers and environmental protectors."[133] However, this argument was a hard sell to both unionists, who worried about their jobs, and environmentalists, who criticized Abzug's acquiescence to construction unions and developers. She believed she had been plenty strong on this issue as a ceaseless critic of the proposed West Side Highway (also known as Westway) along the Hudson River.[134] She approached infrastructure concerns practically, sympathetic to both sides of the development debate as a labor backer and committed environmentalist.

Weighing labor interests and identity-based rights, for Abzug, was not a choice of one or the other. Her insistence that these concerns could be mutually achieved was showcased in her most understated legislative accomplishment. Prompted by disability advocates, Abzug drafted an amendment added to the 1976 Federal Highway Act that slated safety funds earmarked in the bill for the creation of wheelchair ramps. Before this point, these ramps were not widely available, and afterward they became part of the American streetscape.[135] Her former aides see this accessibility measure that also enabled job creation as "an important thing we did—and one for which Bella got little or no credit."[136]

At times, Abzug's determination to stimulate the economy and preserve basic government services led her to set aside social liberationist goals. One decision—to support the Hyde Amendment—has had lasting repercussions. In September 1976, she supported a congressional override of President Ford's veto of the Department of Labor and Department of Health, Education, and Welfare appropriation bill. Opponents of social spending ingenuously attached the Hyde Amendment, which vastly curbed lower-income women's access to abortion, to this bill as a tactic to derail it. While Abzug characterized the Hyde Amendment as "unconstitutional, illegal, and discriminatory," she felt her hands were tied and decided that funding essential social services was the most immediate concern.[137] Uncomfortable with this concession, she teamed with lawyer Sarah Weddington to get a federal court to issue an injunction to put off implementation of the amendment, stalling its blow. But this temporary maneuver did not change the lasting impact of the Hyde Amendment, which effectively ensured that access to abortion would be a privilege, not a right. Accordingly, the politics of "choice" that has come to define women's reproductive rights became linked to the mounting rally for greater personal responsibility of one's economic destiny.

Moynihan believed that Democrats should cultivate political and economic choice—classic liberalism—as their central creed. Abzug remained resolutely committed to the idea that government had a responsibility to provide its citizens with a basic social safety net. As a student activist, she had critiqued the exclusionary features of New Deal social programs. As a legislator, she defended the welfare programs established in the 1930s and 1960s, urging fellow lawmakers to leave Social Security, Medicaid, and other benefits alone. She had hoped that the call for "new politics" would bring forward the next phase of welfare state expansion. While in Congress, she introduced and backed public benefits, health care, and equitable wage campaigns focused on unemployed housewives, agricultural and domestic workers, disabled people, temporary workers, and senior citizens. Congressional advocates achieved piecemeal victories, unable to shift the tide toward austerity.

Abzug still sought to expand social services in a climate of cutbacks. She proposed establishing new agencies such as a Department of Elderly Services. These efforts were futile. Increasingly, progressives hung on to small victories, such as a twelve-month extension Abzug helped negotiate for elderly and disabled Social Security recipients—an estimated 260,0000 in New York City—to be eligible for food stamps in 1974.[138] Mostly, they scrambled to save what services were left, for the city's financial woes had made municipal officials more open to reorienting care toward the private sector. After Nixon's veto of the universal child care bill she had helped draft, Abzug found the constriction of public day care services in New York City particularly demoralizing. In defense of what little existed, she lodged a suit with local child care advocates that helped keep forty-nine city day care centers open in 1976.[139]

The most tragic outcome of the fiscal crisis, in Abzug's view, was the reorganization of the City University of New York, a system of free higher education for 129 years. In June 1976, its tuition-free days came to an end. Abzug saw CUNY as a "symbol of hope and hard work, of free inquiry and limitless opportunity."[140] She joined student and faculty efforts to keep its programs, campuses, open enrollment, and subsidized tuition intact. Personalizing her fight, she called the budget cuts "a smokescreen" to eliminate Hebrew language courses at Hunter College she had helped introduce as a student.[141] Abzug believed what befell CUNY indicated a wider "destruction by abandonment" that would have lasting repercussions.[142] She was not incorrect. The shift away from affordable higher education reflected a widespread scaling down of government commitment to aiding Americans' pursuit of opportunity.

Abzug rightly worried that Moynihan's call for "liberty" over "equality" marked the Democratic Party's reorientation from a party of working people to a party of the white-collar middle class. Abzug argued that the turn away from welfare conveniently coincided with a turn toward inequitable taxation. The system increasingly placed a burden on the lowest income bracket while wealthy Americans took advantage of tax loopholes, what she called "welfare for the rich."[143] Moynihan, she charged, as "an architect of the Nixon-GOP policy of neglect for American cities," bore "some of the responsibility" for the hard times that the urban poor faced.[144] Moynihan disagreed. Pushing back, he called Abzug an obstructionist who welcomed the defeat of the Family Assistance Plan, a bill he helped draft in 1972 that fizzled in the Senate. He countered that Abzug, and progressives like her, encouraged Americans not to take ownership of their own actions and failures.[145] This debate about who was deserving and undeserving, while not clearly dividing along urban-suburban-rural lines, exacerbated tensions and misconceptions about how people lived and prospered in these distinct areas.

This heated political discussion about the government's obligation to its citizens manifested in part because Americans were losing their sense of economic, familial, and national security. Indeed, Americans' increased attention to what came, in this moment, to be described as "family values" was an economic response as much as an expression of social anxiety. The nuclear family model that valorized a male single-earner and housewife at home did not reflect the reality facing most middle-class and working-class American households that now needed two full-time incomes to get by. Economic insecurity was exacerbated by increased numbers of divorces, more single-parent households and common-law unions, and minority groups' demands for recognition and sexual freedom. Aware of these changes under way, Abzug offered a program focused on lessening Americans' painful transition to a new economy and new family structure. Contrastingly, Moynihan stoked the concerns of New Yorkers lamenting the breakdown of the American family and an industrial workforce that were no longer tenable. During the Democratic primary, he introduced family values rhetoric, contending, "The family is under siege."[146]

Moynihan was not subtle in his view that women workers were most to blame. "Dependency of women and children probably will grow," he argued, "because of the shift in the job market away from male-defined jobs."[147] Responding, Abzug spoke of fairness. She reminded that women were one-third of the workers let go during the recent recession and argued that enhancing women's financial standing and workplace opportunity would strengthen the US economy. The 1974 Equal Credit Opportunity Act (ECOA) she helped pass boosted women's economic independence most. For the first time, the law required financial institutions to offer single and married women their own bank accounts, credit cards, mortgages, and school and business loans. Before this landmark law, women were in a sense nonpersons economically, for it was assumed that fathers or husbands handled their financial affairs. Representative Leonor Sullivan (D-MO), chair of the Banking and Currency Committee's Consumer Affairs Subcommittee, introduced the first bill calling for a complete revolution of the banking industry's treatment of women. In May 1972, Abzug followed with a bill that extended beyond Sullivan's design, enhancing its legal enforcement mechanisms; Abzug's version became the leading bill.[148] The Equal Credit Opportunity Act greatly augmented American women's economic rights. But for women who favored the protection of dependency over the uncertainty of independence, this law served as one more indicator that legal benefits they enjoyed were under attack.

The debate that unfolded in New York over a state Equal Rights Amendment made clear that legal feminism was an ideological minefield. "ERA— Equality or Subjugation? Vote NO! on November 4, 1975," read one anti-ERA flyer circulating in New York.[149] Indeed, 1.4 million upstate voters did just so, eclipsing the 914,617 who voted yes in the region. In New York City, while 449,214 voted yes, 310,900 voted no.[150] As a result, it was asked, "Is Abzug tarred by the ERA brush?"[151] "Does the women's movement still have clout?"[152] Facing these questions as the Senate race heated up was not what Abzug would call fun. She brushed aside the state ERA defeat, crediting it to the low turnout among New York City voters—only 25 percent. She also blamed the pro-ERA camp for being outorganized. Abzug's staff exhibited greater worry, recognizing that economic concerns were increasingly framed as identity issues. Paired with antiabortion organizing, the anti-ERA drive read primarily as a cultural challenge. Abzug tried to disentangle these oppositional campaigns, but she did not do so effectively.

New York had become a testing ground for and seedbed of social conservatism. Long Island housewives were among Ellen McCormack's most ardent backers when the Right to Life Party leader ran for president in the Democratic Party in 1976. McCormack did not get far in the primaries, but she gained enough support that she qualified for a Secret Service detail. Antiabortion activists were a nuisance during Abzug's simultaneous campaign. Staff hung on to flyers these protestors passed out noting, "Is this life worth eight cents?"[153] Moynihan cultivated the support of this growing faction within the Democratic Party. Speaking to their concerns, he made clear that he "deplored abortion" but also suggested he would stand by the *Roe v. Wade* decision. Abzug challenged his position, but she also hedged on the issue. She attempted to deflate the emotional punch of this increasingly hot-button concern by suggesting that abortion "is not a political issue . . . it's an intensely personal issue."[154]

Abzug could not get away from bedroom politics because she had helped join the call for civil rights and sexual freedom in the federal arena. Notably, in 1974, she had introduced the first legislation in Congress that focused on gay civil rights. Untouchable, the Equality Act stalled right out of the gate. Regrouping in 1975, she introduced H.R. Resolution 166, which proposed adding "affectional or sexual preference" to Title VII of the 1964 Civil Rights Act.[155] With twenty-three cosponsors, this effort began with more promise but died once it was referred to the House Judiciary Committee for review. Her third try in 1976 had an equally dismal, quick end. Abzug urged Americans to draw on their "fair mindedness . . . and their concern for human rights" to broaden their views on sexuality.[156] This advocacy excited lesbians, gay men, and transsexuals nationally. Those inspired included Harvey Milk, a camera shop owner who made sure to meet Abzug during her West Coast Senate fund-raising sweep, and one year later ran for the San Francisco Board of Supervisors.[157] The effort to open political spaces not only to women but to gay people too had caught on.

"New Yorkers have never had a woman representing them in the Senate," Abzug often proclaimed on the campaign trail.[158] She believed this gender appeal would transcend ideological divides, but representational politics had become toxic. In 1970, her slogan, "The Women's Place Is in the House—the House of Representatives," felt fresh and bold at the upswing of a mass feminist movement and Democratic New Politics. In 1976, feminist women and men remained laser focused on breaking the Senate glass ceiling, with Patsy Mink running for Senate in Hawaii as well. What had changed was the ferocity of the organized resistance feminists faced, intent on rolling back legal advances in civil rights and remedying the seeming deterioration of social values. Resistance to the democratization of electoral politics paralleled a backlash against school integration and affirmative action in higher education. Likewise, the claim of "reverse discrimination" in university admissions and workplace advancement paralleled concern over an erosion of family values.

The slight edge women and racial minorities had gained in office and in the workforce stirred anxiety about the displacement of white, male, heterosexual leadership in all areas—marriage, education, business, and government. Abzug found it particularly rich that Jewish men were among the most adamant challengers of affirmative action in higher education and helped introduce the language of color blindness in critiques of Title IX of the Educational Amendments of 1972. Patsy Mink took the lead in Title IX legislation, driven by her experience being denied entrance into medical school. Abzug signed on as a central sponsor, commiserating with Mink over their difficult time in law school and the male-dominated legal profession. Speaking to Jewish women on this issue, Abzug made clear that Jewish men had prioritized their white male privilege at women's expense. For Jewish women, she argued, "have been and are still being discriminated against as women in hiring and promotion in the colleges and universities."[159]

By highlighting how class was in fact gendered and racialized, Abzug became a symbol of identity politics placed in opposition to the working class, an imagined group defined by whiteness and maleness. Critics of the federal government's remapping of civil rights law in the 1960s and 1970s increasingly dismissed this new landscape by claiming color blindness and disassociating rights from economic parity. During her Senate run, Abzug aimed to heighten public attention to this antirights strategy. She offered an alternative vision of inclusive labor collectivism, which she hoped would counter the widening gulf between race, class, and gender. Her progressive populism was predicated on an insistence that the government respond even more so to Americans' growing diversity, not reverse course. This sell was increasingly difficult as legislators worked to tighten budgets and the electorate that had benefited most from exclusionary policies felt increasingly wronged.

Issues mattered in New York's tight Senate Democratic primary, but so did actions. The *New York Post* (not yet a Rupert Murdoch paper) endorsed Abzug for her "maturity and responsibility in many crucial legislative conflicts," but it was her obstinacy that made a close race tighter.[160] The weekend she stopped by the Duchess County Fair she was understaffed, her closest aides fatigued. A reporter asked her a weighted question, "Will you support Moynihan if you lose?" Abzug answered with an honest "No." Doug Ireland thought it was the wrong answer, later saying, "I told her very early on, 'Look, I don't really give a good crap whether or not you support Pat Moynihan. You simply cannot say in public that you won't support him if he wins.'"[161] Ireland remained convinced that this admission hurt Abzug in the ballot box.

Press adviser Harold Holzer and deputy manager Maggi Peyton were not with Abzug that day, having opted out. They were tired from what one campaign aide described as Abzug's practice of "smiling at voters, and . . . muttering peppery phrases of displeasure at some aspect of staff performance."[162] She had been hard on them the previous day. "We traveled for a hundred weekends in two years, and we still regret that . . . one weekend we didn't go," recalled Holzer.[163] Joe Crangle took advantage of the misstep, suggesting Abzug's repudiation of Moynihan was "all too reminiscent of 1968 when Bella Abzug and others were wringing their hands over the Humphrey-Muskie ticket."[164] Sarah and Victor Kovner countered in a letter to the editor, "The furor in the press over Representative Abzug's reluctance to support a Moynihan candidacy" is "mystifying."[165]

What happened next augmented the blow. The *New York Times* endorsed Moynihan for the Senate. Harold Holzer could not believe his eyes. Nor could Abzug. She furiously underlined her copy of the editorial, writing a question mark next to the sentence "Pat Moynihan strikes us as the most knowledgeable, the most eloquent and, politically, the most believable voice that our city and state could acquire."[166] Ireland believed that Abzug's gaffe "pushed Punch Sulzberger over the line," but the *New York Times* publisher and Moynihan were friendly; Sulzberger had been looking for an excuse to override the editorial board's endorsement of Abzug and did so.[167]

It came as a shock to Opinion Page editor John B. Oakes, who, when he heard of the switch, stopped his car at the nearest phone booth he could find on a drive back from Martha's Vineyard to dictate a rejoinder. "I must express disagreement with the endorsement in today's editorial columns of Mr. Moynihan over four other candidates in the New York Democratic primary contest for the United States Senate," wrote Oakes.[168] This dissenting editorial did little, for the damage was done. Moynihan was so pleased with his *New York Times* endorsement, he carried the clipping in his pocket and pulled it out at final campaign stops. The day after the election, he received a special delivery from Sulzberger. Opening the package, he discovered an apron embossed with the message, "I got my job through the *New York Times*."[169]

As columnist James Wechsler called it, Moynihan's "cliff-hanger of a victory" amounted to "the arithmetic" of three liberals in the race rather than "an endorsement of conservative Democratic doctrine or repudiation of liberalism."[170] Yet, Moynihan had roused enough enthusiasm to capitalize on this arithmetic, and the Abzug campaign had seen this end coming. Her aides and surrogates had tried to pressure Ramsey Clark and Paul O'Dwyer to drop out of the race, but they would not budge. NDC leaders formed the Coalition of Progressive Democrats for Bella Abzug and sent out a last-minute letter to New York mailboxes urging progressives to unite around her candidacy.[171] O'Dwyer "called me to express his regrets" after the loss, Abzug relayed, but she never forgave him.[172] She held a stronger grudge against Clark, for during a debate he had suggested that unequal representation of women in politics need not be part of the conversation. Doug Ireland thought their fund-raising troubles hurt Abzug, believing, "If I had been able to find another hundred thousand dollars for television ads in Buffalo, we would have won."[173] It was tempting to go through these postelection what-ifs, for the electoral difference that made Moynihan the victor and Abzug loser was narrow—he received 329,830 votes and she garnered 317,348.[174]

The Moynihan campaign did not expect Abzug to do so well upstate. She took Buffalo, Joe Crangle's territory, a tribute to her early campaigning in the area and women-led field operation in three-quarters of all New York counties. Irene Drajem, leader of the Greater Democratic Women's Club in Erie County, recruited "475 women" to make "forty thousand phone calls in three weeks."[175] Their effort secured Abzug's county win. It was this kind of outreach that Abzug had advocated in Women Strike for Peace one decade prior and in the National Women's Political Caucus since. Even so, the combined forces of Democratic women and social movement activists did not secure her win. She took Cayuga, Chautauqua, and Chemung, but not Chenango, Clinton, Columbia, Cortland, or the substantial Cattaraugus counties. The sum of these parts tipped the scale toward Moynihan, breaking the draw he and Abzug had in New York City and its suburbs. His inroads with Jewish voters and Scoop Jackson fans helped, but Abzug had garnered significant support among black and Puerto Rican voters.[176]

Abzug expected to win, and she had difficulty accepting the loss. The morning of the primary, Bella and Martin had voted at the Food and Maritime Trade Jobs Hall at 208 West Thirteenth Street. It was Abzug's final nod to being an everywoman for the common man. That night, the orchestra played at her victory party set up at the Embassy Suite of the Summit Hotel, but poll returns dampened the mood. Abzug had prepared only a victory speech, in which she expected to proclaim, "We made it! . . . We're going to have a Senate with one less millionaire, and at least one woman. And believe me, it's about time."[177] Over lunch in the House dining room a few months prior, Ron Dellums had "created the cardinal sin." "I said, 'Suppose you lose,'" he remembered, and "She got totally upset. . . . She totally blistered me out."[178]

Losing by such a slim margin gave Abzug a glimmer of hope that the results were still disputable. On September 21, hundreds in "Bella's Brigade completed one more mission . . . to recanvass the votes registered on the stored, voting machines" throughout the state.[179] The massive effort did not compel the Board of Elections to change the original result. With this avenue closed, Abzug tried to get back in her district's race, enlisting Mary Ann Krupsack to lean on city councilman Ted Weiss to cede his primary win and step aside. When announcing his candidacy, Weiss had publicly suggested he would drop out if Abzug abandoned the Senate bid, and she had assured him that the Senate seat alone was what she was after.[180] Both reneged on these sentiments, and Weiss did not appreciate Krupsack's pressure tactics. He told reporters that she had threatened, "They will hold the male-dominated Democratic Party responsible." Krupsack fired back, noting, I told "him that there was growing concern that women, minorities, the liberal wing might stay home in November because of what had happened to Bella."[181] Abzug explored running on the Liberal Party ticket, but the offer came too late.[182] She had always had a fraught relationship with Liberal Party leader Alex Rose, and she worried about her chances on a third-party ticket. Additionally, she had accrued a considerable debt trying to keep up with Moynihan, who outspent her at the end of the race.[183] Abzug heeded advice to hold out for "a different—and a better—road elsewhere."[184]

THE 1976 NEW YORK DEMOCRATIC SENATE PRIMARY was the greatest disappointment of Bella Abzug's political career. Not so for Daniel Patrick Moynihan. At his victory party, he characterized his win as the "rebirth of a Democratic majority."[185] Defeating James L. Buckley in the general election, Moynihan served in the Senate until 2001. Norman Podhoretz was not as exuberant as his friend after the 1976 primary, conceding, "This campaign against the Left resulted in a less decisive victory than I had expected."[186] The "take back the party" effort attempted by challengers of the Democratic Party's progressive wing helped diminish the influence of New Politics Democrats, whose leftward push since 1968 lost force after 1976. This rightward reorientation, however, did not have the immediate totalizing effect its organizers had hoped. Scoop Jackson's presidential campaign gained enthusiasm, but not at the level of Eugene McCarthy in 1968. President Jimmy Carter, Georgia's evangelical peanut farmer turned governor, was a compromise candidate. His spendthrift, moralistic, centrist politics did not satisfy the Democratic Party's Committee for a Democratic Majority followers or New Politics Democrats. Instead, these wings uncomfortably coexisted as critics of the Carter White House within the party.

Americans exhibited conflicting visions of what US democracy should look like going forward at the twilight of the twentieth century. With postwar affluence waning, the altruistic impulse of doing more for more Americans dampened. And yet, after the Vietnam War, Americans maintained their feeling of superiority and interest in exhibiting global leadership even as battle fatigue made it trickier for national leaders to justify military intervention. Moynihan spoke to this new cultural mood more effectively than Abzug, who would run for office again but would never win. Moynihan's brand of free-market neoliberalism and US-centric, Cold War–driven human rights increasingly held sway in the Democratic Party. In the mid-1970s, Democrats vacillated between promoting national security and promoting privacy, liberty and equality. At the same time, the concepts of "family values" and "color blindness" tried out in the Democratic Party did not become its defining features going forward. The growing discomfort of social conservatives and racists in the Democratic Party demonstrated how completely the rights-centered imperative of New Politics took hold.

Abzug attributed her defeat primarily to the firm grip of patriarchy and white supremacy in US democracy. "Power structures are still very key," she explained, "the heads of power structures . . . still are resisting the change which requires new people, women, and so on, to come in. Those are the fellas we've got to change if we're going to get anything done."[187] She was not incorrect. She and progressive allies had made a dent in "the system" as a disruptive force in the Democratic Party and in the Democratic-controlled Congress, but the basic structures of power remained unbroken. Unwilling to give up her fight, Abzug spent the last years of the 1970s trying to return to elected office. Although this goal remained elusive, she had provided herself with a lifeline to remain in the federal arena by way of a major legislative act—shepherding through federal funding for a domestic International Women's Year conference.

10

INTERNATIONAL WOMEN'S
YEAR AT HOME

ON HER WAY TO THE United Nations World Conference on Women in Mexico City in July 1975, Bella Abzug stopped off in Boston to address 2,000 attendees of a National Women's Political Caucus conference. Speaking over shouts of "Bella for Senate," she rallied NWPC members to go global with their fight for gender parity in politics. She pledged to lead the way at the International Women's Year gathering by urging the UN to deny recognition to nations that showed up without women delegates. Once in Mexico City, she reiterated this promise, telling reporters, "Now 10,000 women from all over the world, including the United States, know they must have representation in their own governments."[1]

As a congressional observer, Abzug had not been deeply involved in the groundwork laid by UN officials, international organizers, or President Gerald Ford's National Commission on the Observance of International Women's Year (NCOIWY). In her later years, Abzug would prioritize global feminist organizing, her journey from the domestic to the international arena not unique. US feminists considered the Ronald Reagan and George H. W. Bush presidencies to be years of retrenchment. Unable to uproot a conservative domestic agenda, they saw the UN as more responsive. They put forward a global feminist creed: "Women's rights are human rights."[2] Abzug helped popularize this concept that would animate the foreign policy aims of Presidents Bill Clinton, George W. Bush, and Barack Obama. In the late 1970s, Abzug did not anticipate making this leap into the global arena, her primary focus domestic politics. At the UN World Conference on

Women, she focused foremost on drawing attention to US feminist goals and holding her nation's government accountable through international pressure. At home, she advocated holding a domestic corollary to the IWY conference to showcase women's leadership abilities and frame women's policy goals. Working with Representative Patsy Mink and additional co-sponsors, Abzug achieved bipartisan legislation that earmarked $5 million to host the National Women's Conference (NWC) to observe IWY in November 1977.

This historic gathering has been cast as both the symbolic climax of "second-wave" feminism and the seedbed of modern conservatism.[3] Undeniably, conservative leader Phyllis Schlafly's success in framing the National Women's Conference as "Bella Abzug's boondoggle" revealed that feminists were losing ground.[4] Enacted in December 1975, NWC appropriations would be among the last legislative victories during this landmark period of legal feminism. Posthumous regret that not more could be done has dampened the euphoric buzz that once filled the convention hall during the NWC. But for those who were there those four days in Houston, Texas, the emotional high remains palpable. Tasked by their government, 2,000 elected delegates debated a twenty-six-plank National Plan of Action as eighty-three dignitaries from fifty-six nations and more than 32,000 domestic observers, including 600 reporters, looked on. All told, preparing for this federally mandated policy convention involved two presidential administrations, prominent appointed commissioners, and more than 152,000 official participants at fifty-six lead-up state and territory meetings. The culminating report, *The Spirit of Houston,* was presented to President Jimmy Carter in March 1978 for further action.[5]

The Houston Conference, as it came to be known, was bigger than its presiding officer, Bella Abzug. Three generations of American women linked across time, suffragists joining children holding "Women on the Move" signs as they rode in strollers pushed along by their mothers. The NWC was the most diverse convention of women in American history to date due to its affirmative action mandate.[6] For Abzug, who strove to create greater openness in US democracy, this diversity modeled the promise of what could be achieved if Congress was truly representative. At the same time, Abzug steered the NWC's program toward a decidedly progressive agenda. Believing the American public and Congress could still be urged leftward, she was not prepared to cede territory.

Figure 10.1 As an official congressional observer, Bella Abzug listened in at a session of the United Nations World Conference on Women held in Mexico City in 1975. Once home, she marshaled legislation through Congress to hold a domestic counterpart, the 1977 National Women's Conference. (Uncredited, Bella Abzug Papers, Box 108, Rare Book and Manuscript Library, Columbia University)

In the late 1970s, Abzug was both notable and notorious. Her place at the helm of the National Women's Conference demonstrated her continued stature within the US feminist movement after leaving elected office. But Abzug still coveted a return to public service. She ran for New York City mayor as she prepared arrangements for the NWC in 1977. During the mayoral race, she made an awkward adjustment to austerity politics, paying lip service to "law and order" rhetoric and emphasizing neighborhood revitalization over redistribution of wealth. This gesturing, more rhetorical than real, did not square with the example of IWY that focused on expanding policy in the area of human rights and economic justice. Moreover, as Abzug stumped for mayor, she was trailed by anti-IWY protesters who accused her personally of feminist social engineering that abused US tax dollars. For someone asking to control New York City's purse, this criticism did not play well.

The National Women's Conference became a lightning rod, pitting feminists against antifeminists, in part because of Abzug's leadership. She was quite purposeful in her intention to link Democratic New Politics and feminism in government, which tinged the bipartisan NWC blue. After Houston, the association with women's rights and Democrats, Abzug and feminist representational politics, was complete. A close circle of like-minded feminist organizers buoyed Abzug as she angled to keep the progressive reformist flame alive through NWC. This self-affirming boost helped her brace opposition but also led her to miscalculate how much political leverage she still had as the political terrain shifted further right.

Legislating the National Women's Conference

Many nations held conferences assessing the status of women before the IWY meeting in Mexico City. It would serve US interests, Abzug stressed, not to fall behind again and to host a follow-up conference timed with the American Bicentennial. In March 1975, she and Patsy Mink introduced the first bills advocating for a domestic IWY conference, seeking to build momentum before the UN World Conference on Women.[7] Once in Mexico City, Representative Margaret "Peggy" Heckler of Massachusetts joined their call. As a Republican congressional observer at IWY, she could put the heat on the Ford White House to support a conference "on the transition of women in America and also on the implementation of existing laws."[8] The US delegation had a difficult time asserting control during deliberations in Mexico City, and Ford aides sought to regain the upper hand in the geopolitical tussle over how to define global human rights.[9] They hoped a US-centered IWY conference could set the tone for the UN's "Decade of Women," a long-term campaign to evaluate women's global status. Ford advisers also looked toward the 1976 presidential campaign and counseled that support of IWY could boost appeal with women voters. As Ford aide Patricia Lindh estimated, "In this election year, Congress is bound to approve some kind of a Conference for women. They would not let 53% of the voters down. . . . I believe that the President should get credit for this initiative."[10]

Abzug saw federal legislation as a means to shape IWY outside the powers of the National Commission on the Observance of International Women's Year, where she did not have great influence. President Ford established this commission by executive order in January 1975 and subsequently awarded most appointments to Republicans. The commission's report, *". . . To Form a More Perfect Union . . .": Justice for American Women,* addressed central feminist concerns such as equal pay for equal work, the ERA, access to abortion, and drawing more "power brokers" into government.[11] Still, the report's breezy tone and emphasis on documenting past change prompted progressive feminists in the Women's Action Alliance to present a bolder alternative, the National Women's Agenda.[12] Not greatly involved in drafting the report or the rebuttal, Abzug focused most on pushing for the establishment of a Department of Women's Affairs, a permanent President's Commission on Women in Government, and a cabinet-level women's adviser. Appointing Abzug to the NCOIWY and as chair of the commission's Government Organization Structure Committee had been a nod to bipartisanship, but there was, as she learned, a limit to this friendliness. Frustrated when her proposal did not take flight, Abzug focused on setting the terms of a National Women's Conference outlined through legislation.[13]

Thirteen congresswomen came together to draft and spearhead the NWC bill, a testament to their collaborative strength and legislative imagination. Understanding that they alone could not drive the NWC bill, they recruited seven congressmen as cosponsors to help pitch the legislation as a civil rights initiative.[14] The final bill extended past Abzug's original design. Initially, she envisioned creating a standing committee not unlike previous presidential women's commissions, tasked to plan a conference to evaluate "women in economic, social, and cultural development," "identify barriers," and "establish a timetable for the achievement of objectives."[15] Bringing more congresswomen to the table had the productive effect of creating a better, more ambitious bill. Patsy Mink favored a White House Conference, seeing this model as an easier sell in Congress with the potential for a larger $10 million budget and as a likely driver of grassroots engagement at preparatory state meetings. Abzug preferred not to give Ford any credit in claiming the NWC as his own.[16] The final bill reflected Abzug and Mink's shared activist and lawyerly instincts. It called for preliminary meetings that fostered localized engagement followed by a national parliamentary convention. The NCOIWY would be the planning engine for the NWC, maintaining elite leadership and executive branch support, while financial assistance for needy participants and a diversity mandate guaranteed delegates would be a cross section of American women.[17]

The law's diversity clause—that delegates be "members of the general public, with special emphasis on the representation of low-income women, members of diverse racial, ethnic, and religious groups, and women of all ages"—made the NWC a model of democratization.[18] Abzug welcomed this visual diversity as well as its accompanying tensions, for she had witnessed the UN's "cultivation of disunity" on the ground in Mexico City and wanted to create a like space. Her speech at the NGO Tribune had been "unmarked by any hostility or demonstration," but shortly after she was done speaking, the room "filled with a group denouncing Latin American detentions, disappearances, and torture and their effects on women and their families."[19] This kind of challenge made the Ford administration nervous, but for Abzug, who loved debate, it was an example of democracy in action.[20] Those in organizations like the National Organization for Women were not pleased when they were passed over for new faces as delegates, but Abzug's goal was not to convert the already converted.[21] She quite intentionally sought to regenerate the feminist movement and expand the feminist wing of the Democratic Party.

The National Women's Conference bill reflected how confident reform Democrats felt in putting forward bold ideas during the Ninety-Fourth Congress that was restive, pliable, and Democratic-controlled in the post-Watergate climate. In September, Chairwoman Abzug used her Government Information and Individual Rights Subcommittee as a forum to hold hearings on the bill. NCOIWY chair Jill Ruckelshaus testified, signaling the Ford White House was behind the venture. Mainstream organizations such as the League of Women Voters, Girl Scouts of America, Business and Professional Women, and the National Council of Negro Women backed the bill, making it seem like a "non-controversial effort to give women an opportunity to discuss their problems."[22] Although, Phyllis Schlafly's boycott letter, in which she characterized the NWC as a lobbying vehicle for the ERA, signaled budding opposition. Sympathetic Congress members decried the earmarked $10 million as excessive and rallied to defeat the bill, voted down on October 20, 233 to 157.[23]

Abzug and her cosponsors did not expect this floor fight and, in the face of defeat, were forced to regroup. At second go, they drew attention to the "substantial majority" that had supported the bill and assured that NWC would not be an unequal "stage for ERA, abortion reform, busing," since "as many [participants] for or against these matters" would attend.[24]

Lobbying their colleagues, they made sure to get out the votes at the next count in December. The moment proved no less tense. Representatives Sam Steiger and Robert E. Baumer (R-MD) argued that $1 million in tax dollars should be enough, since the venture "ought to be funded by the people who are concerned about the issues."[25] In response, Mink introduced a compromise bill drawing down the appropriations to $5 million. With the White House behind the pro-IWY camp, the impasse over funding was finally resolved. On December 10, the House passed the bill 252 to 162, and the Senate soon followed.[26] After Ford signed the bill into law, the Senate Appropriations Committee became the site of a last-ditch effort to derail the NWC. Senator Joseph Montoya (D-NM) delivered a "surprise move," trying to draw down funding to $3 million.[27] At this IWY hearing, a stark ideological contrast to that held by the Abzug Committee, witnesses Nellie Gray of March for Life and Elaine Donnelly of Michigan's Stop ERA argued that the federal women's conference was sacrilegious and antifamily. Senator Birch Bayh (D-IN), an official attendee of IWY in Mexico City, rallied senators to preserve the original amount of $5 million, secured by one vote.[28] It was a nail-biter to the end.

Abzug used all of her political capital as a whip at large and chairwoman to steer this legislation through Congress. When she no longer had a seat at the table, she highlighted her role as the leading drafter of the NWC legislation in her appeal for an appointment to lead this enterprise. This legislative lifeline was tenuous, for she was beholden to the whims of Ford's successor, President Jimmy Carter, who selected her as cochair of the NCOIWY. This position helped Abzug extend her national reach, but it did not ensure her a lasting place in the federal arena or improve her electoral chances. If anything, it strengthened a growing opposition. As the NWC's presiding officer, she came to embody "Big Sister government."[29]

Split Focus: Working for Carter, Running for Mayor

Abzug lost her Senate race in 1976, but that season Democrats still sent a senator from New York to Washington and Democrats gained the White House. During the fall, Abzug had stumped for Carter, despite her concern regarding his "contradictory and confusing" pro-life stance.[30] Senator George McGovern's and Governor Jimmy Carter's waffling on reproductive rights caused grumblings among feminists, but not abandonment. In the same way, Carter aides worried that Abzug's visible support would irk moderate and conservative Democrats, but they calculated her prominence among feminists would reap dividends. Still, it was clear from the first time that Democratic feminists met with Carter and his aides during the 1976 Democratic National Convention that their goodwill would only stretch so far. Abzug mistakenly believed that she could move Carter in her direction, but this would take more effort with Carter than it had with McGovern. A moderate and moralist, Carter was inclined to appease social conservative Democrats as much as feminists, and stood closer to Moynihan than Abzug on domestic and foreign policy.[31]

New York Democrat Midge Costanza served as the essential go-between for Abzug and Carter at the 1976 DNC, easing their relationship and interpreting their interests. Costanza had been active in the NWPC and in Rochester party politics, and she now headed Carter's New York campaign. Perplexed by this choice, Abzug questioned, "Why are you supporting this guy? . . . Hey Costanza, what are ya doin'?" Once Abzug's presidential pick, Arizona representative Morris "Mo" Udall, was out of the running, Costanza worked on bringing Abzug over to Carter's camp. Costanza believed Abzug to be "the most brilliant strategist I had ever met," and advised Rosalynn and Jimmy Carter to take advantage of her skill and sway.[32]

The DNC served as a first meeting of Abzug and Carter. Unlike in 1972, it was now a given that the Democratic nominee would sit down with feminist top brass, although women delegate strength had dipped from 38 to 34 percent.[33] Without the mandate of the McGovern-Fraser Commission in 1976, the Rules Committee waffled on committing to fifty-fifty representation by 1980.[34] A large delegation of Democratic women leaders, including Abzug, pressed Carter to advocate that this goal be a requirement at the next convention. On top aide Hamilton Jordan's advice, Carter hedged on this request but signaled he would support the ERA and high-level women appointments. At a stalemate, Abzug was selected to iron out a deal with Carter, Rules Committee cochair Jane Patterson, and Carter surrogate civil rights organizer Patricia Derian. During final negotiations, Abzug agreed to Carter's language of a "preference" for fifty-fifty representation instead of a "requirement" in exchange for the commitment to appoint women to cabinet-level positions. This concession reflected Abzug's increased willingness to accept piecemeal wins. She publicly proclaimed,

"Our demands have been responded to in full."[35] Some disappointed delegates did not agree.

Abzug believed she could achieve more by nudging Carter within his campaign, and, as she had with McGovern, she focused on increasing women's visibility on his staff. She was brought in to help him offset public criticism that he surrounded himself with "only broad-shouldered men." But Carter advisers worried, "Could Bella handle this?"[36] Mary King and Cooki Lutkefedder, who ran Carter's Committee of 51.3%, named to highlight women's majority, believed Abzug had such clout that she could convince feminists to set aside Carter's abortion problem. Further, Abzug had name recognition and might help with female swing voters. Aide Pat Caddell crunched numbers and showed 2 million more women than men had voted in the 1974 midterms and would be the "crucial group" in 1976.[37] Carter's right-hand man, Hamilton Jordan, fretted about how annoying it was to have to woo "our friends to tell them to help us."[38] Nonetheless, he relented to Carter's directive that he meet with Abzug and her adviser Mim Kelber in Atlanta. Carter had been impressed with Abzug's "highly effective personal appearance" as an opening act at the Women's Agenda Conference in Maryland, where he spoke in early October.[39] She parlayed his appreciation into the reward of a seat on the next plane out to campaign headquarters.

What happened after felt all too familiar. Carter had encouraged the 3,000 women gathered at the Women's Agenda Conference to "be as tough, as militant and as eloquent as you can be."[40] Inside his campaign, however, women were brushed aside when they tried to exert their influence. Promises were made to Abzug and others, but blunders continued at campaign stops. In Indiana, state office candidates Virginia McCardy and Lee Newhauser were seated in the crowd while comparable male contenders were included onstage. "One week ago, Jimmy restated to Bella Abzug his commitment to include women in *every* phase of the Campaign and his administration," Barbara Blum protested internally to Jordan, feeling Carter had paid only lip service to their concerns.[41] As the campaign wrapped up, Carter's staff elected to use Abzug as a surrogate less and less, a noticeable shift captured in one headline noting, "Bella's Curtailed Barnstorm."[42] Carter aides calculated that once she lost her Senate bid, she would only help his chances in the most liberal enclaves.

After Carter won the general election, his advisers did not feel he owed anything to Abzug, but she and her supporters disagreed. His administration would do better than his campaign, with 22 percent of his appointments women.[43] Adviser Stuart E. Eizenstat worried that if Carter did not get in front of the Abzug appointment issue, then "you'll end up with Bella doing something you might not want her to do!"[44] Agreeing, Rick Hutcheson counseled, "She is a smart, tough lady—and that is why so many men resent her. She'll relieve you of your manhood as soon as look at you," but "it is better to have her on your side than against you, if at all possible."[45] President Carter first approached Abzug to direct the Equal Employment Opportunity Commission, but she declined, aware of feminists' efforts to back Eleanor Holmes Norton, who ultimately was selected over male labor leaders' objections. Abzug had higher ambitions, angling to be secretary of transportation, a cabinet-level position.[46] When that did not come through, she lobbied to lead the National Commission on the Observance of IWY.

Abzug's appointment as presiding officer of the National Women's Conference was not a given. Shortly after President Ford signed the bill into law, Abzug held a meeting in her congressional office to talk about next steps, but it was a largely symbolic gesture, since the law she cowrote still left the NCOIWY in charge. Her prospects to commandeer the NCOIWY shifted once Midge Costanza was well placed in the White House as Carter's assistant for public liaison. Abzug impressed upon Costanza, "Naturally, I had to be there."[47] When Republican feminist Elly Peterson caught wind of this possibility, she fretted to Sheila Greenwald of ERAmerica, "Turning that into a Democratic women's caucus with Bella at the head can just murder us."[48] First Lady Rosalynn Carter agreed, anticipating that with Abzug in charge, the ERA ratification campaign could unravel in the South. She urged her husband not to appoint Abzug, aware opposing the former congresswoman had become a rallying point for conservatives and that she had a personality that was hard to control. President Carter recognized these liabilities, but he felt caught between the Democratic Party's family values conservatives and its feminist bloc, which more powerfully weighed in during this search for a presiding officer. Costanza also delivered a strong sell within the White House, arguing that no one was "strong enough and tough enough" or more deserving to lead NWC than Abzug.[49]

In late March, President Carter formerly announced that Abzug would be the NWC's presiding officer. Thrilled, she was nonetheless torn between obligations. One month prior, she had begun a "renewed flurry of activity— meetings with potential campaign workers, and contributors, studies of poll results, talks about strategy" in preparation of a run for New York City mayor.[50] After losing her Senate race, she had instinctively deflected when asked about this prospect, saying, "The mayoralty was never anything I was interested in."[51] But the question lingered in her thoughts as she ruminated over what—and who—might drive the city's rebirth. And so, for the spring and summer of 1977, Abzug found herself torn between these two interests: her singular ambition of returning to public office and her collectivist intention of making the National Women's Conference a historic success.

Abzug and Gloria Steinem leaned on Costanza as she put together a progressive Democratic dream team of labor, women's, lesbian, and racial civil rights leaders on the reconstituted NCOIWY. When Abzug took over, the NCOIWY had already set up the basic design of IWY state meetings and had selected Houston as a conference location.[52] But the issue planks to be considered at these meetings had not been finalized by national commissioners, leaving Abzug to oversee this consequential task. The NCOIWY had to deliberate quickly as the first state meeting was slated to be held in Georgia on May 6 and 7. Commissioner meetings setting this agenda were productive but reflected the wide-ranging backgrounds and concerns represented on the NCOIWY. Those at the table included Gloria Scott, president of the Girl Scouts; Margaret Mealey of the National Council of Catholic Women; LaDonna Harris of the Americans for Indian Opportunity; Sey Kessler, editor of *Redbook* magazine; Carmen Delgado Votaw, president of the National Conference on Puerto Rican Women; Addie Wyatt, active in the Amalgamated Meat Cutters Union; Representatives Margaret Heckler and Elizabeth Holtzman; Rhea Mojica, publisher of *El Clarin*; Rita Elway, founder of the Asian and Pacific Women's Caucus; and Jean O'Leary, codirector of the National Gay Task Force.[53]

Abzug remained laser focused on assuring that topics selected for debate at the state meetings extended the feminist policies promoted in Congress and through the courts during the early 1970s. This legacy concern weighed heavily on Abzug, no longer in Congress and worried about efforts already surfacing to chip away at feminist legislative achievements. Many of the areas highlighted—child care, education, health, employment—had long been within the wheelhouse of women's policy issues. Nonetheless, Abzug and her peers wanted the National Plan of Action to go beyond traditional measures and have an aspirational quality. For this reason, issue recommendations reflected developing advocacy movements including dis-

ability, domestic violence, and sexual assault, and backed the ERA and reproductive rights without great pause. A shared acknowledgment of women's
diverse experience also compelled commissioners to distinguish specific
groups as special-issue areas: rural women, minority women, homemakers,
women in poverty, and older women.[54]

Agreeing in most areas, commissioners divided over whether the National Women's Conference should be a venue to draw attention to and
support lesbian rights. Before Abzug took the reins, the NCOIWY had already discussed whether "lesbianism is a feminist issue," but the question
had been left unresolved and resurfaced as recommendations were finalized.[55] In September 1976, commissioners decided to avoid the issue, but
their guidelines specifying that only topics of "particular concerns for
women" be debated at state meetings implicitly signaled the exclusion of
lesbian rights. Not present at this NCOIWY meeting, Abzug received word
of what unfolded from her aide June Zeitlin, who felt strongly that it was
"imperative" that women's interests be defined broadly and include "particularly gay rights."[56] Again in November, Zeitlin indicated to Abzug that
lesbian activists saw IWY as an opportunity to link sexual freedom and
women's rights. In January 1977, before taking over as presiding officer,
Abzug warned, "We are being wholly incorrect if we push this subject
aside."[57] And yet, when leading her first NCOIWY meeting in April, Abzug
was lukewarm when Commissioners Ruth Abram and Jean O'Leary urged
commissioners to support "sexual or affectual preference" as an issue plank
at state meetings. Midge Costanza, personally close to O'Leary, observed
Abzug's reluctance. "Bella had a hard time with Jean O'Leary on that commission" and "Jean O'Leary felt personally betrayed by Bella Abzug," she
later explained.[58]

It took homophobic resistance exhibited by Commissioner Martha
Griffiths and IWY staff member Catherine East to move Abzug to strongly
back issuing a "sexual preference" workshop booklet. In an April letter to
commissioners drafted by East, Griffiths cautioned, "The women's movement is not strong enough to take on all of society's ills," and protested, "I
simply cannot understand the ready acceptance of homosexuality as a
women's issue."[59] Weighing in, Commissioner Gloria Scott reasoned that
"the Houston Conference must have a point of view," but organizers should
also try to meet "women wherever they are on the continuum of acceptance and pursuit of equality."[60] Abzug decided that the NWC would be

better served as a driver of change on lesbian rights instead of toeing the line. In making this choice, she reinforced her positioning of the NWC as an engine for progressive reform that pushed public debate beyond most Americans' comfort level. As she directed state coordinators, "Our plan of action has to become the nation's action, and if it is to be the nation's action we have to make sure that we are acting in a wholly new way."[61]

By focusing on women's intersectional identity along gender, sexuality, race, and class lines, National Women's Conference organizers prioritized representational over ideological difference. Before becoming a presiding officer, Abzug had questioned at an NCOIWY meeting why religion had been overlooked. "Are we offending people by prohibiting religion as a topic? Being ordained is an intrinsic issue with women in the church," she noted.[62] As a devout Conservative Jew, she understood how religion shaped her politics, but she failed to see the parallel when considering faith-driven opposition to the NWC. Religion had been avoided as a topic at NWC state meetings because the federally funded enterprise had to carefully delineate distinctions between church and state. It annoyed Abzug that the anti-IWY camp refused to abide by these same rules. Lottie Beth Hobbs, an active lay leader in the Church of Christ in Fort Worth, Texas, and founder of Women Who Want to Be Women, dreamed up the idea of holding a simultaneous "pro-family" conference at the Houston Astrodrome that attracted around 16,000.[63] IWY state meetings leading up to the NWC in Houston were frequently disrupted by religious factions seeking to defend their positions and gain representation. The largest upset occurred in Utah, where Mormon affiliates arrived in busloads, "ran the whole thing," and voted in a dozen delegates to be present in Houston.[64] Seething, Abzug scolded Mormon spokesperson Don LeFevre during a heated conference call, characterizing the church's involvement as a violation of the separation of church and state. She believed that women anti-IWY activists were manipulated by religious leaders rather than operating from their own spiritually fired conviction. They were, in Abzug's view, sheep guided by male shepherds who told "their flock to vote 'No' on any recommendation, not just the ERA or abortion."[65]

Abzug gravely underestimated how troublesome anti-IWY opposition would be at state meetings that commenced in May or how quickly challengers would zero in on her. When she delivered keynotes, it became the usual fare for audience members to immediately walk out. Those who remained delivered a chorus of cheers or "no, no."[66] Initially, Abzug dismissed these critics as misguided and a mild irritant but signs of their effective organization emerged. Cleanup crews at IWY state meetings found tape recorders and notebooks mistakenly left behind, evidence of the IWY Citizens' Review Committee's campaign to document proceedings. Texas activist Dianne Edmondson circulated a cassette tape on which she characterized Abzug as a radical architect who wanted to indoctrinate children.[67] State meeting coordinators tried to prepare for this "opposition," to "know where they are at all times," and to anticipate the "what and when of their maneuvers."[68] IWY staff kept a clipping file Abzug helped compile that tracked negative press and challenges at state meetings by affiliates of the Ku Klux Klan, the John Birch Society, and the Church of Jesus Christ of Latter-day Saints (the last of which did not appreciate association with the first).[69]

The antagonism Abzug loathed most was delivered by one person. She waived around a copy of the *Phyllis Schlafly Report* at one NCOIWY meeting, frustrated by Schlafly's vitriolic characterization of the NWC as "federal financing of a foolish festival for frustrated feminists."[70] Schlafly did not name Abzug in her 1977 political tract, *The Power of the Positive Woman,* but her attack was hardly veiled. She urged followers to patriotically support "the legislation, the legislators, and the funding necessary to defend the values of home and country against attack by aggressors who respect neither."[71] Like "reverse discrimination" resisters, "positive women" guarded their feminine way of life. Abzug and other commissioners faced these defenders when visiting Houston ahead of the NWC in November. At the hotel where the preparatory meeting was held, she waded through pickets of protesters with signs telling her, "Bella Go Home."[72]

This backlash intensified as Abzug launched into full-time campaigning for New York City mayor over the summer. On June 1, she kicked off her formal bid by cruising the Avenue of the Americas in a convertible, calling out to passersby, "I'm Bella Abzug. I think I'm going to be your next Mayor. So let's get to know each other."[73] In her announcement speech, she promised to govern "in the activist tradition of Fiorello LaGuardia."[74] Although, Abzug's star-studded, flashy opener suggested entitlement, as did her campaign slogan meant to demonstrate experience and boost confidence: "Elect Congresswoman Abzug. . . . Because she's earned it."[75] She was the early favorite among a venerable and deep pack that included incumbent mayor Abraham Beame, former New York congressional delegation Representative

Herman Badillo, Representative Edward Koch, New York secretary of state Mario Cuomo, prominent Harlem borough president Percy Sutton, and publisher Joel Harnett.[76] Mayor Beame, blamed for the city's near bankruptcy, faced an uphill battle to hang on to his job. He argued that change would be a detriment to the city, but this position was defensive. Abzug and other contenders recognized that their chances hinged on convincing voters that they had the chops to get New York City finances back on track.[77]

Being the presiding officer of the National Women's Conference complicated Abzug's messaging. Eight IWY state meetings were held the week after her mayoral announcement. By the end of the month, nearly half of all states had convened meetings increasingly described in the press as a "dramatic showdown between . . . Christian conservatives" and "lesbians and prostitutes."[78] News stories featured Abzug as the national feminist leader behind the NWC and the main target of conservatives' wrath. Anti-IWY protesters' critique that the NWC was a misuse of taxpayers' money did not aid Abzug's appeal to New York City voters worried about municipal finances. As the Women Caucus for Fiscal Responsibility pointedly asked in one flyer distributed at IWY meetings, "Bella, Can You Spare a Dime?"[79]

Abzug tried to accommodate to the market turn taking hold within the Democratic Party while maintaining her leftist populism. The result was an incongruent melding of messages—"Let's make New York a city of opportunity for all its people" and "Bella Means Business."[80] Percy Sutton, a lawyer who had once represented Malcolm X, offered the strongest critique of money interests during the race, urging New York to "liberate itself from the banks."[81] Abzug softened her rhetoric, excising from one speech an indictment of the "New York Times-Emergency Financial Control Board-Wall Street bankers-Steve Berger vision of New York."[82] She promised to sustain City Hall's social responsibility to its people and build revenue from corporate entities and commercial real estate groups who had avoided paying taxes. She also spoke in wispy terms of stimulating new growth and reducing the city's red tape. When Doug Ireland urged her not to run, she hired Terry O'Connell to manage her campaign; he had worked for George McGovern, but also more centrist Democrats like Scoop Jackson and Jimmy Carter.[83] Bringing O'Connell on board suggests Abzug's awareness that she needed to figure out how to reach the Jackson-Moynihan city voter. Still, she was ill suited to adapt, and her halfhearted overture to business interests undercut her authenticity as a progressive choice.

At her most genuine, Abzug nostalgically looked back to "the city of opportunity" of the early twentieth century.[84] She spoke of her father's Live and Let Live Meat Market on Ninth Avenue, and she returned to 1038 Hoe Avenue in the Bronx to check out her old neighborhood. This previously thriving Jewish enclave had become by 1977 a predominantly African American and Puerto Rican American area blighted with burned-out buildings and empty commercial spaces. Drawing attention to the crime, poverty, and unemployment that befell the neighborhood, Abzug advocated business redevelopment, selling, "It's got land, access to rail and water transportation and thousands of people hungry for a paycheck."[85] She countered the hardened view that New York City's best days had passed, optimistically noting, "I still have that hope."[86]

The race turned dismal on July 13, the day a lightning storm triggered a blackout throughout New York City and looting of private properties as the city was blanketed by darkness. Then not hope, but fear, despair, and rage set the mood. When the lights came on, New Yorkers' awareness of the full scale of loss set in: 3,776 arrests, 2,000 stores damaged, and $1 billion in costs.[87] Abzug had been feeling good about her chances for mayor a few weeks before the blackout. In front of her headquarters, she announced through a bullhorn, "We are winning. We are way ahead in every poll. . . . There is a big out-front feeling."[88] She assured, "I am going to be a good executive, a good conciliator, a good negotiator. I know when to be soft and when to be tough and how to get things done."[89] And she promised to "make City Hall work for women."[90]

After the blackout, journalists openly considered whether "New York is ready for a municipal matriarchy."[91] Gender mattered more when candidates were newly measured by their preparedness and temperament alongside their framing of "law and order." Toughness was an asset, but not Abzug's kind. Her feisty personality now read as unhinged feminine emotion. As Richard Aurelio, who had supported Abzug, openly questioned, "Can you imagine her sitting down with the banks, the unions, the financial board? She'll start screaming at them."[92] Abzug already had to contend with a contingent of male voters, characterized as "Bellaphobes" by reporter Anna Mayo.[93] Polling men on the street in early July, she found that many feared Abzug as mayor because they found her toughness intimidating. In contrast, Ed Koch moved way ahead after the blackout because of his strong critique of Beame, who he charged had "lost control of city services to the municipal unions and now has lost control of the streets."[94] Boosting Koch's case, the *New York Post* (newly acquired by Rupert Murdoch) ran alarmist stories all summer inciting fear about city crime and decay. It was no surprise when the paper eventually endorsed Koch.

While Koch promised tough love, Abzug advocated criminal justice reform and the expansion of neighborhood services. Their positions on capital punishment, him for and her against, became a symbolic measure of the distance between them and an indication that she was "less militant on crime in the streets."[95] Abzug proposed increasing patrol units by 1,500 officers, but her solutions primarily focused on long-term, systemic fixes. She recommended new investment in public schools along with a bifurcated criminal justice system that increased penalties for gun violence and rehabilitation programs for small-time offenders. Responding to the city's arson problem, she proposed hiring 1,000 firefighters to save more buildings that would be turned into industrial parks attracting new environmental industries. Reflecting her socialistic leanings, she returned to the prospect of free tuition at the City University of New York and advocated for the municipal takeover of Con Edison, the electric company servicing New York City.[96] Abzug addressed "law and order," but hers was a different kind than that of conservative calls for more policing and prosecution of criminals. She pressed for greater prosecution of hate crimes and greater police intervention in cases of domestic violence and sexual assault. While she opposed censorship, she promised to clean out the seedy back corners of Times Square where the pornography industry boomed, a stance encouraged by Andrea Dworkin and other antipornography activists involved in her campaign.[97]

As Abzug sought to expand the definition of being tough on crime, Koch delivered a pointed critique of progressives as soft, out-of-touch enablers. He blamed "unions, leftists, and 'poverty pimps'" for the city's problems and characterized Abzug as "a polarizer."[98] The Koch-Abzug face-off was deeply personal, a division that could be traced back to their first sit-down in December 1967 in Abzug's living room. At the time, Koch had been a congressional candidate in pursuit of the endorsement of the 17th CD PAC led by Abzug. All went well initially, according to Koch, for "I opposed the Vietnam War." Where they parted was on "support of Israel's request for arms."[99] Koch later claimed he was for jets for Israel, and Abzug and her PAC were against; Abzug contended that the issue had never come up in conversation. This "he said, she said" became a key source of tension between them that they argued out in the press periodically.[100] Each vied to be New York City's top Jewish advocate, a contest Abzug found annoying because she was more learned and religious. Koch saw Abzug as "a radical" and part of an antiwar "Commie operation," and resented New Politics Democrats' increased influence in reform Democratic circles since the late 1960s.[101] Since then, Village Independent Democrats had uncomfortably split "between the Koch folk and the Bella folk."[102] But by the 1977 mayoral race, the tables were turning, and Koch exploited this advantage. He especially focused in on identity politics, treating Abzug's connection to the feminist movement as her greatest liability.

The week before New York City's blackout, Abzug attended New York's IWY state meeting in Albany. She had not been greatly involved in the planning, but organizers were aware that "because Bella is so prominently identified with this meeting" it needed to be "a smash success, with more than 5,000 women there."[103] Public interest surpassed expectation, with over 11,000 attending to debate one hundred issues and elect eighty-eight delegates.[104] Anti-IWY forces were a visible contingent at this gathering. Members of Operation Wake Up promoted anti-ERA and antiabortion planks in challenge of the Coalition for a Better Slate the NCOIWY backed. Unlikely exchanges occurred during breakout sessions, such as when lesbian feminists explained to Anita Bryant followers "why children cannot catch homosexuality in school, just as they catch the flu." Most focus was directed on floor activity, where Abzug tried to keep debate lighthearted and on track. At one point, she "mounted a chair beside the weary troops" and sang a tune to the crowd as they waited restlessly for a vote to begin.[105] "Bella kept us laughing all night long," recalled *Ms.* editor Joanne Edgar.[106] This reprieve from campaigning buoyed Abzug, but her presence at the New York state meeting solidified her association with IWY. She tried to capitalize on this association by campaigning as a candidate tapped in to social movement organizing who would bring divergent groups together.

If mayor, Abzug hoped to bring a wider selection of issue- and identity-based representatives to the table, as she had once encouraged Mayor John V. Lindsay to do. She proposed a cabinet-level disability advocate, pledging, "When I say that I will work and fight like hell to make New

York live again, I want to make it livable for *all* people."[107] Likewise, she promised to be the mayor to achieve a citywide gay rights antidiscrimination ordinance as these measures came under attack. During Abzug's campaign, Villagers marched in protest when they learned that gospel singer Anita Bryant, heading a "Save our Children" campaign, had successfully pressured for the repeal of a gay civil rights ordinance in Dade County, Florida. Marchers ended their walk in the middle of the night on Abzug's stoop. Awakened by the chanting below, she threw on a bathrobe and went out to console the despondent crowd.[108] It was a natural destination for these longtime supporters and an easy action for Abzug to take. But the impromptu late night assembly was one more indicator that her heart was with neighborhood organizers and movement people, not the city's elite.

Ultimately, it was Abzug's inability to be a chameleon that got her into the most trouble. True to form as a labor lawyer, she weighed in during Mayor Beame's contract negotiations with the Patrolmen's Benevolent Association, defending the police union's right to strike. She called the Taylor Law unconstitutional, rejecting the state law that prohibited public employees from work stoppages. Beame fired back, characterizing Abzug's position as the "height of irresponsibility." She accused him of "getting hysterical."[109] After the blackout and looting that occurred one day later, her position seemed foolhardy. Aware she stepped into a minefield, she solicited advice on how to get above the issue; one counselor encouraged her to avoid restating her position, but he doubted it would be possible to avoid altogether and indeed it was.

Abzug never bounced back. In the Democratic primary in September, she finished fourth behind Ed Koch, Mario Cuomo, and Abraham Beame. She garnered 17 percent of the 900,000 votes (with 40 percent needed for a run-off); she led the vote count only in Manhattan.[110] Abzug had difficulty cornering the Jewish vote next to Koch and Beame, the city's first Jewish mayor. Likewise, she competed with Percy Sutton and Herman Badillo for African American and Hispanic votes, a prospect she worried about before entering the race. Cuomo, boosted by strong backing from Governor Hugh Carey, effectively ran as an establishment candidate playing to the middle. Abzug convinced few voters that she was anything but a progressive Democrat. After this loss, she would stick to this playbill. Abzug was quiet after the election. Her campaign manager Terry O'Connell was not. "Bella could not have won because of this big shift to the conservative," he assessed, "The question is, is this an aberration because of the events of the summer, or a permanent change?"[111]

This very question worried the White House during the final lead-up to the National Women's Conference. President Carter decided to follow the advice of his domestic aide Stuart Eizenstat, who cautioned, "We should have the lowest profile. This appears to be going sour."[112] Carter widened his distance from the NWC after Senator Jesse Helms held anti-IWY ad hoc hearings on Capitol Hill in mid-September. For critics of the NWC, these hearings were "an exciting two days of spiritual unity for several hundred women and a few men dedicated to traditional moral values."[113] For NWC commissioners, the hearings were deeply troubling. In late August, Abzug first learned that Helms might hold hearings, but she was not certain when and was alerted by Helms's aide Carl Anderson only a few days prior. It displeased her immensely that no witnesses had been invited "to discuss the positive value of the state meetings."[114]

With the mayoral race behind her, Abzug delved into final planning for the NWC. She had depended on an army of government employees and grassroots organizers to get the NWC off the ground when distracted by campaigning. Some missteps were made along the way. Most consequentially, she and commissioners were late to hire local staff, and they nearly lost their venue, the Albert Thomas Convention Center, as a result. Attorney Helen Cassidy and NASA engineer Francis "Poppy" Northcutt were recruited a few months out to handle Houston arrangements, selected because they had successfully run a NOW conference there a few years earlier. Abzug positioned her longtime collaborators for key roles in planning the Houston Conference. Congressional aides Linda Dorian and Lee Novick joined the NCOIWY staff; Mim Kelber drafted *The Spirit of Houston* report on the conference with Caroline Bird; and Diana Mara Henry, active in Abzug's mayoral campaign, served as an official photographer in Houston.

Without the immediate prospect of returning to office, Abzug's personal stake in the success of the NWC heightened. Increasingly present and focused on minutiae, she tried the patience of the NCOIWY staff. As Shelah Leader and Patricia Hyatt recalled, "At times the strain became unbearable, and individuals on the staff took turns crying in the bathroom."[115] One month out, Abzug focused on media placement, parliamentary procedure, and preparing floor tellers and security.[116] Her greatest ask of Midge Costanza was not met. Within the White House, Costanza tried to impress

Figure 10.2 In 1973, Bella Abzug introduced legislation to designate the anniversary of women's suffrage as Women's Equality Day. Here, she is pictured celebrating this milestone along with young New Yorkers while running for mayor. (Photo © Bettye Lane, Schlesinger Library, Radcliffe Institute, Harvard University)

upon President Carter the historic importance of attending the NWC, but the anti-IWY mobilization worried him and his male aides. In his letter to Abzug declining the invitation, Carter suggested he had to prepare for a four-continent trip, an excuse that she found unsatisfactory.[117] Disappointed, Abzug settled for the visual weight of clasping hands onstage with three First Ladies—Lady Bird Johnson, Betty Ford, and Rosalynn Carter—during the opening ceremony.

The Unfinished Work of Four Days in Houston

Delegates and observers reminiscing about the National Women's Conference often note with pride, "I was there."[118] "History was made those four days in beautiful steamy Houston," observed Republican Party organizer Elly Peterson shortly after the conference came to a close.[119] Journalist Gloria Steinem expressed a similar sentiment upon returning to New York, noting, "The rest of my life would be divided into pre and post Houston—

like pre and post Kennedy assassination, only for positive reasons, not negative."[120] The experience reenergized Abzug, who wrote to Steinem, "Houston was the landmark for the women's movement we have all hoped for."[121]

Conference organizers understood that they were making history and thought a great deal about how to commemorate the moment. Commissioner Sey Chassler proposed having 2,000 runners participate in a torch relay race from Seneca Falls, New York, to Houston, drawing a line between women's suffrage past and women's rights present. Although a publicity stunt, for the young runners involved it was a moving experience. Abzug ran the last "celebrity mile" of this torch relay, locking arms with three Houston athletes, Michele Cearcy, Peggy Kokernot, and Sylvia Ortiz, selected to showcase the conference's theme of diverse "women on the move."[122] As a former student athlete, Abzug treasured this moment even though it was undercut by local media unkindly noting, "Even the less athletic types, like former Congresswoman Bella Abzug," ran today.[123] Her message still had verve. "Some of us run with a torch," she quipped. "Some of us run for office. Some of us run for equality—but none of us runs for cover."[124]

Speakers during the opening ceremony looked back and forward. Maya Angelou soared as she recited a poem she wrote for the occasion, "To Form a More Perfect Union." Representative Barbara Jordan delivered a resounding appeal for "a domestic human rights program" focused on women, and Liz Carpenter noted how diverse "we are inside this hall and out—women of many faces and voices." Commencing proceedings, Abzug struck a gavel once owned by Susan B. Anthony on loan from the Smithsonian and urged women to lead on "the high road to equality."[125] Her speech, carefully crafted with the help of Mim Kelber, echoed a farewell address that Elizabeth Cady Stanton gave in 1892 before the National American Woman Suffrage Association. Then, Stanton advised, "To guide our own craft, we must be captain, pilot, engineer."[126] Now, Abzug told NWC delegates, "If so many women are concerned today about our status in the family, on the job and in our educational system, it is because more and more women realize that we are responsible for ourselves." Her remarks touted individualism alongside collectivism. Prepping delegates for their proceedings, she encouraged, "Let us agree to disagree, if we must," but remember "our common interests as women who have for too long been treated as merely auxiliary human beings."[127]

Abzug tried to exert more control over deliberations in Houston than the law she helped write allowed. Poppy Northcutt, Helen Cassidy, and the rest of the local arrangements team made sure that accessible bathrooms were constructed, a security detail would be in place, a press room was prepared, and more than 300 volunteers were recruited. They improvised, making executive decisions on the spot, such as using a tampon to light the torch when nothing else worked and recruiting local artists to paint a huge banner stating, "WOMAN," to hang across the stage. When Abzug arrived in town, she grumbled about some of these choices. She was particularly livid that the program, already off to print, included World War I military recruitment posters, which did not sit well with her as a peace activist. She wanted the pages blackened, but it was too late for a change.[128] Abzug was very careful about appearances. The official hotel selected to house conference attendees was involved in a labor dispute, so she booked a room elsewhere. Once the conference began, she leaned on Northcutt to turn over her Hyatt Regency suite in all but name, treating the space as her mission control.[129]

From this command center, Abzug kept watch over floor debates, finessed the schedule of events, and recruited speakers to deliver remarks on prime-time television. She worried about a rank-and-file insurrection, knowing full well that the participants would be the drivers of discussions about the twenty-six issue planks. As Commissioner Carmen Delgado Votaw recalled, "She felt that anything that amended the plan was a threat, because then the delegates could become very active in trying to amend every resolution."[130] Abzug was pleased to see impromptu discussions among delegates convened in hotel alcoves and casual salons set up in the Seneca Falls South exhibit area.[131] Building up to Houston, Chicana activists had formed a Chicana Advisory Committee to press for delegate strength, and African American women drafted a Black Women's Action Plan they presented at the conference. Latina, Native American, Asian American, and African American women came together in Houston to rewrite the inadequately terse proposed minority report; they came to identify their interests as "women of color" in part because of this collaboration. Likewise, rural women and poor women drew attention to poverty and welfare, critiquing feminism void of class as Third World grassroots organizers had done in Mexico City. An effort to unseat the all-white Mississippi delegation that included Dallas Higgins, wife of the state's Grand Dragon of the Ku Klux

Klan, brought an antiracist challenge to the floor.[132] Abzug welcomed this robust debate but sought to orchestrate its unfolding.

Abzug directed the most attention to choreographing the rollout of the Equal Rights Amendment vote. On the first night, 4,000 attendees crammed into a hotel ballroom to mingle with celebrities and political heavyweights at a cocktail party that built excitement for the ERA.[133] Before the conference, commissioners had deliberated over how to order the issues for debate, and all agreed the ERA should receive top billing. They ultimately decided to be more democratic and address proposed planks from A to Z.[134] Uncertain of when the ERA would be discussed, Abzug sought to carefully execute the plank's introduction. She handpicked Ann Richards for the job, a strategic choice as she was white, had married her high school sweetheart, and recently joined the Commissioner's Court of Travis County in Texas, a southern state that had ratified the ERA early. "I was terribly nervous, it would be like a Catholic being summoned to the Pope," Richards recalled of meeting Abzug in her suite. "I want to know more about you Texas," Abzug encouraged; once she was satisfied Richards would suffice, Abzug sent her on her way.[135] Richards kicked off an electric, lengthy floor debate that ran past midnight. Anti-ERA activists had been vocal, but, as Abzug had hoped, using parliamentary procedure kept debate in order. When she called a standing vote, the room was divided; the subsequent teller vote delivered a more definitive result—927 for and 341 against. Satisfied, Abzug blew warm kisses to delegates while saying in parting, "Good night, my loves."[136]

As presiding officer, Abzug instilled order because she wanted to achieve results, but also to demonstrate that the NWC was a model of civility. Over at the "pro-family" rally, California representative Robert K. Dornan called the sight of three First Ladies sitting "along side Abzug, approving of sexual perversion and the murder of young people in America" a national tragedy.[137] Abzug made sure to present a stark contrast. When the abortion plank came up for debate at the NWC, antiabortion delegates rose to speak as supporters unveiled "protect the unborn" banners. "These people have a right to be heard," Abzug declared as she jumped off the stage, microphone in hand.[138] She made this overture because she knew that these "anti" delegates were so few in number that they could not swing the vote. The outcome of the sexual preference plank was more unpredictable. While the resolution had passed at thirty state meetings, lesbian rights was the most controversial issue considered at the NWC. Local newspapers had run an ad timed for the conference that pictured a young girl innocently asking, "Mommy, when I grow up, can I be a lesbian?"[139] This scare tactic, alongside concerted lobbying by lesbian activists at the conference, changed at least one mind. Betty Friedan, who had once warned of a "lavender menace" plaguing the women's movement, spoke unexpectedly in support of the sexual preference plank and helped swing votes that direction.[140] When the plank passed, thousands of purple balloons were released in the convention hall, with the message attached, "We are everywhere."[141]

The only plank that did not pass, a recommendation to establish a cabinet-level Office of Women's Issues, indicated the limits of Abzug's influence. State meetings overwhelmingly rejected this plank, but Abzug insisted that it be voted on at the final convention anyway. "We need full representation in government. . . . Nothing will happen until we get this," she had argued.[142] Friedan suggested at a press conference after the plank failed that some "opposed it fearing that Bella would end up as head of it."[143] Friedan likely harbored lingering hard feelings because Abzug had kept her off the NCOIWY, but Friedan's slight still "stunned" Abzug.[144] Despite this loss, she had much to be pleased about for the NWC proceedings had closed without major conflict and ahead of the allotted timetable. The hundreds of reporters on the scene delivered largely positive reviews. At the closing ceremony, Abzug beamed onstage as Puerto Rican delegates presented her with a homemade palm hat and bouquet of roses. Finally, everyone stood and sang Margie Adam's anthem written for the occasion, "We Shall Go Forth."[145]

Abzug misread the considerable success of the National Women's Conference as increased political clout. President Carter did not treat *The Spirit of Houston* report, presented to him on March 22, 1978, as a mandate for reform.[146] The NCOIWY disbanded after the report's publication as the law required. Abzug and Steinem lobbied hard for the formation of Carter's National Advisory Committee for Women (NACW) to continue the work begun in Houston. "I'm worn out from hearing Bella and Gloria," Costanza told the president.[147] Much like before, she argued that not having a continuation committee and not picking Abzug "would be a bit like not appointing Vernon Jordan after the Black community had request that he serve."[148] Rosalynn Carter delivered her objections once more, maintaining, "The women in Georgia wear pinafores and gloves . . . and Bella doesn't wear pinafores or gloves."[149] Aides Jody Powell, Anne Wexler, and Stuart Eizenstat, who collectively advised Carter to think about his upcoming election, saw Abzug as "a strong card in 1980 when we need the support of the group she represents."[150] Persuaded, the president first offered the co-chair position to Oklahoma state legislator Cleta Deatherage Mitchell. She refused, still frustrated that the sexual preference plank was part of *The Spirit of Houston* report. Abzug's pick, Puerto Rican women's rights advocate Carmen Delgado Votaw, had no such reservations; in June, it was announced that they would lead a forty-member committee.[151]

The wait had been excruciating for Abzug, who had tried for Ed Koch's old seat in the Eighteenth District in the meantime and had not been successful. The Democratic nominee in this special election was decided by an insider vote of the New York Democratic Committee. "I know how to do the job. I've done it. And I think I can do more," she told this group.[152] When an audacious reporter asked how she would overcome her "loser image," Abzug replied, clearly perturbed, "I don't feel like a loser."[153] The Democratic Committee vote went her way, but former councilman Carter Burden, her leading opponent, called foul when six votes in her favor were cast on the wrong color ballot. She lost the next ballot, and this time she contested the outcome, leaving the courts to decide.[154]

When a judge ruled in her favor, Abzug moved on to the general election, where she challenged newcomer Republican Sedgwick William "Bill" Green. Abzug's endorsements from Mayor Koch, Senator Moynihan, and President Carter did not convince East Side voters that she had shifted rightward. A flyer circulated read, "Bella Abzug: Queen of the Lesbos," playing to social conservatives' fears.[155] On Valentine's Day, Abzug received the worst gift that she could, losing by a sliver—29,045 to Green's 29,633. Thrilled, he boasted, "The voters decided that the age of confrontation politics is dead."[156] National and international papers likewise characterized Abzug's loss to "Mr. Nobody" as the "evening shadow" of her political career.[157] Will it "wipe you out?" she was asked. "I would like to suggest to the press that they not write my obituary," she retorted. "As far as I know I'm a 57 year old, alive and well and still kicking and will kick for a long time to come."[158] While so much was true, this election made it clear that Abzug's electoral viability had dissipated and might not rebound.

After this race, Abzug's appointment in the Carter administration was her main access point to the federal arena and a tenuous one from the start.

As Abzug settled into the new offices of the NACW at the Labor Department, Midge Costanza prepared her exit from the White House. Costanza had tired of vying with Carter's male advisers for airtime with the president, as they increasingly persuaded him to exhibit more moderation. Turning to Abzug, she asked her what to do. Sleep on it, go on vacation, Abzug suggested, which was not the response Costanza expected.[159] Pragmatic, Abzug was quite aware that Costanza had provided a necessary buffer between her and the president, a relationship that strained in Costanza's absence. As Carter aide Anne Wexler conceded, Abzug "never really got the respect of the president's people. She was always suspect."[160] Likewise, Abzug did not find Costanza's replacement preferable, believing Sarah Weddington to be a "yes" person despite her feminist credentials as a Texas lawyer who had successfully argued *Roe v. Wade* before the US Supreme Court.

Carter's team saw the NACW primarily as an affirming body formed to signal to the public that the president was good on women's issues. Committee members felt otherwise. They wanted a real commitment of action and face time with the president. Weddington worked toward this end, but a meeting scheduled for fifteen minutes at 1:15 p.m. the day before Thanksgiving was deemed unsatisfactory.[161] NACW members flew to Washington from as far away as Hawaii and gathered one day prior to the meeting between the committee and the president to discuss their agenda. Addie Wyatt raised the view, "I don't think we should go at all," and the group concurred, insulted they had traveled great distances for a photo op.[162] Abzug, who arrived in Washington after NACW members had decided to boycott the meeting, pleaded with the group to reconsider, expecting to be blamed for this decision. Outvoted, she went with the consensus. She and Votaw alerted President Carter that group members saw themselves as domestic advisers, not "just another special interest group pleading for special favors."[163] Votaw and Abzug thought they had made strides during this phone conservation and a follow-up meeting with Eizenstat.[164] As Weddington anticipated, however, the problem would keep "festering."[165]

A conflict was unavoidable. NACW saw the National Women's Conference as the opening salvo of a next phase of women's rights reforms, whereas Carter and his advisers treated it as a culminating point. White House aides thought that a sit-down with the president was unnecessary, while NACW members believed not having this access to be a nonstarter. Weddington recounted that Abzug and Votaw told her, "We have no need to have coffee or tea with you and Anne Wexler and we won't do so."[166] Pressing within the West Wing, Weddington secured time on the president's calendar on January 12.[167] The day before the meeting, the NACW convened in Washington to decide on their agenda. Abzug had not yet arrived. Committee members present voiced their dissatisfaction with Carter's proposed budget that increased military spending and cut social programs. As outsiders drawn to Washington with one purpose in mind—to promote an intersectional agenda for women—they could not be cowed. Instinctively, the NACW drafted a twelve page press release, in which they laid out methodically and pointedly why Carter's anti-inflation policy, "with all its good intentions, will impose additional and disproportionate burdens upon women."[168] Abzug and Votaw had led NACW down this path of most resistance, and this exacting economic critique had been a feature of early correspondence among participants. While she did not help draft the press release, Abzug had publicly critiqued the president for prioritizing the needs of male workers, cutting women-focused social services, and implementing "the highest military spending program in the history of our nation."[169]

When the resulting press release arrived at the White House, the title alone—"President Carter Challenged on Social Priorities by National Advisory Committee for Women"—set off Carter aides.[170] Press secretary Jody Powell promptly took it to communications director Jerry Rafshoon and chief of staff Hamilton Jordan, and "they were angry together."[171] On the spot, they decided Abzug had to be "sacked."[172] The next morning, Carter aides Jordan, Powell, Wexler, Eizenstat, and Weddington, joined by Vice President Walter Mondale's advisor Richard Moe, met to discuss not if Abzug would be fired, but when. Should they do it before or after the scheduled meeting, since reporters had been already invited? At 9:30 a.m. on January 12, 1979, Jordan showed President Carter the press release and presented their recommendation to fire Abzug after the meeting. "Carter agreed. And it was done."[173]

Carter met with NACW members at 2:30 p.m. that day. The conversation that followed is remembered differently depending on which side one was on. "There should be no need for me or my staff to cringe when we see a meeting scheduled with you. I'm a tough politician and I can certainly take criticism, but I thought you were here to work with me. . . . It saps our strength to be confrontational," Weddington recorded Carter stating.[174] "My god, we've just been bawled out by the president of the United States," NOW president Eleanor Smeal recalled thinking. Arkansas ERA organizer Brownie Ledbetter concurred, saying about Carter, "He was literally whining, 'I appointed you. You're my commission. How could you do this to me? I supported you on ERA. I didn't agree with you on abortion, but I let you do your thing. What do my inflation policy and my military policy have to do with women?'"[175] At odds here were Carter's narrow definition of the NACW's domain as limited to traditional "women's issues" versus committee members' more expansive policy interests. Members of the NACW not only felt it was their place to weigh in on austerity policies broadly, but also found it deeply offensive to be pigeonholed. As League of Women Voters officer Nancy Neuman noted, they were not treated as "a group of economic advisors," but rather, "We're to be seen and not heard."[176] The White House put out their own version of the conversation. As one undisclosed aide characterized, "Mrs. Abzug attempted to lecture the President on the duties of the committee and its role in serving the needs of its constituents. She lit into him in front of nearly 40 other people."[177]

After the meeting, Abzug told waiting White House correspondents that the meeting was "very satisfactory" and that "friendship rides a rocky course."[178] She thought that was the end of it, but then an aide unexpectedly stepped into her path and delivered a note from Hamilton Jordan. It read, "Bella: I would like very much to see you briefly after your meeting and press conference."[179] When she arrived, she found Jordan with counsel Robert Lipshutz, who had been called in "to give it a calming, judicial atmosphere."[180] Immediately, Jordan handed Abzug an envelope with a note stating, "To enhance the relationship between the Administration and the Committee and to increase the spirit of consultation, cooperation and partnership, the President believes that new leadership for the Committee will be beneficial."[181] While this dismissal letter was formal and curt, Jordan boiled over, fuming, according to Abzug. "'How dare you write an advance press release before seeing the president," she recalled him accusing. "I begged for an hour to talk with the committee," she recollected, "They were snapping, snapping, it was awful." Abzug made the point that she did not participate in drafting the press release, having arrived on a red-eye after a West Coast speaking engagement. Jordan replied, "You should have been there."[182] To Abzug's question, "Why am I being made a scapegoat?"

Lipshutz countered, "The next thing I know you'll be saying you were fired because you're a Jew."[183] Completely floored, Abzug left the office visibly shaken, pronouncing, "No good, no good at all."[184] Back at her office in the Labor Department, she called Jordan, coaxing, "Let me resign, at least give me that dignity."[185] Abzug never shook how premeditated and callous her firing felt. As her daughter Eve remembered, "She did talk about that all the time. I think she was very sad and angry in a deep way, although it didn't stop her."[186]

Senior aides thought firing Abzug would be "a net plus politically," creating distance between Carter and all but moderate feminists before his re-election campaign.[187] "I suspect a week from now people won't remember anything except that the President fired Bella Abzug. Having a personality conflict with Bella isn't all bad; you have to admit it has a ring of credibility to it," suggested one adviser in talking points circulated within the White House. Carter associates were told to state that "the decision was made some time earlier," even though it was triggered by the NACW press release.[188] Rosalynn Carter publicly called her husband's action the "right thing" to do.[189] Former NCOIWY staff member Catherine East predicted most correctly, "Making a martyr of Bella is no easy task, but Powell and Jordan did it with ease. . . . I would expect that she will campaign for Kennedy."[190]

Carter's team gravely misjudged the reaction to Abzug's firing. Leading feminists coined the event the "Friday Night Massacre" and characterized it as "an act of primordial violence." Steinem called Weddington to alert her, "This means that the entire committee will resign."[191] Weddington tried to coax members to stay, but twenty-seven "deeply shocked" NACW members—more than half of the committee—swore their allegiance to Abzug and exited.[192] She described her dismissal as a sexist act, distinguishing, "When men are fired from the White House, it's usually because they've committed a crime. When women are fired, it's because they've spoken out."[193] Reporters largely agreed, much to the surprise of Carter's advisers. As journalist Ellen Goodman wrote, "Well, the good ole boys of the White House dropped the ax on Abzug with all the style and sensitivity of Attila the Hun."[194] A Harris poll showed 52 percent of Americans rated Carter's action a bad move, and only 29 percent supported the president.[195] Letters of disappointment arrived at the White House. One from the Coalition for Women's Appointments, representing 1 million women in mainstream women's organizations, signaled that many women saw Abzug's firing as an affront to all women. Abzug weathered the slight by traveling the speaking and talk show circuit. Hundreds of letters sent to her echoed one that noted, "You look very well even without your gorgeous hats," praising her hatless appearance on *The Phil Donahue Show*.[196]

BEING FIRED BY PRESIDENT CARTER would definitively mark the conclusion of Bella Abzug's career as an outside agitator working on the inside of the US government. When trying to make sense of this end, she compared the experience to another devastating loss that she carried with her—the execution of her client Mississippian Willie McGee in 1951. News coverage of her firing reminded her of how *Life* magazine had once printed a picture of her as a young lawyer in an article highly critical of the McGee case. "Some friends said, 'Boy, this is worth $50,000 in publicity.' I said, 'yeah, $50,000 *minus*.' Being fired by the president today, you never know. It could be the same thing."[197] Abzug returned to this moment because Carter's firing shook her similarly, and she felt imperiled. Relaying this story to a reporter, Abzug also aimed to signal her resilience as she redoubled her defensive posture. After a decade's hiatus, she renewed her work as a lawyer and grassroots organizer. She remained prominent in Democratic Party politics, retaining influence as a former congresswoman and feminist power broker, but she would not return to office or achieve an appointment akin to leading the NACW.

Abzug's foothold in Congress during her three terms in office had always been fragile, but once she entered the federal legislature, it was hard to imagine working on the outside again. She had been so focused on bringing protest into politics, she had not prepared for an end. In the post–Vietnam War, post-Watergate climate, after the immediate self-reflective flurry of congressional investigation and talk of reform had passed, many Americans reflexively rejected a politics of more—more oversight, more government benefits, and more legal protections. Instead, they desired less—less government in their lives, less federal spending, and less talk of social responsibility. Unable to adapt, Abzug fell out of step with the political times.

The National Women's Conference served as an affirming experience for Abzug as she adjusted to this new climate and braced herself against accompanying losses. It brought her back to the inspiring politics of her youth, reminding her of the time in 1940 when she helped lead Hunter College's all-women legislative congress. In Houston, she moved past this earlier staging exercise to help realize federally mandated women's decision making. The National Women's Conference featured women as astute political actors capable of crafting and deliberating over complex policy proposals, and in turn, fired the imagination of women nationwide. It made many women feel for the first time like they had a tangible stake in a political process in which they were vastly underrepresented. It generated a wide web of impact, inspiring women to seek public office, establish advocacy groups, build new networks, and engage with each other in ways that they had not done previously. And it stirred the partisan passions of its challengers, reminding conservatives what cultural values and policy concerns they most needed to defend.

Abzug's role overseeing this grand expression of civic engagement was the highlight of her public life. She hung on to the spirit of Houston, unsatisfied with leaving the agenda of the National Women's Conference unfinished. But the United States in the 1980s did not offer the promise of progressive reform and structural change that had presented itself one decade prior. At the close of the 1970s, most Americans no longer had an appetite for expansionist policy experimentation or the disruptive talk of remaking US political institutions. The retrenchment politics that took hold instead troubled Abzug greatly but did not unsettle her belief that the Democratic Party could still be a home for progressives. For this reason, she continued to urge leftists to align with Democrats and seek national office to steer the nation toward a more social democratic future.

EPILOGUE

FRANKLY SPEAKING

> Trying to achieve political power without electoral power
> is like unlocking a door and then failing to open it.
>
> —BELLA ABZUG

BELLA ABZUG RENDERED THIS VERDICT in the book she wrote with Mim Kelber, *Gender Gap: Bella Abzug's Guide to Political Power for American Women,* published at the time of President Ronald Reagan's reelection campaign. Political scientists highlighted this "gender gap" when 8 percent less women than men voted for Reagan in 1980, but Abzug had been talking about the difference women could make as swing voters since 1962.[1] Her inability to ultimately harness this gender gap to fully realize a women-led left-liberal new Democratic coalition was deeply disappointing. After the high of the 1977 National Women's Conference, feminists experienced a succession of setbacks culminating in the failure of the Equal Rights Amendment ratification campaign in 1982. As a result, Abzug and Kelber bleakly predicted, "women locked up in an economic ghetto" would lose out further, and an "out-of-control nuclear arms race" would turn into a "nuclear calamity."[2]

After being fired by President Jimmy Carter in 1979, and with few electoral prospects on the horizon, Abzug shed any reluctance she had to temper her progressive pronouncements. That summer, she joined forces with Representatives Patsy Mink and Yvonne Burke (also voted out of office) to establish Women USA. Their most successful venture was a hotline that became an instant hit with feminists, garnering more than 10,000 callers dialing in a month for a "weekly telephone pep talk."[3] One of their first orders of business was to direct women "fed up with inflation" to send their bills to Congress.[4] Women USA, however, had its own financial troubles. The group's legislative director, Margaret Mason, quit within eight months because the promise of resources, staff, and a workplace beyond her efficiency apartment never materialized.[5] Subsequently, Mim Kelber ran Women USA out of Abzug's home for the next three years on funds donated by Arkansas feminist and friend Brownie Ledbetter.

Women USA reached the already converted, and Abzug wanted to amplify her megaphone further. Cable News Network, launched in June 1980, offered wider possibilities. Abzug was among the first political figures in talks with the Atlanta channel headed by entrepreneur Ted Turner about potential programming. Being a television personality appealed, and Abzug pitched a crossfire-style program, a late-night talk show, and women's issues town halls. Instead, she was hired as one of twenty-three inaugural political commentators, selected for her candid, straight-for-the-jugular take on current events. "I love it a lot. . . . I have total freedom," she freely confessed, enjoying this newfound license to be unfiltered.[6] The immediacy of this medium, available nearly around-the-clock, capturing breaking news, and beamed into 4.3 million living rooms by the end of the network's first year, attracted Abzug always on the move. She jotted down quick drafts of her short spots wherever she went, often on the back of Women USA stationery. No issue was too big or small to tackle, from deregulation to real-life Norma Raes. At the end of each commentary, she signed off, "This is Bella Abzug, and I'm not talking through my hat."[7]

Unsurprisingly, Abzug did not recede into the wings after exiting President Carter's administration. Instead, she dug in for a fight to keep the New Politics wing of the Democratic Party front and center during the 1980 race. She used her post at CNN to augment her public critique of Carter during his reelection campaign. On air, she pointedly warned viewers, "Although President Carter has been awarded the nomination by the media, the fact is that he can't be certain of having a majority of the votes until the convention takes place—and that's still 10 weeks away. The President is smiling in public, but he should be worrying in private."[8]

Abzug backed Senator Edward Kennedy when he challenged President Carter as progressives' choice during the Democratic primary, a contest that deeply marred Carter's chances of reelection. Kennedy thought that

Carter had struck the wrong tone in his "malaise" speech delivered on July 15, 1979, in which he diagnosed a national "crisis of confidence" brought on by oil dependency and stagnation. Abzug agreed. In his televised address, Carter warned Americans that the nation was moving down a path of "fragmentation and self-interest."[9] Abzug believed that Carter's call for unity, faith, and redirection came at the cost of abandoning liberalism, diminishing hard-fought legal protections, and sidelining American women. What he saw as discord, she saw as a healthy conversation. Abzug recognized that identity politics had complicated her leadership among feminists, acknowledging going into the 1980 election that "the women's movement is too diverse, democratic and multi-issued to operate in a totally unified, one-voice fashion."[10] But she believed this broadening of participants and interests was a positive measure of greater democratization, not a sign of the nation's breakdown. Likewise, she maintained that cutbacks should not amount to stifling the government's social safety net or deregulating its services when so many Americans were suffering. In her view, Carter prioritized stability over equity, seeking moderation when the intensity of the problems the nation faced required greater imagination. Nor could Abzug get over their personal rift. And so, looking toward the Democratic National Convention, she defiantly criticized Carter and charged, "Women will not be gagged."[11]

In January 1980, Abzug met with Kennedy to iron out the terms of her involvement in his campaign.[12] It was an easy decision to back him, for they were fond of each other, had worked on legislation together while Abzug was in Congress, and had a shared sense of purpose in maintaining focus on progressive issues. Kennedy's challenge of Carter lacked the fortitude and vivacity of a building upset akin to the campaign launched by his brother Robert F. Kennedy or Eugene McCarthy in 1968. But Ted Kennedy's campaigning in Iowa and New Hampshire emboldened him to be "unfettered by concerns" and to unleash his "inner progressive."[13] He charged Carter with introducing "Republican inflation . . . Republican interest rates . . . and Republican economics."[14] Delighted, Abzug pushed the same line during her national stumping for Kennedy in spring and summer. Years later, he called her contribution "very courageous," acknowledging appreciatively, "It certainly did not look like it was going to be a winning cause."[15]

Kennedy's strong showing in the New York, Connecticut, California, and New Jersey primaries ensured that progressive Democrats would be a potent irritant for the Carter campaign at the Democratic National Convention. Abzug worked with the imperfect role she had, voted in as a delegate of New York, but without a place on the Platform Committee or connected Task Forces. Kennedy recruited Abzug to be an informal whip, keeping his delegates in line on the floor. He saw her as "enormously important" in this role, pressuring for planks "on issues of health, on employment, on a number of women's issues."[16]

What happened at the Republican National Convention in Detroit right before the DNC made the stakes higher. Abzug had been on-site, rallying with protesters voicing their concern that the Republican Party had been taken over by social conservatives. The party platform indicated this shift, introducing a plank calling for a right to life constitutional amendment and, for the first time in forty years, omitting a plank endorsing the ERA.[17] When the DNC commenced at Madison Square Garden, Abzug prepared to rally for Kennedy's full economic package, but she prioritized responding to the Republican Party's platform. Negotiations at the 1976 convention ensured that half of the delegates would be women in 1980, and Abzug capitalized on this numerical strength to help secure the passage of two planks beyond Carter's comfort zone. The first required party funding to be withheld from candidates who would not back the ERA, and a second called for government funding of abortions through Medicaid. Pleased with the results, Abzug pronounced, "The White House . . . has always failed to understand 'women's issues,' but they may understand them a bit better today."[18]

This victory came with long-term costs. These planks accentuated the growing gulf between the Republican Party and Democratic Party on social issues. Second, as the National Women's Political Caucus predicted, the frustrating "cycle of hard work, great expectations, some accomplishments, and limited rewards" would continue for Democratic women for some time.[19] Essentially, delegate strength did not immediately equate to a reorganization of the gendered power structure of the party. Democratic leadership retreated from a commitment to greater party democratization, worried about the growing diversity of interests along identity and ideological lines. As a result, party leaders introduced unelected superdelegates with voting powers in 1984 to keep insolent internal challenges akin to McCarthy's, McGovern's, and Robert and Ted Kennedy's in check. This two-tiered power base has endured, although a resurgent push for democratization pressured Democratic leaders in 2018 to restrict superdelegate voting during the first ballot at the convention.[20]

AS MUCH AS ABZUG DID NOT LIKE CARTER, she feared a Reagan presidency more. After the DNC, she joined a band of leftists and liberals actively cautioning their kin to continue pressing Carter, but once he returned to the White House, her pragmatism kicked in. She worried that discord among Democrats would turn the nation over to "radical Right wing groups." Abzug accurately read the Republican Party's platform as a sign that social conservatives were coalescing around one party. While she abhorred "right-to-life" Democrats, she worried about the country's hardening partisan divide. Additionally, she feared that Reagan's Supreme Court appointments could "set back the cause of equality for years to come."[21]

As Abzug expected, feminists had little influence in the federal arena during President Ronald Reagan's years in office. Abzug transitioned to global advocacy over the next decade in pursuit of a new theater of impact. The month before the 1980 DNC, she spent two weeks in Copenhagen at the second UN World Conference on Women. There, she captivated as an "international figure in a big straw hat who was being greeted in many languages with cries of 'Bella!'"[22] By her death on March 31, 1998, she had become so notable in NGO circles that leaders in other countries were called "'the Bella Abzug of Nigeria' or 'the Bella Abzug of Mongolia.'"[23] But it was a return to public office in the United States that she favored, and that remained out of reach. In her wildest "possible dream," she imagined herself "back on Capitol Hill," seated as a member of Congress when "the President, elegant and almost regal in her purple silk dress" delivered her State of the Union address.[24]

Abzug thought about a run each election cycle. In 1982, she briefly tested the prospect of challenging Ted Weiss in Manhattan's Eighteenth District. "For some time now, people have been telling me that one of the ways you send a message to Reagan is to send Bella" to Congress, she averred.[25] Soliciting a few thousand signatures, her petition campaign did not achieve the traction needed for a formidable bid, and she decided, "I am keeping my hat out of the local ring—for now."[26] Again in 1984, she sat out the race. Instead, she used her continued political clout and the occasion of her *Gender Gap* book tour to put the pressure on Democratic Party leaders to put a woman on the presidential ticket. Abzug was not alone in asking, "Why not a woman vice president?" and contributing to a well-organized Women's Presidential Project.[27] The effort persuaded Democratic nominee Walter Mondale, a moderate former senator from Minnesota and Carter's vice president, to select Representative Geraldine Ferraro from Queens, New York, as his running mate. In July, Abzug and other influential Democratic women had met with Mondale and made clear that the DNC would be unpleasant if he did not go this route. While Abzug lobbied state party chairs, governors, senators, and representatives to back Ferraro, those close to Abzug saw this pick as a rejection of her political style. As Ronnie Eldridge wrote in an op-ed, Ferraro may be "smart, charming, good looking and not shrill," but "when Gerry Ferraro speaks . . . she knows and I know and so do all the women who came through the years that somewhere in that voice, hidden but a part of it forever, is Bella Abzug bellowing."[28]

The years of women's organizing that boosted Ferraro's prospects were not lost on Democrats. As one male DNC delegate noted, "They used the vehicles of power effectively. They have developed their networks. They understand the agenda. . . . They have built up their leadership, and they have worked to get people like Ferraro into positions of power."[29] This long-term mobilization of women in politics helped Ferraro but did not secure a win for Mondale. Afterward, Democratic strategist Frank Mankiewicz faulted feminists who "can't deliver their sisters" for Mondale's loss, suggesting they were out of touch and "not talking like most American women are talking."[30] Abzug had a different explanation. She countered that "the powerful arguments that could have been made about Mr. Reagan's dreadful record on women's concerns were submerged in the frantic quest for white male votes, which did not materialize."[31]

The 1984 presidential race brought into stark relief a new reality: Democrats could no longer depend on support from their traditional white, male working-class base. Abzug's solution to this problem was to actively cultivate support from white women and women of color. Doing the math, she knew that if women mobilized collectively, they could swing elections, and she remained convinced that women naturally leaned left of center. Her critique of Democratic leadership went beyond one of gender parity to consider economics as well. She believed Democrats missed the mark during the last decade by ineffectively addressing the wealth stratification and domestic divestment that came with a global capitalist economy. As the new postindustrial, feminized domestic economy took root, Abzug urged Democrats to promote greater equalizing mechanisms and invest in green industries. During the 1980s, she continued to steer Democrats in this direction, encouraging, "I think we could use a rebirth of the human spirit and passion and caring about people who are not as well-off as Mr. Reagan and the people he represents."[32] Instead, the neoliberal strain of deregulation, public-private partnership, and "choice" liberalism that took hold in the Democratic Party in the mid-1970s gained the strongest footing. This market-minded program promoted by the centrist Democratic Leadership Council, formed in response to Reagan's 1984 landslide, carried the party forward. These New Democrats, as they came to be called, did not practice the kind of new politics Abzug and her counterparts had in mind.

Abzug anticipated the needs of a majority-minority US democracy still coming to form because of her intersectional orientation grounded in her Popular Front past. She looked toward a future when the United States would move beyond its self-image as a "melting pot" to a nation proud to be defined by its multiracial, multigendered majority. In the 1960s and 1970s, she tried to articulate and actualize this future, talking of a multifarious Democratic coalition that in the early twenty-first century has not yet been realized. As she transitioned from student activist to political lawyer, she came to see her otherness as a Jew and a woman as linked to her level of educational and workplace opportunity. And as she defended clients marked as "un-Americans" in civil rights and civil liberties cases, she considered how fortunate she was among working mothers to have help at home and financial security. In 1970, she ran on a platform that focused on ending the Vietnam War, addressing urban abandonment, adjusting to a diverse workforce and deindustrializing economy, and expanding women's and gay rights. In the 1980s and 1990s, she still promoted this broad progressive program that fused bread-and-butter issues with the diverse currents of social liberation. She did not believe that "the people's" interests should be narrowly defined by whiteness or maleness.

The economic heart of Abzug's intersectional politics has been overlooked. Part of this was her doing, for once she left office in 1976 and had difficulty making a return, she amplified her call for gender parity in politics within the United States and abroad. Another reason can be traced to political developments beyond Abzug. The neoliberal turn in the Democratic Party and US society at large made it less attractive to foreground her leftist class critique when defining her feminist legacy. Her call for re-distribution of wealth and the protection of all workers proved more challenging than her support of identity politics.

ABZUG TRIED FOR A CONGRESSIONAL COMEBACK one last time in 1986, returning after twenty years to Mount Vernon, New York, to run for a seat in the House of Representatives. "I don't know why she wants to go back there. She's too good for them," Martin told reporters.[33] Bella ignored his misgivings and set up a law office in White Plains. On June 6, she announced her candidacy. "I've been there. I know the ropes, and I know the players," she maintained.[34] For a month, she trekked from Manhattan to Westchester County, reintroducing herself through a door-knocking campaign. On July 19, she was abruptly summoned home. The scene she returned to was one for which she could not prepare.

Martin was dead. He had gone out for a jog and collapsed shortly after his return. "He overcame the [heart] attacks so well it never occurred to me that he could die" of one, Bella later granted. She never quite recovered from her husband's absence after more than forty years together.[35] At sixty-nine, he still worked at Phillips, Appel & Walden, and had just finished writing a new novel about a man's search for his Nazi tormentor. "There she was on the floor next to him," remembered Bella's sister, Helene. "What a scene that was. Berating herself the whole time."[36] Bella herself recalled, "I kept crying, 'What did I do, why was I campaigning in Westchester, why did I run for Congress again, why wasn't I here, how stupid was I, how terrible was I, why wasn't I here to prevent this?'"[37] More than 400 came out to Martin's service at the Riverside Memorial Chapel. "He was the Fred Astaire of Jewish husbands," eulogized actress Renée Taylor, among the entertainers who were close friends.[38] "I don't think that she ever, ever, ever got over the fact that Martin was no longer there. She was a slightly different person," observed Gloria Steinem.[39]

Most expected this setback would mark the end of Bella Abzug's congressional run. Three weeks later, to everyone's surprise, she returned to "carry the struggle without him."[40] Sympathetic journalists noted "a different timbre" in her campaign. "She is listening to her sorrow, and it can be heard wherever she goes or wherever she used to be."[41] She did not win this election, trailing a Reagan backer, incumbent Joe DioGaurdi, by

10 percent. In 1992, another "year of the woman," she flirted one last time with the notion of running for Ted Weiss's former seat. To do so pitted her against Ronnie Eldridge, and it strained their friendship.[42] Mayor David Dinkins gave Abzug her final role in domestic politics, appointing her as chair of the Commission on the Status of Women in New York City. In this position, she directed attention to women's health and environmentalism, raising awareness of breast cancer before realizing she faced this battle personally. In 1994, she underwent a double mastectomy. Afterward, she reassured, "I proceed as though I've got a shot."[43]

Abzug found the greatest purpose in the last years of her life outside the United States as a champion of global women's rights. Her longest collaborator, Mim Kelber, led the way. As a reporter for the *Federated Press,* she had covered the UN's opening conference in San Francisco in 1945. At the UN's Third World Conference on Women in Nairobi, Kenya, in 1985, Abzug chaired the NGO Forum '85's largest breakout session, "Women and Political Power." Representing fifteen nations, eighteen state ministers, legislators, diplomats, and NGO leaders debated a question Abzug continuously came back to: "If women ruled the world would the world be different today, and how?"[44] In this wider arena, Abzug emerged as an adept negotiator, helping women navigate tricky locational politics to iron out common goals. Global advocacy work gave her a focal point to direct her organizing skills and draw on her congressional experience. As *Sisterhood Is Global* author Robin Morgan observed, "She had found another structure— a system she could learn about and get into to change it."[45] Believing international work could give Abzug new flight, Kelber encouraged her friend to join her in global advocacy ventures she initiated. In the mid-1980s, Kelber led an effort to create a diplomatic shadow structure of a few hundred set up to counter the "white male elite obsessed with military supremacy," which in 1987 became the Women's Foreign Policy Council.[46] This project naturally evolved into the NGO she cofounded with Abzug in 1991, the Women's Environment and Development Organization (WEDO).

WEDO took off as an influential NGO just as global focus on women and development expanded and a women's rights imperative formalized in US foreign policy.[47] WEDO's founding conference in Miami in November 1991, the World Women's Congress for a Healthy Planet, attracted 1,500 women from eighty-three nations.[48] Participants drafted the ambitious Women's Action Agenda 21 that echoed the National Plan of Action passed by American women in Houston in 1977. Abzug came to this international work with her national identity intact. Although she steered the US toward a more social democratic model, she nonetheless held US democratic values consecrated in the Constitution as superior. Not slowing down, she instead spent the 1990s jetting to international gatherings of women and chauffeuring between her Greenwich Village apartment and UN headquarters. She complained of the endless meetings but thoroughly enjoyed being at the center of women-focused decision making once again. Abzug's final international voyage of note was to the fourth UN World Conference on Women in Beijing, China, in 1995.

Abzug's health declined at a rapid pace. At seventy-five, she found it difficult to move, but she willed herself onto a plane bound for Beijing. Heavyset and with heart problems, too out of breath and too sore to walk, she depended on others—Robin Morgan, Jo Freeman, Susan Davis—to push her around in a wheelchair. Abzug bounced along muddy paths at the outlying NGO Forum, buoyed by the sight of women's activists' exchanging ideas. Speaking at the Beijing Convention Center, she implored high-level diplomats gathered for these official proceedings to take women seriously. As she reminded, "We have arms—to reach out and be inclusive; legs—to get where we need to go . . . thinking heads—the brain power the world so desperately needs . . . we also have lungs—and we're prepared to keep raising our voices for equality, development and peace."[49] Her final speech in 1998 was before the United Nations, back in Manhattan. The day after she addressed this body, she checked into the hospital for heart surgery, from which she did not recover.

ABZUG KEPT HER MIND moving forward as her body slowed down. Facing physical impairment, she raised her voice in a column she wrote for the *Earth Times* appropriately titled, "Frankly Speaking."[50] It was this commitment to forthright, defiant speech backed by bold, tenacious acts that had made her such a powerful force in US politics.

In the 1980s and 1990s, Abzug did a lot of this speaking on college campuses, seeking to spark the fire of a new generation. "We need to act decisively to limit the government's efforts to victimize the people who can't defend themselves," she told students at CSU-Long Beach in 1981.[51] Abzug lamented that she and New Politics Democrats had not done more in

Congress. She found it troubling that women in politics had not made greater inroads, with women's presence in Congress far from equal to that of men and the patriarchal foundation of US law and political culture still largely intact. Equally regrettable, the national security state she tried to destabilize had proven resilient. An outsider again, Abzug saw "the same gang of crazies" in charge of the Pentagon and the White House.[52] She and other reformers had brought greater transparency to government, but they had not remade its structure or shifted its policy direction to the level they had hoped.

For much of her life, Abzug gained strength by working at the periphery as a defender of the defenseless—workers, racial and sexual minorities, political radicals, new immigrants, and women—in challenge of the status quo. She believed that dissent was an empty vessel, however, if not accompanied by access to and active participation in the political and legal system. US law upheld deep-seated patterns of injustice but also served as a social instrument for change. In her view, it was up to the nation's progressive-minded citizens to agitate until the balance in power leaned toward the many, and the definition of freedom tilted toward justice.

Abzug consistently critiqued leftists who believed "the system" was so broken it was not worth fixing. Reform was not only a liberal device, fixing from the edges. It could be transformative. Protest could be brought into politics. Here, Abzug's leftist worldview and legal background came through most. She favored breaking through rather than breaking up what already existed. She sought radical ends, but did not think radicalism was antithetical to reform. She toiled against the tide, but she wanted to be recognized as the Olympic swimmer who could. She was a collectivist and an individualist, a charismatic feminist leader who wanted to lift women as she climbed.

Abzug believed Democrats could do better, which is why she joined the party despite being a critic of Presidents Kennedy and Johnson. She wanted Democrats to come to grips with the new realities of a more stratified, diverse workforce and economy. She hoped they would abandon their Cold War mentality that allowed for permanent war and a pervasive culture of surveillance. In her last years, she continued to press these positions as a leftist working within Democratic Party ranks rather than returning to third-party politics. This mutually constitutive relationship between liberalism and the Left has refocused the Democratic Party's direction at key junctures.[53]

Progressives such as Abzug became rebel partisans within the Democratic Party because they thought that they could make the greatest difference by engaging electoral politics. They also believed that they could achieve sizable political clout by drawing on grassroots pressure, which offered its own form of organizational and persuasive power outside of party clubs. The heightened state of unrest in the late 1960s and early 1970s stirred many Americans' will for something different. Social movement energy was high. The Vietnam War and the Watergate scandal had galvanized opposition. Voters were primed for change. A small but passionate cadre of activist politicians, boosted by a wider progressive network, capitalized on this opening and entered Congress. Once there, New Politics Democrats helped disrupt the party's establishment, revive congressional might, and secure legislative reforms. Legal feminism advanced in the confluence of New Politics experimentation, but so did laws expanding privacy rights; environmental regulation; disability accommodations; executive oversight; human rights; and workplace, educational, and consumer protections. New Politics Democrats did not achieve the totalizing political realignment they were after, and the party pulled back, opting for moderation in subsequent decades. Nonetheless, their example highlights the regenerative impact of party insurgencies. Their unfinished agenda animates progressives today.

Debate, so essential to the health of a democracy, continues to be the lifeblood of US society. An unabashed dissenter, Bella Abzug embraced the democratic right to speak freely and loudly in public each day of her life. At the core, she was a stubborn idealist who exposed uncomfortable truths because she held her nation in high esteem. She lived out the Jewish maxim *lo dayenu*—it is not good enough, and we will not be satisfied. She urged Americans to go beyond naming social problems to do the hard work of developing and implementing policy solutions. Some of her ideas were workable and some were unrealistic. Some were embraced and some were unpopular. Her story encourages reevaluation of the 1970s not as an era of limits but as an imaginative, expansive period. Ideas churned, new discussions about rights and liberties stirred, because Americans were unsatisfied. Her example suggests that resistance is a fundamental posture of the American character.

ABBREVIATIONS

Manuscript Collections

Ann Arbor, Michigan

Gerald Ford Presidential Library

KL	Kenneth Larazus Files
PLJH	Patricia Lindh and Jeanne Holm Files
RAC	RAC Project Files
RW	Robert K. Wolthuis Files
VLCL	Vernon C. Loen and Charles Leppert Files

Atlanta, Georgia

Jimmy Carter Presidential Library

CL	Cooki Lutkefedder's Subject Files
HJ	Hamilton Jordan Subject Files
LB	Landon Butler Subject Files
OSS	Records of the Office of the Staff Secretary
SE	Stuart Eizenstat Subject Files
SW	Sarah Weddington Subject Files

Manuscript, Archives, and Rare Book Library, Emory University

JC	John M. Coe Papers

Cambridge, Massachusetts

Schlesinger Library on the History of Women in America, Harvard University

BF   Betty Friedan Papers
CE   Catherine East Papers
NWPCP   National Women's Political Caucus Papers

Durham, North Carolina

Rare Book, Manuscript, and Special Collections Library, Duke University

JBM   J. B. Matthews Papers
RM   Robin Morgan Papers

Houston, Texas

Special Collections Library, University of Houston

HNOW   Houston Area NOW Papers
LM   Linda May Papers
MR   Marjorie Randall Papers
NVH   Nikki Van Hightower Papers

Madison, Wisconsin

Wisconsin Historical Society

DA   Donna Allen Papers
NCNPWI   National Conference for New Politics Papers
RKP   Robert Kastenmeier Papers
WSPWI   Women Strike for Peace Papers

New Brunswick, New Jersey

Special Collections and University Archives, Rutgers University

NDCP   New Democratic Coalition Papers
SCP   Shirley Chisholm Papers

New York, New York

American Jewish Historical Society and Yivo Institute

AV   Avukah
JSO   Jewish Student Organizations
YIL   Yivo Institute Library

Archives and Special Collections, Hunter College

HCA   Hunter College Archives

College Archives, Columbia University

YBS   Young B. Smith Central File

Columbia Center for Oral History Archives, Columbia University

BAOH   Reminiscences of Bella Abzug (1995 and 1996)
BDOH   Reminiscences of Ben Davidson (1977)
CBMOH   Reminiscences of Judge Constance Baker Motley (1978)
EKOH   Reminiscences of Edward Koch (1976)
JVOH   Reminiscences of Judith P. Vladeck (2001)
KBOH   Reminiscences of Katherine Berger (1988)
LBOH   Reminiscences of Leonard Boudin (1983)
MKOH   Reminiscences of Mim Kelber (1983)
NWOH   Reminiscences of Nathan Witt (1969)
SMOH   Reminiscences of Sally Falk Moore (2001)

Municipal Archives, New York City

JVLP   Mayor John V. Lindsay Papers (Microfilm)

Rare Book and Manuscript Library, Columbia University

BSA   Bella Abzug Papers
MB   Martha Baker Papers
MKP   Mim Kelber Papers (WEDO)
ZI   Oral Interviews by Mel Ziegler in BSA (1971)

Schomburg Center for Research in Black Culture, New York Public Library

CRCP   Civil Rights Congress Papers

Tamiment Library and Robert F. Wagner Labor Archives, New York University

AU   Abraham Unger Papers
BK   Barbara Kopple: Peekskill Riots Collection
HFP   Henry Foner Papers
JG   Jay Gorney Papers
NLGNY   National Lawyers Guild Papers

Northampton, Massachusetts

Sophia Smith Collection of Women's History, Smith College

CBMP   Constance Baker Motley Papers
GSP   Gloria Steinem Papers
MMK   Mary Metlay Kaufman Papers

Palo Alto, California

Hoover Institution Library and Archives, Stanford University

JCH   J. C. Hurewitz Collection

Princeton, New Jersey

Seeley G. Mudd Manuscript Library, Princeton University

GMP   George McGovern Papers
WFRP   William Fitts Ryan Papers

Swarthmore, Pennsylvania

Swarthmore College Peace Collection

BAWSP   Bella Abzug Collection
WSPP   Women Strike for Peace Papers

Washington, DC

Federal Bureau of Investigation

FBI File   Bella Abzug, 100-102413

Library of Congress

DPMP   Daniel Patrick Moynihan Papers
DSGP   Democratic Study Group Papers
GLP   George Lardner Jr. Papers
HDCR   House Democratic Caucus Records
PMP   Patsy Mink Papers

National Archives and Records Administration

GIIRGO   Government Information and Individual Rights Subcommittee, Government Operations Committee, Record Group 233
SCR   Supreme Court Records

Yorba Linda, California

Richard M. Nixon Presidential Library

AANPL   Anne L. Armstrong Papers
BFRNL   Barbara Franklin Papers
SOH   Staff Oral Histories
WHT   White House Tapes

Interviews by Author

AFG08   Ann Fagan Ginger, April 28, 2008, Berkeley, California
AS07   Amy Swerdlow, November 1, 2007, New York City
BC12   William "Bill" Chafe, October 3, 2012, Phone Interview
CG14   Curtis Gans, January 15, 2014, and February 3, 2014, Phone
         Interviews
CR09   Claire Reed, September 23, 2009, New York City
DA14   Richard "Dick" Aurelio, September 26, 2014, Phone Interview
DMH09   Diana Mara Henry, September 9, 2009, Springfield, Massachusetts
EA12   Eve Abzug, October 26, 2012, New York City
EH14   Eric Hirschhorn, January 6, 2014, Washington, DC
EL15   Elizabeth Langer, September 8, 2015, New York City
EM14   Elizabeth Moynihan, September 4, 2014, New York City
EN15   Esther Newberg, December 9, 2015, Phone Interview
HF07   Henry Foner, November 21, 2007, New York City
HH14   Harold Holzer, September 8, 2014, New York City
HM14   Hal Mayerson, October 30, 2014, Phone Interview
HNM10   Howard N. Meyer, May 5, 2010, Phone Interview
JC14   Jim Crawford, December 9, 2014, Phone Interview
JK14   Jay Kriegel, October 15, 2014, Phone Interview
JL07   Judy Lerner, November 27, 2007, New York City
JN07   Joan Nixon, October 24, 2007, New York City
JS09   Jean Shulman, September 25, 2009, New York City
JW14   Jerome Wilson, January 2, 2014, Phone Interview
JWO15   Judy Wolf, April 9, 2015, Phone Interview
KLK11   Karli and Laura Kelber, June 6, 2011, Brooklyn, New York
LA05   Liz Abzug, August 3, 2005, New York City
LA07   Liz Abzug, February 11, 2007, Phone Interview
MB07   Martha Baker, November 15, 2007, New York City
MB09   Martha Baker, September 23, 2009, Queens, New York
MDF07   Mickey and Dick Flacks, January 19, 2007, Santa Barbara,
         California
MM14   Marilyn Marcosson, January 8, 2014, Washington, DC

NS15   Nancy Stanley, March 29, 2015, Phone Interview
RSH09   Ralph Shapiro, March 17, 2009, New York City
RE14   Ronnie Eldridge, September 8, 2014, New York City
RS14   Rochelle Slovin, September 4, 2014, New York City
SD14   Sid Davidoff, April 18, 2014, Phone Interview
SG09   Sandra Gorney, March 18, 2009, New York City

Publications

AM   *Atlantic Monthly*
ASA   *Avukah Student Action*
BG   *Boston Globe*
BS   *Baltimore Sun*
CL   *Clarion Ledger*
CQ   *Congressional Quarterly*
CQWR   *Congressional Quarterly Weekly Report*
CR   *Congressional Record*
CSM   *Christian Science Monitor*
CT   *Chicago Tribune*
DB   *Daily Breakthrough*
DN   *Daily News*
ET   *Earth Times*
HB   *Hunter Bulletin*
HC   *Hartford Courant*
HE   *Human Events*
JDF   *Jewish Daily Forward*
JDN   *Jackson Daily News*
JP   *Jewish Press*
L   *Life* magazine
LAT   *Los Angeles Times*
MT   *Manhattan Tribune*
ND   *Newsday*
NG   *National Guardian*
NR   *New Republic*
NY   *New York* magazine
NYAN   *New York Amsterdam News*
NYJW   *New York Jewish Week*
NYP   *New York Post*
NYT   *New York Times*
PI   *Philadelphia Inquirer*
PSR   *Phyllis Schlafly Report*
RS   *Rolling Stone*

T	*Time* magazine
TG	*The Guardian*
TNY	*The New Yorker*
TS	*The Sun*
TV	*The Villager*
USNWR	*U.S. News & World Report*
VV	*Village Voice*
WP	*Washington Post*
WSJ	*Wall Street Journal*

Organizations and Institutions

ABA	American Bar Association
ACLU	American Civil Liberties Union
ADA	Americans for Democratic Action
AJC	American Jewish Congress
ALP	American Labor Party
ASU	American Student Union
CCC	Central Coordinating Committee
CCNY	City College of New York
CDA	Coalition for a Democratic Alternative
CDM	Committee for a Democratic Majority
CIO	Congress of Industrial Organizations
CNN	Cable News Network
CPUSA	Communist Party of the United States
CRC	Civil Rights Congress
CU	Columbia University
DNC	Democratic National Convention
DP	Democratic Party
DSG	Democratic Study Group
GAA	Gay Activists Alliance
GLF	Gay Liberation Front
Guild	National Lawyers Guild
HC	Hunter College
HH	Hashomer Hatzair
JDL	Jewish Defense League
JRB	Jeanette Rankin Brigade
JTS	Jewish Theological Seminary
MCPP	Metropolitan Council for Peace Politics
NAACP	National Association for the Advancement of Colored People
NCNP	National Conference for a New Politics
NCPAC	National Conservative Political Action Committee

NDC	New Democratic Coalition
NGO	nongovernmental organization
NOW	National Organization for Women
NWP	National Woman's Party
NWPC	National Women's Political Caucus
NWRO	National Welfare Rights Organization
NYRW	New York Radical Women
NY WSP	New York Women Strike for Peace
RNC	Republican National Convention
SANE	National Committee for a Sane Nuclear Policy
SCLC	Southern Christian Leadership Council
SDS	Students for a Democratic Society
17th CD PAC	Seventeenth District Peace Action Committee
SNCC	Student Nonviolent Coordinating Committee
UFT	United Federation of Teachers
VID	Village Independent Democrats
VVAW	Vietnam Vets Against the War
WEAL	Women's Equity Action League
WEDO	Women's Environment and Development Organization
WEDS	Women's Education of Delegate Selection
WILPF	Women's International League for Peace and Freedom
WRP	ACLU Women's Rights Project
WSP	Women Strike for Peace
YAF	Young Americans for Freedom
YCL	Young Communist League

Government Agencies, Bodies, and Legislation

CIA	Central Intelligence Agency
CRS	Congressional Research Service
DOD	Department of Defense
DOJ	Department of Justice
DOT	Department of Transportation
ECOA	Equal Credit Opportunity Act
EEOC	Equal Employment Opportunity Commission
ERA	Equal Rights Amendment
FBI	Federal Bureau of Investigation
FCC	Federal Communications Commission
FOGI	Foreign Operations and Government Information Subcommittee
FOIA	Freedom of Information Act (1966 and 1974)
FTC	Federal Trade Commission
GIIR	Government Information and Individual Rights Subcommittee

GO	Government Operations Committee
HEW	Department of Health, Education, and Welfare
HUAC	House Un-American Activities Committee
IRS	Internal Revenue Service
IWY	International Women's Year
NACW	National Advisory Committee for Women
NCOIWY	National Commission on the Observance of International Women's Year
NLF	National Liberation Front
NLRB	National Labor Relations Board
NSA	National Security Agency
NSC	National Security Council
NVA	North Vietnamese Army
NWC	National Women's Conference
SA	Special Agent
SAC	Special Agent in Charge
SISS	Senate Internal Security Subcommittee
SS	Secret Service
UN	United Nations
USSC	Supreme Court
WH	White House

NOTES

Introduction

Epigraph: Bella Abzug quoted in Mary McGrory, "The Capitol Letter: Bella Sandpapers the House into Shape," *NY*, April 14, 1957, 7, "Administrative Files—Personal—Campaign 1976, n.d.," Box 64, BSA. Hereafter, folder citations are condensed to the identifier unique to each folder noted after the series and subject (for example, "Campaign 1976, n.d."). I have listed the title noted on the physical folder, which differs at times from the electronic finding aid.

1. Claire Demers, "An Interview with Andy Warhol: Some Say He's the *Real* Mayor of New York," in *I'll Be Your Mirror: The Selected Andy Warhol Interviews,* ed. Kenneth Goldsmith (New York: Carroll and Graf, 2004), 265–273, quoted on 268; Pat Hackett, ed., *The Andy Warhol Diaries* (New York: Twelve, Hachette Book Group, 2014), 53; see also 30, 71, 109, 115.

2. Hackett, *Andy Warhol Diaries,* xii.

3. Some of these Polaroids went to auction at Christie's in 2013. See https://onlineonly.christies.com/s/andy-warhol-christies/bella-abzug-105/201.

4. Leonard McCombe, "Now Women Talk Back: The Politics of '72," *L*, June 9, 1972, 46–50, 46. For the limited scholarship on Abzug, see Judith Nies, *Nine Women: Portraits from the American Radical Tradition* (Berkeley: University of California Press, 2002), 237–268; Alan H. Levy, *The Political Life of Bella Abzug, 1920–1976: Political Passions, Women's Rights, and Congressional Battles* (Lanham, MD: Lexington Books, 2013); Levy, *The Political Life of Bella Abzug, 1976–1998: Electoral Failures and the Vagaries of Identity Politics* (Lanham, MD: Lexington Books, 2013); Masaya Sato, "Bella Abzug's Dilemma: The Cold War, Women's Politics, and the Arab-Israeli Conflict in the 1970s," *Journal of Women's History* 3, no. 2 (Summer 2018): 112–135; Rhodri Jeffreys-Jones, *Changing Differences: Women and the Shaping of American Foreign Policy, 1917–1994* (New Brunswick, NJ: Rutgers University Press, 1995), 131–154; Doris Faber, *Bella Abzug* (New York: Lothrop, Lee and Shepard,

1976); Blanche Wiesen Cook, "Bella Abzug," in *Jewish Women in America,* ed. Paula Hyman and Deborah Dash Moore (New York: Routledge, 1997).

5. Paul Rudnick, October 23, 2016, @PaulRudnickNY, https://mobile.twitter .com/pualrudnickny.

6. "Bella Abzug Park: NYC Parks Announces Renaming of Hudson Yards Park in Honor of Activist, Congresswoman Bella Abzug," March 1, 2019, https://www.nycgovparks.org/parks/hudson-park/pressrelease/21644.

7. Eliza Berman, "Hillary Clinton Has This Woman to Thank for Her Campaign," *T,* April 12, 2015, www.time.com/374970/Hillary-clinton-bella -abzug/.

8. "Look Closely. There's Something Missing," n.d., "Abzug File 1976," Box 52, NDC. For congressional statistics, see http://history.house.gov/Exhibitions -and-Publications/WIC/Historical-Data/Women-Representatives-and-Senators-by -Congress/.

9. "Program of Goals and Action," with notation, n.d., "Background Information," Box 990, BSA.

10. A growing literature on women in politics includes Susan Ware, *Beyond Suffrage: Women in the New Deal* (Cambridge, MA: Harvard University Press, 1981); Susan Hartmann, *From Margin to Mainstream: American Women and Politics since 1960* (New York: McGraw-Hill, 1989); Cynthia Harrison, *On Account of Sex: The Politics of Women's Issues, 1945–1968* (Berkeley: University of California Press, 1988); Catherine E. Rymph, *Republican Women: Feminism and Conservatism from Suffrage through the Rise of the New Right* (Chapel Hill: University of North Carolina Press, 2006); Julie Gallagher, *Black Women and Politics in New York City* (Champaign: University of Illinois Press, 2012); Ellen Fitzpatrick, *The Highest Glass Ceiling: Women's Quest for the American Presidency* (Cambridge, MA: Harvard University Press, 2016); Angie Maxwell and Todd Shields, eds., *The Legacy of Second-Wave Feminism in American Politics* (New York: Palgrave Macmillan, 2018).

11. Before Abzug's at-large whip appointment, women in congressional leadership were limited to chair of the Senate Republican Conference and secretary of the Democratic Caucus, a pattern that held until the mid-1980s. https://history.house.gov/Exhibitions-and-Publications/WIC/Historical-Data /Women-Elected-to-Party-Leadership/.

12. "Who Runs America," *USNWR,* April 19, 1976, 30.

13. Memorandum from Barbara Blum to Jimmy Carter and Rosalynn Carter, July 31, 1976, "Memorandums," Container 298, CL.

14. McGrory, "The Capitol Letter," 7.

15. Tony Hiss, "Dilemma in the New 20th Congressional District—'Bella Should Be There and So Should Ryan,'" *NYT,* June 18, 1972, SM12.

16. Harry Golden, "New Words Enrich Our Lives," *HC,* December 13, 1970, 3A.

17. Abzug quoted in Myra MacPherson, "Bella's Battle Lost: After the Ax, the Bravado Remains," *WP,* January 16, 1979, B1.

18. Mim Kelber to Nat Hentoff, March 24, 1972, 1–7, 4, "General (2)," Box 590, BSA.

19. Doug Ireland quoted in Suzanne Braun Levine and Mary Thom, *Bella Abzug: How One Tough Broad from the Bronx Fought Jim Crow and Joe McCarthy, Pissed Off Jimmy Carter, Battled for the Rights of Women and Workers, Rallied Against War and for the Planet, Shook Up Politics Along the Way* (New York: Farrar, Straus and Giroux, 2007), 76.

20. MM14.

21. Histories of the 1960s have been dominated by participant accounts such as Todd Gitlin, *The Sixties: Years of Hope, Days of Rage* (New York: Bantam Dell, 1987). Notable revisions include David Farber, *The Age of Great Dreams: America in the 1960s* (New York: Hill and Wang, 1994); John McMillian, "'You Didn't Have to Be There': Revisiting the New Left Consensus," in *The New Left Revisited,* ed. John McMillian and Paul Buhle (Philadelphia: Temple University Press, 2003), 1–10.

22. Abzug, National Press Club Speech, July 21, 1971, in *The Bella Abzug Reader,* ed. Mim Kelber and Libby Bassett (New York: Self-published, 2003), 28–32, 31.

23. For representative contrasting views of the US Popular Front, see Nelson Lichtenstein and Robert Korstad, "Opportunities Found and Lost: Labor, Radicals, and the Early Civil Rights Movement," *Journal of American History* 75, no. 3 (December 1988): 786–811; Eric Arneson, "No 'Grave Danger': Black Anticommunism, the Communist Party, and the Race Question," *Labor Studies in Working-Class History of the Americas* 3, no. 4 (2006): 13–52.

24. Arthur M. Schlesinger Jr., *The Vital Center* (Boston: Houghton Mifflin, 1962). For works reconsidering the "vital center," see Jonathan Bell, *The Liberal State on Trial: The Cold War and American Politics in the Truman Years* (New York: Columbia University Press, 2004); Robert Mason and Iwan Morgan, eds., *The Liberal Consensus Reconsidered: American Politics and Society in the Postwar Era* (Gainesville: University of Florida Press, 2017).

25. Historians have treated the 1970s either as a precursor to the "Reagan revolution" or as the last gasp of the "protest sixties." For representative works, see Bruce Schulman, *The Seventies: The Great Shift in American Culture, Society, and Politics* (New York: Da Capo Press, 2002); Laura Kalman, *Right Star Rising: A New Politics, 1974–1980* (New York: W. W. Norton, 2010); Rick Perlstein, *The Invisible Bridge: The Fall of Nixon and the Rise of Reagan* (New York: Simon and Schuster, 2014); Robert O. Self, *All in the Family: The Realignment of American Democracy since the 1960s* (New York: Hill and Wang, 2012). Studies that frame US politics in the 1970s as generative and contested include Michael Stewart Foley, *Front Porch Politics: The Forgotten Heyday of American Activism in the 1970s and 1980s* (New York: Hill and Wang, 2013); Natasha Zaretsky, *No Direction Home: The American Family and the Fear of National Decline* (Chapel Hill: University of North Carolina Press, 2007); Kevin M. Kruse and Julian E. Zelizer, *Fault Lines: A History of the United States since 1974* (New York: W. W. Norton, 2019).

26. Gary Gerstle explains this tension within the American state in *Liberty and Coercion: The Paradox of American Government from the Founding to the Present* (Princeton, NJ: Princeton University Press, 2015).

27. For early use of the term "new politics," see Arnold S. Kaufman, "A Call to Radicalism: Where Shall Liberals Go?," *Dissent* 13, no. 5 (September–October 1966): 555–624.

28. Van Gosse, "A Movement of Movements: The Definition and Periodization of the New Left," in *A Companion to Post-1945 America*, ed. Jean-Christophe Agnew and Roy Rosenzweig (Malden, MA: Wiley-Blackwell, 2006), 277–302.

29. Historians have critiqued studies that divide feminist history into three distinct waves and have decentered the women's liberation movement as the primary engine of postwar women's activism. For this corrective, see Kathleen Laughlin, Julie Gallagher, Dorothy Sue Cobble, Eileen Boris, Premilla Nadasen, Stephanie Gilmore, and Leandra Zarnow, et al., "Is It Time to Jump Ship? Historians Rethink the Wave Metaphor," *Feminist Formations* 22, no. 1 (Spring 2010): 76–135; Nancy Hewitt, ed., *No Permanent Waves: Recasting Histories of U.S. Feminism* (Rutgers, NJ: Rutgers University Press, 2010).

30. Richard Chady to Abzug, February 8, 1976, "General, 1976, Feb. 1," Box 5, BSA; Janice Butler to Abzug, October 11, 1971, "General, 1971 October," Box 2, BSA.

31. Recent studies of liberalism that highlight Abzug as a key figure include Eric Alterman and Kevin Mattson, *The Cause: The Fight for American Liberalism from Franklin Roosevelt to Barack Obama* (New York: Penguin Books, 2012), 263–273; Jeffrey Bloodworth, *Losing the Center: The Decline of American Liberalism, 1968–1992* (Lexington: University Press of Kentucky, 2013), 171–174.

32. "Give the Power Back to the People!," n.d., "General," Box 64, BSA.

33. The following works make clear how New Deal and labor histories centered on white male workers inadequately address the presence and organizing of immigrants, people of color, and women: Dorothy Sue Cobble, *The Other Women's Movement: Workplace Justice and Social Rights in Modern America* (Princeton, NJ: Princeton University Press, 2004); Eileen Boris and Jennifer Klein, *Caring for America: Home Healthcare Workers in the Shadow of the Welfare State* (New York: Oxford University Press, 2012); Kirsten Swinth, *Feminism's Forgotten Fight: The Unfinished Struggle for Work and Family* (Cambridge, MA: Harvard University Press, 2018).

34. For a comparison of 1960s and 1970s policy reforms, see R. Shep Melnick, "From Tax and Spend to Mandate and Sue: Liberalism after the Great Society," in *The Great Society and the High Tide of Liberalism*, ed. Sidney M. Milkis and Jerome M. Mileur (Amherst: University of Massachusetts Press, 2005), 387–410.

35. Kevin P. Phillips, *The Emerging Republican Majority* (New Rochelle, NY: Arlington House, 1969); Richard M. Scammon and Ben J. Wattenberg, *The Real Majority: The Classic Examination of the American Electorate* (New York: Coward-McCann, 1970); Lanny J. Davis, *The Emerging Democratic Majority: Lessons and Legacies from the New Politics* (New York: Stein and Day, 1974).

36. Abzug acknowledged this encouragement in her memoir proposal, Abzug, untitled, n.d., 1–52, 17, in author's possession, generously provided by Mary Marshall Clark in 2004.

37. Bella Abzug with Mel Ziegler, ed., *Bella! Ms. Abzug Goes to Washington* (New York: Saturday Review Press, 1972), 166.

1. Political Ties That Bind

1. Music by Jay Gorney, lyric by Edward Eliscu, "Let's Unite around Bella," n.d., "Bella Abzug," Box 1, JG.

2. "Testimony of Jay Gorney, Accompanied by His Counsel, Bella Abzug," in *Investigation of Communist Activities in the New York City Area—Part 3, Hearing Before the Committee on Un-American Activities, House of Representatives, Eighty-Third Congress, First Session, May 6, 1953* (Washington, DC: US Government Printing Office, 1953), 1370–1377, 1371–1372.

3. Sondra Gorney, *Brother Can You Spare a Dime? The Life of Composer Jay Gorney* (Lanham, MD: Scarecrow Press, 2005), 45.

4. SG09; American Business Consultants, Inc., *Counterattack,* September 22, 1950.

5. "Barry Farber Has No Political Past!," flyer, n.d., "Farber, Barry," Box 64, BSA.

6. Abzug quoted in "Creating a Woman's Life: Conversation between Abzug and Ronnie Eldridge," n.d., Box 1080, BSA (digitized).

7. Daniel Horowitz, *Betty Friedan and the Making of* The Feminine Mystique: *The American Left, the Cold War, and Modern Feminism* (Amherst: University of Massachusetts Press, 1998); Landon R. Y. Storrs, *The Second Red Scare and the Unmaking of the New Deal Left* (Princeton, NJ: Princeton University Press, 2013).

8. Bella Abzug with Mel Ziegler, ed., *Bella! Ms. Abzug Goes to Washington* (New York: Saturday Review Press, 1972), 86.

9. Kelber quoted in Suzanne Braun Levine and Mary Thom, *Bella Abzug: How One Tough Broad from the Bronx Fought Jim Crow and Joe McCarthy, Pissed Off Jimmy Carter, Battled for the Rights of Women and Workers, Rallied Against War and for the Planet, and Shook Up Politics Along the Way* (New York: Farrar, Straus and Giroux, 2007), 16.

10. Abzug, *Bella!,* 84. For Abzug's early years, see Leandra Ruth Zarnow, *Becoming Bella: Bella Abzug, Cold War Dissent, and the Radical Roots of Postwar Feminism,* manuscript-in-progress.

11. W. W. Gill quoted in Evelyn Gonzalez, *The Bronx* (New York: Columbia University Press, 2004), 68–69.

12. Helene Alexander quoted in Levine and Thom, *Bella Abzug,* 4.

13. Savitzky, Bella, Bronx, New York, 8A, District 0403, microfilm 2341211, *Fifteenth Census of the United States, 1930,* Bureau of the Census, accessed via HeritageQuest Online.

14. BAOH, 38.

15. Alexander and Abzug in Levine and Thom, *Bella Abzug,* 8.

16. Norma Baumel Joseph, "Women in Orthodoxy: Conventional and Contentious," in *Women Remaking American Judaism,* ed. Riv-Ellen Prell (Detroit: Wayne State University Press, 2007), 181–210, 183; BAOH, 4.

17. Alexander quoted in Levine and Thom, *Bella Abzug,* 9.

18. Abzug, "Bella Abzug's Chapter in 'First Generation Americans,'" 2, loose document, Box 760, BSA.

19. Alexander quoted in Levine and Thom, *Bella Abzug,* 6.

20. I. Nathan Bamberger, *A Bronx Palace of Torah: Kingsbridge Heights Jewish Center* (Brooklyn: Soncino Press, 2002), ix.

21. BAOH, 17; Alan Mintz, "The Divided Fate of Hebrew and Hebrew Culture at the Seminary," in *Tradition Renewed: A History of the Jewish Theological Seminary,* vol. 2, *Beyond the Academy,* ed. Jack Wertheimer (New York: Jewish Theological Seminary of America, 1997), 81–112, 84.

22. Levi Soshuk and A. P. Gannes, "The Kvutzah and Camp Achvah," *Jewish Education* 20, no. 3 (Summer 1949): 61–69, 66.

23. Alexander quoted in Levine and Thom, *Bella Abzug,* 6.

24. Joseph B. Glass, "Settling the Old-New Homeland: The Decisions of American Jewish Women during the Interwar Years," in *American Jewish Women and the Zionist Enterprise,* ed. Shulamit Reinharz and Mark A. Raider (Waltham, MA: Brandeis University Press, 2005), 192–215, 205; Y. Chazan, *Thirty Years of Hashomer Hatzair,* 1944, 8–9, "Hashomer Hatzair," Box 6, JCH.

25. For the Balfour Declaration, see https://mfa.gov.il/mfa/foreignpolicy /peace/guide/pages/the%20balfour%20declaration.aspx.

26. Mark Raider, *The Emergence of American Zionism* (New York: New York University Press, 1998), 29, 142–146; Yosef Gorny, "Thoughts on Zionism as a Utopian Ideology," *Modern Judaism* 18, no. 3 (October 1998): 240–251, 244.

27. Mordechai Kafri, "Revolutionary Socialism and the Soviet Union," in *Against the Stream: Seven Decades of Hashomer Hatzair in North America,* ed. Ariel Hurwitz (Tel Aviv: Yad Ya'ari, 1994), 207–214, 208.

28. Moshe Furmansky quoted in Aharon Oren, "Confrontations and Ideological Skirmishes," in *Against the Stream: Seven Decades of Hashomer Hatzair in North America,* ed. Ariel Hurwitz (Tel Aviv: Yad Ya'ari, 1994), 203.

29. Aharon Cohen, "Palestine and Arab Aspirations," in *Zionism and the Arab Question: A Collection of Articles from* Youth and Nation (New York: Misrad Bogrim of Hashomer Hatzair, 1944), 24–28, 27, "Hashomer Hatzair," Box 6, JCH.

30. *Pioneer Saga: The Story of Hashomer Hatzair* (New York: Hashomer Hatzair Organization, 1944), 15, "Hashomer Hatzair," Box 6, JCH.

31. BAOH, 15; Maurice Friedman, *Martin Buber: The Life of Dialogue* (New York: Harper and Row, 1960); Jonathan Frankel, *Prophecy and Politics: Socialism, Nationalism, and the Russian Jews, 1862–1917* (London: Cambridge University Press, 1981), 329–363; M. Cohen, "Introduction: Ber Borochov and Socialist Zionism," in *Class Struggle and the Jewish Nation: Selected Essays in Marxist Zionism,* ed. M. Cohen (New Brunswick, NJ: Transaction Books, 1984), 1–34.

32. BAOH, 370.

33. AS07; Amy Swerdlow, "The Impact of Bella Abzug's Youthful Commitment to Labor Zionism on Her Life-Long Political Theory and Practice," March 8, 2000, 1–13, loose document, Box 11, MB.

34. Frederick M. Binder and David M. Reimers, *All the Nations under Heaven: An Ethnic and Racial History of New York City* (New York: Columbia

University Press, 1995), 178; Beth S. Wenger, *New York Jews and the Great Depression: Uncertain Promise* (Syracuse, NY: Syracuse University Press, 1999).

35. "Bella on Bella," *Moment* 1, no. 7 (February 1976): 2, loose document, Box 1101, BSA; BAOH, 15.

36. Shulamit Wittenof, "Adolescence and Maturity," in *Against the Stream,* ed. Ariel Hurwitz (Tel Aviv: Yad Ya'ari, 1994), 187–191, 190.

37. Alexander quoted in Levine and Thom, *Bella Abzug,* 10.

38. Irving Howe, *A Margin of Hope: An Intellectual Biography* (New York: Harvest Books, 1984), 22.

39. Alexander quoted in Levine and Thom, *Bella Abzug,* 6.

40. *Pioneer Saga,* 16.

41. BAOH, 334.

42. BAOH, 25–26, 43.

43. *Program for American Jews* (New York: Avukah, February 1938), 12, 8/47727, YIL; Lawrence Cohen, "History of National Avukah Reveals 15 Years of Growth," *ASA* 1, no. 13 (July 28, 1939): 2, JSO.

44. Robert Cohen, *When the Old Left Was Young: Student Radicals and America's First Mass Student Movement, 1929–1941* (New York: Oxford University Press, 1993), 376n1.

45. BAOH, 361.

46. BAOH, 38.

47. JL07.

48. Helen Eschelbach, "Bella Savitzky, All Around Girl, Plays Harmonica, Bugle Five Ways," *HB* 18, no. 2 (September 24, 1940): 3, HCA.

49. BAOH, 258–259; David Kaufman, "Jewish Education as a Civilization: A History of the Teachers Institute," in *Tradition Renewed: A History of the Jewish Theological Seminary,* vol. 2, *Beyond the Academy,* ed. Jack Wertheimer (New York: Jewish Theological Seminary of America, 1997), 567–629.

50. On Margaret Spahr, see *Columbia Law School Report: Columbia Celebrates 75 Years of Women at the Law School* (New York: Columbia Law School, Fall 2002), 28.

51. "Seek Hebrew, Negro Courses," *HB* 28, no. 11 (December 3, 1940): 1; "Meetings Invalidated," *HB* 28, no. 9, 11/12/40, 1, HCA.

52. *Wistarion* (1941), 18, HCA.

53. "Report of the Elections Committee, May 1940," Folder 1, Box 12, HCA.

54. BAOH, 28; "Rally to 'Save Our Schools' Permanent 'SOS' Organization," *HB* 28, no. 12 (December 17, 1940): 1, HCA; Ellen Schrecker, *No Ivory Tower: McCarthyism and the Universities* (New York: Oxford University Press, 1986), 75–83.

55. Dorothy Schwartz quoted in Maureen McKernan and Johnston D. Kerrhoff, "Hunter College Girls Are Hardworking, Serious, Tolerant," *NYP,* March 18, 1941, 9.

56. "War Branded as Imperialistic at Bronx ASU," *HB* 27, no. 9, November 5, 1939, 1, HCA; Cohen, *When the Old Left Was Young,* 278–298; Eileen Eagan, *Class, Culture, and the Classroom* (Philadelphia: Temple University Press, 1981), 208–211; Charles Chatfield, *For Peace and Justice: Pacifism in America, 1914–1941* (Boston: Beacon Press, 1971), 287–328.

57. BAOH, 125, 372.

58. William Ephaim, "Only Arab, Jewish, Labor Unity Can Solve Crisis in Palestine; Must Fight British Imperialism," *ASA* 1, no. 3 (November 14, 1938): 3, JSO; Monty Noam Penkower, *Decision on Palestine Deferred: America, Britain and Wartime Diplomacy, 1939–1945* (London: Frank Cass, 2002).

59. Abzug (Savitzky), "Armistice Day—and the Last World War," *HB* 28, no. 8 (November 6, 1940): 3, HCA.

60. Cohen, *When the Old Left Was Young,* 289.

61. For contrasting readings, see Harvey Khler, *The Heyday of American Communism: The Depression Decade* (New York: Basic Books, 1984); Doug Rossinow, *Visions of Progress: The Left-Liberal Tradition in America* (Philadelphia: University of Pennsylvania Press, 2008).

62. "Abzug, Mrs. Bella S.," July 1970, Folder 14, Box 1, JBM; "Why the CIA Spied on Bella Abzug," *HE* 35, no. 11 (March 15, 1975): 3–4; "Office Memorandum," SA Paul C. Menton to SAC New York, November 28, 1956, 100-102413-75, FBI File.

63. BAOH, 295.

64. Ellen Schrecker, *Many Are the Crimes: McCarthyism in America* (Princeton, NJ: Princeton University Press, 1998); David Caute, *The Great Fear: The Anti-Communist Purge under Truman and Eisenhower* (New York: Simon and Schuster, 1978).

65. "Shall the Bar Invite 'Creeping Paralysis' of Its Own Thought and Speech?," 1951, Folder 27, Box 56A, NLGNY.

66. BAOH, 80.

67. Young B. Smith to Philip M. Hayden, February 6, 1942, Folder 8, Box 355, YBS.

68. Y. Smith, "Report of the Dean of the School of Law for 1943," April 10, 1944, in *Annual Report of the President and Treasurer to the Trustees with Accompanying Documents for the Academic Year Ending June 30, 1943* (New York: Columbia University, 1943), 3.

69. Karen Berger Morello, *The Invisible Bar: The Woman Lawyer in America 1638 to the Present* (New York: Random House, 1987), 97.

70. JVOH, 12; BAOH, 75.

71. SMOH, 13; Constance Baker Motley in Levine and Thom, *Bella Abzug,* 24.

72. D'Ann Campbell, *Women at War with America: Private Lives in a Patriotic Era* (Cambridge, MA: Harvard University Press, 1984); Susan Hartmann, *The Home Front and Beyond: American Women in the 1940s* (Boston: Twayne, 1982).

73. Abzug quoted in Levine and Thom, *Bella Abzug,* 55.

74. BAOH, 75, 356; LA05.

75. BAOH, 248.

76. N. E. H. Hull, *Roscoe Pound and Karl Llewellyn: Searching for an American Jurisprudence* (Chicago: University of Chicago Press, 1997); Laura Kalman, *Legal Realism at Yale, 1927–1960* (Chapel Hill: University of North Carolina Press, 1986).

77. Jerold S. Auerbach, *Unequal Justice: Lawyers and Social Change in Modern America* (London: Oxford University Press, 1976), 166.

78. BAOH, 144.

79. Whittaker Chambers named Nathan Witt as part of the "Ware Group" Communist cell, and Harold Cammer had received an S-2 discharge during World War II for suspected Communist ties. BOAH, 83, 153; "New Teacher List Asked in Inquiry," *NYT,* February 12, 1941, 23; Cammer Army Disaffection File Dossier No. D8044969, Folder 15, Box 118, NLGNY; Peter H. Irons, *The New Deal Lawyers* (Princeton, NJ: Princeton University Press, 1982), 236–238.

80. BAOH, 84, 87.

81. Cynthia Grant Bowman, "Women in the Legal Profession from the 1920s to the 1970s: What Can We Learn from Their Experience about Law and Social Change?," *Cornell Law Faculty Publications,* paper 12 (2009): 7, http://scholarship.law.cornell.edu/facpub/12.

82. Gilbert J. Gall, *Pursuing Justice: Lee Pressman, the New Deal, and the CIO* (Albany, NY: State University of New York Press, 1999), 186.

83. Abzug quoted in Levine and Thom, *Bella Abzug,* 29, 132.

84. RSH09.

85. BAOH, 386; RSH09.

86. Harold Cammer, "Taft-Hartley and the International Fur and Leather Workers Union," in *The Cold War against Labor,* ed. Ann Fagan Ginger and David Christiano (Berkeley: Meiklejohn Civil Liberties Institute, 1987), 1:404–418.

87. E-mail from Howard N. Meyer to author, May 6, 2010, in author's possession; HNM10.

88. "Attack on Civil Liberties," April 1948, 4, "Smith Act Cases-States, 1947–1954," Box 8, AU.

89. "Chapter Membership," December 31, 1948, Folder 19, Box 56B, NLGNY; "Membership Report," November 1961, Folder 19, Box 56B, NLGNY.

90. House Un-American Activities Committee, *Report on the National Lawyers Guild: Legal Bulwark of the Communist Party* (Washington, DC: Government Printing Office, September 21, 1950); Percival R. Bailey, "The Case of the National Lawyers Guild, 1939–1958," in *Beyond the Hiss Case: The FBI, Congress, and the Cold War,* ed. Athan G. Theoharis (Philadelphia: Temple University Press, 1982), 129–175, 134.

91. Robert Justin Goldstein, *American Blacklist: The Attorney General's List of Subversive Organizations* (Lawrence: University Press of Kansas, 2008), xvi, 63; John H. Fenton, "Brownell Attacks the Lawyers Guild," *NYT,* August 28, 1953, 1. For development of *NLG v. Brownell,* see Folders 11, 12, and 15, Box 31, NLGNY.

92. For instance, Abzug gave $350 during a $25,000 fund drive in 1953; "Return to Reason Appeal," n.d., Folder 11, Box 31, NLGNY.

93. Ralph Shapiro, untitled, n.d., Folder 3, Box 67, MMK.

94. BAOH, 150, 152.

95. AFG08; Michael R. Belknap, *Cold War Political Justice: The Smith Act, the Communist Party, and American Civil Liberties* (Westport, CT: Greenwood Press, 1977); Victor Rabinowitz, *Unrepentant Leftist: A Lawyer's Memoir* (Urbana: University of Illinois Press, 1996).

96. "Testimony of Abraham Unger," in "Executive Sessions of the Senate Permanent Subcommittee on Investigations of the Committee on Government Operations," vol. 3, 83rd Cong., 1st Sess., 1953, http://www.gpo.gov/congress /senate/mccarthy/83871.html.

97. BAOH, 399.

98. LBOH, 189.

99. "Witness List," December 9, 1949, Folder 56, Box 3, BK; BAOH, 287; "U.S. Grand Jury Begins a Super-secret Inquiry," *NYT,* May 23, 1951, 44.

100. BAOH, 289.

101. "Affidavit of Abzug," March 5, 1951, "417 Misc. OT 1950," Box 6562, entry 17, SCR. On McGee's defense, see Craig Zaim, "Trial by Ordeal: The Willie McGee Case," *Journal of Mississippi History,* 65, no. 3 (2003): 215–247; Leandra Ruth Zarnow, "Braving Jim Crow to Save Willie McGee: Bella Abzug, the Legal Left, and Civil Rights Innovation, 1948–1951," *Law and Social Inquiry* 33, no. 4 (Fall 2008): 1003–1041.

102. Alex Heard, *The Eyes of Willie McGee: A Tragedy of Race, Sex, and Secrets in the Jim Crow South* (New York: HarperCollins, 2010); Carl T. Rowan, *South of Freedom* (New York: Alfred A. Knopf, 1952).

103. Patricia Schechter, *Ida B. Wells-Barnett and American Reform, 1880–1930* (Chapel Hill: University of North Carolina Press, 2001); Jacqueline Dowd Hall, *Revolt against Chivalry: Jessie Daniel Ames and the Women's Campaign against Lynching* (New York: Columbia University Press, 1993).

104. Abzug, "Memorandum of Relator," draft, 6, 8, Folder 1, Box 2, AU.

105. John Coe and Abzug, "To the Honorable Harry S. Truman, President of the United States," 7–8, Folder Unknown, Box 36, JC.

106. House Un-American Activities Committee, *Report on Civil Rights Congress as a Communist Front Organization* (Washington, DC: Government Printing Office, 1947). On "acceptable" civil rights policy, see Mary Dudziak, *Cold War Civil Rights* (Princeton, NJ: Princeton University Press, 2000).

107. Zaim, "Trial by Ordeal," 234n85.

108. BAOH, 307; Gerald Horne, *Communist Front? The Civil Rights Congress, 1946–1956* (Rutherford, NJ: Farleigh Dickinson University Press, 1988), 29–51, 84–92; photograph accompanying Larry Rohter, "The Echoes of an Execution Reverberate Loud and Clear," *NYT,* May 5, 2010, https://www.nytimes .com/2010/05/06/arts/television/06radio.html.

109. Fielding Wright quoted in "U.S. Supreme Court Again Dooms Willie McGee," January 17, 1951, Folder 1, Box 91, JBM.

110. Abzug quoted in "Governor to Hear 'Save Willie McGee' Delegation of Ten," *JDN,* July 23, 1950.

111. Abzug to Tom Elliston, May 2, 1951, Reel 10, Slide 571, CRCP; Memo to File, SA Donald P. Adams, January 9, 1951, 100-102413-1, FBI File.

112. BAOH, 138; Virginia Rafferty, "Summary of File References—Abzug: 100-102413," December 17, 1951, 4, Folder 12, Box 148, NLGNY; "Argument of Counsel," March 5, 1951 (Filed March 9, 1951), 35, 41, "417 Misc. OT 1950," Box 6562, entry 17, SCR.

113. Frederick Sullens, "The Low Down on the Higher Ups," *JDN,* March 7, 1951, Folder 2, Box 2, AU.

114. With Abzug notation, Sullens, Folder 2, Box 2, AU.

115. BAOH, 321; Judge Sidney Mize quoted in Charles M. Hills, "Stay of Execution Denied Willie McGee by US Judge," *CL,* May 6, 1951, 1.

116. BAOH, 142, 315. A clip of the execution recording can be heard in "My Grandfather's Execution," *Radio Diaries,* May 7, 2010, https://www.npr.org /templates/story/story.php?storyId=126539134.

117. LA05.

118. MB07; LA05; EA12.

119. "The End of Willie McGee," *L,* May 21, 1951, 44–45.

120. Bella Abzug, Letter to the Editor, *L,* June 11, 1951, 12.

121. BAOH, 313; "Minutes of the Meeting of the National Committee on Civil Rights and Liberties," December 19, 1955, 1, Folder 33, Box 9, NLGNY; Thurgood Marshall to Simon Schachter, 7 / 54, Folder 8, Box 20, NLGNY.

122. "Memorandum Re: Purposes of National Conference," draft, edits by Abzug, 1, "Civil Rights, Historical Material, 1952–53," Box 910, BSA; "Resolution Proposing the Establishment of a National Civil Rights Defense Panel," October 12, 1952, 1, Box 910, BSA; "Conference on Civil Rights Program, October 10–12, 1952," Folder 5, Box 11, AU.

123. I have been unable to find biographical information on Alice Williams. BAOH, 268–270; LA07; EA12.

124. Bella Abzug, "Legislative Proposals in the South against Integration," *Lawyers Guild Review* 16, no. 2 (Summer 1956): 83, 88, 94; AFG08; Michal R. Belknap, *Federal Law and Southern Order: Racial Violence and Constitutional Conflict in the Post-Brown South* (Athens: University of Georgia Press, 1987).

125. Abzug, "National Lawyers Guild Comprehensive Civil Rights Bill Compared with HR 1824 Introduced by Javits, and HR 366 Introduced by Addonizio, which is identical with the Javits Bill," draft, n.d., "Civil Rights, Historical Material, 1952–53," Box 910, BSA.

126. Wendy Brown and Janet Halley, "Introduction," in *Left Legalism / Left Critique,* ed. Wendy Brown and Janet Halley (Durham, NC: Duke University Press, 2002), 1–37, 6.

127. Storrs, *The Second Red Scare*; David K. Johnson, *The Lavender Scare: The Cold War Persecution of Gays and Lesbians in the Federal Government* (Chicago: University of Chicago Press, 2004); Andrea Friedman, *Citizenship in Cold War America: The National Security State and the Possibilities of Dissent* (Amherst: University of Massachusetts Press, 2015).

128. SAC NY to Director, December 7, 1955, 100-102413-59, FBI File; Director (with JEH handwritten initials) to SAC NY, December 28, 1955, 100-102413-60, FBI File.

129. RE14.

130. Arthur J. Sabin, *In Calmer Times: The Supreme Court and Red Monday* (Philadelphia: University of Pennsylvania Press, 1999), 151–172; Belknap, *Cold War Political Justice,* 244–272.

131. "U.S. Abandons Bid to Cite Law Guild," *NYT,* September 13, 1958, 10.

132. "Minutes of the Meeting of the NYC Chapter Board of Directors," February 6, 1952, "File IX: Folder 18," 9, AU.

2. A New Politics

1. Amy Swerdlow reiterated this point in AS07; Amy Swerdlow, *Women Strike for Peace: Traditional Motherhood and Radical Politics in the 1960s* (Chicago: University of Chicago Press, 1993), 17–18, 53.

2. CR09; "2,000 Women Protest New U.N. on Nuclear Testing," *NYT,* November 9, 1961.

3. Michael Kazin, *American Dreamers: How the Left Changed a Nation* (New York: Alfred A. Knopf, 2011), 210; Maurice Isserman, *If I Had a Hammer . . . : The Death of the Old Left and the Birth of the New Left* (New York: Basic Books, 1987).

4. *Beyond the New Left,* ed. Irving Howe (New York: The McCall Publishing Group, 1970).

5. Abzug, "Yes, that women's vote . . . ," draft, n.d., 1–8, 2, Untitled Folder, Box 1005, BSA.

6. Shirley Margolin quoted in Suzanne Braun Levine and Mary Thom, *Bella Abzug: How One Tough Broad from the Bronx Fought Jim Crow and Joe McCarthy, Pissed Off Jimmy Carter, Battled for the Rights of Women and Workers, Rallied Against War and for the Planet, and Shook Up Politics Along the Way* (New York: Farrar, Straus and Giroux, 2007), 65; "East Coast Calling North," n.d., "Literature: 151 East 50th Street (1962–1964)," Box 1, C.1, WSPP.

7. Swerdlow, *Women Strike for Peace,* 51, 77; Andrea Estepa, "Taking the White Gloves Off: Women Strike for Peace and the Transformation of Women's Activist Identities in the United States, 1961–1980" (PhD diss., Rutgers, the State University of New Jersey, 2012), 63; Jo Freeman, "The Tyranny of Structurelessness," *Berkeley Journal of Sociology* 17 (1972–1973): 151–164.

8. Elaine Kuntz to Abzug, February 21, 1978, "Operation Breadbasket," Box 971, BSA.

9. EA12.

10. BAOH, 179.

11. Minutes, December 13, 1961, "Minutes of CCC (1961–1965)," Box 1, C.1, WSPP; Minutes, January 4, 1962, 3, "Minutes of CCC (1961–1965)," Box 1, C.1, WSPP.

12. Letter to Jacqueline Kennedy, October 31, 1961, "Women Strike for Peace Correspondence, 1961–1962," Box 1, WSPWI; Robbie Lieberman, *The Strangest Dream: Communism, Anticommunism, and the U.S. Peace Movement, 1945–1963* (Syracuse, NY: Syracuse University Press, 2000), 121–134.

13. BAOH, 178; 100-NY-102413-123, FBI File.

14. Folly Fodor to Mr. Wharton, November 21, 1961, 1, "WSP Correspondence, 1961–1962," Box 1, WSPWI.

15. Eleanor Garst, Draft WSP Call, n.d., "Women Strike for Peace Correspondence, 1961–1962," Box 1, WSPWI.

16. Swerdlow, *Women Strike for Peace,* 144; "Dagmar Saerchinge Wilson," in Judith Porter Adams, *Peacework: Oral Histories of Women Peace Activists* (Boston: Twayne, 1991), 193–199, 196.

17. John F. Kennedy quoted in Marjorie Hunter, "President Responds to Pickets for Peace," *NYT,* January 16, 1962, 1; Press Release en Route to New York, January 15, 1962, "Memoranda/Reports/Statements/Etc. 1961, Working Documents," Box 5, A.4, WSPP.

18. Untitled Lobbying Guide, January 15, 1962, "Literature: 151 East 50th Street (1962–1964)," Box 1, C.1, WSPP.

19. Abzug, "Report on Summary of Interviews with Officials and Congressmen, Based on Hastily Written Notes Submitted on the Train Coming Back from Washington, January 15, 1962," draft, 15, "Legis. and Political Action Director," Box 1004, BSA.

20. "Guide to Legislative and Political Action," 1962, 1, "Legislative and Political Action Director," Box 1004, BSA.

21. "Report on the National Conference, June 8–10," n.d., 1, "Legislative and Political Action Director," Box 1004, BSA.

22. Eleanor Flexner, *Century of Struggle: The Woman's Rights Movement in the United States,* enl. ed. (1959; Cambridge, MA: Harvard University Press, 1996); Ellen C. Dubois, "Eleanor Flexner and the History of American Feminism," *Gender & History* 3, no. 1 (March 1991): 81–90.

23. Elsa Knight Thompson, "My Personal Impression of the Ann Arbor Conference," n.d., 4, "Abzug, Bella—Notes for Speeches, Etc. (1 of 2)," Box 1, BAWSP.

24. Abzug, Press Release, November 2, 1962, 1, "Literature: 750 3rd Avenue (1961–1963)," Box 1, C.1, WSPP.

25. Abzug, untitled, n.d., 1, "WSP—Related Material about/by Bella Abzug," Box 3, C.1, WSPP.

26. "First WSP Political Pressure Results in Hopes for Effective Action in 1964," *WSP Newsletter* 1, no. 2 (November 1962): 1–3, 2, Folder 4, Box 4, DA.

27. Abzug, "Report of Political and Legislative Action Committee," January 19, 1963, 13, "Minutes of CCC (1961–1965)," Box 1, C.1, WSPP.

28. Lawrence S. Wittner, *Resisting the Bomb: A History of the World Nuclear Disarmament Movement, 1954–1970* (Stanford, CA: Stanford University Press, 1997), 2:469; Wittner, "Gender Roles and Nuclear Disarmament Activism, 1954–1965," *Gender & History* 12, no. 1 (April 2000): 197–222.

29. Marjorie Hunter, "Women Besiege Capitol, Demanding a Test Ban," *NYT,* May 8, 1963, 17; Dorothy Dernstein, "May 7 Mother's Lobby for a Test Ban," "Mother's Lobby for a Test Ban (May 1963)," Box 1, A.4, WSPP.

30. "Twenty-Three New York and New Jersey Women Strike for Peace'ers Fly to Washington, D.C. to meet with Test-Ban Negotiators and Make Presentation," January 25, 1963, "Memoranda/Reports/Statements/Etc. January through June 1963," Box 5, A.4, WSPP.

31. Wittner, *Resisting the Bomb,* 415–441; Robert Kleidman, *Organizing for Peace: Neutrality, the Test Ban, and the Freeze* (Syracuse, NY: Syracuse University Press, 1993), 119–121; Glenn T. Seaborg with Benjamin S. Loeb, *Kennedy, Khrushchev, and the Test Ban* (Berkeley: University of California Press, 1981).

32. Mary Clarke, "Papers," n.d., 1–2, 1, "National Conference 1962, Ann Arbor, MI," Box 3, A.1, WSPP.

33. "Statement on Foreign Policy," draft with Abzug edits, n.d., "Voter Peace Pledge," Box 1005, BSA; Swerdlow, *Women Strike for Peace,* 149–150.

34. "National Conference 1962, Ann Arbor, Michigan," Box 3, A.1, WSPP; "Report on the National Conference, June 8–10," 1–4; MDF07; Estepa, "Taking the White Gloves Off," 51–60.

35. Abzug's handwritten notes quoted here reflect Mickey Flacks's memory of Abzug's argument, MDF07; Abzug, "We are a movement . . . ," n.d., "1: Abzug, Bella—Notes for Speeches, Etc. (2 of 2)," Box 1, BAWSP.

36. MDF07.

37. Mary Clarke, "Papers," n.d., 1–2, 1, "National Conference 1962, Ann Arbor, MI," Box 3, A.1, WSPP.

38. On the Guild's peace conference, see Folder 18, Box 30, NLGNY. See also "Integration Committee," Folder 31, Box 11, NLGNY; J. Betty Bernstein to Abzug, June 25, 1963, Folder 14, Box 46, NLGNY; CR09.

39. Victor Rabinowitz, *Unrepentant Leftist: A Lawyer's Memoir* (Urbana: University of Illinois Press, 1996), 176. Although appointed to the ad hoc disarmament committee, Abzug did not actively help draft its report. "Minutes of Program and Administration Committee Meeting," May 9, 1962, 1–5, 5, Folder 46, Box 13, NLGNY; "Board of Directors Meeting—Minutes," March 20, 1963, Folder 20, Box 56C, NLGNY; *A Summary of Disarmament Documents: 1945–1962* (San Francisco: National Lawyers Guild, 1963).

40. Ann Fagan Ginger and Eugene M. Toobin, "Civil Rights Moves the Guild (1961–1963)," in *The National Lawyers Guild: From Roosevelt through Reagan,* ed. Ann Fagan Ginger and Eugene M. Toobin (Philadelphia: Temple University Press, 1988), 178–179, 179.

41. Abzug quoted in "National Executive Board Meeting Minutes," November 10, 1963, 3.

42. CR09; "Minutes of the CCC," June 26, 1962, 1, "Minutes of CCC (1961–1965)," Box 1, C.1, WSPP.

43. Ernest Goodman quoted in Steve Babson, Dave Riddle, and David Elsila, *The Color of Law: Ernie Goodman, Detroit, and the Struggle for Labor and Civil Rights* (Detroit: Wayne State University Press, 2010), 205; BAOH, 147; Abzug, "Commitment Form," n.d., Folder 8, Box 47, NLGNY; George Crockett and Ernest Goodman, "A Report of CASL," in *The National Lawyers Guild: From Roosevelt through Reagan,* ed. Ann Fagan Ginger and Eugene M. Toobin (Philadelphia: Temple University Press, 1988), 191–192.

44. Bella Abzug, unpublished manuscript, n.d. I read this unfinished memoir at the home of Joan Nixon in 2008.

45. Benita Roth, *Separate Roads to Feminism: Black, Chicana, and White Feminist Movements in America's Second Wave* (Cambridge: Cambridge University Press, 2004).

46. "Guide to Legislative and Political Action," 1962, 2, "Legislative and Political Action Director," Box 1004, BSA.

47. NY WSP Legislative Committee, "To the National Memo," July 1964, 1–2, 1, "Literature: 151 East 50th Street (1962–1964)," Box 1, C.1, WSPP.

48. Doug Rossinow, *Visions of Progress: The Left-Liberal Tradition in America* (Philadelphia: University of Pennsylvania Press, 2008), 138.

49. BAOH, 385; BAOH, 35; Robert Cohen, *When the Old Left Was Young: Student Radicals and America's First Mass Student Movement, 1929–1941* (New York: Oxford University Press, 1993), 319–320. http://select.nytimes.com/gst/abstract.html?res=F40916F73E5E1B7493C2AA178FD85F4D8685F9.

50. Abzug (Savitzky) quoted in "Youth Congress Delegates to Start Peace Clubs," *HB* 28, no. 18 (February 26, 1940): 1, HCA; "Anti-Reds Balked in Floor Scuffles at Youth Session," *NYT,* February 10, 1940, 1; Cohen, 297–304.

51. BAOH, 159; SA George R. Masset to SAC NY, Office Memorandum, November 1, 1956, 100-102413-74, FBI File; Rossinow, *Visions of Progress,* 186–190; Alan Wolfe, "The Withering Away of the American Labor Party," *Journal of the Rutgers University Library* 31, no. 2 (1968): 46–57.

52. Abzug, unpublished manuscript.

53. Abzug, unpublished manuscript.

54. Abzug, "Memo III: Meet the President," n.d., 1–4, 1, "WSP," Box 1005, BSA.

55. Lyndon B. Johnson quoted in Glenn T. Seaborg with Benjamin S. Loeb, *Stemming the Tide: Arms Control in the Johnson Years* (1971; Lexington, MA: Lexington Books, 1987), 95; Paul Y. Hammond, *LBJ and the Presidential Management of Foreign Relations* (Austin: University of Texas Press, 1992), 108–165.

56. Swerdlow, *Women Strike for Peace,* 205; "Report: The Hague Conference," May 1964, Folder 4, Box 4, DA.

57. Abzug, "Why the WSP Is Asking for Public Hearings on the Proposed NATO Multilateral Nuclear Force," 1–5, 4, n.d., "Atomic Energy," Box 963, BSA.

58. "WSP—A Short History of Activities during 1963 and 1964," n.d., 1–2, 1, Folder 4, Box 4, DA; "Four Hundred Women Lobby 80 Congressmen in Mothers' March on Capitol Hill," *WSP Newsletter* 4, no. 2 (May 1964): 1–4, 4, Folder 4, Box 4, DA.

59. "New Republican Slogan Is Used at Convention," *NYT,* July 11, 1964, 8.

60. Barry Goldwater quoted in Rick Perlstein, *Before the Storm: Barry Goldwater and the Unmaking of the American Consensus* (New York: Hill and Wang, 2001), 260.

61. Allan L. Otten, "What Went Wrong? Why GOP Moderates Have Failed to Derail Goldwater," *WSJ,* July 10, 1964, 4.

62. Charles Mohr, "Senator Arrives on the Coast: Goldwater Gives View on Vietnam," *NYT,* July 10, 1964, 1; "Transcript of Goldwater's Speech Accepting Republican Presidential Nomination," *NYT,* July 17, 1964, 10.

63. NY WSP Legislative Committee, "To the National Memo," July 1964, 1–2, 1, "Literature: 151 East 50th Street (1962–1964)," Box 1, C.1, WSPP; Abzug, "In a little over a . . . ," n.d., "Abzug, Bella—Notes for Speeches, Etc. (2 of 2)," Box 1, BAWSP.

64. Rosmarie Tyler Brooks, "Goldwater National Convention Opens as Delegates 'Seig Heil,'" *NYT,* July 14, 1964, 2.

65. Abzug, "Memo I," draft, 3, "Abzug, Bella—Notes for Speeches, Etc. (1 of 2)," BAWSP; "WSP—Agenda—National Conference 1963," n.d., 1–2, "National Conference 1963, Champaign IL," Box 3, A.1, WSPP; Lisa McGirr, *Suburban*

Warriors: The Origins of the New American Right (Princeton, NJ: Princeton University Press, 2001), 111–146; John H. Kessel, *The Goldwater Coalition: Republican Strategies in 1964* (New York: Bobbs-Merrill, 1968).

66. "To the National Memo," 1; Abzug, "In a little over a . . . ," n.d., "Abzug, Bella—Notes for Speeches, Etc. (2 of 2)," Box 1, BAWSP.

67. James McCartney, "It's Ladies' Day at Capitol: Hoots, Howls—and Charm," *Chicago Daily News* in WSP Pamphlet, "So Many Things Have Been Said . . . ," 1–20, 6, 9, n.d., Folder 1, Box 4, DA.

68. Supervisor Cyril J. Ryan to SAC New York, Office Memorandum, September 4, 1962, 100-102413-158, FBI File.

69. McCartney, "It's Ladies' Day at Capitol."

70. Dr. Homer A. Jack, "The Will of the WISP versus the Humiliation of HUAC," 1–4, 1, Folder 1, Box 4, DA.

71. AS07.

72. Abzug, "What Were the Purposes of This Hearing?" draft, n.d., 1–2, Folder 10, Box 1, WSPWI; Swerdlow, *Women Strike for Peace*, 120–121.

73. David Cunningham, *There's Something Happening Here: The New Left, the Klan, and FBI Counterintelligence* (Berkeley: University of California Press, 2004), 6; Wittner, *Resisting the Bomb*, 361; "12 Mt. Vernon Women Join Washington Demonstration," *Daily Argus* clipping, January 17, 1962, 100-102413-148, FBI File.

74. "Testimony of Dagmar Wilson," 213–244, 224, Folder 1, Box 4, DA; *Communist Activities in the Peace Movement (WSP and Certain Other Groups): Hearings before the Committee on Un-American Activities, House of Representatives,* 78th Cong., December 11–13, 1962 (Washington, DC: Government Printing Office, 1963).

75. Bea Freedman, "Minutes of CCC Meeting," August 12, 1964, "Minutes of CCC (1961–1965)," Box 1, C.1, WSPP; "National Conference Minutes," n.d., "National Conference 1964, Winnetka, IL," Box 3, A.1, WSPP.

76. Joint Resolution of Congress H.J. Res 1145, August 7, 1964, http://avalon.law.yale.edu/20th_century/tonkin-g.asp#joint.

77. "Minutes of CCC Meeting," August 12, 1964, 1, "Minutes of CCC (1961–1965)," Box 1, C.1, WSPP.

78. BAOH, 72.

79. Abzug and Audrey Fain, "Testimony of WSP before the Democratic National Platform Committee," August 18, 1964, "July 21, 1976 [mislabeled folder]," Box 1004, BSA.

80. Freedman, "Minutes of CCC Meeting," September 2, 1964, 1, "Minutes of CCC (1961–1965)," Box 1, C.1, WSPP.

81. L. B. Johnson quoted in Robert David Johnson, *All the Way with LBJ: The 1964 Presidential Election* (Cambridge: Cambridge University Press, 2009), 201.

82. Gary Donaldson, *Liberalism's Last Hurrah: The Presidential Campaign of 1964* (Armonk, NY: M. E. Sharpe, 2003), 251.

83. Alice Hamburg, "Policy," "Issues for Discussion-Pre-Conference," October 1965, 1–31, 1, "National Conference 1965, San Francisco, CA," Box 3, A.1, WSPP.

84. "C.C.C. Philadelphia Conference Discussion—Oct. 28, 1964," 1–4, 1, "General Correspondence, NYC (1967-no date)," Box 3, C.1, WSPP.

85. Abzug quoted in Swerdlow, *Women Strike for Peace,* 150.

86. Sidney M. Milkis, "Lyndon Johnson, the Great Society, and the Twilight of the Modern Presidency," in *The Great Society and the High Tide of Liberalism,* ed. Sidney M. Milkis and Jerome M. Mileur (Boston: University of Massachusetts Press, 2005), 34.

87. Lyndon B. Johnson quoted in Fredrik Logevall, *Choosing War: The Lost Chance for Peace and the Escalation of War in Vietnam* (Berkeley: University of California Press, 1999), 299.

88. "Report on Vietnam Lobby," *Memo* 3, no. 13 (February 19, 1965): 2–3, 7, Folder 4, Box 4, DA; "Pickets in Capital Ask Vietnam Talks," *NYT,* February 11, 1965, 6.

89. Jack Valenti quoted in Rhodri Jeffries-Jones, *Peace Now! American Society and the Ending of the Vietnam War* (New Haven, CT: Yale University Press, 1999), 165; Swerdlow, *Women Strike for Peace,* 130; Melvin Small, *Johnson, Nixon, and the Doves* (New Brunswick, NJ: Rutgers University Press, 1988), 35.

90. Abzug, "Vietnam Report," draft, n.d., 1–5, 2, "WSP Political Activity, Cands., Voter Peace Pledge," Box 1005, BSA.

91. "Testimony of WSP at Hearing on Vietnam Called by Congressman William Fitts Ryan in New York City on August 12, 13, 1965," 2–3, attached to Abzug to Freedman, August 24 1965, "Legislative Correspondence (1960–1971)," Box 3, C.1, WSPP.

92. BAOH, 283; LA05; EA12.

93. *USNWR* quoted in Vincent J. Cannato, *The Ungovernable City: John Lindsay and His Struggle to Save New York* (New York: Basic Books, 2001), xii.

94. Abzug, unpublished memoir; Malcolm X, "The Ballot or the Bullet," 1964, www.digitalhistory.uh.edu/disp_textbook.cfm?smtid=3&psid=3624.

95. BAOH, 322–324; LA05; EA12; Russell J. Rickford, *Betty Shabazz: A Remarkable Story of Survival and Faith before and after Malcolm X* (Naperville, IL: Sourcebooks, 2003), 260–264.

96. Liz Abzug quoted in Levine and Thom, *Bella Abzug,* 79.

97. These notes and drafts are often without dates, page numbers, or other designations and are out of order chronologically. See, for instance, "Memoranda/Reports/Statements/Etc. 1961, Working Documents," Box 5, A.4, WSPP.

98. Abzug, "Must use conventional political techniques . . . ," draft, n.d., "Abzug, Bella—Notes for Speeches, Etc. (1 of 2)," BAWSP.

99. Abzug, "Specifically committed to radical change . . . ," draft, n.d., "Abzug, Bella—Notes for Speeches, Etc. (1 of 2)," BAWSP.

100. Abzug, "In a discussion of the . . . ," draft, n.d., 2, "Voter Peace Pledge," Box 1005, BSA.

101. Abzug, "Memorandum on Political Action for WSP and Report on New York Political Action Conference," draft, 1–3, 3, November 1, 1966, "WSP Related Material About/By Bella Abzug," Box 3, C.1, WSPP.

102. Abzug, "BSA-Political," draft, n.d., 7, "Abzug, Bella—Notes for Speeches against the Draft," BAWSP.

103. Bayard Rustin, "From Protest to Politics: The Future of the Civil Rights Movement," *Commentary* 39, no. 1 (January 1965): 25–31, 25, 27–30; John D'Emilio, *Lost Prophet: The Life and Times of Bayard Rustin* (Chicago: University of Chicago Press, 2003).

104. Abzug, "Memorandum on Political Action for WSP," 2–3.

105. For others, see Tom Kahn, "The Problem of the New Left," *Commentary* 42, no. 1 (July 1, 1966): 30–38, 37; Irving Howe, "New Styles in 'Leftism,'" in *Beyond the New Left,* ed. Irving Howe (New York: The McCall Publishing Group, 1970), 19–32; Michael Harrington, "The Mystical Militants," in *Beyond the New Left,* ed. Irving Howe (New York: The McCall Publishing Group, 1970), 33–39.

106. Arnold S. Kaufman, "A Call to Radicalism: Where Shall Liberals Go?," *Dissent* 13, no. 5 (September–October 1966): 555–624, 604. See also Kaufman, *The Radical Liberal: The New Politics: Theory and Practice,* 2nd ed. (New York: Simon and Schuster, 1968); Kevin Mattson, *Intellectuals in Action: The Origins of the New Left and Radical Liberalism, 1945–1970* (University Park: Pennsylvania State University Press, 2002).

107. Alzono L. Hamby draws this connection in *Liberalism and Its Challengers: From F.D.R. to Bush,* 2nd ed. (New York: Oxford University Press, 1992), 277–281.

108. Thomas P. Murphy, *The New Politics Congress* (Lexington, MA: Lexington Books, 1974); James M. Perry, *The New Politics: The Expanding Technology of Political Manipulation* (London: Weidenfeld and Nicolson, 1968); Penn Kimball, *Bobby Kennedy and the New Politics* (Englewood Cliffs, NJ: Prentice-Hall, 1968).

109. Riche, "CCC Minutes," July 27, 1966, "Minutes of CCC (1966–1971)," Box 1, C.1, WSPP; Abzug et al., "Dear Friend," draft, August 1, 1966, "Met. Com. for Peace Politics," Box 1053, BSA.

110. CG14.

3. Office Bound

1. Here I paraphrase Bella Abzug in, "Look Closely" Flier, n.d., "Abzug File 1976," Box 52, NDCP.

2. Rhodri Jeffries-Jones, *Peace Now! American Society and the Ending of the Vietnam War* (New Haven, CT: Yale University Press, 1999), 144.

3. CG14.

4. Casey Hayden and Mary King, "A Kind of Memo," November 18, 1965, Judy Richardson Papers, Digital Collections, Duke University, https://idn.duke.edu/ark:/87924/r43f4mr7p.

5. The original steering committee included Sandra Adickes, Doug Ireland, Dr. Martin Sonenberg, Dr. Harry Lustig, Grace Paley, Dr. Philip Siekevitz, Mort Junger, Phil Jones, Robert Egan, and Miriam Dworkin. BAOH, 164; "What Is the PAC?," n.d., "WSP," Box 1005, BSA.

6. Paul L. Montgomery, "Farbstein Target of Reformers: Clubs Try Practical Approach in Third Attempt to Win," *NYT,* January 25, 1966, 38; Ed Gold, "VID

History and Traditions," February 23, 2007, http://www.villagedemocrats.org
/about/vid-history-and-traditions.

7. "What Is the PAC?"

8. Doug Ireland in Suzanne Braun Levine and Mary Thom, *Bella Abzug: How One Tough Broad from the Bronx Fought Jim Crow and Joe McCarthy, Pissed Off Jimmy Carter, Battled for the Rights of Women and Workers, Rallied Against War and for the Planet, and Shook Up Politics Along the Way* (New York: Farrar, Straus and Giroux, 2007), 76.

9. Ronnie Eldridge quoted in Levine and Thom, *Bella Abzug,* 76–77.

10. Bella Abzug with Mel Ziegler, ed., *Bella! Ms. Abzug Goes to Washington* (New York: Saturday Review Press, 1972), 99.

11. Allard Lowenstein quoted in William Chafe, *Never Stop Running: Allard Lowenstein and the Struggle to Save American Liberalism* (Princeton, NJ: Princeton University Press, 1998), 191.

12. BC12.

13. "Wilson Joins Race for Seat in 17th," *NYT,* April 7, 1966, 36; JW14; and http://jeromelwilson.wordpress.com/about/.

14. Abzug, "How much impact did the . . . ," draft, n.d., 1–8, 4, "Abzug, Bella—Notes for Speeches against the Draft," Box 1, BAWSP; "Divorce Reform Faced Months of Heated Debate, Maneuvering, and Compromise," *NYT,* April 28, 1966, 36.

15. Abzug, "How much impact did the . . . ," 4–5.

16. Abzug, "How much impact did the . . . ," 6–7; handwritten log book, "Abzug, Bella—Involvement with 17th Congressional District Peace Action Committee, 1966–69," BAWSP.

17. JW14. Highlighting similar experiences, BC12; SD14; CG14.

18. Abzug, "How much impact did the . . . ," 4–5. Abzug's influence can be seen in Jerome Wilson, "The War in Vietnam," "WSP," Box 1005, BSA.

19. JW14.

20. Warren Weaver Jr., "House Contents Shake Democrats: Regular Organization Here Upset by Primary Vote," *NYT,* June 30, 1966, 25; "How Districts Voted," *NYT,* June 30, 1966, 25.

21. Thomas Buckley, "Reapportionment in 17th Is Key Factor for Kupferman," *NYT,* October 13, 1966, 38.

22. Wilson for Congress ad quoting *NYT* endorsement on October 26, 1966, in *VV,* November 3, 1966, 15.

23. Abzug, "How much impact did the . . . ," 8; Peter Kinss, "Kupferman Holds Seat in 17th C.D.," *NYT,* November 9, 1966, 33.

24. "7 of 13 Democratic Club Chiefs Back Farbstein for Re-election," *NYT,* April 30, 1966, 14; Thomas P. Ronan, "Farbstein Leads Straus in Poll for Nomination in 19th District," *NYT,* February 19, 1966, 56.

25. Ted Weiss, "Dear Fellow Reformer," Telegram, July 5, 1966, "Campaigns and Candidates—Farbstein, Leonard," Box 504, BSA; "Court Orders New Primary for Democrats in the 19th," *NYT,* August 5, 1966, 11.

26. BC12; Dear Friend," June 25, 1966, "Minutes of CCC (1966–1971)," Box 1, C.1, WSPP; "Farbstein Wins with 51% Vote; Loses West Village," *VV,* October 6, 1966, 3.

27. BC12.

28. NY WSP, "We Need Ted Weiss for Congress," May 15, 1968, "Literature: 799 Broadway (1968)," Box 2, C.1, WSPP. Chafe credits Weiss's larger loss in 1968 to organizers' preoccupation with the presidential race; BC12.

29. Richard Witkin, "Defeat of Weiss Laid to Strategy," *NYT,* September 29, 1966, 42; "Weiss Statement on Farbstein Concerning Jews and Vietnam," September 25, 1966, "Campaigns and Candidates—Farbstein, Leonard," Box 504, BSA.

30. Abzug, "How much impact did the . . . ," 1; T. Buckley, "Vietnam Big Issue in June Primaries: 'Peace Movement' Active in Aiding House Hopefuls," *NYT,* May 8, 1966, 50.

31. Abzug, "Memorandum on Political Action for WSP and Report on New York Political Action Conference," draft, 1–3, 1, November 1, 1966, "WSP—Related Material about/by Bella Abzug," Box 3, C.1, WSPP.

32. Melvin Small, *At Water's Edge: American Politics and the Vietnam War* (Chicago: Ivan R. Dee, 2005), 71; Andrew L. Johns, *Vietnam's Second Front: Domestic Politics, the Republican Party, and the War* (Lexington: University Press of Kentucky, 2010), 119–158.

33. Weaver, "House Contents Shake Democrats," *NYT,* June 30, 1966, 25.

34. Ruth Myers, "Dear National Consultative," n.d., "Literature: 799 Broadway (undated)," Box 2, C.1, WSPP; Jack A. Smith, "15,000 Rally for Peace at Capitol," *NG* 18, no. 33 (May 21, 1966): 1; and, extending this omission, Charles DeBenedetti with Charles Chatfield, *An American Ordeal: The Antiwar Movement of the Vietnam Era* (Syracuse, NY: Syracuse University Press, 1990), 146–148.

35. Abzug, Letter to the Editor, *National Guardian,* draft, May 25, 1966, 1–2, "Voter Peace Pledge," Box 1005, BSA.

36. JW14.

37. DeBenedetti, *An American Ideal,* 170.

38. "A Women's Declaration of Conscience," n.d., Folder 4, Box 4, DA; "CCC Minutes," February 1, 1967, "Minutes of CCC (1966–1971)," Box 1, C.1, WSPP; Amy Swerdlow, *Women Strike for Peace: Traditional Motherhood and Radical Politics in the 1960s* (Chicago: University of Chicago Press, 1993), 159–186; Melvin Small, *Johnson, Nixon, and the Doves* (New Brunswick, NJ: Rutgers University Press, 1988), 116–119.

39. Abzug, "We appear to be near . . . ," attached to "WSP Conference—Proposed Discussion Item," n.d., 1–2, 1, Untitled Folder, Box 1004, BSA.

40. Swerdlow, *Women Strike for Peace,* 176; and for one such debate, "Emergency Meeting 12/14 11 A.M.," n.d., Minutes of CCC (1966–1971)," Box 1, C.1, WSPP.

41. Abzug, "Summary of Report to WSP National Convention," September 21, 1967, "Literature: 799 Broadway (2/67–12/67)," Box 2, C.1, WSPP.

42. I have not found the final version of this statement. Abzug, "A New Wash DC Ordinance . . . ," draft, n.d., 1–2, 2, "Abzug, Bella—Notes for Speeches against the Draft," Box 1, BAWSP.

43. Leah Fritz, "Women for Peace: The Frustration of a Day in Washington," *VV,* September 28, 1967, 5, 38–39; "Bella Abzug—negotiated with police so that

they would not get arrested," on "Women for Peace in Battle," *Memo,* October 1967, 2–4, "WSP," Box 1005, BSA.

44. Abzug, "Is Jail Necessary?," *VV,* October 12, 1967, 41.

45. Dagmar Wilson quoted in, "National Conference WSP," September 21–23, 1967, 8, "National Conference 1967, Washington, D.C.," Box 3, A.1, WSPP.

46. Abzug, "Summary of Report to WSP National Convention."

47. Abzug, "Is Jail Necessary?"; responding to Mina Grossman, "No Woman Power Yet," *VV,* September 28, 1967, 4, 37. See also Abzug, "Civil Disobedience," draft, n.d., 1–15, 1, 5, "Abzug, Bella—Notes for Speeches, Etc. (1 of 2)," Box 1, BAWSP; Elliot M. Zashin, *Civil Disobedience and Democracy* (New York: Free Press, 1972); John F. Bannan and Rosemary S. Bannan, *Law, Morality, and Vietnam: The Peace Militants and the Courts* (Bloomington: Indiana University Press, 1974).

48. MB09.

49. Kathie Sarachild quoted in Alice Echols, *Daring to Be Bad: Radical Feminism in America, 1967–1975* (Minneapolis: University of Minnesota Press, 1989), 57.

50. WSP voted to promote, but not officially sponsor, the JRB; "NY Conference," November 18, 1967, "Regional Conferences," Box 3, A.1, WSPP; Swerdlow, *Women Strike for Peace,* 135–141, 270n30; Alice Echols, "'Woman Power': Exploring the Relationship between the Antiwar Movement and the Women's Liberation Movement," in *Give Peace a Chance,* ed. Melvin Small and William D. Hoover (Syracuse, NY: Syracuse University Press, 1992), 158–170.

51. Abzug, "The Week of January 15, 1968 . . . ," draft, n.d., 1–9, 1, "Misc. Working Documents, NYC (1964–1972)," Box 3, C.1, WSPP.

52. Abzug, "The week of January 15, 1968 . . . ," 4.

53. NYRW, "Burial of the Weeping Womanhood," in *Dear Sisters: Dispatches from the Women's Liberation Movement,* ed. Rosalyn Baxandall and Linda Gordon (New York: Basic Books, 2000), 25.

54. Swerdlow, *Women Strike for Peace,* 140.

55. Katherine Turk, *Equality on Trial: Gender and Rights in the Modern American Workplace* (Philadelphia: University of Pennsylvania Press, 2016).

56. Abzug, "The week of January 15, 1968 . . . ," 4.

57. "New Politics Candidates," n.d., Untitled Folder, Box 1004, BSA; "New Group Seeks to Wed New Politics to New Left," *VV,* June 23, 1966, 38; Paul Hofmann, "New Liberal-Radical Coalition Maps 'Good Society' Platform," *NYT,* June 11, 1966, 12.

58. "Statement of Purpose," n.d., 1–2, 2, NCNPWI.

59. "Resolutions Proposed by the Black Caucus," n.d., NCNPWI; "Resolution on the Middle East—Passed," n.d., NCNPWI; Simon Hall, "On the Tail of the Panther: Black Power and the 1967 Convention of the National Conference for New Politics," *Journal of American Studies* 37, no. 1 (2003): 59–78, 74.

60. Florynce Kennedy and Ti-Grace Atkinson, "The NCNP has taken no stand . . . ," n.d., 1–2, NCNPWI.

61. Jo Freeman, "On the Origins of Social Movements," in *Waves of Protest: Social Movements since the Sixties* (New York: Rowman and Littlefield, 1999), 7–24, http://www.jofreeman.com/socialmovements/origins.htm.

62. Echols, *Daring to Be Bad,* 45–50; Sara Evans, *Personal Politics: The Roots of Women's Liberation in the Civil Rights Movement and the New Left* (New York: Vintage, 1979), 197; Winifred Breines, *The Trouble Between Us: An Uneasy History of White and Black Women in the Feminist Movement* (Oxford: Oxford University Press, 2006), 82–86.

63. Bella Abzug, unpublished memoir, n.d.

64. Abzug, "National Conference WSP," September 21–23, 1967, 1–12, 10–11, "National Conference 1967, Washington, D.C.," Box 3, A.1, WSPP; "Resolutions on Vietnam," n.d., NCNPWI; "Resolution on the Draft," n.d., NCNPWI.

65. My findings align with Eric Leif Davin, *Radicals in Power: The New Left Experience in Office* (Lanham, MD: Lexington Books, 2012); for a different take, Simon Hall, *Peace and Freedom: The Civil Rights and Antiwar Movements in the 1960s* (Philadelphia: University of Pennsylvania Press, 2006), 192.

66. BAOH, 164; "MCPP invites your cooperation . . . ," n.d., "Met Council," Box 1005, BSA.

67. Ireland quoted in Levine and Thom, *Bella Abzug,* 79. See also Richard Marbaum, "Minutes of the August 15, 17th CD PAC Meeting at the Home of Bella Abzug," August 15, 1967, "Abzug, Bella—Involvement with 17th CD PAC, 1966–1969," BAWSP; Tudja Crowder to Abzug, July 14, 1967, "Met. Council," Box 1005, BSA; "Position of the Radical Caucus on Electoral Activity," n.d., NCNPWI; "Resolution by Third Ticket Caucus," Folder 6, Box 3, DA.

68. Abzug, "What about the tactics to . . . ," n.d., Untitled Folder, Box 1004, BSA.

69. Cora Weiss quoted in Thomas Maier, *Dr. Spock: An American Life* (New York: Harcourt Brace, 1998), 232.

70. "Memorandum Report on the Present and Potential Financial Situation," September 1967, Box 3, Folder 4, DA; Marie Runyon to NCNP Former Board Members and Convention Steering Committee, January 5, 1968, Box 3, Folder 1, DA; William F. Pepper, "Continuing Report on the Congressional Investigations," November 15, 1967, Box 3, Folder 1, DA.

71. CG14.

72. Abzug to Linda Stein, October 18, 1967, "WSP," Box 1005, BSA; Abzug, "Want to dump Johnson and end the war?" n.d., Untitled Folder, Box 1004, BSA; Abzug et al., "Dear Friend," n.d., Untitled Folder, Box 1004, BSA; "1968 Presidential Primaries Set in 14 States, D.C.," *CQ,* May 26, 1967, 893–897, Untitled Folder, Box 1005, BSA.

73. "Vietnam Summer Workers Encouraged by Results," *WSP Newsletter,* September 1967, 4, "WSP," Box 1005, BSA; William M. Kutik, "Vietnam Summer Evolves from Phone Call to Nation-Wide Organizing Project," *Harvard Crimson,* May 4, 1967; Michael S. Foley, *Confronting the War Machine: Draft Resistance during the Vietnam War* (Chapel Hill: University of North Carolina Press, 2003), 62–67.

74. Dominick Sandbrook, *Eugene McCarthy and the Rise and Fall of Postwar American Liberalism* (New York: Anchor Books, 2004), 173; LA07.

75. Abzug to Eugene McCarthy, December 11, 1967, 1–2, 1, "Legislative Correspondence, NYC (1960–1971)," Box 3, C.1, WSPP.

76. Mike Mansfield quoted in "LBJ's Critics in Congress See Warning to White House," *BG*, March 13, 1968, 17; "Political Action Committee: Chairman: Bella Abzug," March 5, 1968, "WSP," Box 1005, BSA; CG14; Eugene McCarthy, *Year of the People* (Garden City, NY: Doubleday, 1969), 105.

77. Abzug, "The swift moving events of . . . ," draft, n.d., 1–6, 1, "Dissenting Democrats," Box 1004, BSA.

78. Ronnie Eldridge in Levine and Thom, *Bella Abzug*, 80; "It seems to us that . . . ," draft questions, n.d., "WSP—Related Material about/by Bella Abzug," Box 3, Series C.1, WSPP; Abzug to R. Kennedy, March 3, 1967, Untitled Folder, Box 1004, BSA; WSP to R. Kennedy, May 6, 1966, Untitled Folder, Box 1005, BSA.

79. "Partial List of Senators with Background," n.d., 1–4, 3, "Lobbying against Vietnam (1966)," Box 3, A.4, WSPP.

80. Walter LaFeber, *The Deadly Bet: LBJ, Vietnam, and the 1968 Presidential Election* (Lanham, MD: Rowman and Littlefield, 2005), 30.

81. Walter Cronkite, "We Are Mired in a Stalemate" Broadcast, CBS News, February 27, 1968, http://www.lib.berkeley.edu/MRC/pacificaviet /cronkitevietnam.html.

82. Robert F. Kennedy, "Unwinnable War Speech," February 8, 1968, in *The Tet Offensive and the Media, History and the Headlines,* ABC-Clio, http://www .historyandtheheadlines.abc-clio.com/ContentPages/ContentPage.aspx?entryId =1194576&currentSection=1194544.

83. Eldridge quoted in Levine and Thom, *Bella Abzug,* 80.

84. Abzug, "The swift moving events of . . . ," 2–5.

85. Abzug, "Outline of Meeting, May 3, 1968, Hotel Lancaster," "WSP," Box 1005, BSA.

86. CG14; RE14; CDA, "Statement of Purpose," n.d., "Dissenting Democrats," Box 1004, BSA.

87. Abzug, handwritten note, n.d., "Bella Savitzky, Democratic Convention, 1968: McCarthy for President," Box 966, BSA.

88. Abzug quoted in Levine and Thom, *Bella Abzug,* 81; Abzug, "In 1968 the assassination of . . . ," draft, n.d., 1–18, 15–16, "WSP—Related Material about/by Bella Abzug," Box 3, WSPP; Edward R. Schmitt, *President of the Other America: Robert Kennedy and the Politics of Poverty* (Amherst: University of Massachusetts Press, 2010).

89. Abzug, "The swift moving events of . . . ," 1.

90. "Supporters Seek Election Today: Shadow of Kennedy Hovers over NY Primary," *Globe and Mail,* June 18, 1968, 3.

91. Abzug, *Bella!,* 104.

92. Abzug, "Testimony before the 1968 Platform Committee of the DNC," August 1968, 1–4, 1, "WSP," Box 1005, BSA; "Tentative Witness Schedule–1968 Democratic Platform Hearings," Box 1005, BSA.

93. John Burns quoted in Lewis Chester, Godfrey Hodgson, and Bruce Page, *The Presidential Campaign of 1968* (New York: Viking Press, 1969), 410; "Democratic Search for Accord Goes On," *NYT,* June 28, 1968, 23.

94. Coalition for Politics of the People, "Leading NY Democrats to Take Party Leadership," August 25, 1968, "Abzug, Bella—Notes for Speeches, Etc. (2 of 2)," Box 1, BAWSP; Abzug, "Report of the Commission of the Future of the Coalition," n.d., "Pre-convention Strategy; Alternatives to Humphrey, Platform Lit.," Box 965, BSA.

95. Hughes Commission Report quoted in Byron E. Shafer, *Quiet Revolution: The Struggle for the Democratic Party and the Shaping of Post-reform Politics* (New York: Russell Sage Foundation, 1983), 25 and generally, 13–40.

96. Shafer, *Quiet Revolution,* 4.

97. "All Eyes Are on Chicago," n.d., "Literature: 799 Broadway (1968)," Box 2, C.1, WSPP; David Farber, *Chicago '68* (Chicago: University of Chicago Press, 1988); Small, *At Water's Edge,* 113–124; Theodore H. White, *The Making of the President 1968* (New York: Atheneum, 1969), 284–313.

98. Sociologist Penny Lewis calls this "the 1968-as-peak-argument" in *Hardhats, Hippies, and Hawks: Vietnam Antiwar Movement as Myth and Memory* (Ithaca, NY: Cornell University Press, 2013), 44.

99. Mary Lineham, "Women in the 1968 Eugene McCarthy Campaign and the Development of Feminist Politics," *Journal of Women's History* 29 (Spring 2017): 111–137.

100. Andrea Estepa, "Taking the White Gloves Off: Women Strike for Peace and 'the Movement,'" in *Feminist Coalitions: Historical Perspectives on Second-Wave Feminism in the United States,* ed. Stephanie Gilmore (Urbana: University of Illinois Press, 2008), 84–112; Felicia Kornbluh, *The Battle for Welfare Rights: Politics and Poverty in Modern America* (Philadelphia: University of Pennsylvania Press, 2007).

101. Abzug quoted in Lacey Fosburgh, "Women's Unit Bids Congress Shun War to Aid Human Needs," *NYT,* June 17, 1969, 37; Jean Shulman, "Minutes of CCC Meeting," December 3, 1969, 1–4, 2, "Minutes of the CCC (1966–1971)," Box 1, C.1, WSPP.

102. Abzug quoted in "WSP Demonstrates at Internal Revenue Office Demand No More Taxes to Washington for Vietnam and Missiles," April 15, 1969, "Literature: 799 Broadway (1969)," Box 2, Series C.1, WSP.

103. Robert M. Collins, "The Crisis of 1968 and the Waning of the 'American Century,'" *American Historical Review* 101, no. 2 (April 1996): 396–422; Timothy Conlan, *New Federalism: Intergovernmental Reform from Nixon to Reagan* (Washington, DC: Brookings Institute, 1988).

104. John V. Lindsay quoted in Vincent J. Cannato, *The Ungovernable City: John Lindsay and His Struggle to Save New York* (New York: Basic Books, 2001), 29.

105. Geoffrey Kabaservice, "On Principle: A Progressive Republican," in *Summer in the City: John Lindsay, New York, and the American Dream,* ed. Joseph P. Viteritti (Baltimore: Johns Hopkins University Press, 2014), 27–60, 38; Cannato, *The Ungovernable City,* 19–74.

106. Gloria Steinem, "The City Politic: The White Shirley Chisholm," *NY,* June 22, 1970, 8–9, 9; Joshua Freeman, *Working-Class New York: Life and Labor since World War II* (New York: New Press, 2000), 229, and generally, 228–233.

107. John V. Lindsay quoted in Charles Brecher and Raymond D. Horton, *Power Failure: New York Politics and Policy since 1960* (Oxford: Oxford University Press, 1993), 86.

108. SD14; Richard Dougherty, "Conservative Trend Shows in NY, but It May Not Last," *LAT*, June 19, 1969, A1; Emanuel Perlmutter, "Mailer Epilogue Talks of Badillo: Author Says He May Have Cost Bronx Rival Votes," *NYT*, June 19, 1969, 35; Cannato, *The Ungovernable City*, 405–414.

109. Richard Aurelio quoted in Cannato, *The Ungovernable City*, 414.

110. DA14.

111. RE14.

112. DA14. See also RE14; SD14; "Democratic Unit Backs Lindsay after Melee," *NYT*, July 18, 1969, 4; Kim Phillips-Fein, *Fear City: New York's Fiscal Crisis and the Rise of Austerity Politics* (New York: Metropolitan Books, 2017), 37.

113. SD14.

114. Jean Shulman, "CCC Minutes," October 1, 1969, 1–2, 2, "Minutes of the CCC (1966–1971)," Box 1, C.1, WSPP.

115. "CCC Minutes," July 16, 1969, 1–2, 1, "Minutes of the CCC (1966–1971)," Box 1, C.1, WSPP.

116. Sid Davidoff secured a loan for $7,500 from his mentor Vincent F. Albano Jr., vice president at Century Bank, to run this ad, and Abzug raised the funds to pay him back. "NY spends more on war than on NY," Display Ad 26, *NYT*, July 31, 1969, 15. For drafts, Folder 1221, Box 97, Reel 109, JVLP.

117. Max Frankel, "Lindsay and the Future: His Task and National Voting Trends Indicate His Opportunities Are Small," *NYT*, November 6, 1969, 37.

118. SD14.

119. Abzug to John V. Lindsay, "A Proposal for a New York City Urban Priorities Division," n.d., 1–2, "Abzug, Bella—Notes for Speeches, Etc. (1 of 2)," BAWSP. Aurelio had no recollection of this proposal coming before Lindsay or Abzug's appointment being considered; DA14.

120. SD14.

121. Phillips-Fein, *Fear City*, 38 and, generally 34–44.

122. BAOH, 228–230; "Lindsay Assigns Job to Democrat: Brown, Counsel to Seingut, Named to Albany Post," *NYT*, December 19, 1969, 51.

123. Abzug quoted in Levine and Thom, *Bella Abzug*, 82.

124. Abzug, "Womanpower for Peace," draft, October 31, 1967, "Literature: 799 Broadway (February 1967–December 1967)," Box 2, C.1, WSPP.

125. In her unpublished memoir, Abzug suggested she decided in 1968 to run for office.

126. Abzug quoted in Karen Foerstel and Herbert N. Foerstel, *Climbing the Hill: Gender Conflict in Congress* (Westport, CT: Praeger, 1996), 68.

127. "New York spends more on the war than on New York."

128. David Hapgood to Abzug, August 10, 1969, "General Correspondence, NYC (1967-No Date)," Box 3, C.1, WSPP.

4. Campaign for the People

1. Jimmy Breslin, "Is Washington Ready for Bella Abzug? Is Anybody?," *NY*, October 5, 1970, http://nymage.com/news/politics/48260/index.html.

2. Breslin, "Is Washington Ready for Bella Abzug?"

3. Audre Lorde, "New York City 1970," in *I Speak of the City: Poems of New York,* ed. Stephen Wolf (New York: Columbia University Press, 2007), 215–217.

4. Pete Hamill, "A Woman's Place," *NYP,* June 4, 1970, Same Titled Folder, Box 1028, BSA; Gloria Steinem, "The City Politic: The White Shirley Chisholm," *NY,* June 22, 1970, 8–9, 8.

5. Abzug, "I am announcing today my . . . ," March 13, 1970, 1–3, 2, "General," Box 64, BSA.

6. Letty Cottin Pogrebin quoted in Suzanne Braun Levine and Mary Thom, *Bella Abzug: How One Tough Broad from the Bronx Fought Jim Crow and Joe McCarthy, Pissed Off Jimmy Carter, Battled for the Rights of Women and Workers, Rallied Against War and for the Planet, and Shook Up Politics Along the Way* (New York: Farrar, Straus and Giroux, 2007), 131.

7. Joshua Freeman likewise observes that Al Shanker brought the "tough guy" back to New York politics in *Working-Class New York: Life and Labor since World War II* (New York: New Press, 2000), 223.

8. I expand the ideological trajectory of populism presented in Michael Kazin, *The Populist Persuasion: An American History* (Ithaca, NY: Cornell University Press, 1998).

9. Abzug quoted in "Issue Summary for Canvassers," n.d., 2, "Issue Statements," Box 64, BSA.

10. Abzug credited Jerry Rowe with devising this slogan; BAOH, 423.

11. "Give the Power Back to the People!," n.d., "General," Box 64, BSA.

12. Nancy MacLean, "Postwar Women's History: The 'Second Wave' or the End of the Family Wage?," in *A Companion to Post-1945 America,* ed. Jean-Christophe Agnew and Roy Rosenzweig (Malden, MA: Blackwell, 2002), 235–259, 254. MacLean draws on Nancy Fraser, *Justice Interruptus: Critical Reflections on the "Post-Socialist" Condition* (New York: Routledge, 1997).

13. Abzug, "Woman Activist, N.D.C. Founder to Oppose Farbstein," March 13, 1970, 1–4, 1, 3, "General," Box 64, BSA.

14. "A 'Bomb Factory?': The House on 11th Street: Digging Up the Debris," *VV,* March 12, 1970, 1.

15. Abzug, "Dear Sir," April 4, 1969, "General Correspondence (1967-Date)," Box 3, Series C.1, WSP.

16. Joe Flaherty, "Crazies at Peace Forum: The New Purists: Water Gun Wrath," *VV,* April 3, 1969, 1, 24.

17. Abzug, "Dear Sir."

18. BAOH, 204.

19. Abzug, "A Message to the Second Congress to Unite Women from Bella Abzug, Candidate for Congress, 19th C.D.," n.d., "General," Box 64, BSA.

20. Abzug, "Woman Activist, N.D.C. Founder to Oppose Farbstein." Key WSP affiliates in the campaign included Claire Reed, Ruth Myers, Amy Swerdlow, Judy Lerner, Mim Kelber, Jean Shulman, Sylvia Martin, Shirley Margolin, Lynn Lane, and Lorraine Gordon.

21. Abraham Unger, "Dear Bella: Congratulations," March 17, 1970, Folder 2, Box 16, AU.

22. Martin Abzug quoted in "Abzug: Maturity Is the Key," *WP*, February 12, 1971, C1; BAOH, 218–220, 423–424; Letty Pogrebin in Levine and Thom, *Bella Abzug*, 103.

23. MM14; RS14.

24. Nick Browne, "The Bella Blitz: 'I'm Going to Washington,'" *VV*, July 2, 1970, Same Titled Folder, Box 1028, BSA.

25. MM14. Campaign aides included Joan Metcalfe, Sandy Turner, Art Woodstone, Ted Johnson, Eileen Jennings, Ed Savage, Harold Mayerson, Eric Hirschhorn, Ross Graham, Marilyn Marcosson, and Dora Friedman.

26. Christine Boyer et al., "Straight Down Christopher Street: A Tale of the Oldest Street in Greenwich Village," in *Greenwich Village: Culture and Counter-culture*, ed. Rick Beard and Leslie Cohen Berlowitz (New Brunswick, NJ: Rutgers University Press, 1993), 36–53, 36.

27. Martin Duberman, *Stonewall* (New York: Plume of Penguin Books, 1993), 202.

28. "Bella Abzug Launches Primary Campaign, Opens Campaign Headquarters with the First Child Care Center," April 20, 1970, "4/30/70—HQ Opening," Box 1028, BSA.

29. Vivien Leons, "For Whom the Bella Tolls," *MT*, May 23, 1970, "5/23/70 Man-Trib 'Nursery Rhymes with Abzug,'" Box 1028, BSA.

30. "Leonard Farbstein Democrat for Congress," n.d., "Lobby—18/7/30," Box 64, BSA.

31. Warren Farrell, "Profile of 19th Congressional District, NY," n.d., loose document, Box 1031, BSA.

32. Abzug quoted in Grace Lichtenstein, "Farbstein Faces a Strong Challenge by Bella Abzug," *NYT*, June 6, 1970, 30.

33. "Congressional Candidate Applauds City Efforts to End Sabbath Bias Plans Campaign to Provide Mechanism for Filing Grievances," June 3, 1970, "6/3/70 Sabbath Bias," Box 1028, BSA.

34. Abzug, "In 1968 the assassination of . . . ," draft, n.d., 1–18, 15–16, "WSP—Related Material About/By Bella Abzug," Box 3, WSPP; "Before the June 1969 Mayoralty Primary," draft, n.d., 1–7, "Abzug, Bella—Notes for Speeches, Etc. (1 of 2)," Box 1, BAWSP.

35. "New Face in the Council: Carol Hutter Greitzer," *NYT*, January 29, 1969, 23; Judy Klemesrud, "Now the Councilman Wants Voters to Know She's a Woman," *NYT*, May 13, 1969, 36.

36. Abzug, "In 1968 the assassination of . . ."

37. BAOH, 423–424; "Democratic Coalition Plans to Interview Candidates," *NYT*, January 28, 1970, 34; Sandra L. Russell, "Club Presidents' Caucus on Pre-Primary Procedure for 19th CD," July 31, 1970, "Reform Designation," Box 64, BSA.

38. Media representation of Abzug's male opponents focused on their leadership attributes and résumé, an inequity that frustrated her campaign. Joe Flaherty, "Wonder Woman Throws Her Bonnet in the Ring," *VV*, March 19, 1970, 3; Nat Hentoff, "Forces and Counter-forces," *VV*, March 12, 1970, 22; "Nat Hentoff's In last week's . . . ," n.d., "Reform Designation," Box 64, BSA.

39. Abzug, "Woman Activist, N.D.C. Founder to Oppose Farbstein," 1, 3; BAOH, 220–221.

40. RS14.

41. BOAH, 201–202.

42. Raley Benet, "Politics: Mrs. Abzug Wins VID Nomination," *TV,* April 9, 1970, "4/9/70 on VID nom.," Box 1028, BSA.

43. Sandra L. Russell, "Club Presidents' Caucus on Pre-primary Procedure for 19th CD," March 21, 1970, 1–6, 2, "Reform Designation," Box 64, BSA.

44. Saul Rudes quoted in Russell, "Club Presidents' Caucus on Pre-primary Procedure for 19th CD," 4.

45. Shirley Chisholm quoted in Shulman et al., "Dear Friend," March 3, 1970, "Signature Requirements," Box 64, BSA.

46. Abzug, "Dear 19th Congressional District Voter," draft, April 6, 1970, "Letters," Box 64, BSA.

47. Abzug, "Dear 19th Congressional District Voter."

48. M. Abzug quoted in Margaret Crimmins, "Lower Manhattan's Bella Abzug Rasps It Like It Is," *WP,* July 5, 1970, G1.

49. Doug Ireland quoted in Levine and Thom, *Bella Abzug,* 87.

50. Hamill, "A Woman's Place."

51. Peter Riegert quoted in Cynthia Robins, "Profile: Peter Riegert: From Pickles to Pinter: Protean Star of ACT's Season-Opener Got Late Start in Career," September 18, 2001, http://www.sfgate.com/politics/article/PROFILE-Peter-Riegert-From-pickles-to-Pinter-2876807.php.
Riegert quoted in Budd Mishkin, "One on 1: Actor Peter Riegert," August 9, 2005, http://www.ny1.com/content/shows/one_on_1_archives_qz/54310/one-on-1--actor-peter-riegert/?ap=1 (accessed in 2014, no longer available).

52. "Official Schedule/Tuesday, 5/19/70," 1–2, 2, "Canvassing," Box 64, BSA.

53. Zero Mostel et al., "Dear Friend," n.d., Loose Document, Box 1032, BSA.

54. "Village Gate Opens for Bella Gala," June 9, 1970, "6/9/70 Village Gate," Box 1028, BSA; "Fundraising for Bella Abzug at Village Vanguard Sunday Night," n.d., "May 4—Promo. of Village Vanguard Party," Box 1028, BSA; "More Celebrities to Attend Streisand Party for Bella Abzug," June 8, 19, "6/8/70 Streisand Update," Box 1028, BSA.

55. Streisand quoted in Rita Reif, "Barbra Streisand's 5-Story Compromise," *NYT,* June 5, 1970, 47.

56. Phyllis Schlafly quoted in Donald Critchlow, "Conservatism Reconsidered: Phyllis Schlafly and Grassroots Conservatism," in *The Conservative Sixties,* ed. David Farber and Jeff Roche (New York: Peter Lang, 2003), 108–126, 119; Critchlow, *Phyllis Schlafly and Grassroots Conservatism: A Woman's Crusade* (Princeton, NJ: Princeton University Press, 2005), 196.

57. Margaret Scherf, "More Women Seen in New Congress," *LAT,* October 19, 1970, C2.

58. Susan Brownmiller, "'Sisterhood Is Powerful': A Member of the Women's Liberation Movement Explains What It's All About," *NYT,* March 15, 1970, 230; Minda Bikman, "An Insider's View: The Ladies' Invasion of Man's Home Journal," *VV,* March 26, 1970, 7.

59. BAOH, 219.

60. Ruth Rosen, *The World Split Open: How the Modern Women's Movement Changed America* (New York: Penguin Books, 2000), 231–239.

61. "Who Bella Abzug Is—Her Roots, Her Achievements and Her Commitments," n.d., 1–2, "Hard Hat Piece—Cup of Coffee," Box 1028, BSA; "This Is Bella Abzug," n.d., loose document, Box 1032, BSA.

62. Abzug quoted in Diana Lurie, "Living with Liberation," *NY*, August 31, 1970, 22–34, 24; Abzug, "Women in Political Life," 1–4, 3, "Campaign Material," Box 1029, BSA.

63. Shulamith Firestone quoted in Joyce Antler, *You Never Call! You Never Write! A History of the Jewish Mother* (Oxford: Oxford University Press, 2007), 154.

64. Robin Morgan, "Goodbye to All That," in *Dear Sisters: Dispatches from the Women's Liberation Movement,* ed. Rosalyn Baxandall and Linda Gordon (1970; New York: Basic Books, 2000), 53–57.

65. Abzug quoted in Lurie, "Living with Liberation," 24.

66. Antler, *You Never Call! You Never Write!,* 151, 149–168; Joyce Antler, *Jewish Radical Feminism: Voice from the Women's Liberation Movement* (New York: New York University Press, 2018).

67. BAOH, 215.

68. "New York City Feminist Groups & Contacts," n.d., "Reform Designation," Box 64, BSA.

69. Brownmiller quoted in Levine and Thom, *Bella Abzug,* 107.

70. AS07; JL07; RE14.

71. Ireland quoted in Levine and Thom, *Bella Abzug,* 99; Arthur Bell, "Gay Is Political and Democrats Agree," *VV*, August 13, 1970, 1; Robert O. Self, *All in the Family: The Realignment of American Democracy since the 1960s* (New York: Hill and Wang, 2012), 94–95.

72. Arthur Evans quoted in Dudley Clendinen and Adam Nagourney, *Out for Good: The Struggle to Build a Gay Rights Movement in America* (New York: Simon and Schuster, 1999), 49.

73. Kevin J. Mumford, "The Trouble with Gay Rights: Race and the Politics of Sexual Orientation in Philadelphia, 1969–1982," *Journal of American History* 139 (June 2011): 49–72, 55.

74. Jim Owles to Dan Collins, July 15, 1970, "Homosexual Rights," Box 8, NDCP.

75. Ireland quoted in Levine and Thom, *Bella Abzug,* 99.

76. Abzug, "Questionnaire for Candidates in the General Election 1972," May 1, 1972, "Correspondence 1970–1974," Box 152, BSA; Memorandum from Don to Abzug, October 22, 1970, Box 152, BSA.

77. Peter Fisher to Abzug, n.d., "Correspondence, 1971," Box 150, BSA; and Mary Visiliodes to Abzug, March 9, 1971, "Voting Rights," Box 157, BSA.

78. Stan Brossette to Abzug, February 26, 1971, "Correspondence 1970–1974," Box 152, BSA.

79. RE14.

80. "New York's Fiscal Situation," May 1, 1969, 14, "Fiscal Crisis-General (2)," Box 467, BSA.

81. "Who Bella Abzug Is—Her Roots, Her Achievements and Her Commitments," n.d., 1–2, "Hard Hat Piece—Cup of Coffee," Box 1028, BSA.

82. Abzug quoted in Crimmins, "Lower Manhattan's Bella Abzug Rasps It Like It Is," G1.

83. Unnamed cab driver quoted in Crimmins, "Lower Manhattan's Bella Abzug Rasps It Like It Is."

84. HM14.

85. Andrew Battista makes this cogent argument in *The Revival of Labor Liberalism* (Urbana: University of Illinois Press, 2008).

86. Browne, "The Bella Blitz"; "Troops Kill Four Students in Antiwar Riot at Ohio College: Guards' Gunfire Wounds 11 at Kent State," *LAT,* May 5, 1970, 1.

87. "We call on you . . . ," n.d., "Abzug, Bella," Box 41, NDC.

88. Abzug quoted in "Anti-war Rally Held in Wall Street by Congressional Candidate Bella Abzug," May 6, 1970, 1–2, "5/6/70 Anti-war Rally on Wall Street," Box 1028, BSA; Joseph Lelyveld, "Protests on Cambodia and Kent State Are Joined by Many Local Schools," *NYT,* May 6, 1970, 20.

89. Lindsay's endorsement was a surprise to some reform Democrats and caused a rift in the Village Independent Democrats club. Lindsay quoted in Edward C. Burks, "Lindsay Assails War Policy; Stresses Peaceful Dissent," *NYT,* May 7, 1970, 24; Lindsay to Abzug, June 8, 1970, Campaign Scrapbook, Box 1032, BSA; Judith Michaelson, "Mayor for Bella," *NYP,* June 9, 1970, "New York Post: Mayor for Bella and Eikernberry, 6/9/70," Box 1028, BSA.

90. Michael Drosnin, "After 'Bloody Friday,' New York Wonders If Wall Street Is Becoming a Battleground," *WSJ,* May 11, 1970, 10; Joshua Freeman, "Hardhats: Construction Workers, Manliness, and the 1970 Pro-war Demonstrations," *Journal of Social History* 26, no. 4 (Summer 1993): 725–744; Sandra Scanlon, *The Pro-war Movement: Domestic Support for the Vietnam War and the Making of Modern American Conservatism* (Amherst: University of Massachusetts Press, 2013), 202–209.

91. Lindsay quoted in "Lindsay Cites Police 'Breakdown,'" *BG,* May 10, 1970, 5.

92. Pete Hamill, "The Revolt of the White Lower Middle Class," *NY,* April 14, 1969, 24–29.

93. "Hellraiser Heads for Congress," clipping, n.d., "NY Post 6/27 'Hellraiser Heads for Congress' Post-Primary," Box 1028, BSA.

94. Abzug and unnamed workers quoted in Nick Browne, "Mrs. Abzug & the Hardhats: Reason Had Nothing to Do with It," *VV,* May 21, 1970, 9–10. This clipping appeared in Abzug's FBI file at 100-102413-250.

95. "Bella Abzug Equates 'Breakdown in Civilization' with Killing in South," May 18, 1970, 1–2, "Statements and Activities," Box 150, BSA; "Two Die as Police Fire on Dormitory: Windows Shot Out: 10 Wounded at Jackson, Mississippi Negro College," *LAT,* May 15, 1970, 1; Freeman, *Working-Class New York,* 238.

96. "Bella!" n.d., Loose Document, Box 1032, BSA.

97. "The Lettuce of Wrath," August 13, 1970, "United Farm Workers," Box 417, BSA; "Congressional Candidate Joins Village Residents in Redeeming U.S. Savings Bonds to Protest Indochina War," May 27, 1970, "5/27/70—C.C. Joins Village Residents," Box 1028, BSA; "Congressional Candidate Marches with

Tenants Evicted by 'Phone Company,'" May 21, 1970, "May 21—Cong. Cand. Marches," Box 1028, BSA.

98. "Who Bella Abzug Is—Her Roots, Her Achievements and Her Commitments," n.d., 1–2, 2, "Hard Hat Piece—Cup of Coffee," Box 1028, BSA

99. "The War in Cambodia: Remarks of Leonard Farbstein," *CR* offprint, April 28, 1970, "Farbstein," Box 64, BSA; Richard M. Nixon, "Address to the Nation on the Situation in Southeast Asia," April 30, 1970, http://www.presidency.ucsb.edu/ws/?pid=2490.

100. "Barbra Streisand Campaigns with Bella Abzug," *NYT,* clipping, Same Titled Folder, Box 1028, BSA.

101. Hamill, "A Woman's Place"; Farrell, "Profile of 19th Congressional District, NY."

102. Abzug, "Mid East," draft, n.d., 1–7, 1, 3, "Abzug, Bella—Notes for Speeches against the Draft," BAWSP.

103. Robert Aronson, "Political Morning," *VV,* June 18, 1970, "Village Voice: Political Meeting," Box 1028, BSA.

104. William B. Quandt, *Decade of Decisions: American Policy toward the Arab-Israeli Conflict, 1967–1976* (Berkeley: University of California Press, 1977), 88.

105. Abzug quoted in Browne, "The Bella Blitz."

106. Pamela E. Pennock, *The Rise of the Arab American Left: Activists, Allies, and Their Fight against Imperialism and Racism, 1960s–1980s* (Chapel Hill: University of North Carolina Press, 2017).

107. Unnamed volunteer quoted in Jonathan Rynhold, *The Arab-Israeli Conflict in American Political Culture* (Cambridge: Cambridge University Press, 2015), 142.

108. Browne, "The Bella Blitz."

109. Abzug and Lowenstein quoted in Edith Spiegel, "The Great Abzug Upset: A Most Happy Bella," June 27, 1970, 10, "Press Clippings—1970," Box 111, BSA; Victory Speech, digitized in BSA.

110. "Women's Lib Now Has Congress Candidate," *BG,* June 25, 1970, 2.

111. Herman Badillo quoted in Thomas Poster, "Badillo Enjoys Bravos, Hails Mrs. Abzug's Win," *DN,* June 25, 1970, 36; "Herman Badillo Apoya a Bella Abzug," n.d., "6/25/70 El Dario-Herman Badillo," Box 1028, BSA.

112. ". . . and End of Powellism," *NYT,* June 25, 1970, Same Titled Folder, Box 1028, BSA.

113. Saul Friedman, "There'll Be Fireworks from the Radical Left," *PI,* July 14, 1970, Same Titled Folder, Box 1028, BSA

114. Shulman, "Dear WSPer," n.d., "Literature: 799 Broadway (undated)," Box 2, C.1, WSPP; "Bella and the Boys," *NYP,* June 24, 1970, 3.

115. Ted to Abzug, May 25, 1970, "WOR (FCC Case)," Box 64, BSA; Alan Ehrenhalt, "Must Quit or Give Equal Time: TV Men in Politics Pose a Problem," *WP,* September 24, 1970, E12.

116. Barry Farber, "My Dear Mrs. Abzug," August 24, 1970, "Farber, Barry," Box 64, BSA; Frank Lynn, "Farber-Abzug Campaign Opens on Flowery Note," *NYT,* August 25, 1970, 33.

117. Linda Charlton, "The Feminine Protest: Liberation Movement, a Liberal-Radical Blend, Seeks 'Equality' in Many Ways," *NYT,* August 28, 1970,

20. Representative of Abzug's role, "Speech by Bella Abzug for Women's Liberation Anniversary Rally, August 26," August 26, 1970, 1–5, "Statements and Releases," Box 599, BSA; "Women's Strike for Equality Meeting," July 29, 1970, "National Women's Strike Coalition, 8/26/70," Box 990, BSA.

118. Farber quoted in Lynn, "Farber-Abzug Campaign Opens on Flowery Note."

119. "Barry Farber: A Profile," n.d., 1–2, 1, "Farber, Barry," Box 64, BSA.

120. Abzug quoted in Mary Perot Nichols, "Runnin' Scared," VV, August 20, 1970, 3; Memo from Ben D. Shaw to Ed Savage, n.d., "Farber, Barry," Box 64, BSA.

121. Abzug quoted in Gil Scott, "Bella and Barry Enliven Politics," CSM, November 2, 1970, 5; "Barry Farber Has No Political Past!," flyer, n.d., "Farber, Barry," Box 64, BSA.

122. SA Thomas J. Devine to SAC NY, December 7, 1970, 100-102413-272, FBI File.

123. Penn Kemble, "Who Needs the Liberals?," Commentary 50, no. 4 (October 1970): 57–64, 63. For Abzug surrogates' response, see Paul O'Dwyer to Norman Podhoretz, October 19, 1970, "Newspaper Speakers Campaign Clippings," Box 1029, BSA; Saul Rudes, "Bella Abzug's Stand: To the Editor," NYT, November 2, 1970, 46.

124. HF07; "Statement of Henry Foner," n.d., Folder 3, Box 6, HFP; "Court Upholds Farber as Liberals' Candidate," NYT, June 17, 1970, 36. For Liberal Party–Farber staff crossover, see Irving Schiffer to "Dear Friends," September 10, 1970, "Farber, Barry," Box 64, BSA.

125. Alice O'Connor, "The Privatized City: The Manhattan Institute, the Urban Crisis, and the Conservative Counterrevolution in New York," Journal of Urban History 34, no. 2 (January 2008): 333–353, 334; Irving Kristol and Paul Weaver, "Who Knows New York? Notes on a Mixed-Up City," Public Interest, no. 16 (Summer 1969): 59.

126. Campaign volunteer Eva Lederman mentioned this photo in an oral interview found in Box 11, MKP; I have not been able to locate it.

127. Barnard L. Collier, "Attempts to Open Schools Are Tense," NYT, October 18, 1968, 50; Jerald Podair, The Strike That Changed New York: Blacks, Whites, and the Ocean Hill–Brownsville Crisis (New Haven, CT: Yale University Press, 2002).

128. Al Shanker quoted in Nat Hentoff, clipping, VV, July 2, 1970, 24, "Village Voice Hentoff 7/2/70," Box 1028, BSA.

129. "Statement of Bella S. Abzug, Democratic Candidate for Congress, 19th District Delivered at a Public Hearing of Local School Board #1," August 26, 1970, Same Titled Folder, Box 1028, BSA; Abzug, "Statement by Rep. Bella Abzug," September 18, 1976, "Unions," Box 1033, BSA.

130. "Statement by Congresswoman Bella Abzug," Press Release, September 2, 1976, "For Concord," Box 1055, BSA; LA05; EA12.

131. Richard D. Kahlenberg, Tough Liberal: Albert Shanker and the Battles over the Schools, Unions, Race, and Democracy (New York: Columbia University Press, 2007), 157; Podair, The Strike That Changed New York.

132. "To America, Barry Farber Is 'The Voice of New York,'" n.d., "Farber, Barry," Box 64, BSA.

133. Victor Lasky, "Say It Straight: Israel Aid Is Main Issue in N.Y. House Seat Fight," *JP*, September 11, 1970, "9/11/70 Jewish Press: 'Say It Straight' by Victor Lasky," Box 1028, BSA.

134. Farber, "Charges Bella Called Him a Liar," transcription, October 21, 1970, "WOR (FCC Case)," Box 64, BSA.

135. Meir Kahane, "The Story of Bella," *JP* 29, no. 44 (October 30, 1970), reprint, 1–2, "Statements, Notes, Etc.," Box 292, BSA; Concerned Citizens to Defeat Abzug, "Bella Abzug Spells Disaster for Jews," Loose Document, Box 1032, BSA.

136. Abzug and Esther Smith quoted in Grace Lichtenstein, "The Abzug-Farber Contest: Plenty of Color," *NYT,* October 30, 1970, 48.

137. MM14; Barbera Leder to Abzug, October 31, 1970, "Farber, Barry," Box 64, BSA.

138. Ireland quoted in Marlene Nadle, "'Listen Buckley . . .': Bella in the Backroom," *VV,* November 12, 1970, 50.

139. Nichols, "Runnin' Scared," 3; and HM 14.

140. RS14.

141. Abzug quoted in Nadle, "'Listen Buckley . . . ,' 50.

142. "Congressional Vote in the City," *NYT,* November 5, 1970, 41.

143. BAOH, 208.

144. "Abzug TV," n.d., "WOR Spots," Box 64, BSA.

145. Abzug, "Speech Delivered by Bella Abzug to CCC of WSP," December 5, 1970, 1–9, 4, "CCC, WSP, 5 December 1970," Box 759A, BSA.

146. Ireland, Letter to the Editor, *VV,* January 20, 1971, 1–2, 1, "Issues Convention," Box 12, NDC.

147. John Kenneth Galbraith, *Who Needs the Democrats* (Garden City, NY: Doubleday, 1970), 86.

148. Abzug quoted in Jim Gash Radio Show transcript, November 29, 1970, "Bella Abzug—Transcripts," Box 1031, BSA.

149. Ronnie Eldridge quoted in "Hellraiser Heads for Congress," clipping, n.d., "NY Post 6/27 'Hellraiser Heads for Congress' Post-Primary," Box 1028, BSA.

5. Not One of the Boys

1. Barbara Carlson, "Mrs. Abzug Gives Portent of Future," *HC,* January 22, 1971, 7.

2. "Bella Won't Be One of the Boys," n.d., "Literature: 799 Broadway (1971)," Box 2, C.1, WSPP.

3. "Text of 'Set the Date' Resolution (House Resolution #54)," in "For Insertion into CR 1/25 (Tuesday)," 1–4, 4, "Sponsored by Abzug," Box 388, BSA.

4. "Bella's First Appearance on the Steps of the Capitol, 1971," audio recording, digitized, BSA.

5. "'State of the Congress' Message by Our Woman in Washington or Bella Give 'Em Hell," *Memo* 1, no. 4 (1971): 15, loose document, Box 7, MB.

6. Bella Abzug with Mel Ziegler, ed., *Bella! Ms. Abzug Goes to Washington* (New York: Saturday Review Press, 1972), 35.

7. Abzug quoted in Marty Racine, "The Only One Talking Is," *Bugle-American,* October 22, 1976, 20–23, 21, "1976 Clippings," Box 1044, BSA.

8. Abzug quoted in Mary McGrory, "Bella Abzug—New House Rebel," *BG,* January 26, 1971, 21.

9. "Rep. Bella S. Abzug's Speech to California Democratic Council," April 2, 1971, "Democratic Council, 4/2/71," Box 759A, BSA.

10. Julian Zelizer, *On Capitol Hill: The Struggle to Reform Congress and Its Consequences, 1948–2000* (Cambridge: Cambridge University Press, 2004), 92; Zelizer, "Bridging State and Society: The Origins of 1970s Congressional Reform," *Social Science History* 24, no. 2 (Summer 2000): 379–393.

11. Michael P. Harrington, "Cracking the Seniority Wall," *NYT,* January 18, 1971, 39.

12. John A. Lawrence, *The Class of '74: Congress after Watergate and the Roots of Partisanship* (Baltimore: Johns Hopkins University Press, 2018), 19.

13. Richard L. Lyons, "House GOP, Democrats Loosen Seniority Knot," *BG,* January 21, 1971, 1; Minutes, January 19–20, 71, Folder 7, Box 3, HDCR.

14. Mim Kelber to Morton Stavis, December 23, 1970, 1–2, "Rules, House," Box 174, BSA.

15. Susan Tolchin and Martin Tolchin, *Clout: Womanpower and Politics* (New York: Coward, McCann, and Geoghegan, 1974), 24.

16. Abzug, Interviewed by Mel Ziegler, n.d., March 14, 1971, 18, Loose Documents, Box 63A, BSA. This transcript is incomplete and includes multiple interviews. Sometimes identifying information such as the tape side or number of transcript date is not noted, and some pages are numbered with two separate designations. I have tried to provide as much identifying information as possible. Hereafter, I reference as ZI, Date or Tape, Page Number(s). For example, Abzug, ZI, March 14, 1971, 18.

17. Judith Nies McFadden, "Women's Lib on Capitol Hill," *Progressive,* December 1970, 22–25, 22, 23, Folder 10, Box 564, PMP; "Bella Abzug's Legislative Report to Women's Panel at NDC Conference in NY, Washington Irving HS, NY," February 7, 1971, "Statements on the Issues A–W (2)," Box 1033, BSA; Rachel Laura Pierce, "Capitol Feminism: Work, Politics, and Gender in Congress, 1960–1980" (PhD diss., University of Virginia, 2014).

18. Fred Lembeck, "Hauling the Line in Bella's Office," *TV,* November 6, 1975, 5, "Press Clippings," Box 1046, BSA.

19. EN15.

20. Abzug quoted in Richard L. Madden, "NY's Freshmen in Congress Get a Head Start on Homework," *NYT,* December 26, 1970, 3, 8; Abzug, ZI, February 1971, 1.

21. EN15.

22. Esther Newberg quoted in, "Middletown Woman Commands Big Job," *HC,* January 21, 1971, 48A.

23. Initial staff included mail coordinator Ever Terry, receptionist Emily Collins, and constituent coordinator Sharon Oper, NS15; Abzug, ZI, February 1971, 3; JWO15.

24. JC14.

25. The first New York staff included Mim Kelber, Claire Reed, Steve Max, Dora Friedman, Howard Brock, Sylvia Epstein, and Ed Serepede. Edith Evans Asbury, "Mrs. Abzug Opens a District Office," *NYT,* February 13, 1971, 11.

26. "Women in Congress, 1917–2019: Service Dates and Committee Assignments by Member, and Lists by State and Congress," April 9, 2019, CRS, https://fas.org/sgp/crs/misc/RL30261.pdf.

27. Abzug met with Wilbur Mills, Tip O'Neill, Olin Teague, and James Watts and considered an outside letter-writing pressure campaign. "Bella's Statement to Washington Heights–Child Care Coalition," January 28, 1971, "Speeches, Statements, Testimony, Cong. Record," Box 140, BSA; Abzug, ZI, February 1971, 9–10; "January 26: Appointments with Leadership and Ways and Means Members," "Correspondence, 1971 Jan–Feb.," Box 108, BSA.

28. Abzug, "Speech for the Jewish Center of Kew Garden Hills," n.d., 4, 9, "Statements, Activities, Notes, and Memos," Box 398, BSA; David E. Rosenbaum, "House Committee Assignments to Liberals Are Rebuff to Top Southern Democrats," *NYT,* February 1, 1971, 18.

29. Abzug quoted in Minutes, February 3, 1971, 20, Folder 8, Box 3, HDCR.

30. Shirley Chisholm, *Unbought and Unbossed* (Boston: Houghton Mifflin, 1970), 81; Minutes, February 3, 1971, 13; Thomas P. Murphy, *The New Politics Congress* (Lexington, MA: Lexington Books, 1974), 82–85, 118–119; Zelizer, *On Capitol Hill,* 126–132; Susan J. Carroll, "Committee Assignments: Discrimination or Choice?," in *Legislative Women: Getting Elected, Getting Ahead,* ed. Beth Reingold (Boulder, CO: Lynne Rienner, 2008), 135–156.

31. "General Information on House Committees," November 11, 1970, Folder 2, Box 43, DSGP.

32. One example is Don Fraser's (D-MN) bid for the Ways and Means Committee, which he lost 119 to 104. Abzug, ZI, February 1971, 6–7; Abzug, "Caucus," note, n.d., "Notes, 1971–1972 and N.D.," Box 68, BSA; Marjorie Hunter, "House Democrats Uphold Seniority by 30-Vote Margin," *NYT,* February 4, 1971, 1.

33. Abzug quoted in Richard L. Madden, "2 in House Upset by Assignments; Mrs. Abzug and Badillo Get Unwanted Committees," *NYT,* January 29, 1971, 12; Abzug, ZI, February 1971, 16.

34. Abzug, ZI, March 1971, 17–19; "Subcommittees of the Committee on Government Operations Jurisdiction," n.d., "Correspondence," Box 519, BSA; "House Committees: Government Operations," *CQWR* 29, no. 17 (April 23, 1971): 897.

35. "EDA Statement—Bella S. Abzug," n.d., "Notes, Memoranda, and Statements," Box 520, BSA; Chairman John A. Blatnik to Abzug with her handwritten rankings, February 9, 1971, "Public Works—Correspondence," Box 519, BSA; Blatnik to Abzug, March 9, 1971, "Public Works—Correspondence," Box 519, BSA; "House Committees: Public Works," *CQWR* 29, no. 17 (April 23, 1971): 902–903.

36. Kelber to Stavis, December 23, 1970.

37. EH14; John A. Farrell, *Tip O'Neill and the Democratic Century* (Boston: Little, Brown, 2001), 295.

38. Carl Albert with Danney Goble, *Little Giant: The Life and Times of Speaker Carl Albert* (Norman: University of Oklahoma Press, 1990), 339.

39. Jonathan C. Randal, "Allies Hint of Saigon Move into Laos," *WP*, February 5, 1971, A14; Abzug, Untitled, February 12, 1971, "Press Releases," Box 382, BSA; Martin Weil, "Antiwar Leaders 'Outraged' over Laos, Protests Planned," *WP*, February 9, 1971, A12; Jeffrey Kimball, *Nixon's Vietnam War* (Lawrence: University Press of Kansas, 1998).

40. Richard Bolling quoted in Minutes, March 31, 1971, 5, Folder 11, Box 3, HDCR; Spencer Rich, "Senate Democrats Adopt Total Pullout Resolution," *WP*, February 24, 1971, A1; Adam Clymer, "House Doves Seek Year-End Viet Pullout," *TS*, March 15, 1971, A5; Marjorie Hunter, "Democratic Whip Asks U.S. Pullout," *NYT*, March 30, 1971, 7; Hunter, "House Democrats Ask Pullout by '73," *NYT*, April 1, 1973, 1.

41. Drinan, Dellums, and Abzug quoted in Mary McGrory, "Elbow Room—and a Warning," *BG*, April 4, 1971, B6.

42. Abzug quoted in Minutes, April 21, 1971, 4, Folder 12, Box 3, HDCR; Minutes, April 19, 1972, Folder 24, Box 3, HDCR.

43. Abzug, ZI, March 19, 1971, 5–6; Abzug, ZI, Tape 15, Side A, 10-424; "Mrs. Abzug: Mr. Speaker I object . . . ," n.d., "Week of 27 Sept. 1971 OEO, Resolution of Inquiry, Vietnam Elections," Box 645, BSA; Roland Evans Jr. and Robert Novak, "Mitchell Set to Run Campaign: Laird Draws Few," *WP*, March 28, 1971, B7; David R. Boldt, "Rep. Jacobs' Tactic on DC Delays House," *WP*, April 22, 1971, B4.

44. Abzug introduced a like resolution but requested to have it withdrawn to enhance their collective effort. Minutes, April 19, 1972, HDCR; Abzug to DSG members, April 17, 1972, DSGP; Spencer Rich and Mary Russell, "Debate over Bombing Rages on Capitol Hill," *WP*, April 20, 1972, A1; John W. Finney, "Democrats on House Unit Favor Pullout," *NYT*, May 11, 1972, 19; Finney, "End-War Measure Beaten in House by 228–178 Vote," *NYT*, August 11, 1972, 1.

45. Pat Kruse to Congressmen Phillip Burton et al., February 11, 1971, Folder 1, Box 106, RKP.

46. For a representative tour, see "BSA's Schedule Friday, 4/30/71–Monday, 5/10/71," "1972 March–December," Box 108, BSA.

47. Representatives James Abourezk, Robert Drinan, Parren Mitchell, John F. Seiberling, and Paul Sarbanes were selected to join the Group. Kruse to Burton et al., June 10, 1971, Folder 1, Box 106, RKP; Kruse to Group, October 27, 1971, Folder 1, Box 106, RKP.

48. Burton paraphrased in Honorable Abner J. Mikva, Interviewed by Stephen J. Pollak, 1996–1999, Oral History Project, Historical Society of District of Columbia Circuit, 134; see also 307–308; http://dcchs.org/AbnerJMikva /abnerjmikva_complete.pdf.

49. Mikva interview, 168.

50. JWO15.

51. "Testimony of Bella S. Abzug before the Gallagher Sub-committee of the House Foreign Affairs Committee," n.d., 1–4, 2, "Resolution of Inquiry," Box 173, BSA.

52. Susan Hartmann, *From Margin to Mainstream: American Women and Politics Since 1960* (New York: Alfred A. Knopf, 1989), 95–96.

53. Abzug, ZI, Tape 12, Side B, n.d., 27.

54. Abzug, ZI, March 14, 1971, 8.

55. Daniel Crystal to Abzug, February 11, 1971, 1–2, 1, "Resolution of Inquiry," Box 173, BSA; "Precedents for Resolution of Inquiry," n.d., "Congress, US—Resolution of Inquiry," Box 173, BSA; Abzug, "The Resolution of Inquiry: Too Long Neglected," n.d., "Res. of Inquiry, Abzug, Statements, Legis., Etc.," Box 273, BSA; Louis Fisher, *The Politics of Executive Privilege* (Durham, NC: Carolina Academic Press, 2004), 135–159.

56. H.R. Res. 491, 92nd Cong., 1st Sess., June 21, 1971, "Sponsored by Abzug," Box 388, BSA; and for connected resolutions, H.R. Res. 490, "Sponsored by Abzug," Box 388, BSA; H.R. Res. 489, "Sponsored by Abzug," Box 388, BSA; H. Res. 691, "Sponsored by Abzug," Box 388, BSA.

57. "BSA Schedule—Wed., 2/17," "1971 Jan–Feb.," Box 108, BSA.

58. I am indebted to Tom Wells for sharing his transcript, "Bella Abzug, 11/9/96, phone." See also Wells, *Wild Man: The Life and Times of Daniel Ellsberg* (New York: Palgrave Macmillan, 2001); Daniel Ellsberg, *Secrets: A Memoir of Vietnam and the Pentagon Papers* (New York: Viking, 2002), 356–366.

59. "Testimony of Bella S. Abzug before the Gallagher Sub-committee of the House Foreign Affairs Committee," 1, 3.

60. "Meeting between President Nixon and John N. Mitchell, H. R. ("Bob") Haldeman, and John D. Ehrlichman in the Oval Office between 5:09 pm and 6:46 pm on 6/22/71," Conv. No. 527-12, WHT.

61. Nixon quoted in "Transcript #1: Part of a Conversation between President Nixon and H. R. Haldeman in the Oval Office between 12:26 pm and 1:02 pm on 5/7/71," Conv. No. 495-18#1, WHT.

62. Howard N. Meyer, "My Dear M. Chairwoman," n.d., "Berrigan Case," Box 499, BSA.

63. Glen Elsasser, "Top Justice Aide Backs FBI Probe," *CT,* April 8, 1971, 10.

64. "Statement by the Honorable Bella S. Abzug (D-NY): Remarks Introducing Resolution Investigation FBI," April 7, 1971, 1–2, 1, "FBI Investigation, 4/7/71," Box 759, BSA.

65. "Statement by Congresswoman Bella S. Abzug to Conference on the State of Civil Liberties in the USA Today," May 23, 1971, 1–2, 1, "Statements on Issues A-W (1)," Box 1033, BSA.

66. "Testimony of Congresswoman Bella S. Abzug before the House Armed Services Committee," June 28, 1971, "Resolution of Inquiry," Box 173, BSA.

67. Abzug, *CR* 117, no. 166, Part II, November 4, 1971, "Abzug—Statements," Box 275, BSA. On Abzug as a "new internationalist," see Robert B. Johnson, *Congress and the Cold War* (Cambridge: Cambridge University Press, 2006).

68. "Testimony of Congresswoman Bella S. Abzug before the House Armed Services Committee," June 28, 1971, "Resolution of Inquiry," 1–4, 3, Box 173, BSA.

69. Abzug, H.R. Res. 638, 92nd Cong., 1st Sess., October 6, 1971, "Sponsored by Abzug," Box 388, BSA; H.R. Res. 918, 92nd Cong., 2nd Sess., April 11, 1972, "Sponsored by Abzug," Box 388, BSA; Abzug, et al., H.R. Res 1367, 93rd Cong., 2nd Sess., September 18, 1974, "Notes and Memos," Box 273, BSA; "The Resolution of Inquiry: Too Long Neglected," n.d., "Abzug, Statements, Legis., Etc.," Box 273, BSA.

70. A 2017 CRS report indicates the resolution of inquiry was used most frequently between 1971–1976 and 2003–2006: https://www.everycrsreport .com/reports/R40879.html. For its recent employment in challenge of the Trump administration, see Seth Millstein, "What Is a Resolution of Inquiry? Jerrold Nadler Is Requesting Info on Donald Trump," February 9, 2017, *Bustle,* https://www.bustle.com/p/what-is-a-resolution-of-inquiry-jerrold-nadler-is -requesting-info-on-donald-trump-37067.

71. Crystal to Abzug, February 9, 1971, 1–4, 3, "Congress, U.S., Rules, House," Box 174, BSA.

72. Abzug quoted in Sarah Evans, *Tidal Wave: How Women Changed America at Century's End* (New York: Free Press, 2003), 67; Memorandum from Stanley to Abzug, May 14, 1971, "Week of 5/17/71," Box 642, BSA; Nixon, "Veto of the Accelerated Public Works Bill," June 29, 1971, http://library.cqpress .com/cqalmanac/document.php?id=cqal71-869-26707-1255194; Nixon, "Remarks on Signing the Emergency Employment Act of 1971," July 12, 1971, http://www.presidency.ucsb.edu/ws/index.php?pid=3074.

73. "BSA's Women's Work (First Six Months in Office—Partial List)," June 30, 1971, 1–2, 1, "Legislative Accomplishments, 92nd Congress," Box 727, BSA.

74. Abzug, ZI, February 1971, 27; "BSA Schedule—3/25–4/1: Sat. 3/27—Barnstorming Day—WSP," "1971 March–December," Box 108, BSA.

75. Abzug, "Speech Delivered by Bella Abzug to CCC of WSP," December 5, 1970, 1–9, 1, "CCC, WSP, 5 December 1970," Box 759A, BSA.

76. Abzug quoted in David E. Rosenbaum, "House May Pass Service Pay Raise," *NYT,* March 31, 1971, 6.

77. Abzug quoted in Robert C. Maynard, "Abolition of Draft Is Pressed on the Hill," *WP,* March 2, 1971, A2; Bernard D. Nossiter, "Vietnam Oil Find a Whopper—of a Tale," *BG,* April 11, 1971, A30; "House Approves Two-Year Extension of the Draft," *CQWR* 29, no. 14 (April 2, 1971): 735–737.

78. Jan Barry Crumb to Abzug, January 18, 1971, "Winter Soldier Investigation," Box 393, BSA; Crawford to Abzug with her notes, February 3, 1971, "Winter Soldier Investigation," Box 393, BSA; Crawford, Memorandum for the Record, February 9, 1971, ibid.; "1. House Armed Services Comm . . . ," "Notes, 1971–1972 and N.D.," Box 68, BSA; Abzug, ZI, March 14, 1971, 3–4 and March 26, 1971, 24–25; "Congresswoman Bella Abzug Supports Demands for Congressional Hearings on War Crimes in Vietnam," February 5, 1971, "General," Box 393, BSA; Andrew E. Hunt, *The Turning: A History of the Vietnam Veterans against the War* (New York: New York University Press, 1999).

79. Abzug, ZI, March 19, 1971, 11; Ronald V. Dellums with H. Lee Halterman, *Lying Down with the Lions: A Public Life from the Streets of Oakland to*

the Halls of Power (Boston: Beacon Press, 2000), 61; Laura "X" Murra, e-mail correspondence with author, May 25, 2017, in author's possession.

80. Abzug, ZI, April 12, 1971, 6.

81. "On the Hill," photo accompanying Thomas Oliphant, "Arlington Cemetery Gates Barred to Mothers, Vet with Wreaths," *BG,* April 20, 1971, 1.

82. John Kerry, "Transcript: Kerry Testifies before Senate Panel, 1971," excerpt posted on April 25, 2006, http://www.npr.org/templates/story/story.php ?storyId=3875422.

83. Vinny Giardina to Abzug, April 21, 1971, "General, 1970; 1971 Jan.–Aug.," Box 1, BSA.

84. JC14; James H. Pasto to Abzug, March 14, 1972, "Correspondence, 1970–1972, n.d.," Box 422, BSA; Memorandum from Crawford to Abzug, October 17, 1972, "Notes, Statements, and Memoranda," Box 422, BSA.

85. Arthur Egendorf, "Dear VVAW member," n.d., "Veterans Correspondence, 1970–1973," Box 434, BSA; Abzug, "Dear Concerned Veteran," May 31, 1971, Box 434, BSA; "Proposal on Setting Up a Task Force on Veterans Problems," n.d., "Notes, Memoranda, and Statements," Box 434, BSA.

86. Abzug, Fletcher Thompson, G. V. Montgomery, and John G. Schmitz quoted in "Peace Demonstrators: 'Congress Has the Power,' " *CQWR* 29, no. 18 (April 30, 1971): 959–962, 960–961.

87. HM14; "People's Peace Treaty Con. Res.," Box 388, "General," Box 393, BSA.

88. Abzug quoted in John W. Finney, "3 Representatives Decry Arrests on Capitol Steps," *NYT,* May 6, 1971, 38.

89. Abzug, ZI, Tape 12, Side A, n.d., 2; JWO15; NS15.

90. "On Monday May 3 after repeated . . . ," n.d., "1971–1972—Capitol Steps / May Day Cases," Box 116, BSA; "Wednesday May 5 was the day . . . ," Box 116, BSA; "1,000 Held in Protest at Capitol: Arrest Total Reaches 11,000 in This Week's Anti-war Activities," *TS,* May 6, 1971, A1.

91. Abzug, ZI, Tape 12, Side A, n.d., 2, 6; Abzug, "The Constitution versus Law Enforcement," *CR* reprint, May 11, 1971, "Statements and Activities," Box 150, BSA.

92. Andrea A. Warren et al. to Abzug, attached to Memorandum from Crawford to Linda Dorian, August 3, 1971, 1–2, 1, "Military," Box 629, BSA; Heather Marie Stur, *Beyond Combat: Women and Gender in the Vietnam War Era* (Cambridge: Cambridge University Press, 2011).

93. Abzug quoted in "Women Assail Nixon Abortion Directive," *TS,* April 8, 1971, A3; Carol T. Foreman to Abzug, April 7, 1971, "Military," Box 605, BSA.

94. Memorandum to Abzug, October 1, 1971, 1–2, 2, "Women's National Abortion Action Coalition," Box 605, BSA.

95. Abzug et al., "HR 10240," 92nd Cong., 1st Sess., July 30, 1971, 1–3, 2, "Legislation—92nd and 93rd Congress," Box 604, BSA; BAOH, 259–261; David Garrow, *Liberty and Sexuality: The Right to Privacy and the Making of* Roe v. Wade (Berkeley: University of California Press, 1998).

96. Mary Vasiliodes to Abzug, March 9, 1971, "Voting Rights," Box 157, BSA; Lillian Faderman, *The Gay Revolution: The Story of the Struggle* (New York: Simon and Schuster, 2015), 231–237.

97. Anonymous to Abzug, January 30, 1971, "Correspondence 1970–1974," Box 152, BSA; this letter was quoted in "Testimony by Congresswoman Bella S. Abzug before City Council's General Welfare Committee on Bill #475," October 18, 1971, 1–5, 4, "Statements and Activities," Box 153, BSA.

98. "Statement by Congresswomen-Elect Bella S. Abzug to NY State Assembly Hearing on the Problems of Homosexuals," January 7, 1971, 1–3, 1, 2, "Statements and Activities," Box 153, BSA.

99. Abzug to Lindsay, April 8, 1971, "Folder 173: Congress (2) 1971," Box 14, Reel 67, JVLP.

100. "Service Plan of Abzug," *NYAN,* March 13, 1971, 31; "Some District Activities of Congresswoman Bella S. Abzug (19th CD)," n.d., "Statements and Releases," Box 444, BSA.

101. I have excised typos in this quote for readability. "Primary function has been to . . . ," n.d., "Notes and Activities," Box 444, BSA; "1,000 Constituents Get Help, Advice," *Congresswoman Bella S. Abzug* 1, no. 1 (June 1971): 1–4, 4, "National Constituents," Box 65, BSA.

102. Abzug paraphrased in "Staff Meeting," December 20, 1971, 1–8, 2–4, "Abzug, Checklists and Staff Reports," Box 44, BSA.

103. Joan Gregg to Abzug, April 3, 1971, "Correspondence," Box 179, BSA.

104. For women labor unionists' first visits, see "BSA Schedule—Wed., Feb. 3, 1971," "Administrative Files—Public Activities—Schedules, 1971 January–February," Box 108, BSA; "In NY Office: Thursday, April 8, 1971," "Administrative Files—Public Activities—Schedules, 1971 March–April," Box 108, BSA. For building complaint files, see "Notes, Memos, Statements, and Activities," Box 358, BSA. For Abzug's speech before NWRO, see "Notes, Memoranda, Statements, Releases and Activities," Box 590, BSA. For early environmentalism, see Abzug, "A Bold Program for Clean Water," *The Progressive,* October 1971, 27, Box 760, BSA.

105. Patsy Mink, "Women in the Field of Politics," n.d., 1–8, 3, Folder 10, Box 564, PMP; Claudia Dreifus, "Mink Is a Girl's Best Friend," March 1972, *Juris Doctor,* 16–17, 49, Folder 1, Box 565, PMP; Judy Tzu-Chun Wu and Gwendolyn Mink, *Patsy Takemoto Mink: Feminist Politics, U.S. Citizenship, and Post–World War II Liberalism* (New York: New York University Press, forthcoming).

106. Abzug, ZI, March 19, 1971, 10; Jon E. Purmont, *Ella Grasso: Connecticut's Pioneering Governor* (Middletown, CT: Wesleyan University Press, 2012).

107. Mrs. Benjamin M. Robinson to Abzug, July 19, 1971, "Women's Rights," Box 157, BSA; Abzug, ZI, February 1971, 23; Anastasia Curwood, "Black Feminism on Capitol Hill: Shirley Chisholm and Movement Politics, 1968–1984," *Meridians* 13, no. 1 (2015): 204–232; Barbara Winslow, *Shirley Chisholm: Catalyst for Change* (Boulder, CO: Westview Press, 2014).

108. Deborah Dinner, "The Universal Childcare Debate: Rights Mobilization, Social Policy, and the Dynamics of Feminist Activism, 1966–1974," *Law and History Review* 28, no. 3 (August 2010): 577–628, 615.

109. "Statement of Congresswoman Shirley Chisholm before the Select Committee on Education of the House Committee on Education and Labor on

Preschool Education and Day Care," March 4, 1970, 1–11, 1, 2, 5, "General," Box 141, BSA.

110. "Statement by Rep.-Elect Bella Abzug at White House Conference on Children," n.d., 1–3, 2, 3, "Speeches, Statements, Testimony, and CR Remarks," Box 140, BSA.

111. Unnamed quoted in "RBML BA 24 Hour Child Care Hearing 2.22.1971 A," digitized audio, BSA.

112. Abzug quoted in "RBML BA 24 Hour Child Care Hearing 2.22.1971 B," digitized audio, BSA.

113. Stanley to Abzug, "High Points of Chisholm-Abzug Child Care Bill," n.d., 1–4, 3, "Legislation," Box 140, BSA; Abzug, "I am pleased to be here . . . ," May 18, 1971, 1–10, 9, "Speeches, Statements, Testimony, Congressional Record Remarks," Box 140, BSA; Abzug, "Comprehensive Child Care," CR reprint, May 18, 1971, "Speeches, Statements, Testimony, CR," Box 140, BSA.

114. Robert O. Self, *All in the Family: The Realignment of American Democracy since the 1960s* (New York: Hill and Wang, 2012), 128.

115. Nixon, "387—Veto of the Economic Opportunity Amendments of 1971," December 9, 1971, http://www.presidency.ucsb.edu/ws/?pid=3251.

116. NS15. Wolf and Stanley cotaught an inaugural course on women and law at George Washington University in 1976.

117. "Testimony of the Honorable Bella S. Abzug (D-NY) before the House Judiciary Committee," March 24, 1971, 1–4, 1, "Women: Equal Rights Amendment—Abzug Notes, Memoranda, and Statements," Box 615, BSA. For Abzug's critique of protective labor legislation, see Abzug to Gordon A. Thomas, June 14, 1971, "Correspondence," Box 417, BSA.

118. Martha Griffiths circulated this article to all House members. Barbara A. Brown, Thomas I. Emerson, Gail Falk, and Ann E. Freedman, "The Equal Rights Amendment: A Constitutional Basis for Equal Rights for Women," *Yale Law Journal* 80, no. 5 (April 1971): 871–985, 878.

119. "Testimony of the Honorable Bella S. Abzug (D-NY) before the General Labor Subcommittee of the House Education and Labor Committee," March 18, 1971, 1–3, 1, 2, "Correspondence, Notes, and Statements," Box 627, BSA; Herbert Hill, "Black Workers, Organized Labor, and Title VII of the 1964 Civil Rights Act: Legislative History and Litigation Record," in *Race in America: The Struggle for Equality*, ed. Herbert Hill and James E. Jones Jr. (Madison: University of Wisconsin Press, 1993), 263–344, 318.

120. "Bella Abzug Demands Immediate Cancellation of All AT&T Contracts with Federal Government and Congressional Investigation of Government Enforcement of Sex Discrimination Prohibitions," December 2, 1971, 1–2, 1, "Am. Telephone and Telegraph Company," Box 627, BSA. For representative advocacy and visits, see Abzug et al. to EEOC, April 7, 1971, "Correspondence, Incoming—General, 1971 April," Box 1, BSA; Francis Weltraut to Abzug, October 25, 71, Box 1, BSA.

121. Eileen Shanahan, "A.T.&T. to Grant 15,000 Back Pay in Job Inequities," *NYT,* January 19, 1973, 69.

122. Jeffrey Bloodworth, *Losing the Center: The Decline of American Liberalism, 1968–1992* (Lexington: University Press of Kentucky, 2013), 155; Memorandum, July 18, 1973, "Chron File—July 1973," Box 11, BFRNL.

123. Clipping attached to Mrs. Fred Ingalls to Abzug, April 3, 1971, "Correspondence," Box 630, BSA.

124. Abzug to Miss Ellen Perry, April 3, 1971, "General, 1971 Jan.–Mar.," Box 1, BSA.

125. Abzug, "Women Are Harassed Daily for Title Designation," CR reprint, July 22, 1971, "Correspondence," Box 630, BSA; "Right of Married Women to Retain or Regain Their Birth Names," September 1972, "Women's Rights," Box 157, BSA.

126. Karen Foerstel and Herbert Foerstel, Climbing the Hill: Gender Conflict in Congress (New York: Praeger, 1996), 127.

127. "Women Representatives and Senators by Congress, 1917–Present," http://history.house.gov/Exhibitions-and-Publications/WIC/Historical-Data /Women-Representatives-and-Senators-by-Congress/.

128. "Bella Abzug's Legislative Report to Women's Panel at NDC Conference in New York, Washington Irving HS, New York," February 7, 1971, "Statements on the Issues A–W (2)," Box 1033, BSA.

129. Mary McGrory, "The Two Congresses: One Docile, Other Seething," BG, September 8, 1971, 19.

130. Abzug, ZI, n.d., Tape 12, Side B, 29–30.

131. Abzug, "The Cold War is being liquidated . . . ," n.d., "Notes, 1971–1972 and N.D.," Box 68, BSA.

132. Richard L. Madden, "Ms. Abzug Finding Mr.'s Rule House," NYT, October 11, 1971, 37.

6. Year of the Woman

1. Robert W. Dietsch, "Bella Abzug Beware: The 1971 Gerrymander," NR, May 29, 1971, 20–22, 20; Abzug, ZI, Tape 13, Side B, 2 (372); Baker v. Carr, 369 U.S. 186 (1962); J. Douglas Smith, On Democracy's Doorstep: The Inside Story of How the Supreme Court Brought "One Person, One Vote" to the United States (New York: Hill and Wang, 2014).

2. "The Hand That Rocks the Ballot Box," ABC News Special, "Women," Box 991, BSA; Susan Tolchin and Martin Tolchin, Clout: Womanpower and Politics (New York: Coward, McCann, and Geoghegan, 1974), 15, 29.

3. "Women's World, World's Day," NYT, August 28, 1971, 24.

4. Flora Davis, Moving the Mountain: The Women's Movement in America since 1960 (New York: Simon and Schuster, 1991), 184–204; Susan Carroll, "Women's Rights and Political Parties: Issue Development, the 1972 Conventions, and the NWPC" (master's thesis, Indiana University, 1975); Rona F. Feit, "Organizing for Political Power: The NWPC," in Women Organizing: An Anthology, ed. Bernice Cummings and Victoria Schuck (Metuchen, NJ: Scarecrow Press, 1979), 184–208.

5. Byron Shafer contends Phyllis Segal gave Abzug the idea to focus on delegate mobilization, but her work on this front preceded NWPC; Byron E. Shafer, Quiet Revolution: The Struggle for the Democratic Party and the Shaping of Post-reform Politics (New York: Russell Sage Foundation, 1983), 466. See also

Abzug, "'New Politics' Speech: Outline of NWPC Founding and Activity at Conventions," n.d., "Notes, Memoranda, Statements, and Activities," Box 502, BSA.

6. "Fact Sheet on Women in the Electorate," n.d., Box 168, GSP.

7. George Meany quoted in Robert O. Self, *All in the Family: The Realignment of American Democracy since the 1960s* (New York: Hill and Wang, 2012), 250.

8. "Speech by Congresswoman Bella S. Abzug to NWPC," July 10, 1971, 1–3, "Statements and Releases," Box 599, BSA; "Adopted Report of the Workshop on the Future Structure of the NWPC," n.d., "NWPC: Structure Committee," Box 990, BSA; Abzug, "National Policy Council," handwritten notes, "Background Information," Box 990, BSA.

9. Roslyn Willett to Abzug, April 28, 1971, "General, 1971 April," Box 1, BSA; "Those Who Have Been Approached by Betty Friedan and Have Agreed to Serve as Conveners of the Caucus," n.d., "NWPC 1971," Box 1054, BSA; Abzug, "The National Democratic Party and the Status of Women," *CR* reprint, April 6, 1971, "Background Information," Box 990, BSA.

10. Liz Carpenter quoted in Marjorie J. Spruill, *Divided We Stand: The Battle over Women's Rights and Family Values That Polarized American Politics* (New York: Bloomsbury USA, 2017), 26.

11. Letty Pogrebin, "Suggested Agenda: National Women's Caucus: June 9 Meeting," n.d., 1–2, 1, "Politics—NWPC—Background Information," Box 990, BSA; Ronnie Feit, "Dear Conveners," June 23, 1971, Folder 7, Box 1, NWPCP.

12. Pogrebin quoted in Levine and Thom, *Bella Abzug,* 143.

13. Abzug, ZI, Tape 13, Side A, 6–8 (434–436), 13 (368); Bella Abzug with Mel Ziegler, ed., *Bella! Ms. Abzug Goes to Washington* (New York: Saturday Review Press, 1972), 177; Pogrebin in Suzanne Braun Levine and Mary Thom, *Bella Abzug: How One Tough Broad from the Bronx Fought Jim Crow and Joe McCarthy, Pissed Off Jimmy Carter, Battled for the Rights of Women and Workers, Rallied Against War and for the Planet, and Shook Up Politics Along the Way* (New York: Farrar, Straus and Giroux, 2007), 142; Vera Glaser, "Harriet Cipriani," notes, June 18, 1971, Folder 1, Box 17, CE.

14. Daniel Horowitz, *Betty Friedan and the Making of* The Feminine Mystique: *The American Left, The Cold War, and Modern Feminism* (Amherst: University of Massachusetts Press, 1998).

15. Betty Friedan, "The Next Step: Women's Participation—Human Liberation," July 10, 1971, 1–4, 1, "Background Information," Box 990, BSA.

16. Eleanor Smeal quoted in Levine and Thom, *Bella Abzug,* 140; Tim O'Brien, "Women Organize for More Power," *WP,* July 11, 1971, A1; Eileen Shanahan, "Women Organize for Political Power: 200 Women Organize for Political Power and Vote to Disavow Any Racist Candidate of Either Sex," *NYT,* July 11, 1971, 1.

17. Friedan quoted in "NWPC Organizing Conference, First Session," July 10, 1971, 5, Folder 4, Box 1, NWPCP.

18. "Resolution on Racism," n.d., 1–2, 1, "Background Information," Box 990, BSA.

19. Abzug in "NWPC Organizing Conference, First Session," 26–27.

20. George McGovern to Abzug, July 22, 1971, "BSA Speeches, 1972," Box 992, BSA.

21. Abzug to Donald M. Fraser, July 15, 1971, "Organizations, 1971," Box 65, BSA.

22. DNC Commission on the Rules chair James O'Hara was less receptive to Abzug's parity demands; she also pressed for on-site day care at the DNC. Abzug to James G. O'Hara, July 23, 1971, "Background Information," Box 990, BSA; Fraser to Abzug, July 23, 1971, "Organizations," Box 992, BSA; Tim O'Brien, "Democratic Party Reform: Now It Has to Be Put into Practice: Process of Reform," *WP*, August 8, 1971, A2; Shafer, *Quiet Revolution*, 396–459.

23. Fred Dutton quoted in Shafer, *Quiet Revolution*, 475; "Friends of the Caucus," *WP*, August 26, 1971, C2.

24. Abzug, "Role of NWPC in Electoral Campaigns and Other Campaigns to Achieve Equal Representation in All Levels of Government, Legislative, Executive and Judiciary," n.d., 1–6, "NWPC," Box 513, BSA; Abzug, "Pol. Goals," notes, October 22, 1971, "Notes, 1971–1972, ND," Box 68, BSA; "Delegate Selection," n.d., "NWPC Delegate Selection Task Force—Fraser Letter," Box 992, BSA; "A Proposal for Securing Full Participation by Women in the Presidential Nominating Process of the Major Parties," n.d., "NWPC Delegate Selection Task Force—Fraser Letter," Box 992, BSA.

25. Abzug et al. to Lawrence O'Brien, November 8, 1971, "O'Brien—NWPC Meeting 11/18/71, Dole Letter 11/2/71," Box 991, BSA; Eileen Shanahan, "Caucus to Seek Equal Number of Women Convention Delegates," *NYT*, November 10, 1971, 36.

26. "Meeting with NWPC Task Force and O'Brien & Co.," November 18, 1971, "O'Brien—NWPC Meeting 11/18/71, Dole Letter 11/2/71," Box 991, BSA; Segal to Members of Delegation of Women to Chairman Larry O'Brien with Abzug notes, November 18, 1971, "Women—NWPC Delegate Selection Task Force—Fraser Letter," Box 992, BSA.

27. Gwendolyn Mink and Donald Fraser quoted in Shafer, *Quiet Revolution*, 481.

28. William Chapman, "Delegations: More Women," *WP*, November 19, 1971, C1.

29. Doris Meissner quoted in Shafer, *Quiet Revolution*, 481.

30. Nixon and William P. Rogers quoted in "Women's Caucus Target of White House Jokes," *NYT*, July 14, 1971, 17.

31. Abzug quoted in "Mrs. Abzug Hits Remarks by President," *WP*, July 15, 1971, A7.

32. Joan Hoff downplays Barbara Hackman Franklin's role, focusing on male advisers' response to women's political demands in *Nixon Reconsidered* (New York: Basic Books, 1994), 98–114; Lee Stout, *A Simple Matter of Justice: The Untold Story of Barbara Franklin and a Few Good Women* (University Park: Pennsylvania State University Press, 2012); Janet M. Martin, *The Presidency and Women: Promise, Performance, and Illusion* (College Station: Texas A&M University Press, 2003), 123–166.

33. Nixon and unidentified quoted in "Meeting between Nixon and H. R. Haldeman, Robert J. Dole, and William E. Timmons in the Oval Office between

10:29 am and 11:07 am on 7/20/71," Conversation No. 540-7, "Nixon Presidential Materials Staff: Tape Subject Log," WHT.

34. Abzug to Franklin, August 30, 1971, "Bella Abzug Issue," Box 41, AANPL.

35. Franklin, Interview by Timothy Naftali, July 26, 2007, 1–14, 4, SOH.

36. "So What's Wrong with Me?," *Daily News,* July 14, 1971, 45, "Bella Abzug Issue," Box 41, AANPL.

37. Memorandum from Franklin to Fred Malek, June 18, 1971, 1–2, 2, "Malek Memoranda (5 of 6)," Box 1, BFRNL; Memorandum from Franklin to Malek, November 22, 1972, 1–2, 1, "Memos to White House Staff Members (3 of 10)," Box 1, BFRNL.

38. Franklin, "Caucus," n.d., "NPWC (1 of 4)," Box 65, BFRNL; P. Nixon to Lorraine Beebe, April 17, 1972, "NWPC (2 of 4)," Box 65, BFRNL; "Operating Committee Meeting-Agenda," September 27, 1971, Folder 11, Box 168, GSP; Franklin, Interview by Timothy Naftali and Paul Musgrave, March 7, 2007, 1–39, 14, SOH.

39. Memorandum from Charles Colson to Henry Kissinger, February 1, 1972, "NWPC [2 of 2]," Box 15, BFRNL.

40. "Women in Politics" Cover, *L,* June 9, 1972.

41. Phil Tracy, "The Battle of Bella & Bill," *VV,* June 8, 1972, http://www.villagevoice.com/news/the-battle-of-bella-abzug-and-bill-ryan-6716645.

42. Pete Hamill, "West Side Story," n.d., "B. A. Press," Box 216, WFRP.

43. Judith Michaelson, "Ryan & Bella on the Streets," *NYP,* May 11, 1972, 16.

44. Bertha McGowan to Abzug, March 20, 1972, "Correspondence," Box 172, BSA.

45. Julia Edwards to Linda Adler, May 23, 1972, 1–2, 2, "Edwards, Julia, Wash. DC 1972," Box 128, GMP.

46. Anonymous quoted in Art Buchwald, "Woman Nominee Not in the Cards," *WP,* October 26, 1971, B1; Laura Kalman, *The Long Reach of the 1960s: LBJ, Nixon, and the Making of the Contemporary Supreme Court* (Oxford: Oxford University Press, 2017), 252–306.

47. Abzug, "Speech to Texas Bills of Rights Foundation 11/21/71 by Congresswoman Bella S. Abzug (D, NY)," n.d., 1–16, 1, 5, 6, 9, "Censure," Box 489, BSA. For Ruth Bader Ginsburg's similar experience, Jane DeHart, *Ruth Bader Ginsburg: A Life* (New York: Alfred A. Knopf, 2018).

48. Serena Mayeri, *Reasoning from Race: Feminism, Law, and Civil Rights Revolution* (Cambridge, MA: Harvard University Press, 2011).

49. Ginsburg brief quoted in Mayeri, *Reasoning from Race,* 61, and see generally, 58–63.

50. *Reed v. Reed,* 404 U.S. 71 (1971).

51. Abzug, "Equal Rights for Men and Women," *CR* reprint, October 6, 1971, 1–3, "Notes, Memoranda, and Statements," Box 615, BSA; Richard L. Lyons, "House Passes Resolution on Women's Rights Amendment," *BG,* October 13, 1971, 2.

52. It is does not appear Abzug delivered the testimony prepared for this hearing, "Testimony of Bella S. Abzug before Subcommittee No. 5 of the House Judiciary Committee on HR 7624," July 21, 1971, 1–5, 2, 4, "Notes, Memoranda,

Statements and Activities," Box 502, BSA; Abzug to Kelber, note, n.d., "Notes, 1971–1972, and ND," Box 68, BSA; "House Subcommittee No. 5, Committee on the Judiciary, *Congressional Districting,* 92nd Cong., 1st Sess., July 21–22, 29, 1971. Abzug added notes especially to Robert G. Dixon Jr., "The Warren Court Crusade for the Holy Grail of 'One Man, One Vote,'" in *The Supreme Court Review,* ed. Philip B. Kurland (Chicago: University of Chicago Press, 1969), 219–270, "Printed," Box 173, BSA.

53. Barbara Palmer and Dennis Simon, "Breaking the Political Glass Ceiling: Incumbency, Redistricting, and the Success of Women Candidates," *Thomas Jefferson Law Review* 31 (2008): 29–52.

54. "Statement by Congresswoman Bella S. Abzug (D-Man) at New Conference at 252 Seventh Ave., NY, NY," February 16, 1972, "Statements, Notes, Memos," Box 172, BSA.

55. Abzug quoted in *Newsmakers,* transcript, March 5, 1972, 1–15, 6, "TV, 1970–1974," Box 111, BSA.

56. "Transcript of Interview of Congresswoman Bella S. Abzug by Mr. Watson on Channel 13, TV, at 10:00 PM on 2/18/72," 1–4, 3, 4, "TV, 1970–1974," Box 111, BSA.

57. Memorandum from Kelber to Abzug, March 3, 1972, 1–2, 2, "Statements, Notes, Memo.," Box 172, BSA.

58. Abzug quoted in Flora Lewis, "Reform vs. Tradition: A Future in Congress for Bella Abzug?," *WP,* March 8, 1972, A20.

59. Howard Keats to Abzug, March 9, 1972, "Correspondence," Box 172, BSA.

60. Abzug and Barry Gray quoted in "Barry Gray Show—WMCA," January 20, 1972, "Notes, Memoranda, Statements, and Activities," Box 502, BSA.

61. Abzug, "Role of NWPC in Electoral Campaigns . . . ," 5; Abzug, "1. Too big an issue for . . . ," handwritten note, n.d., "Women—NWPC State Caucuses (Misc.)," Box 992, BSA; Virginia Allan, "Dear Editor," January 1972, "Drafts, ND, and 1972," Box 111, BSA.

62. Shirley Chisholm, *The Good Fight* (New York: Harper and Row, 1973), 74; "BSA Statement at Chisholm's Press Conference," January 25, 1972, "Drafts, ND, and 1972," Box 111, BSA.

63. Abzug, "Role of NWPC in Electoral Campaigns . . . ," 5.

64. Francis X. Clines, "Look What They Did to Bella Abzug!," *NYT,* March 12, 1972, E3.

65. Jeffrey to Abzug, March 20, 1972, "Amnesty," Box 1030, BSA.

66. J. Richard and Michele Forman to Abzug, March 13, 1972, "Correspondence," Box 172, BSA.

67. "Abzug District Presupposing Staten Island Gets No Part of the Lower East Side," n.d., "General," Box 173, BSA; "This tabulation is made on . . . ," February 29, 1972, Box 173, BSA.

68. Kelber to Nat Hentoff, March 24–26, 1972, 1–7, 1–3, "General (2)," Box 590, BSA.

69. Abzug, "Dear Friend," March 30, 1972, 1–2, "1972," Box 64, BSA; Abzug, "I have decided to run . . . ," draft with handwritten comments, n.d., "Statements

and Releases," Box 444, BSA; "Mrs. Abzug Reported Planning to Challenge Ryan for His Seat," *NYT,* March 21, 1972, 47; Eileen Shanahan, "Equal Rights Amendment Is Approved by Congress," *NYT,* March 23, 1972, 1.

70. Ross Graham quoted in Larry Simonberg, "Save Seat for Bella, Women Urge," *Staten Island Advance,* March 2, 1972, 1, "Correspondence," Box 172, BSA; "State Democratic Committee Passes Resolution Supporting Rep. Bella Abzug's Position on Redistricting Issue," February 22, 1972, "Statements, Notes, Memos," Box 172, BSA; "McGovern, Lindsay Back Abzug District," *NYT,* February 19, 1972, 16.

71. Abzug, "Murphy—137,000 people . . . ," note, n.d., 1–3, 3, "'72 Redistricting," Box 1031, BSA.

72. Joseph Kraft, "The City Politic: Ryan's Totter," *NY,* January 24, 1972, 8.

73. See the grouping of March 1972 memos in "Ben F. Riverdale," Box 487, WFRP.

74. William Fitts Ryan quoted in "Rep. Ryan to Run in Revised 20th District," *NYT,* March 16, 1972, 27; Ryan, handwritten note, n.d., "WFR Announcement," Box 487, WFRP.

75. Abzug, "The House of Semi-Representatives," *NYT,* March 29, 1972, 43.

76. Abzug, *Newsmakers* Transcript, March 5, 1972, 1–15, 6, "TV, 1970–1974," Box 111, BSA.

77. Nat Hentoff, "Giving Politics Back Its Bad Name," *VV,* March 30, 1972, http://www.villagevoice.com/news/bella-abzug-and-predatory-politics-nat-hentoff-6668823.

78. Tracy, "The Battle of Bella & Bill."

79. Shana Alexander, "The City Politic: Bella Abzug Is No Gentleman," *NY,* May 1, 1972, 10–11, 10.

80. Irene Davall to Dear Sir, June 1, 1972, 4, clipping, "B. A. Press," Box 216, WFRP; Jean Fause to Ryan, Rita, *ET,* December 15, 1971, Untitled Folder, Box 487, WFRP; "The Ryan Platform on Women's Issues," n.d., "N.Y. Times," Box 487, WFRP.

81. Abzug quoted in "Mrs. Abzug to Run against Liberal to Give Voters a Choice of 'Two Goods,'" *TS,* March 22, 1972, A6; Abzug quoted in "Bella Abzug," n.d., Untitled Folder, Box 487, WFRP.

82. On Ryan, see Frederick H. Gardner, "Silhouette: William F. Ryan," *Harvard Crimson,* December 6, 1962, http://www.thecrimson.com/article/1962/12/6/william-f-ryan-pnew-yorks-only/.

83. "A New Politics: This Year We Can Make It Happen!" n.d., "B. A. Literature," Box 216, WFRP.

84. "Statement in Support of Congressman William F. Ryan Issued by the Citizens Committee (In Formation) for the Re-election of William F. Ryan," April 5, 1972, "Endorsements," Box 216, WFRP.

85. Hamill, "West Side Story."

86. Ryan, "Eleven years ago . . . ," 4, Untitled Folder, Box 487, WFRP.

87. Abzug quoted in Alfred E. Clark, "Mrs. Abzug Opens Drive for 51st State," *NYT,* June 2, 1971, 46; "Bella Abzug, Rep. Ryan, Borough Presidents Sutton and Abrams, Others Will Launch City-Statehood Petition Campaign at Rally, Sat., June 26," n.d., "Releases," Box 460, BSA; "NY Cong. Bella Abzug and

William F. Ryan on 'Let's Find Out,'" WCBS News Radio 88, May 28, 1972, 1–14, 2, 10, "1972," Box 64, BSA.

88. Ryan quoted in Steven R. Weisman, "Mrs. Abzug Joins Ryan in Debate: Leadership, Not Issues, Is Focus of Polite Clash," *NYT,* April 29, 1972, 29.

89. "Dear Colleague" and attached "Summary of Amnesty Legislation Proposed by Bella S. Abzug," April 19, 1972, "Correspondence, 1971–1972, ND," Box 423, BSA; "Bella Abzug Calls on Army to Act Equitably and Openly in 'Desertion' Case of Sgt. Herndon," *WP,* March 25, 1972, A2.

90. Swerdlow to Kelber, handwritten, n.d., , "Paris, 1972," Box 383, BSA; "Meeting with Madame Binh," draft transcript, n.d., Box 383, BSA; Binh to the Honorable Members of the U.S. Congress, April 20, 1972, Box 383, BSA; "Interview with Madame Nguyen Thi Binh by Representative Patsy S. Mink," April 21, 1972, Folder 5, Box 510, PMP; "Reps. Abzug, Mink Meet Mme. Binh," *WP,* April 22, 1972, A13.

91. Corky Trinidad, "I knew letting her talk . . . ," clipping, *Statesman,* May 3, 1972, Folder 7, Box 510, PM.

92. John Conyers Jr. to the Editors, draft, n.d., "General," Box 492, BSA; "Congresswoman Bella Abzug Says: Impeach 'Emperor' Nixon! Stop the War!" n.d., "Statements (Misc.) and Activities," Box 492, BSA; Joseph Crown and William Standard, "Memorandum of Law on Impeachment," with Abzug notations, n.d., "Memoranda of Law, Briefs, Legal Papers," Box 494, BSA; "McCarthy, Abzug Urge Congress to Impeach," *BG,* May 10, 1972, 33; "Protests on Nixon Decision Mounting: House Members Say They Will Start Impeachment Legislation," *LAT,* May 9, 1972, 2.

93. "Ryan Supporters Score Mrs. Abzug: Some Leading Politicians Back His Primary Drive," *NYT,* April 6, 1972, 37; Nat Hentoff, "Getting 'Into' Fairness with Bella," *VV,* May 4, 1972, 13, clipping, "B. A. Press," Box 216, WFRP.

94. Kenny Schaeffer, "Report on How the Issue of Candidate's Health Has Been Handled in Four Elections, and Recommendations for Bill Ryan's Campaign," n.d., 1–3, 3, "TV—Debate—Notes," Box 487, WFRP.

95. Ryan, "I am presenting a group . . . ," handwritten notes, 1–2, 2, "WFR Announcement," Box 487, WFRP.

96. "Our Congressman Ryan. His record speaks louder," n.d., "June 1972 WFR Lit," Box 487, WFRP.

97. "If ever there was an . . . ," n.d., "CBS Poll," Box 216, WFRP. Abzug dismissed the Ryan campaign's accusation that her canvassers participated in a whisper campaign; Abzug to Editor, June 12, 1972, "Correspondence, 1970–1973," Box 111, BSA; Abzug to Arthur Sulzberger, June 14, 1972, Box 111, BSA; Abzug, "Whisper Campaign Denied," *NYT,* June 15, 1972, 40.

98. "Dear Brothers and Sisters," n.d., "Endorsements," Box 216, WFRP.

99. Jack Shor, "I think that in speeches . . . ," n.d., "TV—Debates—Notes," Box 487, WFRP.

100. Judith Michaelson, "Bella Reaches All for 20th CD Support," n.d., clipping, "B. A. Press," Box 216, WFRP.

101. Peter Fisher copied Abzug on this letter, writing, "P.S. Good to see you in the streets with us yesterday, Bella. Fight!" Fisher to Ryan, April 13, 1972, "Correspondence 1970–1974," Box 152, BSA.

102. Francis X. Clines, "Ryan-Abzug," *NYT,* June 21, 1972, 29.

103. Abzug quoted in David Lamb, "Loses to Another Liberal: 'I'll Still Be Around,' Bella Abzug Says," *LAT,* June 21, 1972, A18.

104. Abzug quoted in Marjorie Hunter, "House Democrats Score Party Reform Proposals: Bitterly Divided Caucus Votes 105 to 50 to Denounce Plan as 'Not in the Best Interests of the Party,'" *NYT,* June 29, 1972, 28.

105. Abzug quoted in Mary McGrory, "The Shattering of a Myth," *BG,* May 7, 1972, 6A; "Bella Abzug Calls for McGovern Victory in California Primary," June 1, 1972, "McGovern, George and Sargent Shriver (and Thomas Eagleton)," Box 504, BSA.

106. Abzug to Dan Collins, June 2, 1972, with "Proposed Democratic Party Platform Plank on Indochina" attached, "Abzug, Bella," Box 41, NDCP; "Clifford Terms War Key '72 Issue: Tells Democratic Platform Panel Here GOP Offers a 'Perpetual' Conflict," *NYT,* June 23, 1972, 18.

107. Plank quoted in Bruce Miroff, *The Liberal's Moment: The McGovern Insurgency and the Identity Crisis of the Democratic Party* (Lawrence: University Press of Kansas, 2007), 217; Denis G. Sullivan, *The Politics of Representation: The Democratic Convention 1972* (New York: St. Martin's Press, 1974), 100.

108. Abzug quoted in "National Democratic Party Platform Committee," June 26, 1972, 1–2, "National Convention and Platform, 1972," Box 506, BSA. Abzug drew on "Homosexual Rights," in "New Democratic Coalition, Platform 1972," 22–23, "Platform Committee and Drafts," Box 965, BSA; and "Discussion of Rights," n.d., Box 965, BSA. For McGovern assessment, see "Positions on Platform Minority Planks," n.d., "DNC: Platform Committee Convention Deliberations 1972," Box 157, GMP.

109. "Statement by Congresswoman Bella Abzug at Press Conference on the Abortion Rights Act of 1972," May 2, 1972, 1–3, 1, "Statements and Releases," Box 602, BSA; "1972 Democratic Platform Committee, Schedule of Events," June 22–27, 1972, "Platform Committee and Drafts," Box 965, BSA.

110. Vera Glaser, "Doris Meissner," June 21, 1972, Folder 2, Box 17, CE.

111. Memorandum from Amanda J. Smith to McGovern Organizers, July 1972, "Women," Box 107, GMP.

112. McGovern, Press Release, May 6, 1972, 1–3, 3, "Abortion 1972," Box 91, GMP.

113. Shirley MacLaine, "Women, the Convention and Brown Paper Bags," *NYT,* July 30, 1972, SM14; MacLaine, *You Can Get There from Here* (New York: W. W. Norton, 1975), 47–48.

114. MacLaine, "Women, the Convention and Brown Paper Bags"; Memorandum from Pat Caddell, n.d., "Abortion—1972," Box 91, GMP; "Abortion," n.d., Box 91, GMP.

115. Amendment quoted in Joseph Kraft, "McGovern Makes Room," *WP,* June 29, 1972, A21.

116. MacLaine quoted in David S. Broder, "Display of Unity: Harmony Emerges among Party Platform Drafters," *WP,* June 28, 1972, A1; "Rights of Women," in ". . . For the People: The Platform of the Democratic Party 1972," 5, "Platform Committee and Drafts," Box 965, BSA; Abzug, "The singular success of women . . . ," n.d., 1–5, "Women," Box 991, BSA.

117. Anne Kunze to McGovern, July 28, 1972, 1–7, 5, Box 128, GMP.

118. Frank Lynn, "Few NY Leaders to Be Delegates: More Than 90% of the 278 at Democratic Convention to Be Political Unknowns," *NYT,* July 4, 1972, 1.

119. "The New Delegate," in Official DNC Program "Democrats in Convention, 1972," July 10–13, 1972, 122–125, "Platform, 1972," Box 506, BSA.

120. Midge Costanza quoted in Levine and Thom, *Bella Abzug,* 144.

121. Abzug quoted in Ellen Goodman, "Democratic Women Hear Unity Cry at Caucus," *BG,* July 10, 1972, 15.

122. Friedan quoted in Myra McPherson, "Women's Groups in Disagreement on Convention Eve," *WP,* July 10, 1972, A8.

123. McGovern quoted in Warren J. Weaver, "South Carolina Vote Balks Women's Bid," *NYT,* July 11, 1972.

124. Memorandum from Eli Segal to George McGovern, n.d., "Women," Box 107, GMP.

125. Richard G. Stearns quoted in Hunter S. Thompson, *Fear and Loathing on the Campaign Trail '72* (New York: Simon and Schuster, 1973), 265, 273, 281.

126. Vera Glaser, "Phyllis Segal," notes, June 29, 1972, 1–2, 1, Folder 2, Box 17, CE; Miroff, *The Liberal's Moment,* 72–74, 207–208.

127. Abzug quoted in MacLaine, "Women, the Convention and Brown Paper Bags." For NWPC challenges after South Carolina, see Nan Robertson, "Democrats Feel Impact of Women's New Power," *NYT,* July 15, 1972, 1.

128. Gary Hart quoted in Miroff, *The Liberal's Moment,* 208.

129. Stearns quoted in Thompson, *Fear and Loathing on the Campaign Trail,* 265, 273, 281.

130. Bill Dougherty quoted in Thompson, 287.

131. Eugene Walsh, Steinem, MacLaine, and Abzug quoted in Goodman, "Abortion Plank—a Family Feud," *BG,* July 13, 1972, 1.

132. John S. Carroll, "Democrats Give McGovern What He Wants in Shaping Party Platform," *TS,* July 13, 1972, A6; Myra McPherson, "Sisters v. Sisters: Abortion Battle Turns Bitter," *WP,* July 13, 1972, A1.

133. Abzug quoted in John Adam Moreau, "Activists OK Women Plank of Democrats," *CT,* July 14, 1972, 7.

134. Elizabeth Frapello, "The Ticket That Might Have Been . . . Vice-President Farenthold," *Ms.,* January 1973, 74–76, 116–120, 119.

135. Eldridge and Midge Miller came up with the vice president idea, and Doris Meissner suggested Sissy Farenthold as an option. Vira Katz quoted in David Lamb, "Spirits Revived: It Was Late When the Yawns Ended," *LAT,* July 14, 1972, A1; Memorandum from Meissner to Abzug, June 9, 1972, "Democratic Convention, 1972: Platform Committee and Drafts," Box 965, BSA.

136. R. Lafayette to Abzug, July 21, 1972, "Correspondence," Box 502, BSA.

137. Norman Podhoretz, "Issues: Between Nixon and the New Politics," *Commentary* 54, no. 3 (September 1972): 4–8, 6, 8.

138. Abzug quoted in Barbara J. Keys, *Reclaiming American Virtue: The Human Rights Revolution of the 1970s* (Cambridge, MA: Harvard University Press, 2016), 116.

139. MM14; Michael Knight, "Rep. William Ryan, West Side Liberal, Is Dead of Cancer," *NYT,* September 18, 1972, 1.

140. NWPC statement quoted in Thomas P. Ronan, "Mrs. Ryan to Seek Husband's Seat," *NYT,* September 27, 1972, 31; Ronan, "Both Mrs. Ryan and Mrs. Abzug Pick Up Backing in 20th District," *NYT,* September 29, 1972, 31; Edward Ransel, "City Post Is Quit by Mrs. Eldridge: Lindsay Adviser to Manage Rep. Abzug's Campaign," *NYT,* October 10, 1972, 35; William E. Farrell, "Mrs. Abzug Wins Party Approval to Succeed Ryan: New Democratic Candidate for Congress Chosen by 20th District Leaders," *NYT,* October 2, 1972, 1.

141. "Welfare Story Evokes Denial by Bella Abzug," *HC,* October 1, 1972, 31.

142. Priscilla Ryan quoted in "Abzug Wins NY District Nomination," *BG,* October 2, 1972, 8; William E. Farrell, "Liberals Nominate Mrs. Ryan to Run for Husband's House Seat," *NYT,* October 3, 1972, 96; and HF07.

143. Abzug, P. Ryan, and Eldridge quoted in Tolchin and Tolchin, *Clout,* 161, 167, 169, 173; P. Ryan quoted in "Candidates' Personalities Are Issue in Abzug-Ryan Race in 20th District," *NYT,* November 3, 1972, 41; Al Shanker, "Display Ad 221: Where We Stand," *NYT,* November 5, 1972, E9.

144. Christopher Lydon, "Shriver Feels Candidacy Was Not Put to Fair Test," *NYT,* November 5, 1972, 53; Maurice Carroll, "Bella Abzug Re-elected by Wide Margin," *NYT,* November 5, 1972, 36.

145. Steven J. Roberts, "Democrats Face Fight for Control: Bloc of Officials and Labor Leaders Considers Steps to Recapture the Party," *NYT,* November 9, 1972, 1.

146. "Commenting on Senator George McGovern . . . ," draft press release, n.d., "Women—NWPC Delegate Selection," Box 992, BSA.

147. McGovern, Press Release, June 9, 1971, "Women," Box 107, GMP; Abzug to Hart, August 11, 1972, "McGovern/Shriver," Box 965, BSA.

148. Hart to Abzug, August 18, 1972, "McGovern/Shriver," Box 965, BSA.

149. Judy Brown Sheerer to Abzug, August 29, 1972, "McGovern/Shriver," Box 965, BSA.

150. Abzug, "Memo on Women's Role in McGovern-Shriver Campaign," September 11, 1972, 1–2, "McGovern/Shriver," Box 965, BSA.

151. Miroff, *The Liberal's Moment,* 214.

152. Memorandum from Hart to All State Coordinators, September 22, 1972, "Women," Box 107, GMP; Memorandum from Hart to State Coordinators, October 3, 1972, Box 107, GMP; "Women's Advisory Council Names State Coordinators for McGovern," October 12, 1972, "Women," Box 107, GMP; Xandra "Sandy" Kayden to Sophia Peterson, September 18, 1972, "West Virginia," Box 131, GMP.

153. Eileen Shanahan, "Women's Unit Broke and Split on Future," *NYT,* August 28, 1972, 36.

154. Friedan quoted in Frank Swertlow, "Friedan, Steinem Air Split," *BG,* July 20, 1972, 39; Dierdre Carmody, "Feminists Rebut Friedan Charges: Say 'Female Chauvinism' Attack Was Unfortunate," *NYT,* July 20, 1972, 29.

155. Steinem, "Policy Council Dominated by Superstars," Folder 13, Box 168, GSP; Brownie Ledbetter, Notes, October 9, 1973, Folder 14, GSP; Elizabeth Duff, "Women's Caucus Boos Bella, a Founder," *PI,* February 12, 1973, 1-A.

156. Martha McKay quoted in "Transcript of NWPC Meeting," October 20, 1973, "1973," Box 111, BSA.

157. Shafer, *Quiet Revolution,* 462.

158. Penn Kemble and Josh Muravchik, "The New Politics and the Democrats," *Commentary* 54, no. 6 (December 1972): 78–84, 78.

159. Thomas P. Murphy, *The New Politics Congress* (Lexington, MA: Lexington Books, 1974), 86–87; "The New Congress: Its Members and Its Mood," *CQWR* 31, no. 1 (January 1, 1973): 13.

160. "Democrats: Another Step toward Congressional Clout," *CQWR* 31, no. 2 (January 13, 1973): 67.

7. Performing Political Celebrity

1. RE14.

2. LA05; EA12; Dorothy Collin, "Trash Tells All: Those Garbage Snatchers Are Back!," *CT,* July 13, 1975, 2.

3. "Rep. Abzug Resting Following Surgery," *WP,* January 4, 1972.

4. Ruth B. Mandel, *In the Running: The New Woman Candidate* (New Haven, CT: Ticknor and Fields, 1981), 34.

5. Maurice Carroll, "Bella Abzug Re-elected by Wide Margin," *NYT,* November 5, 1972, 36.

6. Jennifer E. Manning, Ida A. Brudnick, and Colleen J. Shogan, "Women in Congress: Historical Overview, Tables, and Discussion," CRS, April 29, 2015, https://fas.org/sgp/crs/misc/R43244.pdf.

7. Lynn Povich, *The Good Girls Revolt: How the Women of Newsweek Sued Their Bosses and Changed the Workplace* (New York: Public Affairs, 2016); Patricia Bradley, *Mass Media and the Shaping of American Feminism, 1963–1975* (Jackson: University Press of Mississippi, 2003).

8. Abzug quoted in Douglas Murphy, "'Battling Bella' Puts on Her 'Image' Hat," *LAT,* November 20, 1972, D1.

9. George Frazer, "Ugh, as in Abzug," *BG,* May 12, 1972, 31.

10. Ken Auletta, "'Senator' Bella—Seriously," *NY,* August 11, 1975, 27–34, 27.

11. Robert Self, "Bodies Count: The Sixties Body in American Politics," in *The Long 1968: Revisions and New Perspectives,* ed. Daniel J. Sherman, Ruud van Dijk, Jasmine Alinder, and A. Aneesh (Bloomington: Indiana University Press, 2013), 239–269, 264.

12. I am indebted to Jonathan Soffer for sharing his full transcript of this interview. Jim Capalino quoted in Soffer, *Ed Koch and the Rebuilding of New York City* (New York: Columbia University Press, 2010), 100.

13. Bella Abzug with Mel Ziegler, ed., *Bella! Ms. Abzug Goes to Washington* (New York: Saturday Review Press, 1972), 42.

14. Abzug, ZI, Tape 14, Side A, 1 (386).

15. Belinda Robnett, *How Long, How Long? African-American Women in the Struggle for Civil Rights* (New York: Oxford University Press, 1997); Barbara Ransby, *Ella Baker and the Black Freedom Movement: A Radical Democratic Vision* (Chapel Hill: University of North Carolina Press, 2003).

16. For one such exchange, see "Creating a Woman's Life," audio recording, digitized, BSA.

17. Abzug quoted in Joseph B. Treaster, "Harriman Calls for Nixon Defeat," *NYT,* February 22, 1971.

18. Abzug, ZI, Tape 13, Side B, n.d., 6 (376).

19. Sidonie Smith, "Autobiographical Discourse in the Theaters of Politics," *Biography* 33, no. 1 (Winter 2010): v–xxvi, xx; Abzug, *Bella!;* EN15.

20. Shirley Chisholm, *Unbought and Unbossed* (Boston: Houghton Mifflin, 1970).

21. Abzug, "Speech for the Jewish Center of Kew Garden Hills," December 18, 1970, 1–12, 4, "Statements, Activities, Notes, and Memoranda," Box 398, BSA; Abzug, *Bella!,* 3.

22. Abzug's papers include an incomplete transcript of these sessions. In the finished book, Mel Ziegler ordered some events out of chronology for effect, edited language, and interlaced language from media appearances, speeches, and CR excerpts. Ziegler to Kristine White, March 10, 1976, Appendix in White, "A Burkeian Analysis of Selected Speeches of Bella Abzug" (master's thesis, University of the Pacific, 1977), A1; "Sun. Jan 24," "1971 Jan–Feb.," Box 108, BSA; on Ziegler, see "Dean Steve Coll in Conversation with Co-founders of Banana Republic," Columbia Journalism School, September 30, 2014, https://www.youtube.com/watch?v=MPI63l2rcK8.

23. Abzug, ZI, Tape 29, Side A, n.d., 1 (767).

24. Abzug, ZI, Tape 4, March 19, 1971, 7; Tape 29, Side A, n.d., 4 (770).

25. I have altered "Now, look please, Don't *hoch* me a *chinuk,*" as reflected on the original transcript, to provide an accurate transliteration. Abzug, ZI, Tape 19, Side A, n.d., 14 (543).

26. Abzug, ZI, Side B, n.d., 3, 6 (549–550).

27. Smith, "Autobiographical Discourse in the Theaters of Politics," ix.

28. My copy of *Bella! Ms. Abzug Goes to Washington,* purchased used from Amazon.com, has this autograph designation.

29. Stephanie Harrington, "O Congress," *NYT,* July 2, 1972, BR5.

30. I looked at the full run of Abzug's general correspondence and the majority of subject area correspondence, analyzing for patterns in tone and form. While Abzug preferred personalized responses, form letter responses were used more frequently in her second and third terms. Annette Pickett to Abzug, February 28, 1971, "General, 1971 Jan.–Mar.," Box 1, BSA; Janice Butler to Abzug, October 11, 1971, "General, 1971 Sept.–Dec.," Box 2, BSA.

31. Jan Donovan to Abzug, March 10, 1971, "General, 1971 Jan.–Mar.," Box 1, BSA.

32. Sidney M. Gilbert to Abzug, January 23, 1974, "General, 1974, Jan.–Mar.," Box 3, BSA.

33. David Lippman to Abzug, n.d., "General, 1971 Sept.–Dec.," Box 2, BSA.

34. Joan and Leo Laskoff to Abzug, April 5, 1971, "General, 1971 April," Box 1, BSA; Roslyn Pulitzer to Abzug, March 24, 1971, "General, 1971 Jan.–Mar.," Box 1, BSA; Anita M. Goldstein to Abzug, December 19, 1973, "General, 1973," Box 3, BSA.

35. Abzug, ZI, Tape 3, March 14, 1971, 10.

36. Esther Newberg set up this classification system and directed staff to treat these as dead letters. By 1972, Abzug's office began the practice of replying. "Start to file 'hate' letters . . . ," n.d., "Abusive Mail, 1970 and n.d.," Box 9, BSA.

37. Edna Thalit to "My Dear Young Lady," May 7, 1971, "Abusive Mail, 1971 (1)," Box 9, BSA; Anonymous to Abzug, notation on clipping, May 3, 1971, Box 9, BSA; Anonymous to Abzug, May 19, 1971, Box 9, BSA; "A Taxpayer" to Abzug, May 8, 1971, "Abusive Mail, 1971 (2)," Box 9, BSA.

38. Mrs. I. M. Watkins to Abzug with clipping, June 16, 1971, "Abusive Mail, 1971 (2)," Box 9, BSA; Anonymous to "Dear Rep.," June 17, 1971, Box 9, BSA.

39. Harold O. Bernet to Abzug, July 15, 1971, "Abusive Mail, 1971 (2)," Box 9, BSA.

40. "A military man's mother's definition . . ." to Abzug, May 5, 1971, "Abusive Mail, 1971 (1)," Box 9, BSA.

41. L. Law to "Dear 'Alice,'" May 7, 1971, "Abusive Mail, 1971 (1)," Box 9, BSA.

42. Shana Alexander, "The City Politic: Bella Abzug Is No Gentleman," NY, May 1, 1972, 10–11, 10.

43. CG14; Marlene Nadle, "'Listen Buckley . . .': Bella in the Backroom," VV, November 12, 1970, 1, 50.

44. Ireland quoted in Suzanne Braun Levine and Mary Thom, Bella Abzug: How One Tough Broad from the Bronx Fought Jim Crow and Joe McCarthy, Pissed Off Jimmy Carter, Battled for the Rights of Women and Workers, Rallied Against War and for the Planet, and Shook Up Politics Along the Way (New York: Farrar, Straus and Giroux, 2007), 80; EN15.

45. EL15.

46. EN15.

47. KLK11.

48. Abzug, ZI, Tape 3, March 14, 1971, 9; Tape 16, Side B, 11 (458); Tape 17, Side A, 11 (484).

49. Ireland quoted in Fred Lembeck, "Hauling the Line in Bella's Office," TV, November 6, 1975, 5, "Press Clippings," Box 1046, BSA.

50. EL15.

51. Lembeck, "Hauling the Line in Bella's Office"; Eugene Brown, "In the Shadows—Jobs on Capitol Hill," clipping, n.d., "Press Clippings," Box 1046, BSA.

52. EH14.

53. Abzug paraphrased in "Staff Meeting," December 20, 1971, 1–8, 1, 2, "Abzug, Checklists and Staff Reports," Box 44, BSA; Abzug to staff, December 4, 1973, "Administrative Files—Memoranda, 1973 and ND, Confidential," Box 69, BSA; Eric Hirschhorn, "How to Be a Legislative Assistant in 10 Easy Lessons," n.d., "Office Procedure Manual," Box 66, BSA.

54. MM14; EH14.

55. Abzug quoted in Rhoda Amon, "Bella Abzug: 'I Don't Just Go Along,'" LI, November 16, 1976, 12–32, 32, "Press Clippings," Box 1046, BSA; Richard Yafee, "There Is Mr. Abzug! Plus 2 Daughters and a 30-Year Marriage," NYJW, December 13, 1975, 14; Eric Aiken, "What Congress Is Worth: Some Legislators

Disclose Their Investments, Incomes," *Barron's National Business and Financial Weekly,* November 2, 1974, 5.

56. MM14.

57. EN15.

58. JS09; DMH09; MM14; JN07.

59. Abzug, ZI, Tape 3, March 14, 1971, 10.

60. Martin Abzug quoted in Mary Daniels, "Martin Abzug Isn't . . . Bella's Little Man," *CT,* July 23, 1972, E8.

61. M. Abzug in Mary Daniels, " 'Beauty Secret': Fat Gets the Brushoff," *CT,* December 28, 1975, WA4.

62. M. Abzug quoted in Daniels, "Martin Abzug Isn't . . . Bella's Little Man."

63. M. Abzug quoted in Myra MacPherson, "Abzug: Maturity Is the Key," *WP,* February 12, 1972, C1; MacPherson, *The Power Lovers: An Intimate Look at Politicians and Their Marriages* (New York: Ballantine Books, 1976).

64. EA12.

65. M. Abzug quoted in MacPherson, "Abzug: Maturity Is the Key"; and B. Abzug responding, *Bella!,* 75, 90.

66. EA12; Abzug, "Martin, What Should I Do Now?," *Ms.,* July–August 1990, 94–96, 95; Mandel, *In the Running,* 64–65.

67. B. Abzug to Mary A. Synder, June 13, 1974, "Correspondence, 1974," Box 598, BSA.

68. SD14.

69. M. Abzug, "An Instant Libber," *LAT,* November 2, 1975, D14.

70. M. Abzug quoted in MacPherson, "Abzug: Maturity Is the Key"; the Abzugs quoted in Diana Lurie, "Living with Liberation," *NY,* August 31, 1970, 22–34, 24.

71. Levine and Thom, *Bella Abzug,* 25n; EA12.

72. Myra MacPherson, " 'Everybody Is People,' " *WP,* May 3, 1972, B1.

73. EA12.

74. Patricia Schroeder quoted in Levine and Thom, *Bella Abzug,* 156.

75. Abzug quoted in Judith Michaelson, "Ryan & Bella on the Streets," *NYP,* May 11, 1972, 16.

76. Abzug, ZI, Tape 19, Side A, 1 (530); Tape Three (2), March 19, 1971, 15.

77. See schedules in "1971 Jan.–Feb.," Box 108, BSA.

78. Tony Hiss, "Dilemma in the New 20th Congressional District—'Bella Should Be There and So Should Ryan,' " *NYT,* June 18, 1972, SM12.

79. These adjectives are highlighted from representative press: Douglas Murphy, " 'Battling Bella' Puts on Her 'Image' Hat"; Norman Mailer, "The Prisoner of Sex," *Harper's,* March 1971, 41–92, 45; Auletta, " 'Senator' Bella—Seriously"; Patricia Burstein, "The Full-Throttle, High-Decibel Life of Bella Abzug," *People,* March 24, 1975, http://www.people.com/people/archive/article /0,,20065068,00.html.

80. After hearings in both chambers, the newsman's privilege bill lost traction by spring 1973 after being opposed by Nixon. *DSG Staff Bulletin,* January 22, 1973, 3, Folder 7, Box 44, DSGP; "Newsman's Privilege: Action Stalled on Shield Bill," *CQ Almanac 1973,* 29 (Washington, DC: Congressional Quarterly, 1974), 383–388.

81. Daniel Schorr to Abzug, March 20, 1976, "Bella—Campaign Endorsements and Flak," Box 1045, BSA.

82. Mary McGrory, "Bella Abzug—New House Rebel," *BG,* January 26, 1971, 21; Abzug, *Bella!,* 235.

83. *Ms.,* July 1972; *Ms.,* December 1975.

84. Grace Lichtenstein to Abzug, July 19, 1971, "General, 1971 July," Box 1, BSA.

85. Maria Braden, *Women Politicians and the Media* (Lexington: University Press of Kentucky, 1996), 5.

86. Abzug, *Bella!,* 19; Abzug, ZI, Tape 11, Side A, n.d., 2 (297).

87. "Worst-Dressed," clipping, January 10, 1975, "Printed—Clippings about Abzug," Box 760, BSA; Abzug, "Answers to Asbury Park Press Written Interview," n.d., 1–3, 2, "Speeches, Statements, Releases, Drafts, ND-1972," Box 111, BSA.

88. EKOH.

89. Beth Ann Krier, "A Devoted Clan: Hats Off to the Hatted," *LAT,* August 16, 1972, H1.

90. Maurice Carroll, "Bella Abzug Re-elected by Wide Margin," *NYT,* November 8, 1972, 36.

91. Linda Charlton, "An Alleged GOP Partisan Temporarily Pulls Mrs. Abzug's Hat Out of the Ring," *NYT,* July 6, 1972, 27.

92. Maxine Cheshire, "VIP: Giving Crown Jewels for Christmas," *WP,* December 15, 1970, B1.

93. Abzug, "Speech for the Jewish Center of Kew Garden Hills," December 18, 1970, 1–12, 4, "Statements, Activities, Notes, and Memoranda," Box 398, BSA.

94. Abzug quoted in "Senate and House Warmings," *WP,* January 22, 1971, B1.

95. Abzug, *Bella!,* 29.

96. Wyneta Jane Driscoll to Abzug, August 16, 1971, "General, August 1971," Box 1, BSA.

97. Abzug quoted in "David Steinberg Talks with Congresswoman Bella Abzug (D-NY) and Helen Gurley Brown, Editor of Cosmopolitan," *David Frost Show,* January 15, 1971, 23, "Bella Abzug, Transcripts," Box 1031, BSA.

98. Abzug, ZI, Tape Eleven, Side A, 2 (297); "My Favorite Crash Diet," *Cosmopolitan,* February 1973, 114, loose document, Box 760, BSA.

99. EN14.

100. Spiro Agnew quoted in "Names and Faces in the News," *BG,* March 6, 1971, 2.

101. Mailer, "The Prisoner of Sex," 44.

102. Abzug, *Bella!,* 72.

103. Abzug, ZI, Tape Four (2), March 26, 1971, 20.

104. Memorandum from Marcosson to Abzug, February 20, 1973, "Memoranda 1973–1974," Box 68, BSA.

105. Auletta, "'Senator' Bella—Seriously," 13.

106. Amon, "Bella Abzug."

107. Susan J. Douglas, *Where the Girls Are: Growing Up Female with the Mass Media* (New York: Random House, 1994); Victoria Hesford, *Feeling Women's Liberation* (Durham, NC: Duke University Press, 2013).

108. "Women Talk Back," *L,* June 9, 1972, 46.

109. Abzug quoted in Alexander, "The City Politic," 11.

110. Handwritten draft response to Letter to the Editor by Irene Davall, "B. A. Press," Box 216, WFRP.

8. Government Wrongs and Privacy Rights

1. "Spies Bug Abzug Phone: A Strange Voice Says: 'Keep the Tape Going,'" clipping, *City Reporter,* November 1972, 1, "Abzug-Bugging of Phones-Nov. '72, City Reporter article on Abzug," Box 1029, BSA.

2. Paul Van Souder to Abzug, October 1, 1972, "Bugging Incident, 10/1972," Box 66, BSA.

3. "Summary of Investigation," Investigation, Inc., n.d., "Office, General, Bugging Incident, 10/1972," Box 66, BSA; "Charge by Mrs. Abzug," *NYT,* October 11, 1972, 27; Memorandum on the Watergate Break-In and Bugging from McGovern-Shriver Political Research, September 22, 1972, "McGovern, George and Sargent Shriver (and Thomas Eagleton)," Box 504, BSA.

4. SAC NY to Director J. Edgar Hoover, September 23, 1970, 1–3, 3, 100-102413-264, FBI File; and for continued surveillance, 100-102413-275 to 100-102413-434, FBI File.

5. "New Congress Prepares to Convene," *CQWR* 33, no. 2 (January 11, 1975): 63; Bella Abzug, "Bella's Eye View of Her Party's Future," *Ms.,* April 1974, 64–65, 65.

6. Carl Albert quoted in and see generally, James L. Sundquist, *The Decline and Resurgence of Congress* (Washington, DC: Brookings Institute, 1981), 1.

7. Bella Abzug with Mel Ziegler, ed., *Bella! Ms. Abzug Goes to Washington* (New York: Saturday Review Press, 1972), 109.

8. Sarah E. Igo, *The Known Citizen: A History of Privacy in Modern America* (Cambridge, MA: Harvard University Press, 2018), 223, generally 221–263.

9. John M. Crewdson, "CIA Opened Bella Abzug's Mail, Kept 20-Year File," *NYT,* March 6, 1975, 77.

10. See, for instance, Lillian Hellman, *Scoundrel Time* (Boston: Little, Brown, 1976); and on new McCarthyism, Alice Kessler-Harris, *A Difficult Woman: The Challenging Life and Times of Lillian Hellman* (New York: Bloomsbury Press, 2012), 287–301.

11. Abzug to David R. Zuckerman, May 23, 1973, "Nixon, Richard Milhous—Correspondence," Box 489, BSA.

12. Abzug quoted in GIIR, *CIA Exemption in the Privacy Act of 1974,* 94th Cong., 1st Sess., March 5 and June 25, 1975, 1–346, 27; James J. Kilpatrick, "Commentary, WTOF," March 19, 1975, "Correspondence, 1975–1976," Box 111, BSA.

13. Abzug quoted in Thomas Oliphant, "Massive, Orderly Protest Staged during Inaugural," *BG,* January 21, 1973, 1.

14. "Cong. Bella Abzug's Speech at NCC Mtg.," March 12, 1973, 1–5, 1, 2, "National Consultative (Aug. 70–73)," Box 1, A.1, WSPP.

15. "An Introspective and Angry Congress Begins Its Work," *CQWR* 31, no. 1 (January 6, 1973): 3–12, 5.

16. Abzug quoted in Betty Medsger, "NW Peace Rally Hears of Despair, Horror," *WP*, January 4, 1973, H6.

17. Minutes, January 2, 1973, HDCR; Minutes, January 22, 1973, HDCR; Minutes February 1, 1973, HDCR; Robert V. Remini, *The House: The History of the House of Representatives* (Washington, DC: Library of Congress, 2006), 433–434.

18. "Statement of Hon. Bella Abzug of New York: Hearings before the Subcommittee on National Security Policy of the House Committee on Foreign Affairs," March 1973, 286, "Statements, Notes, and Memoranda," Box 518, BSA.

19. "Impoundment of Funds: Constitutional Crisis Ahead," *CQWR* 31, no. 5 (February 3, 1973): 213.

20. Abzug quoted in Anthony Ripley, "Capitol Protest Scores Fund Cuts," *NYT*, February 21, 1973, 26; Abzug, "Testimony on Impoundment Bills," April 3, 1973, "Impoundment," Box 496, BSA; Beverly Gage, "Deep Throat, Watergate, and the Bureaucratic Politics of the FBI," *Journal of Policy History* 24, no. 2 (2012): 157–183.

21. John A. Lawrence, *The Class of '74: Congress after Watergate and the Roots of Partisanship* (Baltimore: Johns Hopkins University Press, 2018), 42–44; Sundquist, *The Decline and Resurgence of Congress,* 199–237.

22. Paul McCloskey quoted in "Congress: Views on Reaching the End of the Tunnel," *CQWR* 31, no. 4 (January 27, 1973): 166–170, 166.

23. Abzug, "Remarks: War Powers," November 7, 1973, "Statements, Notes, and Memoranda," Box 518, BSA; "House Passes Its Toughest War Powers Resolution Ever," *CQWR* 31, no. 29 (July 21, 1973): 2024–2025; "Congress Overrides Nixon's Veto of War Powers Bill," *CQWR* 31, no. 45 (November 10, 1973): 2985–2986; Robert David Johnson, *Congress and the Cold War* (Cambridge: Cambridge University Press, 2006), 192–193; Louis Fisher, "War Power," in *The American Congress: The Building of Democracy,* ed. Julian E. Zelizer (Boston: Houghton Mifflin, 2004), 687–702.

24. H. R. Haldeman quoted in "Meeting between President Nixon and H. R. Haldeman in the Executive Office Building between 4:16 pm and 5:46 pm on February 13, 1973," Conversation No. 410-14, "Nixon Presidential Materials Staff: Tape Subject Log," WHT.

25. Abzug, "Opening Remarks for Amnesty Meeting (Abzug Chairing)," May 4, 1973, 1–6, 4, "Statements, Releases," Box 424, BSA; "As We Rejoice in the Homecoming of the Prisoners of War," *BG*, February 19, 1973, 13.

26. Abzug, "Political Prisoners in South Vietnam," n.d., 1–17, 2, "Statements, Notes, and Memos," Box 391, BSA. For leftists' use of "Nixon-as-Hitler," see David Greenberg, *Nixon's Shadow: The History of an Image* (New York: W. W. Norton, 2003), 98–100.

27. Abzug quoted in Marjorie Hyer, "Rep. Abzug Scores Nixon at Protest," *WP*, January 17, 1973, B7; BAOH, 264–265.

28. Natasha Zaretsky, *No Direction Home: The American Family and the Fear of National Decline* (Chapel Hill: University of North Carolina Press, 2007), 25–70; "House Votes Fund Cutoff for U.S. Bombing of Cambodia," *CQWR* 31, no. 19 (May 12, 1973): 1170.

29. "Crusade Ends for Bella Abzug," *HC*, August 16, 1973, 29; Memorandum from Eleanor Garst to Abzug, August 4, 1973, 1–6, 1, "SE Asia, 1973, General," Box 383, BSA; "Documents Received by Cong. Abzug in Saigon August 1973," n.d., "Statements, Notes, and Memos," Box 391, BSA; "WSP Document Misuse of Tax Funds for Saigon's Police and Prison Systems," June 11, 1973, "Organizations," Box 391, BSA; Abzug to Les Whitten, September 19, 1973, "Thanh, Ngo Ba," Box 391, BSA.

30. Nixon Speech via Cable, August 15, 1973, "General," Box 383, BSA.

31. "Transcript of a Recording of a Meeting of March 1, 1973 between President Nixon and John Dean from Approximately 9:18 to 9:45 am in the Oval Office," Conversation No. 886-3, 1–21, 1, 3–4, WHT, https://www.nixonlibrary.gov/forresearchers/find/tapes/watergate/wspf/866-003.pdf.

32. "Follow up on Watergate," April 27, 1973, "Notes, Memoranda, Statements," Box 386, BSA; Memorandum from Mark to Abzug and Eric Hirschhorn, April 26, 1973, "Notes and Memoranda," Box 492, BSA; Memorandum from Hirschhorn to Abzug, May 23, 1973, "Notes, Memoranda, Statements," Box 489, BSA.

33. "Watergate: Capital's Unwholesome Preoccupation," *CQWR* 31, no. 17 (April 28, 1973): (1007.

34. Stanley I. Kutler, *The Wars of Watergate: The Last Crisis of Richard Nixon* (New York: W. W. Norton, 1990), 382.

35. For the full run of staff memos covering the Senate Watergate Committee hearings, "Watergate, Hearings and Testimony," Box 497, BSA; Memorandum from Hirschhorn and Elizabeth Langer to Abzug, June 4, 1973, "Notes and Memoranda," Box 492, BSA; Memorandum from Langer to Abzug re: Identification of Issues for DSG Impeachment Task Force, n.d., Box 492, BSA.

36. "Abzug Proposes Investigation of President Possibly Leading to Impeachment: Reacts to Watergate Speech," May 1, 1973, "Press Releases and Form Letters," Box 492, BSA; Memorandum from Hirschhorn to Abzug, May 8, 1973, "General," Box 497, BSA; "Moss Hints Impeachment in Seeking House Probe," *BG,* May 10, 1973, 12; Abzug, "The President's 'Explanation,'" *CR,* May 23, 1973, H 16806–H16807, H16807.

37. James M. Naughton, "GOP Quorum Call Halts McCloskey's Impeachment Speech," *NYT,* June 7, 1973, 35.

38. Abzug, "The Conduct of the President," *CR,* June 12, 1973, H19264–H19268, H19264–H19266; "Watergate: Magruder Implicates Top Officials," *CQWR* 31, no. 24 (June 16, 1973): 1486–1497, 1494.

39. Abzug and Albert quoted in Marjorie Hunter, "Inquiry Is Urged on Impeachment: Mrs. Abzug Asks House to Study Legal Grounds," *NYT,* June 13, 1973, 34.

40. Robert Drinan quoted in "Watergate: Continued Hearings by a Tired Committee," *CQWR* 31, no. 31 (August 4, 1973): 2110–2134, 2123; "Watergate:

A Historic Constitutional Confrontation," *CQWR* 31, no. 30 (August 28, 1973): 2031–2051.

41. Elizabeth Holtzman with Cynthia L. Cooper, *Who Said It Would Be Easy? One Woman's Life in the Political Arena* (New York: Arcade, 1996), 41.

42. Abzug, "Impeach the President," *CR*, October 23, 1973, H34820; Memorandum from Langer to Abzug re: Summary of Impeachment Activities, October 24, 1973, "Notes and Memoranda," Box 492, BSA; John C. Culver et al. to "Dear Colleagues," October 23, 1973, Folder 3, Box 45, DSGP; *DSG Staff Bulletin*, October 23, 1973, 3, Box 45, DSGP; Oliphant, "Impeachment: What's Happened, What's to Come?," *BG*, October 28, 1973, 1.

43. *U.S. v. Nixon*, 418 U.S. 683 (1974).

44. David W. Dennis quoted in Richard Lyons and William Chapman, "Judiciary Committee Approves Article to Impeach President Nixon, 27 to 11," *WP*, July 28, 1974, A1.

45. Abzug, Untitled, *NYT*, October 18, 1973, 47; Abzug to "Dear Colleague" with Draft Impeachment Resolution, September 26, 1973, "Press Releases and Form Letters," Box 492, BSA; "House Democrats Ask Thorough Probe of Ford's Qualifications," *LAT*, October 17, 1973, 2; Kutler, *The Wars of Watergate*, 391–414.

46. Abzug, "Legislation Providing for Special Presidential Election Introduced," *CR*, November 1, 1973, H35702–H35704.

47. Abzug, "A Pearl Harbor Attack on Our System of Equal Justice," unpublished draft, n.d., 1–4, 1, "Statements, Legislation, Etc.," Box 273, BSA; Abzug et al., H.R. Res. 1367, 93rd Cong., 2nd Sess., September 18, 1974, "Notes and Memos," Box 273, BSA; "Abzug's Pardon Questions," *WP*, October 18, 1974, A11; Seymour M. Hersh, "The Pardon: Nixon, Ford, Haig, and the Transfer of Power," *AM*, 8/83, www.theatlantic.com/magazine/archive/1983/08/the-pardon /305571/.

48. William L. Hungate quoted in Paul Houston, "Panel Sends Questions to Ford on Nixon Pardon; Hearings Due," *LAT*, September 19, 1974, A21; Abzug, "Conversation with Bill Hungate," notes, "Notes and Memos," Box 273, BSA; Hungate to Ford, September 17, 1974, "Resolution of Inquiry, General," Box 273, BSA.

49. Ford to Hungate, September 20, 1974, "Notes and Memos," Box 273, BSA.

50. Gerald Ford, *A Time to Heal: The Autobiography of Gerald Ford* (New York: Harper and Row, 1979), 196–197.

51. John Marsh quoted in Mary McGrory, "No Oath, Two Hours, and No Ms. Abzug," *BG*, October 5, 1974, 6.

52. Abzug quoted in Bob Kuttner, "House Democrats Urge Further Pardon Probe," *WP*, October 18, 1974, A10; "Further Questions for President Ford's Appearance on October 17 Suggested by Ms. Abzug," n.d., "Notes and Memos," Box 273, BSA.

53. *U.S. v. Nixon*, 418 U.S. 683 (1974).

54. "Dissenting Views of Hon. Bella S. Abzug," in Moorhead, "Amending the Freedom of Information Act to Require That Information Be Made Available to

Congress," House Committee Report No. 93-990, 93rd Cong., 2nd Sess., 1–41, 37–38, "Freedom of Information," Box 152, BSA; Moorhead et al., H.R. Res. 12471, Report No. 93-876, January 31, 1974, 93rd Cong., 2nd Sess., "Government Operations: (HR 12471) to Amend Section 552, of Title 5, United States Code, Known as the Freedom of Information Act," Box 695, BSA.

55. "Executive Privilege Issue Splits House Committee," *CQWR* 32, no. 16 (April 20, 1974): 998–999; *Freedom of Information Act and Amendments of 1974 (PL 93-502): Source Book: Legislative History, Texts, and Other Documents,* Joint Committee Print, 94th Cong., 1st Sess., March 1975.

56. Katherine A. Scott suggests that most on Ford's staff saw FOIA as "obnoxious" and supported the veto, but opinions were more varied; *Reining in the State: Civil Society and Congress in the Vietnam and Watergate Eras* (Lawrence: University Press of Kansas, 2013), 131–132. Memorandum from Philip W. Buchen to Kathy Tindle, October 16, 1974, "LE HR 12471 Freedom of Information Act Amendments (4)," Box 28, KL.

57. Igo, *The Known Citizen,* 249.

58. Richard Nixon, "Address on the State of the Union Delivered before a Joint Session of Congress," January 30, 1974, http://www.presidency.ucsb.edu/ws/index.php?pid=4327.

59. Ed Koch, Don Edwards, and Moorhead to Dear Colleagues, March 20, 1974, "General," Box 155A, BSA; "Privacy: Committees Probe Ways to Curb Data Use," *CQWR* 32, no. 10 (March 9, 1974): 683; Scott, *Reining in the State,* 117–135.

60. "Rep. Abzug's Statement on Privacy Legislation before FOGI," February 26, 1974, 1–5, 5, "Abzug—Notes, Etc.," Box 155A, BSA; "Memorandum from Langer and Fran Temko to Abzug: Questions for Mr. Koch," February 19, 1974, Box 155A, BSA.

61. "Testimony of Honorable Bella S. Abzug before the FOGI Subcommittee of the House Government Operations Committee," May 16, 1974, 1–8, 3, "Abzug—Notes, Etc.," Box 155A, BSA; "Comparison of Privacy Bills—13872 (BSA), 14493 (Goldwater), 13303 (Koch)," n.d., Box 155A, BSA; Abzug, HR 13872, April 2, 1974, "Bills Printed," Box 156, BSA.

62. Ford, "Statement by the President," October 9, 1974, "Invasion of Privacy," Box 623, GIIRGO.

63. "Testimony of Honorable Bella S. Abzug before the FOGI Subcommittee," 6.

64. Abzug, "Special Order on Privacy," *CR,* April 2, 1974, H2492–H2493, H2493, "General," Box 155A, BSA.

65. Memorandum from Moorhead to Members, May 14, 1974, "General," Box 155A, BSA; "Memo on Mark-Up Session on Privacy Legislation," June 27, 1974, "Abzug, Notes, Etc.," Box 155A, BSA; Abzug to Moorhead, September 9, 1974, "Invasion of Privacy," Box 623, Box 623, GIIRGO.

66. "Privacy: A Year-End Report," *WP,* December 26, 1974, A24.

67. Whip Brochure, "Congress, US, House Rules," Box 174, BSA; Moorhead to Abzug, July 12, 1974, "Abzug," Box 609, GIIRGO; Jack Brooks to Abzug, February 5, 1975, "Office Matters—Proposed Budget and Agenda—94th," Box 9, GIIRGO.

68. "As the Old Order Begins to Crumble on Capitol Hill," *USNWR,* February 3, 1975, 23.

69. Mary McGrory, "The Capitol Letter: Bella Sandpapers the House into Shape," *NY,* April 15, 1975, 7, "Campaign 1976, n.d.," Box 64, BSA; Abzug quoted in Lawrence, *The Class of '74,* 89; profiling the class of '74, 50–71.

70. Abzug, "The White House is clearly not satisfied . . . ," handwritten draft, n.d., 1–4, 1, "Notes and Memoranda," Box 492, BSA.

71. It is unclear why this article went unpublished. Abzug, "No More Watergates! Many More Women!," draft, n.d., 1–11, 1, 3, Folder 9, Box 153, GSP.

72. B. J. Phillips, "Recognizing the Gentleladies of the Judiciary Committee," *Ms.,* November 1974, 70–74, 71, 74.

73. Jules Witcover, "Women Candidates Capitalizing on Clean Political Image," *WP,* June 16, 1974, L1; "Women Candidates: Many More Predicted for 1974," *CQWR* 32, no. 15 (April 13, 1974): 941–944; Susan Tolchin and Martin Tolchin, *Clout: Womanpower and Politics* (New York: Coward, McCann, and Geoghegan, 1974), 29.

74. Phil Sharp quoted in Lawrence, *The Class of '74,* 193; see also 87–89.

75. William Gildea, "Fishbait at the Door: The Power of the Odd Job," *WP,* February 17, 1974, M1.

76. Minutes, December 2, 1974, Folder 34, Box 4, HDCR; Minutes, December 4, 1974, Folder 1, Box 5, HDCR; Barbara Sinclair, *Legislators, Leaders, and Lawmaking: The US House of Representatives in the Postreform Era* (Baltimore: Johns Hopkins University Press, 1995), 40, 52–54.

77. Sundquist, *The Decline and Resurgence of Congress,* 327.

78. Muriel Dobbin, "Abzug Mail Was Opened by CIA," *BS,* March 6, 1975, "HRNS CIA, Colby's Statement, 3/5/75," Box 18, GIIRGO; Rhodri Jeffreys-Jones, *The CIA and American Democracy,* 2nd ed. (New Haven, CT: Yale University Press, 1989), 194–215; John Prados, *William Colby and the CIA: The Secret Wars of a Controversial Spymaster,* 2nd ed. (Lawrence: University Press of Kansas, 2009), 297–330.

79. William Colby and anonymous quoted in Seymour M. Hersh, "Huge CIA Operation Reported in U.S. against Antiwar Forces, Other Dissidents in Nixon Years," *NYT,* December 22, 1974, 1, 26, 26. For Colby's briefing, see Colby to Ford, December 24, 1974, "John Marsh Files—Intelligence Series (7)," Box 37, RAC.

80. "Rep. Bella Abzug Describes Rockefeller Panel on CIA as 'Coverup' Operation: Will Introduce Bill Requiring Destruction of Illegal Files Held by CIA on Estimated 10,000 Americans," January 6, 1975, 1–2, 1, "Abzug Statements and Activities—1976," Box 155A, BSA; Memorandum from Moorhead to FOGI Members, January 22, 1975, "Mtg. Colby Briefing re: Privacy Act of 1974, 1/23/75," Box 18, GIIRGO; "FOGI Subcommittee, January 1975," n.d., "Subcommittee—Monthly Reports, 1975–1976," Box 9, GIIRGO.

81. John M. Crewdson, "CIA Opened Bella Abzug's Mail, Kept 20-Year File," *NYT,* March 6, 1975, 77.

82. "Statement W. E. Colby Director of Central Intelligence before GIIR," March 5, 1975, 1–22, 5, "HRNS—CIA and Secret Service Exemptions in Privacy Act, 3/13/1975," Box 18, GIIRGO.

83. "Statement by Rep. Bella S. Abzug (D-N.Y.), Chairwoman, House Subcommittee on Government Information and Individual Rights," March 7, 1975, 1–2, 1, "BSA Statement re. CIA File on Her-3/7/75," Box 5, GIIRGO. For disclosures during the 1949 Judith Coplon case, see Athan Theoharis, *Spying on Americans: Political Surveillance from Hoover to the Huston Plan* (Philadelphia: Temple University Press, 1978), 100–105.

84. Abzug quoted in GIIR, *CIA Exemption in the Privacy Act of 1974,* 94th Cong., 1st Sess., March 5 and June 25, 1975, 1–346, 10, 81; "CIA, FBI Investigations," *CQWR* 33, no. 10 (March 8, 1975): 11.

85. Colby quoted in GIIR, *CIA Exemption in the Privacy Act of 1974,* 11–12.

86. For a reiteration, see William Colby and Peter Forbath, *Honorable Men: My Life in the CIA* (New York: Simon and Schuster, 1978), 404.

87. GIIR, *CIA Exemption in the Privacy Act of 1974, 9, 67–68, 74–76.*

88. Colby quoted in GIIR, *CIA Exemption in the Privacy Act of 1974,* 84.

89. Colby, *Honorable Men,* 403.

90. Colby quoted in Loch K. Johnson, *A Season of Inquiry: The Senate Intelligence Investigation* (Lexington: University Press of Kentucky, 1985), 7.

91. Colby, *Honorable Men,* 403.

92. Russell Baker, "Social Distinctions," *NYT,* March 11, 1975, 35.

93. "Speech by Rep. Bella S. Abzug before the Federal Bar Association Seminar at the Mayflower Hotel," March 22, 1975, 1–15, "Abzug—Notes, Memos, Statements," Box 155A, BSA.

94. James J. Kilpatrick, "Commentary, WTOF," March 19, 1975, "Correspondence, 1975–1976," Box 111, BSA. In contrast, "CIA vs. Bella & WSP," n.d., "Lit. 799 Broadway (1973–1979)," Box 2, C.1, WSP.

95. Eugene C. Pulliam, "Bella as Snow White," *Indianapolis News,* March 13, 1975, 10, attached to "Representative Bella Big Hat Abzug, D-NY," March 18, 1975, "Abusive Mail—1975 (3)," Box 10, BSA.

96. "Why the CIA Spied on Bella Abzug," *HE* 35, no. 11 (March 15, 1975): 3.

97. Abzug to John Hammond of the *Democrat & Chronicle,* March 26, 1975, "Correspondence, 1975–1976," Box 111, BSA.

98. Anonymous to Abzug, January 15, 1976, "Abusive Mail—1976," Box 10, BSA.

99. "Nauseated" to Abzug, May 5, 1975, "Abusive Mail—1975 (1)," Box 10, BSA.

100. Anonymous to Abzug, April 11, 1975, "Abusive Mail—1975 (3)," Box 10, BSA.

101. "Representative Bella Big Hat Abzug, D-NY."

102. Frank Church quoted in Johnson, *A Season of Inquiry,* 15; Kathryn Olmsted, *Challenging the Secret Government: The Post-Watergate Investigations of the CIA and FBI* (Chapel Hill: University of North Carolina Press, 1996); David F. Schmitz, "Congress Must Draw the Line: Senator Frank Church and the Opposition to the Vietnam War and the Imperial Presidency," in *Vietnam and the American Political Tradition: The Politics of Dissent,* ed. Randall B. Woods (Cambridge: Cambridge University Press, 2003), 121–148.

103. Nicholas M. Horrock, "Intelligence Hearings: Inquiries Seem Mired in Data after 9 Months, with Goals Unclear," *NYT,* October 10, 1975, 21.

104. Olmsted, *Challenging the Secret Government,* 4.

105. Abzug to Democratic Steering and Policy Committee Members, February 3, 1975, "Government Information," Box 161, BSA; "Minutes of the Organizational Meeting, GIIR," February 19, 1975, "Meeting, Organizational, Transcripts, 2/19/1975," Box 18, GIIRGO; "Jurisdiction and Security-Related Activities of the GIIR Subcommittee," n.d., "Office Matters—Proposed Budget and Agenda—94th," Box 9, GIIRGO.

106. "Rep. Bella Abzug Describes Rockefeller Panel on CIA as 'Coverup' Operation," 2; Seymour M. Hersh, "Democrats Vote Wide CIA Study by Senate Panel," *NYT,* January 21, 1975, 69.

107. Memorandum from Redacted (Likely Richard Ober) to General Scowcroft, June 26, 1975, "Philip Buchen Files—Intelligence Series (18)," Box 36, RAC.

108. Abzug, Sam Steiger, and Colby quoted in *CIA Exemption in the Privacy Act of 1974,* 112–113, 116, 200; George Lardner Jr., "Colby Defends CIA's Congress Files," *WP,* June 26, 1975, A1; Robert L. Jackson, "CIA Has Files on 75 Congressmen, Not Just Four, Colby Acknowledges," *LAT,* June 26, 1975, 24.

109. The Houston memorandum is not to be confused with the "Huston Plan," a cross-agency spying program investigated by the Church Committee in September 1975. Memorandum from Lawrence R. Houston to William P. Rogers, March 1, 1954, "Press Clippings re: CIA Hearing 6/25/75," Box 22, GIIRGO; "6/25/75—CIA Hearings, List of Requested Information," n.d., "Hearings—Justice Oversight," Box 22, GIIRGO; Abzug notes, "CIA—Three Functions," "HRNS CIA Exemption under the Privacy Act 6/25/75," Box 22, GIIRGO.

110. Colby quoted in John Crewdson, "Church Doubts Plot Links to Presidents," *NYT,* July 19, 1975, 1.

111. Tim Ingram, Memorandum, June 26, 1975, "Hearings—Justice Oversight," Box 22, GIIRGO. For Abzug's CIA bill, see Memorandum from Abzug to GIIR Members, June 23, 1975, "HRNS CIA Exemption under the Privacy Act 6/25/75," Box 22, GIIRGO.

112. Memorandum from Ingram to Abzug, July 14, 1975, "Hearings—Justice Oversight," Box 22, GIIRGO; George L. Cary to Ingram, July 16, 1975, "HRNGS—Justice and CIA Agreement, 7/22–23/75," Box 22, GIIRGO; John S. Warner to Kevin Maroney, July 8, 1975, Box 22, GIIRGO; Abzug to Warner, July 18, 1975, "John Marsh Files—Intelligence Series (4)," Box 37, RAC; Colby to Brooks, July 19, 1975, Box 37, RAC.

113. Cary to Marsh, September 30, 1975, "Michael Raoul-Duval Files—Intelligence Series (1)," Box 39, RAC.

114. Memorandum from Cary to Marsh, October 11, 1975, 1–3, 1, "John Marsh Files—Intelligence Series (9)," Box 37, RAC.

115. Frank Church quoted in Olmsted, *Challenging the Secret Government,* 104, and see generally, 94–104.

116. Memorandum from Abzug to GIIR Members, October 6, 1975, with attached letters Colby to Abzug, August 15, 1975; Abzug to Colby, September 26,

1975; Colby to Abzug, October 3, 1975, "HRNS—Puttaporn Caucus, 9/11/75," Box 23, GIIRGO; Johnson, *A Season of Inquiry,* 78. On press coverage, see, for instance, "Abzug Unit Fails to Get Secret CIA Documents," *WP,* August 2, 1975, A2.

117. Frank Van Riper, "Find US Agents Spy on Embassies' Cables," *DN,* July 22, 1975, 1; Nicholas M. Horrock, "National Security Agency Reported Eavesdropping on Most Private Cables," *NYT,* August 31, 1975, 1; Robert P. Haley, "New Charges Broaden Issue of US Security vs. Privacy," *CSM,* September 2, 1975, 3.

118. Olmsted, *Challenging the Secret Government,* 105; "Shamrock," October 29, 1975, "NSA," Box 27, GIIRGO; Johnson, *A Season of Inquiry,* 99, 103–104.

119. "Western Union International: Additional Notes (To Those Included in the Summary)," n.d., "HEAR—Cable and Telex Interception, 10/23/75," Box 23, GIIRGO; "Memorandum for the Record: Robert Fink Meeting with Thomas Algie and Lawrence J. McKay, 9/10/75," n.d., Box 23, GIIRGO; "Memorandum for the Record," September 15, 1975, Box 23, GIIRGO; "Mr. E. Brod," September 16, 1975, Box 23, GIIRGO; "Memorandum for the Record on Western Union," n.d., Box 23, GIIRGO; "Background Memorandum for Oversight Hearings of GIIR on the Interception of Non-verbal Communications by Intelligence Agencies," October 23, 1975, Box 23, GIIRGO; Theoharis, *Spying on Americans,* 94–132; Frank J. Donner, *The Age of Surveillance: The Aims and Methods of America's Intelligence System* (New York: Alfred A. Knopf, 1980), 275–277. For the NSA's self-assessment, see "Shamrock," n.d., "John Marsh Files—Intelligence Series (CODEWORD)," Box 33, RAC.

120. Robert S. Fink, "Notes for Record on Conversation with Joe R. Craig," October 19, 1975, 1–2, 1, "HEAR—Cable and Telex Interception, 10/23/75," Box 23, GIIRGO.

121. Bob Woodward, "Messages of Activists Intercepted," *WP,* October 13, 1975, A1.

122. Peter C. Stuart, "Message 'Snooping' Probed: NSA Intercepted Private Cablegrams?," *CSM,* October 24, 1975, 3.

123. Nicholas M. Horrock, "Ford Aides Seek to Modify Laws on Spying Method," *NYT,* October 15, 1975, 1.

124. "Statement of Chairwoman Bella S. Abzug for Hearing on the Interception of Non-verbal Communications by Federal Agencies, before GIIR," 3; Memorandum from Ingram, Hirschhorn, and Fink to Abzug, October 21, 1975, "Abzug—Notes, Memos, Statements," Box 155A, BSA; "2 Western Union Aides Say US Machine Copied Cables," *HC,* October 24, 1975, 1; GIIR, *Interception of Nonverbal Communications by Federal Intelligence Agencies,* 94th Cong., 1st and 2nd Sess., October 23, 1975, and February 25, March 3, and October–November 1976.

125. Obituary notice for Esther Savitzky, *NYT,* October 28, 1975, "Miscellaneous Personal," Box 963, BSA; Rese Debref to Abzug, July 13, 1975, "Miscellaneous Personal," Box 963, BSA.

126. George Lardner Jr., "NSA Intercepted Messages of 1,600 Americans Abroad," *WP,* October 30, 1975, A2; Horrock, "NSA Chief Tells of Broad Scope

of Surveillance," *NYT,* October 30, 1975, 1; Olmsted, *Challenging the Secret Government,* 102–105.

127. Memorandum from Abzug to Brooks, February 18, 1976, "GIIR, Correspondence," Box 161, BSA.

128. Olmsted, *Challenging the Secret Government,* 140.

129. Olmsted, *Challenging the Secret Government,* 140.

130. Walter Pincus, "House Bars Pike Panel CIA Report," *WP,* January 30, 1976, A1; "Abzug Intelligence Activities," n.d., "Abzug—Notes, Memos, Statements," Box 155A, BSA; Olmsted, *Challenging the Secret Government,* 155–167.

131. Abzug to Brooks, February 18, 1976, "Hearing and Meeting Files—2/25–3/11/76 (Cable Interception Hearings)," Box 27, GIIRGO.

132. "Abzug Matter," n.d., "John Marsh Files—Intelligence Series (CODE-WORD)," Box 33, RAC.

133. Memorandum from Buchen to Ford, February 17, 1976, "Philip Buchen Files—Intelligence Series (19)," Box 36, RAC; Memorandum from Ford to Donald S. Rumsfeld and Edward H. Levi, February 17, 1976, "Hearing and Meeting Files—2/25–3/11/76 (Cable Interception Hearings)," Box 27, GIIRGO; Memorandum from Ingram for the Record, February 18, 1976, "NSA," Box 27, GIIRGO.

134. Abzug quoted in Rhodri Jeffreys-Jones, *The FBI: A History* (New Haven, CT: Yale University Press, 2007), 186.

135. Memorandum from Ted Jacobs to Abzug, March 2, 1976, 1–3, 3, "Memorandum—Staff, Etc.," Box 9, GIIRGO.

136. Hirschhorn to Abzug, March 19, 1976, "NSA," Box 27, GIIRGO; "June 1976," "Subcte.—Monthly Reports (1975–1976)," Box 9, GIIRGO.

137. Edward H. Levi quoted in attachment to Michael M. Uhlmann to Hirschhorn, March 12, 1976, "NSA," Box 27, GIIRGO.

138. Abzug quoted in "Abzug Panel Passes Government in the Sunshine Bill," January 21, 1976, Box 5, GIIRGO.

139. Hirschhorn to Roy Wilkins, January 21, 1976, 1–2, 2, "1976 July," Box 7, GIIRGO; "Points of Contention," n.d., "Meet. Subcte. 2/10/76 HR11656 Clean. Sunshine Bill," Box 26, GIIRGO; "HR 11656," February 3, 1976, 94th Cong., 2nd Sess., "Sunshine (Gov't in the Sunshine) Bill," Box 156, BSA; Memorandum from Hirschhorn to Abzug, July 29, 1976, "1976 July," Box 7, GIIRGO.

140. Memorandum from Hirschhorn to Abzug, April 14, 1976, 1–3, 2, "Memoranda—Staff, Etc.," Box 9, GIIRGO.

141. "Opening Statement of Chairwoman Bella S. Abzug, at Hearings on HR 10315 and HR 9868 before GIIR," November 6, 1975, 1–3, 2, "Hear. HR 10315—Sunshine Legislation 11/6 and 11/7–1975," Box 24, GIIRGO.

142. Abzug to "Dear Editorial Writer," March 15, 1976, "Meet. Subcte. 2/10/76 HR11656 Clean. Sunshine Bill," Box 26, GIIRGO; Pub. L. 94-409.

143. "FOI how to do it" letters are designated in chronological correspondence files, Boxes 6–8, 94th Cong., GIIRGO. See also ACLU pamphlet "The Privacy Act: How It Affects You, How to Use It," n.d., "Abzug—General," Box 155A, BSA; *The Privacy Report* 8 (March 1974), "Abzug—General," Box 155A, BSA;

"Openness in Government," Federal Bar Association conference transcript, n.d., Folder 7, Box 83, GLP.

144. Igo, *The Known Citizen*, 259.

145. "Speech by Rep. Bella S. Abzug before the Federal Bar Association Seminar at the Mayflower Hotel," 9.

146. For instance, historian Athan Theoharis went back to GIIR transcripts when researching FBI record-keeping practices and intelligence FOIA exemptions. Theoharis to Ingram, Folder 3, Box 90, GLP; Theoharis, "The Freedom of Information Act versus the FBI," in *A Culture of Secrecy: The Government versus the People's Right to Know*, ed. Athan Theoharis (Lawrence: University Press of Kansas, 1998), 16–36.

147. Abzug quoted in "Abzug Asks Government Inform Subjects of Files," February 24, 1976, Box 5, GIIRGO.

148. In 2007, I looked at these case files at the Tamiment Library in unprocessed form. Abzug to Bush, June 22, 1976, "1976 June," Box 7, GIIRGO; Michael Krinsky to Abzug, June 28, 1976, "Corres. Misc. A76-D76," Box 14, GIIRGO; Bush to Abzug, July 8, 1976, Box 14, GIIRGO; Emma E. Pullen, "CIA Sued for Spying on Radicals," *BG*, October 29, 1975, 44; Traci Yodder, "Breach of Privilege: Spying on Lawyers in the United States," April 2014, https://www.nlg.org/wp-content/uploads/2016/09/Breach-of-Privilege -COLOR_3.pdf.

149. See, for instance, SAC, New York to Director, FBI, December 7, 1955, 100-102413-59, FBI File; and Director, FBI (with JEH handwritten initials) to SAC, NY, December 28, 1955, 100-102413-60, FBI File.

150. "Periscope: Hoover's Secrets," *Newsweek*, April 28, 1975, 15; Memorandum from Fink to Ingram, November 15, 1975, "Hear. 12/1/75—FBI Do Not File," Box 25, GIIRGO; "Memorandum Regarding Hearings of the Subcommittee on FBI Record-Keeping, 'Do Not File' Files, and the Files Maintained in the Offices of the Late Director J. Edgar Hoover," November 14, 1975, Box 25, GIIRGO; Jacobs, "Memo on Telephone Conversation with L. Patrick Gray (203-446-8080) Regarding Hoover Files," November 20, 1975, "Hear. FBI Record-Keeping 12/1/75," Box 25, BSA; GIIR, *Inquiry into the Destruction of Former FBI Director J. Edgar Hoover's Files and FBI Recordkeeping*, 94th Cong., 1st Sess., December 1, 1975.

151. Abzug quoted in "Abzug Panel Probes FBI Records," December 1, 1975, 1–3, 2, Box 5, GIIRGO.

152. Edward M. Kennedy quoted in Suzanne Braun Levine and Mary Thom, *Bella Abzug: How One Tough Broad from the Bronx Fought Jim Crow and Joe McCarthy, Pissed Off Jimmy Carter, Battled for the Rights of Women and Workers, Rallied Against War and for the Planet, and Shook Up Politics Along the Way* (New York: Farrar, Straus and Giroux, 2007), 165.

153. Sundquist, *The Decline and Resurgence of Congress*, 335.

154. Abzug to William O. Douglas, November 13, 1975, "Miscellaneous Personal," Box 963, BSA.

9. Running for a Democratic Future

1. "Factors to Be Considered in Decision on Senate Race," n.d., 1–3, "Polls," Box 1053, BSA.

2. This view has been the leading sentiment of Abzug friends, family, and former staff I have interviewed.

3. Robert Mason, *Richard Nixon and the Quest for a New Majority* (Chapel Hill: University of North Carolina Press, 2004); Dominic Sandbrook, *Mad as Hell: The Crisis of the 1970s and the Rise of the Populist Right* (New York: Anchor Books, 2012).

4. John A. Lawrence, *The Class of '74: Congress after Watergate and the Roots of Partisanship* (Baltimore: Johns Hopkins University Press, 2018).

5. "Look Closely" flyer, n.d., "Abzug File 1976," Box 52, NDCP.

6. "My Man Moynihan," bumper sticker, Folder 3, Box 1, Part IV, DPMP.

7. Eric Alterman and Kevin Mattson, *The Cause: The Fight for American Liberalism from Franklin Roosevelt to Barack Obama* (New York: Penguin Books, 2012), 272; Patrick Andelic, "Daniel Patrick Moynihan, the 1976 NY Senate Race, and the Struggle to Define American Liberalism," *Historic Journal* 57, no. 4 (2014): 1111–1133.

8. "Ford to City: Drop Dead," *DN*, October 30, 1975, 1; Roger Biles, *The Fate of Cities: Urban America and the Federal Government, 1945–2000* (Lawrence: University Press of Kansas, 2011).

9. Ken Bode and William Straus, "The NY Senate Race: Five Is a Crowd," *NR*, August 21, 1976, 12–15; "Rep. Abzug Seeks to Stop Arms Sales to Saudi Arabia by Oct. 1," September 8, 1976, "September 1976 Senate Release," Box 1048, BSA.

10. "Jackson Candidacy: Already Well Organized; Politics Log," *CQWR* 33, no. 6 (February 8, 1975): 311.

11. Maurice Carroll, "Democrats Vie, Openly and Otherwise, for Right to Challenge Buckley," *NYT*, November 20, 1975, 86.

12. Maurice Carroll, "Hirschfeld, a Businessman, Off to Fast TV Start in Democratic Race for Senate," *NYT*, January 19, 1976, 19.

13. Frank Lynn, "Clark Candidacy Announced Here," *NYT*, March 16, 1976, 26; Edward C. Burks, "O'Dwyer Formally Enters Race for Nomination for U.S. Senate," *NYT*, April 24, 1976, 60; Francis X. Clines, "Paul O'Dwyer, New York's Liberal Battler for Underdogs and Outsiders, Dies at 90," *NYT*, June 25, 1998.

14. Memorandum from Adrienne Sheehan to Herman Kane, March 26, 1976, "Report of Findings of Voter Attitudes, NY Democratic Senatorial Primary Election—March, 1976," Box 1024, BSA.

15. David Burke to unknown, April 15, 1976, Folder 12, Box 383, Part I, DPMP. For endorsement effort, see "Bella Gets Krupsak Support," *Harold Statesmen,* May 19, 1976, 2, "Press Clippings," Box 1044, BSA; "Senate Bid: Women Politicians Backing Bella Abzug," clipping, n.d., Box 1044, BSA; Abzug to Rangel, April 1, 1976, "NY Senate Primary—1976," Box 1052, BSA; "Region: Buffalo Area . . . ," call sheets, n.d., "Upstate Misc. to Sort," Box 1043, BSA.

16. EKOH, 388, 408–412; Koch to Moynihan, January 14, 1976, Folder 8, Box 383, Part I, DPMP; Joseph Crangle to Moynihan, February 18, 1976, Folder 5, DPMP.

17. EM14.

18. Frank Lynn, "State Democrats Select O'Dwyer, Qualify 3 Others," *NYT*, June 16, 1976, 81.

19. Sam Fredman quoted in Lynn, "O'Dwyer Is Backed for U.S. Senate Seat; Moynihan Wavering," *NYT*, June 3, 1976, 1.

20. Frank Lynn, "Voter Turn Out Light," *NYT*, September 15, 1976, 1.

21. Gil Troy, *Moynihan's Moment: America's Fight against Zionism as Racism* (Oxford: Oxford University Press, 2012), 44.

22. EM14.

23. Godfrey Hodgson, *The Gentleman from New York: Daniel Patrick Moynihan: A Biography* (Boston: Houghton Mifflin, 2000), 51.

24. Hodgson, 14; Joseph E. Hower, "'The Sparrows and the Horses': Daniel Patrick Moynihan, the Family Assistance Plan, and the Liberal Critique of Government Workers, 1955–1967," *Journal of Policy History* 28, no. 2 (2016): 256–289; Daniel Patrick Moynihan, *The Negro Family: The Case for National Action*, 1965, https://www.dol.gov/oasam/programs/history/webid-meynihan.htm.

25. Report quoted in Troy, *Moynihan's Moment*, 50; Peter Kihss, "'Benign Neglect' on Race Is Proposed by Moynihan: Moynihan Urges 'Benign Neglect' of Racial Issues," *NYT*, March 1, 1970, 1.

26. Michael Harrington, "The Welfare State and Its Neoconservative Critics," *Dissent* (Autumn 1973): 435–454.

27. Hodgson, *The Gentleman from New York*, 12.

28. H. Carl McCall, "Benign Neglect for Moynihan," *NYAN*, February 28, 1976, A3.

29. "Bye, Bye Bella . . . Tune Bye, Bye Blackbird," n.d., "For Concord," Box 1055, BSA; Damon Stetson, "Shanker Assails Mrs. Abzug; She Denies His 'Scab' Charge," *NYT*, September 3, 1976, B17; William F. Buckley, "Where Was Bella Abzug When the Teachers Struck?," *BG*, September 11, 1976, 11.

30. Frances Fitzgerald, "The Warrior Intellectuals: A Philippic against Daniel P. Moynihan and the Augurs on the Right," clipping, n.d., "National Friends of BSA (Forms)," Box 1056, BSA; Richard Chady to Abzug, February 8, 1976, "General—1976, Feb. (1)," Box 5, BSA.

31. "Press Release: Daniel P. Moynihan, Announcement of Candidacy for the United States Senate from the State of NY," June 10, 1976, 1–6, 2, "DPM," Box 1057, BSA; EM14.

32. Jesse Helms, "Dear Friend," n.d., 1–2, 2, attached to Richard Chady to Abzug, February 8, 1976, "General—1976, Feb. (1)," Box 5, BSA; Laura Kalman, *Right Star Rising: A New Politics, 1974–1980* (New York: W. W. Norton, 2010), 25–27; Kim Phillips-Fein, *Invisible Hands: The Making of the Conservative Movement from the New Deal to Reagan* (New York: W. W. Norton, 2009), 213–225; William A. Link, *Righteous Warrior: Jesse Helms and the Rise of Modern Conservatism* (New York: St. Martin's Press, 2008), 192–194.

33. James Roach, "A Nemo to Jese Healms," *NYT*, May 18, 1976, 26.

34. Karen DeYoung, "Special Groups Donate to Spellman, Burchman," *WP*, October 12, 1976, C4.

35. "A Special Report on the Political Action Program of the Committee for Survival of a Free Congress," n.d., "Corresp.," Box 502, BSA. For Abzug's awareness of this campaign, see Abzug to Beaulak Beakett, April 19, 1976, "Congress, US, Corresp. (2)," Box 160, BSA; and liberal response to this campaign, "There's a New Enemies List . . . and Some of Your Best Friends Are on It," Fall 1976, "Bella—Campaign Endorsements and Flak," Box 1045, BSA.

36. Joseph D. Ragan quoted in Athelia Knight, "Vote Record in Tune, Fisher Says," *WP*, September 14, 1976, C1.

37. "Threat against Congresswoman Abzug," June 13, 1975, "Miscellaneous Personal," Box 963, BSA.

38. EM14.

39. Elliott Abrams to Moynihan, June 30, 1976, Folder 5, Box 383, Part I, DPMP.

40. "Democratic voters may resent the intrusion . . . ," n.d., "DPM," Box 1057, BSA; "Statement by Abzug Campaign Manager Douglas Ireland on Radio Spot on Moynihan and Nixon," September 3, 1976, "Moynihan Commercial Yanked, 11 pm 9/3/76," Box 1053, BSA. For the Abzug campaign "dirt" file, see "Backgrounder: Daniel P. Moynihan," n.d., "Addl. Moynihan," Box 1052, BSA.

41. Hodgson, *The Gentleman from New York,* 16.

42. Elizabeth Moynihan confirmed what "people said about her" during my interview with her; EM14.

43. EM14; "Yip-Pie Protest," *HC,* September 6, 1976, 12; Jon Margolis, "Mud Flies in NY: Foppish Moynihan vs. Battling Bella," *CT,* September 9, 1976, 2.

44. Ann Pincus, "Is Bella as Badass as They Say?," *VV,* May 10, 1975, "Press Clippings," Box 1046, BSA.

45. "Moynihan Is a Fighter," flyer, n.d., "Senate Candidates," Box 1051, BSA.

46. "Bella Shows Her Brass," clipping, n.d., "State Committee," Box 1045, BSA; Memorandum from Robert D. Squier to Abzug for Senate Committee, July 23, 1976, Untitled Folder, Box 1042, BSA.

47. Abzug to Timothy Crouse, August 5, 1976, "NY Senate Primary-1976," Box 1052, BSA; Crouse, "Ruling Class Hero: How Pat Moynihan Became a Credit to His Race," *RS,* August 12, 1976, "Moynihan—Rolling Stone's," Box 1056, BSA.

48. Ireland quoted in Maurice Carroll, "Teams Differ, Game's Same for 5 in Senatorial Primary," *NYT,* August 14, 1976, 48.

49. Harold Holzer quoted in Suzanne Braun Levine and Mary Thom, *Bella Abzug: How One Tough Broad from the Bronx Fought Jim Crow and Joe McCarthy, Pissed Off Jimmy Carter, Battled for the Rights of Women and Workers, Rallied Against War and for the Planet, and Shook Up Politics Along the Way* (New York: Farrar, Straus and Giroux, 2007), 171. For precampaign local press coverage, see Untitled Folder, Box 1044, BSA; Untitled II; and "Press Clippings," Box 1046, BSA.

50. Abzug paraphrased by Gloria Steinem in Levine and Thom, *Bella Abzug,* 174.

51. "Pass a Buck to Bella," n.d., "Women for Bella," Box 1054, BSA.

52. "Abzug on Coast-to-Coast Fundraising Swing This Week," July 20, 1976, "July 1976, Senate Release," Box 1042, BSA; "'Ice Cream for Bella' Fundraiser Features MacLaine and Tomlin," Box 1042, BSA; Sally Quinn, "NY Democrats Gathering Stars for the NY Democratic Primary," *WP,* September 14, 1976, B1.

53. "Gay Group Formed to Help Elect Bella Abzug to US Senate," July 8, 1976, "July 1976, Senate Race," Box 1042, BSA; "Hispanics for Bella Abzug Launch Voter Registration Drive," August 29, 1976, "Hispanic Voter Drive, 8/29/76," Box 1047, BSA; "For Immediate Release: NWPC Endorses Abzug Bid for US Senate," n.d., "Aug '76," Box 1052, BSA; "Lawyers for Bella," Box 1046, BSA; "Clubs Supporting Bella," n.d., "Local Races Sept/1976," Box 1046, BSA; "NDC People for Bella," May 8, 1976, "El Dario," Box 1051, BSA.

54. Other key staff included David Burke, Harold Holzer, Lynne Abraham, Bob Ortiz, Jerry Skurnik, Steve Max, Ed Serrapede, Judy Colp, Carol Bellamy, Arnie Weiss, Bonnie Lobel, and Dorothy Samuels; for the final leg, Sid Davidoff directed a team that included Peter Arevallo, Patti Goldman, Gene Grossman, Jean Wolcott, and Sally Grant Morse. "Let's start from scratch, although . . . ," n.d., 2–6, 2, "Lists for O'Neill Breakfast," Box 1043, BSA. See also Harold Holzer, "Remembering Maggi Peyton," *NYT,* October 27, 2016; Ruth B. Mandel, *In the Running: The New Woman Candidate* (New Haven, CT: Ticknor and Fields, 1981), 229.

55. EM14.

56. EM14; "Protesting Graduates Walk Out on Moynihan," *WP,* June 12, 1976, A4. For representative speeches, see Folders 1–5, Box 384, Part I, DPMP.

57. Abzug quoted in Maurice Carroll, "Senate Hopefuls in First Debate: Five Democratic Candidates Expound on Qualifications to Fill Buckley's Seat," *NYT,* August 23, 1976, 1.

58. Memorandum from Robert Wolthuis to Marsh, January 21, 1975, "Memo File: Jan.–Feb. 1975," Box 3, RW.

59. Troy, *Moynihan's Moment,* 56.

60. Daniel P. Moynihan, "The United States in Opposition," *Commentary* 59, no. 3 (March 1975): 31–44, 31; Barbara J. Keys, *Reclaiming American Virtue: The Human Rights Revolution of the 1970s* (Cambridge, MA: Harvard University Press, 2016), 217–221.

61. Moynihan quoted in Troy, *Moynihan's Moment,* 57, see generally, 56–59.

62. "Speech by Rep. Bella Abzug to 51st Convention, Columbia Scholastic Press Assn., Hotel Commodore," March 15, 1975, 1–17, 3, "HRNS-CIA and Secret Service Exemptions in Privacy Act, 3/13/75," Box 18, GIIRGO; Abzug quoted in Philip A. McCombs, "US Visitors See Cambodia on Run," *WP,* March 2, 1975, 23.

63. Memorandum from Robert K. Wolthuis to Friedersdorf, March 3, 1975, "Memo File: March 1975," 1–4, 3, Box 3, RW.

64. "A Report from Bella Abzug on Congress and South Vietnam," April 25, 1975, "HR 6096 (Vietnam Evacuation)," Box 389, BSA; Robert David Johnson, *Congress and the Cold War* (Cambridge: Cambridge University Press, 2006), 208–209.

65. For a clip of such coverage, see https://www.cbsnews.com/pictures/fall-of -saigon-vietnam-anniversary/13/.

66. Gerald Ford quoted in J. Y. Smith and Abzug in accompanying photo, "100 Picket at White House against A-Weapon," *WP*, July 9, 1975, 47; "Campaign for Survival. "From the Office of Congresswoman Bella S. Abzug," May 9, 1975, "Survival Campaign," Box 501, BSA; Michael Stewart Foley, *Front Porch Politics: The Forgotten Heyday of American Activism in the 1970s and 1980s* (New York: Hill and Wang, 2013), 121–149.

67. Ford quoted in Yanek Mieczkowski, *Gerald Ford and the Challenges of the 1970s* (Lexington: University Press of Kentucky, 2005), 295.

68. "Statement by Rep. Bella S. Abzug on Cambodia," draft, May 14, 1975, "Mayaguez Incident," Box 387, BSA.

69. "Big Nuclear Test Is Held in Nevada," *NYT*, May 15, 1975, 26.

70. Samuel Moyn, "The Return of the Prodigal: The 1970s as a Turning Point in Human Rights History," in *The Breakthrough: Human Rights in the 1970s,* ed. Jan Eckel and Samuel Moyn (Philadelphia: University of Pennsylvania Press, 2014), 1–14, 3.

71. Keys, *Reclaiming American Virtue,* 3; Sarah B. Snyder, *Human Rights Activism and the End of the Cold War: A Transnational History of the Helsinki Network* (Cambridge: Cambridge University Press, 2011).

72. Daniel P. Moynihan, *Counting Our Blessings: Reflections on the Future of America* (Boston: Little, Brown, 1980), 91.

73. Representative Robert Kasten (R-WI) initiated action on this issue when he learned that the Corps of Engineers did not assign Jewish employees to Saudi Arabia, and the matter was referred by government operations chair Jack Brooks to the Abzug Committee. Abzug quoted in *Discriminatory Overseas Assignment Policies of Federal Agencies,* 94th Cong., 1st and 2nd Sess., April 8–9, 1975 and July 27, 1976, 14.

74. Rhodri Jeffreys-Jones, *Changing Differences: Women and the Shaping of American Foreign Policy, 1917–1994* (New Brunswick, NJ: Rutgers University Press, 1995), 144. See also Keys, *Reclaiming American Virtue,* 120–126.

75. Salim Yaqub, *Imperfect Strangers: Americans, Arabs, and U.S.–Middle East Relations in the 1970s* (Ithaca, NY: Cornell University Press, 2016); Douglas Little, *American Orientalism: The United States and the Middle East since 1945* (Chapel Hill: University of North Carolina Press, 2008).

76. Thomas Borstelmann, *The 1970s: A New Global History from Civil Rights to Economic Equality* (Princeton, NJ: Princeton University Press, 2012), 208–214.

77. Hashomer Hatzair position quoted in Michael Staub, *Torn at the Roots: The Crisis of Jewish Liberalism in Postwar America* (New York: Columbia University Press, 2002), 287.

78. Staub, *Torn at the Roots,* 144.

79. "I Look Forward with Great . . . ," n.d., "Trip, 1971," Box 292, BSA.

80. "List of Guests at Party of Mrs. Ora Namir, General Secretary, Working Mothers' Association," n.d., "Trip, 1971," Box 292, BSA; "Bella Abzug—the US Congresswoman," translation, *Ha'aretz,* August 11, 1971, 13, Box 292, BSA;

"Visit to Israel," August 9–15, 1971, "Trip, 1973," Box 292, BSA; Abzug, ZI, Tape 28, Side B, 1 (753)–13 (765); "Statement to Subcommittee on Europe," draft, November 6, 1971, 1–4, 3, "Legislative Accomplishments, 1971–1976," Box 727, BSA.

81. Masaya Sato, "Bella Abzug's Dilemma: The Cold War, Women's Politics, and the Arab-Israeli Conflict in the 1970s," *Journal of Women's History* 30, no. 2 (Summer 2018): 112–135, 118.

82. Abzug, ZI, Tape 28, Side B, 8 (760).

83. Abzug, "A New Foreign Aide Bill," *CR* reprint, November 4, 1971, "Foreign Affairs—Foreign Aid—Abzug, Statements," Box 275, BSA.

84. Kelber drafted this response despite disagreement, Abzug to Myron Holtzman, January 10, 1974, "Correspondence," Box 291, BSA.

85. "Representative Abzug Calls for Immediate Cease Fire in Arab-Israeli War: Deplores Shocking Aggression on Yom Kippur," October 9, 1973, "Statements, Notes, and Memoranda," Box 291, BSA; Linda Greenhouse, "News of Conflict Given at Yom Kippur Prayers," *NYT,* October 6, 1973, 12.

86. Judith A. Kinghoffer, *Vietnam, Jews and the Middle East: Unintended Consequences* (New York: St. Martin's Press, 1999).

87. Abzug irked Ed Koch and Ben Rosenthal by releasing these Israeli POW images alone and then asking Representatives Marjorie Holt and Patricia Schroeder to help her with publicity. Abzug, "Golda," n.d., "Statements, Notes, and Memoranda," Box 291, BSA; "Evidence," handwritten notes, n.d., "Prisoners of War," Box 293, BSA; "Photos Termed Israeli Evidence of Syrian Atrocities," *NYT,* November 27, 1973, 16; Abzug, Marjorie Holt, and Patricia Schroeder to "Dear Colleagues," November 29, 1973, "Prisoners of War," Box 293, BSA; EKOH, 387; "Memorandum of Telephone Conversation, Bella Abzug/Secretary Kissinger," October 29, 1973, 4:23 p.m., 1–2, 1, The Kissinger Telephone Conversations: A Verbatim Record of US Diplomacy, 1969–1977, Digital National Security Archive.

88. "Statement of Bella Abzug, Co-plaintiff in Arab Boycott Suit against Secretaries of Commerce and Interior," November 17, 1975, "Arab Boycott Suit," Box 135, BSA.

89. KLK11; Mike, Jeanne, and Eric Holtzman to Abzug, November 27, 1973, "Correspondence," Box 291, BSA; "Congresswoman Bella Abzug's Record: Support of Israel and the Rights of Soviet Jewry," 1–5, 1, n.d., "Legislative Accomplishments, 1971–1976," Box 727, BSA.

90. Ruth Gage-Colby and Elaine Eldridge to Jacob K. Javits, May 25, 1975, "WILPF," Box 294, BSA; "Bella Abzug Has Resigned from the Leftist Women's Organization Because of Its Opposition to Aid for Israel," *JDF,* June 18, 1975, Box 294, BSA; Abzug to Meyer Sticker, June 17, 1975, Box 294, BSA.

91. Abzug to members of Temple Shalom Senior Youth Group, March 13, 1974, "Correspondence," Box 399, BSA.

92. Abzug, ZI, Tape 16, Side B, 14 (471); LA07.

93. "Speech by Congresswoman Bella Abzug to National Council of Jewish Women, Area Four, Northeastern District, New York," October 6, 1974, "Statements and Releases," Box 599, BSA.

94. Abzug, "Rabbi Sally Priesand: One-Minute," November 23, 1973, "Memoranda, 1973, nd," Box 69, BSA.

95. "Declaration of Mexico on the Equality of Women and Their Contribution to Development and Peace," 1975, in *Report of the World Conference of the International Women's Year, Mexico City, 19 June–2 July 1975* (New York: United Nations, 1976), 2–8, 3, 6.

96. Abzug quoted in Richard Yaffe, "Women's Year Parley Distorted by UN Males, Says Bella," *NYJW,* July 19, 1975, 20; "Statement by Rep. Bella S. Abzug on the Declaration of Mexico," n.d., "Abzug—Notes, Memoranda, Statements, Activities," Box 619, BSA.

97. Abzug to the Editor, *T,* July 10, 1975, "Abzug—Notes, Memoranda, Statements, Activities," Box 619, BSA; Jocelyn Olcott, *International Women's Year: The Greatest Consciousness-Raising Event in History* (Oxford: Oxford University Press, 2017), 161–164; Joyce Antler, *Jewish Radical Feminism: Voices from the Women's Liberation Movement* (New York: New York University Press, 2018), 315–347.

98. Sato, "Bella Abzug's Dilemma," 115, 121–125.

99. Mrs. Pam Bates to Abzug, January 12, 1976, "China," Box 283, BSA; Abzug, Transcript, December 27, 1975, "Transcript and Itinerary," Box 964, BSA.

100. EM14.

101. Moynihan quoted in Olcott, *International Women's Year,* 218–219.

102. Moynihan quoted in Troy, *Moynihan's Moment,* 6, 150, and see generally, 132–157.

103. "Bella-Moynihan Platform Clash," *NYP,* June 14, 1976, Untitled Folder, Box 1046, BSA.

104. Abzug quoted in Keys, *Reclaiming American Virtue,* 235.

105. "Statement by Representative Bella Abzug on UN Vote on Israel," November 11, 1975, 1–2, "Zionism Resolution," Box 280, BSA.

106. Norman Podhoretz quoted in Thomas L. Jeffers, *Norman Podhoretz: A Biography* (Cambridge: Cambridge University Press, 2010), 189.

107. Frank Lynn, "Democrats in Senate Race Wooing New York's Jews," *NYT,* October 9, 1976, 47.

108. MB07.

109. Troy, *Moynihan's Moment,* 133, 135.

110. "An Abzug Assault on Multinationals: 'Women Exploited,'" *NYT,* July 2, 1975, 35; "Remarks by Rep. Bella Abzug at IWY Conference, Mexico City," July 2, 1975, 1–7, 4, "Notes, Memoranda, Statements, Activities," Box 619, BSA; Olcott, *International Women's Year,* 207.

111. "Statement by Rep. Bella Abzug on Moynihan Labor Announcement," July 21, 1976, Folder Titled Same, Box 1049, BSA; "Rep. Abzug Says She Demonstrates 'Broadest Coalition of Labor Support'; Announces Endorsement of Amalgamated Clothing & Textile Workers," August 30, 1976, "Amalgamated Endorsement," Box 1047, BSA.

112. "Issues-Oriented Media Events," n.d., "Media Misc.," Box 1044, BSA; "Rep. Bella Abzug to Survey Harbor Cleanup Aboard 70-Foot Sailing Yawl

'Petrel' in of Sail Press Preview Cruise Friday, July 2," June 29, 1976, Folder Titled Same, Box 1048, BSA.

113. Hodgson, *The Gentleman from New York,* 35.

114. Eric Porter, "Affirming and Disaffirming Actions: Remaking Race in the 1970s," in *America in the Seventies,* ed. Beth Bailey and David Farber (Lawrence: University Press of Kansas, 2004), 50–74.

115. Louis Harris, Patrick Caddell, Peter Hart, and Abzug quoted in "Democratic Left Urged to Take Radical Posture, *WP,* March 16, 1975, 7.

116. Bruce F. Berg, *New York City Politics: Governing Gotham* (New Brunswick, NJ: Rutgers University Press, 2007), 58, and generally, 58–87.

117. Abzug's office considered this influential memo; Paul Posner, "Federal Grant Programs: Costs to New York City," 1–7, 1, "Fiscal Crisis—General (2)," Box 467, BSA.

118. Selwyn Raab, "Not Much Is Certain, Except Dirty Streets: When a City Cuts Back Hard," *NYT,* July 27, 1975, E6.

119. Ed Koch to New York Democratic Delegation, July 14, 1975, "New York City and State Congressional Delegations," Box 469, BSA; "Rep. Bella Abzug Proposes Voluntary Campaign by New Yorkers to Bail Out City, Ranging from Day's Past to Interest-Free Loans from NYC Banks, Reps. Reuss, Young, Dr. Rivlin Join in Community Conference on Recession," May 17, 1975, "Abzug—Statements, Notes, Memoranda, Activities," Box 403, BSA.

120. Considering the local roots of the neoliberal turn, see Benjamin Holtzman, *The Long Crisis: New York City and the Path to Neoliberalism* (Oxford: Oxford University Press, forthcoming).

121. Kim Phillips-Fein, *Fear City: New York's Fiscal Crisis and the Rise of Austerity Politics* (New York: Metropolitan Books, 2017), 168–176.

122. Phillips-Fein, *Fear City,* 200, and generally, 177–202.

123. "Major Legislative Accomplishments, 1971–1976," n.d., "Legislative Accomplishments—1971–1976," Box 727, BSA.

124. "Statement by Rep. Bella Abzug on President Ford's Veto of Public Works Bill," July 6, 1976, "July 1976, Senate Release," Box 1042, BSA. For Abzug's advocacy of the Public Works Employment Act of 1976, see Box 523, BSA.

125. "Bella Abzug Works for *ALL* New Yorkers," n.d., "Briefings," Box 1043, BSA.

126. "Rep. Abzug Proposes Program to End 'Regional Recession' Plaguing Northeast," June 28, 1976, "July 1976, Senate Race," Box 1042, BSA.

127. "Speech by Rep. Bella S. Abzug to Overseas Press Club," April 20, 1976, 1–8, 2, "Udall, Morris," Box 505, BSA.

128. Moynihan, "The United States in Opposition," 41.

129. Moynihan quoted in "Capitalism's World Struggle: An Interview with UN Ambassador Daniel Patrick Moynihan," *Nation's Business* 64, no. 2 (February 1976): 20.

130. "Congresswoman Bella Abzug's Record: A New National Energy Policy," n.d., 1–6, 4, "Legislative Accomplishments, 1971–1976," Box 727, BSA; "Congresswoman Bella Abzug's Record: Jobs for All Americans," n.d., Box 727, BSA.

131. "Congresswoman Abzug Outlines Steps to Reduce High Energy Costs in Northeast: Proposes Crash Development of Solar Energy in the State," September 8, 1976, "September 1976 Senate Release," Box 1048, BSA; "Rep. Abzug Introduces Bill to Protect Workers Hit by Plant Shutdowns in Environmental Cases," May 10, 1976, Folder Titled Same, Box 1049, BSA.

132. Memorandum from Kelber to Abzug, December 16, 1975, "Westway, Mass Transit, and Railroads," Box 1045, BSA; "Bella Gets Gold Token of Appreciation for Aid to NYC Mass Transit," July 29, 1976, "July 1976, Senate Race," Box 1042, BSA; "Statement against Beame Shuffle Repeal," n.d., Box 1045, BSA; Memorandum from Carolyn S. Konheim et al. to Abzug, n.d., Box 1045, BSA; William W. Buzbee, *Fighting Westway: Environmental Law, Citizen Activism, and the Regulatory War That Transformed New York City* (Ithaca, NY: Cornell University Press, 2004), 22–30.

133. "Rep. Abzug Says She Will Fight for Increased National Commitment to Mass Transit in NY State," November 10, 1976, "September 1976 Senate Releases," Box 1048, BSA.

134. Abzug, "Letter to Carey/Beame on Westway," draft, n.d., Box 1045, BSA; Marcy Benstock to Abzug, October 24, 1975, Box 1045, BSA.

135. "To Require That State Highway Safety Programs Make Provision for Curb Ramps for the Handicapped," July 1, 1976, "Legislation," Box 558, BSA; "Congress Clears Compromise Highway Bill," *CQWR* 34, no. 16 (April 17, 1976): 941–943.

136. EH14.

137. "Veto of Labor-HEW Funds Bill Overridden," *CQWR* 34, no. 40 (October 2, 1976): 2684; J. Brooks Flippen, *Jimmy Carter, the Politics of Family, and the Rise of the Religious Right* (Athens: University of Georgia Press, 2011), 91.

138. For Abzug's shepherding of H.R. Res. 15124, see Box 541, BSA.

139. Memorandum from Marsha to Bella, "Accomplishments Notebook," August 14, 1974, Box 541, BSA; "Statement by Rep. Bella S. Abzug at Announcement of Legal Action to Prevent Shutdown of Day Care Centers July 1," June 21, 1976, "BSA Announcement of Legal Action to Prevent Shutdown of Day Care Centers July 1, 1976," Box 1047, BSA.

140. "Statement by R. Bella S. Abzug (D-L, Man.-Bronx) at Board of Higher Education Hearing on Proposed Reorganization of City University," March 8, 1976, 1–4, 1, "Abzug—Statements, Notes, Memos," Box 203, BSA; Edward B. Fiske, "Tuition Imposed at City U., Ending a 129-Year Policy," *NYT,* June 2, 1976, 1; Phillips-Fein, *Fear City,* 242–255.

141. Abzug to Jacqueline Wexler, draft, "Correspondence, 1975–1976," Box 398, BSA.

142. "Statement by R. Bella S. Abzug (D-L, Man.-Bronx) at Board of Higher Education," 4.

143. "Rep. Abzug Asks for Prosecution of US Firms Collaborating with Arab Boycott," July 12, 1976, 1–2, 2, "July 1976, Senate Race," Box 1042, BSA; "Bella's Tax Program," May 15, 1976, "Abzug—Notes, Memoranda, Statements and Activities," Box 549, BSA.

144. "Abzug Charges Moynihan Must Bear Some of Responsibility for Nixon-Agnew Urban Policies," September 2, 1976, "September 1976 Senate Release," Box 1048, BSA.

145. "Moynihan Assails Abzug for Votes against Welfare Reform," August 20, 1976, "August 20, 1976—Moynihan Welfare Attack on BSA, and BSA Response," Box 1047, BSA.

146. Andelic, "Daniel Patrick Moynihan," 1125.

147. Moynihan, "The Liberal's Dilemma: A Professor's Stump Speech That Worked," *NR*, January 22, 1977, https://newrepublic.com/article/104073/the -liberals-dilemma.

148. ECOA Amendments that Abzug sponsored during her Senate race further accounted for the intersectional concern of "secondary discrimination." Abzug quoted in "How Can Women Achieve Their Legal Rights to Property and Credit?," in "Women as Economic Equals: Conference Proceedings, March 21, 1973, Shoreham Hotel, Washington, DC" (San Francisco: National Bank Americard Inc., 1973), 45–55, 45, 52; "Congresswoman Bella Abzug's Record: More Consumer Protection," n.d., "Legislative Accomplishments, 1971–1976," Box 727, BSA; "Statement of Representative Bella S. Abzug before the Federal Reserve Board Regarding Implementation of the ECOA Amendments of 1976 (Public Law 94–239)," n.d., "Abzug—Notes, Memoranda, Statements and Releases," Box 609, BSA.

149. Western NY Chapter, Knights of Columbus, "ERA—Equality or Subjugation?," advertisement, November 3, 1975, "NY State," Box 615, BSA.

150. "Vote on ERA," clipping, *NYT,* November 6, 1975, "NY State," Box 615, BSA.

151. Dick Zander, "Is Abzug Tarred by the ERA Brush?," *Newsday,* November 7, 1975, "Press Clippings," Box 1046, BSA.

152. Pete Hamill, "Does the Women's Movement Still Have Clout?," *VV,* November 17, 1975, "Press," Box 1046, BSA; Abzug's response, "The Women's Movement Is Still Moving," *VV,* December 22, 1975, 33, "Women—Equal Rights Amendment—NY State," Box 615, BSA.

153. "Is This Life Worth 8¢?," n.d., Untitled Folder, Box 1042, BSA; Stacie Taranto, *Kitchen Table Politics: Conservative Women and Family Values in New York* (Philadelphia: University of Pennsylvania Press, 2017), 129–161.

154. Moynihan paraphrased and Abzug quoted in Maurice Carroll, "5-Way Senate Race in NY Heads for a Weary Finish," *NYT,* September 13, 1976, 1.

155. Abzug aides shifted the language "sexual orientation or marital status" to "affectional preference" after input from activists. Memorandum from Marcosson to Abzug, September 23, 1974, "Abzug—Notes and Memos," Box 153, BSA; Memorandum from Jay to Abzug, December 4, 1974, Box 153, BSA; "Dear Colleague," January 22, 1975, "Statements and Activities," Box 153, BSA; "HR 166," 94th Cong., 1st Sess., January 14, 1975, "Statements and Activities," Box 153, BSA.

156. "Statement by Bella S. Abzug on Supreme Court Ruling on Homosexual Conduct," draft, March 30, 1976, 1–2, 2, "Statements and Activities," Box 153, BSA; Chai R. Feldblum, "The Federal Gay Rights Bill: From Bella to ENDA," in *Creating Change: Sexuality, Public Policy, and Civil Rights,* ed. John D' Emilio,

William B. Turner, and Urvashi Vaid (New York: St. Martin's Press, 2000), 149–187.

157. Eric Walther, biographer of Harvey Milk, shared this photograph in Folder 11, Box 19, Harvey Milk Archives and Scott Smith Collection, GLC 35, James C. Hormel LGBTQUIA Center, San Francisco Public Library, San Francisco, California.

158. "Rep. Abzug Says She Expects Women's Representation Issue to Help Her in Tuesday's Democratic Primary," September 13, 1976, "September 1976 Senate Releases," Box 1048, BSA.

159. "Speech by Congresswoman Bella Abzug on Quotas at Democratic Women's Club," draft, March 13, 1973, 1–18, 2, "Civil Rights and Human Rights—Discrimination, Affirmative Action," Box 151, BSA; Nancy MacLean, *Freedom Is Not Enough: The Opening of the American Workplace* (Cambridge, MA: Harvard University Press, 2008).

160. "Abzug for Senate," flyer, September 13, 1976, "Briefings," Box 1043, BSA; James A. Wechsler, "How Famous a Victory?," *NYP,* September 16, 1976, Untitled Folder, Box 1055, BSA.

161. Ireland quoted in Levine and Thom, *Bella Abzug,* 176; Ronald Smothers, "Mrs. Abzug Urged to Retract Repudiation of Moynihan," *NYT,* September 1, 1976, 27.

162. Sally Grant Morse, "Campaign Saturday with Bella: An Advanceperson's Adventure & Journal: The Senate Primary 1976," n.d., 1–14, 7, Folder 14, Box 156, GSP.

163. Holzer quoted in Levine and Thom, *Bella Abzug,* 177.

164. Crangle quoted in Ray Herman, "Crangle Raps Bella on Moynihan Stand," clipping, *Buffalo Courier,* September 1, 1976, "Concord," Box 1055, BSA. Rowland Evans and Robert Novak, openly favoring Moynihan, boosted Crangle in "Moynihan: Breaking Myths," *WP,* September 13, 1976, A23.

165. Sandra "Sarah" S. Kovner and Victor A. Kovner, "Opportunist to the End," *NYT,* September 9, 1976, 38.

166. "Moynihan for Senate," with Abzug notations, *NYT,* September 10, 1976, Untitled Folder, Box 1056, BSA; HH14.

167. Ireland quoted in Levine and Thom, *Bella Abzug,* 176.

168. Abzug wrote, "This disclaimer was deliberately printed the following day," on John B. Oakes, "Moynihan Endorsement," *NYT,* September 11, 1976, Untitled Folder, Box 1056, BSA; Oakes in Levine and Thom, *Bella Abzug,* 178.

169. EM14. See also Andelic, "Daniel Patrick Moynihan," 1128.

170. Abzug liked this article so much, she reprinted it as a final "Bella Abzug for Senator" campaign flyer; Wechsler, "How Famous a Victory?"

171. "Today we are announcing formation . . . ," n.d., "Lists for O'Neill Breakfast," Box 1043, BSA; "Concerned Democrats Urge Progressives to Unite behind Abzug Candidacy," September 10, 1976, "Concerned Dems. Sept. 10, 1976," Box 1049, BSA.

172. Bella Abzug with Mim Kelber, *Gender Gap: Bella Abzug's Guide to Political Power for American Women* (Boston: Houghton Mifflin, 1984), 184.

173. Ireland quoted in Levine and Thom, *Bella Abzug,* 180; "Madison North: Spot Television Schedule: Bella Abzug," August 30, 1976, "Media Misc. (III)," Box 1044, BSA.

174. The upstate totals were Moynihan, 69,754; Abzug, 65,839; Hirschfeld, 10,039; Clark, 30,287; and O'Dwyer, 10,181. Lynn, "Voter Turn Out Light"; "How They Voted throughout the City," *NYP,* September 15, 1976, 27.

175. Irene Drajem paraphrased in Mandel, *In the Running,* 247.

176. Lynn, "Voter Turn Out Light."

177. "Statement by Rep. Bella S. Abzug, Summit Hotel," September 14, 1976, 1–3, 1, 3, "DPM," Box 1057, BSA; Robert McG. Thomas Jr., "Moynihan and Abzug Supporters Hold Their Spirits in Abeyance," *NYT,* September 15, 1976, 28.

178. Dellums quoted in Levine and Thom, *Bella Abzug,* 170.

179. Morse, "Campaign Saturday with Bella," 14.

180. Joyce Purnick, "Weiss Says He'll Seek Abzug's Job," *NYP,* May 20, 1976, "Abzug, Bella Savitzky—Press Clippings, 1976: Senate Race," Box 1054, BSA.

181. Ted Weiss and Mary Ann Krupsack quoted in Maurice Carroll, "Weiss Spurns Plea to End Bid for Senate Left by Mrs. Abzug," *NYT,* September 22, 1976, 1.

182. Thomas P. Ronan, "Liberal Party Split on Senate Race," *NYT,* September 25, 1976, 36; Foner to D. Harrington, October 9, 1976, Folder 3, Box 4, HFP; Harrington to Foner, October 5, 1976, Box 4, HFP; Foner and Harrington in Levine and Thom, *Bella Abzug,* 181.

183. Abzug raised more initially, with $250,000 in comparison to Moynihan's $100,000 by July 1976, but by the end of the race Moynihan outspent Abzug three to one according to her camp. Scant financial records have been preserved. Sam Roberts, "A Tale of Two Cities: How Long Will the Spirit of the Garden Survive Here?," *DN,* July 19, 1976, 28, "Press Clippings," Box 1044, BSA; "Dear Friend," draft, n.d., "Women for Bella List," Box 1057, BSA.

184. Memorandum from Arthur to Abzug, September 21, 1976, 1–4, 2, 4, "Election," Box 1049, BSA.

185. Moynihan quoted in Wechsler, "How Famous a Victory?"

186. Norman Podhoretz, *Breaking Ranks: A Political Memoir* (New York: Harper and Row, 1979), 357.

187. Abzug quoted in Marty Racine, "The Only One Talking Is," *Bugle-American,* October 22, 1976, 20–23, 21, "1976 Clippings," Box 1044, BSA.

10. International Women's Year at Home

1. Carol Kleiman, "Wait'll Next Time: Bella," *CT,* June 30, 1975, 2; Viola Osgood, "Women Urged to Take Bigger Role in World Affairs," *BG,* June 28, 1975, 3; "Rep. Bella Abzug Tells NWPC Boston Meeting World Survival Is 'Women's Issue,' Calls for Peace Initiatives at Mexico City IWY Conference," June 27, 1975, "Notes, Memoranda, Statements, Activities," Box 619, BSA.

2. Karen Gardner, *Shaping a Global Women's Agenda: Women's NGOs and Global Governance, 1925–1985* (Manchester: Manchester University Press, 2010).

3. Marjorie J. Spruill, *Divided We Stand: The Battle Over Women's Rights and Family Values That Polarized American Politics* (New York: Bloomsbury USA, 2017); Doreen J. Mattingly and Jessica L. Nare, "'A Rainbow of Women': Diversity and Unity at the 1977 U.S. International Women's Year Conference," *Journal of Women's History* 26, no. 2 (2014): 89–112.

4. Phyllis Schlafly, "The Ripoff of the Taxpayers Known As: The Commission on International Women's Year or, Bella Abzug's Boondoggle," *PSR* 9, no. 6, sect. 2, January 1976, 1, Folder 30, Box 18, CE.

5. *The Spirit of Houston: An Official Report to the President, the Congress and the People of the United States* (Washington, DC: US Government Printing Office, 1978), 114–115; Shelah Leader and Patricia Hyatt, *American Women on the Move: The Inside Story of the National Women's Conference, 1977* (Lexington, MA: Lexington Books, 2016), 76, 86.

6. Thirty-five percent of delegates identified as nonwhite. For demographic analysis, see Alice Rossi, *Feminists in Politics: A Panel Analysis of the First National Women's Conference* (Cambridge, MA: Academic Press, 1982).

7. Abzug was the sole sponsor of H.R. Res. 4346, 94th Cong., 1st Sess., March 6, 1975, "Legislation—Printed," Box 621, BSA; Abzug, "International Women's Year," *CR,* March 6, 1975, E946; Patsy Mink, "Remarks in the U.S. House of Representatives Concerning a White House Conference on Women in 1976," March 10, 1975, Folder 6, Box 562, PMP.

8. Margaret Heckler quoted in "Elsewhere in the News . . . International," *BG,* June 30, 1975, 2.

9. Jocelyn Olcott, "Empires of Information: Media Strategies for the 1975 International Women's Year," *Journal of Women's History* 24, no. 4 (Winter 2012): 24–48; Spruill, *Divided We Stand,* 52.

10. Memorandum from Patricia Lindh to Ralph Malvik, October 15, 1975, "NWC (IWY, 1976) (2)," Box 11, PLJH.

11. NCOIWY, ". . . *To Form a More Perfect Union . . .": Justice for American Women: Report of the National Commission on the Observance of International Women's Year* (Washington, DC: US Government Printing Office, 1976), 40–47.

12. Cynthia Harrison, "Creating a National Feminist Agenda: Coalition Building in the 1970s," in *Feminist Coalitions: Historical Perspectives on Second-Wave Feminism in the United States,* ed. Stephanie Gilmore (Urbana: University of Illinois Press, 2008), 19–47.

13. Spruill, *Divided We Stand,* 68; "IWY Government Organization Structure Committee, Rep. Bella S. Abzug, Chairwoman, Discussion Issues for Permanent Government Structure on Women's Affairs," n.d., "National Commission Meeting Feb. 26, 1976 (1)," Box 28, PLJH; Memorandum from Abzug to Commissioners, February 20, 1976, Box 28, PLJH; "Reactions to Draft Proposal: Govt Org Structure," n.d., "Gov't Organization Structures—General," Box 624, BSA.

14. The leading sponsors of this bill on the House side were Abzug, Lindy Boggs, Yvonne Burke, Shirley Chisholm, Cardiss Collins, Millicent Fenwick, Margaret Heckler, Elizabeth Holtzman, Martha Keys, Helen Meyner, Patsy Mink, Patricia Schroeder, and Gladys Spellman. The additional sponsors who

signed on in September were Barbara Jordan, Shirley Neil Pettis, John Conyers, Michael Harrington, Andrew Maguire, Pete McCloskey, Toby Moffett, John Moss, and Leo Ryan. Abzug et al., "H.R. 9924," 94th Cong., 1st Sess., September 30, 1975, Legislation Printed," Box 621, BSA.

15. H.R. Res. 4346, 6.

16. Lillian Rymarowicz to Abzug, July 17, 1975, "Correspondence and Dear Colleagues," Box 621, BSA; Eric Hirschhorn to Co-sponsors of H.R. 9924, December 9, 1975, Box 621, BSA; Abzug et al., "H.R. 8903," 94th Cong., 1st Sess., July 24, 1975, "Legislation Printed," Box 621, BSA; Mink, "Remarks in the U.S. House of Representatives Concerning a White House Conference on Women in 1976"; Judy Tzu-Chun Wu, "Envisioning the National Women's Conference: Patsy Takemoto Mink and Pacific Feminism," in *Suffrage at 100: Women's Uneven Road in American Politics since 1920,* ed. Stacie Taranto and Leandra Zarnow (Baltimore, MD: Johns Hopkins University Press, 2020).

17. For implementation of this delegate support, see Barbara Langham to Nikki Van Hightower, April 6, 1977, Folder 23, Box 5, NVH.

18. "H.R. 9924," 3; Sec. 3, A.2, PL 94.167.

19. Abzug, "Report on 'The Tribune Speakout,'" n.d., 1–7, 7, "General," Box 619, BSA; Jocelyn Olcott, *International Women's Year: The Greatest Consciousness-Raising Event in History* (Oxford: Oxford University Press, 2017), 7.

20. Olcott, *International Women's Year,* 5.

21. This sentiment was expressed at the "Mixed Outcomes of the 1977 IWY Conference" roundtable at the fortieth anniversary conference of the NWC held at the University of Houston in November 2017; http://www.uh.edu/class /mcgovern/national-women-conference/conference-schedule/.

22. Abzug to "Dear Sisters," October 21, 1975, "Correspondence and Dear Colleagues," Box 621, BSA; GIIR, *National Women's Conference,* 94th Cong., 1st and 2nd Sess., September 30, 1975; "Testimony of Jill Ruckelshaus, Presiding Officer of the National Commission to Observe IWY, 1975 on HR 8903 before GIIR," September 30, 1975, "NWC (IWY, 1976) (1)," Box 11, PLJH. For hearing planning documents and H.R. Res. 8903 drafts, see "Abzug—Notes, Memoranda, and Statements, Releases, BSA Conferences, National," Box 620, BSA.

23. "Statement by Phyllis Schlafly, National Chairman, Stop ERA, Before GIIR," September 30, 1975, "Hearings and Testimony," Box 621, BSA; "House Rejection: Women's Conference, *CQWR* 33, no. 43 (October 25, 1975): 3; Eileen Shanahan, "Antifeminist Says Federal Funds Aid Equal Rights Group," *NYT,* June 5, 1975, 40; *CQ,* October 25, 1975, 2267, "NWC (IWY, 1976) (1)," Box 11, PLJH.

24. Abzug to Dear Colleague, November 3, 1975, "Correspondence and Dear Colleagues," Box 621, BSA; Abzug et al. to Dear Colleague, December 9, 1975, "Correspondence and Dear Colleagues," Box 621, BSA.

25. Sam Steiger quoted in clipping, *CR,* December 10, 1975, H12196, "NWC (IWY, 1976) (2)," Box 11, PLJH; Steiger and Bob Baumer to Dear Colleagues, December 8, 1975, "Correspondence and Dear Colleagues," Box 621, BSA.

26. "Final Action: Women's Conference," *CQWR* 33, no. 52 (December 27, 1975): 2893–2894.

27. Memorandum from Lynn to Gerald Ford with Ford notations, October 30, 1975, "NWC (IWY, 1976) (2)," Box 11, PLJH; Abzug et al. to Dear Colleague, May 6, 1976, "Correspondence and Dear Colleague," Box 621, BSA.

28. Birch Bayh to Montoya, April 15, 1976, "Abzug—Notes, Memos, and Statements," Box 621, BSA; Malvik to Lindh et al., December 16, 1975, "NWC (IWY, 1976) (2)," Box 11, PLJH; Abzug et al. to "Dear Senator," April 28, 1976, "IWY, Conferences, National—Legislation—Corresp., 'Dear Colleagues,'" Box 621, BSA.

29. "Ford, Congress Increase Funds for Militant Women's Lobby," *HE* 36, no. 22 (May 29, 1976): 1.

30. Abzug to Jimmy Carter, May 3, 1976, "Carter Campaign," Box 963, BSA.

31. Susan Hartmann, "Feminism, Public Policy, and the Carter Administration," in *The Carter Presidency: Policy Choices in the Post–New Deal Era,* ed. Gary M. Fink and Hugh Davis Graham (Lawrence: University Press of Kansas, 1998), 224–243; J. Brooks Flippen, *Jimmy Carter, the Politics of Family, and the Rise of the Religious Right* (Athens: University of Georgia Press, 2011).

32. Abzug paraphrased in and Midge Costanza quoted in Doreen J. Mattingly, *A Feminist in the White House: Midge Costanza, the Carter Years, and America's Culture Wars* (Oxford: Oxford University Press, 2016), 69, 71; Abzug, "The leading liberal cand. is Morris Udall . . . ," note, n.d., "Independent Slate," Box 1055, BSA.

33. Louise Sweeny, "Abzug: 3 Women Good V-P Picks," *CSM,* July 2, 1976, 7; Dorothy Collin, "No Longer Babes in Politics," *CT,* July 6, 1976, B1.

34. Sweeny, "Abzug: 3 Women Good V-P Picks."

35. Abzug quoted in Eileen Shanahan, "Compromise Reached on Women's Role," *NYT,* July 13, 1976, 1; Hamilton Jordan, "Proposed substitute language for Rules . . . ," notes, July 9, 1976, "Women's Meeting with Carter at Convention, 7/11/76," Box 300, CL; Mim Kelber, "Meeting with Carter," July 11, 1976, "Women's Mtg. w/Jimmy Carter July 1976 (Handwritten Notes by MK)," Box 995, BSA; "Summary of Women's Caucus Meetings with Governor Carter, July 11 & 12," n.d., "Democratic Convention, 1976," Box 967, BSA; Gloria Steinem, "The City Politic: Kissing with Your Eyes Open: Women and the Democrats," *NY,* July 26, 1976, 6.

36. Memorandum from Cooki Lutkefedder to Landon Butler, September 17, 1976, 5, "Committee of 51.3%," Box 202, LB.

37. Memorandum from Mary King, Cooki Lutkefedder, and Anita Nelam, September 9, 1976, 1–2, 1, "Abortion," Box 294, CL; Memorandum from King, Lutkefedder, and Nelam to Butler and Fran Voorde, September 17, 1976, 1–7, 1, "Committee of 51.3%," Box 202, LB.

38. Jordan, handwritten note on Memorandum from King, Lutkefedder, and Nelam to Jordan, September 7, 1976, 1, "Memorandums," Box 296, CL.

39. Bella Abzug with Mim Kelber, *Gender Gap: Bella Abzug's Guide to Political Power for American Women* (Boston: Houghton Mifflin, 1984), 50.

40. Carter quoted in Bill Peterson, "Carter Vows Fight for Women's Rights," *WP*, October 3, 1976, 1.

41. Memorandum from Barbara Blum to Jordan et al., October 11, 1976, "Memorandums," Box 296, CL.

42. Rowland Evans and Robert Novak, "Bella's Curtailed Barnstorm," *WP*, October 21, 1976, A15; "Game Plan," October 4, 1976, 3, "Memorandums," Box 296, CL.

43. Flippen, *Jimmy Carter*, 120.

44. Stuart E. Eizenstat to Jordan, February 10, 1977, "Presidential Appointments, 1976–77 [CF, O/A 414]," Box 51, HJ.

45. Rick Hutcheson to Jordan, February 16, 1977, "2/16/77 (1)," Box 7, OSS.

46. Telegram from Tip O'Neill et al. to Carter, December 22, 1976, "Carter," Box 966, BSA; Frank Lynn, "Aides of Carter Talk about Job for Mrs. Abzug," *NYT*, January 9, 1977, 15; Marie Brenner, "What Makes Bella Run?," *NY*, June 20, 1977, 54–64, 64.

47. Abzug with Kelber, *Gender Gap*, 56; "Summary: Women's Conference Meeting on Guidelines," January 30, 1976, "Notes, Memoranda, Statements, Releases, BSA Conferences, National," Box 620, BSA; Novick to Abzug, "Women's Conferences," n.d., "Corresp., 'Dear Colleagues,'" Box 621, BSA.

48. Elly Peterson quoted in Spruill, *Divided We Stand*, 125.

49. Costanza quoted in Mattingly, *A Feminist in the White House*, 147; Spruill, *Divided We Stand*, 122–125.

50. Maurice Carroll, "Mrs. Abzug Weighing Race for Mayoralty: Friends Expect Her to Announce Democratic Bid—Former Aide of Hers Joins Beame Effort," *NYT*, February 1, 1977, 28.

51. Abzug quoted in Judy Klemesrud, "Mrs. Abzug, Out of Race, Won't Talk about Future," *NYT*, September 16, 1976, 35.

52. Spruill, *Divided We Stand*, 117.

53. Spruill, *Divided We Stand*, 119–121; Mattingly, *A Feminist in the White House*, 74, 148.

54. The full issue planks concerned Arts and Humanities, Battered Women, Business, Child Abuse, Child Care, Credit, Disabled Women, Education, Elective and Appointive Office, Employment, the ERA, Health, Homemakers, Insurance, International Affairs, Media, Minority Women, Offenders, Older Women, Rape, Reproductive Freedom, Rural Women, Sexual Preference, Statistics, Welfare, and the Continuing Committee of the Conference. For Houston Women's March's reevaluation of these planks in 2017, see https://docs.google.com/forms/d /12HMYO3cMr08loCFAl0WoNy3RwIEb6D_AJzYzXDNo8e4/viewform?edit _requested=true.

55. Leader and Hyatt, *American Women on the Move*, 24–25.

56. June Zeitlin quoted in Leader and Hyatt, 24.

57. Abzug quoted in Leader and Hyatt, 25; Memorandum from Zeitlin to Abzug, November 10, 1976, "IWY Memo—Nov. 1976," Box 982, BSA.

58. Costanza quoted in Spruill, *Divided We Stand*, 131, and generally, 130–132, 195–196; Leader and Hyatt, *American Women on the Move*, 28–29; for incomplete minutes and agendas, see Folders 2 and 3, Box 18, CE.

59. Catherine East left the NCOIWY staff in September, siding with Martha Griffiths on this issue. Memorandum from Martha Griffiths to Presiding Officer and Members of the NCOIWY, April 14, 1977, 1–5, 2, Folder 10, Box 20, CE; East to Abzug, August 29, 1977, Folder 18, Box 20, CE.

60. Gloria D. Scott to Abzug, April 18, 1977, 1–4, 1, 3, Folder 10, Box 20, CE.

61. "Remarks of Bella S. Abzug, Presiding Officer, National Commission on the Observance of IWY to Informal Meeting of IWY State Coordinators," April 29, 1977, 1–4, 2, Folder 29, Box 18, CE.

62. Abzug quoted in Leader and Hyatt, *American Women on the Move*, 26.

63. Spruill, *Divided We Stand*, 86–88, 236–237.

64. John M. Crewdson, "Mormon Turnout Overwhelms Women's Conference in Utah," *NYT*, July 25, 1977, 27; Spruill, *Divided We Stand*, 174.

65. Abzug quoted in *CR*, September 22, 1977, excerpted in "Summary Sheet of Press Reports on the Tactics of Radical Right Wing Groups," 1–7, 7, Folder 30, Box 18, CE; Jack Anderson and Les Whitten, "Abzug's Run-In with the Mormons," *WP*, December 28, 1977, B16.

66. Abzug quoted in Meg O'Connor, "Women's Year Panel Supports ERA," *CT*, June 13, 1977, 3.

67. Spruill, *Divided We Stand*, 167–169.

68. Linn Galagher Stitt, AAUW Action Alert, 1–2, 2, June 15, 1977, Folder 1, Box 6, NVH; Spruill, *Divided We Stand*, 135–139, 186–188.

69. "Summary Sheet of Press Reports on the Tactics of Radical Right Wing Groups," 7.

70. "Federal Financing of a Foolish Festival for Frustrated Feminists," *PSR* 10, no. 10, sect. 2, May 1977, 1, Folder 30, Box 18, CE; Spruill, *Divided We Stand*, 145–149.

71. Phyllis Schlafly, *The Power of the Positive Woman* (New Rochelle, NY: Arlington House, 1977), 167, and generally, 166–176; Jane DeHart, "Gender on the Right: Meanings behind the Existential Scream," *Gender & History* 3, no. 3 (Autumn 1991): 246–267.

72. Photograph by Janice Blue accompanying Carol Bartholdi, "Return of the Minute Women," *Daily Breakthrough*, November 18, 1977, 5, University of Houston Digital Library, http://digital.lib.uh.edu/collection/feminist/item/4155 /show/4123; Linda Gillian, "Women's Conference Leaders Picketed," *LAT*, July 16, 1977, A14.

73. Abzug quoted in Maurice Carroll, "Mrs. Abzug Puts on Her Campaign Hat," *NYT*, January 2, 1977, 1.

74. Abzug, "City Club Speech," June 17, 1977, "Mayor, Speeches, Issues," 1–12, 12, Box 1029, BSA.

75. "Elect Congresswoman Abzug. Your Democratic Candidate. Vote Row B!," flyer, n.d., "New York City Mayoral 1977, Bella Literature," Box 1058, BSA.

76. For a full accounting of this race, see Jonathan Mahler, *Ladies and Gentlemen, The Bronx Is Burning: 1977, Baseball, Politics, and the Battle for the Soul of a City* (New York: Picador, 2005).

77. Charles Brecher and Raymond D. Horton with Robert A. Cropf and Dean Michael Mead, *Power Failure: New York City Politics and Policy since 1960* (New York: Oxford University Press, 1993), 95.

78. Spruill, *Divided We Stand*, 164.

79. It is unclear if this group realized that Abzug's former client Jay Gorney composed the original song "Brother, Can You Spare a Dime?" "Bella, Can You Spare a Dime?," flyer, n.d., Folder 30, Box 18, CE.

80. "Bella for Mayor: 'Let's Make New York a City of Opportunity for All Its People,'" n.d., Untitled Folder, Box 1068, BSA; "A Proposal for Economic Development in New York City" on "Bella Means Business" stationary, July 28, 1977, "Economic Development," Box 1066, BSA. Jonathan Soffer adroitly highlighted Abzug's inconsistency in messaging in *Ed Koch and the Rebuilding of New York City* (New York: Columbia University Press, 2010), 128.

81. Percy Sutton quoted in Soffer, *Ed Koch and the Rebuilding of New York City*, 125.

82. "Speech by Bella Abzug to NDC Nominating Meeting," draft, May 15, 1977, 1–4, 1, "General and Miscellaneous," Box 1067, BSA. For City Hall's diminishing social obligation, see Kim Phillips-Fein, *Fear City: New York's Fiscal Crisis and the Rise of Austerity Politics* (New York: Metropolitan Books, 2017), 301–316.

83. Ireland quoted in Andy Humm, "Two Pivotal Elections: What the 1977 Mayoral Race Can Tell Us about 2103," May 19, 2013, http://www.gotham gazette.com/index.php/elections/4241-a-pivotal-election-looking-back-at-the -1977-mayoral-race; "Staff Notes," n.d., "Memos—Inter Office," Box 1058, BSA; Carroll, "Mrs. Abzug Weighing Race for Mayoralty," 28.

84. Abzug quoted in "Bella for Mayor," flyer, n.d., "New York City Mayoral 1977, Bella Literature," Box 1058, BSA.

85. Abzug, "I'll Take Manhattan . . . The Bronx and Staten Island Too . . . ," *RS*, no. 249 (October 6, 1977): 54–57, 55.

86. Abzug quoted in "Bella for Mayor."

87. Robert D. McFadden, "'Disaster Status Given NY and Westchester to Speed Loans: Services Resume after Blackout," *NYT*, July 16, 1977, 1. For the Abzug campaign assessment of the blackout, "Memo: Looting, Blackout, and Police Manpower," n.d., "Briefings #2," Box 1068, BSA.

88. Abzug quoted in Maurice Carroll, "Mrs. Abzug Sprints While Rivals in Mayoral Race Pace Themselves," *NYT*, June 22, 1977, 27. For the Abzug campaign's tracking of polls up and down, see "Polls," Box 1070, BSA.

89. Abzug, "City Club Speech," June 17, 1977, "Mayor, Speeches, Issues," 1–12, 12, Box 1029, BSA.

90. Ruth Bader Ginsburg et al. to "Dear Friend," n.d., Folder 9, Box 517, RM; "Bella Abzug Fights for New York's Neighborhoods and the Neighborhoods Are Fighting for Bella," flyer, n.d., Box 517, RM.

91. Marie Brenner, "What Makes Bella Run?," *NY*, June 20, 1977, 54–64, 54.

92. Aurelio quoted in Carey Winfrey, "In Search of Bella Abzug," *NYT*, August 21, 1977, 190.

93. Anna Mayo, "Why Men Fear Bella," *VV*, July 4, 1977, 11.

94. Koch quoted in Frank Lynn, "Blackout and Looting Emerging as Issues in Mayoral Campaign," *NYT,* July 21, 1977, 27.

95. Jack W. Germond and Jules Witcover, "New York Blackout Was a Blessing in Disguise for Beame," *TS,* July 19, 1977, A15.

96. Abzug quoted in "What Bella Wants. Jobs for All," flyer, n.d., "NYC Mayoral 1977, Bella Literature," Box 1058, BSA; "New York's Stake in Full Employment," n.d., "September 6—Full Employment Paper," Box 1059, BSA; Memorandum from Dinni Gordon to Abzug, May 12, 1977, "Briefings #1," Box 1068, BSA; "Bella on Crime," n.d., "Crime—Capital Punishment," Box 1067, BSA; E. J. Dionne Jr., "Study of Takeover of Con Ed Is Urged: Citing 'Highest Rates and Lowest Reliability,' Mrs. Abzug Asks City Council to Back Inquiry DelBello Seeks Takeover," *NYT,* July 31, 1977, 36; Maurice Carroll, "Mrs. Abzug Revives City U. Tuition Issue," *NYT,* June 21, 1977, 33.

97. Abzug to Andrea Dworkin, February 27, 1976, "Snuff," Box 963, BSA; "Bella Abzug, Joined by Diverse Group of Women, Links Pornography Industry to 'Crime Wave Against Women': Outlines Anti-Porno Program," July 26, 1977, "Pornography," Box 1067, BSA.

98. Koch quoted in Francis X. Clines, "About New York: Koch on the Candidates," *NYT,* June 2, 1977, 30; Koch quoted in Soffer, *Ed Koch and the Rebuilding of New York City,* 129, and see generally, 121–144.

99. EKOH, 376; Abzug, "As you are undoubtedly aware . . . ," November 24, 1967, "17th CD PAC," Box 1004, BSA; Koch to Abzug, December 15, 1967, Box 1004, BSA; "1. What steps do you advocate . . . ?," n.d., "WSP," Box 1005, BSA.

100. Bella Abzug, "Bella Abzug on Mayor Koch," *NYT,* April 15, 1984; Edward Koch, *Mayor: An Autobiography* (New York: Simon and Schuster, 1984), 37–39.

101. EKOH, 375, 378; Soffer, *Ed Koch and the Rebuilding of New York City,* 76–80.

102. MB07.

103. Memorandum from Jan Levy to Kelber and Abzug, March 20, 1977, "NY State Women's Meeting," Box 982, BSA; "Plans for First New York State Women's Meeting Announced: Thousands Expected to Gather in Albany July 8–10," March 22, 1977, Box 982, BSA; Abzug to "Dear Friend," February 3, 1977, "IWY NY State Meeting 1977," Box 982, BSA.

104. Jennifer Dunning, "Women's Parley Opens in Albany," *NYT,* July 9, 1977, 16; "Feminists Prevail in Most States: Politics Dominates Women's Year Talks," *LAT,* July 11, 1977, B4.

105. Janice Prindle, "Running to Stay in Place," *VV,* July 18, 1977, 11.

106. Joanne Edgar quoted in Spruill, *Divided We Stand,* 179.

107. "Bella S. Abzug Promises Cabinet-Level Office for Handicapped, and to Make City Buildings Accessible to Them," August 19, 1977, "Handicapped," Box 1067, BSA; "Issue Paper on the Handicapped," n.d., 1–4, 4, "Handicapped," Box 1067, BSA.

108. Dudley Clendinen and Adam Nagourney, *Out for Good: The Struggle to Build a Gay Rights Movement in America* (New York: Simon and Schuster, 1999), 310.

109. Abzug and Beame quoted in Frank Lynn, "Mrs. Abzug's Opponents Denounce Defense of Right of Police to Strike," *NYT*, July 13, 1977, 18; "A Report from Bella Abzug: What I Really Said about Police and the 'Right' to Strike," July 15, 1977, "Unions," Box 1067, BSA; Bertrand B. Pogrebin to Abzug, July 20, 1977, "Briefings #2," Box 1068, BSA.

110. Frank Lynn, "Beame Finishes Third," *NYT*, September 9, 1977, 1; Lee Dembart, "Abzug Defeat Laid to 3 Candidates and Length of Primary Campaign," *NYT*, September 10, 1977, 15.

111. Terry O'Connell quoted in Dembart, "Abzug Defeat Laid to 3 Candidates and Length of Primary Campaign."

112. Stuart Eizenstat, notation on Memorandum from Beth Abramowitz to Eizenstat, July 22, 1977, "Women's Issues [O/A 6348] (5)," Box 323, SE.

113. Rosemary Thompson quoted in Spruill, *Divided We Stand*, 201, and see generally, 198–202.

114. Abzug to Carl Anderson, September 12, 1977, 1–3, 1, Folder 18, Box 19, CE.

115. Leader and Hyatt, *American Women on the Move*, 35.

116. "Executive Committee Minutes," October 19, 1977, Folder 3, Box 18, CE.

117. Carter to Abzug, October 27, 1977, "(NACW) Items Pre 1-12-79," Box 13, SW; Lee Novick to Costanza, July 27, 1977, "(NACW) Items Pre 1-12-79," Box 13, SW; Abzug to Carter, May 12, 1977, "(NACW) Items Pre 1-12-79," Box 13, SW; Mattingly, *A Feminist in the White House*, 153–156.

118. "Sharing Stories" NWC Oral Histories, November 2018, Special Collections, M. D. Anderson Library, University of Houston, Houston, Texas.

119. Elly M. Peterson, "Report on Houston," November 25, 1977, 1–8, 1, Folder 17, Box 20, CE.

120. Steinem to Susan, December 1, 1977, Folder 2, Box 142, GSP.

121. Abzug to Steinem, December 5, 1977, Folder 2, Box 142, GSP.

122. "Torch Relay Fact Sheet," August 22, 1977, Folder 12, Box 7, NVH; "Texas Schedule," n.d., 3 pp., Folder 12, Box 7, NVH.

123. Local news clip featured in the documentary *Sisters of '77* (Cynthia Salzman Mondell and Allen Mondell, 2005).

124. Abzug quoted in *The Spirit of Houston*, 129.

125. For Maya Angelou's, Barbara Jordan's, Liz Carpenter's, and Bella Abzug's remarks, see *The Bella Abzug Reader*, ed. Mim Kelber and Libby Bassett (New York: self-published, 2003), 127–134.

126. Elizabeth Cady Stanton made this address to the National American Woman Suffrage Association upon resigning; Stanton, "The Solitude of Self," 1892, http://voicesofdemocracy.umd.edu/elizabeth-cady-stanton-the-solitude-of-self-speech-to-the-house-judiciary-committee-18-february-1892/.

127. Bella Abzug, "Bella Abzug Opens the Plenary Session," in *The Bella Abzug Reader*, 128.

128. Leader and Hyatt, *American Women on the Move*, 73–76; "IWY Office Opens, Seeks Volunteers," clipping, n.d., Folder 4, Box 1, MR; "American Women on the Move" program, n.d., Folder 16, Box 1, MR.

129. Poppy Northcutt relayed this story to participants at a National Endowment for the Humanities Summer Seminar that I codirected at the University of Houston in June 2017.

130. Carmen Delgado Votaw quoted in Suzanne Braun Levine and Mary Thom, *Bella Abzug: How One Tough Broad from the Bronx Fought Jim Crow and Joe McCarthy, Pissed Off Jimmy Carter, Battled for the Rights of Women and Workers, Rallied Against War and for the Planet, and Shook Up Politics Along the Way* (New York: Farrar, Straus and Giroux, 2007), 207.

131. "Seneca Falls South, Something New, Something Different," program, Folder 13, Box 1, LM; Leader and Hyatt, *American Women on the Move,* 81–83.

132. Spruill, *Divided We Stand,* 221–222; "Unseat the Mississippi Delegation," Women for Racial and Economic Equality, n.d., Folder 14, Box 3, HNOW. For the Chicana Advisory Committee, see Box 9, Martha Cotera Papers, Benson Library, UT-Austin, Texas. Forthcoming work on the National Women's Conference include a volume edited by Judy Wu on Asian American delegates and Laura Lovett on African American participants. Activist Loretta Ross suggests the phrase "women of color" was first introduced at this conference, https://www.makers.com/videos/55474ed9e4b042cdf6207d6a.

133. "We Invite You to Join Us . . . ," November 18, 1977, Folder 14, Box 1, LM; Leader and Hyatt, *American Women on the Move,* 74.

134. Leader and Hyatt, *American Women on the Move,* 71.

135. Ann Richards quoted in *Sisters of '77.*

136. Abzug quoted in *The Spirit of Houston,* 152; Memorandum from Linda May to Linda and Margaret, September 18, 1977, Folder 13, Box 1, LM; Parliamentary Committee, n.d., Folder 13, Box 1, LM; Delegate Seating Plan, (Both Sides), Folder 13, Box 1, LM.

137. Robert K. Dornan quoted in Pat Reed, "Pro-family Groups Ink Proposals," *DB,* November 20, 1977, 4, Houston and Texas Feminist and Lesbian Newsletters, University of Houston Digital Library, http://digital.lib.uh.edu/collection/feminist/item/663/show/634.

138. Abzug quoted in *The Spirit of Houston,* 163.

139. *The Spirit of Houston,* 127.

140. Betty Friedan quoted in *The Spirit of Houston,* 166.

141. Anna Quindlen, "Women's Conference Approves Planks on Abortion and Rights for Homosexuals," *NYT,* November 21, 1977, 44; *The Spirit of Houston,* 165–166.

142. Abzug quoted in Leader and Hyatt, *American Women on the Move,* 71.

143. Friedan quoted in Spruill, *Divided We Stand,* 226. See also "Plank 26," in *The Spirit of Houston,* 97.

144. Sally Quinn quoted in Spruill, *Divided We Stand,* 224.

145. Leader and Hyatt, *American Women on the Move,* 101–107.

146. "Note: At the Request of . . . ," March 22, 1978, "Remarks Nat'l Women's Comm. Presentation to Carter," Box 986, BSA.

147. Costanza quoted in Levine and Thom, *Bella Abzug,* 214.

148. Costanza memo quoted in Mattingly, *A Feminist in the White House,* 177, and generally, 168–175.

149. This exchange is relayed secondhand, Abzug with Kelber, 65; Spruill, *Divided We Stand*, 265–266.

150. Memorandum from Eizenstat, Jody Powell, and Anne Wexler to Carter, April 24, 1978, "4/24/78 (2)," Box 72, OSS.

151. Peggy Rainwater to Abzug, May 19, 1978, Untitled Folder, Box 986, BSA; "Executive Order 12050," April 4, 1978, "Women's Advisory Committee [CF, O/A 647]," Box 57, HJ.

152. Abzug to "Dear Member of the County Committee," December 6, 1977, Loose Documents, Box 1032, BSA.

153. Abzug quoted in Frank Lynn, "Mrs. Abzug Announces Candidacy for Koch's East Side House Seat," *NYT,* December 20, 1977, 29; Lee Lescaze, "Abzug Facing Little-Known Opponent Today," *WP,* February 14, 1978, A6.

154. Abzug quoted in Frank Lynn, "Mrs. Abzug Presses for Nomination for House Seat," *NYT,* January 17, 1978, 22; "Missing Abzug Aide Cost Her 290.5 Votes," *NYT,* January 17, 1978, 22; Lynn, "Burden Is Nominated to Seek House Seat Surrendered by Koch," *NYT,* January 16, 1978; Lynn, "Recount Reaffirms Abzug Candidacy," *NYT,* January 21, 1978, 1.

155. Harold Holzer quoted in Levine and Thom, *Bella Abzug,* 188.

156. S. William Green quoted in Frank Lynn, "Mrs. Abzug Defeated Narrowly by Green; Garcia Wins in Bronx," *NYT,* February 15, 1978, 19.

157. John Keifner, "Evening Shadows Grow on a Political Life," *NYT,* February 15, 1978, A22.

158. Abzug quoted in "Bitter after Upset, Abzug Hits the Press," *HC,* February 16, 1978, 5.

159. Abzug and Votaw to "Dear Senator," draft with Abzug notations, n.d., Untitled Folder, Box 986, BSA; "President's Advisory Committee on Women Urges Senate to Vote on ERA Extension before Recess," September 21, 1978, Untitled Folder, Box 986, BSA; Mattingly, *A Feminist in the White House,* 190.

160. Anne Wexler quoted in Martin Schram, "The Story behind Bella's Departure," *WP,* January 17, 1979, A1.

161. Abzug and Votaw to Carter, October 6, 1978, "(NACW) Items Pre 1-12-1978," Box 13, SW; "Weddington: NACW Meeting," Binder, October 4–5, 1978, "(NACW) Items Pre 1-12-79," Box 13, SW; Weddington to Abzug and Votaw, November 16, 1978, "(NACW) Items Pre 1-12-79," Box 13, SW; Votaw and Abzug to Carter, November 21, 1978, 1–2, Untitled Folder, Box 986, BSA; Abzug and Votaw to Weddington, November 17, 1978, "(NACW) Items Pre 1-12-1978," Box 13, SW.

162. Addie Wyatt quoted in Abzug with Kelber, *Gender Gap,* 68.

163. Votaw and Abzug to Carter, November 21, 1978, 1, "President's Advisory Committee and State Coalitions to Commemorate 'Houston Plus One,'" November 14, 1978, "Natl. Advisory Committee," Box 986, BSA; "Minutes of the 11/21–22/78 Meeting," draft, "Advisory Committee, Dec. 78," Box 987, BSA; Weddington to Votaw, December 18, 1978, "Firing," Box 988, BSA.

164. Abzug with Kelber, *Gender Gap,* 63–75; Memorandum from Beth Abramowitz to Eizenstat, December 20, 1978, "(NACW) Items Pre 1-12-79," Box

13, SW; Memorandum from Jane Wales to Wexler, December 19, 1978, "(NACW) Items Pre 1-12-79," Box 13, SW.

165. Memorandum from Weddington to Fran Voorde et al., November 22, 1978, "(NACW) Items Pre 1-12-79," Box 13, SW.

166. Memorandum of Weddington to Voorde, Wexler, and Eisenstadt, December 16, 1978, "(NACW) Items Pre 1-12-1978," Box 13, SW.

167. Request marked "disapproved," "Meeting with IWY Commissioners and Staff," December 22, 1977, "(NACW) Items Pre 1-12-1978," Box 13, SW; Weddington to Abzug and Votaw, January 8, 1979, "(NACW) Items Pre 1-12-79," Box 13, SW.

168. Abzug and Votaw, "Statement to President Carter," January 12, 1979, 1–14, 1, 2, "Women's Advisory Committee [CF, O/A 647]," Box 57, HJ.

169. "The NWC, a Turning Point in American Women's Long Struggle for Equality—Message from the President of the United States," CR reprint, September 27, 1978, H 10860, Untitled Folder, Box 986, BSA; "Economic Justice for Women Resolution: Speech by Bella Abzug at Democratic Mid-term Conference," December 10, 1978, "Democratic Convention, 1980," Box 968, BSA.

170. "President Carter Challenged on Social Priorities by National Advisory Committee for Women," January 12, 1979, 3 p.m., 1–4, 1, "Women's Advisory Committee [CF, O/A 647]," Box 57, HJ.

171. Schram, "The Story behind Bella's Departure."

172. Mayra MacPherson, "Bella's Battle Lost: After the Ax, the Bravado Remains," WP, January 16, 1979, B1

173. Schram, "The Story behind Bella's Departure"; "Wexler Reportedly at Front in Hiring, Firing of Abzug," HC, January 18, 1979, 20.

174. Memorandum from Weddington to White House Senior Staff, January 16, 1979, 5–8, 6, "(NACW) Items on 1-12-79," Box 14, SW; "Agenda for Meeting of NACW," January 12, 1979, "(NACW) Items on 1-12-79," Box 14, SW.

175. Eleanor Smeal and Brownie Ledbetter quoted in Levine and Thom, Bella Abzug, 218, 219.

176. Nancy Neuman quoted in Eleanor Randolph, "Uncivil War Flares over Bella Abzug: Reasons for Ouster Clouded by Emotions," CT, January 19, 1979, 1.

177. Anonymous quoted in Terence Smith, "Carter, in Angry Exchange, Ousts Bella Abzug from Women's Unit," NYT, January 13, 1979, 1.

178. Abzug quoted in Smith, "Carter, in Angry Exchange, Ousts Bella Abzug from Women's Unit," 1.

179. Note from Jordan to Abzug, January 12, 1979, "Women's Advisory Committee [CF, O/A 647]," Box 57, HJ.

180. Robert J. Lipshutz, Exit Interview by Marie Allen, September 29, 1979, 1–26, 22, WH, https://www.jimmycarterlibrary.gov/library/exitInt/Lipshutz.pdf.

181. Jordan to Abzug, January 12, 1978, "BSA Misc. Letters Etc.," Box 986, BSA. The press release issued the next day echoed Abzug's dismissal letter, "The commitment of this Administration . . . ," January 13, 1979; Memorandum from Greet Dewald to Weddington, January 16, 1979, "(NACW) Items on 1-12-79," Box 14, SW.

182. Jordan paraphrased and Abzug quoted in MacPherson, "Bella's Battle Lost," B1.

183. Lipshutz paraphrased in Alice Bonner, "Abzug Colleagues Resign to Protest Ouster by Carter," *WP*, January 14, 1979, A1. Lipshutz confirmed this exchange in Lipshutz, Exit Interview by Marie Allen, 21–22.

184. Abzug quoted in Smith, "Carter, in Angry Exchange, Ousts Bella Abzug from Women's Unit," 1.

185. Abzug as paraphrased in Levine and Thom, *Bella Abzug*, 221.

186. Eve Abzug quoted in Levine and Thom, 222.

187. Martin F. Nolan, "Jordan and Abzug and Abrasiveness," *BG*, January 16, 1979, 10.

188. Randolph, "Uncivil War Flares over Bella Abzug"; "Abzug: Talking Points," n.d., "(NACW) Items on 1-12-79," Box 14, SW.

189. Rosalynn Carter quoted in "First Lady Seconds Carter in Dismissing Bella Abzug," *LAT*, January 15, 1979, B2.

190. East to R. Carter, January 29, 1979, "(NACW) Historical Predecessor," Box 13, SW.

191. Author unknown, "The member of the Democratic . . . ," n.d., "Natl. Advisory Committee—Memo on BA's Firing," Box 987, BSA; Memorandum of call from Steinem to Weddington, n.d., "(NACW) Items on 1-12-79," Box 14, SW.

192. Mailgram from Smeal et al. to J. Carter, January 13, 1979, "Firing," Box 988, BSA; Memorandum from Weddington to White House Senior Staff, January 16, 1979, "(NACW) Items on 1-12-79," Box 14, SW; Georgia Dullea, "White House Fails to Mend Fences with Key Women's Groups," *NYT*, January 20, 1979, 22.

193. Abzug quoted in Mim Kelber, "Bella Speaks," *Black American* 18, no. 9 (n.d.): 32, "Bella's Firing by Carter—Responses: Cartoons / Articles," Box 988, BSA.

194. E. Goodman, "Bella Bella-Cosity," *TS*, January 26, 1979, A15. See also Judy Mann, "The Abzug Affair: A White House Signal," *WP*, January 17, 1979, C1; D. Broder, "Costanza, Abzug Go Out the Hard Way: For Women, Humiliation in the White House," *LAT*, January 17, 1979. Rowland Evans and Robert Novak were less sympathetic in "Bella Abzug's Dismissal: An 'Inescapable Reaction to Rudeness,'" *WP*, January 17, 1979, A13.

195. Louis Harris, "Carter Rating Down Sharply on All Fronts," clipping, *Detroit Free Press*, February 20, 1979, Box 988, BSA.

196. Abzug suggested she received "thousands and thousands of letters" upon being fired, but it was hundreds. See Boxes 921–923, BSA. Quoted here, Mrs. Lily Ann (Weiss) Wood to Abzug, February 5, 1979, "California II," Box 988, BSA; ADA et al. to Carter, January 19, 1979, "Firing," Box 988, BSA; Joy Horowitz, "Bella Abzug: A Woman in Motion: Former Official Explains Firing from Women's Committee," *LAT*, January 24, 1979, E1.

197. Abzug quoted in MacPherson, "Bella's Battle Lost."

Epilogue

Epigraph: Bella Abzug with Mim Kelber, *Gender Gap: Bella Abzug's Guide to Political Power for American Women* (Boston: Houghton Mifflin, 1984), 12.

1. Carol M. Mueller, "The Empowerment of Women: Polling and the Women's Voting Bloc," in *The Politics of the Gender Gap: The Social Construction of Political Influence,* ed. Carol M. Mueller (Newbury Park, CA: Sage, 1988), 16–36, 16. For representative "gender gap" coverage, see Juan Williams, "Reagan's Aides Say Gender Gap Is GOP Problem," *WP,* September 19, 1983, A1. When writing *Gender Gap,* Abzug and Kelber discussed starting a think tank with academics including Ruth Mandel, Catharine Stimpson, and Ethel Klein. "Women's Meeting: 'Think Tank,'" Box 986, BSA.

2. Abzug with Kelber, *Gender Gap,* 4–6.

3. "Women USA 'A Ringing Success,' 170,000 Women Call for Information on Women's Rights Issues," n.d., "Women USA—Instructions for Taping Hotline Messages," Box 1007, BSA; "Three Women Leaders Announce Formation of 'Women USA,'" April 11, 1979, "Women USA Cerrell Press Releases," Box 1007, BSA.

4. Abzug, "Dear Friend," October 1, 1979, "Women USA Inflation Mailing (Send Your Bills to Congress) Oct. 79," Box 1006, BSA.

5. Margaret Mason to Abzug, September 11, 1980, "Women USA— Margaret Mason, Memos," Box 1008, BSA; Memorandum from Abzug to Mink et al., November 11, 1980, "Women USA—Memo to Co-directors Nov. 11, 1980," Box 1008, BSA.

6. Abzug quoted in Judy Flander, "Commentators Clamor for Attention at CNN," clipping, *On Cable,* November 1981, "Cable News Network Agreement," Box 1020, BSA; Memorandum from Abzug to Burt Reinhardt, n.d., "Cable News Network Agreement," Box 1020, BSA; "Agreement," October 25, 1979, Box 1020, BSA; Kevin M. Kruse and Julian E. Zelizer, *Fault Lines: A History of the United States since 1974* (New York: W. W. Norton, 2019), 139–142.

7. For full commentary, see Boxes 1019 and 1020, BSA.

8. Abzug, "CNN Spot," June 5, 1980, "CNN, June 1980–Sept. 1980," Box 1019, BSA.

9. Jimmy Carter, "A Crisis of Confidence," July 15, 1979, https://millercenter.org/the-presidency/presidential-speeches/july-15-1979-crisis-confidence-speech. Kevin Mattson, *"What the Heck Are You Up To, Mr. President?": Jimmy Carter, America's "Malaise," and the Speech That Should Have Changed the Country* (New York: Bloomsbury USA, 2009); Jon Ward, *Camelot's End: Kennedy vs. Carter and the Fight That Broke the Democratic Party* (New York: Twelve, Hachette Book Group, 2019), 139–144.

10. Abzug, Confidential Memo, December 21, 1979, 1–2, 1, "Democratic Convention, 1980," Box 968, BSA.

11. "Ellie," n.d., "Press Conference," n.d., "Women's Division, Coalition for Women's Rights," Box 967, BSA.

12. Abzug to Edward Kennedy, January 18, 1980, "Meetings and Correspondence with Sen. Kennedy (Jan. 1980)," Box 1007, BSA.

13. Ward, *Camelot's End,* 202, 203.

14. Ted Kennedy quoted in Ward, *Camelot's End,* 203.

15. Ted Kennedy quoted in Suzanne Braun Levine and Mary Thom, *Bella Abzug: How One Tough Broad from the Bronx Fought Jim Crow and Joe McCarthy, Pissed Off Jimmy Carter, Battled for the Rights of Women and Workers, Rallied Against War and for the Planet, and Shook Up Politics Along the Way* (New York: Farrar, Straus and Giroux, 2007), 226.

16. Kennedy quoted in Levine and Thom, *Bella Abzug,* 226; Potter to Abzug, March 30, 1980, "Delegates, Speech (EMK), Literature," Box 969, BSA; Kennedy to "Dear Delegate," July 4, 1980, "Platform Info and Literature," Box 968, BSA; "Statement by Bella Abzug, NWPC," April 10, 1980, "Democratic Platform Committee, 10 April 1980," Box 968, BSA.

17. Ronald L. Soble and Larry Green, "Convention Mood Differs: Symbol of ERA Protest Evokes Memories of '68," *LAT,* July 15, 1980, 1.

18. Abzug quoted in Karlyn Barker and Bill Peterson, "The Women Delegates: Some Victories but a Sense of Frustration, Division," *WP,* August 13, 1980, A14; Abzug, loose notes, n.d., "8 August: Press Conference—Coalition for Women's Rights," Box 967, BSA; "Substitution for Minority Plank #10" with Abzug edits, n.d., "DNC: Women's Division; Coalition for Women's Rights," Box 967, BSA; "Coalition for Women's Rights Strategy Meeting," August 9, 1980, Box 967, BSA; "Convention Coalition for Women's Rights Calls for Changes on ERA and Abortion Platform Planks," September 8, 1980, Box 967, BSA.

19. NWPC, "Democratic Women Are Wonderful: A History of Women at Democratic National Conventions," 1–33, 33, "Democratic Convention, 1980," Box 968, BSA; Mildred Jeffrey, "The number of dates missing . . . ," July 1983, Box 968, BSA; Marybel Batjer to NWPC Steering Committee, November 11, 1980, "Women '80, Candidates and Women's Issues," Box 968, BSA.

20. Astead W. Herndon, "Democrats Overhaul Controversial Superdelegate System," *NYT,* August 25, 2018, https://www.nytimes.com/2018/08/25/us/politics/superdelegates-democrats-dnc.html.

21. Abzug, "That our children need in . . . ," handwritten draft statement, n.d., "Democratic Convention—1980," Box 969, BSA.

22. Georgia Dullea, "Women at World Parley Discuss the Meaning of Political Power," *NYT,* July 21 1980, A15.

23. Levine and Thom, *Bella Abzug,* xi.

24. Abzug with Kelber, *Gender Gap,* 7.

25. Abzug quoted in Sharon Rosenthal, "Abzug Weighs Another Comeback Bid," *HC,* June 6, 1982, A9.

26. Abzug quoted in "Moynihan Opponent Files for Primary," *NYT,* August 11, 1982, B3.

27. Bella Abzug, "Why Not a Woman Vice President?," *NYT,* November 10, 1983, G7. See also Alison Muscatine, "Women to Meet with Mondale on Choice of Running Mate," *WP,* June 28, 1984, A12; Howell Rainess, "Mondale's Tough Choice: His Aides Try to Alleviate 'Super Pressure' to Pick a Woman, and Feminists Are Split," *NYT,* July 3, 1984, A1.

28. Ronnie Eldridge, "In Praise of Shrillness," *NYT,* August 3, 1984, A23.

29. David Mixner quoted in Kay Mills, "Drive Began in Women's Restroom, Ended in Political Board Room," *LAT,* July 19, 1984, 5.

30. Frank Mankiewicz quoted in David Farrell, "Democrats' Misguided Bows to Feminist Groups," *BG,* December 3, 1984, 19.

31. Bella Abzug and Mim Kelber, "Despite the Reagan Sweep, a Gender Gap Remains," *NYT,* November 23, 1984, A35.

32. Abzug quoted in Mark Matthews, "Fans Rally Around Legend as Abzug Tries for House," *TS,* October 6, 1986, 1A.

33. Martin Abzug quoted in Kempton, "A Touching Softness in a Force of Nature," clipping, *ND,* n.d., Folder 1, Box 518, RM.

34. Abzug quoted in James Feron, "Abzug Running for Congress from District in Westchester," *NYT,* June 6, 1986, D18.

35. Bella Abzug, "Martin, What Should I Do Now?," *Ms.* July–August 1990, 94–96, 95; William G. Blair, "Martin Abzug, 69, a Stockbroker Who Wrote Three Novels," *NYT,* July 19, 1986, 14.

36. Helene Alexander quoted in Levine and Thom, *Bella Abzug,* 244.

37. Abzug, "Martin, What Should I Do Now?," 95.

38. Renee Taylor quoted in "All-Star Farewell to Bella's Hubby," clipping, *NYP,* July 21, 1986, "Bella-65th Birthday Party, 7/24/1985," Box 2, MB.

39. Gloria Steinem quoted in Levine and Thom, *Bella Abzug,* 245.

40. Abzug to "Dear Friend," flyer, n.d., Folder 1, Box 518, RM.

41. Murray Kempton, "A Touching Softness in a Force of Nature," clipping, *NYN,* n.d., Folder 1, Box 518, RM; Elizabeth Kolbert, "Abzug Beaten by Dio-Guardi in House Race," *NYT,* November 5, 1986, B13.

42. Todd S. Purdum, "Democrats Nominate Nadler to Succeed Weiss in House," *NYT,* September 9, 1992, A1; Abzug to "Dear Member of the Democratic County Committee," September 18, 1992, Folder 2, Box 518, RM; "Bella Abzug Announces Candidacy for Vacant Seat in 8th CD," September 19, 1992, Box 518, RM; RE14.

43. Abzug quoted in "Viewpoints: 'I Proceed as Though I've Got a Shot,'" clipping, n.d., loose document, Box 11, MB.

44. Abzug, "I am writing to you . . . ," draft letter, n.d., loose document, Box 8, MKP; Elaine Sciolino, "As Their 'Decade of Women' Ends, Women Take Stock," *NYT,* July 10, 1985, A1; Brooke W. Kroeger, "Decade for Women Conference: Bella Steals the Show: If Women Ruled the World," *ND,* July 19, 1985, C1.

45. Robin Morgan quoted in Levine and Thom, *Bella Abzug,* 266.

46. Bella Abzug and Mim Kelber, "Let's Use 'Wise Women,'" reprinted in *The Bella Abzug Reader,* ed. Mim Kelber and Libby Bassett (New York: self-published, 2003), 263–264; on the Women's Foreign Policy Council, see 264–282.

47. Valerie M. Hudson and Patricia Leidl, *The Hillary Doctrine: Sex and American Foreign Policy* (New York: Columbia University Press, 2015). WEDO remains active: www.wedo.org.

48. For conference preparation and proceedings, see Box 12 and Box 15, MKP.

49. Abzug, "Take the Brackets Off Women's Lives," September 19, 1995, reprinted in *The Bella Abzug Reader,* 349–351, 350.

50. For a representative column, see Bella Abzug, "Gender Justice: No Turning Back," *ET,* May 31–June 14, 1995, reprinted in *The Bella Abzug Reader,* 342–343.

51. Abzug quoted in Rebecca Trounson, "Reaganomics Hurt the Weak, Abzug Says: Ex-congresswoman Calls Administration a 'Ruthless Crowd,'" *LAT,* November 19, 1981, LB8.

52. Abzug quoted in "Thousands March on Pentagon to Protest Aid to El Salvador," *HC,* May 4, 1981, A1.

53. Michael Kazin, "What Liberals Owe to Radicals," in *Liberalism for a New Century,* ed. Neil Jumonville and Kevin Mattson (Berkeley: University of California Press, 2007), 119–130, 120.

ACKNOWLEDGMENTS

Biography is a special kind of beast. It requires spending an unusual amount of time with one person, thinking about singularity and representativeness, the banal and extraordinary in life. Along this absorbing journey, I have benefited from the generosity of many fellow historians, librarians, students, and interested audiences who have listened as I shared my latest discoveries and tried out ideas. These exchanges shaped this book considerably.

I am a biographer today because of other practitioners of this craft. Daniel Horowitz was my first great history teacher and shared his love for intellectual history with such care that I could not help but join him in the enterprise. In Santa Barbara, Jane De Hart brought me into her process as she completed what will stand as the definitive biography of Justice Ruth Bader Ginsburg. She expressed immediate delight when I first shared that I might write about Bella Abzug, and she has continued to be a pilot and champion. Nelson Lichtenstein encouraged me to dig into the early years, think deeply about Jewishness, and draw out a more complicated story of labor and the American Left. Laura Kalman convinced me to look more critically at both human foibles and triumphs and to find the law in biography. Eileen Boris brings life to all that she does as a tireless, courageous activist and historian whose theoretical sophistication and passion inform every page. I have been fortunate to be among her disciples and continue to learn from her example. Two others stand out most as I have transitioned from student to scholar. At Stanford, I worked alongside another great biographer, Estelle Freedman, whose stories of her journey down this path left an imprint on my own. And in Houston, I have had the great joy of collaborating with Nancy Beck Young, who shared her deep knowledge of congressional and political history and her mutual interest in crafting life stories.

At the University of Houston, my colleagues have been generous and inspiring. Kristina Neumann has affirmed for me what exhilaration can come from teaching and how research is richer for it. Rachel Quinn has imprinted in me a better sense of how to bridge ideas and community. I have valued conversation about this work and so much more with Natalia Milanesio, Mark Goldberg, Monica Perales, Jimmy Schafer, Cihan Muslu, Rick Mizelle, Kristin Wintersteen, Abed Takriti, Eric Walther, Julie Cohn, Kairn Klieman, Wes Jackson, Hannah Decker, Sarah Fishman, Todd Romero, Alexey Golubev, Raul Ramos, Phil Howard, Marty Melosi, Renee Knake, Sarah Luna, and Laura Oren. Participants in the Center for Public History workshop were incisive readers who helped me hone my analysis of Bella Abzug as a political celebrity. Christopher Haight was a wonderfully precise and skilled research assistant. In my graduate professionalization course, I have learned as much about the craft of history and the art of teaching from future historians as I hope I have imparted. Teaching students in the Women, Gender, and Sexuality Studies program about the politics of archives has also inspired me to think differently about the life of historical texts. Students at Stanford University in courses on biography, women's history, and the law shaped my thinking on these subjects.

The Stanford women and gender reading group enlivened my days there and broadened my thinking; thank you to Estelle Freedman, Katherine Marino, Allyson Hobbs, Annelise Heinz, and Natalie Marine-Street. My framing as a political biographer took greater shape at a writing seminar on gender and biography I attended at the Radcliffe Institute at Harvard University in 2007. Nancy Cott guided our workshop ably, and our group's enthusiasm for each other's works in progress propelled me forward as I completed this book over the next decade. I have valued being a repeat participant in a dynamic feminist legal biography writing workshop organized by Constance Backhouse and Jane DeHart and connected to the American Society for Legal History. Additionally, I benefited immensely from participation in a lively speaker series hosted by the Tamiment Library and convened by Marilyn Young.

Friends who hit the books with me despite all of that Santa Barbara sunshine have left an imprint. Andrea Thabet was the best roommate one could imagine, and I gained so much from lighthearted and profound conversation with Elizabeth Shermer, Justin Bengry, Megan Bowman, Julia Brock, Bianca Murillo, Andrea Gill, John Sciarcon, John Munro, Matthew

Sutton, Carolyn Herbst-Lewis, and Laura Izuel. So many historians have offered comments on my manuscript as it progressed as conference papers, workshop drafts, talks, and chapters. Thank you to Nancy MacLean, Michael Parrish, Landon Storrs, Serena Mayeri, Patricia Schechter, Ellen Schrecker, Judy Tzu-Chun Wu, Linda Gordon, Leslie Dunlap, Tomiko Brown-Nagin, Pnina Lahav, Barbara Babcock, Felice Batlan, Marlene Trestman, Franca Iacovetta, and Jim Walker. Others provided advice and consolation over coffee, in elevators, and across the table. Thank you to Felicia Kornbluh, Lisa Levenstein, Leigh Ann Wheeler, Nancy Hewitt, Ronnie Grinberg, Natasha Zaretsky, Stephanie Gilmore, Marjorie Spruill, Joanne Meyerowitz, Julie Gallagher, Hasia Diner, Alice O'Connor, Ann Plane, Jill Fields, Lori Clune, Kitty Sklar, Dorothy Sue Cobble, Helen Horowitz, Tom Dublin, Sara Dubow, Shira Kohn, Rachel Kranson, Mary Ziegler, and Nina Dayton. Writers working in similar areas have provided source leads that came at the perfect time, including Jocelyn Olcott, Judy Tzu-Chun Wu, Eric Walther, Shelah Leader, Alan Wald, Robert Cohen, Gilbert Gall, Judith Nies, Tom Wells, Thomas Maier, and Jonathan Soffer. It was a pleasure to trade leads and talk shop with filmmaker Jeff Lieberman as we neared the ends of our respective projects. Katherine Turk read portions of this book as we began to imagine our project on the history of women's history, and Stacie Taranto gave me space to finish things up as we collaborated on a postsuffrage collection.

Archivists I have worked with are the stars of this project. I have spent more than a decade returning happily to the Rare Book and Manuscript Library at Columbia University and have received wonderful support, especially from Mary Marshall Clark, Jennifer Lee, Tara Craig, Susan Hamson, Whitney Bagnall, and Sabrina Sondhi. I remain appreciative that the library digitized select audio files from the Bella Abzug Papers. At New York University, Gail Malmgreen, Janet Levy, Peter Filardo, and K. Kevyne Baar of the Tamiment Library were expert aides. Vince Lee has been a collaborator and guide at University of Houston Special Collections, and movement archivist Laura X has been a champion. Thank you to all other delightful library staff at archives I have visited for offering assistance and a friendly welcome.

This book was championed by Sandra Dijkstra and Elise Capron before it had form, and I am grateful for their expertise and constant enthusiasm. Harvard University Press took things from there with Joyce Seltzer, assisted by Brian Distelberg, providing practiced direction and encouragement, and James Edwin Brandt seeing the project to the finish line. My ideas gained depth and precision because of two fine-tuned anonymous readings of the manuscript. The final prose was sharpened ably by Susan Ecklund and Kimberly Giambattisto.

Thank you to Christopher Tomlins, Kathleen Laughlin, and Jacqueline Castledine as well as anonymous readers who helped me develop my interpretation of the Willie McGee case. Chapter 1 builds on ideas first discussed in "Braving Jim Crow to Save Willie McGee: Bella Abzug, the Legal Left, and Civil Rights Innovation, 1948–1951," *Law and Social Inquiry* 33, no. 4 (Fall 2008): 1003–1041; and "The Legal Origins of 'The Personal Is Political': Bella Abzug and the Sexual Color Line in Cold War Civil Rights Law," in *Breaking the Wave: Women, Their Organization, and Feminism, 1945–1985,* eds. Kathleen Laughlin and Jacqueline Castledine (New York: Routledge, 2010).

Abzug would not have been portrayed as richly without the remembrances provided by those who knew her, and I am grateful to all I have interviewed, a list that goes beyond those featured in my abbreviations guide. I am especially grateful for the care that Liz Abzug and Eve Abzug took to share their memories of their mother while giving me space to form my own understanding. Liz has been encouraging beyond anything I expected.

I am fortunate to have received support from fine institutions and foundations. A summer stipend provided by the National Endowment for the Humanities aided me during this project's last stage, as did generous grants from the University of Houston and the Women's Caucus of the Association for Jewish Studies. Postgraduate support provided by the American Council of Learned Societies and the Center for the United States and the Cold War at New York University helped me extend my study forward in time, and deepen my analysis, among inspiring intellects. An affiliation at the Centre for the Study of the United States at the Munk School of Global Affairs, University of Toronto, likewise offered an intellectual home. In the early stages of this project, I received votes of confidence and generous support from the Charlotte W. Newcombe Foundation, the Woodrow Wilson National Fellowship Foundation, the Hadassah-Brandeis Institute, and the Jewish Women's Caucus of the National Women's Studies Association. I benefited from sustained funding from the graduate division, the history department, and the affiliated history association at the University of California, Santa Barbara, and from the University of California's Labor and Employment Research Fund. Grants provided by the Schlesinger Library at Harvard University, the Sophia Smith Collection at Smith College, and the Feinstein Center for American Jewish History at Temple University enabled me to spend extended time digging in archives.

My research trips have always been more enjoyable because of welcoming friends. In New York and elsewhere, I have been grateful for the couches and companionship offered by Katie Forst, Kari Detwiler Beck, Ellie Shermer, Sarah and Judah Stevenson, Lesley Kroupa and Chris Kearns, Corinne Gill and Eoin Kenny, Jill Zwaanstra, Julia Brock, and Tamara Gagnolet and Mike Barth. My dear friends Suzanne Schaffner and Gwen Guzman Rose continue to be spirit sisters. Dana Weiner and Amy Milne-Smith remind me of why historians make great friends.

My family, the Zarnow, Feuer, and Sbardellati clan, have been so patient as I completed this project, always asking how it was going with genuine interest over the years. This support has carried me through. My sister, Suzanne, and brother, Marek, have been important anchors. My parents, Beverly and Gary, read drafts very early on, offered advice along the way, and never ceased to believe in the story I set out to tell. My grandparents, Raymond and Beatrice, and Jack and Marian, always asked how Bella was doing, reminisced about their memories of the fiery lady with the hat, and cheered me on. It saddens me especially that Nana Bea, who had such a love for words and tough grammar radar, could not see this completed book. Aunt Kathy and Uncle Matt opened their home when I taught at Stanford, and I cherish our dinner conversations that often gravitated to where I was with this project. Aldo was always nearby as I wrote this book and a much loved little guy. Most of all, I want to thank John Sbardellati, a fine historian I greatly admire, who read more drafts and heard more about where things were with Bella than he probably bargained for or imagined was possible. We have traveled throughout North America together, John, but with you, I am always home.

INDEX

Page references in italics indicate a figure.